T0180259

Communications
in Computer and Information Science 1286

Guangquan Xu · Kaitai Liang ·
Chunhua Su (Eds.)

Frontiers in Cyber Security

Third International Conference, FCS 2020
Tianjin, China, November 15–17, 2020
Proceedings

 Springer

Editors
Guangquan Xu (iD)
Tianjin University
Tianjin, China

Chunhua Su (iD)
University of Aizu
Aizuwakamatsu, Japan

Kaitai Liang (iD)
Delft University of Technology
Delft, The Netherlands

ISSN 1865-0929   ISSN 1865-0937 (electronic)
Communications in Computer and Information Science
ISBN 978-981-15-9738-1   ISBN 978-981-15-9739-8 (eBook)
https://doi.org/10.1007/978-981-15-9739-8

This Springer imprint is published by the registered company Springer Nature Singapore Pte Ltd.
The registered company address is: 152 Beach Road, #21-01/04 Gateway East, Singapore 189721, Singapore

Preface

This volume contains the papers from the Third International Conference on Frontiers in Cyber Security (FCS 2020). The event was organized by the School of Cybersecurity, Tianjin University, China, which started in 2018, and brings together individuals involved in multiple disciplines of cyber security in order to foster exchange of ideas.

In recent years, cyber security threats have increased rapidly. All kinds of extremely dangerous attack behaviors expose common users to risks including privacy leakage, property loss, etc. Cyber security has also received increasing attention from researchers. The development of cyber security requires extensive communication. The permanent theme of the FCS conference series in "Cyber Security." The conference aims to introduce security concepts and technology achievements from the international forefront in the field of information security. Using the latest development trends and innovative technology of cyber security, the FCS conference provides a good platform for researchers and practitioners to exchange the latest research achievements and discuss questions relating to network security, system security, cryptography, trust management, privacy protection, information hiding, computer forensics, content security, and their applications. FCS keeps pace with international security innovation concept and provides theoretical and technical support for the international cyber space development.

Since it was first held at the University of Electronic Science and Technology of China in 2018, the FCS conference series has been held for three years. In these three years, hundreds of researchers have exchanged ideas with each other at the FCS conference, which has promoted the development of cyber security. In 2020, FCS was held in Tianjin, China, and organized by Tianjin University which is one of the most important research institutes in China. FCS 2020 received 143 papers and accepted 39 papers finally, including 10 short papers. Four papers were assigned to each reviewer and on average each paper received five reviews. The type of peer review was double blind in order to promote transparency. The conference has gotten great attention from all over the world and the participants are from different countries, such as, China, Japan, The Netherlands, Denmark, the USA, etc. During the COVID-19 pandemic, the conference needed to comply with relevant epidemic prevention regulations. For the health of the participants, some overseas participants needed to participate in the conference online, which was a big challenge.

According to the accepted papers, the 14 topics of FCS 2020, classified by reviewers, included the following fields: IoT Security, Artificial Intelligence, Blockchain, Cryptography, Cyber-Physical Systems Security, Database Security, Depth Estimation, Mobile Security, Network Security, Privacy, Program Analysis, Quantum Cryptography, Steganography, and Web Security.

The proceedings editors wish to thank the dedicated Scientific Committee members and all the other reviewers for their contributions. We also thank Springer for their trust and for publishing the proceedings of FCS 2020.

September 2020   Guangquan Xu
                                                                  Kaitai Liang
                                                                  Chunhua Su

Organization

Steering Committee

Baocang Wang	Xidian University, China
Chunhua Su	University of Aizu, Japan
Fagen Li	University of Electronic Science and Technology of China, China
Guangquan Xu	Tianjin University, China
Kai Chen	Institute of Information Engineering, Chinese Academy of Sciences, China
Kaitai Liang	Delft University of Technology, The Netherlands
Mingwu Zhang	Hubei University of Technology, China
Robert H. Deng	Singapore Management University, Singapore
Tsuyoshi Takag	The University of Tokyo, Japan
Weizhi Meng	Technical University of Denmark, Denmark
Xiaojiang Du	Temple University, USA

General Chairs

Xiaohong Li	Tianjin University, China
Xiaojiang Du	Temple University, USA
Xiaosong Zhang	University of Electronic Science and Technology of China, China

Program Committee Chairs

Guangquan Xu	Tianjin University, China
Kaitai Liang	Delft University of Technology, The Netherlands
Chunhua Su	University of Aizu, Japan

Program Committee Members

Arun Kumar Sangaiah	Vellore Institute of Technology, India
Baocang Wang	Xidian University, China
Bok-Min Goi	Universiti Tunku Abdul Rahman, Malaysia
Budi Arief	University of Kent, UK
Chhagan Lal	University of Padova, Italy
Chunhua Su	University of Aizu, Japan
Debasis Giri	Maulana Abul Kalam Azad University of Technology, India
Debiao He	Wuhan University, China

Deqing Zou	Huazhong University of Science and Technology, China
Ding Wang	Peking University, China
Fagen Li	University of Electronic Science and Technology of China, China
Fangguo Zhang	Sun Yat-sen University, China
Gautam Srivastava	Brandon University, Canada
Guangquan Xu	Tianjin University, China
Hao Wang	Norwegian University of Science and Technology, Norway
Hequn Xian	Qingdao University, China
Honggang Qi	Chinese Academy of Sciences, China
Hongyu Yang	Civil Aviation University of China, China
Huaqun Wang	Nanjing University of Posts and Telecommunications, China
Jianxin Li	Beihang University, China
Jiliang Li	University of Göttingen, Germany
Jingqiang Lin	State Key Laboratory of Information Security, Chinese Academy of Sciences, China
Joonsang Baek	University of Wollongong, Australia
Junfeng Xu	China Information Technology Security Evaluation Center, China
Kai Chen	Chinese Academy of Sciences, China
Kaitai Liang	Delft University of Technology, The Netherlands
Mande Xie	Zhejiang Gongshang University, China
Meng Shen	Beijing Institute of Technology, China
Mingwu Zhang	Hubei University of Technology, China
Muhammad Khurram Khan	King Saud University, Saudi Arabia
Qianhong Wu	Beihang University, China
Riccardo Spolaor	University of Oxford, UK
Shanchen Pang	China University of Petroleum, China
Shaojing Fu	National University of Defense Technology, China
Shaoying Liu	Hiroshima University, Japan
Shui Yu	University of Technology Sydney, Australia
Shujun Li	University of Kent, UK
Si Chen	West Chester University, USA
Song Han	Zhejiang Gongshang University, China
Stjepan Picek	Delft University of Technology, The Netherlands
Tao Li	Nankai University, China
Tao Song	China University of Petroleum, China
Wei Wang	Beijing Jiaotong University, China
Weizhe Wang	Tianjin University, China
Weizhi Meng	Technical University of Denmark, Denmark
Willy Susilo	University of Wollongong, Australia
Wojciech Mazurczyk	Warsaw University of Technology, Poland
Xiaochun Cheng	Middlesex University, UK

Xiaofei Xie   Nanyang Technological University, Singapore
Xiaoheng Deng   Central South University, China
Xiaoming Li   Tianjin University, China
Zheli Liu   Nankai University, China
Zhengjun Jing   Jiangsu University of Technology, China

Publicity Chairs

Hao Peng   Zhejiang Normal University, China
Hongyu Yang   Civil Aviation University of China, China
Weizhi Meng   Technical University of Denmark, Denmark
Yong Ding   Peng Cheng Laboratory, China

Organization Committee Chairs

Tao Song   Tiangong University, China
Tie Qiu   Tianjin University, China
Shanchen Pang   Tiangong University, China
Zheli Liu   Nankai University, China

Organization Committee Members

Ao Liu   Tianjin University, China
Chenchen Sun   Tianjin University, China
Jian Liu   Tianjin University, China
Junjie Wang   Tianjin University, China
Zhongwei Li   Nankai University, China

Contents

Cyber-Physical Systems Security

Cryptography

Database Security

Depth Estimation

Mobile Security

IoT Security

IoT Security

Blockchain-Based CP-ABE with Publicly Verifiable Outsourced Decryption in IoT

Mande Xie, Jifei Hu, and Haibo Hong$^{(\boxtimes)}$

School of Computer and Information Engineering, Zhejiang Gongshang University,
Hangzhou, China
honghaibo1985@163.com

Abstract. Attribute based encryption (ABE) was used to ensure confidentiality and access control in IoT as a preeminent cryptographic primitive. However, the traditional ABE with outsourced decryption cannot achieve public verifiability for decryption results. In this paper, blockchain technology is appplied to realize the publicly verifiability in our CP-ABE scheme. Furthermore, our scheme has many characteristics: white box traceability, malicious users revocability and updatability of ciphertext. Lastly, we present the security analysis and demonstrate the performance of our scheme. The results show that our scheme is IND-CPA secure under the standard model and also has high efficiency.

Keywords: IoT · CP-ABE · Fog computing · Outsourced decryption · Blockchain

1 Introduction

Over the last decades, there has been growing development in Internet of Things (IoT). We have witnessed the application of the Internet of Things in various fields, including medicine, transportation, industry 4.0 and manufacturing [1–3]. In traditional IoT systems, sensitive data is stored on cloud servers and it is distributed to IoT devices. Firstly, due to the large amount of data transferred between the IoT device and the cloud server, the cloud server will suffer from transmission delays and service degradation [4–6]. Secondly, sensitive data need to be encrypted before uploading to cloud server. Lastly, it is necessary to support fine-grained access control when sharing sensitive data.

According to the first problem, fog computing located between the cloud infrastructure and IoT devices, and fog-enabled IoT architectures guarantee that the enables real time devices and applications can have less delay and sufficient computing resources [7–9].

Moreover, attribute based encryption (ABE) was used to ensure confidentiality and access control in cloud as a preeminent cryptographic primitive to solve the second and third problems, which was first proposed by Sahai and Waters [10]. There exists two forms of attribute based encryption: ciphertext-policy attribute-based encryption (CP-ABE) [11] and key-policy attribute-based

© Springer Nature Singapore Pte Ltd. 2020
G. Xu et al. (Eds.): FCS 2020, CCIS 1286, pp. 3–18, 2020.
https://doi.org/10.1007/978-981-15-9739-8_1

encryption (KP-ABE) [12]. Overall, data owners can define its own data access policy in the CP-ABE, which is considered to be more suitable than KP-ABE in the context of the Internet of Things (IoT).

As described above, it is necessary to study a practicable scheme that can solve the problems mentioned above.

1.1   Contributions

In our paper, we develop a blockchain-Based CP-ABE with publicly verifiable outsourced decryption in fog-enabled IoT. Our main contributions and technologies are summarized as follows:

(1) We develop a new system which combines blockchain, CP-ABE, cloud computing and the fog computing in IoT.

(2) Our scheme has white-box traceability as well as identify malicious users who give away their secret keys. Once the malicious user is traced, we can update the ciphertext in time to provide forward security. In addition, our scheme provides an efficient revocation mechanism that allows data user (DU) to be revoked from the system once the malicious user is caught.

(3) Our scheme delegates part of the user's decryption capabilities to a fog node (FN) with a transformation key. In addition, we utilize the blockchain technology to achieve public verifiability of outsourced decryption.

(4) We also evaluate the security and performance of our system. As a result, our scheme is selective CPA-secure under the standard model. And it is found to be efficient by comparison with other schemes.

1.2   Related Work

In this section, we introduced some related work about CP-ABE and blockchain-based outsourced computation.

Recently, there have been many extensions to CP-ABE. For example, Liu [13] proposed a white-box traceable CP-ABE scheme, Soon afterwards, Ning [14] maked some improvement. Then, Liu [15] proposed a traitor tracing and revocation CP-ABE. But in [15], it cannot support forward security. Later, the scheme [16] have both white-box traceability and user revocation as well as ciphertext updatable.

However, due to the limited storage and computing capacities of IoT devices, the traditional CP-ABE schemes was not suitable. To address this problem, Green [17] first developed a CP-ABE with outsourced decryption which can eliminate a lot of decryption operations. After that, Lai [18] improved the scheme [17], which supported verifiability of decrypted results. Following this, there are many new CP-ABE which possess different efficiency classification and security classification. Nevertheless, most existing schemes' outsourced decryption [19,20] cannot realize public verifiability, that means, once the dispute occurs, it must be submitted to a third party for arbitration through revealing data user' secret key. Hence, the CP-ABE with outsourced decryption technology should be equipped with public verifiability.

Furthermore, to improve transparency and resist data tampering, some works utilizing blockchain technology to achieve verifiability of outsourced computing. Kumaresan [21] proposed a protocol that verifying the correctness of outsourced computing results through blockchain to pay a deposit in advance. Guo [22] send the encrypted electronic medical data to the blockchain to realize the tamper-proof modification of the sensitive data. Also, Azaria [23] realized secure access to medical data through the control of smart contracts. Huang [24] proposed a protocol which based on a trusted third-party to implement blockchain-based outsourcing computing. However, none of these schemes could support the verifiability of outsourced computing.

2 Preliminaries

2.1 Linear Secret Sharing Schemes (LSSS)

Suppose that $\mathbb{A}$ is a access structure. A LSSS can be expressed as $\mathbb{A} = (\mathbf{M}, \rho)$. $\mathbf{M}$ is a $l \times n$ matrix, and ρ is a function that can map $\mathbf{M}_i$ to an attribute. There exists two algorithms as follows:

- **Share** $((\mathbf{M}, \rho), s)$: We randomly choose $r_2, ..., r_n$ and a secret $s \in \mathbb{Z}_p$. Then, we denote $v = (s, r_2, ..., r_n)$ as a column vector. And $\lambda_i = \mathbf{M}_i \cdot v$ is a share of the secret s where λ_i belongs to a attribute.
- **Reconstruction** $(\lambda_1, \lambda_2, ..., \lambda_l, (\mathbf{M}, \rho))$: The constants $\{c_i \in \mathbb{Z}_p\}_{i \in I}$ where $I = \{1, 2, ...l\}$, and we can recover secret s through $\sum_{i \in I} c_i \lambda_i = s$.

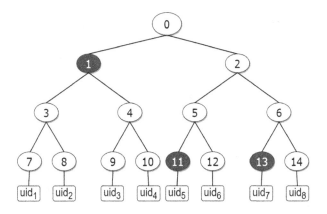

Fig. 1. An example of binary tree.

2.2 Binary Tree

Our scheme was based on breadth-first search and has the following six characteristics:

1. Leaf nodes in the tree is connected to a user identity uid. Therefore, we set the number of users as $|Num| = 2^d$ where d is a depth in our binary tree.
2. We describe the $path(uid)$ as the path from root node to the leaf nodes.
3. Then, $cover(L)$ is a cover list, and it possess the minimum number of nodes that can contains all users, and none of these users exist in revocation list L.
4. When we consider the intersection of $path(uid)$ and $cover(L)$, we can know there exists only one element in this intersection.
5. LN is described as a set of leaf nodes in the $cover(L)$.
6. $depth(x)$ is expressed as the depth of node x, and we set $depth(root) = 0$.

Given a simple example in Fig. 1, we can know $path(uid_3) = \{0, 1, 4, 9\}$ and $|Num| = 2^d = 2^3 = 8$, we set the revocation list $L = \{uid_6, uid_8\}$, so $cover(L) = \{1, 11, 13\}$, $LN = \{11, 13\}$, and the intersection $path(uid_3) \cap cover(L) = \{1\}$.

2.3   Complexity Assumptions

Definition 1 (decisional q-BDHE problem): Let p be a prime order of bilinear group $\mathbb{G}$ and let $d, s \in \mathbb{Z}_p^*$. Also, set g as a generator of bilinear group, then.

$$\vec{y} = (g, g^s, g^d, ..., g^{d^q}, g^{d^{q+2}}, ..., d^{d^{2q}})$$

The decisional q-BDHE problem is defined to distinguish $e(g, g)^{d^{q+1}s} \in \mathbb{G}_T$ from a random element Z in $\mathbb{G}_T$.

The advantage for all PPT algorithm $\mathcal{A}$ that solve the decisional q-BDHE problem as:

$$\left| Pr[\mathcal{A}(\vec{y}, e(g, g)^{d^{q+1}s}) = 0] - Pr[\mathcal{A}(\vec{y}, Z) = 0] \right|$$

this advantage is negligible with respect to the security parameter λ.

Definition 2 (l-SDH problem): Given an $(l+1)$-tuple $(g, g^x, g^{x^2}, ..., g^{x^l})$, the l-SDH problem is to find a pair $(f, g^{1/(x+f)}) \in \mathbb{Z}_p \times \mathbb{G}$

If an adversary can solve the the l-SDH problem, then it has an advantage at least ϵ:

$$\left| Pr[\mathcal{A}(g, g^x, g^{x^2}, ..., g^{x^l}) = (f, g^{1/(x+f)})] \right| \geq \epsilon$$

Definition 3 (DL problem): Let p be a prime order of bilinear group $\mathbb{G}$ and let $x \in \mathbb{Z}_p$. Also, set g as a generator of bilinear group. Given a turple $(\mathbb{G}, p, g, g^x)$, DL problem is to find a element $x \in \mathbb{Z}_p$. The advantage that adversary $\mathcal{A}$ can solve the DL problem is defined as:

$$\left| Pr[\mathcal{A}(\mathbb{G}, p, g, g^x) = x] - \frac{1}{2} \right|$$

3   System Overview

In this section, the system model is first described, then present the framework and the traceability model as well as the security model.

3.1 System Model

As shown in Fig. 2, Our system has the following six entities: Trust Authority (TA), Data Owner (DO), Fog Nodes (FN), Cloud Storage Providers (CSP), Data Users (DU), Consortium Blockchain (CB). Then the details are described as follows:

Trust Authority (TA): A TA is considered to be completely trusted. TA generates parameters PK and MSK for our system. Then, TA possess a revocation list L and a binary tree T_{tree}. Moreover, TA just send the revocation list L and minimum cover list $cover(L)$ to fog nodes (FN) and data owner (DO) respectively instead of making the entire binary tree public to cloud and data owner (DO), it champions data users' privacy. After that, TA can generate a decryption key SK and send it to DU as well as be able to update a ciphertext in time after a new user is added to the revocation list.

Data Owner (DO): A DO can design the access structure for the message to be encrypted, and encrypts the message by using our scheme. Then, uploads the ciphertext to the FN;

Fog Nodes (FN): The FN were assumed to be semi-trusted (honest but curious). FN maintains a user revocation list L, when DU request the data, DU send the request to a FN. If the DU does not exist in the L as well as the attribute set S matches the access structure $\mathbb{A}$, FN forwards the request to TA. Lastly, FN plays a role that packages some crucial key information to the blockchain.

Cloud Storage Providers (CSP): The CSP is also considered semi-trusted. And is responsible for storing the ciphertext from FN, then it also return the ciphertext storage location $Adress_{CT}$ to FN.

Data Users (DU): A DU is identified by a uid, issues its data request and data verify by transferring data descriptions to a fog node.

Consortium Blockchain (CB): The CB is composed of distributed fog nodes (FN), A FN stores information on the blockchain through smart contracts, such as: the hash of ciphertext, updated ciphertext, public key.

3.2 System Framework

We design nine algorithms in this paper:

Setup$(\lambda, U) \rightarrow (PK, MSK)$: The setup algorithm responsible for TA inputs two parameters: an implicit security parameter λ and an attribute universe U. TA will generate a global public key PK and a master key MSK.

Encrypt$(PK, m, \mathbb{A}, cover(L)) \rightarrow (CT)$: A DO executes the encryption algorithm to generate ciphertext CT. The algorithm requires a public key PK, a message m, a LSSS access structure $\mathbb{A}$ and a cover list $cover(L)$ as input.

KeyGen$(MSK, uid, S) \rightarrow (SK)$: This algorithm accepts three inputs: a master key MSK, an user identity uid, and an attribute set S. It outputs an secret key SK. This algorithm is also run by TA.

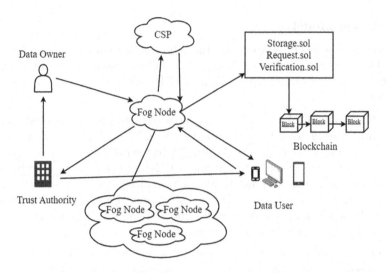

Fig. 2. System architecture of scheme.

Decrypt$(CT, SK) \rightarrow (m)$: The decryption algorithm accepts two inputs: a ciphertext CT and a secret key SK. It outputs a message m. The algorithm is usually run by DU.

OutKeyGen$(SK) \rightarrow (TK, RK)$: The outsourcing key generation algorithm accepts only one inputs: a secret key SK. It outputs a transformation key TK and an retrieving key RK. The algorithm is also run by DO.

Transform$(PK, CT, TK) \rightarrow (CT')$: The transformation algorithm accepts three inputs: a public key PK, a ciphertext CT and a transformation key TK. It outputs a transformation ciphertext CT'. The algorithm is run by FN.

OutDecrypt$(RK, CT, CT') \rightarrow (m)$: The outsourcing decryption algorithm accepts three inputs: a retrieving key RK, a ciphertext CT, and a transformation ciphertext CT'. It outputs a message m. The algorithm is run by DU.

Trace$(PK, cover(L), SK) \rightarrow (uid$ or $\perp)$: The traceability algorithm accepts three inputs: a public key PK, a cover list $cover(L)$ and a secret key SK. It outputs the uid or $\perp$. The algorithm is run by TA.

CTUpdate$(PK, CT, cover(L')) \rightarrow (CT'')$: The ciphertext updating algorithm accepts three inputs: a public key PK, a ciphertext CT and a latest revocation list L'. It outputs an updated ciphertext CT''. The algorithm is run by TA.

4   Our Construction

In our scheme, the ciphertext CT was divided into two component, One is the access structure ciphertext component which is associated with the $\mathbb{A}$. Meanwhile, another is related to the $cover(L)$ named cover list ciphertext component.

Then, the secret key SK was divided into two components: secret key component associated with the uid and secret key component associated with the S. Our construction is based on [16] and [18].

Setup$(\lambda, U) \rightarrow (PK, MSK)$: The algorithm accepts two inputs: an implicit security parameter λ and an attribute universe U. It chooses a bilinear map $(\mathbb{G}, \mathbb{G}_T, e, p)$ where g is a generator of $\mathbb{G}$, and p is a prime order of $\mathbb{G}$ and $\mathbb{G}_T$. We denote L and $\mathcal{T}_{tree}$ as a revocation list and binary tree, respectively. We stick the identities of users to the leaf nodes of our binary tree. Then we denote d as the depth of the tree. Thus, we can figure out that the users' max number is $|Num| = 2^d$ and nodes' number is $2|Num| - 2$. Then, this algorithm performs as follows:

1. Chooses $\alpha, a \in \mathbb{Z}_p$ as well as $g, u, v, d, h \in \mathbb{G}$ randomly.
2. For all $i \in U$, TA picks a random numbers $s_i \in \mathbb{Z}_p^*$ and computes $T_i = g^{s_i}$;
3. TA adopts a hash function $H \colon \mathbb{G} \to \mathbb{Z}_p^*$ which maps messages m and random message m' to an element of $\mathbb{Z}_p^*$.
4. In this stage, the algorithm firstly selects random elements $n_j \in \mathbb{Z}_p$ for each node in the binary tree $\mathcal{T}_{tree}$, then computes $N = \{n_j\}_{j=0}^{2|Num|-2}$. it also calculates $Q = \{q_j | q_j = g^{n_j}\}_{j=0}^{2|Num|-2}$ in the end.
5. TA selects a probabilistic encryption scheme (Enc, Dec), which is a symmetric encryption maps uid from $\{0, 1\}^*$ to $\mathbb{Z}_p$. Each time it run the Enc algorithm with its symmetric key k, it can return different results.

Therefore, the resulting public parameters is:

$$\{PK = u, v, d, h, H, g, g^a, e(g, g)^\alpha, \{T_i\}_{i \in U}, Q = \{q_j | q_j = g^{n_j}\}_{j=0}^{2|Num|-2}\}$$

The corresponding master key is:

$$\{MSK = k, \alpha, a, N = \{n_j\}_{j=0}^{2|Num|-2}\}$$

Encrypt$(PK, m, \mathbb{A}, cover(L)) \rightarrow (CT)$: The algorithm inputs a public parameters PK, a message $m \in \mathbb{G}_T$ and an access structure $\mathbb{A} = (\mathbf{M}, \rho)$, where $\mathbf{M}$ is an $l \times n$ access matrix and ρ can map $\mathbf{M}_i$ to a attribute. Then DO picks two secret exponent $s, s' \in \mathbb{Z}_p$ at random, After that it set two random vectors $v = (s, v_2, ..., v_n)$ and $v' = (s', v_2', ..., v_n')$ where $v_2, ..., v_n$ and $v_2', ..., v_n'$ are chosen randomly. For each row $\mathbf{M}_i$ of $\mathbf{M}$, the algorithm chooses $r_{1,i}, r_{2,i} \in \mathbb{Z}_p^*$ randomly, After that, it also calculates $\lambda_i = \mathbf{M}_i \times v$ and $\lambda_i' = \mathbf{M}_i \times v'$. In the end, DO chooses a random message $m' \in \mathbb{G}_T$ to achieve verifiability of the scheme.

Our ciphertext generation process is as follows:

1. First, our algorithm generates the ciphertext component related to the access structure :

$$\tilde{C} = u^{H(m)} v^{H(m')} d,$$
$$C_1 = m \cdot e(g, g)^{\alpha s}, C_1' = g^s, C_1'' = g^{as}, C_{1,i} = h^{\lambda_i} T_{\rho(i)}^{-r_{1,i}}, D_{1,i} = g^{r_{1,i}},$$
$$C_2 = m' \cdot e(g, g)^{\alpha s'}, C_2' = g^{s'}, C_2'' = g^{as'}, C_{2,i} = h^{\lambda_i'} T_{\rho(i)}^{-r_{2,i}}, D_{2,i} = g^{r_{2,i}}$$

2. When receiving the latest $cover(L)$ from TA, DO can generate the ciphertext component associated with the $cover(L)$:

$$\{\{R_x = q_x^s\}_{x \in cover(L)}, \{R_x' = q_x^{s'}\}_{x \in cover(L)}\}$$

So the CT is as follows:

$$CT = \{\tilde{C}, C_1, C_1', C_1'', C_{1,i}, D_{1,i}, C_2, C_2', C_2'', C_{2,i}, D_{2,i}, R_x, R_x', \mathbb{A}\}$$

Algorithm 1: The transaction that store information related to ciphertext

---

Input: CT, PK;

Output: The Storage transaction related to the $Storage.sol$;

1 initialization

2 **if** *FN receives a ciphertext CT and a PK* **then**

3 | FN computes the hash: $H(CT)$ and $H(PK)$;

4 | FN sends CT to Cloud Server Provider(CSP);

5 | CSP return the $Address_{CT}$ which denotes the ciphertext storage location used to search ciphertext;

6 | FN stores the $\{H(PK), H(CT), Address_{CT}\}$ in the transaction.

7 | FN generate the storage transaction;

As show in Algorithm 1, Once FN receives the ciphertext of DO, FN will call the smart contract which named $Storage.sol$. After this transaction is generated, FN will broadcasts it to other Fog Nodes in Blockchain for consensus verification. Note that, $H(CT)$ is used to protect the ciphertext from malicious CSP.

Algorithm 2: The transaction that users access request a ciphertext

---

Input: user identity uid, user attribute set S, revocation list L;

Output: 1 or 0;

1 initialization;

2 **while** *variable j not at end of L* **do**

3 | **if** $uid == L[j]$ **then**

4 | | return 0;

5 | **else**

6 | | **if** S *satisfies* $\mathbb{A}$ **then**

7 | | | return 1;

8 | | | FN forwards the request to TA;

9 | | **else**

10 | | | return 0;

11 | | | FN rejects user's request;

12 | | **end**

13 | **end**

14 **end**

If there exists a user in the system who wants to request data, the user will submit a request to a FN, and then the FN will call this smart contract which named *Request.sol*, if this algorithm return 0, FN will reject the user's access request. Otherwise, TA receives the request from FN, and the request carries user attribute set S and user identity uid. The process is described as Algorithm 2.

KeyGen$(MSK, uid, S) \rightarrow (SK)$: This algorithm accepts three inputs: a master key MSK, a user identity uid, and an attribute set S. Then, TA randomly picks a numbers $b \in \mathbb{Z}_p^*$ and use a probabilistic encryption function Enc to generate the value f, where f is randomly distributed in $\mathbb{Z}_p$, It can be expressed by the equation as $f = Enc_k(l_x)$, the k is the secret key, l_x is a leaf node, and the user is connected to this node. As the result, it will generate a decryption key SK.

The specific algorithm is as follows:

1. First computes the secret key component associated with the S:
   $\{K_1 = f, K_2 = g^{\frac{\alpha+ab}{a+f}} h^b, K_3 = g^b, K_4 = g^{ab}, \{K_i = T_i^{(a+f)b}\}_{i \in S}\}$
2. As we know above, we assign a user to a leaf node l_x. Then TA select a number $w \in \mathbb{Z}_p$ uniformly at random. According to the user identity uid, we can obtain the node x that $x \in path(uid) \cap cover(L)$, and we set $E_x = R_x = q_x^s$ and $E_x' = R_x' = q_x^{s'}$, then algorithm calculates secret key component related to the uid as follows:
   $\{(K_5 = g^{ab} q_{l_x}^w), K_6 = g^w, K_7 = E_{l_x} = (R_x)^{\frac{n_{l_x}}{n_x}} = q_{l_x}^s, K_8 = E_{l_x}' = (R_x')^{\frac{n_{l_x}}{n_x}} = q_{l_x}^{s'}\}$

Finally DU obtains the secret key as:

$$SK = \{K_1, K_2, K_3, K_4, K_i, K_5, K_6, K_7, K_8\}$$

Decrypt$(CT, SK) \rightarrow (m)$: This algorithm accepts two inputs: a ciphertext CT and a secret key SK. There exists constants c_i and c_i' that $\sum_{i \in I} c_i \lambda_i = s$ and $\sum_{i \in I} c_i \lambda_i' = s'$, where $I = \{i | \rho(i) \in S\}$. Then DU does as follows:

$$Y_1' = \frac{e(K_2, C_1'^{K_1} \cdot C_1'')}{\prod_{i \in I}(e(K_3^{K_1} \cdot K_4, C_{1,i}) \cdot e(K_{\rho(i)}, D_{1,i}))^{c_i}} \cdot \frac{e(K_6, K_7)}{e(C_1', K_5)} = e(g, g)^{\alpha s}$$

$$Y_2' = \frac{e(K_2, C_2'^{K_1} \cdot C_2'')}{\prod_{i \in I}(e(K_3^{K_1} \cdot K_4, C_{2,i}) \cdot e(K_{\rho(i)}, D_{2,i}))^{c_i}} \cdot \frac{e(K_6, K_8)}{e(C_2', K_5)} = e(g, g)^{\alpha s'}$$

and computes $m = C_1 / Y_1'$ and $m' = C_2 / Y_2'$, If $\tilde{C} \neq u^{H(m)} v^{H(m')} d$, it will returns $\perp$. Otherwise, it returns m.

OutKeyGen$(SK) \rightarrow (TK, RK)$: This algorithm inputs a secret key SK, then it picks a number z at random and set $K_1' = K_1, K_2' = K_2^{1/z}, K_3' = K_3^{1/z}, K_4' = K_4^{1/z}, K_i' = K_i^{1/z}, K_5' = K_5^{1/z}, K_6' = K_6^{1/z}, K_7' = K_7, K_8' = K_8$.

Lastly, it outputs a transformation key to FN:

$$TK = \{K_1', K_2', K_3', K_4', K_i', K_5', K_6', K_7', K_8'\}$$

and a retrieving key it itself:

$$RK = \{z\}$$

Transform$(PK, CT, TK) \rightarrow (CT')$: This algorithm inputs a public key PK, a ciphertext CT, and a transformation key TK. Then it does as follows:

1. FN computes:

$$W_1' = \frac{e(K_2', C_1'^{K_1'} \cdot C_1'')}{\prod_{i \in I}(e(K_3'^{K_1'} \cdot K_4', C_{1,i}) \cdot e(K_{\rho(i)}', D_{1,i}))^{c_i}} \cdot \frac{e(K_6', K_7')}{e(C_1', K_5')} = e(g, g)^{\alpha s/z}$$

$$W_2' = \frac{e(K_2', C_2'^{K_1'} \cdot C_2'')}{\prod_{i \in I}(e(K_3'^{K_1'} \cdot K_4', C_{2,i}) \cdot e(K_{\rho(i)}', D_{2,i}))^{c_i}} \cdot \frac{e(K_6', K_8')}{e(C_2', K_5')} = e(g, g)^{\alpha s'/z}$$

2. Then, FN sets the transformed ciphertext as:

$$CT' = \{\tilde{W} = \tilde{C}, W_1 = C_1, W_1', W_2 = C_2, W_2'\}$$

Then FN sends the CT' to a user who with the identity uid.

OutDecrypt$(RK, CT, CT') \rightarrow (m)$: On input a CT, a CT' and an RK, if $\tilde{W} \neq \tilde{C}$ or $W_1 \neq C_1$ or $W_2 \neq C_2$, it output $\perp$,Then the algorithm computes:

$$m = \frac{W_1}{W_1'^z}$$

$$m' = \frac{W_2}{W_2'^z}$$

After that, DO calculates $V_1 = u^{H(M)}, V_2 = v^{H(m')}$ and sends the V_1 and V_2 to a FN, then FN calls the smart contract which named $Verification.sol$, through this smart contracts we can achieve the public verifiability in our scheme. Then the algorithm principle of this smart contract is as follows:

Algorithm 3: The transaction that check the result of outsourcing decryption

---

Input: $\tilde{W}, V_1, V_2, d, uid$;

Output: 1 or 0;

1   initialization

2   **if** $uid \in L$ **then**

3   ⌊ **return** 0;

4   **else if** $uid \notin L$ **then**

5   **if** $\tilde{W} = V_1 V_2 d$ **then**

6   ⌊ **return** 1;

7   **else**

8   ⌊ **return** 0;

Trace$(PK, cover(L), SK) \rightarrow (uid$ or $\perp$): First, We need to examine whether SK is well-formed. That is to say, our secret key needs to meet the following conditions:

Key Sanity Check

$$K_1 \in \mathbb{Z}_p, K_2, K_3, K_4, K_i, K_5, K_6, K_7, K_8 \in \mathbb{G}. \tag{1}$$

$$e(g, K_4) = e(g^a, K_3) \neq 1. \tag{2}$$

$$\exists i \in U, \ e(T_i, K_3^{K_1} K_4) = e(g, K_i) \neq 1. \tag{3}$$

If SK is well-formed, we can believe that SK conforms to the description of Key Sanity Check above, then we give a decryption privilege of the attribute set:

$$S_w = \{i \in S \wedge e(T_i, K_3^{K_1} K_4) = e(g, K_i) \neq 1\}.$$

After that, the algorithm will perform the following steps:

1. Recover user's identity through decryption algorithm $Dec(l_x)$.
2. The algorithm will sets the LN to a set of leaf nodes in minimum cover set $cover(L)$, then search l_x in the LN: if l_x exists in LN, it return the uid which is associated with the l_x. Otherwise, it return a special identity uid^* which will never exist in LN.
3. Add the uid to the L and update the revocation list to $L' = L \cup \{uid\}$.

If SK dissatisfies the description of Key Sanity Check above, this algorithm will return $\perp$.

CTUpdate$(PK, CT, cover(L')) \rightarrow (CT'')$: The trust authority TA chooses v uniformly at random, then it computes $Q' = \{q_j^v\}_{j=0}^{2|Num|-2}$. After that, TA sets $\{C = \tilde{C}, C_1 = C_1, C_1' = C_1', C_1'' = C_1'', C_{1,i} = C_{1,i}, D_{1,i} = D_{1,i}, C_2 = C_2, C_2' = C_2', C_2'' = C_2'', C_{2,i} = C_{2,i}, D_{2,i} = D_{2,i}\}$ and recalculates the $\{R_x\}$ and $\{R_x'\}$, and update ciphertext as follows:

$$CT'' = \{C, C_1, C_1', C_1'', C_{1,i}, D_{1,i}, C_2, C_2', C_2'', C_{2,i}, D_{2,i}, R_x, R_x', \mathbb{A}\}$$

After that, TA sends the CT'' and the update revocation list L' to a FN, then FN will update ciphertext to CSP. After that, FN recalculate the hash $H(CT'')$ and calls the smart contract $Storage.sol$ as above.

5 Security Analysis

5.1 Traceability

Theorem 1. *Our scheme is traceable based on the l-SDH assumption and $q < l$.*

Proof. Given an $(l+1)$-tuple $(g, g^x, g^{x^2}, ..., g^{x^l})$, the l-SDH problem is to find a pair $(c, g^{1/(x+c)}) \in \mathbb{Z}_p \times \mathbb{G}$. We let $l = q + 1$, assumed that adversary $\mathcal{A}$ can make q key queries. Set $\{A_j = \bar{g}^{a^j}\}_{j=0}^{j=l}$. Then simulator $\mathcal{B}$ do as follows:

Setup: $\mathcal{B}$ selects q random numbers $f_1, f_2, ..., f_q \in \mathbb{Z}_p^*$, $\alpha, \alpha_0, \alpha_1, ..., \alpha_q \in \mathbb{Z}_p$ and $u, v, d, h \in \mathbb{G}$, set $fun(y)$ as:

$$fun(y) = \prod_{j=1}^{q}(y + f_j) = \prod_{j=0}^{q} \alpha_j y^j$$

Then $\mathcal{B}$ will do the following:

1. Set $g = \sum_{j=0}^{q}(A_j)^{\alpha_j} = \bar{g}^{fun(a)}$ and $g^a = \sum_{j=0}^{q+1}(A_j)^{\alpha_{j-1}} = \bar{g}^{fun(a)\cdot a}$.
2. For each i in attribute universe U, chooses random numbers $s_i \in \mathbb{Z}_p^*$ and computes $T_i = g^{s_i}$;
3. $\mathcal{B}$ adopts a hash function $H: \mathbb{G} \rightarrow \mathbb{Z}_p^*$ which maps messages m and random message m' to an element of $\mathbb{Z}_p^*$.
4. Firstly, selects random elements $n_j \in \mathbb{Z}_p$ for each node in the binary tree $\mathcal{T}_{tree}$, then computes $N = \{n_j\}_{j=0}^{2|Num|-2}$. it also calculates $Q = \{q_j | q_j = g^{n_j}\}_{j=0}^{2|Num|-2}$ in the end.

Then we set the PK as:

$$\{PK = u, v, d, h, H, g, g^a, e(g,g)^\alpha, \{T_i\}_{i \in U}, Q = \{q_j | q_j = g^{n_j}\}_{j=0}^{2|Num|-2}\}$$

Key Query: $\mathcal{A}$ queries secret key after $\mathcal{A}$ sends the $\{uid_j, S\}$ to $\mathcal{B}$, let $fun_j(y)$ as:

$$fun_j(y) = \frac{fun(y)}{y + f_j} = \prod_{i=1, i \neq j}^{q}(y + f_i) = \prod_{i=0}^{q-1} \beta_i y^i$$

$\mathcal{B}$ set:

$$\sigma_j = \prod_{i=0}^{q-1}(A_i)^{\beta_i} = \bar{g}^{fun_j(a)} = \bar{g}^{fun(a)/(a+f_j)} = g^{1/(a+f_j)}$$

then, $\mathcal{B}$ randomly selects $b \in \mathbb{Z}_p$ and computes the secret key and return the result to $\mathcal{A}$. The secret key is as follows:

$$\{K_1 = f_j, K_2 = (\sigma_j)^{\alpha + \alpha b} h^b, K_3 = g^b, K_4 = (g^a)^b, \{K_i = (g^a \cdot g^{f_j})^{s_i b}\}_{i \in S}\}$$

We select a number $w \in \mathbb{Z}_p$ uniformly at random. According to the user identity uid, we can obtain the node x that $x \in path(uid) \cap cover(L)$, and we set $E_x = R_x = q_x^s$ and $E_x' = R_x' = q_x^{s'}$, then $\mathcal{B}$ calculates as follows:

$$\{K_5 = g^{ab} y_{l_x}^w, K_6 = g^w, K_7 = E_{l_x} = (R_x)^{\frac{n_{l_x}}{n_x}} = q_{l_x}^s, K_8 = E_{l_x}' = (R_x')^{\frac{n_{l_x}}{n_x}} = q_{l_x}^{s'}\}$$

Finally, $\mathcal{B}$ return the secret key to $\mathcal{A}$ as:

$$\{K_1, K_2, K_3, K_4, K_i, K_5, K_6, K_7, K_8\}$$

Key Forgery: Adversary $\mathcal{A}$ sends a SK^* to $\mathcal{B}$. Then, there exists two cases as follows:

- If $\mathcal{A}$ loses the game, a solution of l-SDH problem is found by computing a turple $(f, \tau) \in \mathbb{Z}_p \times \mathbb{G}$ randomly via $\mathcal{B}$.
- If $\mathcal{A}$ wins the game, a solution of l-SDH problem is found by computing a turple $(K_1, \bar{g} \overline{a + K_1})$ via $\mathcal{B}$.

Provided that the protocol in [16] is traceability, our scheme is traceability.

5.2 IND-CPA Security and Verifiability

Theorem 2. *If the decisional q-BDHE assumption holds, the basic CP-ABE scheme is selective CPA-secure.*

Proof. Suppose that, the advantage of adversary $\mathcal{A}$ is non-negligible. Then, the simulator $\mathcal{B}$ can wins the game with non-negligible advantage. Given $y = (g, g^s, g^d, ..., g^{d^q}, g^{d^{q+2}}, ..., g^{d^{2q}})$. The game does as follows:

Init: $\mathcal{A}$ submits a challenged cover list $cover(L^*)$ and a challenged access structure $\mathbb{A}^*$.

Setup: Simulator $\mathcal{B}$ does as follows:

1. Selects $\alpha' \in \mathbb{Z}_p^*$, then computes $e(g, g)^\alpha$ where $\alpha = \alpha' + d^{q+1}$.
2. For all attribute $i \in U$, $\mathcal{B}$ chooses a random number $z_i \in \mathbb{Z}_p$. After that, set the $T_i = g^{z_i} g^{dM_{i,1}^*}, ..., g^{d^{n^*} M_{i,n^*}^*}$ if $\rho^*(i) \in U$ where $i \in \{1, 2, ..., l^*\}$. Otherwise, $T_i = g^{z_x}$.
3. Then picks random $a, u, v, d \in \mathbb{Z}_p$ and a hash function H, then computes g^a and $h = g^d$.
4. Let $J_{R^*} = \{j \in path(uid) | uid \in R^*\}$ and randomly picks a number $u_j \in \mathbb{Z}_p^*$. Then, set $q_j = g^{d^j + u_j}$ if $j \in J_{R^*}$. Otherwise, set $q_j = g^{d^q + u_j}$.

   Hence, the PK is:
   $\{PK = u, v, d, h, H, g, g^a, e(g, g)^\alpha, \{T_i\}_{i \in U}, Q = \{q_j | q_j = g^{n_j}\}_{j=0}^{2|Num|-2}\}$
   and send it to $\mathcal{A}$.

Phase 1: In this phase, $\mathcal{A}$ makes a private key query on a series of tuples (uid, S), and $\mathcal{B}$ does as follows:

1. If $S \in \mathbb{A}^* \wedge uid \notin L^*$, then outputs $\perp$
2. Otherwise, $\mathcal{B}$ chooses three random numbers $b, f, w \in \mathbb{Z}_p$ and computes:
   $K_1 = f, K_2 = g^{\frac{\alpha + \alpha b}{a + f}} h^b, K_3 = g^b, k_4 = g^{ab}, K_i = T_i^{(a+f)b}, K_5 = g^{\alpha b} q_{l_x}^w, K_6 = g^w, K_7 = q_{l_x}^s$

Challenge: $\mathcal{A}$ returns two messages m_0, m_1, then $\mathcal{B}$ picks $\gamma \in \{0, 1\}$ and computes CT^*. After that, $\mathcal{A}$ receives the CT^* sent by $\mathcal{B}$.

Phase 2: The same as Phase 1.

Guess: $\mathcal{A}$ submits $\gamma' \in \{0, 1\}$.
Our scheme is selective CPA-secure based on the analysis in [16].

Theorem 3. *Assume the basic CP-ABE scheme is selective CPA-secure, our scheme with outsourced decryption is selective CPA secure as well.*

Proof. According to the analysis in [18], our scheme with outsourced decryption is selective CPA secure.

Theorem 4. *Our scheme with outsourced decryption is verifiable if DL assumption holds.*

Proof. According to the analysis in [18], our scheme is verifiable.

6 Performance Evaluation

In terms of functionality and efficiency, we evaluate our scheme in Table 1 and Table 2. For simply, we denote P, E, N as a pairing computing, an exponentiation computing and the size of the $cover(L)$. Then, we set l as the amount of rows in the **M**, Respectively, $|S|$ was expressed as the amount of attributes in the SK, $|I|$ was expressed as the amount of attributes in the SK which satisfies $\mathbb{A}$. We also define:

$$t_1 = \sum_{x' \in cover(L')} (depth(x') - 1 - depth(x))$$

$$t_2 = |I| + d - depth(x)$$

$$t_3 = 2|Num| - 2 + N$$

As shown in Table 1, our scheme has many characteristics: white box traceability, malicious users revocability, updatability of ciphertext, publicly verifiability as well as security under the standard model. Moreever, according to Table 2 we can know that the decryption of our scheme is efficient.

Table 1. Properties comparison.

Schemes	[13]	[15]	[16]	[18]	[20]	Ours
Traceability	✓	✓	✓	×	×	✓
Revocation	×	✓	✓	×	×	✓
Ciphertext updating	×	×	✓	×	×	✓
Outsourced decryption	×	×	×	✓	✓	✓
Public verifiability	×	×	×	×	×	✓
Security in standard model	✓	✓	✓	✓	×	✓

Table 2. Efficiency comparison.

Schemes	[13]	[15]	[16]	[18]	[20]	Ours
Enc	$(2+2l)E$	$(7l+1)E$	$(2l+N+3)E$	$(6l+6)E$	$(l+3)E$	$(6l+N+8)E$
OutDec	×	×	×	$2\|I\|E+(4\|I\|+2)P$	$(2l+2)E+(2l+2)P$	$(4\|I\|+2)E+(4\|I\|+6)P$
Dec	$(\|I\|+1)E+(2\|I\|+1)P$	$(3\|I\|+9)P$	$(t_2+2)E+(2\|I\|+3)P$	$4E$	$1E$	$4E$
CTUpdate	×	×	t_1E	×	×	t_3E
Trace	$2E$	×	$2E+(2\|S\|+2)P$	×	×	$2E+(2\|S\|+2)P$

7 Conclusions

We utilize blockchain technology to achieve public verifiability in traditional CP-ABE. Furthermore, we also prove the security and verifiability in this paper. And through performance evaluation, it can be known that our scheme is multi-functional and high-efficiency, which is practical in IoT.

References

1. Bandyopadhyay, D., Sen, J.: Internet of things: applications and challenges in technology and standardization. Wirel. Pers. Commun **58**(1), 49–69 (2011). https://doi.org/10.1007/s11277-011-0288-5
2. Xu, G., Zhao, Y., Jiao, L., et al.: TT-SVD: an efficient sparse decision making model with two-way trust recommendation in the AI enabled IoT systems. IEEE Internet Things J. 1 (2020)
3. Xu, G., Liu, B., Jiao, L., et al.: Trust2Privacy: a novel fuzzy trust-to-privacy mechanism for mobile social networks. IEEE Wirel. Commun. **27**(3), 72–78 (2020)
4. Lu, R., Zhu, H., Liu, X., et al.: Toward efficient and privacy-preserving computing in big data era. IEEE Netw. **28**(4), 46–50 (2014)
5. Xu, G., Wang, W., Jiao, L., et al.: SoProtector: safeguard privacy for native SO files in evolving mobile IoT applications. IEEE Internet Things J. **7**(4), 2539–2552 (2020)
6. Li, L., Xu, G., Jiao, L., et al.: A secure random key distribution scheme against node replication attacks in industrial wireless sensor systems. IEEE Trans Ind. Inform. **16**(3), 2091–2101 (2020)
7. Ni, J., Zhang, K., Lin, X., et al.: Securing fog computing for internet of things applications: challenges and solutions. IEEE Commun. Surv. Tutor. **20**(1), 601–628 (2017)
8. Xu, G., Zhang, Y., Jiao, L., et al.: DT-CP: a double-TTPs-based contract-signing protocol with lower computational cost. IEEE Access. **7**, 174740–174749 (2019)

9. Xu, G., Zhou, W., Sangaiah, A.K., et al.: A security-enhanced certificateless aggregate signature authentication protocol for InVANETs. IEEE Netw. **34**(2), 22–29 (2020)
10. Sahai, A., Waters, B.: Fuzzy identity-based encryption. In: 24th Annual International Conference on the Theory and Applications of Cryptographic Techniques, pp. 457–473. ACM, Aarhus (2005)
11. Bethencourt, J., Sahai, A., Waters, B.: Ciphertext-policy attribute-based encryption. In: IEEE Symposium on Security and Privacy, pp. 321–334. IEEE, Berkeley (2007)
12. Goyal, V., Pandey, O., Sahai, A., et al.: Attribute-based encryption for fine grained access control of encrypted data. In: 13th ACM Conference on Computer and Communications Security, pp. 89–98. ACM, Alexandria (2006)
13. Liu, Z., Cao, Z., Wong, D.: White-box traceable ciphertext-policy attribute-based encryption supporting any monotone access structures. IEEE Trans. Inf. Foren. Secur. **8**(1), 76–88 (2013)
14. Ning, J., Cao, Z., Dong, X., Wei, L., Lin, X.: Large universe ciphertext-policy attribute-based encryption with white-box traceability. In: Kutyłowski, M., Vaidya, J. (eds.) ESORICS 2014. LNCS, vol. 8713, pp. 55–72. Springer, Cham (2014). https://doi.org/10.1007/978-3-319-11212-1_4
15. Liu, Z., Wong, D.: Practical attribute-based encryption: traitor tracing, revocation and large universe. Comput. J. **59**(7), 983–1004 (2016)
16. Liu, Z., Duan, S., Zhou, P., et al.: Traceable-then-revocable ciphertext-policy attribute-based encryption scheme. Future Gener. Comput. Syst. **93**, 903–913 (2019)
17. Gree, M., Hohenberger, S., Waters, B., et al.: Outsourcing the decryption of ABE ciphertexts. In: Proceedings of the 20th USENIX Conference on Security, p. 34. ACM, San Francisco (2011)
18. Lai, J., Deng, R., Guan, C., et al.: Attribute-based encryption with verifiable outsourced decryption. IEEE Trans. Inf. Foren. Secur. **8**(8), 1343–1354 (2013)
19. Li, J., Wang, Y., Zhang, Y., et al.: Full verifiability for outsourced decryption in attribute based encryption. IEEE Trans. Serv. Comput. **13**(3), 478–487 (2017)
20. Huang, X., Li, J., Li, J., et al.: Securely outsourcing attribute-based encryption with checkability. IEEE Trans. Parallel Distrib. Syst. **25**(8), 2201–2210 (2014)
21. Kumaresan, R., Bentov, I.: How to use bitcoin to incentivize correct computations. In: Proceedings of the 2014 ACM SIGSAC Conference on Computer and Communications Security, CCS, USA, pp. 30–41 (2014)
22. Guo, R., Shi, H., Zheng, D., et al.: Flexible and efficient blockchain-based ABE scheme with multi-authority for medical on demand in telemedicine system. IEEE Access **7**, 88012–88025 (2019)
23. Azaria, A., Ekblaw, A., Vieria T., et al.: MedRec: using blockchain for medical data access and permission management. In: 2016 2nd International Conference on Open and Big Data (OBD), pp. 25–30. IEEE, Vienna (2016)
24. Huang, H., Chen, X., Wu, Q., et al.: Bitcoin-based fair payments for outsourcing computations of fog devices. Future Gener. Comput. Syst. **78**, 850–858 (2018)

DNS Rebinding Detection for Local Internet of Things Devices

Xudong He[1], Jian Wang[1(✉)], Jiqiang Liu[1], Zhen Han[1], Zhuo Lv[2],
and Wei Wang[1,3]

[1] Beijing Key Laboratory of Security and Privacy in Intelligent Transportation,
Beijing Jiaotong University, Beijing, China
wangjian@bjtu.edu.cu
[2] State Grid Henan Electric Power Research Institute, Zhengzhou, China
[3] Division of Computer, Electrical and Mathematical Sciences and Engineering
(CEMSE), King Abdullah University of Science and Technology (KAUST),
Thuwal 23955-6900, Saudi Arabia

Abstract. Smart home technology makes the living environment comfortable and safe. However, threats in the smart home environment bring more new challenges. As a typical attack method, DNS rebinding seriously threatens the data privacy and the security of smart home devices. Aiming at detecting this attack and minimizing its effect as much as possible, we use simulation experiments to model the DNS rebinding attack scenarios. Based on the analysis of the key factors of the experiments, a DNS rebinding attack detection model is proposed. When devices in a smart home environment meet the detection model, they may be vulnerable to DNS rebinding attacks. Our simulation experimental results show that the smart home devices in the detection model are vulnerable to DNS rebinding attacks. Finally, we put forward some defensive measures.

Keywords: Smart home · DNS rebinding · IoT · TTL · Attack
detection

1 Introduction

In the smart home system environment, the technology of computer, network communication, and the sensor is adapted to combine the electrical equipment related to home life with the network master station which provides the service [1,2]. Communicate within the LAN, call the interface, can be completed by mature protocol standards such as FTP, HTTP, ZigBee, RFID, etc. [3]. For

This work was supported in part by the Natural Science Foundation of China under Grants 61672092, in part by the Fundamental Research Funds for the Central Universities of China under Grants 2018JBZ103, the Fundamental Research Funds for the Central Universities 2019YJS033, Major Scientific and Technological Innovation Projects of Shandong Province, China (No. 2019JZZY020128).

G. Xu et al. (Eds.): FCS 2020, CCIS 1286, pp. 19–29, 2020.
https://doi.org/10.1007/978-981-15-9739-8_2

the manufacturer, the open API interface gives the user some control of the local area network freedom. The API service interface implements the functions of the IoT device through protocol calls and parameter passing. It is a good choice for the linkage of devices implemented by different manufacturers. Because vendors open up API services interfaces that control freedom. The Internet of things devices and sensors devices include smart toys, smart home devices, smart cameras and more. We have recently witnessed many Internet of Things privacy and security issues [4,5]. Many security problems will have a serious impact on personal safety [6]. Therefore, these security issues have aroused great concern. Attacks on Internet of things, including children's security and privacy, and so on [7]. In addition, IoT devices are used to attack the Internet environment. For example, the 2016 Mirai botnet destroyed Internet of things devices and launched one of the most destructive DDoS attacks in the history of the Internet [8]. Armis, a cyber security company, recently issued another warning after discovering the Bluetooth protocol vulnerability "BlueBorne" in 2017, saying that about 500 million smart devices are still affected by old-fashioned attacks such as DNS rebinding [9]. In the smart home environment, the intrusion of sensitive devices such as cameras or constant temperature devices will have a serious impact on people's privacy and even personal safety. DNS rebinding is a form of computer attack [10]. In this attack, a malicious Web page causes the visitor to run a client script that attacks computers elsewhere on the network. The same-origin policy specifies that clientside scripts only allow access to resources on the same host that serve the script [11]. In theory, the same-origin policy can prevent this kind of attack from happening. But comparing domain names is an important part of implementing this policy, and DNS rebinding can bypass this protection by abusing the DNS. There is a browser device or a client that can access a network link in a smart home environment. When such a device inadvertently accesses a malicious site controlled by an attacker, the attacker loads the JS code for the malicious site. It is possible to control the malicious DNS server back and forth domain query, and send malicious request data to the device service interface in the environment, so as to control the devices in the LAN [12]. IoT devices are vulnerable to the threat of DNS rebinding. In this paper, the DNS query process and DNS rebinding attack process are simulated by simulation experiment. We will abstract the DNS rebinding attack detection model in the local Internet of things device scenario. The contribution of this paper is as follows:

- Through experiments, it is proved that this attack really exists, and the attack process is reproduced.
- The key factors of DNS rebinding attack in smart home environment are put forward for the first time, and the key factors are discussed, which provides a powerful basis for preventing such attacks.
- The DNS rebinding attack detection model in smart home environment is proposed for the first time. Target IoT device is under the detection model, it is proved by experiments that the TTL value and JS loading frequency in the IoT rebinding attack in the smart home environment are important factors. We can use them as a basis for detecting attacks.

The rest of the paper is organized as follows: In Sect. 2, we introduce related work on this topic. In Sect. 3, we describe the DNS rebinding detection model. In Sect. 4, Through experiments, it is proved that DNS rebinding attack exists in Smart home. The experimental validation of the model is presented. In Sect. 5, we summarize the contribution of the article and put forward the future work.

2 Related Work

This section mainly describes the related work to the key conditions involved in DNS rebinding attacks.

2.1 Domain Name System and DNS Rebinding Attack

Domain name system as a distributed database which maps domain name and IP address to each other, it can make it easier for people to access the Internet. The frequency of resource record updates in the DNS is determined by the TTL. They concluded that DNS scalability was not threatened by the TTL value of 0 resource records. TTL (Time-To-Live), which is the lifetime of a domain name resolution record in the DNS server [13,14].

There is a kind of attack called DNS rebinding in threatening the security of DNS system and users. In 1996, Princeton computer Science Laboratory first implemented DNS rebinding attack [16]. This attack is very harmful [17]. The attack process is shown in the Fig. 1.

Fig. 1. DNS rebinding attack

The DNS rebinding attack subverts the browser's same-origin policy and converts it into an open network proxy. These attacks can be used to bypass firewalls and are highly effective for sending spam and spoofing payper click advertisers [15]. This attack can also be used to compromise a private network by giving the victim's Web browser access to the computer with a private IP address and returning the results to the attacker.

DNS rebinding uses the victim host as a proxy to transmit the content of the target server to the attacker. Because the local victim host is used to access the target server, it is difficult for the intranet firewall to provide effective protection. Xin Hongming et al. studied the influence of DNS rebinding on routers and the protection strategy [18]. Pandiaraja proposed a new technique by using a security proxy with a hash function. Rebinding attacks can be avoided by using this technique. It provides a secure environment for the DNS to communicate with other DNS. While the source DNS is receiving a response from any DNS it will authenticate all the receiving packets and then sends the data to the client [19].

2.2 API and JavaScript Security

Predecessors have also studied the security of JavaScript to a certain extent, Gupta, S. et al. [20] they proposed an injectionbased and clusterbased cleanup framework, JS-SAN (JavaScript SANitizer), to mitigate JavaScript code injection vulnerabilities. Because of the urgent need for the security and services of Internet of things devices, the problem of API security has attracted people's attention. Despite the development of security technology, hackers still seem to be able to find security vulnerabilities in software applications to make their attacks successful [21–23]. Lack of security and availability is one of the main factors that programmers often make mistakes in developing the application programming interface (API) for applications, which can easily lead to security vulnerabilities [24]. Wijayarathna et al. evaluated the availability of Java secure Sockets extension (JSSE) API. Their findings provide useful insights into how to design, develop, and improve TLS API [25]. Kai Mindermann et al. believe that many encryption software libraries are not easy to use, and that there are many ways to improve (encrypt) API, in such a way as to improve the robustness of existing API [26].

2.3 DNS Rebinding in IoT

DNS rebinding attacks are very harmful. Existing mechanisms cannot prevent all types of DNS rebinding attacks. Siva Brahmasani et al. proposed a twolevel solution [27], the first level is to use the IP address returned by the DNS response to reverse the comparison of the corresponding domain name with the original domain name, and the second level is to compare each IP address returned by the DNS response in the HTTP response content. The proposed solution can detect and prevent all subsequent DNS rebinding attacks. In the local Internet of things smart device environment, JavaScript security and API security are very important. In this environment, the Internet of things devices are vulnerable to DNS rebinding attacks even behind the firewall. Acar, G et al. described the attack scenario [28], which allows the victim to visit the attacker's Web site and communicates with an Internet of things device with an open HTTP server on the local network. However, they did not give a formal description of the attack model, and finally did not give a specific defense method. By using a Remote Code Execution vulnerability [29] or simple credentials, which are still common in many home devices, the attacker can gain control of the entire internal network. Based on the previous research on DNS rebinding attack, we reproduce DNS rebinding attack in simulated local Internet of things environment.

3   DNS Rebinding Attack Detection Model in Smart Home

This section describes the attack process and necessary parameters of the DNS rebinding attack. Through the analysis of the process and parameters, we abstract the attack detection model of the attack process.

3.1   DNS Rebinding Attack Process and Necessary Factors

This section describes the DNS rebinding attack process of smart home devices in a local Internet of things environment, as shown in the following Fig. 2. The devices include DNS server, Attacker web server and Target IoT device.

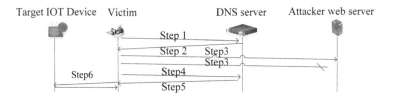

Fig. 2. DNS rebinding attack process

Step 1: The attacker controls a site to cause the victim to issue a DNS request.
Step 2: The attacker controlled DNS server responds to the victim's DNS request.
Step 3: JS fragments continue to make requests to malicious domain names.
Step 4: Do the DNS query again.
Step 5: Return the IP address of the target IoT device.
Step 6: The victim keeps making requests to the target device.

The victim's computer receives this malicious DNS response. The browser sends a POST request to API . At this point, the JavaScript code continuously sends POST or GET requests in JSON format to the target IoT to control the device.

3.2   Necessary Factors Analysis

In the course of this attack, there are three prerequisites: external malicious DNS server, internal springboard Web browser and internal IoT device address. After satisfying these three conditions, we can form a complete DNS rebinding attack in the smart home environment.

External Malicious DNS Server. The external malicious DNS server builds the attack model in the smart home device, and the malicious DNS server plays an essential role. It responds to the domain name query request and points the IP to the target device.

Internal Springboard Web Browser. Springboard Web browser is an important part of building attack model in smart home devices. In the process of DNS rebinding, it communicates with the external network as the initiator of the request to the external network.

Internal IoT Device Discovery. At present, there are many security problems of IoT devices in smart home environment. It easily contributes the device to be the target of DNS rebinding attack. In the constructed attack model, the discovery of the internal device IP address and the interface are the key issues [30], which are the core of detecting this attack.

3.3 DNS Rebinding Attack Detection Model

After satisfying the necessary conditions for DNS rebinding, we model the DNS rebinding for a single attack, as shown in the Fig. 3.

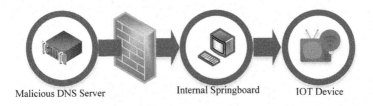

Malicious DNS Server   Internal Springboard   IOT Device

Fig. 3. DNS rebinding attack model

In the process of building the attack model, we found several key factors, including the DNS query response time (Affected by TTL), JS load frequency, and the response time of the victim page.

(1) The DNS query response time that between springboard and malicious DNS server affect the domain name of the internet and the request corresponding time of the IP returned by the malicious attack.

(2) JS load frequency between the springboard and the IoT device affects the discovery of the service interface of the IoT device. Malicious JS code loading frequency is too fast, increasing the pressure on local IoT device services, and easily blocking normal request links. The request frequency is too low, malicious JS code can not efficiently explore the effective port of IoT device service.

(3) The victim's page response time is related to the efficiency of DNS query, and the most intuitive feeling feedback to the attacker is that the loading speed of the page. The value of TTL and the JS loading frequency play an important role in DNS rebinding attacks.

4 Simulation Experiment

According to our attack detection model, the attack of DNS rebinding in the environment of the Internet of things is simulated.

4.1   Simulation Network Structure and Process

The environment built by the experiment is shown in the Fig. 4.

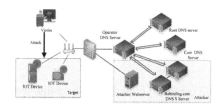

Fig. 4. Lab environment topology diagram

We used a total of eight machines to do simulation experiments. The information are shown in the Table 1.

Table 1. Resource of devices.

Device name	IP address	OS	Software	Service	Port
Victim	192.168.100.22	win7	Chrome	ssh	22 53
IoT Device	192.168.100.25	CentOS	Bind	ssh DNS	22 53
Attacker Webserver	172.17.10.11	CentOS	Apache	ssh apache	22 80
Rebinding.com DNS M Server	172.17.10.6	CentOS	Bind	ssh DNS	22 53
Rebinding.com DNS S Server	172.17.10.7	CentOS	Bind	ssh DNS	22 53
Operator DNS Server	172.17.10.8	CentOS	Bind	ssh DNS	22 53
Com DNS Server	172.17.10.5	CentOS	Bind	ssh DNS	22 53
Root DNS server	172.17.10.4	CentOS	Bind	ssh DNS	22 53

In order to better illustrate, we designed the experiment. The structure as shown in the Fig. 5.

Step 1: The victim accesses a malicious domain named www.rebinding.com built in Attacker Web Server. The ComDNS server and the RebindingDNS server to get the IP address (172.17.0.11) corresponding to the built service domain name on the webserver.

Step 2: The victim requests a web server with a IP address of 172.17.0.11 through the domain name, and the web server returns the result of the request, which contains a snippet of JavaScript that contains malicious behavior. The value of TTL in the Rebinding DNS server is set T seconds.

Step 3: The JS code snippet runs on the victim's machine and sends a request for JSON format data at intervals t seconds to the Attacker DNS server.

Step 4: The victim device fails the cache after T(the value of TTL) seconds and perform step 1 again. However, the IP address returned to the victim this

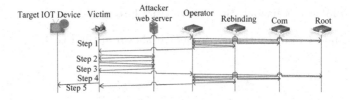

Fig. 5. Smart home DNS rebinding process

time is the address of the target IoT device in the same network segment as him, such as 192.168.100.25.

Step 5: JavaScript reloads the request www.rebinding.com/settemp interface, the victim makes repeated requests to the Internet of things device with IP address 192.168.100.25.

4.2   Analysis of Experimental Results

In the experiments, we analysis TTL value T and JavaScript loading interval t respectively. We also analyzed whether the IP address responds and the time it took for the victim's web page to load the response.

The respective values of the TTL and JavaScript variables are in seconds, and the result of a random look at whether IP binds successfully in the server is shown in the Table 2 (S is rebinding success, F is rebinding failure).

Table 2. Rebinding result

JS	TTL						
	1	15	30	60	900	1800	3600
1	S	S	S	S	F	S	S
15	S	F	S	S	F	F	S
30	S	S	F	F	S	S	S
60	S	F	F	F	F	F	F
900	S	F	F	F	F	F	F
1800	S	F	S	S	F	F	F
3600	S	F	F	S	F	F	F

To observe the response time of the victim's web page loaded, the values of the TTL and JS variables are set to the same values as in Table 2. We analyzed the load time of the victim web page as shown in the Fig. 6.

The Z-axis in the three-dimensional coordinate system of the figure is the time of the page response. Combining the results of Table 2 and Fig. 6, we can draw a conclusion that the smaller the TTL, the faster the JavaScript loading frequency, the higher the success rate of DNS rebinding attacks, and the slower the response speed of the page.

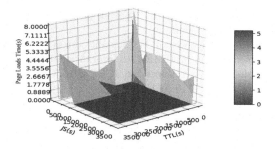

Fig. 6. Result of web page loads time

4.3 Precautionary Suggestions

Some scholars have proposed an automatic model to analyze attack behavior through mixed analysis of flow based and graph based network traffic behavior [31]. In order to protect the privacy and security of users in the vehicle network of the Internet of things, some scholars have proposed a solution based on block chain [32].

In this paper, the following suggestions can be given to detect DNS rebinding attacks in the Internet of things environment.

(1) Excluding the network speed, when the user uses a similar browser page, whether the page access speed is significantly reduced.

(2) The code on the local Internet of things device is detected whether there are frequent requests for services under a domain name by JavaScript fragments.

(3) Detect the service interface provided by the local Internet of things sensitive equipment, such as thermostat, camera and so on, whether there is abnormal traffic. Whether the device has a normal request that cannot respond.

5   Conclusion

In this paper, we found that local Internet of things devices are more vulnerable to DNS rebinding attacks because of their weak level of protection. We reproduce this kind of attack through the simulation experiment. We also quantitatively analyze the TTL value of DNS rebinding attack and the loading frequency of client JavaScript. Finally, it is found that the TTL value and the loading frequency of JS are the key factors of this attack. We propose a DNS rebinding attack detection model in smart home environment, including internal springboard, malicious DNS server and target Internet of things devices. Finally, We have put forward some preventive suggestions. The following work will focus on the defense method of multi-device attack threat model and the edge security in the local network.

References

1. Panwar, N., Sharma, S., Mehrotra, S., Krzywiecki, L., Venkatasubramanian, N.: Smart home survey on security and privacy. CoRR, abs/1904.05476 (2019)

2. Tong, X., Fang, B., He, Y., Zhang, Y.: Analysis on the development of internet of things smart home. Mobile Commun

3. Chirila, S., Lemnaru, C., Dînsoreanu, M.: Semantic-based IoT device discovery and recommendation mechanism. In: IEEE 12th International Conference on Intelligent Computer Communication and Processing, ICCP 2016, Cluj-Napoca, Romania, 8–10 September 2016, pp. 111–116. IEEE (2016)

4. Castro, R.R., López, J., Gritzalis, S.: Evolution and trends in IoT security. IEEE Comput. **51**(7), 16–25 (2018)

5. Wang, W., Wang, X., Feng, D., Liu, J., Han, Z., Zhang, X.: Exploring permission-induced risk in android applications for malicious application detection. IEEE Trans. Inf. Foren. Secur. **9**(11), 1869–1882 (2014)

6. Xu, T., Wendt, J.B., Potkonjak, M.: Security of IoT systems: design challenges and opportunities. In: Chang, Y.-W. (ed.) The IEEE/ACM International Conference on Computer-Aided Design, ICCAD 2014, San Jose, CA, USA, 3–6 November 2014, pp. 417–423. IEEE (2014)

7. McReynolds, E., Hubbard, S., Lau, T., Saraf, A., Cakmak, M., Roesner, F.: Toys that listen: a study of parents, children, and internet-connected toys. In: Mark, G., et al. (eds.) Proceedings of the 2017 CHI Conference on Human Factors in Computing Systems, Denver, CO, USA, 06–11 May 2017, pp. 5197–5207. ACM (2017)

8. Wikipedia. 2016 dyn cyberattack (2016). https://en.wikipedia.org/wiki/2016_Dyn_cyberattack

9. Armis. DNS rebinding exposes half a billion IoT devices (2018). https://armis.com/dns-rebinding-exposes-half-a-billion-iot-devices-in-the-enterprise/

10. Johns, M., Lekies, S., Stock, B.: Eradicating DNS rebinding with the extended same-origin policy. In: King, S.T. (ed.) Proceedings of the 22th USENIX Security Symposium, Washington, DC, USA, 14–16 August 2013, pp. 621–636. USENIX Association (2013)

11. Karlof, C., Shankar, U., Tygar, J.D., Wagner, D.A.: Dynamic pharming attacks and locked same-origin policies for web browsers. In: Ning, P., di Vimercati, S.D.C., Syverson, P.F. (eds.) Proceedings of the 2007 ACM Conference on Computer and Communications Security, CCS 2007, Alexandria, Virginia, USA, 28–31 October 2007, pp. 58–71. ACM (2007)

12. NPM. Whonow dns server. https://www.npmjs.com/package/whonow

13. Yi, W., Janne, T., Mikael, L.: An analytical model for DNS performance with TTL value 0 in mobile internet. In: Ning, P., di Vimercati, S.D.C., Syverson, P.F. (eds.) TENCON 2006 IEEE Region 10 Conference, pp. 1–4. IEEE (2006)

14. Cohen, E., Kaplan, H.: Proactive caching of DNS records: addressing a performance bottleneck. Comput. Netw. **41**(6), 707–726 (2003)

15. Jackson, C., Barth, A., Bortz, A., Shao, W., Boneh, D.: Protecting browsers from DNS rebinding attacks. ACM Trans. Web **3**(1), 2:1–2:26 (2009)

16. Princeton University. DNS attack scenario. http://sip.cs.princeton.edu/

17. Dean, D., Felten, E.W., Wallach, D.S.: Java security: from hotjava to netscape and beyond. In: 1996 IEEE Symposium on Security and Privacy, 6–8 May 1996, Oakland, CA, USA, pp. 190–200. IEEE Computer Society (1996)

18. Xin, H., Wang, Y., Zhao, R.: Research on the influence of DNS rebinding on router and its protection strategy. Chengdu Inst. Inf. Eng. **29**(6) (2014)

19. Pandiaraja, P., Parasuraman, S.: Applying secure authentication scheme to protect dns from rebinding attack using proxy. In: 2015 International Conference on Circuits, Power and Computing Technologies [ICCPCT-2015], pp. 1–6. IEEE (2015)

20. Gupta, S., Gupta, B.B.: JS-SAN: defense mechanism for html5-based web applications against javascript code injection vulnerabilities. Secur. Commun. Netw. **9**(11), 1477–1495 (2016)
21. Fahl, S., Harbach, M., Muders, T., Smith, M., Baumgärtner, L., Freisleben, B.: Why eve and mallory love android: an analysis of android SSL (in)security. In: Yu, T., Danezis, G., Gligor, V.D. (eds.) The ACM Conference on Computer and Communications Security, CCS 2012, Raleigh, NC, USA, 16–18 October 2012, pp. 50–61. ACM (2012)
22. Fahl, S., Harbach, M., Perl, H., Koetter, M., Smith, M.: Rethinking SSL development in an appified world. In: Sadeghi, A.-R., Gligor, V.D., Yung, M. (eds.) 2013 ACM SIGSAC Conference on Computer and Communications Security, CCS 2013, Berlin, Germany, 4–8 November 2013, pp. 49–60. ACM (2013)
23. Georgiev, M., Iyengar, S., Jana, S., Anubhai, R., Boneh, D., Shmatikov, V.: The most dangerous code in the world: validating SSL certificates in non-browser software. In: Yu, T., Danezis, G., Gligor, V.D. (eds.) The ACM Conference on Computer and Communications Security, CCS 2012, Raleigh, NC, USA, 16–18 October 2012, pp. 38–49. ACM (2012)
24. Wurster, G., van Oorschot, P.C.: The developer is the enemy. In: Bishop, M., Probst, C.W., Keromytis, A.D., Somayaji, A. (eds.) Proceedings of the 2008 Workshop on New Security Paradigms, Lake Tahoe, CA, USA, 22–25 September 2008, pp. 89–97. ACM (2008)
25. Wijayarathna, C., Arachchilage, N.A.G.: Why Johnny can't develop a secure application? A usability analysis of java secure socket extension API. Comput. Secur. **80**, 54–73 (2019)
26. Mindermann, K., Wagner, S.: Usability and security effects of code examples on crypto apis. In: McLaughlin, K., et al. (eds.) 16th Annual Conference on Privacy, Security and Trust, PST 2018, Belfast, Northern Ireland, Uk, 28–30 August 2018, pp. 1–2. IEEE Computer Society (2018)
27. Brahmasani, S., Sivasankar, E.: Two level verification for detection of DNS rebinding attacks. Int. J. Syst. Assur. Eng. Manag. **4**(2), 138–145 (2013)
28. Acar, G., Huang, D.Y., Li, F., Narayanan, A., Feamster, N.: Web-based attacks to discover and control local iot devices. In: Proceedings of the 2018 Workshop on IoT Security and Privacy, IoT S&P@SIGCOMM 2018, Budapest, Hungary, 20 August 2018, pp. 29–35. ACM (2018)
29. MSRC: Prevent a worm by updating remote desktop services (cve-2019-0708). https://msrc-blog.microsoft.com/2019/05/14/prevent-a-worm-by-updating-remote-desktop-services-cve-2019-0708/
30. Feng, X., Li, Q., Wang, H., Sun, L.: Acquisitional rule-based engine for discovering internet-of-thing devices. In: 27th USENIX Security Symposium USENIX Security 18), pp. 327–341 (2018)
31. Wang, W., Shang, Y., He, Y., Li, Y., Liu, J.: Botmark: automated botnet detection with hybrid analysis of flow-based and graph-based traffic behaviors. Inf. Sci. **511**, 284–296 (2020)
32. Li, L., et al.: Creditcoin: a privacy-preserving blockchain-based incentive announcement network for communications of smart vehicles. IEEE Trans. Intell. Transp. Syst. **19**(7), 2204–2220 (2018)

Low-Speed Injection Attack Detection on CAN Bus

Chundong Wang[1,2], Chuang Li[1,2(✉)] [ID], Tongle An[1,2], and Xiaochun Cheng[3]

[1] Key Laboratory of Computer Vision and System, Ministry of Education,
Tianjin University of Technology, Tianjin 300384, China
michael3769@163.com, lyc5117@hotmail.com, luoye_atl@163.com
[2] Tianjin Key Laboratory of Intelligence Computing and Novel Software Technology,
Ministry of Education, Tianjin University of Technology, Tianjin 300384, China
[3] Department of Computer Science, Middlesex University, London NW4 4BT, UK
Xiaochun.cheng@gmail.com

Abstract. The car CAN (Controller Area Network) bus message injection attacks seriously affects various functions of the safety of cars, life and property. However, low-speed injection attack is detection inconspicuous in a majority of existing researches. This paper proposes a self-contained low-speed injection attacks detection system including whole detection process and principle. This paper first analyzes the feasibility of low-speed injection attacks; then we propose to use LOF (Local Outlier Factor) to detect the injection attack, and compare with the previous detection algorithms. Experimental results show that our algorithm has obvious advantages in detection rate over the previous algorithms.

Keywords: Anomaly detection · Controller Area Network · Local Outlier Factor · Periodic error · Data mining

1 Introduction

With the rapid development of intelligent networked vehicles, the safety of automobiles has gradually attracted researchers' attention, especially the safety inside the vehicles [1–6]. When designing the vehicle's internal bus, the researchers being to consider only partial security. However, the threats from external network access have caused serious damage to IOV security. Among them, the most concerned point of the researchers is the intrusion detection of the car bus.

The key equipment (e.g. Brake systems, Engine) in the car are connected by CAN (Controller Area Network) bus. The safety detections inside cars have

Supported by NSFC: The United Foundation of General Technology and Fundamental Research (No. U1536122), the General Project of Tianjin Municipal Science and Technology Commission under Grant (No. 15JCYBJC15600), and the Major Project of Tianjin Municipal Science and Technology Commission under Grant (No. 15ZXDSGX00030).

G. Xu et al. (Eds.): FCS 2020, CCIS 1286, pp. 30–43, 2020.
https://doi.org/10.1007/978-981-15-9739-8_3

Table 1. Data frame format of CAN 2.0 Bs.

SOF	ID	Control	Data	CRC	ACK	EOF
1 bit	11 bits	6 bits	0–64 bits	16 bits	1 bit	1 bit

always focused on the intrusion detection of CAN bus by analyzing physical characteristics or message format of CAN bus (Table 1). Cho et al. [7] proposed a clock-based anomaly Intrusion Detection System (IDS), which measures and uses the time interval for periodically transmitting information as the fingerprint of the ECU (Electronic Control Unit). The resulting fingerprint is constructed by using a Recursive Least Squares (RLS) algorithm to construct the ECU clock behavior. Based on this standard, CIDS uses Cumulative sum (CUSUM) to detect and identify abnormal changes, and its core is still clock-based. Similar to [8] and [9], time intervals are used as features to detect anomalies.

Existing papers based on traffic anomaly detection, including intrusion detection based on bus features and intrusion detection based on machine learning [10–16], can detect high frequency or large data insertion injection attacks, and rarely detect injection data. But this type of attack can also threaten vehicle safety. At this time, the abnormal data are small, and the abnormality detection based on the traffic is generally not detected. In addition, most existing works assume that the period of the message is fixed and used as a fingerprint, but existing research does not consider the situation in which the message period changes due to actual conditions.

In this paper, considering the periodic variation, the injection attacks with less data volume is detected, and finally a good detection effect is achieved. So, we have two contribution:

1) This paper analyzes the feasibility and harm of low-speed injection attacks;
2) This paper proposes a new detection method: it can detect low-speed injection attacks.

The main contents of this paper are as follows. In Sect. 2, we introduce and analyzes different detection methods for injection attacks. In Sect. 3, The article analyzes the possibility of low-speed injection attacks. In Sect. 4, The article proposes a detection model and introduces the detection process. In Sect. 5, We introduce the detection principle for low-speed injection attacks. Further, we use experiments to verify the feasibility of the detection algorithm, conduct comparative experiments and analyze in Sect. 6. Finally, we summarize the article in Sect. 7.

2 Related Work

Recently, machine learning technology has become more and more mature, and many researchers have gradually applied related algorithms to bus intrusion detection. For example, the Kang et al. [15] uses Deep Neural Networks (DNN) to detect intrusion behavior, among which DNN parameters. It is trained by probability-based feature vectors extracted from the in-vehicle network grouping. Literature [16] uses information entropy as a feature structure of the Gradient Lifting Decision Tree (GBDT), and realizes the detection of abnormal messages. Markovitz et al. [17] proposes a semantic perceptual anomaly detection model for CAN bus traffic. In the learning phase, the field is characterized according to the classifier, and the model is built according to the field type. The model can detect the abnormal traffic on the CAN bus very well. The traffic on the port is abnormal. Kang et al. [18] use the voltage of the ECU (Electronic Control Unit) as fingerprint information, which not only achieves a high intrusion detection rate, but also realizes identification of the ECU.

Marchetti et al. [19] propose an anomaly detection algorithm based on CAN bus message ID sequence, which can identify attacks based on malicious injection. However, in the face of one or several malicious message injections, the detection rate depends on the probability distribution. In short, this type of attack has a limited effect. For example, as described in the article, when the insertion rate is low, the anomaly detection rate of the four IDs is relatively low. Marchetti et al. [20] uses the concept of entropy in information theory to calculate the information entropy of the message, and this theory can determine whether the message is forged to achieve the purpose of detecting anomalies. However, this detection method aims at all message injection attacks and only works under high-rate attacks; while the low-speed injection attack with the same ID is effective, this method requires several exception detectors to be executed in parallel (one for each ID). However, the overhead of resource consumption is quite heavy.

3   The Feasibility Analysis of Low-Speed Injection Attacks

3.1   CAN Message

In order to distinguish the independence and uniqueness of each message on the CAN bus, the ID of the message must be unique on a bus; later, the ID of the message is determined by the priority of the message, which also indicates the priority of the message on the bus.

When a message is sent on the CAN, the level on the bus is read and compared to the data that it wants to send when each message sends an ID portion. This is called bus arbitration. If node A sends a recessive bit (usually 1) and reads a dominant bit (usually 0), then A will realize that a message with a higher priority than itself is being sent on the bus, losing its right to send, waiting to send it the next time.

For the bus-based message arbitration mechanism, when message A and message B collide (simultaneous transmission), there will be two cases: A wins or B wins. Considering the presence of an attacker, when malicious message A and normal message B are simultaneously sent, there are generally three cases:

1) A has a high priority, wins arbitration, and B message is sent the next time. That is, message A is injected successfully, and message B is delayed transmission, which does not affect normal message transmission.
2) B has a high priority and wins arbitration. Message injection fails.
3) The IDs of A and B are the same, and they are sent at the same time. An error occurs in the data field, and an increment of the error counter occurs [21].

3.2 Principle of Attack

If an attacker conducts low-speed injection attacks, there are generally two purposes:

(1) Random message injection, to destroy normal communication. First, it listens, collects the data sent on the CAN bus, and then randomly performs message injection. In order to avoid most of the current detection methods, low-frequency, irregular message injection is required. It is called the random injection attack in this article.
(2) In order to control the vehicle, targeted injection of information is carried out. The attacker listens to the target message on the bus and calculates the message period. In the next step, the attacker has two attack methods according to the purpose of the attack:

A. The message is sent on time according to the calculated period. In order to cause the malicious message to collide with the normal message, the message is invalidated, and eventually the normal communication is destroyed.

B. The attacker calculates the time at which the next message is sent, avoiding the point in time for message insertion. The purpose is to stagger the malicious message and the normal message, to make the malicious message take effect, and finally disrupt the normal communication, so that the vehicle performs unexpected actions. For example, send a command to open the door during high-speed driving. This behavior can implement bus-off attack [11].

The success rate of these two attack methods depends on the attacker's understanding of the communication process. In order to achieve the second attack purpose, the attacker needs to have bigger computing power and deeper understanding of the communication process than the first one. With the improvement of hardware (ECU) and the development of the industry, these are not problems. So, the impact of low-speed injection attacks on vehicles has become possible. This paper is useful for the detection of these two kinds of aggression.

4 Detection Model

The detailed flow of data from sending to detection is displayed in the Fig. 1.

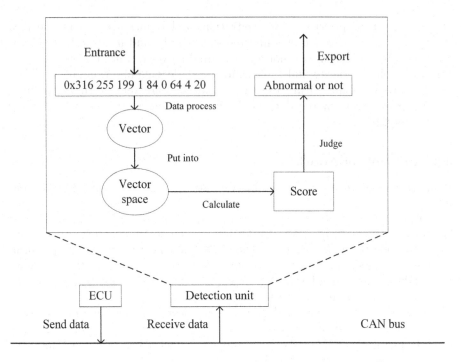

Fig. 1. Detection process.

4.1 Data Process

The data used in this article are all standard data sets [22]. Once the data is available, the data is processed first, so that all data are normalized and formatted. The format of the data collected at the beginning is as follows:

0x123:8:fec05dc05d0708b8

For ease of calculation and analysis, we convert the data to a decimal number:

291:254,192,93,192,93,7,8,184

Among them, the third part of the data field has a total of 64 bits, which is divided into 8 parts, each part is 8 bits, and then converted into a decimal number.

According to the previous section, the CAN bus data in the car can be divided into two parts: The first part the ID number, there are many ECUs on the bus, generally only one ID number can be issued by an ECU, so the ID number can be used as a description dimension of the data point; The second part is the data field, which is the specific content of the message. In this paper, it is divided into eight parts, which are eight other dimensions of the data point. In addition, since the data on the bus is generally sent periodically, the cycle can also be an important dimension. In this paper, the current ID is predicted, and the probability that the ID appears at this time is taken as a reference dimension.

So far, we have obtained data descriptions for 10 dimensions. They are: period T, identifier I and data fields D_1, D_2, D_3, D_4, D_5, D_6, D_7 and D_8.

4.2   Low-Speed Injection Attacks Detection

On the bus, the data transmission is exclusive. The detection unit only needs to read the detection abnormality frame by frame, and the detection result can be obtained before the complete data transmission ends. The detection principle is described in detail later.

5   Detection Principle

The normal communication process on the bus is shown in the Fig. 2.

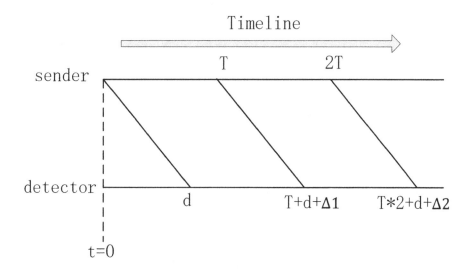

Fig. 2. Message simulation.

In the Fig. 2, $t = 0$ is the first data time point sent by the sender, T is the transmission period, and the d that is the time a message is uploaded from the ECU to the bus is the reception delay, depending on the length of the packet that is generally fixed. When the ECU on the bus sends a message, due to the influence of the transmission environment-such as the transmission speed of the bus and the performance of the ECU, the time when the receiver receives the data and the theoretical time always have a certain discrepancy, which is Δ in the above figure. Although Δ_1 and Δ_2 are not equal in the figure, due to hardware factors, the values of the two variables will always be in a small range.

The attacker is unable to inject data with an abnormal ID number, they will consider injecting data of the same ID for destruction and interference. The general attack process is as follows:

a) The attacker listens and periodically detects the data of an ID number on the bus.
b) Calculate the sending period of the message
c) Calculate the time you want to send based on the time of the last message at the appropriate time
d) Inject packet on time

When an attacker injects a packet in this way, there are two situations: Malicious messages and normal messages are misaligned due to random perturbations in the periodicity of the message; malicious messages and normal messages fail to be sent due to the message collision mechanism of the CAN bus.

A message is misplaced, the following occurs in the Fig. 3.

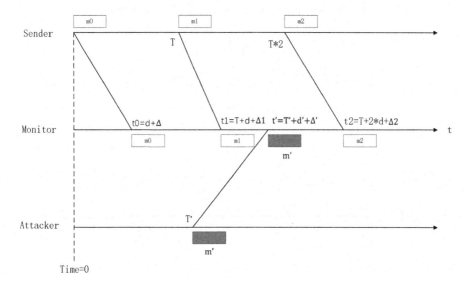

Fig. 3. Message misplacement.

The sender of the normal message has a transmission period of T, the delay of the message that the listener receives the ID is d, and the listener will randomly perturb Δ when it receives each message. When $T = 0$, the attacker has calculated the transmission period T' of the message m according to the previous message, and then sends an attack message at the time T'. The propagation delay of the attacker sending the message is d', and the random disturbance is Δ'. At this point, the listener receives four messages: m_0, m_1, m', m_2, at times t_0, t_1, t', t_2, respectively. For the listener, four messages are sent.

In this way, when the listener detects the message period of this ID, the calculation cycle will be different for the messages m_1 and m': the message m' is close to m_1, so the calculated period is very short; When calculating the period of the message m_2, since the time after the occurrence of m is later, the obtained value will be different from the normal period, that is, it will be smaller. This difference is more pronounced if the period of each message is more stable.

When two messages collide, the following happens in the Fig. 4.

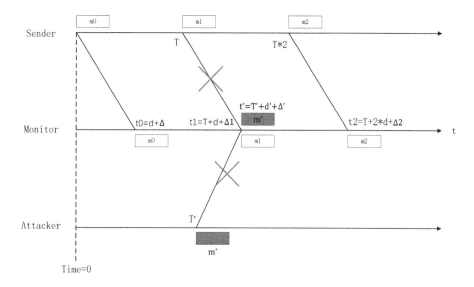

Fig. 4. Message collision.

As shown in the Fig. 4, when messages m_1 and m' collide, both messages fail to be sent. The listener only receives two messages at times t_0 and t_2.

Thus, when the listener detects the message period of the ID, the message m_1 collides with the malicious message m', the m_1 transmission fails, and the existence of m_1 is not detected. The calculated period of m_2 will be twice the normal period.

According to the above detection principle, we use the LOF (Local Outlier Factor) algorithm [23] in the outlier detection algorithm to detect periodic packets. When low-speed injection attacks occur, the cycle of the message has changed, the location of the message in the data space is farther from the normal data points, and the LOF algorithm can find these anomalies accurately and quickly.

6   Experimental Results and Analysis

6.1   Abnormal Insertion

In order to perform anomaly detection experiments, we use two different types of low-speed injection attacks:

a) Random injection attack: Random insert data.
b) Replay attack: The attacker listens for messages on the bus and then sends the packet according to the detected ID period

All the data in this paper comes from the CAN bus when the vehicle is driving normally.

6.2   Abnormal Detection

Using the 20,000 data in the static state as a template, use the LOF algorithm to get the Fig. 5.

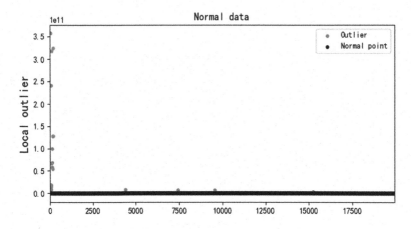

Fig. 5. Normal data outliers.

We have intercepted a piece of data. Each ID number has a small period when it first appears. In this experiment, it is treated as 0, which must be an outlier, so the outliers starting from the figure can be omitted. There are three outliers with small outliers in the middle of the graph, which can be regarded as normal systematic errors with an error rate of 0.015%.

a) randomly extract and insert from the vehicle speed data

We extract 10 and 100 strips from the vehicle speed data and insert them separately. After running the LOF algorithm, we get the Fig. 6.

There are more outliers in the two graphs. The abnormal rate on the top is about 0.045%, which is 3 times the normal. The abnormal rate on the below is 0.35%, which is 23 times the normal conditions. Therefore, when randomly inserting less data, it is easy to detect whether the data on the bus is abnormal by using the LOF algorithm.

b) perform cycle detection and insert the message

In this experiment, we extract the data of the same ID number in the collected data and then format it. In addition, simulate an attack node for message insertion.

When a malicious message is inserted, the message is misplaced. The LOF algorithm results are in the Fig. 7.

In the Fig. 7, there are two abnormal points, and the above abnormal point ID and the following abnormal point ID are just approaching, which is consistent with our expectation.

When a malicious message is inserted, no misalignment occurs, that is, two messages collide, and the LOF algorithm results are in the Fig. 8.

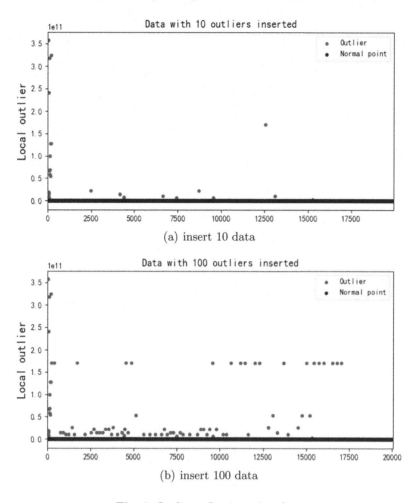

Fig. 6. Outliers after inserting data

In the Fig. 8, only one abnormal point appears, which is also in line with our expectations.

c) brief summary

During the detection of a specific ID message injection, if the normal message and the malicious message do not collide, then two of the messages will become outliers in the LOF algorithm. The local outlier factor of the first point is relatively large, and the second one is relatively small. The value of the second local outlier is largely dependent on the error value (disturbance value) of this message as it travels over the bus. The smaller the error value, the smaller the second local outlier factor. When the error value is small, the probability that a normal message collides with a malicious message is greater. Only when the error value is within a certain range can an attacker escape the detection of the

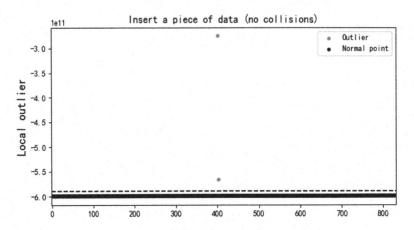

Fig. 7. Outliers after a message misplacement.

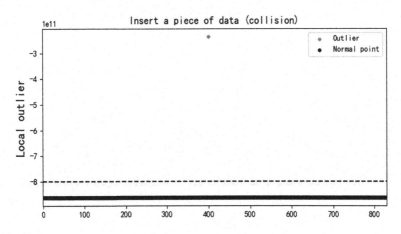

Fig. 8. Outliers after a message collision.

LOF algorithm. But the attacker does not know the error value of a certain message, so it is hard to evade detection.

6.3   Contrast Experiment

In this paper, algorithm based on sequence (AS) [19], information entropy algorithm (IEA) [20] and LOF algorithm are used for comparative experiments. The sequence-based algorithm is to create a two-dimensional array associated with ID Numbers. If adjacent messages appear in normal messages, fill in 1 at the corresponding position in the array. During the detection process, it is judged whether the position of the serial number in the matrix is 1 or not. For example, after serial number A is serial number B., write 1 in column A and row B of the array. Detection based on information entropy is calculating the information entropy of packet within a certain time window.

There are three attack windows in this article: 0.1s, 0.5s and 1s. The selection of the time window has no effect on the detection results of AS and LOF. In this paper, only the detection results with attack window of 1s are displayed for two algorithms. In the experiment, there are seven different levels of data volume for inserting data: 0.1%, 1%, 3%, 5%, 8%, 10% and 20%. The detection results of the three algorithms are shown in Table 2 and Table 3.

Table 2. Random injection attack.

		0.1%	1%	3%	5%	8%	10%	20%
AS	1s	99.2	99	99	99.1	99.1	99	99.1
IEA	1s	100	100	100	100	100	100	100
	0.5s	0	100	100	100	100	100	100
	0.1s	NULL	0	0	0	100	100	100
LOF	1s	90.1	86.7	83.2	80.1	79	78.8	77

Annotate: The number unit in the table is %.

Table 3. Replay attack.

		0.1%	1%	3%	5%	8%	10%	20%
AS	1s	50	51.4	51.6	51.8	51.9	51.9	52
IEA	1s	0	0	0	100	100	100	100
	0.5s	0	0	0	0	100	100	100
	0.1s	NULL	0	0	0	0	0	0
LOF	1s	90.1	86.7	83.2	80.1	79	78.8	77

Annotate: The number unit in the table is %.

As can be seen from Table 2, the detection of the random injection attacks by the LOF algorithm is worse than the other two algorithms. However, as can be seen from Table 3, the LOF algorithm is significantly better than the AS. Compared with the IEA, the LOF algorithm is better when the insertion data is below 3%. When it is higher than 3%, the detection effect of the IEA depends on the detection window. The detection effect of the LOF algorithm is independent of the detection window, so it is better than the IEA.

In general, when the inserted data is less than 20%, the LOF algorithm is superior to the other two algorithms in detecting the replay attack, and is worse than the other two algorithms in detecting the random injection attacks. The data inserted by the random injection attacks have a greater impact on the entire communication process, calculating information entropy and contrasting two-dimensional array are more sensitive to random injection attacks, so the two methods have better detection effects on random injection attacks. The LOF algorithm detection does not depend on the attack behavior, which is only related to the amount of data inserted, so the detection effect of the two attacks is basically the same.

The purpose of the two attack methods is different. The random injection attack is for the communication system, and the replay attack is to achieve certain functions. Detection of replay attacks is more important.

7   Conclusions

This paper describes the low-speed injection attacks from the uniqueness of each state message of the vehicle, and introduces the purpose and principle of the two related attacks: the random injection attack and the replay attack. The density-based outlier detection algorithm LOF algorithm in data mining is used to detect these two attacks. For the replay attack in low-speed insertion attacks, a good detection result is finally obtained.

With the development of attack technology, the attacker's means are more sophisticated. Message anomalies are not only reflected in traffic, but data content can also be forged by attackers. In order to face endless attacks, it is not enough to detect anomalies only from the aspect of traffic. It is also necessary to detect various attacks from the data content. This is our next research goal.

References

1. Malik, K.R., Ahmad, M., Khalid, S., Ahmad, H., Jabbar, S.: Image and command hybrid model for vehicle control using Internet of Vehicles. Trans. Emerg. Telecommun. Technol. **31**(5), e3774 (2020)
2. Sajjad, M., et al.: CNN-based anti-spoofing two-tier multi-factor authentication system. Pattern Recogn. Lett. **126**, 123–131 (2019)
3. Chen, C., Liu, X., Qiu, T., Sangaiah, A.K.: A short-term traffic prediction model in the vehicular cyber-physical systems. Future Gener. Comput. Syst. **105**, 894–903 (2020)
4. Aloqaily, M., Otoum, S., Al Ridhawi, I., Jararweh, Y.: An intrusion detection system for connected vehicles in smart cities. Ad Hoc Netw. **90**, 101842 (2019)
5. Al Ridhawi, I., Otoum, S., Aloqaily, M., Jararweh, Y., Baker, T.: Providing secure and reliable communication for next generation networks in smart cities. Sustain. Cities Soc. **56**, 102080 (2020)
6. Lv, Z., Mazurczyk, W., Wendzel, S., Song, H.: Recent advances in cyber-physical security in industrial environments. IEEE Trans. Ind. Inf. **15**(12), 6468–6471 (2019)
7. Shin, K.G., Cho, K.T.: Fingerprinting electronic control units for vehicle intrusion detection. In: 25th USENIX Security Symposium (USENIX Security 16), Austin, TX, USA (2019)
8. Song, H.M., Kim, H.R., Kim, H.K.: Intrusion detection system based on the analysis of time intervals of CAN messages for in-vehicle network. In: 2016 International Conference on Information Networking (ICOIN), pp. 63–68. IEEE, Kota Kinabalu (2016)

9. Gmiden, M., Gmiden, M.H., Trabelsi, H.: An intrusion detection method for securing in-vehicle CAN bus. In: 17th International Conference on Sciences and Techniques of Automatic Control and Computer Engineering (STA), pp. 176–180. IEEE, Sousse (2016)
10. Taylor, A., Sylvain L., Nathalie J.: Anomaly detection in automobile control network data with long short-term memory networks. In: 2016 IEEE International Conference on Data Science and Advanced Analytics (DSAA), pp. 130–139. IEEE, Montreal (2016)
11. Ullah, F., Naeem, H., Jabbar, S., Khalid, S., Mostarda, L.: Cyber security threats detection in internet of things using deep learning approach. IEEE Access **7**, 124379–124389 (2019)
12. Amrollahi, M., Hadayeghparast, S., Karimipour, H., Derakhshan, F., Srivastava, G.: Enhancing network security via machine learning: opportunities and challenges. In: Choo, K.-K.R., Dehghantanha, A. (eds.) Handbook of Big Data Privacy, pp. 165–189. Springer, Cham (2020). https://doi.org/10.1007/978-3-030-38557-6_8
13. Mohammadi Rouzbahani, H., Karimipour, H., Rahimnejad, A., Dehghantanha, A., Srivastava, G.: Anomaly detection in cyber-physical systems using machine learning. In: Choo, K.-K.R., Dehghantanha, A. (eds.) Handbook of Big Data Privacy, pp. 219–235. Springer, Cham (2020). https://doi.org/10.1007/978-3-030-38557-6_10
14. Skowron, M., Artur, J., Wojciech, M.: Traffic fingerprinting attacks on internet of things using machine learning. IEEE Access **7**, 20386–20400 (2020)
15. Min-Joo, K., Je-Won, K., Tieqiao, T.: Intrusion detection system using deep neural network for in-vehicle network security. PLoS ONE **11**(6), e0155781 (2016)
16. Tian, D., et al.: An intrusion detection system based on machine learning for CAN-bus. In: Chen, Y., Duong, T.Q. (eds.) INISCOM 2017. LNICST, vol. 221, pp. 285–294. Springer, Cham (2018). https://doi.org/10.1007/978-3-319-74176-5_25
17. Markovitz, M., Avishai, W.: Field classification, modeling and anomaly detection in unknown CAN bus networks. Veh. Commun. **9**, 43–52 (2017)
18. Cho, K.T., Kang, G.S.: Viden: attacker identification on in-vehicle networks. In: Proceedings of the 2017 ACM SIGSAC Conference on Computer and Communications Security, pp. 815–828. ACM, Dallas (2017)
19. Marchetti, M., Dario S.: Anomaly detection of CAN bus messages through analysis of ID sequences. In: 2017 IEEE Intelligent Vehicles Symposium (IV), pp. 1577–1583. IEEE, Los Angeles (2017)
20. Marchetti, M., Stabili, D., Guido, A., Colajanni, M.: Evaluation of anomaly detection for in-vehicle networks through information-theoretic algorithms. In: 2016 IEEE 2nd International Forum on Research and Technologies for Society and Industry Leveraging a better tomorrow (RTSI), pp. 1–6. IEEE, Bologna (2016)
21. Cho, K.T., Kang G.S.: Error handling of in-vehicle networks makes them vulnerable. In: Proceedings of the 2016 ACM SIGSAC Conference on Computer and Communications Security, pp. 1044–1055. ACM, Vienna (2016)
22. TU-CRRC. http://tucrrc.utulsa.edu/Publications.html. Accessed 3 Apr 2019
23. Breunig, M.M., Kriegel, H.P., Ng, R., Sander, J.: LOF: identifying density-based local outliers. In: Proceedings of the 2000 ACM SIGMOD International Conference on Management of Data, pp. 93–104. ACM, Dallas (2000)

User Similarity-Aware Data Deduplication Scheme for IoT Applications

Yuan Gao[1,2], Hequn Xian[1,2(✉)] (iD), and Yan Teng[1]

[1] Qingdao University, Qingdao 266071, China
xianhq@qdu.edu.cn
[2] State Key Laboratory of Information Security, Institute of Information Engineering,
Chinese Academy of Sciences, Beijing 100093, China

Abstract. As an important technology in cloud storage, deduplication is widely used to reserve network bandwidth and storage resources. While deduplication brings us convenience, there are also security risks that we have to confront. If internal data from organizations are treated in the same way of ordinary data, deduplication may lead to unexpected data leakage and other issues. A user similarity-aware data deduplication algorithm is proposed which can properly handle internal data uploaded by group users. This scheme can recognize the situation that uploaders with similar attributes hold the same data in the process of deduplication. The goal of our scheme is to ensure that the participation of group users will not change the current popularity of uploaded data. In the aspect of attribute distance calculation, we divide attribute types and introduce specific attribute distance calculation methods for each type. We determine user category by comparing the similarities of their attributes. Finally, the counting method of uploaded data is adjusted adaptively according to the current popularity status of data and user categories. This scheme can avoid potential internal data leakage caused by deduplication. Through experiment evaluation, we show that our scheme is efficient, and is of great scalability and practicability.

Keywords: Deduplication · Attribute similarity · Attribute distance calculation

1 Introduction

With the advent of the information age, everyone is linked to a large amount of data. It takes a lot of time and resources for people to store and maintain these data. As a mainstream and very popular storage technology, cloud storage solves these problems well. Statistics show that up to 60% of the data in cloud storage are redundant [1]. It means that a large amount of cloud storage space and storage resources are occupied by redundant data. This greatly increases the Cloud Service Provider (CSP) storage and maintenance costs. In order to reduce operating costs, to reserve storage space and to improve the performance, some CSP may delete data that users rarely access without their knowledge [2, 3]. In fact, the main reason for the existence of redundant data in cloud storage is that identical data are repeatedly uploaded by different users. Therefore, a large number of deduplication schemes have been proposed [4–6].

© Springer Nature Singapore Pte Ltd. 2020
G. Xu et al. (Eds.): FCS 2020, CCIS 1286, pp. 44–52, 2020.
https://doi.org/10.1007/978-981-15-9739-8_4

Please note that the first paragraph of a section or subsection is not indented. The first paragraphs that follows a table, figure, equation etc. does not have an indent, either.

According to different purposes and emphases of deduplication, existing deduplication schemes are mainly divided into the following categories: online and offline, file-level and block-level, user-aware and user-agnostic [7]. Different deduplication techniques have different computational processing methods and they have their respective advantages and disadvantages. However, all of the deduplication schemes share a common purpose, which is to eliminate duplicate data distributed in storage system and optimize the utilization of storage space. Besides storage efficiency, the use of deduplication technology can reduce the amount of data that need to be transmitted s, so it can save a lot of network bandwidth for data transmission operations [8]. In the currently known deduplication schemes, popularity detection is a very important processing method [9]. Unlike normal deduplication, popularity based schemes does not process every data copy on the CSP, a predetermined threshold is usually set for the uploaded data and the amount of actual storage of each data in the cloud is detected to determine whether that copy needs deduplication or not. When the amount of duplicate copies of a certain data reaches or exceeds the predetermined threshold, the data are to be popular. The CSP only performs deduplication on popular data. Popularity based deduplication schemes not only eliminate data with high popularity, but also ensure the security of private data with low popularity. For example, in the secure deduplication scheme proposed by Pasquale Puzio et al. [10], the data block-level popularity detection problem is mentioned for the first time, which can further reserve cloud storage space and network bandwidth. At the same time, the application of convergence encryption in this paper better secure data security of the upload user's data. A secure encrypted deduplication scheme for offline delivery of encryption keys was proposed by Zhang et al. [11], which constructed a query label of data popularity through elliptic curve, and securely transmits the encryption key using broadcast encryption technology. Improved convergence encryption algorithm is adopted for popular data in their scheme, which improves the query efficiency of data popularity.

There are many other types of deduplication methods. In the security cross-user deduplication [12], when the CSP carries out deduplicate on data with client encryption, only query labels with high popularity can be detected. This operation reduces the network traffic and computation of cloud storage servers. Meanwhile, the deduplication across the user is guaranteed to secure uploaded data better and save more cloud storage space. The MRN-CDE deduplication scheme not only better resists poison attacks [13], but also solves the problem of real-time information authentication and replay attacks. A similarity-aware cryptographic deduplication scheme is proposed by Zhou et al. [14], which uses similarity to reduce the deduplication message locking encryption computing consumption. This scheme supports flexible access control by revocation. In addition, it also combines source-based similar segment detection and target-based duplicate block checking to handle attacks and ensure deduplication efficiency.

Deduplication achieves efficient utilization of limited storage space [15, 16] and is widely adopted by the CSP. Though deduplication technology brings us efficiency and convenience, there are also some information security risks. Most of the existing deduplication technologies do not take into account a practical problem - internal data leakage problems caused by deduplication of internal data. The main reason for this situation is that different users who upload the same data to the CSP may come from the same company or organization, who share similar security attributes. If the company has a large employee population, the amount of cloud storage for that data will soon reach or exceed the predetermined threshold. In this case, if we treat and deduplicate the data in ordinary ways, it may lead to internal data leakage and other security issues. Therefore, the potential security risks caused by deduplication need further consideration.

In this paper, we propose a new secure deduplication scheme for group users, a user similarity-aware deduplication algorithm, which can effectively solve the problem of internal data leakage.

2   System Model and Objectives

2.1   System Model

The system model based on threshold adaptive deduplication scheme is mainly constructed for group users. The system is composed of clients and the CSP. The clients are divided into data uploader and data viewer. Among them, when the client uploads data to the CSP, it is regarded as a data uploader. When it sends a request for viewing data to the CSP, it is regarded as a data viewer. The CSP is mainly responsible for detecting the popularity status of the uploaded data, and adjusting the counting method adaptively according to the actual situation. The operation process of our scheme can be summarized as follows. 1) Users first generate the upload data ciphertext and query labels, and send them to the CSP. 2) The CSP performs duplicate data detection operations by comparing the query labels. 3) The CSP calculates the attribute similarity between uploading users and all users who have uploaded the data to the cloud before. 4) The CSP dynamically adjusts the counting method according to the similarity degree of attributes between the uploading user and existing users. 5) The CSP checks the current popularity status of the data and decides whether to perform deduplication or not.

2.2   Design Goals

By dynamically adjusting the counting based on attribute similarity, the scheme can solve the problem of internal data leakage caused by deduplication. The design goals are as follows:

- Confidentiality of upload data: In order to protect user privacy, upload data need to be encrypted.
- Computability of attribute distances: specific calculation methods for various types of attribute distances should be given.
- Adaptability of dynamic counting: the counting mode should be adjusted dynamically according to the actual situation to ensure the adaptability of the scheme.

3 Scheme Design

3.1 Background Set

M different upload users who have uploaded the same data to the CSP are regarded as a set of users, and are denoted by $A = \{A_i \mid i = 1, 2, \ldots, M\}$. Each user has m different attributes, such as IP address type, age, hobby type, reputation interval and other user attributes. Set each user's property to collection $B = \{B_j \mid j = 1, 2, \ldots, m\}$. At the same time, each attribute of user A_i is quantified to obtain an attribute vector $a_i = \{a_{i1}, a_{i2}, \ldots, a_{im}\}^T$. Let the uploading user be A_0, then there is $A_0 = \{a_{01}, a_{02}, \ldots, a_{0m}\}$. The distance matrix formed by A_0 and the attribute distance of all users in user set A_i, denoted as $C = \{c_{ij}\}_{m*M}$. In order to overcome the influence of different attribute dimensions on the calculation results, we normalize the distance matrix C and convert it into a standard matrix $R = \{r_{ij}\}_{m*M}$, where $r_{ij} = (c_{ij} - c_{i\min})/(c_{i\max} - c_{i\min})$, $c_{i\max}$ is the maximum distance value between A_0 and all former upload users in the ith attribute, $c_{i\min}$ is the minimum distance value of A_0 and all former upload users in the ith attribute.

The proposed method can better handle the application scenarios with group users, and can better protect the security of intra-group data compared with the existing deduplication scheme. When an uploading user A_0 uploads the encrypted data F to the CSP, the CSP can check whether the cloud has stored the data by using the query label generated with elliptic curve. The CSP calculates the attribute similarity of all known users A_i with data F and A_0, and compares whether A_0 is a group user. Finally, the CSP dynamically adjusts the count based on the category of A_0, always ensuring that the current popularity status of the uploaded data will only change due to the addition of individual users. Based on the threshold value and the current number of data, the CSP decides whether to perform deduplication or not. The scheme is divided into the following three parts: attribute similarity calculation, file upload, dynamic adjustment count.

In order to calculate the similarity between uploading users, it is an effective way to calculate the attribute distance between uploading users and to check whether two different users belong to the same group. In most traditional attribute distance calculation schemes, the calculation can be carried out only when the attribute value is a specific value. The calculation formula usually adopts the Euclid distance formula and the Haiming distance formula. These formulas are only valid for the attribute of the numerical value after the numerical conversion. However, when the attribute is not a numerical value, it may not be quantified as an accurate value. It can only be quantified as a less certain fuzzy number or only the fuzzy interval that it belongs to. This makes the traditional similarity calculation methods not applicable in our scheme. Therefore, our scheme adopts a new improved attribute distance calculation method [17], and uses different attribute distances for different types of attribute values. The calculation method makes the results more precise.

3.2 Data Type

According to different situations after attribute quantification, the attributes are divided into the following six types [17].

- Numeric. For attribute values such as age, such attributes are usually represented by a certain value after numerical conversion.
- Specific symbol. Such attributes are usually represented by a specific symbol.
- Determined interval. Such attribute are usually represented by a range with defined boundaries after numerical transformation.
- Fuzzy number. The number of such attributes cannot be quantified to a certain value and can only be represented by approximate numbers.
- Fuzzy interval. The number of such attributes cannot be quantified as a certain interval and can only be represented by an interval with no defined boundaries.
- Fuzzy semantics. Such attributes are often semantic variables. Each semantic variable corresponds to a fuzzy set and a membership function.

3.3 Data Upload

When the uploading user A_0 uploads encrypted data F to the CSP, the CSP performs a similarity calculation according to A_0 and each user A_i associated with F, and determines whether A_0 is a group user. According to the category of A_0, the data upload operation is divided into the following two cases: A_0 is an individual user or A_0 is a group user. In this paper, only the popularity count of non-popular data is discussed, when $\text{count}(F) < T$, the data upload operation is as follows, which is shown in Fig. 1.

First, the uploading user A_0 uploads F and its query label H to the CSP, and the CSP performs duplication check with H. If it is not the first copy, the CSP calculates the attribute similarity between A_0 and user A_i who owns F, and determines the category of A_0. If A_0 is recognized as an individual user, value of $\text{count}(F)$ is incremented by 1. Then, the CSP checks whether to carry out deduplication on F according to the new value of $\text{count}(F)$. If A_0 is recognized as a group user, the CSP cannot directly add 1 to $\text{count}(F)$, but needs to dynamically adjust the increment to ensure that the current popularity status of the data will only change due to the participation of individual users. This mechanism better ensures the security of the internal data of the group. When F becomes popular data, the CSP can directly deduplicate F by querying the label, which can reduce computational and communication overhead.

3.4 Dynamic Adjustment Count

According to the calculation of the similarity between the uploading user A_0 and the existing user A_i on the CSP, we can determine whether A_0 is a group user. The CSP checks the number of users whose similarity with A_0 is greater than the distance threshold parameter f (where f is in the range of $(0, 1)$). If the number is less than or equal to the group user threshold parameter z (z is a fixed integer). Therefore, A_0 is considered as an individual user, and contribute 1 to the value of $\text{count}(F)$ when the popularity is counted. Otherwise, it is regarded as a group user and we adopt the counting method of fitting growth curve to dynamically adjust the popularity to ensure that the participation of group users does not change the current popularity of uploaded data status. The specific formula is as follows:

$$\text{count}(F) = \frac{T}{1 + ae^{b(\text{count}(F)+1)}} \tag{12}$$

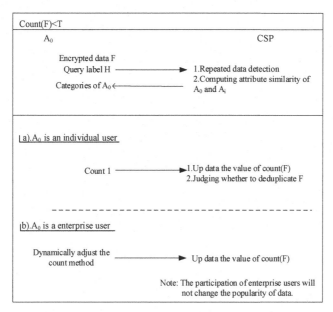

Fig. 1. Data upload process.

The value of $count(F)$ will only be infinitely close to T, but will never exceed T, and T is the established popularity threshold.

4 Experiment and Analysis

We use the PBC [24], GMP [25], PBC_bce [26] and OPENSSL [27] libraries. Key operations are implemented with C++ language. To implement AES encryption, we use the standard functions provided by the OPENSSL library. We use the CERNET IaaS cloud server for deployment, which is configured with 8 GB RAM, 4 core CPU, and 160 GB storage space. The practical feasibility of this scheme is proved from the aspects of time consumption and accuracy of the classification process.

4.1 Classification Accuracy

We selected 1000 records from UCI's public data set—"YouTube Spam Data Set" as the experimental data. The ratio of group users and individual users were about 6:4. We used Fuzzy-C-Means clustering algorithm with high public recognition to cluster them. The final result of C-means clustering serves as an evaluation reference for experimental classification accuracy. In this experiment, threshold parameter z is set to 3, and different classification accuracy is obtained by adjusting the size of the distance threshold parameter f. The results are shown in Fig. 2.

As can be seen from the result, with the increase of the value of f, the classification accuracy of individual users increases gradually, while that of group users decreases. The overall classification accuracy increases first and then decreases with the increase

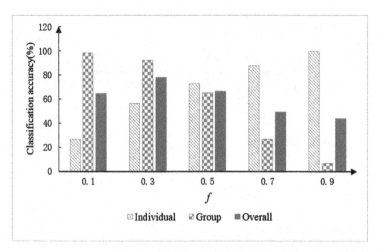

Fig. 2. Classification accuracy.

of the value of f. Through repeated experiments, it is concluded that when f is about 0.412, the overall classification accuracy is the highest, about 85.67%.

4.2   Performance Comparison

By uploading 1000 data of 10 MB, the total time cost of our scheme is calculated and compared with that of other schemes, namely the perfectDedup scheme, the common popularity threshold-based deduplication scheme and the Xu-CDE scheme. The experimental results are shown in Fig. 3. Results show that our design does not cause additional time overhead while improving the security of the deduplication operation.

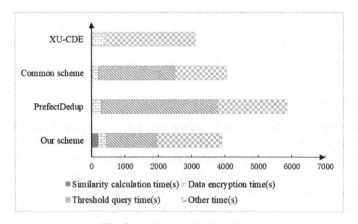

Fig. 3. Performance comparison.

5 Conclusions

In this paper, we propose a user similarity-aware deduplication algorithm. When tracking the popularity of data, the CSP compares the attributes of the uploading user with those of the users who already uploaded the data in the cloud to determine whether the uploading user is a group user. The CSP uses different adaptive counting methods for the uploaded data according to the category of users, thus effectively protecting the internal data security. For the first time, the scheme applies user attribute detection to improve the security of deduplication, and presents different types of attribute distance calculation methods in detail. This scheme can guarantee the security of internal data in the application scenarios where there is a large amount of group users. Through experiment comparison and analysis, it can be concluded that our scheme is applicable and efficient.

References

1. Mcsharry, P.E., Little, M.A., Rodda, H.J.E., et al.: Quantifying flood risk of extreme events using density forecasts based on a new digital archive and weather ensemble predictions. Q. J. R. Meteorol. Soc. **139**(671), 328–333 (2013)
2. Wang, C., Chow, S.M., Wang, Q., et al.: Privacy-preserving public auditing for secure cloud storage. IEEE Trans. Comput. **62**(2), 362–375 (2013)
3. Wang, Q., Wang, C., Ren, K., Lou, W.J., Li, J.: Enabling public auditability and data dynamics for storage security in cloud computing. IEEE Trans. Parallel Distrib. Syst. **22**(5), 847–859 (2011)
4. Yuan, H.R., Chen, X.F., Jiang, T., et al.: DedupDUM: secure and scalable data deduplication with dynamic user management. Inf. Sci. **456**, 159–173 (2018)
5. Jayapandian, N., Md Zubair Rahman, A.M.J.: Secure deduplication for cloud storage using interactive message-locked encryption with convergent encryption, to reduce storage space. Braz. Arch. Biol. Technol. **61**, e17160609 (2018)
6. Stanek, J., Kencl, L.: Enhanced secure thresholded data deduplication scheme for cloud storage. IEEE Trans. Dependable Secure Comput. **15**(4), 694–707 (2018)
7. Fu, Y.J., Xiao, N., Liu, F.: Research and development on key techniques of data deduplication. J. Comput. Res. Dev. **49**(1), 12–20 (2012)
8. Diao, K., Papapanagiotou, I., Hacker, T.J.: HARENS: hardware accelerated redundancy elimination in network systems. In: IEEE International Conference on Cloud Computing Technology & Science (2017)
9. Stanek, J., Sorniotti, A., Androulaki, E., et al.: A secure data deduplication scheme for cloud storage. IBM Corporation (2014)
10. Puzio, P., Molva, R., Önen, M., Loureiro, S.: PerfectDedup: secure data deduplication. In: Garcia-Alfaro, J., Navarro-Arribas, G., Aldini, A., Martinelli, F., Suri, N. (eds.) DPM/QASA -2015. LNCS, vol. 9481, pp. 150–166. Springer, Cham (2016). https://doi.org/10.1007/978-3-319-29883-2_10
11. Zhang, S.G., Xian, H.Q., Liu, H.Y., et al.: Research on encrypted deduplication method based on offline key transfer in cloud storage environment. Net info Secur. **7**, 66–72 (2017)
12. Liu, J., Asokan, N., Pinkas, B.: Secure deduplication of encrypted data without additional independent servers. In: ACM SIGSAC Conference on Computer & Communications Security. ACM (2015)
13. Yang, C., Ji, Q., Xiong, S.C., et al.: New method for file deduplication in cloud storage. J. Commun. **38**, 25–33 (2017)

14. Zhou, Y., Dan, F., Wen, X., et al.: SecDep: a user-aware efficient fine-grained secure deduplication scheme with multi-level key management (2015)
15. Meyer, D.T., Bolosky, W.J.: A study of practical deduplication. ACM Trans. Storage **7**(4), 1–20 (2012)
16. Yang, Y., Zheng, X., Guo, W., et al.: (Revised Version) privacy-preserving smart IoT-based healthcare big data storage and self-adaptive access control system. Inf. Sci. **479**, 567–592 (2018)
17. Zhu, L.F., Dong, Z.H., Xu, L.Y.: Similarity measurement for retrieval based on hybrid attribute distance. J. Tongji Univ. **43**(7), 1089–1096 (2015)
18. Cao, B.Y.: Fuzzy Mathematics and System. Science Press, Beijing (2005)
19. Peng, Z.Z., Sun, W.Y.: Fuzzy Mathematics and Applications. Wuhan University Press, Wuhan (2007)
20. Hu, Q.Z., Zhang, W.H.: Research and Application of Interval Number Theory. Science Press, Beijing (2010)
21. Bao, Y.E., Peng, X.Q., Zhao, B.: The interval number distance and completeness based on the expectation and width. Fuzzy Syst. Math. **27**(6), 133–139 (2013)
22. Xingui, H.: Semantic distance and fuzzy users' view in fuzzy databases. Chin. J. Comput. **12**(10), 757 (1989)
23. Leydesdorff, L., Bornmann, L.: How fractional counting of citations affects the impact factor: normalization in terms of differences in citation potentials among fields of science (2011)
24. Lynn, B.: The pairing-based cryptographic library (2015). http://crypto.Stanford.edu/pbc/
25. Loukides, M., Oram, A.: Programming with GNU Software, vol. 86, no. 3, pp. 350–359. O'Reilly & Associates (1997)
26. Steiner, M.: The PBC_bce broadcast encryption library (2006). https://crypto.stanford.edu/pbc/bce/
27. Hu, X.T., Qin, Z.P., Zhang, H., Hao, G.S.: Research and improved implementation of AES algorithm in OpenSSL. Control Autom. **25**(12), 83–85 (2009)

Artificial Intelligence

Analysis Model of Node Failures and Impact for AANET

Lixia Xie[1]([⊠]) [iD], Liping Yan[1] [iD], Guangquan Xu[2] [iD], and Jiyong Zhang[3]

[1] Civil Aviation University of China, Tianjin 300300, China
lxxie@126.com
[2] Tianjin University, Tianjin 300350, China
[3] Swiss Federal Institute of Technology in Lausanne, 1015 Lausanne, Switzerland

Abstract. To effectively analyze the impact of node failures on the AANET (Aeronautical Ad Hoc Network) and improve the network invulnerability, an analysis model of node failures and impact for AANET is proposed. The main business of AANET is identified and the business network is established based on the business process, the physical network is built according to the real-time AANET, and the business-physical network mapping relationship is used to establish the interdependent networks. Then, the business node volume and network volume are defined and the business node weight is calculated. At the same time, the weight of the physical node is determined by the aggregation degree. Finally, a link survivability calculation module is given and a traffic reallocation strategy based on link survivability is proposed and apply to this model. The experiments show that the model proposed in this paper can accurately analyze the degree of the failure and improve the network invulnerability more effectively than other node failures analysis model.

Keywords: AANET · Node failures · Interdependent networks · Failure propagation model · Link survivability

1 Introduction

AANET is a complex network built on all kinds of aircraft and some base stations, which can cover the business needs of aviation and integrate various communication systems, functional networks, and business systems. On the one hand, the proposal of AANET strengthens the connection between aircraft [1]. On the other hand, it makes the network face more serious node failure risk. Therefore, it is important to analyze the node failures in AANET and propose an optimal network traffic reallocation strategy to improve the network invulnerability.

Jose et al. [2] proposed an effective cascade failure control algorithm based on communication delay but did not concern the communication network coupled with the power grid. Buldyrev et al. [3] proposed a fully dependent dependency network model, in which there is one-to-one correspondence between nodes of two networks. However,

© Springer Nature Singapore Pte Ltd. 2020
G. Xu et al. (Eds.): FCS 2020, CCIS 1286, pp. 55–64, 2020.
https://doi.org/10.1007/978-981-15-9739-8_5

the one-to-multi relationship between nodes of the two networks is not considered. Wang et al. [4] proposed an improved complex network model for risk assessment of power-communication interdependent networks but did not allocate corresponding weights for different nodes. Zhang [5] proposed that effective evaluation of the importance of nodes could improve the robustness of the network. It also shows that the network can effectively prevent cascading failures in real life if important nodes are protected. Chen [6] proposed a cascading failure model of interdependent networks with different coupling preferences under targeted attack. However, it is not considered that the failed nodes can be restored to working nodes by corresponding means. Han [7] proposed a new cascading failure model with adjustable parameters based on the weighted scale-free network. Peng [8] gave the analysis that affects the security of the information system during the failure process of deliberate attack strategy. But the model lacks consideration about random attacks.

Motivated by those above, in this paper, we propose an analysis model of node failures and impact for AANET. The main contributions of this paper are listed as follows:

a. To describe AANET accurately, we build the business-physical interdependent networks and propose an analysis model that describes the node failures propagation process based on failure propagation model. First, two states of nodes are defined: working node and failed node. Second, the network traffic reallocation mechanism is analyzed. Finally, the failure propagation model is used to obtain the degree of network cascade effect and judge the network destruction degree.

b. Based on a failure propagation model, we propose a traffic reallocation strategy based on link survivability to improve the network invulnerability. First, the link survivability is calculated by combining the node failure rate and distance between nodes. Then, select available optimal links according to link survivability. Finally, the failed node traffic is reallocated by the weight of the neighbor nodes.

The rest of this paper is organized as follows. Section 2 recommends the business-physical interdependent networks building module. In Sect. 3, the node failures analysis model based on failure propagation model is proposed. Section 4 proposes a traffic reallocation strategy based on link survivability. In Sect. 5, the experimental comparisons are carried out and the results are analyzed. Finally, Sect. 6 gives the conclusions.

2   The Business-Physical Interdependent Networks Building Module

In this Section, a two-layer network model is constructed to describe the various business and association relations of the AANET.

2.1   Business Network

Business network G_B is a directed weighted network, expressed as $G_B = (V_B, E_B, W_B)$, where V_B represents the set of business nodes; E_B represents the set of edges, indicating the information interaction between business nodes; W_B represents the set of business node weight, which is determined by the business volume. The following is the calculation process of business node weight W_B:

Define that the network volume is C_B and the total business that the network can handle per unit time is T_B. The business volume of link j is S_j, the shortest path length of the network is $\bar{d}_B$, the shortest path length between node N_u and node N_v is $d_{u,v}$, then:

$$T_B = \sum_{i=1}^{E_B} S_j \tag{1}$$

$$\bar{d}_B = \frac{2}{V_B(V_B - 1)} \sum_{u=1}^{V_B-1} \sum_{v=u+1}^{V_B} d_{u,v} \tag{2}$$

$$C_B = \frac{T_B}{d_B} = \frac{\sum\limits_{j=1}^{E_B} S_j}{d_B} \tag{3}$$

Define that the business volume handled by nodes per unit time is C_u, the weight of business nodes can be calculated as:

$$W_B = \frac{C_u}{C_B} \tag{4}$$

Thus, the business network can be represented by the matrix $A_B = [a_{ij}]_{n \times n}$, where the diagonal element a_{ii} is the weight of the business nodes, and the non-diagonal element is the connection relationship between the nodes. If there is an information interaction between nodes, $a_{ij} = 1$, otherwise $a_{ij} = 0$.

2.2 Physical Network

Physical network G_P is an undirected weighted network, expressed as $G_P = (V_P, E_P, W_P)$, where V_P represents a set of physical nodes (aircraft); E_P represents the set of edges, indicating the communication links between aircraft; W_P represents the set of physical node weights, which are determined by the aggregation degree [9]. The calculation process of physical node weight is as follows:

Calculate the aggregation degree α of G_P:

$$\alpha = \frac{n - 1}{\sum\limits_{u \neq v \in V_P} d_{u,v}} \tag{5}$$

where n is the number of all nodes in the network, $n \geq 2$, $d_{u,v}$ represents the shortest distance between node N_u and N_u.

Thus, the node weight w_u can be calculated as:

$$w_u = 1 - \frac{\alpha(G_P)}{\alpha(G_P \times N_u)} \tag{6}$$

where $G_P \times N_u$ represents the graph after the N_u is shrunk. The shrinking N_u refers to the fusion of all k_u nodes connected with the node N_u, namely a new node replaces the $k_u + 1$ nodes. The edges originally associated with them are now associated with the new node.

Thus, the physical network can be represented by the matrix $B_P = [B_{ij}]_{n \times n}$, where the diagonal element b_{ii} is the weight of the physical node, and the non-diagonal element is the communication link between the nodes. If there is a communication link between nodes, $b_{ij} = 1$, otherwise $b_{ij} = 0$.

2.3 Business-Physical Interdependent Networks

According to the above analysis, the business nodes are coupled by the physical nodes. If the physical node N_P has multi-functions, there are corresponding multi-business nodes. Meanwhile, there is a one-to-multi dependency edge between the physical network and the business network. A physical node may be the basis of multiple business nodes, and a business node must rely on a physical node to function normally. $E_C = [e_{ij}]_{P \times B}$ represents the set of dependent edges between two-layer networks. If there is a dependent edge between physical node N_P and business node N_B, $e_{ij} = 1$, otherwise $e_{ij} = 0$.

In summary, a business-physical dependent network model for AANET can be built, represented by multiple groups $BP = \Theta (G_B, G_P, E_C)$.

3 Analysis Model Based on Failure Propagation Model

In this Section, a failure propagation model is selected to analyze node failures.

3.1 Traffic Reallocation Mechanism

When node failure occurs, the traffic on the failed node needs to be reallocated to adjacent nodes. Assume that the reallocation of the process is not uniformly distributed, but based on the weights between nodes. Define the increase of the traffic on the neighbor node N_j is ΔL_j:

$$\Delta L_j = \frac{w_i L}{\sum_{S \in (N_n \in i)} w_S} \tag{7}$$

where, w_i is the weight of N_i, and N_i is the failed node. L represents the traffic that needs to be redistributed. w_s represents the weight of the neighbor nodes. Node weights are concerned with traffic reallocation to better analyze the failure propagation process. The bigger the node weight, the easier it is to propagate traffic. In the process of traffic reallocation, the traffic should be given priority to nodes with high weight, which can effectively reduce the scope and possibility of further node failures.

3.2 Failure Propagation Model

The failure propagation model [10] divides nodes in the network into two types: W (Working) and F (Failed). Defined that $W(t)$ is the number of working nodes at t time and $F(t)$ is the number of failed nodes at t time. When the working node fails due to its overload, it will be transformed into a failed node. The failed nodes can also be converted into working nodes after being repaired by corresponding means.

In the failure propagation model, each failed node is converted to a working node by conversion rate γ. Each working node is converted to a failed node by failed rate β, which can be expressed as

$$\begin{cases} W(t_1) + F(t_1) \xrightarrow{\beta} F(t_2) + F(t_2) \\ F(t_1) \xrightarrow{\gamma} W(t_2) \end{cases} \tag{8}$$

This model is characterized by the fact that the rates are influenced by both $W(t)$ and $F(t)$. Therefore, the proportion of working nodes and failure nodes in the network changes with time can be described by the following differential equation:

$$\begin{cases} \frac{dW}{dt} = -\beta WF + \gamma F \\ \frac{dF}{dt} = \beta WF - \gamma F \\ W(0) = N - F_0 \\ F(0) = 0 \end{cases} \tag{9}$$

where N represents the number of total nodes, βWF represents the number of increased nodes during the propagation from working nodes to failed nodes, γF represents the number of nodes increased during the propagation from failed nodes to working nodes, F_0 represents the number of failed nodes when the network started.

Finally, the ratio f is used in this paper to represent the node failure effect degree. The higher the value is, the worse the network security status is. Therefore, the operator of the effect value is:

$$f = \frac{F(t)}{N} \tag{10}$$

In this paper, the degree of node failure effect can be determined by the value of f. It is shown in Table 1.

Table 1. Network node failure effect degree.

f	[0, 0.2]	(0.2, 0.4]	(0.4, 0.6]	(0.6, 0.8]	(0.8, 1]
Degree	Very Minor	Minor	Moderate	Major	Very Major

4 Traffic Reallocation Strategy Based on Link Survivability

In this Section, we proposed a traffic reallocation strategy based on link survivability to improve the network invulnerability.

4.1 Link Survivability Calculation Module

Link survivability is proposed to measure the stability of a link between two aircrafts in a physical network. Link survivability is determined by the distance between nodes and the node failure rate. Assuming that all nodes in the network have available positioning information, the distance between the two nodes is estimated through mathematical modeling, and the corresponding calculation process is as follows:

Define that the longitude and latitude coordinates of N_A and N_B are (A_j, A_w) and (B_j, B_w), and the earth radius R is taken as 6371 km. Then the distance between the two nodes is:

$$d_{A,B} = R \times \arccos[\cos A_w \times \cos B_w \times \cos(A_j - B_j) + \sin A_w \times \sin B_w] \quad (11)$$

Using the inverse distance weighted interpolation method, the link weight $w_{A,B}$ between node N_A and N_B is:

$$w_{a,b} = \frac{1}{d_{A,B}^{\mu}} \quad (12)$$

where $\mu > 0$.

Thus, link survivability can be expressed as

$$\sigma = w_{A,B} \times \beta \quad (13)$$

where β represents the probability that a working node is converted into a failure node.

4.2 Traffic Reallocation Strategy Based on Link Survivability

When a node fails in the network, the traffic on the failed node needs to be reallocated to other neighboring work nodes. In this paper, the workflow design of the optimal traffic reallocation algorithm based on link survivability is presented as follows.

Step 1. The available neighbor nodes are stored in set N, the link information between failed nodes and neighbor working nodes is stored in set L, and the distance $d_{A,B}$ between nodes is calculated by using the link information stored in set L.

Step 2. The weight $w_{A,B}$ of each available link is calculated by inverse distance weighted interpolation.

Step 3. Calculate link survivability σ based on Eq. (11–13) and the average link survivability $\bar{\sigma}$

Step 4. Select available links according to link survivability σ.

Step 5. Calculate the weight w_i of available nodes and distribute the traffic to each available node according to the weight w_i.

5 Experiment and Analysis

To verify the validity of this model, it is applied to the AANET of a domestic airport. Taking the ADS-B data of March 5, 2019, as an example, the application process of the node failure model is illustrated below. From this AANET, the number of business network nodes and links are $V_B = 25$, $E_B = 24$, and the number of physical network nodes and links are $V_P = 50$, $E_P = 96$. According to the mapping relationship between two-layer nodes, a business-physical interdependent networks model can be constructed. The network initialization parameters are set as shown in Table 2.

Table 2. Network initialization parameters

Parameter	Initial value	Parameter	Initial value	Parameter	Initial value
γ_1	0.4	γ_2	0.4	μ	0.5
β_1	0.6	β_2	0.6		

5.1 Calculate Node Weight

Calculate the Business Node Weight. According to the calculation method of network traffic described in Sect. 2.1, the total network traffic at this time can be calculated as $C_B = 82\ 973.85829$. Based on Eq. (4), the weight of business node is (see in Table 3):

Table 3. The weight of business node

No.	Weight	No.	Weight	No.	Weight
1	0.046130	11	0.004301	21	0.020930
2	0.049077	12	0.001501	22	0.057807
3	0.039373	13	0.010067	23	0.019462
4	0.031319	14	0.068827	24	0.059738
5	0.090923	15	0.101915	25	0.043774
6	0.091858	16	0.004329		
7	0.012851	17	0.038345		
8	0.011890	18	0.039458		
9	0.032172	19	0.032919		
10	0.005130	20	0.085900		

Calculate the Physical Node Weight. According to the method described in Sect. 2.2, the importance of physical network nodes is calculated as the weight of physical nodes, and the results are shown in Table 4.

Table 4. The weight of the physical node

No.	Weight	No.	Weight	No.	Weight	No.	Weight	No.	Weight
1	0.953455	11	0.906528	21	0.879105	31	0.893799	41	0.926799
2	0.858166	12	0.879962	22	0.884467	32	0.838961	42	0.880508
3	0.861346	13	0.871528	23	0.947392	33	0.880623	43	0.825233
4	0.872374	14	0.883541	24	0.952314	34	0.885750	44	0.900037
5	0.855380	15	0.845832	25	0.862411	35	0.853717	45	0.899340
6	0.840138	16	0.830429	26	0.858166	36	0.936378	46	0.915638
7	0.898922	17	0.909773	27	0.856616	37	0.856060	47	0.874517
8	0.864464	18	0.818002	28	0.840904	38	0.843213	48	0.817346
9	0.843866	19	0.929349	29	0.86260	39	0.875039	49	0.878512
10	0.873670	20	0.832370	30	0.889279	40	0.832714	50	0.867661

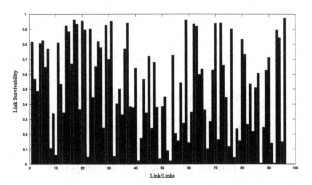

Fig. 1. Value of link survivability

5.2 Calculate the Link Survivability

According to Sect. 5, the physical network has 96 links. Then, based on the link survivability calculation module, the survivability of each link is shown in Fig. 1.

5.3 Analysis of Node Failures for Different Attack Modes

Random Attacks. Under the random attack, the ML (Motter-Lai) model [6], the WR (Weight based Redistribution) [7] model, the FP (Failure Propagation) model [10], and the model proposed in this paper are respectively used to analyze the node failure and impact on AANET. The results are shown in Fig. 2.

When the network is attacked randomly, no matter which kind of interdependent networks node failure model is used, the network will be affected at the beginning, and the affected degree will increase, and then become stable. Compared with other models,

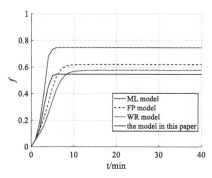

Fig. 2. The degree of network node failures of random attacks

the final state of our model is "Moderate". Obviously, the loss of the network caused by the model proposed in this paper is significantly lower than that of other models, and the stability of the network is also significantly improved.

Deliberate Attacks. The four models are attacked respectively by deliberate attacks. The results are shown in Fig. 3.

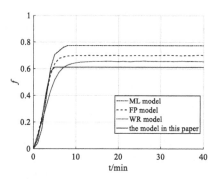

Fig. 3. The degree of network node failures of deliberate attacks

The final state of the four models is "Major". But the loss of the network caused by the model proposed in this paper is significantly lower than other models. It also can be seen from the comparison that under the condition of deliberate attack intensity, the influence of deliberate attacks on the network is obviously greater than that of random attacks. This is due to the high traffic of the key nodes themselves, and once the failure occurs, other nodes will be difficult to carry the reallocated traffic, thus generating node effect and causing large-scale damage to the network easily and rapidly. The reasons why this happened are as follows.

a.   The model proposed in this paper takes into account the actual factors of the network. The crash of the network is not only the interaction between the physical nodes but also the interaction between the two layers of nodes, which means the physical nodes are controlled by the business nodes. Therefore, this paper increases the consideration of the AANET business network, which makes the model more consistent with the actual situation.

b. AANET is a highly dynamic and self-organizing network, so this paper proposes a link survivability strategy based on the distance between physical nodes. Assign smaller weights to distant nodes and larger weights to near nodes. Combined with the failure rate of network nodes to obtain the link survivability. The traffic reallocation path is optimally selected to make the network better reduce network losses and improve the invulnerability of the network after being attacked.

6 Conclusion

In this paper, the analysis model of node failures and impact for AANET is proposed. The business node weight is calculated through the node volume and network volume, and the physical node weight is calculated according to the node aggregation degree. The failure propagation model is used to analyze the failure process of the network, and the value of the effect caused by the node failures on the network is obtained and the degree of the network affected is judged. Finally, this paper proposes a traffic reallocation strategy based on link survivability. The link is selected according to the overall consideration of link survivability and node failure rate. The traffic is reallocated by node weight. The experiment shows that compared with other model, the model proposed in this paper has better stability and invulnerability.

References

1. Kumar, V.: Aircraft ad-hoc network (AANET). Int. J. Adv. Res. Comput. Commun. Eng. 3(5), 6679–6684 (2014)
2. Jose, C.G.: Control of communications-dependent cascading failures in power grids. In: 2019 IEEE Power & Energy Society General Meeting (PESGM), Atlanta, p. 1 (2019)
3. Sergey, V.B.: Catastrophic cascade of failures in interdependent networks. Nature 1025–1028 (2010)
4. Wang, Z.: Cascading risk assessment in power-communication interdependent networks. Physica A: Statal Mech. Appl. 540 (2019)
5. Zhang, L.: Study on the cascading failure model of double-layer coupling network, In: 2018 Chinese Control and Decision Conference (CCDC), Shenyang, pp. 4586–4590 (2018)
6. Chen, Z.: Cascading failure of interdependent networks with different coupling preference under targeted attack. Chaos Solitons Fractals 7–12 (2015)
7. Han, L.: Cascading failure model of weighted scale-free networks. J. Softw. 28(10), 2769–2781 (2017)
8. Peng, H.: Cascading failures and security assessment of information physics system under intentional attack strategy. J. Zhengzhou Univ. 51(03), 13–21 (2019)
9. Wu, J.: Evaluation method for node importance based on node contraction in complex networks. Syst. Eng.-Theory Practice 26(11), 79–83 (2006)
10. Gong, W.: Research on the stability and control of computer virus network communication model. Wireless Internet Technol. 24–25 (2015)

Deep Attention Model with Multiple Features for Rumor Identification

Lina Wang[1,2(✉)], Wenqi Wang[1,2], Tong Chen[1,2], Jianpeng Ke[1,2], and Benxiao Tang[1,2]

[1] Key Laboratory of Aerospace Information Security and Trusted Computing, Ministry of Education, Wuhan University, Wuhan, China
{lnwang,wangwenqi_001,chentong,kejianpeng,tangbenxiao}@whu.edu.cn
[2] School of Cyber Science and Engineering, Wuhan University, Wuhan 430072, China

Abstract. With the rapidly development of social networks and advances in natural language processing (NLP) techniques, rumors are extremely common and pose potential threats to community. In recent years, massive efforts are working on detecting rumors by using various techniques like simply investigating the content of texts, exploring the abnormality of propagation. However, these techniques are not ready to fully tackling this emerging threats due to the dynamic variations of rumors in a period of time. In this paper, we observed that the user feedback provides a clean signal for determining the trend of rumors, thus we combine the text content and the improved representation of network topology to characterize the dynamic features of rumors in a period of time. In detection, we employ a deep attention model with proposed features for spotting the minor differences between legitimate news and rumors. Experimental results show that our approach give an accuracy more than 94.7% in detecting rumors and outperforms previous approaches. Our studies also give a new insight that user interactions could be working as an important asset in rumor identification.

Keywords: Attention mechanism · Representation learning · Rumor identification · Multiple Features

1 Introduction

Nowadays, online social networks have greatly promoted the communication between humans, resulting in an explosive growth of various information. They have also become important ways for ordinary people to obtain external knowledge. However, this convenience also promotes the widespread of rumors. Recently, there is no standard definition of what a rumor is. DiFonzo et al. [8] define rumor as unverified and instrumentally relevant information statements in circulation that arise in contexts of ambiguity, danger or potential threat. Gupta et al. [11] regard rumor as uncertain or deliberately forged information. Matsuta et al. [19] point that a rumor spreads like an infectious disease. According to the multiple features we used, a rumor is defined here as the information with

© Springer Nature Singapore Pte Ltd. 2020
G. Xu et al. (Eds.): FCS 2020, CCIS 1286, pp. 65–82, 2020.
https://doi.org/10.1007/978-981-15-9739-8_6

harmful content, abnormal topology structure of networks, and disparate feedback (*i.e.*, inquiry and correction signals by users [31]). Rumors have negative influence on public security and stability of society. They not only damage the credibility of social media, but also destroy the orderly development of society. For example, someone said that high concentration alcohol could prevent coronavirus disease outbreaking in 2019 (COVID-19), leading to the death of hundreds of Iranians. Therefore, effective rumor identification methods are urgently needed to deal with this issue.

Recently, the majority of rumor identification methods extract features (*e.g.*, text content [25], propagation patterns [17], and user profiles [28]) to train machine learning models to distinguish rumors from non-rumors. However, rumors can not be described accurately by using one or a few features among them. Text content-based methods usually ignore the dynamic structure of the propagation process and highly rely on the characteristics of information content. Propagation-based methods are limited by the artificially constructed features and the learning representation ability of models. The effects are not as good as expected. User profiles-based methods require high accuracy and a large amount of training data. They ignore the role of content in propagation, so that the results may have some deviations.

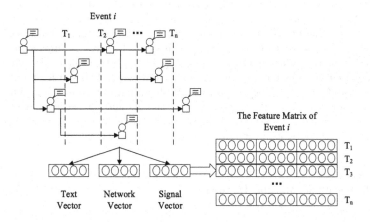

Fig. 1. Feature representation of an event in the propagation cycle. The propagation of event i is divided into n time periods. We extract the relevant features in each time period and splice them to form a feature matrix for training.

To deal with this issue, we use text content, topology structure of networks, and user feedback signals to represent the characteristics of an event in the propagation cycle. Then, we introduce the attention mechanism, which can find the elements closest to detection task from the input sequence to help classify the text, to a deep learning model for rumor identification. The framework of our method is shown in Fig. 1, and our contributions are summarized as follows:

- We combine user feedback signals with text content and topology structure of networks to characterize the features of an event for rumor identification task.
- We propose a representation learning method for network nodes based on the space-time similarity and improve the Struct2vec method to make it more suitable for the propagation process of events on online social networks.
- Our method achieves a relatively good result with 94.2% accuracy. It also performs better in the early detection of rumors than some works.

2   Related Works

Rumor identification is a hot research topic in various disciplines, and there exist a lot of relevant studies. Most of them utilize different features for distinction. Hence, the selection and extraction of features are significant to rumor identification. Takahashi et al. [25] found the differences in vocabulary distribution between rumors and non-rumors and use this feature for detection. Sun et al. [24] extracted 15 features related to content, users profiles, and multimedia to identify event rumors. Ma et al. [16] recognized the deficiencies of user profiles, content and propagation characteristics, and introduced the time series of information to improve the detection efficiency. Wu et al. [27] proposed a graph-kernel based hybrid support vector machine (SVM) classifier to utilize the propagation structure of the messages, which was ignored in prior works. All these works are based on traditional machine learning methods, and the features are extracted manually which are time-consuming and labor-intensive.

Recently, deep learning (DL) has achieved great performance in various natural language processing tasks. Therefore, researchers have tried to use DL-based models to identify rumors and received better results. Ma et al. [15] first used a recurrent neural network (RNN) to learn the vector representation of information-related texts over different periods. RNN-based rumor detection is faster and more accurate than the methods at the time. Chen et al. [6] introduced a self-attention mechanism based on the work of [15] to capture contextual variations of relevant posts over time. Yu et al. [29] proposed a novel method based on convolutional neural network (CNN), which can flexibly extract key features and shape high-level interactions among them. Yuan et al. [30] extracted the global structural information and combined with the semantic information for detection. Huang et al. [12] trained a graph convolutional network with graph structural information in the user behavior, which was not considered in other works.

3   Preliminaries

3.1   Description of Rumor Identification

Rumor identification is to determine whether the information of an event transmitted on social networks is a rumor or not. It can be seen as a two-category problem. The formal definition of this task is as follows:

For a given set $E = \{e_1, e_2, \ldots, e_i, \ldots, e_h\}$ with h events and a label set $L = \{l_1, l_2\}$, e_i stands for a set of messages related to the i-th event in E. Each event contains n pieces of information m_i, timestamp t_i and related attributes f_i. Thus, an event is composed of some time-series information, which is symbolized as $e_i = \{(m_{i1}, t_{i1}, f_{i1}), \ldots, (m_{ij}, t_{ij}, f_{ij}), \ldots, (m_{in}, t_{in}, f_{in})\}$ $(j = 1, 2, \ldots, n)$. The labels l_1 and l_2 represent rumor and non-rumor respectively. The rumor identification task is to map e_i into a corresponding category by learning a pre-trained classification model F, i.e., F: $e_i \rightarrow l$, $l \in \{l_1, l_2\}$. The input of the model is the event e_i, and the output is a discriminant label for the event.

3.2   Division of an Event

Division of the overall propagation phase can be seen as a transformation from a complete cycle into a series of different periods. For example, the messages in the set m_i of event e_i is divided into n intervals according to the timestamp t_{ij}, where n is the number of intervals, and j ranges from 1 to n. The time-series division of an event cycle is divided below.

We assume that the earliest timestamp in the event e_i is $startTime_i$, and the latest timestamp is $endTime_i$. e_i is divided into n intervals at equal length as shown in (1).

$$T_{ij} = \frac{j}{n} * endTime_i + \frac{n-j}{n} * startTime_i \tag{1}$$

where T_{ij} is the end time of the j-th period in the linear division of e_i.

But the distribution of information in an event has a significant long-tail phenomenon. It indicates that most of the information is concentrated in the early stage of propagation. Then the number of information about the event drops sharply with time. To eliminate the long-tail phenomenon, we obtain the logarithmic intervals by nonlinear division instead of linear division. Hence, the interval of the latter period becomes larger and larger. The distribution of the data in each period has a good consistency. The calculation process of nonlinear division is shown in (2).

$$t_{ij} = (endTime_i - startTime_i + 1)^{\frac{T_{ij} - startTime_i}{endTime_i - startTime_i}} + startTime_i - 1 \tag{2}$$

where t_{ij} is the end time of the j-th period in the logarithmic interval division of e_i.

3.3   Propagation of an Event

Due to the complexity of network topology, the representations of propagation process in existing methods have two main problems. One is the incomplete use of propagation features. Existing researches tend to focus on one aspect of the propagation process, so that the information disseminated throughout its cycle is not fully learned. For example, researchers only use the time-series features [15,16] or content features [9,18]. They intentionally ignore the complexity of network topology. Thus, the dynamic variability of online social networks is lack of consideration. The other one is a lack of quantitative expression for user opinion [14,26]. Because the semantic representation of potential topics is limited by short text corpus, the feedback information and user opinions of events(i.e. user feedback signals) in the networks are not well quantified. In response to the two problems, our method takes better use of the dynamic feature and user feedback signals to represent the propagation process of an event on online social networks.

4 The Multiple Features

The multiple features consist of text content, network topology, and user feedback signals. In this section, we introduce the constructions of network topology and user feedback signals.

4.1 Text Content

On online social network, text content includes two forms: one is the content of the message published by the original publisher, and the other is the reposting of the former by some users, *i.e.*, a copy of the original message. There is no difference in their contents, so that researchers usually regard them as the same one to study the characteristics of the words, symbols and uncertainties they contain. In this paper, we convert the text content into a vector according to word2vec, and then combine the features of topology feedback signals to construct a feature matrix for rumor identification.

4.2 Network Topology

Struct2vec [21] is a framework for learning latent representations of network nodes. Inspired by it, we propose a representation learning method for network nodes based on the space-time similarity. We have done some improvements on the Struct2vec. The attributes of node feature, the similarity of ordered degree sequence and the average passive response time which are not considered in Struc2vec are used in our method.

4.3 Definition of the Similarity Between Nodes

Figure 2 is a diagram of node similarity on online social networks. We assume that the thickness of the edge between two nodes in Fig. 2 represents the degree of influence. The size of a node represents its characteristic properties, such as the number of fans. Generally, node u and node v are not similar in an open social network according to the similarity assumption of neighbors. Because they are not directly connected and do not share any neighbor nodes. In that case, the probability that u and v appear in the same walk sequence by the traditional representation algorithm is almost zero. But u and v will have some similarities from the perspectives of spatial structure, degree of influence and node attributes. The degrees of u and v are 5 and 4 respectively. They are connected to other parts of the network through 2 nodes from spatial structure. Both u and v only have high influence on individual nodes in the view of influence. From the view of node attributes, the sizes of node u and node v are similar. The distributions of their neighbor nodes also have some similarities. Hence, it can be said that u and v are similar.

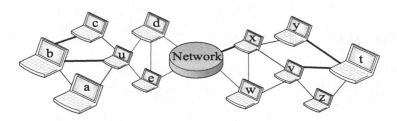

Fig. 2. Diagram of node similarity on social network. Each icon represents a node and they are connected by the networks.

Therefore, principles of the similarity between nodes in a directed graph with node attributes are defined as follows. First, the more similar the feature attributes of nodes are, the higher the similarity is. If their neighbor nodes also have similar distributions, the similarity of them will increase. Second, the closer the degrees of two nodes are, the higher the similarity is. If their neighbor nodes also have similar degrees, the similarity will increase. Third, the closer the average passive response time between two nodes is, the higher the similarity is. The passive response time of a node is better to describe its influence or similarity on social networks than the response time.

Structural Similarity of Loop Nodes. Given a directed graph $G = \langle V, E \rangle$ with node attributes, the directed edge e_{ij} represents the forwarding behavior of node i for node j. Let $R_k(u)$ denote the set of nodes with the shortest distance k to node u, where $R_0(u)$ represents the node u itself. $R_1(u)$ represents the directly connected neighbor set of u. Let D_i denote the indegree of node i. The loop structure refers to the part with a loop in the directed cycle graph(DCG). The definition of k-hop loop structure similarity $f_k(u, v)$ for given nodes u and v is in (3).

$$f_k(u, v) = f_{k-1}(u, v) + g(S(R_k(u), S(R_k(v)))) \cdot$$
$$\sum_c \alpha_c g(F_c(R_k(u)), F_c(R_k(v))) \tag{3}$$

where $k \geq 0$ and $f_{-1} = 0$. α_c is the weight of feature c. $g(S_1, S_2)$ is the sequence similarity calculated by the dynamic time warping algorithm [4] for sequence S_1 and sequence S_2. The sequence $S(V)$ is calculated in (4).

$$S(V) = sort([D_1 \cdot e^{-\Delta t_1}, \ldots, D_n \cdot e^{-\Delta t_n}]) \tag{4}$$

where e is the natural constant. Δt_i is the average passive response time of node i. $sort$ is the function for ascending order according to their values. The ordered sequence $F_c(N)$ of the feature c in node set N is calculated in (5).

$$F_c(N) = sort([c_1, \ldots, c_n]) \tag{5}$$

Construction of Hierarchically Weighted Graph. The distance of the local loop structure between two nodes is calculated by (3). Then we construct a hierarchically weighted graph M based on random walk sampling by the method in [21]. M is made up of $(k^* + 1)$ layers. Each layer in M is composed of all the nodes in $G = \langle V, E \rangle$. Nodes in the set V are pairwise connected without directions. The current layer represents the jump probability based on the nearest k-hop loop distance of the nodes, where $k = 0, \ldots, k^*$. The weights $w_k(u, v)$ of the edge between u and v in the k-th layer are calculated in (6).

$$w_k(u, v) = e^{-f_k(u,v)} \tag{6}$$

Nodes belonging to different levels are connected by directed edges. Hence, each node is connected with its corresponding upper node and lower node. The definition of weight on a directed edge connected to the upper node is shown in (7).

$$w(u_k, u_{k+1}) = \log(\Gamma_k(u) + e) \tag{7}$$

The definition of weight connected to the lower node is shown in (8).

$$w(u_k, u_{k-1}) = 1. \tag{8}$$

where $\Gamma_k(u)$ is the number of edges in k-th layer that are connected to the node u with weights greater than the average. The calculation process is shown in (9):

$$\Gamma_k(u) = \sum_{v \in V} 1 \cdot bool((w_k(u, v) > \bar{w}_k)) \tag{9}$$

$bool$ is the boolean function, and $\bar{w}_k$ is the average weight of all edges for the k-th layer.

Node Sampling Based on the Biased Random Walk. To catch the node sequences, we sample on the hierarchically weighted graph M using a biased random walk. Each sampling is decided according to the pre-set probability walking at the current, upper or lower layer. Each time the sampled nodes are more inclined to select similar nodes to current ones in local structure, influence, and other features.

If it walks at the current layer, we assume that it is the k-th layer. The probability from node u to node v is shown in (10).

$$p_k(u, v) = \frac{e^{-f_k(u,v)}}{Z_k(u)} \tag{10}$$

where $Z_k(u) = \sum_{v \in V, v \neq u} e^{-f_k(u,v)}$. It is the normalization factor for node u in k-th layer.

If it walks at the upper layer, the $(k+1)$-th layer is selected with the probability shown in (11).

$$p_k(u_k, u_{k+1}) = \frac{w(u_k, u_{k+1})}{w(u_k, u_{k+1}) + w(u_k, u_{k-1})} \tag{11}$$

If it walks at the lower layer, the $(k-1)$-th layer is selected with the probability shown in (12).

$$p_k(u_k, u_{k-1}) = 1 - p_k(u_k, u_{k+1}) \tag{12}$$

Representation of Network Topology. The sequence H_S for global user nodes is obtained by biased random walk sampling on the probabilistic jump of M. The following construction of network topology is shown in Fig. 3. There are T nodes in the graph $G = \langle V, E \rangle$, where $T \in \{u_1, u_2, \ldots, u_T\}$. This model is used to predict the central nodes for a given node sequence, and then these central nodes are linked to form the network topology. The optimization objective is shown in (13).

$$\frac{1}{T} \sum_{t=i}^{T-i} \log p(u_t \mid u_{t-i}, \ldots, u_{t+i}) \tag{13}$$

where i represents the size of a sliding window. $p(u_t \mid u_{t-i}, \ldots, u_{t+i})$ is the output of the model. The prediction result is shown in (14).

$$p(u_t \mid u_{t-i}, \ldots, u_{t+i}, \mathbf{S}) = \frac{e^{y_{u_t}}}{\sum_j e^{y_j}} \tag{14}$$

y_j is the non-normalized likelihood probability of node j calculated in (15).

$$y = b + Uh(u_{t-i}, \ldots, u_{t+i}; H) \tag{15}$$

U and b are parameters of the output layer. h is averaged by the node vectors in H.

4.4   Feedback Signals

Feedback signals are the feedback information of users for an event, and they have an obvious time effect. The information about the same event will lead to different sub-events which stand for various point of views. The changes of views are related to the mode of propagation [17]. Hence, feedback information of users can help us to have a better understanding of the event.

The user feedback signals have achieved significant results on rumor identification [2,24]. But the usage of this feature often has two problems, which are incomplete collection [31] and poor scalability. To overcome these problems, we efficiently use this feature and propose a mining method based on seed words.

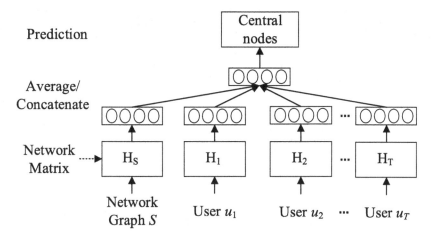

Fig. 3. Training model of network structure vector. H_i represents the node sequence obtained by sampling the i-th node, where i ranges from 1 to T.

Our approach utilizes the word vectors [23] pre-trained in the external corpus (*e.g.*, Wikipedia). It extends the scope of semantic sources and ensures the accuracy of feedback signals in the overall semantic space. The corresponding algorithm is shown in Algorithm 1.

Generation of Seed Words: The regular expression of inquiry and correction signals [31] is used as the initial generation method. The information content of datasets is regularly matched to obtain the initial seed words.

Matching Calculation of Inquiry and Correction Signals: In the process of finding a match, each seed word is separately calculated to find a word whose cosine similarity in the pre-trained word vectors P is greater than a threshold.

Construction of Feedback Signals: All the seed words obtained in the previous steps are seen as the word set Q of feedback signals. The information sequence of event e_i is divided into n periods by the nonlinear segmentation method. The information text sequence $d_{i1}, d_{i2}, \ldots, d_{in}$ from e_i in each nonlinear period is obtained. Then matching process between the text sequence d_{ij} of the event e_i in the j-th period and the word set of feedback signals is carried out by Aho-Corasick [1].

5   Model

In this section, we analyze the influence of multiple features on online social networks and design an attention model for rumor identification. The basic architecture of our model is shown in Fig. 4.

Input Layer. The network topology $(w_{i1}, w_{i2}, \ldots, w_{in})$, user feedback signal $(s_{i1}, s_{i2}, \ldots, s_{in})$ and text content $(d_{i1}, d_{i2}, \ldots, d_{in})$ of event e_i in each non-linear period are used as the input data.

Algorithm 1. Mining algorithm of user feedback signals

Input: event set $E = e_1, e_2, \ldots, e_m$, number of iterations γ, number of event periods
$\quad$ n, similarity threshold t, pre-training word vector set P
Output: feedback signal matrix S for each period of the event
1: $Q \leftarrow$ RexMatch(E)
2: **for** iter$\leftarrow 1, \ldots, \gamma$: **do**
3: $\quad$ $L \leftarrow |Q|$
4: $\quad$ **for** $j \leftarrow 1, \ldots, L$: **do**
5: $\quad\quad$ $U_j \leftarrow$ GetSimilarWords($Q[j], t, P$)
6: $\quad\quad$ $Q \leftarrow$ AddWord(Q, U_j)
7: $\quad$ **end for**
8: **end for**
9: **for** $i \leftarrow 1, \ldots, m$: **do**
10: $\quad$ $d_{i1}, d_{i2}, \ldots, d_{in} \leftarrow$ Split(e_i, n)
11: $\quad$ **for** $j \leftarrow 1, \ldots, n$: **do**
12: $\quad\quad$ $S_{ij} \leftarrow$ AhoCorasick(d_{ij}, Q)
13: $\quad$ **end for**
14: **end for**
15: **return** S

Embedding Layer. The multiple features are structured as input to the embedding layer. Then the heterogeneous features are normalized.

Encoder Layer. The output of the embedding layer is processed by the encoding layer to obtain time-series information of the event.

Attention Layer. The attention layer weights the obtained information from the encoding layer to get related content of the event in the propagation process.

Output Layer. The output of the attention layer is used as an input of a fully connected layer for predicting the category of event.

5.1 Embedding Layer

Due to the multiple features of the event come from different feature domains, they are not suitable as the direct inputs to the model. Therefore, the primary role of the embedding layer in the network architecture is to transform them into vectors. Then, these vectors are standardized and aggregated as inputs for an encoding layer. The input of an embedding layer is the original feature data x_t shown in (16) of the event at period t, including the network topology vector w_t, the user feedback signal vector s_t and the text vector d_t.

$$x_t = aggregate(d_t, w_t, s_t) \tag{16}$$

where $aggregate$ is the function to connect the vectors.

$\quad$ The output of an embedding layer acts as the input c_t for the encoding layer at period t. The calculation process is shown in (17).

$$c_t = tanh(W_a x_t + b_a) \tag{17}$$

where W_a is the weight matrix and b_a is the bias. $tanh$ is the activation function.

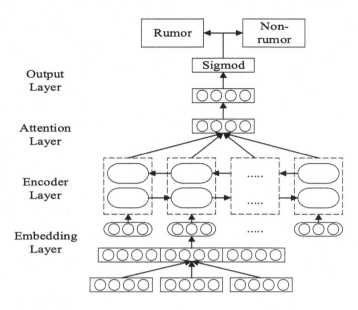

Fig. 4. Basic architecture of the model

5.2   Encoding Layer

To obtain the relationship of response time between the rumor and the event in general propagation process, the Bi-directional Gated Recurrent Unit [7] (Bi-GRU) model is adopted in this layer. Bi-GRU can gain long-term dependence on the data. It also has the flexibility to handle variable-length inputs. Hence, it is suitable for capturing information about event propagation in time-series relation. The calculation of the encoding layer is shown in (18):

$$
\begin{cases}
h_t = (\overrightarrow{h_t}, \overleftarrow{h_t}) \\
\overrightarrow{h_t} = \overrightarrow{GRU_1}\,(c_t), t = 1, \ldots, n \\
\overleftarrow{h_t} = \overleftarrow{GRU_1}\,(c_t), t = n, \ldots, 1
\end{cases}
\tag{18}
$$

where $\overrightarrow{h_t}$ represents the output value of the forward part at period t and $\overleftarrow{h_t}$ represents that of the backward part. h_t is used as an input to the successor network. $\overrightarrow{GRU_1}$ and $\overleftarrow{GRU_1}$ are the forward and backward propagation process respectively.

5.3   Attention Layer

This layer introduces the attention mechanism [3] by adding different weights to the output sequence $(h_1, h_2, \ldots, h_n)$. By weighting the output of the encoding layer, more context information of the original data can be utilized while aligning the input and output. The input of attention layer is h_t and the output v_e is calculated in (19):

$$\begin{cases} u_t = tanh(W_c h_t + b_c) \\ a_t = \dfrac{e^{u_t^T u_c}}{\sum_j e^{u_j^T u_c}} \\ v_e = \sum_j a_j h_j \end{cases} \qquad (19)$$

where W_c is the weight matrix and b_c is the bias. u_c represents the initial random weight of the attention layer. a_t represents the attention weight of the potential information in Bi-GRU. The attention module in the network structure is used for automatically learning the attention weight a_t. It can capture the correlation between h_t and the hidden state of the decoder. Then, these attention weights are used to construct the content vector v_e. The output of an attention layer is used as the input of a fully connected layer for the final rumor discrimination. In addition, it can also be used as an independent analysis of events.

5.4   Output Layer

The final output discrimination of the output layer is shown in (20).

$$\hat{L}_e = \sigma(W_e v_e + b_e) \qquad (20)$$

where $\hat{L}_e$ represents the predicted category of the event. σ is the activation function. W_e is the weight matrix and b_e is the bias. We use the cross-entropy loss function to measure the difference between the predicted category and the ground-truth category. The Adam optimization algorithm [13] is used for training iteration as shown in (21).

$$Loss = -\frac{1}{N} \sum_{j=1}^{N} [L_j \ln \hat{L}_j + (1 - L_j) \ln(1 - \hat{L}_j)] + \frac{\lambda}{2} ||\theta||_2^2 \qquad (21)$$

where N represents the total number of samples in the training set and L_j represents the ground-truth category of the j-th event. θ is a set of parameters for the model. λ is a hyper-parameter.

6   Experiments

6.1   Dataset

We use the classic dataset which has been applied in the work of [15,17,22,29] on the rumor detection. It is divided into Weibo data and Twitter data. But the Twitter data only provides the ID of each event, and the contents need to be obtained through the official interface. Some of them can not be obtained due to access rights or non-existence. After statistics, about fifteen percent of Twitter data has lost. To carry out a complete experimental comparison on the same dataset, we use Weibo data to conduct experiments. The entire dataset has a total of 2313 rumors and 2351 non-rumor samples, and each of them contains a number of information.

6.2   Baselines

In order to verify the effectiveness of our method, we compare with some benchmark models on the same dataset. They are described as follows:

DT-Rank [31]: This method obtains feature information by regular matching and text clustering. The clusters of samples are sorted by various statistical features.

SVM-TS [16]: This method uses the support vector machine (SVM) as a classification model. It utilizes time-dependent propagation features which are connected with event features as inputs of the model.

DTC [5]: This method uses the decision tree as the classification model. The characteristics they used are the number of microblog posts, the average number of followers, and so on.

GRU-2 [15]: This method uses term frequency–inverse document frequency (TF-IDF) to represent text information of each period. The classification model is the Bi-GRU.

CAMI [29]: This method is different from GRU-2. It uses segment vectors to represent text information. The model it used is a convolutional neural network (CNN).

6.3   Experiment of Representation Learning Method for Network Nodes

To verify the validity of the representation learning method for network nodes proposed in this paper, we analyze the existing methods and compare the performance of them with the same training model. We extract the vectors of network nodes by representation learning methods as the training data. Then we train an extra DNN model to evaluate the effectiveness of these methods. The experimental results are shown in Table 1.

From Table 1, we can see that the Struc2vec model performs better than Deepwork and Node2vec. Struc2vec is not based on the hypothesis of neighbor similarity but the spatial structure similarity. However, it is still not as effective as our representation learning method of network nodes on the training model. Besides, the models [10,20,21] are not well applied to directed graphs with node attributes and edge weights. They are designed without considering the characteristic attributes of user nodes and the time attributes of events on online social networks.

Table 1. Experiments on representation methods of network nodes

Method	Category	Accuracy	Precision	Recall rate	F1 score
Struct2vec [21]	R	0.785	0.762	0.823	0.791
	N		0.811	0.747	0.777
Deepwalk [20]	R	0.618	0.671	0.699	0.685
	N		0.691	0.662	0.676
Node2vec [10]	R	0.723	0.702	0.766	0.733
	N		0.747	0.679	0.712
Ours	R	**0.828**	**0.802**	**0.865**	**0.833**
	N		**0.857**	**0.790**	**0.822**

6.4 Experiment of Rumor Identification

In order to verify the effectiveness of our method, we compare with some benchmark models on the same dataset. The experimental results are shown in Table 2. From Table 2, we can see that our method perform better than these state-of-art works in rumor identification task. We also compare the effect of feedback signals, which show a difference of nearly 3% points.

The rumor identification task not only needs to have the judgment after overall propagation cycle of an event, but also needs to verify the authenticity of the information in the early stage. Accurate discrimination during the early period of an event plays an extremely important role in warning, containment, and blocking of rumors on social networks. Hence, experiments are conducted to verify if our method works in the early propagation of rumors.

The average time for the official media of Sina Weibo to refute rumors is 72 h [15,16,29]. Hence, we select 9 time points within 72 h and train the discriminant models respectively. The experimental results of our method are shown in Table 3. We can see that our method achieves a high accuracy in the early detection of rumors. As the propagation of events, the accuracy of rumor identification is gradually increased and it tends to be stable around the point of 24 h.

Figure 5 is a performance comparison between the proposed method and the existing methods at different time points in the early detection of rumors. The experimental results show that our method is better than others in the early detection of rumors. Even though the CAMI has a high detection rate in the initial stage of the event, but its effect is not as good as our method with the time changes.

Table 2. Experiments on rumor identification by different methods

Method	Category	Accuracy	Precision	Recall rate	F1 score
DT-Rank [31]	R	0.732	0.738	0.715	0.726
	N		0.726	0.749	0.737
SVM-TS [16]	R	0.857	0.839	0.885	0.861
	N		0.878	0.830	0.857
DTC [5]	R	0.831	0.847	0.815	0.831
	N		0.815	0.847	0.830
GRU-2 [15]	R	0.910	0.876	0.956	0.914
	N		0.952	0.864	0.906
CAMI [29]	R	0.933	0.921	**0.945**	0.933
	N		**0.945**	0.921	0.932
Ours (except feedback)	R	0.915	0.902	0.913	0.922
	N		0.887	0.907	0.936
Ours (all features)	R	**0.947**	0.944	0.927	0.935
	N		0.930	**0.945**	**0.938**

Table 3. Early detection of rumors

Deadline	Category	Accuracy	Precision	Recall rate	F1 score
1 h	R	0.821	0.816	0.823	0.820
	N		0.825	0.818	0.821
3 h	R	0.873	0.882	0.857	0.869
	N		0.863	0.887	0.875
6 h	R	0.905	0.880	0.934	0.906
	N		0.931	0.875	0.902
12 h	R	0.924	0.908	0.941	0.924
	N		0.940	0.906	0.923
24 h	R	0.934	0.928	0.939	0.933
	N		0.939	0.928	0.934
36 h	R	0.933	0.936	0.927	0.932
	N		0.929	0.937	0.933
48 h	R	0.938	0.929	0.946	0.937
	N		0.946	0.929	0.937
72 h	R	0.940	0.933	0.941	0.937
	N		0.941	0.934	0.938
96 h	R	0.938	0.953	0.917	0.935
	N		0.922	0.955	0.940

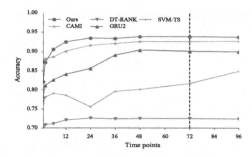

Fig. 5. Comparisons in the early detection of rumors

7   Conclusion and Future Work

In this paper, we creatively propose a new point of view based on the multiple features for rumor identification task and achieve a relatively good result. Our method also performs better in the early detection of rumors than some works. Besides, we propose a representation learning method for network nodes based on the space-time similarity. This method can also be used for other time-series tasks on social networks like public opinion monitoring and influence analysis of user. But there exists some shortcomings. Our method is slightly better than the best one for rumor identification in the propagation cycle of an event. The time for training and testing needs several days. In the future, we will do some improvements to the model for optimizing the performance of our model and reducing training time. At the same time, the loss of spatial information in network topology and the representation method of network nodes can also be optimized.

Acknowledgement. This work was partly supported by the National Natural Science Foundation of China under No. U1836112, the National Key R&D Program of China under No. 2016YFB0801100, the National Natural Science Foundation of China under No. 61876134 and U1536204.

References

1. Aho, A.V., Corasick, M.J.: Efficient string matching: an aid to bibliographic search. Commun. ACM **18**(6), 333–340 (1975)
2. Al-Khalifa, H.S., Al-Eidan, R.M.: An experimental system for measuring the credibility of news content in Twitter. Int. J. Web Inf. Syst. **7**(2), 130–151 (2011)
3. Bahdanau, D., Cho, K., Bengio, Y.: Neural machine translation by jointly learning to align and translate. In: Proceedings of the International Conference on Learning Representations (2015)
4. Bemdt, D.J., Clifford, J.: Using dynamic time warping to find patterns in time series. In: Proceedings of AAA1-94 Workshop on Knowledge Discovery in Databases, vol. 10, pp. 359–370 (1994)

5. Castillo, C., Mendoza, M., Poblete, B.: Information credibility on Twitter. In: Proceedings of the 20th International Conference on World Wide Web, pp. 675–684 (2011)
6. Chen, T., Wu, L., Li, X., Zhang, J., Yin, H., Wang, Y.: Call attention to rumors: deep attention based recurrent neural networks for early rumor detection. In: Ganji, M., Rashidi, L., Fung, B., Wang, C. (eds.) PAKDD 2018, pp. 40–52. Springer, Heidelberg (2018). https://doi.org/10.1007/978-3-030-04503-6_4
7. Cho, K., et al.: Learning phrase representations using RNN encoder-decoder for statistical machine translation. In: Proceedings of the Conference on Empirical Methods on Natural Language Processing (2014)
8. DiFonzo, N., Bordia, P.: Rumor, gossip and urban legends. Diogenes **54**(1), 19–35 (2007)
9. Friggeri, A., Eckles, D., Adamic, L.: Rumor cascades in social networks. In: Proceedings of the International AAAI Conference on Weblogs and Social Media (2014)
10. Grover, A., Leskovec, J.: node2vec: Scalable feature learning for networks. In: Proceedings of the 22nd ACM SIGKDD International Conference on Knowledge Discovery and Data Mining, pp. 855–864. ACM (2016)
11. Gupta, M., Zhao, P., Han, J.: Evaluating event credibility on Twitter. In: Proceedings of the 2012 SIAM International Conference on Data Mining, pp. 153–164 (2012)
12. Huang, Q., Zhou, C., Wu, J., Mingwen, W.: Deep structure learning for rumor detection on Twitter. In: Proceedings of the International Joint Conference on Neural Networks (2019)
13. Kingma, D.P., Ba, J.: Adam: A method for stochastic optimization. In: Proceedings of the 3rd International Conference for Learning Representations (2015)
14. Liu, X., Nourbakhsh, A., Li, Q., Fang, R.: Real-time rumor debunking on Twitter. In: Proceedings of the 24th ACM International Conference on Information and Knowledge Management (2015)
15. Ma, J., et al.: Detecting rumors from microblogs with recurrent neural networks. In: Proceedings of the 25th International Joint Conference on Artificial Intelligence, pp. 3818–3824 (2016)
16. Ma, J., Gao, W., Wei, Z., Lu, Y., Wong, K.F.: Detect rumors using time series of social context information on microblogging websites. In: Proceedings of the 24th ACM International on Conference on Information and Knowledge Management, pp. 1751–1754 (2015)
17. Ma, J., Gao, W., Wong, K.F.: Detect rumors in microblog posts using propagation structure via kernel learning. In: Proceedings of the 55th Annual Meeting of the Association for Computational Linguistics, pp. 708–717 (2017)
18. Margolin, D., Keegan, B., Hannak, A., Weber, I.: Get back! you don't know me like that: the social mediation of fact checking interventions in Twitter conversations. In: Proceedings of the International AAAI Conference on Weblogs and Social Media (2014)
19. Matsuta, T., Uyematsu, T.: On the distance between the rumor source and its optimal estimate in a regular tree. In: arXiv preprint arXiv:1901.03039 (2019)
20. Perozzi, B., Al-Rfou, R., Skiena, S.: Deepwalk: online learning of social representations. In: Proceedings of the 20th ACM SIGKDD International Conference on Knowledge Discovery and Data Mining, pp. 701–710 (2014)
21. Ribeiro, L.F.R., Savarese, P.H.P., Figueiredo, D.R.: struc2vec: Learning node representations from structural identity. In: ACM SIGKDD Conference on Knowledge Discovery and Data Mining (2017)

22. Ruchansky, N., Seo, S., Liu, Y.: CSI: a hybrid deep model for fake news detection. In: Proceedings of the 26th ACM International Conference on Information and Knowledge Management (2017)

23. Song, Y., Shi, S., Li, J., Zhang, H.: Directional skip-gram: explicitly distinguishing left and right context for word embeddings. In: Proceedings of the 2018 Conference of the North American Chapter of the Association for Computational Linguistics: Human Language Technologies, vol. 2, pp. 175–180 (2018)

24. Sun, S., Liu, H., He, J., Du, X.: Detecting event rumors on sina weibo automatically. In: Ishikawa, Y., Li, J., Wang, W., Zhang, R., Zhang, W. (eds.) APWeb 2013. LNCS, vol. 7808, pp. 120–131. Springer, Heidelberg (2013). https://doi.org/10.1007/978-3-642-37401-2_14

25. Takahashi, T., Igata, N.: Rumor detection on Twitter. In: The 6th International Conference on Soft Computing and Intelligent Systems, and The 13th International Symposium on Advanced Intelligence Systems. IEEE (2012)

26. Wang, S., Terano, T.: Detecting rumor patterns in streaming social media. In: Proceedings of the 2015 IEEE International Conference on Big Data (2015)

27. Wu, K., Yang, S., Zhu, K.Q.: False rumors detection on Sina Weibo by propagation structures. In: 2015 IEEE 31st International Conference on Data Engineering, pp. 651–662 (2015)

28. Yang, F., Liu, Y., Yu, X., Yang, M.: Automatic detection of rumor on Sina Weibo. In: Proceedings of the ACM SIGKDD Workshop on Mining Data Semantics, pp. 1–7 (2012)

29. Yu, F., Liu, Q., Wu, S., Wang, L., Tan, T.: A convolutional approach for misinformation identification. In: Proceedings of the Twenty-Sixth International Joint Conference on Artificial Intelligence, pp. 3901–3907 (2017)

30. Yuan, C., Ma, Q., Zhou, W., Han, J., Hu, S.: Jointly embedding the local and global relations of heterogeneous graph for rumor detection. In: Proceedings of the IEEE International Conference on Data Mining (2019)

31. Zhao, Z., Resnick, P., Mei, Q.: Enquiring minds: early detection of rumors in social media from enquiry posts. In: Proceedings of the 24th International Conference on World Wide Web, pp. 1395–1405 (2015)

Defending Poisoning Attacks in Federated Learning via Adversarial Training Method

Jiale Zhang[1]([X]), Di Wu[2], Chengyong Liu[1], and Bing Chen[1]

[1] College of Computer Science and Technology, Nanjing University of Aeronautics
and Astronautics, Nanjing 211106, China
{jlzhang,lhoien,cb_china}@nuaa.edu.cn
[2] School of Computer Science, University of Technology Sydney,
Sydney 2007, Australia
di.wu-16@student.uts.edu.au

Abstract. Recently, federated learning has shown its significant advantages in protecting training data privacy by maintaining a joint model across multiple clients. However, its model security issues have not only been recently explored but shown that federated learning exhibits inherent vulnerabilities on the active attacks launched by malicious participants. Poisoning is one of the most powerful active attacks where an inside attacker can upload the crafted local model updates to further impact the global model performance. In this paper, we first illustrate how the poisoning attack works in the context of federated learning. Then, we correspondingly propose a defense method that mainly relies upon a well-researched adversarial training technique: pivotal training, which improves the robustness of the global model with poisoned local updates. The main contribution of this work is that the countermeasure method is simple and scalable since it does not require complex accuracy validations, while only changing the optimization objectives and loss functions. We finally demonstrate the effectiveness of our proposed mitigation mechanisms through extensive experiments.

Keywords: Federated learning · Poisoning attacks · Label-flipping · Pivotal training

1 Introduction

Driven by big data and distributed computing technologies, such as mobile edge computing [1], federated learning has attracted significant attention recently from both academia and industries [2]. It presents a distributed training strategy by maintaining a global model across multiple devices and a central server. This

Supported in part by the National Key Research and Development Program of China, under Grant 2019YFB2102000, in part by the National Natural Science Foundation of China, under Grant 61672283, and in part by the Postgraduate Research & Practice Innovation Program of Jiangsu Province under Grant KYCX18_0308.

global model trains each participant's private training data locally, and then the server collects local model parameters to update the global model iteratively. Since the private training data never leave the participants' devices, federated learning shows the big innovation in protecting users' training data privacy [3,4]. Besides, another big innovation in federated learning is that the global model is updated by using the designed model average algorithm, which can benefit from a wide range of unbalanced data distribution among diverse participants.

However, existing attack proposals [5,6] found that the federated learning framework is vulnerable to the poisoning attacks launched by the malicious participants for the following reasons: 1) there are many participants in the federated learning system, which is likely to contain one or more malicious users; 2) the authenticity of some user updates cannot be verified because the server cannot see the user's local data and training process; 3) there may be great differences among local updates generated by multiple users, which brings great difficulties to anomaly detection; 4) the access model of federated learning is white box, so internal attackers can easily observe the model structure, learning algorithm and multiple versions of global model parameters. Moreover, such a poisoning attack could bring serious security threatens form machine learning applications, such as face recognition, word prediction, and natural language processing [7].

For defending the above-mentioned poisoning attacks, existing solutions are mainly coming to three categories: 1) identifying the poison data points from the assumed trusted datasets [8–10] 2) reducing the negative effects of poison data trough robust losses [11–13]; 3) verifying each local model updates in the distributed setting [14,15]. For example, Mozaffari-Kermani et al. [8] proposed to distinguish the poison and benign data points by assuming a golden model to evaluate the validation accuracy for training data. Han et al. [11] presented the stronger-convex losses for SGD methods to enhance the robustness of model parameters on noised labels. However, the defense mechanism of the above analysis is based on the assumption that attacker or server already has the same distributed verification data set as the training data, which is impractical in federated learning since the training data is not shared among participants.

To address this problem, we presented an efficient defense mechanism, called federated adversarial training (FAT), which utilize the *pivotal property* of adversarial training method [16,17] to improve the robustness of conventional federated learning model with poisoned local model updates. Compared with the existing poisoning defense mechanisms [8–14], FAT does not need access to the participants' raw datasets and computes only on the received weight changes from all the participants' local models. The main idea of FAT is that the server can distinguish the difference among received local gradients by creating an extra predictive model to predict which participant a certain gradient belongs to, while the federated model is modified to prevent this discriminating behavior, thus eliminating the influence that poisoned local updates have on the global model. The main contributions of this paper can be summarized as follows:

– We demonstrate that the federated learning framework is essentially vulnerable to poisoning attacks launched by malicious users. Then, we show the details on how to construct the poisoning attacks in federated learning by using the label-flipping method to generate poison data records.

- We also propose a new poisoning defense strategy, which improves the robustness of conventional federated learning protocol by integrating the pivotal learning technique.
- We conduct extensive experiments on two benchmark datasets in federated learning environment. Evaluation results show that the proposed defense method can efficiently mitigate poisoning attack without impact the main tasks of federated learning.

The remainder of this paper is organized as follows. In Sect. 2, we introduce the preliminaries, including federated learning and pivotal training method. In Sect. 3, we present the construction of poisoning attack in federated learning using label-flipping method. Section 4 details the federated adversarial training strategy and performance evaluation is depicted in Sect. 5. Finally, Sect. 6 concludes the paper.

2   Preliminaries

2.1   Federated Learning

Federated learning [3] is a novel distributed framework that maintains a joint model across multiple participants and trains this model in a decentralized manner. Compared with conventional centralized machine learning as a service framework, such a localized training method can directly protect each participant's data privacy from leakage of any untrusted entities. According to the standard federated learning framework as shown in Fig. 1, all the participants are basically followed with a common objective, so that the structure of shared model can be unified by the server. At each iteration, clients first download the initialized model from the server and then adopt the distributed selective stochastic gradient descent (DSSGD) to complete the local training task:

$$L_{t+1} = L_t - \eta \cdot \nabla_{L_t} \mathcal{L}(L_t, b), \tag{1}$$

where L_t indicates the local model parameters assigned by the central server after the t-th communication round, $\mathcal{L}(L_t, b)$ denotes loss function under the local model parameters L_t and the local minibatch size b, and η is the learning rate. Then, the local updates, i.e., parameter change of the i-th user, can be calculated as follow:

$$\Delta L_{t+1}^i = L_{t+1}^i - L_t^i, \tag{2}$$

which were sent back to the server. After receiving those local parameters, the server will execute the model average algorithm to update the shared model using Eq. 3.

$$G_{t+1} = G_t + \frac{1}{N} \sum_{i=1}^{N} \Delta L_{t+1}^i, \tag{3}$$

where G_t denotes global parameter at the t-th iteration. The aforementioned steps will be iteratively executed until the global model training is completed.

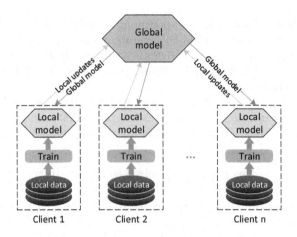

Fig. 1. Standard federated learning framework

2.2 Pivotal Training Method

In 2017, Louppe et al. [16] proposed the pivotal training method, which enables a learning model pivot on the sensitive attributes. In another word, the predictions of a model trained using pivotal learning method is *independent* of the sensitive attributes embedded in training data. We call this kind of adversarial training as *pivotal learning*. Assume that $x \in X$ are the training samples, $y \in Y$ are the corresponding labels, and $s \in S$ are sensitive attributes. Similar to GAN, the structure of pivotal learning comprises two neural network models f and g, where model f takes x as inputs and outputs a target label y, and model g takes inputs from the *logits* $r \in \mathbb{R}^{|\mathcal{R}|}$ of model f (the outputs of second-to-last layer of neural network) and predicts the sensitive attributes. As with GAN, those two model are trained simultaneously, in which g is trained to predict the sensitive attributes by giving the *logits* value from f. Equation 4 gives the value function of the pivotal learning.

$$E(\theta_f, \theta_g) = \mathcal{L}_f(\theta_f) - \mathcal{L}_g(\theta_f, \theta_g), \tag{4}$$

where $\mathcal{L}_f$ and $\mathcal{L}_g$ are the expected value of the negative log-likelihood of $Y|X$ under models f and of $S|r$ under model g, respectively. The adversarial training property between f and g is reflected in the optimization objectives, in which f aims to minimize its own prediction task loss and maximize the error of g, while g is trained to minimize the loss of predicting sensitive attribute S. Then, the optimize of the above value function is to find the minimax solution:

$$\tilde{\theta}_f, \tilde{\theta}_g = \arg\min_{\theta_f} \max_{\theta_g} E(\theta_f, \theta_g). \tag{5}$$

where the stochastic gradient descent is normally used for solving Eq. 5. In the remainder of this work, we apply pivotal training method to mitigate the poisoning attacks in the context of federated learning.

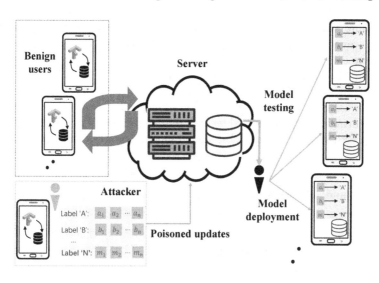

Fig. 2. Poisoning attack flow (label-flipping & backdoor)

3   Poisoning Against Federated Learning

In federated learning, attackers have the ability to observe model structure, learning algorithms, and sharing multiple versions of global model parameters. At the same time, the attacker can also modify the model hyperparameters arbitrarily, control the local training process, and change the local model update generated. In the federal learning system, the poisoning attacker first downloads the global model parameters to update his local model, and then he trains this new local model on the poisoned training data and uploads the generated local parameters to the server. After model averaging, the global model will achieve high accuracy on poisoned samples, while the main tasks (non-poisoned samples) will not be affected, thereby achieving the purpose of corrupting the global model.

In this paper, we mainly consider the label-flipping poisoning attack scenario, which denotes that malicious users are able to inject the crafted attack points into the training data by flipping the target classes' labels, thus making the trained model deviate from the original prediction boundaries. As shown in Fig. 2, the attacker tries to generate poisoned local update by training the global model on his crafted training dataset where the label of class M was flipped as 'N' and the remaining samples' labels are unchanged. When this poisoned update are pooled with other participants' local updates, the global model will classify the attacker-targeted samples in class M as the attacker-chosen label 'N'. Backdoor attack requires an attacker to train a targeted DNN model on his poisoned training data with some specific hidden patterns. These attacker-chosen patterns were defined as the backdoor trigger that making learning model produces unexpected results in the prediction phase.

Poisoning attack is launched to achieve the purpose of destroying the global model. However, this simple attack method is not effective in the federal learning, because the central server will average and aggregate all received local updates through Eq. 3, thereby reducing the impact of poison local updates on the global model. To mitigate the performance degradation of poisoning attack model, we introduce a scale factor S to expand the gradient changes of the attacker's local model, ensuring that the poisoned local updates keep surviving during the model averaging. By this way, the attacker's local model updates can be formulated as Eq. 6.

$$\Delta \hat{L}_{t+1}^p = S(L_{t+1}^p - \eta_{adv} \nabla \mathcal{L}(L_t^p, b_p)), \tag{6}$$

where η_{adv} and b_p are attacker's local learning rate and local batch size, respectively.

4 Adversarial Defense Mechanism

4.1 Main Idea and Design Goals

For efficiently mitigating the poisoning attacks as described in Sect. 3, we propose a novel defense algorithm called *federated adversarial training* (FAT) based on the pivotal learning method [16], with the goal of improving robustness of the conventional federated learning protocol. The key insight of FAT is that *the diversity of attackers' poisoned gradients are very different from victims' normal local updates*. Especially when the attacker calculates the gradient updates by training his local model on the generated poison data [18]. Correspondingly, the *logits* of the attacker's local model are showing significant differences compared with other victims', thus we use logits to represent the attacker's poisoned gradients as well as sensitive attributes.

Inspiring by the pivotal learning method (as shown in Sect. 2.2), our FAT algorithm consists of two classification models f_1 and f_2, in which f_1 is a modified global model used to generate logits, and f_2 is deployed at the server side to predict which participant a certain logits belongs to. Here, we assume that each participant has a unique identifier before the learning algorithm gets started. For the optimization objectives of f_1 and f_2, f_2 is trained to minimize its prediction task error (i.e., predict correct identifier), while f_1 is trained to minimize its own classification error (i.e., federated learning objective) and maximize f_2's objective function. In this way, f_1 replaces the original global model G to execute the federated classification task and trained adversarially with f_2, thus eliminating the influence that poisoned logits have on the global model. The robust federated adversarial training framework is shown in Fig. 3.

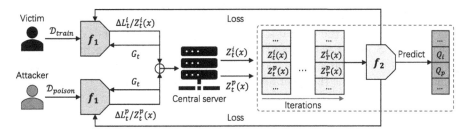

Fig. 3. Structure of federated adversarial training for defending poisoning attacks.

4.2 Defense Methodology

We now explain the theoretical results of FAT algorithm. In a federated learning protocol, each participant is assigned with an initialized global model to begin the local training process. Here, the attacker has no privilege to change the prescribed local training algorithm. Thus, FAT can adopt the modified global model f_1 to synchronously collect the gradient updates (include the logits) generated by all the participants. We illustrate the federated adversarial training algorithm based on the following perspectives: optimization goal of the whole learning system, loss functions of two models f_1 and f_2, gradient descent for solving the optimization problem, and the detailed training procedure in federated learning scenario.

Federated Adversarial Training: We emphasize that our proposed defense algorithm is suitable to federated learning system since FAT does not change the overall learning procedure except with modifying the optimization objectives and loss functions. We now give an explanation about how FAT algorithm be applied in federated learning protocol.

When the central server $\mathcal{S}$ starts to bootstrap the federated learning system, it first initializes a probabilistic classification model f_2 secretly which aims to find the optimal solution on predicting the participants' identifiers Q. Then, it further creates a global model with deliberated learning objective and loss function as with model f_1, whose main purpose is to minimize the error of its own classification task and maximize the error of f_2's prediction task. After that, $\mathcal{S}$ assigns the modified global model f_1 to the selected participants at the beginning of first communication round. Intuitively, each participant's local model W^i is the same model structure as f_1, which is trained to generate the local gradient updates ΔW based on minibatch stochastic gradient descent method. Note that, the training data sampling for each local batch $b \in \mathcal{B}$ is the same with conventional federated learning protocol [3] and the updating of local model f_1 in FAT can be formalized as:

$$W^i_{t+1} = W_t - \eta' \cdot \nabla_{W_t} \mathcal{L}_{f_1}(W_t, b), \tag{7}$$

where the gradient descending $\nabla_{W_t} \mathcal{L}_{f_1}(W_t, b)$ process is modified as Louppe's min-max game [16] to achieve adversarial training property. Correspondingly, the required local gradient updates can be easily calculated as $\Delta W_{t+1}^i = W_{t+1}^i - W_t^i$, which is sent back to the central server along with the identifiers $i \in Q$. For the executions of $\mathcal{S}$ after receiving all the gradient updates ΔW_{t+1}^i, $\mathcal{S}$ first trains f_2 on these gradient updates by ascending the gradient based on Louppe's min-max game [16], then it runs the federated average step as

$$G_{t+1}' = G_t' + \frac{1}{n_t'}\sum_{i \in [n_t]} \Delta W_{t+1}^i, \tag{8}$$

where n_t' is the number of selected participants. Finally, $\mathcal{S}$ publishes a new global model G_{t+1} along with f_2's loss to the participants for starting a new communication round $t + 1$. The aforementioned procedures are executed iteratively until the global model f_1 has high performance on classification task of labels $Y \in \mathbb{R}^{|\mathcal{Y}|}$ and f_2 performs poorly on prediction task of participants' identifier $Q \in \mathbb{R}^{|\mathcal{Q}|}$.

5   Experimental Evaluation

5.1   Experimental Settings

To evaluate the effectiveness of the poisoning attack and our proposed defense mechanism, we conduct exhaustive experiments of classification tasks on two classical datasets, i.e., MNIST and Fashion-MNIST. For all the experiments in this section, we distributed the training data set equally to participants (including attackers). These two datasets are all have 10 classes with different images (hand-writing images for MNIST and fashion images for FMNIST) and the total number of samples are 70000's grayscale images with 28×28 input size. When datasets are divided in this way, a class may be owned by different clients, which can be regarded as the *worst-case* of label-flipping poisoning attack.

For the experimental environments, we implement a federated learning prototype by using the PyTorch framework, which has been widely adopted in machine learning algorithms. All the experiments are done on a RHEL7.5 server with NVidia Quadro P4000 GPU with 32 GB RAM, and Ubuntu 16.04LTS OS. For the attack strategy, we here use the label-filliping method to construct the poisoned data and further train the local model on those crafted datasets. The neural network models used in our experiment are Convolutional Neural Networks (CNN). For the classifier (global model) and adversarial model f_1, they share the same network structure which consists of 6 convolution layers and 1 dense layer. The kernel size of the first three convolutional layers are set to 4×4 and last three convolutional layers are 3×3. For the adversarial model f_2, we apply a simple neural network with two dense layers and the activation functions applied to all the CNN model are ReLU and LReLU, respectively. The detailed network structures for MNIST and FMNIST datasets are shown in Table 1. Besides, we also define two evaluation indexes, i.e., *poisoning task accuracy* P_{acc} and *main task accuracy* M_{acc}, to quantify our experimental results. The impact parameters in our experimental evaluations are defined as: scale factor S and number of attackers A.

Table 1. Model architectures for classifier and adversarial models.

Items	MNIST, FMNIST, classifier, f_1 model	f_2 model
Models	Conv(1,64,4)+LReLU	
	Conv(64,64,4)+LReLU	
	Conv(64,64,4)+LReLU	FC(200)+ReLU
	Conv(64,128,3)+LReLU	FC(200)+ReLU
	Conv(128,128,3)+LReLU	FC(200)+ReLU
	Conv(128,128,3)+LReLU	FC(10)+Softmax
	Avgpooling(2,2)	
	FC(11)+Softmax	

Table 2. Fixed attacker number.

Settings		Total clients: **33**, Each round sampling: 10, Attacker: 1			
Scale factor		$S = 10$	$S = 20$	$S = 30$	$S = 40$
MNIST	P_{acc}	**0.5287** ± 0.002	**0.7392** ± 0.004	**0.7848** ± 0.004	**0.9080** ± 0.007
	M_{acc}	**0.9641** ± 0.0003	**0.9629** ± 0.001	**0.9584** ± 0.005	**0.9574** ± 0.0003
FMNIST	P_{acc}	**0.6311** ± 0.003	**0.7129** ± 0.002	**0.8061** ± 0.001	**0.9265** ± 0.003
	M_{acc}	**0.9543** ± 0.004	**0.9580** ± 0.006	**0.9607** ± 0.004	**0.9529** ± 0.007

5.2   Performance of Poisoning Attack

In our poisoning attack evaluations, we mainly consider the label-flipping attack in the context of federated learning to demonstrate the effectiveness of the poisoning attack model. As depicted above, the indexes involved in our experiments are P_{acc} and M_{acc}, in which the former one represents the correct classification rate of attacker-targeted classes from the final global model and the latter one means the classification results apart from the poisoned samples. Here, we mainly evaluate the classification accuracy on both main task and poisoning task under different impact parameter settings, i.e., different attacker number and scale factor, where one of the parameters is variable, the other is fixed.

Firstly, we design a set of experiments to evaluate the impact of scale factor S to the poisoning attack model, where the number of attackers is fixed to 1. In order to illustrate our experimental results intuitively, we run 100 rounds of federated learning protocol after the attacker begins to submit the poisoned local update, and then take the average value of all accuracy results under four scale factor settings (i.e., $S = 10, 20, 30, 40$). The mean accuracy of poisoning and main task accuracy with different scale factors for two datasets are shown in Table 2, it is easy to see that the poisoning attack model can achieve a minimum poisoning task accuracy of 52.87% and maximum of 92.65%. This is mainly because we set attackers to train their local models for multiple stages, thus increasing the impact of poisoning gradient on other participants' local updates.

Table 3. Fixed scale factor.

Settings		Total clients: **33**, Each round sampling: 10, Scale factor: 20			
Attackers		A = 3	A = 4	A = 5	A = 6
MNIST	P_{acc}	**0.7996** ± 0.003	**0.7947** ± 0.002	**0.8885** ± 0.005	**0.9253** ± 0.004
	M_{acc}	**0.9510** ± 0.004	**0.9504** ± 0.003	**0.9630** ± 0.005	**0.9362** ± 0.003
FMNIST	P_{acc}	**0.7635** ± 0.001	**0.8109** ± 0.004	**0.8642** ± 0.004	**0.9041** ± 0.006
	M_{acc}	**0.9526** ± 0.0002	**0.9607** ± 0.003	**0.9568** ± 0.001	**0.9562** ± 0.006

In addition, the number of attackers will significantly affect the accuracy of training phase and poisoning task because the training phase is distributed among multiple participants in joint learning. Therefore, we evaluate the impact of multiple attackers by comparing the accuracy of the poison and main tasks of the two datasets, where scale factor is fixed at 20 and the number of attackers changes from 3 to 6. As shown in Table 3, we can see that the mean accuracy of poisoning tasks have a significant increasing trend compared with fixed attacker number setting in Table 2. It can be demonstrated that the attacker number has a positive impact on poisoning task accuracy since the poisoned updates account for a large proportion of all the local updates.

5.3 Defense Mechanism Evaluation

To evaluate our proposed defense mechanism, FAT, we choose two attack settings that have performed the best poisoning task accuracy, which are single attacker ($A = 1$) with scale factor 20 ($S = 20$) and 5 attackers ($A = 5$) with scale factor 10 ($S = 10$), In our code, each participant identifiers are chosen by unique local model ID, i.e., 10 IDs for each communication round. Recall that given a model update of f_1, the goal of f_2 is to predict which party that the update belongs to. We experiment this by implementing two models with distinct loss functions while one model's loss is keeping fixed when another model is trained. Unlike a previous defense method described in [15], we use the last layer of model f_1's weights as model f_2's input which is more practical than inputting only a uniform probability vector since weights can be great representatives of each participant's training samples including poisoning records.

Here, we run 100 communication rounds after the attack launched to measure the poison and main task accuracy of image classifications on MNIST and FMNIST datasets. Figure 4 shows the results of our defined four indexes in the context of federated learning, which are 1) main task accuracy without federated adversarial training; 2) main task accuracy with federated adversarial training; 3) poisoning task accuracy without federated adversarial training; 4) poisoning task accuracy without federated adversarial training. As shown in Figs. 4(a) and 4(b), the difference of main task accuracy with and without adversarial training is quite small (below 8.7%), which means the involved adversarial training method has little effect on the accuracy of federated learning. Besides, for two

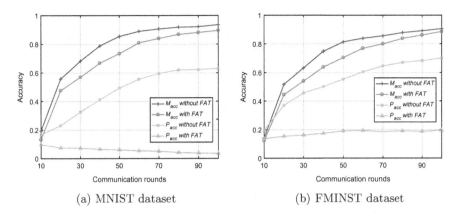

(a) MNIST dataset   (b) FMINST dataset

Fig. 4. Effectiveness of FAT on MNIST and FMNIST datasets

datasets, the poisoning task accuracy with adversarial training method is substantially low than 20%, while rapidly up to about 60% in standard federated learning settings without adversarial training.

6   Conclusion

In this work, we proposed the federated adversarial training, i.e., FAT, method to defense the poisoning attack model in the context of federated learning. Firstly, we demonstrate that the federated learning framework is essentially vulnerable to poisoning attacks launched by malicious users. Then, we give a formal describe how to construct the poisoning attacks in federated learning by taking a label-flipping attack as an example. Finally, we proposed a federated adversarial training method to mitigate such an active attack by integrating pivotal learning into local training procedures. The extensive experimental results on two benchmark datasets, MNIST and FMNIST, demonstrated the effectiveness of the poisoning attack model and our proposed defense strategy.

Acknowledgment. This work was supported in part by the National Key Research and Development Program of China under Grant 2019YFB2102000, in part by the National Natural Science Foundation of China under Grant 61672283, and in part by the Postgraduate Research & Practice Innovation Program of Jiangsu Province under Grant KYCX18_0308.

References

1. Ribeiro, M., Grolinger, K., Capretz, M.A.: MLaaS: machine learning as a service. In: Proceedings of ICMLA, pp. 896–902 (2015)
2. Lim, W.Y.B.: Federated learning in mobile edge networks: a comprehensive survey. IEEE Commun. Surv. Tutorials (2020)

3. McMahan, H.B., Moore, E., Ramage, D., Hampson, S., y Arcas, B.A.: Communication-efficient learning of deep networks from decentralized data. In: Proceedings of AISTATS, pp. 1–10 (2017)
4. Yang, Q., Liu, Y., Chen, T., Tong, Y.: Federated machine learning: concept and applications. ACM Trans. Intell. Syst. Technol. **10**(2), 1–19 (2019)
5. Jagielski, M., Oprea, A., Biggio, B., Liu, C., Nita-Rotaru, C., Li, B.: Manipulating machine learning: Poisoning attacks and countermeasures for regression learning. In: Proceedings of IEEE S&P, pp. 19–35 (2018)
6. Melis, L., Song, C., De Cristofaro, E., Shmatikov, V.: Exploiting unintended feature leakage in collaborative learning. In: Proceedings of IEEE S&P, pp. 691–706 (2019)
7. Nasr, M., Shokri, R., Houmansadr, A.: Comprehensive privacy analysis of deep learning: passive and active white-box inference attacks against centralized and federated learning. In: Proceedings of IEEE S&P, pp. 793–753 (2019)
8. Mozaffari-Kermani, M., Sur-Kolay, S., Raghunathan, A., Jha, N.K.: Systematic Poisoning attacks on and defenses for machine learning in healthcare. IEEE J. Biomed. Health Inform. **19**(6), 1893–1905 (2015)
9. Shen, S., Tople, S., Saxena, P.: Auror: defending against poisoning attacks in collaborative deep learning systems. In: Proceedings of ACSAC, pp. 508–519 (2016)
10. Baracaldo, N., Chen, B., Ludwig, H., Safavi, J.A.: Mitigating poisoning attacks on machine learning models: a data provenance based approach. In: Proceedings of ACM AISec, pp. 103–110 (2017)
11. Han, B., Tsang, I.W., Chen, L.: On the convergence of a family of robust losses for stochastic gradient descent. In: Frasconi, P., Landwehr, N., Manco, G., Vreeken, J. (eds.) ECML PKDD, pp. 665–680. Springer, Heidelberg (2016). https://doi.org/10.1007/978-3-319-46128-1_42
12. Steinhardt, J., Koh, P.W., Liang, P.S.: Certified defenses for data poisoning attacks. In: Proceedings of NIPS, pp. 3517–3529 (2017)
13. Wang, B., et al.: Neural cleanse: identifying and mitigating backdoor attacks in neural networks. In: Proceedings of IEEE S & P, pp. 707–723 (2019)
14. Zhao, Y., Chen, J., Zhang, J., Wu, D., Teng, J., Yu, S.: PDGAN: a novel poisoning defense method in federated learning using generative adversarial network. In: Wen, S., Zomaya, A., Yang, L.T. (eds.) ICA3PP 2019. LNCS, vol. 11944, pp. 595–609. Springer, Cham (2020). https://doi.org/10.1007/978-3-030-38991-8_39
15. Hayes, J., Ohrimenko, O.: Contamination attacks and mitigation in multi-party machine learning. In: Proceedings of NIPS, pp. 6604–6616 (2018)
16. Louppe, G., Kagan, M. and Cranmer, K.: Learning to pivot with adversarial networks. In: Proceedings of NIPS, pp. 981–990 (2017)
17. Huang, L., Joseph, A.D., Nelson, B., Rubinstein, B.I., Tygar, J.D.: Adversarial machine learning. In: Proceedings of ACM AISec, pp. 43–58 (2011)
18. Zhang, J., Chen, J., Wu, D., Chen, B., Yu, S.: Poisoning attack in federated learning using generative adversarial nets. In: Proceedings of IEEE Trustcom, pp. 374–380 (2019)

Multi-type Source Code Defect Detection Based on TextCNN

Xiaomeng Wang$^{(\boxtimes)}$, Zhibin Guan, Wei Xin, and Jiajie Wang

China Information Technology Security Evaluation Center, Beijing, China
xiao_meng_wang@163.com

Abstract. Classical static analysis for defect detection usually depends on code compilation or virtual compilation, which meanwhile requires high professional experience. The existing deep learning-based code defect analysis methods are mostly binary classification methods, in which the type of defects cannot be accurately judged. Under the condition of without compiling the project, a new multi-classification method was proposed which can achieve multi-type, cross function and cross file defect detection of source code. The core parts were word2vec and TextCNN, which were training based on abstract syntax tree, code attribute graph and program slices. The public data set SARD and open source projects were used to verify the performance of the method. The results show that this method is able to tackle 60 categories of source code defect classification task, which is superior to the existing methods in terms of model evaluation parameter precision, recall and $F1$ by 95.3%, 84.7%, 89.7% respectively.

Keywords: TextCNN · Word2vec · Multi-classification · Program slice · Defect detection

1 Introduction

Vulnerabilities are the core cause of cyberspace security incidents. As an important category of vulnerability, software source code defects seriously threaten cyber security. Therefore, source code review at various stages of the software development life cycle facilitate the detection and repair of defects early. Due to the over-reliance on experience and participation, even senior analysts may find only one critical defect after long time analysis and mining. With the success of deep learning, data mining,etc., academia try to use deep learning for static code review such as defect pattern learning, clone detection, and bug analysis [3,9–12]. The proposed multi-type source code defect detection method based on Text Convolution Neural Network (TextCNN) aims to exploit the latent semantic features, contained in the source code abstract syntax tree and code attribute

This paper was supported by National Natural Science Foundation of China (NSFC) [U1836209],[U1736110], [U1936211].

graph, to train multi-type source code defects detection model for judging multi-type source code defects.

The organizational structure of this paper is as follows: The second part introduced the related research of deep learning in the field of source code defect detection; the third part illustrated the proposed method, including data preprocessing, data representation, and TextCNN; the fourth part explained the experimental environment, the experimental results and analysis; the last section summarized the advantages and disadvantages of the proposed method and showed the future work in brief.

2   Related Work

For deep learning-based methods, the source code is essentially text information. Without relying on expert knowledge, deep learners can mine the semantic information and logical relationship in the source code and obtain the pattern of the defective code. Russell et al. developed the function-level defect detection based on deep learning for C/C++ open source software code [12], which did not consider the defects appeared in level of cross-function or cross-file. Li Zhen et al. proposed a deep learning method for vulnerability detection of source code slices, recommended to apply Bidirectional-LSTM in vulnerability detection on source code gadget combining program data flow and control flow, ignored convolutional neural networks and other comparative analysis [6,7]. Harer et al. adopted machine learning methods for data-driven vulnerability detection of C/C++ source code [5], and compared the effects of applying to source code and compiled code. Duan Xu et al. implemented the source code defect detection method VulSniper based on the attention mechanism [4].ZhouYaqin et al. implemented a source code defect detection system Devign based on graph neural network [13].

Due to the high requirements for prior knowledge and the lack of large-scale labeled data sets covering various types of vulnerabilities, the existing deep learning-based methods often rely on artificially created, simpler vulnerability data sets, such as the Software Assurance Reference Dataset (SARD) [1] maintained with the US National Standards Institute of Technology. The lack of data restricts the ability to detect source code vulnerabilities of deep learning.

3   Methodology

In this paper, text convolutional neural network was applied to detect source code defects, which is applicable for defect classification in various granularity such as across functions, files, and project levels. The overall architecture was shown in Fig. 1, which is mainly consist of data preprocessing, data representation and TextCNN model.

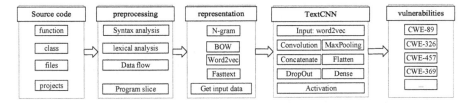

Fig. 1. Principle and process of the proposed method.

3.1 Data Preprocessing

The cause of TextCNN succeed in text classification attributed to the ability of learning the logical relationships among context. Source code is essentially text information, and its logical relationship, part-of-speech and other characteristics are reflected through the data flow, control flow and other dependence structures. This method attempted to retrieve code logical features with the assistance of data flow analysis.

Data flow describes the possible declare, definition, reference or call of various variables and functions at a certain point of the program in source code. Data flow was generally extracted from a control flow graph of the code, which mainly has two methods: forward analysis and backward analysis. Many source code analysis applications have introduced data flow analysis techniques as core engineer, such as Fortify, Checkmarx, etc. In this paper, the open source tool joern [2] is used to extract the code's abstract syntax tree and data flow information based on grammatical and lexical analysis to generate program slice data. Taking backward slicing as an example, the generated data is shown in Fig. 2. The slice is reversed to obtain the data flow relationship related to function *strcpy()* and its variables *(data, source)*.

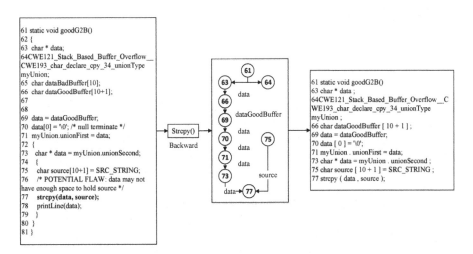

Fig. 2. Program slice and example.

3.2   Data Representation

Data preprocessing is an important step in natural language processing. For text analysis tasks, the text is firstly expressed as a vector by one-hot encoding and word embedding. The vector generated by one-hot encoding is a high-dimensional sparse binary vector and does not contain semantic information. The word embedding technology contributes to low-dimensional dense vectors. The distance between the word vectors can measure the similarity of different words, and the sum of the word vectors matches the semantic relationship of the words with correlation analysis by cosine similarity, Euclidean distance and so on. For example, the vectors like "female"-"queen" and "male"-"king" generated by word2vec [8] are very similar. Therefore, word2vec was employed to represent the source code slices.

In this article, x represents a code unit, where in a given code fragment X is a collection of code units, as shown in Eq. 1.

$$X = \{x^1, x^2, ..., x^n\}. \tag{1}$$

Each code unit can be expressed as a d-dimensional vector v, then the code segment X can be expressed by the matrix M^{r*d}, seen as Eq. 2, where r indicates the number of code units.

$$M^{r*d} = [v^1, v^2, ..., v^r]^T. \tag{2}$$

$Vocab$ represents the set of vector expressions of all code units. The vector expression of code unit i in the test code can be obtained from $Vocab$ through the function $Lookup$, referring to Eq. 3.

$$V^i = Lookup\,(i, Vocab)\,. \tag{3}$$

The examined code fragment X^j contains l code units, X will be mapped to a $l*d$ dimensional matrixas following Eq. 4.

$$M^{j,n*d} = [v^1, v^2, ..., v^l]^T. \tag{4}$$

3.3   Text Convolution Neural Network

The sight in this paper is inspired by the TextCNN model proposed by Kim [8]. TextCNN utilizes a variety of data such as one-hot encoding or word embedding as input. In order to preserve the context of the code, this article uses the code vector $Matrix\,(X)$ pre-trained by word2vec as input. Convolutional layers, pooling layers, etc. referred to the network model proposed by Kim. The network structure of TextCNN is shown in Fig. 3:

In the first layer of the model, each sample is mapped to an $n*d$-dimensional matrix M. Assuming that the number of samples to be tested is N, then samples S from all code segments can be expressed as Eq. 5

$$M^{1,L} = [M^1, M^2, ..., M^N]^T. \tag{5}$$

The softmax activation function in the last layer of TextCNN is used to calculate the probability of the category, and to judge which class the sample X belongs to. Assuming that all samples can be divided into $K(K = 0, 1, 2, ..., k)$ categories, the probability $p(y = k|X)$, which indicates the predicted label of each sample, can be expressed as Eq. 6.

$$p(y = k|X) = \frac{\exp\left(w_k^T x + b_k\right)}{\sum_{k'=0}^{K} \exp\left(w_{k'}^T x + b_{k'}\right)}. \tag{6}$$

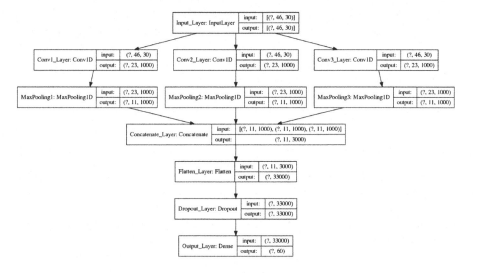

Fig. 3. TextCNN structure.

Among them, the weights w_k and bias b_k are shared and need to be trained all the time.

4   Experiment and Evaluation

4.1   Experiment Environment

The computer used in the experiment uses two E5–2683-v4 CPUs, the main frequency is 2.1 GHz, the graphics card is consist of two titan Xp, the hard disk capacity is 2T, and the memory size is 256 G. The experiments were carried on Linux 18.04 × 64, the development language is python3.7, the model was written by keras, and the backend kernel is tensorflow 1.14.0.

4.2   Dataset Preparing

The dataset used in the experiment includes SARD and real project source code. SARD contains more than 170,000 programs such as C, C++, Java, PHP and C#, covering more than 150 categories of defects. It contains a large number of test cases, and each test case has "metadata" to mark and describe it. Test cases are marked as "good", "bad" or "mixed". The "bad" test case contains one or more specific defects. The "good" test case is a repaired version of the "bad" test case and can be used to check for false positives. The "mixed" test case has both the defective code and the corresponding repaired code. SARD C/C++ testcases were chosen to train and valid model in this paper.

In addition, the actual data from open source projects is added to the experimental dataset, such as openssl, firefox, etc., and the slice information of the source code of the project is extracted according to the scan results of the project's historical vulnerabilities by source code defect detection tools like cppcheck, fortify, etc. All test cases are annotated according to CWE numbers.

There are 60 types of defects involved in this experiment, where the number of positive samples is 173221 and the number of negative samples is 147470.

4.3   Experimental Settings

The parameter setting mainly includes word2vec and TextCNN.

On training Word2vec, multiprocessing was implented to increase the training speed in parallel. Each code unit is trained as a vector with d = 30, the size of the sliding word window is 5, the learning rate is 0.01, the sampling rate is 0.01, and the number of iterations is 5.

The input samples of TextCNN are code fragments, generated by program slice, and each code fragment is composed of several code units. All code fragments are padded with same length L. The value of L is the length of the code segment with the most code units, in this way $L = 802$. The step size of the convolutional layer is 2, the size of the convolution kernel is 3, 4, 5 respectively, and the activation function is relu. The maxpooling is used in pooling layer, the pooling scale is 2, the down sampling rate is set to 0.3, and the loss function is categorical_crossentropy, which is defined as Eq. 7.

$$loss = - \sum_{i=1}^{n} \hat{y}_{i1} \log y_{i1} + \hat{y}_{i2} \log y_{i2} + ... + \hat{y}_{im} \log y_{im}. \qquad (7)$$

The softmax activation function is used to achieve multi-class task in the final output layer.

4.4   Evaluation

Confusion matrix is a general application indicator that helps to understand the performance of classifiers in machine learning and deep learning. The matrix describes the mix between actual and predicted categories, namely True Positive

(TP), False Negative (FN), False Positive (FP) and True Negative (TN). TP indicates the case where the defect code function is classified as a defect code. The FN generation indicates that the defect code is classified as a normal code. FP indicates the case where normal codes are classified as defective codes. TN represents the case where normal codes are classified as normal codes. This article uses three comprehensive evaluation indicators based on confusion matrix, including recall, precision, and $F1$.

$$recall = \frac{TP}{TP + FN} \tag{8}$$

$$precision = \frac{TP}{TP + FP} \tag{9}$$

$$F1 = \frac{2 * (recall * precision)}{recall + precision} \tag{10}$$

4.5   Result and Analysis

In order to verify the effectiveness of the method in this paper, the proposed method was compared with the existing learning-based methods from the three dimensions of the above evaluation parameters. The results are as follows Table 1.

Table 1. Comparison of experimental results (%).

Methods	Precision	Recall	F1
Vuldeepecker [7]	91.9	50.5	65.2
SySeVr [6]	84.2	87.9	86.0
This paper	95.3	84.7	89.7

Compared with other deep learning-based source code defect detection methods, sight in this paper has the following advantages:

(1) The accuracy is improved by 3.4% and 11.1% compared to Vuldeepecker and SySeVr respectively; the recall rate is increased by 34.2% compared to Vuldeepecker; $F1$ is increased by 24.5% and 3.7% compared to Vuldeepecker and SySeVr.
(2) The word embedding vector d = 30, smaller than Vuldeepecker and SySeVr, that are all larger than 200. This method saves more computing resources and improves the learning efficiency.
(3) The number of applicable defect categories is more than others, Vuldeepecker is designed for binary classification, SySeVr is up to 40 categories, and the proposed method is applicable to 60 different defect categories, which can be extended to more than 100.

5   Conclusion and Future Work

Combine static analysis and deep learning technology, TextCNN were deployed to automatically learn potential defect patterns in the source code based on data flow and program slice, supporting cross-function and cross-file code defect detection methods and relieving the high dependence on expert experience and the compilation environment. Through the verification of the public data set SARD and multiple real code projects such as firefox and openssl, it is shown that the method in this paper is effective. In terms of evaluation parameters, the average accuracy is 95.3%, up to 98.4%, the recall rate is 84.7%, the F1 evaluation parameter is 89.7%, the type of source code defects detected is 60 categories, and the overall effect is better than the existing deep learning-based source code defect detection methods.

Along with the achievements,there are some shortcomings in this procedure including only considers representing the context information by dataflow slices, just carried experiments on C/C++ language, etc. In the future work, the code context representation method can be extended to considering the control flow, software measurement meta-information and implementing on more program languages including Java, Php, etc.

References

1. https://samate.nist.gov/SRD/index.php
2. https://joern.readthedocs.io/en/latest/index.html
3. Bian, P., Liang, B., Zhang, Y., Yang, C., Shi, W., Cai, Y.: Detecting bugs by discovering expectations and their violations. IEEE Trans. Softw. Eng. **45**(10), 984–1001 (2019)
4. Duan, X., et al.: Vulsniper: focus your attention to shoot fine-grained vulnerabilities. In: Proceedings of the Twenty-Eighth International Joint Conference on Artificial Intelligence, IJCAI-19, pp. 4665–4671. International Joint Conferences on Artificial Intelligence Organization, July 2019
5. Harer, J.A., et al.: Automated software vulnerability detection with machine learning. CoRR abs/1803.04497 (2018)
6. Li, Z., et al.: Sysevr: a framework for using deep learning to detect software vulnerabilities. CoRR abs/1807.06756 (2018)
7. Li, Z., et al.: Vuldeepecker: a deep learning-based system for vulnerability detection. CoRR abs/1801.01681 (2018)
8. Mikolov, T., Sutskever, I., Chen, K., Corrado, G., Dean, J.: Distributed representations of words and phrases and their compositionality. In: Proceedings of the 26th International Conference on Neural Information Processing Systems - Volume 2, pp. 3111–3119. NIPS'13, Curran Associates Inc., Red Hook, NY, USA (2013)
9. Svajlenko, J., Roy, C.K.: Cloneworks: a fast and flexible large-scale near-miss clone detection tool. In: 2017 IEEE/ACM 39th International Conference on Software Engineering Companion (ICSE-C), pp. 177–179 (2017)
10. Wang, S., Liu, T., Tan, L.: Automatically learning semantic features for defect prediction. In: 2016 IEEE/ACM 38th International Conference on Software Engineering (ICSE), pp. 297–308 (2016)

11. Guan, Z., Wang, X., Xin, W., Wang, J., Zhang, L.: A survey on deep learning-based source code defect analysis. In: 2020 5th International Conference on Computer and Communication Systems (ICCCS), pp. 167–171, May 2020
12. Zhou, C., Li, B., Sun, X., Guo, H.: Recognizing software bug-specific named entity in software bug repository. In: 2018 IEEE/ACM 26th International Conference on Program Comprehension (ICPC), pp. 108–10811 (2018)
13. Zhou, Y., Liu, S., Siow, J., Du, X., Liu, Y.: Devign: effective vulnerability identification by learning comprehensive program semantics via graph neural networks. In: Advances in Neural Information Processing Systems 32, pp. 10197–10207. Curran Associates, Inc. (2019)

Noninvasive Research on Cardiac Electrical Activity by Non-Gaussian Prior Bayesian Matching Pursuit

Lu Bing[1], Yudong Li[2], and Wen Si[1,3(✉)]

[1] Faculty of Business Information, Shanghai Business
School, Shanghai 201400, People's Republic of China
betty20006@163.com
[2] School of Business Economics, Shanghai
Business School, Shanghai 201400, People's Republic of China
lydmm_2002@163.com
[3] Department of Rehabilitation, Huashan Hospital, Fudan University,
Shanghai 200040, People's Republic of China
siwen@fudan.edu.cn

Abstract. It is an important branch of biometrics security to obtain the cardiomagnetic signal non-invasively. In our study, the problem of sparse cardiac current source reconstruction is studied using Bayesian matching pursuit with non-Gaussian prior. The characteristics of cardiac electrical activity by source imaging are analyzed. We use goodness of fit (GoF) and root mean square error (RMSE) to measure the reconstruction ability of the source reconstruction method. The trajectory during QRS complex and T-wave segment can preliminarily reveal the conduction features of electrical excitation and effective electrophysiological information in ventricular depolarization and repolarization. The experimental results verify that our method with the source solution non-Gaussian or unknown prior is available for cardiomagnetic signal's inverse problem and cardiac sparse source imaging.

Keywords: Bayesian matching pursuit · Non-Gaussian prior · Sparse source · Cardiac electrical activity · Biometrics security

1 Introduction

At present, the mortality rate of heart diseases is high and the cure rate is low, which has become a problem that plagues the medical profession. Therefore, it is of great significance for the research and early diagnosis of heart diseases. Common detection methods for heart diseases include electrocardiography (ECG), echocardiography, coronary angiography (CAG), magnetic resonance imaging (MRI) and computerized tomography (CT), etc. From the perspective of biometrics security, there are few reports on completely non-invasive, non-contact imaging of cardiac electrical activity and early diagnosis of heart diseases. It is known that action currents in the heart produce a weak

G. Xu et al. (Eds.): FCS 2020, CCIS 1286, pp. 104–110, 2020.
https://doi.org/10.1007/978-981-15-9739-8_9

magnetic field, which can be recorded by cardiomagnetic signal [1]. With the rapid development of superconducting quantum interference device (SQUID) measurement technology, the accuracy of cardiomagnetic signal has been continuously improved, enabling the measurement of weak cardiac magnetic field signals with high spatial and temporal resolution [2, 3]. Cardiomagnetic signal is the result of measuring the magnetic signal generated by the bioelectric current on the surface of the external thoracic cavity, providing a new means for non-invasive diagnosis of heart diseases [4–6].

The study of cardiac electrical activity and its characteristic quantification have important significance in theory and application to the analysis of heart function and the diagnosis of heart diseases. Where, the measured magnetic signal is used to generate sources of the current/magnetic model, called source reconstruction, which is involved of an inverse problem [7]. Source reconstruction can locate the position, orientation and intensity of the current source that generates the magnetic signal, and can better visualize the electrical activity of the heart. In the past ten years, scholars from all over the world have not only continuously innovated in source models and various methods, but also gradually made use of source reconstruction results for diagnosis of heart diseases. However, how to obtain current sources that are in line with electrophysiological significance still faces theoretical and application challenges.

In this paper, non-Gaussian Bayesian matching pursuit (BMP) framework is used to obtain sparse sources and analyze the characteristics of electrical activity conduction. The results of QRS complex and T-wave segment current source reconstruction are achieved by solving inverse problem in a healthy cardiomagnetic signal subject. The characteristics of cardiac electrical activity revealed by source imaging are discussed. The effectiveness of the method is verified by various evaluation indicators. The purpose of this paper is to study new possibility of cardiac current source reconstruction and extract electrophysiological characteristics.

The organization of this paper contains 5 sections. We introduce inverse problem of cardiomagnetic signal in Sect. 2. Section 3 details our method. Section 4 contains cardiomagnetic signal source reconstruction and electrical activity imaging. We have some conclusions in Sect. 5 finally.

2 Inverse Problem

Traditional inverse problem studies can be seen as compression sensing (CS) [8]. In the inverse problem solving, the relationship between the heart magnetic field and the source points in the distributed source space (i.e., the lead field matrix) is used. The sparse method is then to decompose the signal into a given lead field matrix to solve the optimal sparse solution under various conditions. The sparse solution contains spatial location, intensity, and direction information of the sources. Sparse source imaging is obtained by the obtained sparse source information, and thus the spatio-temporal information such as the distribution or the trajectory of the sources is visualized. For current source reconstruction in cardiomagnetic signal, CS framework intends to recover sparse signals in underdetermined system as follows [8],

$$B = AX + V \tag{1}$$

where, $X \in \mathbb{R}^N$, and $B \in \mathbb{R}^M$ are the unknown sparse source signal and the magnetic field data respectively. $A \in \mathbb{R}^{M \times N}$ is a lead field matrix, also known as a dictionary, representing transfer coefficients from each source to each measure location. The number of unknown elements N is much larger than the number of observations M. $V \in \mathbb{R}^M$ is the additive Gaussian noise.

3 Method

Similar to the CS theory, the Bayesian method solves the sparse signal reconstruction problem in (1). Suppose signal to be measured is K-sparse, and its support set is θ. Unlike the CS method, the Bayesian method also requires the sparse vector X to have some fixed probability and statistical properties that can be decomposed into the following forms [8].

$$X = Be_X \odot G_X \tag{2}$$

where, Be_X obeys Bernoulli distribution, independently taking values from 1, 0 with probability p and 1-p, which determines the non-zero position of X. G_X obeys independent and identical distribution, describing the statistical properties of X's non-zero entries. The probability that the vector X to be measured takes any support set θ is,

$$\Pr(\theta) = p^{|\theta|}(1-p)^{N-|\theta|} \tag{3}$$

When $p \ll 1$, X is a sparse vector, and spatity $K \approx pN$.

According to Bayesian theory, $\Pr(\theta|B)$ can be expressed as [8],

$$\Pr(\theta|B) = \frac{\Pr(B|\theta)\Pr(\theta)}{\Pr(B)} \tag{4}$$

Support set θ_{MAP} of MAP probability is defined as [8],

$$\theta_{MAP} = \arg \max_{\theta} \Pr(\theta|B) \tag{5}$$

For (1), MMSE and MAP estimation of X are [8],

$$\widehat{X}_{MMSE} = E[X|B] = \sum_{\theta} \Pr(\theta|B)E[X|B, \theta] \tag{6}$$

$$\widehat{X}_{MAP} = E[X|B, \theta_{MAP}] = E\left[X\middle|B, \arg \max_{\theta} \Pr(\theta|B)\right] \tag{7}$$

where, $\Pr(B|\theta)$ and $E[X|B, \theta]$ are two key factors vary from traditional BMP with Gaussian prior. Since G_X is a non-Gaussian distribution, B is mapped to the orthogonal complement space constituted by column vectors of A_θ. Define the projection matrix $P_\theta^\perp$ as [8, 9],

$$P_\theta^\perp = I - A_\theta \left(A_\theta^H A_\theta\right)^{-1} A_\theta^H \tag{8}$$

Then, $P_\theta^\perp \mathbf{B} = P_\theta^\perp \mathbf{V}$, is Gaussian vector with zero mean, and its covariance is,

$$\sum_{\mathbf{B}} = \mathrm{E}\left[\left(P_\theta^\perp \mathbf{V}\right)\left(P_\theta^\perp \mathbf{V}\right)^H\right] = P_\theta^\perp \sigma_V^2 P_\theta^{\perp H} = \sigma_v^2 P_\theta^\perp \tag{9}$$

Then, the conditional probability of $\mathbf{B}|\theta$ can be approximated as [8, 9],

$$\Pr(\mathbf{B}|\theta) \approx \exp\left(-\frac{1}{2\sigma_v^2} P_\theta^\perp \mathbf{B}^2\right) \tag{10}$$

Since $\mathbf{X}|\theta$ is non-Gaussian and the distribution probability function is unknown, it is impossible to directly solve $\mathrm{E}[\mathbf{X}|\mathbf{B}, \theta]$. Best linear unbiased estimate (BLUE) is used for approximation [8, 9],

$$\mathrm{E}[\mathbf{X}|\mathbf{B}, \theta] = \left(\mathbf{A}_\theta^H \mathbf{A}_\theta\right)^{-1} \mathbf{A}_\theta^H \mathbf{B} \tag{11}$$

4   Cardiomagnetic Signal Source Imaging

Given the cardiomagnetic signal measurements and the forward solutions informed in the lead field according to Maxwell's equations, it is possible to achieve inverse solution and reconstruct current sources as they evolve. According to the current source trajectory, electrical excitation conduction paths can be explored.

4.1   Data Preparation

We adopt measured 36-channel cardiomagnetic signal in single-cycle for source reconstruction. Measurement and acquired signal is shown in Fig. 1. The data is acquired by Shanghai Institute of Microsystem and Information Technology. During a cardiac cycle, QRS complex and T-wave segment are corresponding to the processes of ventricular depolarization and repolarization, respectively. Throughout the cardiac cycle, we select QRS complex and the T-wave segment as the analysis object.

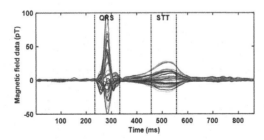

Fig. 1. The cardiomagnetic signal waveform of a group of healthy subject in a single cardiac cycle, where, QRS complex: (234–333) ms; T-wave segment: (457–556) ms.

4.2 Source Imaging

Source feature analyses for QRS complex are shown in Fig. 2. For every single time, current source with the highest dipole moment intensity (named as dominant current source) is displayed for cardiac electrical activity analysis. The QRS complex is divided into four parts: begin-Q (blue color), Q-R (green color), R-S (yellow color), and S-end (red color), by solid lines to observe and analyze the conduction process of cardiac electrical activity during this time period. As can be seem from Fig. 2, the current sources reconstructed in the QRS complex are located in the middle area of the measurement surface, and the range is approximately (14×10) cm^2. The depths of the reconstructed current sources vary from 3 to 10 cm.

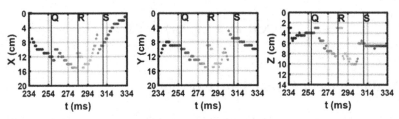

Fig. 2. Spatio-Temporal movement of the current sources in QRS complex along X, Y, Z direction (depth).

Source feature analyses for T-wave segment are shown in Fig. 3. T-wave segment is the ventricular repolarization phase. Compared with the depolarization phase, the magnetic field pattern of the entire T-wave segment changes very slowly, this is related to the slow process of electrical excitation during this period. It can be seen from Fig. 3 that the positions and the directions of the T-wave segment reconstruction current sources are relatively stable, within the range of (5×6) cm^2. The depths of the reconstructed current sources vary from 3 to 9 cm. The entire conduction process is basically consistent with the ventricle repolarization.

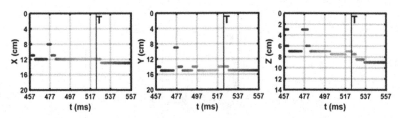

Fig. 3. Spatio-Temporal movement of the current sources in T-wave segment along X, Y, Z direction (depth).

4.3 Statistics

Two indicators including goodness of fit (GoF) and root mean square error (RMSE) are used to measure the reconstruction ability [10].

$$\text{GoF} = \sqrt{1 - \frac{\sum_{i=1}^{M}(B_{zi} - B_{si})^2}{\sum_{i=1}^{M} B_{zi}^2}} \tag{12}$$

$$\text{RMSE} = \sqrt{\frac{1}{M} \sum_{i=1}^{M}(B_{zi} - B_{si})^2} \tag{13}$$

where, B_{zi} is the reconstructed magnetic field, and B_{si} is the measured data at the measuring point. M is the magnetic field measurement point. GoF is a relatively straightforward evaluation criterion for similarity. It measures the degree of similarity between the reconstructed and measured signal in terms of percentage. The value ranges from 0 to 1. In general, the better the reconstruction effect, the closer the value is to 1. RMSE is used to measure the deviation between the reconstructed and measured signal. Usually the better the reconstruction, the smaller the value. The GoF and RMSE evaluations are shown in Table 1. It can be seen that the GoF coefficients of the healthy person at the Q, R, S and T points are all above 90%, and RMSEs retain relatively small values. The average of GoFs for QRS complex and T-wave segment (indicated by Avr_QRS and Avr_T) can achieve 94.40% and 92.91%, respectively, while average RMSEs are 3.5702 pT and 3.9782 pT, respectively.

Table 1. GoF and RMSE of the typical features.

Cardiomagnetic signal	Time (ms)	GoF (%)	RMSE (pT)
Healthy	Q (257)	95.68	2.2462
	R (284)	97.59	8.5553
	S (310)	96.67	1.8680
	T (523)	91.67	4.9727
Total	Avr_QRS	94.40	3.5702
	Avr_T	92.91	3.9782

5 Conclusion

In this paper, an improved sparse method is used for non-invasive research on the current sources from healthy subject in consideration of biometrics security. The location and direction characteristics of the reconstructed current sources are analyzed, and useful electrophysiological characteristics are extracted. The study finds that the reconstructed current source trajectories of the healthy subject coincide with the ventricle electrical excitation conduction, similar to the previous studies. Although some useful preliminary results have been obtained in this study, it is a very valuable work to improve the calculation time in the future, further, it requires a large amount of statistics and analysis to distinguish between healthy people and patients and help diagnose heart diseases.

Acknowledgment. The authors would like to express their gratitude to Prof. Shiqin Jiang, Ph.D Dafang Zhou, Ph.D Chen Zhao for academic exchange and great support during this project. The authors are also grateful to Shanghai Institute of Microsystem and Information Technology, for kindly providing the data. This work is supported by the Natural Science Foundation of Shanghai (Grant No. 18ZR1427400), the Shanghai Business School 'Phosphor' Science Foundation, and the Natural Science Foundation of Shanghai (Grant No. 18ZR1427500).

References

1. Baule, G., Mcfee, R.: Detection of the magnetic field of the heart. Am. Heart J. **66**(1), 95–97 (1963)
2. Wang, J., Yang, K., Yang, R., Kong, X., Chen, W.: Squid gradiometer module for fetal magnetocardiography measurements inside a thin magnetically shielded room. IEEE Trans. Appl. Supercond. **29**(2), 1–4 (2019)
3. Shanehsazzadeh, F., Kalantari, N., Sarreshtedari, F., Fardmanesh, M.: Environmental noise cancellation for high-TC SQUID-based magnetocardiography systems using a bistage active shield. IEEE Trans. Appl. Supercond. **27**(7), 1–6 (2017)
4. Sun, W., Kobayashi, K.: Estimation of magnetocardiography current sources using reconstructed magnetic field data. IEEE Trans. Magn. **53**(11), 1–4 (2017)
5. Iwakami, N., Aiba, T., Kamakura, S., Takaki, H., Kusano, K.: Identification of malignant early repolarization pattern by late qrs activity in high-resolution magnetocardiography. Annals of Noninvasive Electrocardiology (2020)
6. Shin, E.S., Park, J.W., Lim, D.S.: Magnetocardiography for the diagnosis of non-obstructive coronary artery disease. Clin. Hemorheol. Microcirc. **69**(1–2), 9–11 (2018)
7. Salido-Ruiz, R.A., Ranta, R., Korats, G., Cam, S.L., Louis-Dorr, V.: A unified weighted minimum norm solution for the reference inverse problem in EEG. Comput. Biol. Med. **115**, 103510 (2019)
8. Donoho, D.L.: Compressed sensing. IEEE Trans. Inf. Theory **52**(4), 1289–1306 (2006)
9. Yi, L.: Fast Time-varying Channel Estimation for OFDM Systems Based on Compressed Sensing [ph.d thesis]. Beijing Institute of Technology (2015)
10. Pewsey, A.: Parametric bootstrap edf-based goodness-of-fit testing for sinh–arcsinh distributions. TEST **27**(1), 147–172 (2017). https://doi.org/10.1007/s11749-017-0538-2

Video Investigation Analysis System Enhanced by Explicable Model

Jun Xing[1], Guangquan Xu[2], and Chengbo Yin[1(✉)]

[1] Big Data College, Qingdao Huanghai University, Qingdao, China
`fumulan_cn@163.com`, `ycb1004@126.com`
[2] College of Intelligence and Computing, Tianjin University, Tianjin, China

Abstract. In view of problems of the existing video investigation systems that there are single data collection methods, low efficiency of viewing video clues, less means of actual combat application, and contact and combination of multiple cases which are not effective enough, a multi-source sensing data fusion system is constructed, and an explicable model is applied to enhance the human-machine fusion decision-making. According to actual profession requirements, an application platform of video investigation actual combat is structured, and a framework design of video investigation analysis system is proposed that can be enhanced by explicable models, which can improve the efficiency of video investigation work. Finally, the system implementation approach is pointed out, which is based on core products of relevant mainstream manufacturers.

Keywords: Video investigation · Explicable model · Human-machine fusion decision-making · Structured analysis · Knowledge graph

1 Introduction

Along with new changes of the principal contradiction in our society, new requirements have been put forward for criminal surveillance, and it is necessary to comprehensively strengthen the video investigation ability of the criminal investigation department of the public security organs, so as to realize equipment professionalization, intelligent application and practical combat function. However, following problems mainly exist in the existing video investigation systems: Speed of video data acquisition is slow speed, single methods and inefficiency. Inefficiency manual ways are mainly relied on to view video clues. There are few deep applications of video clues, and only common image comparison and video structured analysis are generally carried out. Multi-case connection and combination can not be effectively realized.

To effectively solve the existing problems of video investigation systems, this article is based on the solutions of existing mainstream manufacturers of video investigation system, and an improved video investigation analysis system are put forward from the point of improving capacities of multi-source heterogeneous data resource service, intelligent video image analysis, big data retrieval and mining and multiple business application processing. Besides, explicable model is used to enhance human-machine

© Springer Nature Singapore Pte Ltd. 2020
G. Xu et al. (Eds.): FCS 2020, CCIS 1286, pp. 111–117, 2020.
https://doi.org/10.1007/978-981-15-9739-8_10

fusion decision-making, which can improve practical combat application ability of video investigation analysis system.

2 Multi-source Sensing Data Fusion System

Video detection analysis system for processing the data, according to the needs of police department detective, is derived from multiple channels, a bayonet is personnel, vehicles bayonet, 2 it is structured camera at the end of every unit area, security monitoring, 3 it is setting outlook camera at an altitude of the commanding heights, four is the air motor unmanned aerial vehicle (uav), five is the police law enforcement to carry mobile police terminal, six is used to locate the MAC detection device, seven is offline video data, pictures, etc.

These collected structured, semi-structured and unstructured data are transmitted to the data fusion system through wired or wireless communication. After data preprocessing and data standardization, they are saved in distributed storage, and various forms of fusion computing and knowledge extraction are carried out on the big data platform. The multi-source perception data fusion system is constructed as shown in the figure below: (Fig. 1)

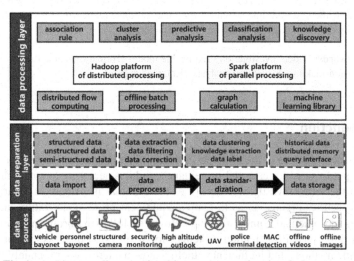

Fig. 1. Architecture diagram of multi-source perception data fusion system.

3 Human-Machine Fusion Decision Based on Explicable Model

At present, the mainstream video investigation system is mainly based on the structural analysis of collected video, image, text and other data, supplemented by routine professional applications, to assist police officers on analysis and decision-making. However, human's subjective factors has not really introduced into the system as input data to output human-machine fusion decision results.

Explicable AI technologies will be developed for new or improved machine learning technologies to produce more explicable models, which will be translated into understandable and useful explicable conversation combined with advanced human-machine interface technologies for users. Rich sources are provided by entities, concept, properties and relations in knowledge graph for explanation. Distributed representation of knowledge graph is input into deep learning models, and the methods that are similar to attention mechanism are used to choose explicable elements of knowledge graph. Besides, subjective factors are introduced into explicable process, and this kind of discrete data of knowledge graph are numeralize and effectively integrated into the statistic learning model. Finally, real human-machine fusion decision-making will be achieved. The relevant principle is shown as the figure below: (Figs. 2 and 3)

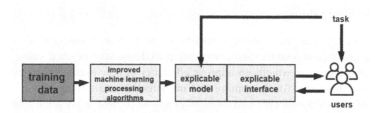

Fig. 2. Schematic diagram of explicable AI technology.

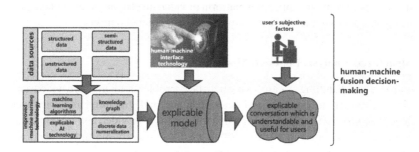

Fig. 3. Schematic diagram of human-machine fusion decision-making system.

4 Practical Combat Application Platform of Video Investigation

As application part of the video investigation analysis system, the actual combat application platform of video investigation takes multi-source data as the core, actual criminal investigation as purpose, and profession application as the key point, including several modules such as structured analysis, video investigation, technology and tactics, case video library and system management.

4.1 System Architecture

Video investigation analysis systems are constructed on public security private network, and multi-source data are taken as the core of actual combat application platform of video investigation. Platforms of province, city, district and county levels are mainly constructed, which are based on a shared video monitoring platform, accessing to multi-source real-time monitoring videos, history video resources to analysis system of videos and images. The security border is crossed by analytical data through converging and transmitting nodes of video image library, and these data are input into actual combat application systems video investigation in public security private network, which can realize surveillance application, carry out dynamic portrait recognition, video investigation, case video library, analysis and study for personnel and vehicles, make it come true as dynamic deployment and control, path query, alarm convergence, collaborative surveillance and deep analysis and study etc.

4.2 Case Video Library

Criminal investigation case, video and statistical resources are integrated by case video library for correlation analysis and comparative analysis, and the case video files are managed and classified, which can improve efficiency of case management greatly and provide video resources for the coming case investigation and solving.

Data of case video library and ones of practical combat application platform of video investigation can be intercommunicated, and video review and case connection and combination can be seamlessly connected. Import of multi-source video, image and text data can be realized by local off-line uploading, monitoring platform import, import of practical combat application platform of video investigation. Knowledge graph technology is used to realize case description and target label option.

4.3 Structured Analysis Function Module

In the process of handling a case, we often face problems of massive video targets screenings, different video scenes and quick searches, and structured analysis function module is specially used for application scenarios of massive video and secondary analysis of images, which are suitable for various media sources of multiple scenarios, big differences. Functional interface is shown as the figure below: (Fig. 4)

Real-time analysis is conducted on massive data collected by multi-type fronts through structured analysis module, and secondary analysis is done on target detection, attribute analysis and feature extraction for offline images and videos.

4.4 Video Investigation Function Module

Video investigation function mainly realizes case center study & judgment and intelligent analysis. Case center study & judgement mainly includes case management and analysis of case connection and combination. Intelligent analysis mainly includes means of viewing, study and judgment of investigation, and control.

Fig. 4. Structured analysis interface.

4.5 Technology and Tactics Methods Function Module

The function of technology and tactics is the weapon for criminal investigation department to investigate and handle cases, mainly including technology and tactics of personnel, vehicle and probe, and key area control, track library and so on.

5 Overall Architecture Design and Implementation Approach

By means of explicable AI technology integrated with human subjective factors, the improved video investigation analysis system can realize human-machine fusion decision-making, and improve video investigation functions, so as to focus on profession, and conduct practical combat. Meanwhile, hardware and software requirements can be supported by products of relevant mainstream manufacturers at present in the aspect of system implementation.

5.1 Architecture Design of Enhanced Video Investigation Analysis System

The analysis and decision-making ability of case connection and combination can be enhanced by explicable AI algorithms based on knowledge graph and human-machine fusion decision-making algorithms in the improved video investigation analysis system. At the same time, this system can be used to meet the requirements of case investigation departments and help solve the case quickly through multi-source data fusion processing, enhanced performance of big data computing platform, practical application functions improvement of video investigation, etc. (Fig. 5)

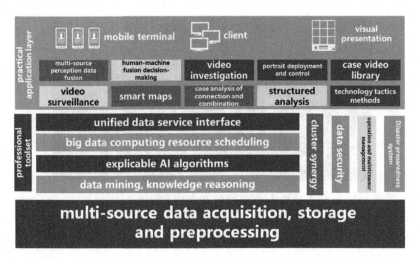

Fig. 5. Architecture diagram of enhanced video investigation analysis system.

5.2 System Implementation Approach

The realization of video investigation and analysis system enhanced by explicable AI needs to integrate hardware and software products of several relevant manufacturers, such as Hikvision, Huawei, Kedacom, Dahua, Netposa and YISA, etc., and secondary development of algorithm on this basis will be carried out. As long as unified access standards and data standards are followed, products of these different manufacturers can be integrated, and then the core platform can be integrated for development, which can realize smooth running of the whole system.

6 Conclusion

Based on shortcomings of the existing video investigation system and pain points in actual case handling by criminal investigation departments, an improved video investigation analysis system is studied in this article. By construction of multi-source perception data fusion system, a variety of data needed to handle cases are imported and processed for fusion, so as to prepare data for analysis and decision-making. Explicable AI technology is used to enhance human-machine fusion decision-making, and improve rapidity and precision of decision-making. Based on actual profession requirements, practical combat application platform of video investigation is built to make system application more close to criminal investigation profession. Finally, a architecture design of video investigation analysis system enhanced by explicable AI is proposed, and the way to realize the system is pointed out based on the core products of relevant mainstream manufacturers, which provides an improved idea and method for improving efficiency of video investigation.

References

1. Xiao, Y.: Concept and Technology of Knowledge Graph. Electronic Industry Press, Beijing (2020)
2. Chen, D., Cai, J., Huang, Y.: Prospect of fuzzy systems for interpretable AI and big data. J. Intell. Sci. Technol. 1(04), 327–334 (2019)
3. Guo, T., Han, C.: Explanation of artificial intelligence mechanism and Discussion on mathematical methods [J/OL]. Chinese science: Numbers:1–38 (2020) http://kns.cnki.net/kcms/det ail/11.5836.O1.20200527.1602.002.html
4. Guangquan, X., et al.: A security-enhanced certificateless aggregate signature authentication protocol for InVANETs. IEEE Netw. 34(2), 22–29 (2020). https://doi.org/10.1109/mnet.001. 1900035
5. Lv, Y.: Design and Implementation of Data Monitoring Platform based on Multi-data Sources and Business Process Analysis [Master's thesis]. Beijing University of Posts and Telecommunications, Beijing (2019)
6. Zhen, T., Junlin, L., Weili, W., Yuanfu, X., Jing, C., Safeng, L.: Device state perception method based on multi-source monitoring data [J/OL]. J. Power Syst. Autom. pp. 145–150 (2020) https://doi.org/10.19635/j.cnki.csu-epsa.000452
7. Xiao, G., Ma, Y., Liu, C., Jiang, D.: A machine emotion transfer model for intelligent human-machine interaction based on group division. Mech. Syst. Signal Process. 142, 106736 (2020)
8. Peng, C., Yue, D.: Intelligent sensing, neural computing and applications. Neurocomput. 397, 381–382 (2020)

Blockchain

Application of Blockchain Technology to the Credit Management of Supply Chain

Rong Tan[1,2], Yudong Li[1], Jing Zhang[1], and Wen Si[1(✉)]

[1] Faculty of Business Information, Shanghai Business
School, Shanghai 201400, People's Republic of China
tanrong529@gmail.com, lydmm_2002@163.com, zhangjing25@163.com,
siwen@fudan.edu.cn
[2] Tehua Postdoctoral Programme, Beijing 100029, People's Republic of China

Abstract. Blockchain technology has been extensively applied to Supply Chain Management (SCM). Based on technological innovations such as distributed ledgers, symmetric encryption, authorization, consensus mechanisms, and smart contracts, blockchain technology overcomes the traditional limitations of information gap, traceability, transaction transparency, and credit problems in SCM. In this paper, a platform for SCM is established and analyzed from the perspective of blockchain technology. This paper provides important reference for the construction of supply chain logistics information systems and the design of supply chain application systems for credit management.

Keywords: Blockchain · Distributed ledger · Supply chain management · Credit management

1 Introduction

Supply chain management is a crucial process of optimization that leads to lower costs and higher profits for companies. It creates a sustainable, competitive advantage while maximizing customer value [1–4]. SCM integrates suppliers, manufacturers, distributors, and customers into a complete functional network by comprehensively controlling logistics, capital flow, and information flow (Fig. 1). Of these, capital flow is the most important component of the supply chain. Logistics and information flow serve as the material basis and guarantee of the supply chain separately. The normal operation of a supply chain relies on complete, accurate, and reliable information flow from each of the various links of the supply chain. Only stable, reliable, credible, unalterable, and traceable data can ensure the security of capital flow and guarantee benefits to all the participants in a supply chain [5].

Due to the growing difficulties in SCM, this business field usually copes with challenges that are complicated to solve [6, 7]. Within the global business supply chain, traceability and credit management play the most decisive roles in the advancement of its sustainability [8, 9]. As a distributed, decentralized, traceable, and tamper-resistant ledger technology, blockchain has been widely used in various fields including supply chain

© Springer Nature Singapore Pte Ltd. 2020
G. Xu et al. (Eds.): FCS 2020, CCIS 1286, pp. 121–132, 2020.
https://doi.org/10.1007/978-981-15-9739-8_11

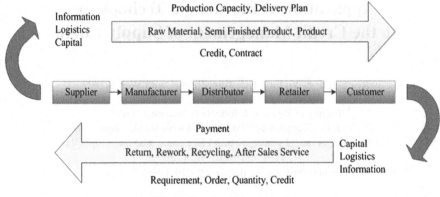

Fig. 1. Supply chain network

management, identity authentication, credit investigation, public charity, etc. Blockchain technology has significantly promoted the development of a range of industries and has created tremendous social benefits [10–16].

New technologies are prone to suffer technical problems and external attacks. Although blockchain technology can significantly reduce management risks, enhance stability, and improve the security of supply chain finance, some risks are difficult to identify due to blockchain bifurcation and pseudo-decentralization [17–20]. Therefore, it is necessary to study methods of strengthening financial supervision and risk control as a way to improve credit management of supply chain finance.

2   Credit Risk Analysis of Supply Chain Management

Credit risks are major obstacles to the development of supply chain management [21]. It is important to explore the essence of supply chain management from the perspective of ecological systems and to handle the credit risks of supply chain management by establishing risk prevention mechanisms.

In an era when Internet technology develops rapidly, supply chain finance differs greatly from traditional finance in terms of the credit risks it presents. There are a number of reasons for this:

- Core enterprises in the supply chain are likely to experience credit or qualification problems due to poor management, thereby generating credit risks.
- Financing enterprises in the supply chain are mostly small and medium-sized enterprises. Such enterprises are generally characterized by incomplete qualifications, poor transparency, capital shortage, weak risk control, bad management, and low credit.
- Participants in the supply chain come from different fields and locales, and this aggravates the risks of information asymmetry and poor contact.
- Information in the supply chain is easily falsified, generating new risks.

More than 90% of supply chain financial risks are credit risks manifested as customer fraud, including disputes over the ownership of shares, implicit liabilities, capital withdrawals, unrelated diversified investments, and undesirable qualities of actual stakeholders.

Overall, supply chain financial risks are generated under the influence of both external and internal factors. Externally, supply chain finance is influenced by macroeconomic cycles, financial supervision policies, and financial costs. For example, many enterprises will suffer serious credit risks due to management difficulties and high financing costs during economic cycle fluctuations, especially during economic downturns. In addition, the risks will involve a wide range. Non-financial enterprises engage in business financing after obtaining related qualifications under legal supervision, changing the participants in supply chain financing. However, these non-financial enterprises tend to be affected by changes in financial supervision policies, such as policy tightening and strengthened supervision, that are not conducive to the development of supply chain financial activities. Business profits and the financing costs of supply chain finance are affected differently by market liquidity and the capital environment. Specifically, financing costs increase while business profits decrease during tight liquidity conditions. In severe cases, capital shortage occurs and financing costs fail to be recovered.

Internally, supply chain financial risks are mainly attributed to the different financing modes adopted at different stages such as procurement, sales, and inventory. Although the adoption of different financing modes brings about high profits, the management risks are increased accordingly. For example, supply chain management risks are directly influenced by the correlation between business activities and the closed operation of capital flow. For this reason, businesses in the same field should establish smooth and close cooperation with each other during the procurement, sales, distribution, and inventory stages. To an extent, the credit status of downstream enterprises reflects their ability and willingness to pay debts. Therefore, the various stages of the supply chain should be closely correlated and effectively integrated. Otherwise, management mechanisms or supply chain risks will run out of control. In addition, both financing guarantees and capital flows in financial management will generate financial risks. Specifically, enterprises rely on their excellent credit and the supply chain to participate in financing. As financing scale and leverage gradually increase, the refinancing business will inevitably be influenced and financial risks will be intensified. Supply chain enterprises provide financing services for small and medium-sized enterprises via credit sales and advance payments. Consequently, advance expenditure and the delayed recovery of funds will put tremendous financial pressure on these small and medium-sized enterprises. A large amount of credit sales and advance payments leads to significant capital outflows and long recovery periods, eventually resulting in poor capital liquidity and accumulation. Once such financing channels are blocked, supply chain enterprises face the risks of capital rupture.

3 Applications and Advantages of Blockchain Technology in Supply Chain Finance

The credit problems of traditional supply chain finance have become increasingly prominent due to changes in market operation mechanisms and the expansion of demands [22–24]. The main problems that affect the innovative development of supply chain finance are as follows:

- *Limitations of credit substitution credibility*

Supply chain finance develops business financing through credit substitution, thereby amplifying the credit of core enterprises. Financial resources tend to gravitate towards core enterprises. The information management of small and medium-sized enterprises is asymmetric, which amplifies the credit risk in disguised form. Therefore, there are serious limitations to developing supply chain finance based on this kind of credit substitution relationship. The risks will be aggregated and intensified, which is not conducive to the healthy development of innovations in supply chain finance.

- *Limitations of credit management systems*

At present, innovative management modes of supply chain finance mainly include the cooperative financing modes of banks and third-party logistics enterprises, and the structural trade financial business models of traditional firms. Although the new model has solved some defects of supply chain financing, there are also insufficient drivers of innovation to find new ways to investigate information such as the net worth of collateral, original price, quality, model, underwriters, and sales targets, etc.

- *Limitations of technology integration methods*

At the bank and enterprise level of supply chain finance, it is difficult to obtain symmetric transaction information for reasons that include incomplete information and unsmooth business connections. The basic innovation of information technology can hardly be solved. The limitations on technological innovation mean that the continuous promotion of supply chain business financing has led to many risks.

- *Credit limitations on trading processes*

Supply chain finance emphasizes the transparency and authenticity of each link in the supply chain. As a practical matter, this means that efforts to design supply chain financial solutions must focus on the credit status of core enterprises, the stability of transaction relationships, and the degree to which core companies cooperate. However, due to the strong professionalism of logistics products, its value assessment affects the control of collateral. The opacity of the transaction process not only increases management cost but also restricts the normal development of supply chain business financing.

Blockchain supply chain finance is a concern for stakeholders at multiple levels, including (Fig. 2):

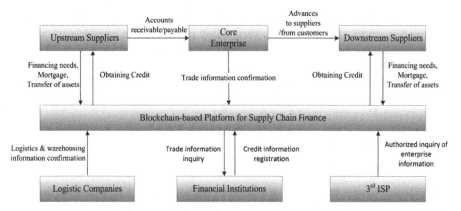

Fig. 2. Business flow of blockchain-based platforms for supply chain finance

- *Core enterprises*, which generally possess core competencies, provide financing to upstream and downstream distributors and suppliers.
- *Upstream and downstream enterprises* are mostly small and medium-sized. They mostly rely on the credit of core enterprises to develop business financing and enjoy low-cost financing services, thereby optimizing cash flow and improving capital turnover efficiency.
- *Financial institutions* are, in this context, mainly institutions with controllable asset risks and transparent information, such as commercial banks, micro-loan companies, factoring companies, and P2P companies.
- *Other service providers* that mainly include ERP, warehousing, logistics, and financial technology enterprises. They tend to expand the business and provide services based on their technical and/or resource advantages.

In a block supply chain, the core enterprise and the upstream and downstream enterprises form a complete financial ecological structure by authorizing the sharing of platform data. The core enterprises or financial institutions have a standard enterprise information management system by which they obtain relevant system authorizations, realize connections with system business, and get relevant enterprise data. By contrast, the upstream and downstream small and medium-sized enterprises have no such complete information management system. The system obtains authorization from the core enterprises in the system and then obtains information data from a third-party platform.

In this financial ecosystem, the system coordinates cooperation between all involved parties through data sharing. In actual operation, not all parties participate in the unified chain. The leader gradually expands the ecology from a certain aspect.

The introduction of blockchain technology has solved many of the limitations of a traditional supply chain:

- *Blockchain solves the problems of difficult supply chain financing and high operating costs.*

After the introduction of blockchain, digital bills are transparent and freely split, and commercial credits can be transmitted and traced to make up for any trust gap between the two parties to a transaction. The blockchain confirms contractual relationships with equality, fast access, traceability, and verifiability in real-time to provide personalized service. This enables small and medium-sized enterprises that previously could not be financed to obtain financing easily. Only about 15% of enterprises in traditional supply chains can obtain financing. After blockchain technology is introduced, the proportion of enterprises that can obtain financing rises to about 85%, increasing capital transfer efficiency and decreasing capital costs.

- *Blockchain has established more business models for supply chain finance and has solved the difficulty of capital flow.*

A blockchain changes the records, transactions, and contracts of supply chain financial transactions and eliminates the barriers to trust. Participants can be platforms, companies, individuals, factoring organizations, intermediary financial institutions, or algorithm companies. The programmability of the blockchain can be personalized to meet the demands of different consumers.

- *Blockchain has established a very reliable trust relationship and solved the problem of financing credit risk.*

Blockchain decentralized storage technology not only ensures data security but also provides a unified and traceable data source to ensure the transparency of supply chain information. In a blockchain, the various parties of supply chain management, product quality, price, origin, and other information, due to the characteristics of the decentralized bookkeeping structure, other parties may not have ownership control data. The transaction is unalterably encrypted. Credit risk control is thus greatly improved, and the encryption security level is enhanced. The blockchain provides real-time transaction status for supply chain finance with improved transparency, which helps to establish a more reliable and stable supply chain financial ecosystem and strengthen trust relationships.

In the supply chain, a blockchain is most suitable for transaction scenarios in which suppliers, core companies, banks, and financial institutions coexist. Blockchain technology can identify assets such as accounts receivable, bills, and warehouse receipts through tamper-resistant and transparent data. It can realize asset transactions such as factoring, discounting, and pledges by reducing intermediate links and facilitating financing. It can leave data deposits in the form of electronic contracts, key data, and identity information to prevent risks such as ticket fraud and repeated pledges via the creation of permanent audit trails. For these reasons, blockchain technology has the following significant advantages in supply chain financing:

- *Improved multi-agent cooperation space*

Blockchain distributed ledger technology has established a good platform for the multiparty collaborative environment of the supply chain. The information in the chain cannot be modified. The decentralization of trust and benefits forms a basis of cooperation and reduces credit risks and cooperation costs among the participating entities. Reconciliation between multiple agencies makes transactions more convenient.

- *Multi-level credit transfer enhances direct trading relationships*

The blockchain establishes a trading relationship between various levels in the supply chain and expands the service scope of supply chain finance by virtue of its ability to facilitate credit transfers between the core enterprise and upstream and downstream enterprises.

- *Digital circulation of assets*

The traditional silver ticket cannot be split or transferred, which limits the flexibility of transactions. The use of digital assets solves the difficulty of splitting and transferring. Participants can easily transfer the relevant assets to obtain cash flow according to their needs.

- *Intelligent processes*

Both parties to a transaction automatically complete the contract through systematic intelligent contracts, and the payment is thereby strongly protected. This reduces waste in interactions, improves efficiency, and reduces errors.

Through blockchain technology, supply chains can become more transparent and large-scale synergy can become easier, thereby improving traceability and security, promoting trust and honesty, and preventing the implementation of problematic practices, with a net effect of strengthening the economy.

4 Application of Blockchain to Supply Chain Financial Credit Management

The application of blockchain technology to the credit management of supply chain finance aims to fully utilize its distributed, decentralized, trustworthy, traceable, and tamper-resistant advantages. This section focuses on the utilization of these technical advantages in the design of credit management system structures for supply chain finance.

4.1 Blockchain Design

Blockchain technology uses a distributed network with multi-party participation of all nodes to ensure the credibility of information. A long-chain mechanism (generally requiring about 5-6 nodes) is adopted in the blockchain. After confirming the long-chain information, the short-chain is automatically revoked. The use of a delay confirmation decreases the possibility of a faster transaction, thus ensuring the reliability of the transaction.

The sidechain mode of blockchain is a hybrid design in which side chains use a decentralized two-way anchoring technology known as SPV (Simplified Payment Verification,) while the main chain uses drive chain mode. Both of these improve security through different unlocking methods. The user sends the digital asset to an address on the main chain, locks the main chain asset, and then sends the SPV certificate to the sidechain for verification. Similarly, the main chain also takes the soft fork RootStock to establish the side chain and increase the function and value of the digital currency. The element chain realizes the mutual conversion of digital currency between the main chain and the side chain, thus providing innovative technical features such as evidence separation, new operation codes, private transactions, relative lock times, and signature coverage amounts. Moreover, the Ethereum blockchain platform design with an open-source smart contract function and cryptocurrency is used to handle point-to-point contracts and further enhance system security. The side chain design mode solves the problem of network congestion under high transaction volume. Users can download relevant sidechains as needed, which effectively reduces invalid synchronization data and improves the efficient operation of the Lisk network.

The digitization of intelligent contracts under blockchain technology is the key to improving their efficiency. It can avoid malicious modifications and interference in normal contract execution and can increase cost-effectiveness. The blockchain smart contract application model is designed to meet the following goals:

- Define the authentication method for all main chain node participants.
- After account verification, define the commercial agreement in code form by writing a smart contract to maintain the normal transaction.
- Permit participants to sign smart contracts through their respective accounts, and perform corresponding operations according to business needs in the subsequent process, thus triggering the execution of contracts.

Under this system the blockchain design achieves data sharing, encryption ensures tamper resistance and data privacy protection, and digital contracts and distributed storage technologies solve business-level problems at a technical level, making them more flexible and objective. It does so in a number of ways. First, the data trust problem is solved. The blockchain makes use of cryptography and digital signatures. The consensus protocol guarantees that the participant's data in blockchain form is combined with the data change history after the data signature is confirmed. Meanwhile, a copy is held, and data credibility is improved. Second, the contractual agreement is implemented objectively and automatically. The smart contract guarantees that the computer program will automatically execute the contract as long as the trigger condition is met, granting high objectivity. Last of all, blockchain gives the transaction history traceability, non-repudiation, and non-tamperability of queries, and ensures that multi-level credit transmission is carried out under the real identity of the participating entities.

4.2 Establishment of a Supply Chain Logistics Information Model Based on Blockchain

The information flow of the supply chain consists of all the information regarding the activities carried out by the enterprises at each node. The main body of this information is the nodes of the participating parties. The logistics of managing this information includes the processes of generating, storing, transmitting, developing, utilizing, and disposing of these information resources.

The supply chain logistics information ecosystem is a chain-dependent relationship composed of the information flows of the four types of information subjects: producers, communicators, users, and decomposers in supply chain information activities. In the blockchain-based supply chain logistics information ecosystem, the blockchain acts as a foundation layer, avoiding the decentralization effect. Each chain of nodes in the data layer constitutes a mesh data path, and only authorized nodes can obtain other nodes and sensors. The public key effectively protects the network topology from external attack. The consensus layer sensor sends data with a private key digital signature, which makes it more difficult for attackers to falsify the data, thereby improving information security. This blockchain-based design for the supply chain logistics information ecosystem increases the advantages of data confidentiality, resistance to attack, self-repairing toughness, and operational ecology, making the ecosystem more stable and harmonious.

The decentralized nature of blockchain technology is manifested in the maintenance of the database by distributed entities. Multi-agent information sharing creates a multi-level, diversified, and multi-functional chain organization of information. The subjects have equal rights and obligations of information storage and exchange. The chain structure constitutes a consensus mechanism. On this basis, each block forms a continuous "chain" for the permanent storage of information data. The decentralized trust mechanism eliminates the opportunity cost caused by a lack of trust between subjects.

These mechanisms of decentralization and common trust have made the blockchain the technical basis for large-scale collaboration tools that have solved complex transaction cost problems and multi-agent information-sharing problems in supply chain logistics information resource management. Supply chain management aims to minimize system costs. Through blockchain technology, supply chain logistics information management realizes a "point, chain, and network" chain management mode. To wit:

- **"Point"**: Blockchain technology has opened the channel for node enterprises to enter the Internet of Things. Through identification technology, intelligent sensing, and information exchange, extension across the Internet meets the needs of blockchain technology operation. Each node interacts to support the establishment and improvement of network consensus mechanisms.
- **"Chain"**: As behavioral entities, node enterprises are interconnected through blockchain technology. This reduces the opportunity cost caused by lack of trust, and facilitates cooperation, information sharing, and benefit distribution in supply chain management.
- **"Network"**: Decentralized and distributed coexistence technology realizes the block coupling of each node enterprise in the supply chain, forming an extended chain. The generation of information flow, capital flow, and logistics constitute the neural network of the supply chain.

4.3 Application of Architecture System Design to the Block Supply Chain

The block supply chain application architecture consists of an application layer, an extension layer, and a protocol layer. The service contents of each layer are shown in Table 1.

Table 1. Service contents of block supply chain application architecture

Layers	Service contents				
Application layer (service platform)	Gateway	Service	Node network	SDK	Tool
Expansion layer (component model)	Consensus Network	Ledger	Persistence engine	Contract engine	
Protocol layer (blockchain protocol)	Ledger Status	Historical proof	Ledger operation set	Contract instruction set	

The application layer is similar to software in a computer, or a browser in the browser/server architecture. Neither the protocol layer nor the extension layer can truly understand and verify the application layer. In fact, the application layer can hardly be used by third-party developers. Therefore, we adopt a completely open-source approach and develop application layers through blockchain technology to expand applications.

The expansion layer is similar to the drive program of the computer. There are two types of practical extension layer design techniques. The first is to use trading markets to implement the exchange of cryptocurrency. The second is the extension of a certain direction for manufacturers such as third-party organizations. Programmable contracts (smart contracts) are typical applications developed at the expansion layer.

The protocol layer is similar to the computer operating system, and it is the basis of the block supply chain transaction. It can be further decomposed into the network layer and the storage layer. The cryptographic signature and the distributed algorithm implement peer-to-peer network coding, cryptographic signature, the network layer consensus algorithm, and data storage. With the improvement of the underlying protocol, any block-paying technology can be easily used for any products requiring third-party payment. Any information that needs confirmation, credit, and traceability can be implemented through blockchain.

Because of the limitations in storage capacity of blockchain systems, different services are encapsulated into functional modules in the design of blockchain. Through the interactive communication of the module interface, different encryption methods are used to encrypt and record the data in the block, thereby increasing the safety of the design. Therefore, our application platform structure design module is divided into four parts: a rights management module, a digital assets management module, a digital assets transaction module, and a credit management module. The rights management module implements the management of user rights, including background review of user information, authority granting, risk assessment, and warnings on the platform. The digital asset management module implements offline applications, asset registration, online audits, online asset management, etc. For example: in an audit of bulk goods warehouse receipts, the quantity and quality of the information in the warehouse receipts are audited. After the offline assets are frozen, third-party institutions evaluate the goods, and then generate and monitor the digital assets with offline asset details and valuations. After the smart contract pays the management fee, the offline assets will be released. The digital asset trading module handles the transaction management functions of digital assets, such as digital asset listing transaction management, trading product splitting, automatic matching transactions, digital asset financing, and asset changes. The credit management module comprehensively manages user behavior, social credit, credit generation, platform display, etc., and provides different operation rights according to users' credit.

Through comprehensive optimization design, supply chain financial applications based on blockchain technology have the advantages of block data storage in which the scale of data storage can be continuously expanded. In order to reduce the financial risks associated with the supply chain, the platform models analyze and evaluate the data on the blockchain using big data technology, and give reasonable credit rating recommendations to build an integrity platform. The big data credit analysis module collects a large amount of user business information to establish an enterprise credit information system, which is tracked and published by the platform dynamically in real-time. Therefore, enterprise credit information is embedded in the supply chain financial services, which greatly strengthens the system's capacity to manage credit risk. The trust mechanism promotes incentives for companies in each node to participate in financing and reduces financing risks.

5 Conclusions

The combination of blockchain and supply chain management has greatly promoted the management of supply chain credit and has effectively made up for the deficiency of trust in each node enterprise. The model proposed in this paper makes full use of the multi-entity and decentralization features of blockchain, as well as symmetric encryption, authorization technology, consensus mechanisms, and technological innovation in smart contracts to solve the problems of trust and security in supply chain management.

However, future supply chain services will develop into a multi-chain structure. Capital structure, customer structure, and risk structure will all undergo great changes. The supply chain financing of the B2B platform and the supply chain financial model of "platform + platform" will gradually rise. Supply chain financial services and supply chain services will be separated. The "chain +" characteristics of supply chain finance will be highlighted. The continuous development of blockchain integrating into supply chain innovation can ensure that the credit management risks of supply chain finance are controllable, and this will help to build a more reliable and safe economic system.

References

1. Fahimnia, B., Tang, C.S., Davarzani, H., Sarkis, J.: Quantitative Models for Managing Supply Chain Risks: A Review. Eur. J. Oper. Res. **247**(1), 1–15 (2015)
2. Li, S., Ragu-Nathan, B., Ragu-Nathan, T.S., Subba Rao, S.: The impact of supply chain management practices on competitive advantage and organizational performance. Omega **34**(2), 107–124 (2006)

3. Dubey, R., et al.: Big data analytics and organizational culture as complements to swift trust and collaborative performance in the humanitarian supply chain. Int. J. Prod. Econ. **210**, 120–136 (2019)
4. Han, J.H., Wang, Y., Naim, M.: Reconceptualization of information technology flexibility for supply chain management: an empirical study. Int. J. Prod. Econ. **187**, 196–215 (2017)
5. Carter, C.R., Rogers, D.S., Choi, T.Y.: Toward the theory of the supply chain. J. Supply Chain Manage. **51**(2), 89–97 (2015)
6. Fan, H., Li, G., Sun, H., Cheng, T.: An information processing perspective on supply chain risk management: antecedents, mechanism, and consequences. Int. J. Prod. Econ. **185**, 63–75 (2017)
7. Baryannis, G., Validi, S., Dani, S., Antoniou, G.: Supply chain risk management and artificial intelligence: state of the art and future research directions. Int. J. Prod. Res. **57**(7), 2179–2202 (2018)
8. Zhu, S., Song, J., Hazen, B.T., Lee, K., Cegielski, C.: How supply chain analytics enables operational supply chain transparency. Int. J. Phys. Distrib. Logistics Manage. **48**(1), 47–68 (2018)
9. Lamming, R.C., Caldwell, N.D., Harrison, D.A., Phillips, W.: Transparency in supply relationships: concept and practice. J. Supply Chain Manage. **37**(3), 4–10 (2001)
10. Abeyratne, S.A., Monfared, R.P.: Blockchain ready manufacturing supply chain using distributed ledger. Int. J. Res. Eng. Technol. **5**(9), 1–10 (2016)
11. Saberi, S., Kouhizadeh, M., Sarkis, J., Shen, L.: Blockchain technology and its relationships to sustainable supply chain management. Int. J. Prod. Res. **57**(7), 2117–2135 (2019)
12. Wang, Y., Singgih, M., Wang, J., Rit, M.: Making sense of blockchain technology: How will it transform supply chains? Int. J. Prod. Econ. **211**, 221–236 (2019)
13. Dolgui, A., Ivanov, D., Sokolov, B.: Ripple effect in the supply chain: an analysis and recent literature. Int. J. Prod. Res. **56**(1–2), 414–430 (2018)
14. Cole, R., Stevenson, M., Aitken, J.: Blockchain technology: implications for operations and supply chain management. Supply Chain Manage. Int. J. **24**(4), 469–483 (2019)
15. Yang, C.: Maritime shipping digitalization: blockchain-based technology applications, future improvements, and intention to use. Trans. Res. Part E **131**, 108–117 (2019)
16. Chong, A.Y.L., Lim, E.T., Hua, X., Zheng, S., Tan, C.W.: Business on chain: a comparative case study of five blockchain-inspired business models. J. Assoc. Inf. Syst. **20**(9), 9 (2019)
17. Whipple, J.M., Griffis, S.E., Daugherty, P.J.: Conceptualizations of trust: can we trust them? J. Bus. Logistics **34**(2), 117–130 (2013)
18. Mao, D., Fan, W., Hao, Z., Li, H.: Credit evaluation system based on blockchain for multiple stakeholders in the food supply chain. Int. J. Environ. Res. Public Health **15**(8), 1627–1647 (2018)
19. Kshetri, N.: Blockchain's roles in meeting key supply chain management objectives. Int. J. Inf. Manage. **39**, 80–89 (2018)
20. Kamble, S., Gunasekaran, A., Arha, H.: Understanding the blockchain technology adoption in supply chains-Indian context. Int. J. Prod. Res. **57**(7), 2009–2033 (2018)
21. Montecchi, M., Plangger, K., Etter, M.: It's real, trust me! establishing supply chain provenance using blockchain. Bus. Horiz. **62**, 283–293 (2019)
22. Catallini, C.: How blockchain applications will move beyond finance. Harvard Business Review 2 (2017). https://hbr.org/2017/03/howblockchain-applications-will-move-beyond-fin ance
23. Hofmann, E., Strewe, U.M., Bosia, N.: Supply Chain Finance and Blockchain Technology. SF. Springer, Cham (2018). https://doi.org/10.1007/978-3-319-62371-9
24. Beck, R., Avital, M., Rossi, M., Thatcher, J.B.: Blockchain technology in business and information systems research. Bus. Inf. Syst. Eng. **59**(6), 381–384 (2017)

Data Auditing for the Internet of Things Environments Leveraging Smart Contract

Fang Peng[1,2], Hui Tian[1,2(✉)], Hanyu Quan[1], and Jing Lu[3]

[1] College of Computer Science and Technology, National Huaqiao University,
Xiamen 361021, China
fpeng323@stu.hqu.edu.cn, {htian,quanhanyu}@hqu.edu.cn
[2] Wuhan National Laboratory for Optoelectronics, Wuhan 430074, China
[3] Network Technology Center, National Huaqiao University, Xiamen 361021, China
jlu@hqu.edu.cn

Abstract. Cloud storage has been proposed to be integrated with the Internet of Things (IoT) to provide more intelligent and powerful services through sharing and analyzing the IoT data. However, how to assure the integrity of IoT data outsourced in the cloud is still an open challenge. A number of auditing schemes have been proposed in recent years, but most of them introduce a credible auditor to perform auditing work instead of the user. However, the absolutely credible auditor is an ideal hypothesis. Thus, we propose a new public auditing scheme, which introduces the smart contract to replace the auditor to perform the auditing task. Since the essence of smart contracts is a piece of public code posted on the blockchain, our scheme can solve the credit problem of the auditor compared with the traditional public auditing model. The proposed scheme streamlines the auditing processes to reduce the computational overheads of the user and cloud. The security of the proposed scheme is rigorously proved. In addition, the results of the performance evaluation show that our scheme can effectively realize the security auditing, and outperforms the existing schemes in computational overheads.

Keywords: Cloud storage · Public auditing · Internet of Things

1 Introduction

The Internet has penetrated into every aspect of people's lives because of the development of techniques. A growing number of physical objects will be connected to the Internet at an unprecedented rate realizing the idea of the Internet of Things (IoT) [1], which is considered to be the third wave of the world's information industry after computers and the Internet. IoT has realized the perception and communication capabilities of objects by using existing technologies such as Wireless Sensor Network, Radio Frequency Identification, and Intelligent Embedding Technology [2, 3]. This, in turn, changes the way people interact with each other, objects, and the environment. As we all known, the IoT has created a world of connected things in which they can pass data and interact with each other. Thus, smart applications in various industries, including the Internet of Vehicles (IoV), Smart Cities, Smart Healthcare, and Smart Agriculture [4], can be developed

© Springer Nature Singapore Pte Ltd. 2020
G. Xu et al. (Eds.): FCS 2020, CCIS 1286, pp. 133–149, 2020.
https://doi.org/10.1007/978-981-15-9739-8_12

based on the IoT data, which makes the digital representation of the real world possible [5].

It can be seen that the data generated in the IoT scenario contains enormous commercial and social values. There are many mature techniques to solve the data security problems during the transmission phase [6–9]. As an important branch of cloud computing, cloud storage is one of the important ways to solve massive data storage and management [10]. At present, many cloud service providers (CSPs) have proposed different cloud-based IoT solutions, and cloud management on data has become an inevitable requirement of the IoT scenario. Figure 1 shows the domain-specific application of data in the cloud-based IoT scenario. There is no doubt that data integrity is the basis for upper-level applications to obtain valuable information. Any incorrect or incomplete data can have an impact on the results of the data analysis, which in turn affects the final decision and the user experience. Although the cloud platform brings great convenience to the storage and management of IoT data, it is undeniable that cloud storage also faces a series of security challenges [19], especially in terms of data integrity and privacy. First, the CSP is more vulnerable to both internal and external security threats due to its opened and shared nature. Second, some dishonest CSPs may try to conceal the fact of data corruption for their own interest once they have suffered Byzantine failures. Therefore, it is necessary to verify the integrity of outsourced data. Based on this, many auditing schemes have been proposed.

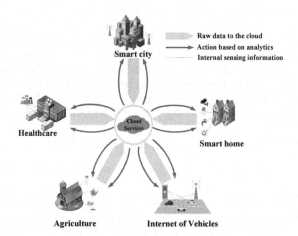

Fig. 1. The domain-specific application of IoT data in a cloud computing environment.

Introducing a credible third-party auditor (TPA) to perform auditing tasks on behalf of data users is a preferred option for most schemes. However, it has many inherent weaknesses in terms of a trust model [11, 12]. First, the TPA is an idealized entity that is difficult to find in real life. Second, since the data users, the CSP, and the TPA are each located in different trust domains, any two parties may initiate a collusion attack against the rest party. Finally, as a centralized entity, external attacks or internal management failures can cause the TPA system to be interrupted. To solve the above problems, we consider changing the traditional cloud auditing framework and using the smart contracts of the blockchain to carry out the auditing process. The idea of decentralization of blockchain provides new research ideas for solving the problem of mutual trust by using a distributed network structure, cryptography, and consensus mechanism [13]. In Ethereum, smart contracts are presented in the form of computer programs and published on blockchain [14]. In this paper, we present an auditing scheme called DALSC (Data auditing leveraging smart contracts) that specifically addresses the integrity verification requirements of IoT data. The DALSC scheme is based on blockchain technology and leverages smart contracts to audit IoT data stored in the cloud. Specifically, the contributions of this work are as follows.

1. We propose an effective cloud auditing scheme, DALSC, which replaces TPA's auditing work by leveraging smart contracts in the blockchain. DALSC provides an open and transparent auditing environment and reduces the user's verification overhead.
2. We propose an auditing log record mechanism to achieve the solidification of auditing evidence by writing auditing results and related information into the public blockchain. Since the smart contracts and auditing logs on the blockchain are publicly stored, the non-repudiation and traceability of the services are guaranteed.
3. Security analysis and performance evaluations show that the scheme we proposed is safe, efficient, and reliable.

The remainder of this article is organized as follows. We describe the system model and design goals in Sect. 2. Then, we present a detailed description of our scheme DALSC in Sect. 3. The security analysis and the performance evaluation of the proposed scheme are presented in Sect. 4. Section 5 gives overviews about the related work. Finally, we draw conclusions in Sect. 6.

2 Problem Statement

2.1 System Model

We consider designing a public auditing model with four different entities. As shown in Fig. 2, there are data users, CSPs, Smart Contracts, and Blockchains.

- Data Users (DUs): This type of entity contains both the owner of the data and the consumer of the data. The data owner uploads the original IoT data to the CSP for storage, and the data user uses the cloud computing technology to analyze and process the data. To ensure the integrity of the data, the data user has the right to initiate a verification request before using the data.
- Cloud Service Providers (CSPs): The CSP provides a large amount of storage space and efficient computing power for data users. The most important thing is that the CSP needs to respond to DUs' auditing challenges in time to prove that data is stored securely.
- Blockchain: The blockchain provides a transparent auditing environment with nodes consisting of at least two entities mentioned above. Relevant information for each audit will be packaged to log and stored publicly on the blockchain.

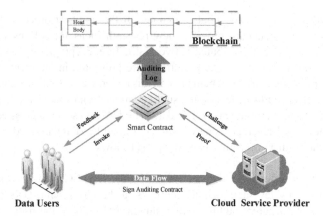

Fig. 2. System model of our scheme.

- Smart Contracts (SCs): The SC is a computerized protocol implemented in an informational manner to publicly verify audit results and provide timely feedback to the DU.

2.2 Threat Model

We assume that the potential threats in the above auditing model mainly stream from malicious data users, CSP, and online opponents. Specifically, malicious data users may deliberately provide erroneous data tags during the audit process. Then even if the CSP correctly stores the data, it will not pass the integrity verification. In this way, malicious data users can refuse to pay CSP service fees or even ask the CSP to make compensation. CSP is considered semi-honest, which means CSP can provide users with scalable on-demand data outsourcing services, but can deliberately hide data corruption events for their own benefit. Finally, there may be malicious nodes on the blockchain that attempt to tamper with or falsify smart contracts to undermine audit work, whether for commercial or personal reasons. However, this behavior is impossible from the perspective of the design and maintenance mechanism of the blockchain. Therefore, we are not discussing malicious online opponents here. To cover up the fact of data corruption, CSP may further launch the following attacks:

(1) Forge attack. CSP attempts to pass the verification by forging the data blocks and corresponding tags.
(2) Replacing attack. CSP attempts to pass the verification by replacing a corrupted block and its tag with another block and its corresponding tag.
(3) Replay attack. CSP attempts to pass the verification through the proofs generated previously.
(4) Collusion attack. CSP may collude with the TPA to obtain their challenged information specified by the CSP, and thus it can replace the damaged one with the normal data block and its tags.

2.3 Security Assumptions

Discrete Logarithm (DL) Problem. Let G_1 be a cyclic group with the large prime order q. For given $P, Q \in G_1$, it is computationally intractable to compute $n \in Z_q^*$ to make $Q = nP$. For any probabilistic polynomial-time adversary $\Re$, the probability of solving the DL problem is negligible, namely,

$$Pr(\Re_{DL}(P, Q \in G_1) \to n \in Z_q^*, \ s.t. \ P = nQ) \leq \varepsilon \tag{1}$$

Computation Diffie-Hellman (CDH) Problem. Let G_1 be cyclic groups of a large prime order q. Given $P, Q, R \in G_1$, where $Q = xP, R = yP$ which $x, y \in Z_q^*$ are two unknown elements. It's computationally intractable to compute xyP. For any probabilistic polynomial-time adversary $\Re$, the probability of solving the CDH problem is negligible, namely,

$$Pr(\Re_{CDH}(xP, yP \in G_1) \to xyP \in G_1 : \forall x, y \in Z_q) \leq \varepsilon \tag{2}$$

3 Proposed Scheme

3.1 Preliminaries

Bilinear Pairing. Let q be a large prime number. Suppose G_1 and G_T are additive group and a multiplicative group with the same order q, respectively. A map is called a bilinear pairing if all the following three conditions hold [15, 24].

(1) Bilinear. For two random points $S, T \in G_1$ and two random elements $a, b \in Z_q^*$. We can get $e(aS, bT) = e(S, T)^{ab}$.
(2) Nondegeneracy. There is a point $S \in G_1$ that $e(S, S) \neq 1$.
(3) Computability. For any two random points $S, T \in G_1$, $e(S, T)$ can be calculated efficiently in polynomial time.

Homomorphic Verifiable Authenticator (HVA). Homomorphic Verifiable Authenticator (HVA): HVA is widely employed as a building block for public auditing, which allows a public auditor to verify the integrity without accessing or downloading the original data. In this sense, HVA can be considered as homomorphic verifiable signatures. In addition to being unforgeable, HVA also meets the following properties [21]:

(1) *Blockless verifiability.* The proof information constructed by the HVT allows the auditor to verify the integrity of the data without retrieving the original data.
(2) *Homomorphism.* It is assumed that both G and H are two groups of large prime numbers q, operations "$\oplus$" and "$\otimes$" are operations defined in G and H and respectively. If the mapping function $f : G \to H$ satisfies the homomorphism, then $\forall h_1, h_2 \in G, f(h_1 \oplus h_2) = f(h_1) \otimes f(h_2)$.
(3) *Non-malleability.* Let σ_1 and σ_2 be labels of data blocks m_1, m_2 respectively, and $\beta_1, \beta_2 \in Z_q^*$ are two random numbers. For a given block $m' = \beta_1 m_1 + \beta_2 m_2$, if the user does not know the corresponding private key, the valid label σ' of the data block m' cannot be derived through σ_1 and σ_2.

Smart Contract. A smart contract is a computerized transaction protocol that executes the terms of a contract. The general objectives are to satisfy common contractual conditions (such as payment terms, liens, confidentiality, and even enforcement), minimize exceptions both malicious and accidental, and minimize the need for trusted intermediaries [17]. Take the implementation of the Ethereum Smart Contract as an example. Typically, smart contracts are compiled into a piece of bytecode in a specific binary format (i.e., Ethereum virtual machine bytecode) and deployed by an account into the blockchain. A smart contract usually provides many functions or application binary interfaces (ABIs) that can be used to interact with it. These ABIs can be executed by sending a transaction from an account or sending a message from another contract. They can also be executed by invoking a call function without sending a transaction or message [18].

3.2 Algorithmic Description

Our scheme, to be detailed in the next Section, consists of three modules: Storage module, Contract module, and Auditing module. The storage module is designed to perform outsourcing operations of IoT data between the DU and the CSP. The contract module provides the process of signing and deploying smart contracts. The audit module gives a solution to the integrity verification of outsourced data.

Storage Module. This module is composed of the *KeyGen, TagGen, Storage* algorithms.

- $(pk, sk) \leftarrow KeyGen()$: The user run this algorithm to generate their public/secret key. They make pk public and keep sk secret.
- $(F, \vartheta, \Phi) \leftarrow TagGen(F, sk)$: Data owners run this algorithm to generate data tags Φ and file signature ϑ.

Contract Module. This module is composed of the *Initialization, ConSign, ConGen* algorithms.

- $\omega_{DU,CSP} \leftarrow ConSign(ASC, sk)$: The algorithm signs an auditing contract ASC for data file F between DU and CSP.
- $(SC, Addr_{SC}) \leftarrow ConGen()$: This algorithm generates a smart contract SC and a contract address $Addr_{SC}$. The DU can invoke the auditing function of the smart contract through the contract address.

Auditing Module. This module is composed of the *Challenge, ProofGen, Verification* algorithms.

- $chal \leftarrow Challenge()$: The algorithm is mainly run by the challenge function of the SC and outputs the challenge information.
- $\varphi \leftarrow ProofGen(F, chal, \Phi)$: This algorithm is run by the CSP. It takes the file F, data tags Φ and the challenge information $chal$ as input. And responses the integrity proof φ.

Table 1. Notations and descriptions.

Notation	Description
G/G_T	Multiplicative cyclic groups
e	Bilinear map
H	A secure hash function
g/u	Generators of G
sk_x/pk_x	Key pair of entity x
$SIG(T, sk)$	Sign on T using key sk
ϑ	The signature of data file
σ_i	Tag of data block m_i
Φ	Tag collection of data blocks
$Addr_x$	Blockchain address of x
ASC	Auditing contract
CF/VF	Challenge/Verification function
$chal$	Challenge information
φ	Proof information

- $\{True/False\} \leftarrow Verificaton(\varphi, chal, pk)$: This algorithm is run by the verification function of the *SC*. It takes the public key *pk*, the challenge information *chal* and proof φ as input, and outputs TRUE if the integrity of the file is verified as correct, or FALSE otherwise.

3.3 The Detailed Scheme

This section details the working principle of DALSC, including storage modules, contract modules, and auditing modules. Table 1 provides a description of the key notations used in DALSC. Note that the storage module and contract module need only be executed once at creation time, and the audit module can be executed multiple times.

Suppose we give the system security parameters κ and $S = (p, G, G_T, e)$ where S is a bilinear map group system. Let G and G_T be two multiplicative cyclic groups of a large prime order p, and $e : G \times G \rightarrow G_T$ be a bilinear map. g and u are the generators of G. H is a secure hash function such that $H : \{0, 1\}^* \rightarrow G$. Assume that the file F to be outsourced to the CSP is divided into n blocks, i.e., $F = \{m_{\cdot}, m_2, \ldots, m_n\}$. The construction of the storage module is as follows:

KeyGen (**Key Generation**): In this algorithm, each DU selects random number $\alpha, \beta \in Z_p^*$ and computes $Y = g^\alpha, W = g^\beta$. Their key pair is $sk = (\alpha, \beta)$, and $pk = (g, u, Y, W)$. They keep sk secret and publishes $\{pk, e, H, G, G_T\}$ public.

TagGen (**Tag Generation**): In this algorithm, the data owner first computes a file signature ϑ for the file where file's identifier is *ID*.

$$\vartheta = ID \,||\, SIG(ID, sk). \tag{3}$$

where $SIG(ID, sk)$ is performed for the signature on file ID with DO's secret key. For each block m_i, the data owner generates a tag σ_i that:

$$\sigma_i = H(\vartheta \| i)^\alpha \cdot (u^{m_i})^\beta. \tag{4}$$

Let the set of all blocks' tags be $\Phi = \{\sigma_i | 1 \le i \le n\}$. The data owner uploads $\{F, \Phi, \vartheta\}$ to the CSP.

Storage: Once receiving information from data owners, the CSP should check the validity of all the block tags by running algorithms in the verification phase, and verify the signature ϑ under the public key. The CSP stores file F only the authentication metaset Φ generated is valid. While the verification passes, output TRUE and save them; otherwise output FALSE and request the data owner to sends the correct block tags.

Initialization: DU and CSP register the blockchain client to obtain the corresponding address $Addr_{DU}$ and $Addr_{CSP}$.

ConSign (Contract Signing): Taking the file F as an example, this algorithm signs an auditing contract ASC for F between DU and CSP. The ASC contains terms agreed by both parties, such as auditing requirements, default clauses, etc. Then, DU signs ASC with sk to get ω_{DU}.

$$\omega_{DU} = SIG(ASC, sk). \tag{5}$$

DU send $\{ASC, \omega_{DU}\}$ to the CSP for checking. After the verification is completed, the CSP also signs ω_{DU} and returns $\omega_{DU,CSP}$ to DU, which

$$\omega_{DU,CSP} = SIG(\omega_{DU}, sk). \tag{6}$$

Finally, DU broadcasts ASC and $\omega_{DU,CSP}$ to blockchain for saving.

ConGen (Contract Generation): DU completes the deployment of smart contract SC on the blockchain by issuing smart contract codes and then gets an address $Addr_{SC}$. Information such as file identifier ϑ, challenge function CF and verification function VF are written in SC.

Challenge: DU gets challenge information by calling the challenge function CF of SC. First, select a c-element subset $I = \{j | 1 \le j \le c\}$ from set $\{1, 2, \ldots, n\}$ randomly. For each $j \in I$, pick a random element $v_j \in Z_p$ and let $V = \{v_j | j \in I\}$. Second, choose a random element $\ell \in Z_p$. At this time, $chal = \{I, V, \ell\}$ is sent to the CSP as challenge information.

ProofGen (Proof Generation): While receiving the challenge information, the CSP would produce a response proof of data storage correctness as follows. First, the CSP calculating τ by using the ℓ.

$$\tau = H(\ell). \tag{7}$$

To generate $\xi \in G_T$, the random number λ is selected which $\lambda \in Z_p$.

$$\xi = e(u^\lambda, W). \tag{8}$$

Finally, compute the tag proof and data proof of the challenge data block. The specific steps are as follows.

$$\sigma = \prod_{j \in I} \sigma_j^{v_j}. \tag{9}$$

$$\eta = \lambda + \tau \sum_{j \in I} m_j \cdot v_j. \tag{10}$$

After completing the above calculation, the CSP responses the proof $\varphi = \{\xi, \sigma, \eta\}$ to the verification function *VF* for data integrity detection by calling the smart contract *SC*.

Verification: To perform the verification, *VF* first computes the hash values τ. Further, it can verify the proof by checking the following equation:

$$\xi \cdot e(\sigma^\tau, g) \overset{?}{=} e(\prod_{j \in I} H(\vartheta \| j)^{\tau \cdot v_j}, Y) \cdot e(u^\eta, W). \tag{11}$$

If the above equation holds, the TRUE is sent to the DU, and the information related to this auditing, such as the timestamp, intermediate parameters, and auditing result, etc., is packaged into an auditing log and stored in the Blockchain. Otherwise, the SC will throw an exception and generate a failed auditing log to store.

4 Security Analysis and Performance Evaluation

4.1 Security Analysis

In this section, we formally prove the security of our scheme based on the threat model in Sect. 2.2.

Theorem 1: If all entities are authentic and the scheme DALSC can execute normally, then the CSP can pass the verification.

Proof: We prove the correctness of our scheme as follows:

$$\xi \cdot e(\sigma^\tau, g) = e(u^\lambda, W) \cdot e(\sigma^\tau, g)$$
$$= e(u^\lambda, W) \cdot e((\prod_{j \in I} \sigma_j^{v_j})^\tau, g)$$

$$= e(u^\lambda, W) \cdot e(\prod_{j \in I} (H(\vartheta \,||\, j)^\alpha \cdot (u^{m_j})^\beta)^{v_j \tau}, g)$$

$$= e(u^\lambda, W) \cdot e(\prod_{j \in I} H(\vartheta \,||\, j)^{v_j \tau}, g^\alpha) \cdot e(\prod_{j \in I} (u)^{m_j v_j \tau}, g^\beta)$$

$$= e(u^\lambda, W) \cdot e(\prod_{j \in I} H(\vartheta \,||\, j)^{v_j \tau}, Y) \cdot e(u^{\tau \sum_{j \in I} m_j v_j}, W)$$

$$= e(u^{\lambda + \tau \sum_{j \in I} m_j v_j}, W) \cdot e(\prod_{j \in I} H(\vartheta \,||\, j)^{v_j \tau}, Y)$$

$$= e(\prod_{j \in I} H(\vartheta \,||\, j)^{v_j \tau}, Y) \cdot e(u^\eta, W).$$

Theorem 2: The BLS-based Homomorphic Verifiable Authenticator cannot be forged by any adversary if the Computational Differ-Hellman assumption in the bilinear group holds.

Proof: This theorem shows that it is computationally infeasible to falsify BLS-based homomorphic verification labels. As shown by the safety analysis of Wang et al. [31], the HVA scheme has proven to be effective and unforgeable because the BLS is safe when the CDH problem in the bilinear group is difficult [32]. Therefore, the detailed certification process is omitted here.

Theorem 3: This scheme can effectively resist the forgery attack of CSP. That is to say, it is difficult for CSP to try to pass audit verification by forging valid evidence information.

Proof: In response to the challenge information $chal = \{I, V, \ell\}$ received from SC, the CSP shall calculate the corresponding certification information $\varphi = \{\xi, \sigma, \eta\}$. If the value of ξ is incorrect, Eq. (9) does not hold even if the other content in the proof information is correct. Therefore, it is not necessary for the CSP to give an incorrect value of ξ. In addition, if the user's private key is unknown, the BLS-HVTs cannot be falsified, which can be proved by existing related documents. In summary, we only need to prove the unforgeable of the tag proof set σ and the data proof set η of the challenge data block.

(1) The Unforgeability of σ. To prove this hypothesis, the following game is designed: In response to the received challenge information, the CSP provides a forged proof message $\varphi' = \{\xi, \sigma', \eta\}$, where

$$\sigma = \prod_{j \in I} \sigma_j^{v_j} \neq \sigma' = \prod_{j \in I} \sigma_j'^{v_j}. \tag{12}$$

Equation (10) shows that for $j \in I$, there is $\sigma_j \neq \sigma_j'$. If the CSP can still pass the auditing verification, the CSP wins; otherwise, it fails. Suppose CSP wins the game, then

$$\xi \cdot e(\sigma'^\tau, g) = e(\prod_{j \in I} H(\vartheta \,||\, j)^{\tau \cdot v_j}, Y) \cdot e(u^\eta, W).$$

The correct proof information satisfies the following equation

$$\xi \cdot e(\sigma^\tau, g) = e(\prod_{j \in I} H(\vartheta \,||\, j)^{\tau \cdot v_j}, Y) \cdot e(u^\eta, W).$$

According to the property of the bilinear map, for any j belonging to I, $\sigma_j = \sigma'_j$ holds. However, this conclusion contradicts the assumption. That is to say, the aggregation label σ cannot be forged.

(2) The Unforgeability of η. To prove this hypothesis, the following game is designed: In response to the received challenge information, the CSP provides a forged proof message $\varphi^* = \{\xi, \sigma, \eta^*\}$, where

$$\eta = \lambda + \tau \sum_{j \in I} m_j \cdot v_j \neq \eta^* = \lambda + \tau \sum_{j \in I} m_j^* \cdot v_j. \qquad (13)$$

Inequality (11) shows that $m_j \neq m_j^*$. If the CSP can still pass the auditing verification, the CSP wins; otherwise, it fails. Suppose CSP wins the game, then

$$e(u^{\eta^*}, W) = e(u^{\lambda + \tau \sum\limits_{j \in I} m_j^* \cdot v_j}).$$

The correct proof information satisfies the following equation

$$e(u^\eta, W) = e(u^{\lambda + \tau \sum\limits_{j \in I} m_j \cdot v_j}).$$

According to the property of the bilinear map, it can be derived

$$\lambda + \tau \sum_{j \in I} m_j \cdot v_j = \lambda + \tau \sum_{j \in I} m_j^* \cdot v_j.$$

Obviously, this conclusion contradicts the previous assumptions. In other words, η cannot be forged.

Theorem 4: In our scheme, it is impossible to retrieve any data content from the auditing log stored in Blockchain, and there is no collusion attack.

Proof: Leveraging the similar security analysis of [19], the reliability of the HVT is based on the CDH problem. And we added a random value λ when aggregating data proofs. Therefore, our scheme can preserve the privacy of the owner's data. At the same time, *SC* plays the role of TPA in the traditional public audit program, and the audit process is open and transparent. Therefore, there is no possibility that any party between the third-party auditor and the user or the CSP will initiate a collusion attack against the other party.

4.2 Performance Evaluation

In this section, we evaluate the performance of our scheme from two aspects, namely property comparison and the computational cost.

Theoretical Analysis. Table 2 shows the property comparison of the state-of-the-art against the proposed scheme. From the comparison of existing properties, our scheme supports public auditing without the involvement of TPA. Since smart contracts are publicly uploaded, any data user or IoT data user can verify the validity of the auditing results at any time. And each auditing log is stored on the blockchain to form a solidification of evidence.

Table 2. Property comparison with exiting schemes.

Scheme	Public auditing	TPA participation	Smart contract based	Traceability
LPCA [28]	Y	Y	N	N
USPA [29]	Y	Y	N	N
RDA [30]	N	N	N	N
DALSC	Y	N	Y	Y

Table 3 shows the computational overhead of our solution on the client side and the cloud server. Let n be the total number of data blocks. Let t represents the number of data blocks being challenged. H represents the average execution time of the hash function H. Let ε is the average execution time of the exponentiation operation on group G. Let M_1, M_t be the average execution times of the multiplication operations on group G and G_T respectively. Let ρ be the bilinear pairing operation. The computational overheads are mainly in the *TagGen*, *ProofGen* and *Verification* algorithms. In the *TagGen* algorithm, the data owner generates tags for all data blocks, the computation cost is $n(M_1 + 3\varepsilon + H)$. In the *ProofGen* algorithm, the overhead is mainly spent on calculating the label aggregation value σ and the data aggregation value η. The CSP performs pairing and hashing operations for once time. The number of exponentiation operations and exponentiation operations are $t(2M_1 + \varepsilon)$.

Table 3. Computation overhead of our scheme.

	TagGen	ProofGen	Verification
DU	$n(M_1 + 3\varepsilon + H)$	–	–
CSP	–	$\rho + t(2M_1 + \varepsilon) + H$	–
SC	–	–	$3\rho + t(H + M_1) + 2M_T + (3 + t)\varepsilon$

Experiment Evaluation. This article performs simulation experiments on HP workstations. All encryption algorithms are implemented by using Pairing-Based Cryptography (PBC) in the Python environment. All the algorithms in the scheme run on HP workstations with an Intel (R) Core (TM) i5-6600 CPU of 3.30 GHz, 2133 MHz of 2×4 GB DDR4 and a 7200 rpm 2 TB Serial ATA hard drive with 64 MB of cache. The experiment uses an elliptic curve of MNT d159, and the length of the group is 160 bits. In addition, the size of the data blocks in the experiment was 4 KB, and all the experimental results were the average of 20 trials.

Figure 3 shows the relationship between the computational overhead of the tag generation and the number of data blocks. Figure 4 shows the computational overhead of the verification phase and the audit phase in the case of the different number of challenge blocks. It is not difficult to see that the computation time of the CSP and SC is very short, and the computational overhead of generating tags is acceptable because the data tags can be generated once in the life cycle of the data audit for a long time. Although the computational overhead of the proof and verification phase increases linearly as the number of data blocks increases. However, according to the sampling test, the verifier selects 460 data blocks in a large number of data blocks for verification. When this file has 1% data block error, it can detect data errors with 99% probability.

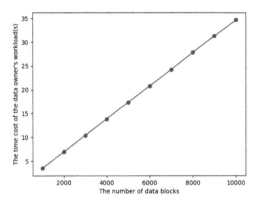

Fig. 3. Relationship between tag generation time and number of data blocks.

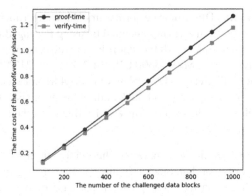

Fig. 4. The relationship between proof and verification time and the number of challenge blocks.

5   Related Work

Cloud data auditing enables remote security assessment of data on cloud storage platforms. On the one hand, it enhances the security capability of the cloud platform, and on the other hand, it builds a bridge of mutual trust between users and CSPs. According to the identity of the auditors, the auditing model can be classified into private auditing [10, 20] and public auditing [21–26]. In 2007, Juels et al. proposed a Proofs of Retrievability (POR) scheme based on a private auditing model [10] in which the user acts as an auditor and completes the auditing process by interacting with the CSP through multiple times. However, this model has many drawbacks. First, the results are given by the user alone, since the user and the CSP are located in different domains of trust, the auditing results are difficult to convince both entities. Second, frequent computational and communicational operations undoubtedly add to the burden on users. Based on this, Ateniese et al. pioneered the PDP (Provable Data Possession) scheme [16] based on the public auditing model. This scheme is believed to be the first scheme to provide blockless and public verification at the same time. It can generate probabilistic proofs that the CSP possesses the user's data and aggregate the tags of the sampled blocks into a single value by using homomorphic verifiable tags (HVT). When 1% of the cloud data is damaged, the auditor can send a challenge message of size 460 to identify the data integrity problem with a probability of 99%.

To fulfill different data auditing demands, many novel schemes have been presented. Ateniese et al. [22] implemented some dynamic operation functions by improving the PDP model. Although the scheme improves the verification efficiency by leveraging symmetric encryption and hash function, it does not realize the random verification in the true sense. Erway et al. [23] proposed a PDP-based public auditing scheme that supports dynamic data updates by introducing a Rank-based Authenticated Skip List. Subsequently, Wang et al. [24] proposed a public auditing scheme based on the BLS signature, which uses Merkle Hash Tree (MHT) as the authentication data structure to support the dynamic update of data. Although they all guarantee the statelessness of auditors in public auditing, they cause large computational and communication overhead during the data validation and update phases. Zhu et al. [25] designed an Index Hash

Table (IHT) for public auditing programs to support dynamic data auditing. Tian et al. [21] and Shen et al. [26] proposed a public auditing scheme based on Dynamic Hash Table (DHT) and public auditing based on Double Linked Info Table (DLIT). Both have achieved smaller computational and communication overhead than scheme [23, 24]. Wang et al. [27] proposed a privacy-preserving public auditing scheme which assumed that the TPA was semi-trusted and honestly executed the auditing scheme whilst being curious about the data. This scheme can prevent the TPA from learning the content of cloud user data during the auditing process.

However, most of the above schemes believe that TPA will perform the auditing work honestly and credibly. In fact, TPA may launch security attacks on users for various reasons [11]. For example, TPA who is irresponsible can always generate a good integrity report without performing verification to avoid resource consumption. Besides, malicious auditors may collude with CSP to generate deviation verification results to deceive users for profits. Of course, TPA may also collude with users to defame CSP for compensation with the reason for data damaging. To solve the above problems, we introduced smart contracts and hoped to achieve mutual trust between the entities in the auditing through blockchain technology. The auditing scheme we proposed will be more reliable and robust than the others.

6 Conclusion

Nowadays, the IoT environment demands data collection and the ability to analyze it by using intelligent algorithms. These depend greatly on the quality and reliability of data. In this paper, we will investigate the integrity auditing of IoT data in cloud scenarios to address the challenges faced by the IoT technique. We propose a public auditing scheme based smart contract, DALSC, which eliminates the role of TPA in traditional auditing models by introducing smart contracts. The scheme signs auditing contracts between the DU and CSP and pushes the auditing process by invoking the function of the contract. The scheme protects both the server and the user by the nonrepudiation record on the blockchain. By storing the auditing log on the blockchain, the proposed scheme could trace all of the auditing histories and allow all data files to be verified by any data owner or user at any time. The theoretical analysis demonstrates that our scheme is secure and efficient.

Acknowledgements. This work was supported in part by the Natural Science Foundation of China under Grant No. U1405254, Natural Science Foundation of Fujian Province of China under Grant No. 2018J01093, Open Project Program of Wuhan National Laboratory for Optoelectronics under Grant No. 2018WNLOKF009, The Scientific Research Funds of Huaqiao University (No. 605-50Y19028), and Subsidized Project for Postgraduates' Innovative Fund in Scientific Research of Huaqiao University.

References

1. Al-Fuqaha, A., Guizani, M., Mohammadi, M., Aledhari, M., Ayyash, M.: Internet of Things: a survey on enabling technologies, protocols, and applications. IEEE Commun. Surv. Tutor. **17**(4), 2347–2376 (2015)

2. Gubbi, J., Buyya, R., Marusic, S., Palaniswami, M.: Internet of Things (IoT): a vision, architectural elements, and future directions. Futur. Gener. Comput. Syst. **29**(7), 1645–1660 (2013)
3. Kelly, S.D.T., Suryadevara, N.K., Mukhopadhyay, S.C.: Towards the implementation of IoT for environmental condition monitoring in homes. IEEE Sens. J. **13**(10), 3846–3853 (2013)
4. Reyna, A., Martín, C., Chen, J., Soler, E., Diaz, M.: On blockchain and its integration with IoT. Challenges and opportunities. Futur. Gener. Comput. Syst. **88**, 173–190 (2018)
5. Mohanty, S.P., Choppali, U., Kougianos, E.: Everything you wanted to know about smart cities: the Internet of Things is the backbone. IEEE Consum. Electron. Mag. **5**(3), 60–70 (2016)
6. Capkun, S., Buttyán, L., Hubaux, J.P.: Self-organized public-key management for mobile ad hoc networks. IEEE Trans. Mob. Comput. **2**, 52–64 (2003)
7. Chuang, M.C., Lee, J.F.: TEAM: trust-extended authentication mechanism for vehicular ad hoc networks. IEEE Syst. J. **8**(3), 749–758 (2013)
8. Yang, X., Lin, J., Yu, W., Moulema, P.M., Zhao, W.: A novel enroute filtering scheme against false data injection attacks in cyber-physical networked systems. IEEE Trans. Comput. **64**(1), 4–18 (2013)
9. Lin, J., Yu, W., Zhang, N., Yang, X., Zhang, H., Zhao, W.: A survey on Internet of Things: architecture, enabling technologies, security and privacy, and applications. IEEE Internet Things J. **4**(5), 1125–1142 (2017)
10. Juels, A., Kaliski Jr., B.S.: PORs: proofs of retrievability for large files. In: Proceedings of the 14th ACM Conference on Computer and Communications Security, pp. 584–597. ACM (2007)
11. Xue, J., Xu, C., Zhao, J., Ma, J.: Identity-based public auditing for cloud storage systems against malicious auditors via blockchain. Sci. China Inf. Sci. **62**(3), 1–16 (2019). https://doi.org/10.1007/s11432-018-9462-0
12. Armknecht, F., Bohli, J.M., Karame, G.O., Liu, Z., Reuter, C.A.: Outsourced proofs of retrievability. In: Proceedings of the 2014 ACM SIGSAC Conference on Computer and Communications Security, pp. 831–843. ACM (2014)
13. Nakamoto, S.: Bitcoin: a peer-to-peer electronic cash system (2008). http://bitcoin.org/bitcoin.pdf
14. Wood, G.: Ethereum: a secure decentralised generalised transaction ledger. Ethereum Proj. Yellow Pap. **151**, 1–32 (2014)
15. Liu, C., Ranjan, R., Zhang, X., Yang, C., Georgakopoulos, D., Chen, J.: Public auditing for big data storage in cloud computing–a survey. In: 2013 IEEE 16th International Conference on Computational Science and Engineering, pp. 1128–1135. IEEE (2013)
16. Ateniese, G., et al.: Provable data possession at untrusted stores. In: Proceedings of the 14th ACM Conference on Computer and Communications Security, pp. 598–609. ACM (2007)
17. Tapscott, D., Tapscott, A.: Blockchain revolution: how the technology behind bitcoin is changing money, business, and the world. Portfolio (2016)
18. Zhang, Y., Kasahara, S., Shen, Y., Jiang, X., Wan, J.: Smart contract-based access control for the Internet of Things. IEEE Internet Things J. **6**(2), 1594–1605 (2018)
19. Srinivasan, M., Sarukesi, K., Rodrigues, P.: State-of-the-art cloud computing security taxonomies: a classification of security challenges in the present cloud computing environment. In: Proceedings of the International Conference on Advances in Computing, Communications and Informatics, pp. 470–476. ACM (2012)
20. Shacham, H., Waters, B.: Compact proofs of retrievability. In: Pieprzyk, J. (ed.) ASIACRYPT 2008. LNCS, vol. 5350, pp. 90–107. Springer, Heidelberg (2008). https://doi.org/10.1007/978-3-540-89255-7_7
21. Tian, H., Chen, Y., Chang, C.C., Jiang, H., Huang, Y.: Dynamic-hash-table based public auditing for secure cloud storage. IEEE Trans. Serv. Comput. **10**(5), 701–714 (2015)

22. Ateniese, G., Di Pietro, R., Mancini, L.V., Tsudik, G.: Scalable and efficient provable data possession. In: Proceedings of the 4th International Conference on Security and Privacy in Communication Networks, p. 9. ACM (2008)
23. Erway, C.C., Küpçü, A., Papamanthou, C., Tamassia, R.: Dynamic provable data possession. ACM Trans. Inf. Syst. Secur. **17**(4), 15 (2015)
24. Wang, Q., Wang, C., Li, J., Ren, K., Lou, W.: Enabling public verifiability and data dynamics for storage security in cloud computing. In: Backes, M., Ning, P. (eds.) ESORICS 2009. LNCS, vol. 5789, pp. 355–370. Springer, Heidelberg (2009). https://doi.org/10.1007/978-3-642-04444-1_22
25. Zhu, Y., Ahn, G.J., Hu, H., Yau, S.S.: Dynamic audit services for outsourced storages in clouds. IEEE Trans. Serv. Comput. **6**(2), 227–238 (2011)
26. Shen, J., Shen, J., Chen, X., Huang, X., Suailo, W.: An efficient public auditing protocol with novel dynamic structure for cloud data. IEEE Trans. Inf. Forensic Secur. **12**(10), 2402–2415 (2017)
27. Wang, C., Chow, S.S.M., Wangm, Q.: Privacy-preserving public auditing for secure cloud storage. IEEE Trans. Comput. **62**(2), 362–375 (2011)
28. Han, J., Li, Y., Chen, W.: A Lightweight And privacy-preserving public cloud auditing scheme without bilinear pairings in smart cities. Comput. Stand. Interfaces **62**, 84–97 (2019)
29. Zhao, H., Yao, X., Zheng, X.: User stateless privacy-preserving TPA auditing scheme for cloud storage. J. Netw. Comput. Appl. **129**, 62–70 (2019)
30. Zang, L., Yu, Y., Xue, L., Li, Y., Ding, Y., Tao, X.: Improved dynamic remote data auditing protocol for smart city security. Pers. Ubiquit. Comput. **21**(5), 911–921 (2017). https://doi.org/10.1007/s00779-017-1052-y
31. Wang, Q., Wang, C., Li, J., Ren, K., Lou, W.: Enabling public auditability and data dynamics for storage security in cloud computing. IEEE Trans. Parallel Distrib. Syst. **22**(5), 847–859 (2011)
32. Boneh, D., Lynn, B., Shacham, H.: Short signatures from the Weil pairing. J. Cryptol. **17**(4), 297–319 (2004)

Design a Proof of Stake Based Directed Acyclic Graph Chain

Haibo Tian$^{(\boxtimes)}$, Huizhi Lin, and Fangguo Zhang

Guangdong Province Key Laboratory of Information Security Technology,
School of Data and Computer Science, Sun Yat-Sen University,
Guangzhou 510275, Guangdong, People's Republic of China
{tianhb,isszhfg}@mail.sysu.edu.cn, 921334116@qq.com

Abstract. The concept of blockchain comes from the Bitcoin system where transactions are organized in blocks. However, blocks are not necessary. Researchers have found ways to use a directed acyclic graph (DAG) to build a chain without blocks. Currently, these chains still rely on some kinds of proof of work, which is not environmentally friendly. We here design a DAG chain with a proof of stake for independent nodes in the Internet. We split nodes into two categories. One is client nodes that produce only normal net transactions (NNTs). The other is chain nodes where active chain nodes are selected periodically based on their stakes and aspirations to participate in the chain management. Active chain nodes produce chain transactions (CTs) that may include hashes of NNTs. CTs form the DAG chain, which helps an ordering process of the NNTs. With the ordering ability of transactions from client nodes, the chain naturally supports global state transition. With a brief analysis, we found that the theoretical performance limitation of the chain depends only on the bandwidth and computation power of chain nodes.

Keywords: DAG chain · Stakes · Transactions · State transition

1 Introduction

A chain is a list of ordered transactions agreed by some independent nodes. Bitcoin blockchain [14] could be viewed as a special kind of chain. Transactions in Bitcoin are ordered by a block and the block is ordered in a main blockchain. Ethereum blockchain [23] also has a main chain that includes ordered blocks and each block includes ordered transactions. One of the difference of the Ethereum blockchain and the Bitcoin blockchain is the rule to select a main chain. The off-chain blocks in Ethereum contribute to their main chain selection algorithm. To further use transactions in off-chain blocks, inclusive blockchain protocols

Supported by the National Key R&D Program of China (2017YFB0802500), Natural Science Foundation of China (61972429), Natural Science Foundation of Guangdong Province of China (2018A0303130133).

[11] are proposed where blocks form a DAG. Transactions in the IOTA project [17] directly form a DAG.

A DAG chain is a chain in the form of a DAG. A vertex in a DAG is a block or a transaction. The block or transaction includes hashes of previous blocks or transactions, which are directed edges of a DAG. An edge between two vertexes implies an order of the vertexes. Roughly, all edges of a DAG may reveal the order among most vertexes. A DAG chain is attractive since it allows many nodes to produce blocks or transactions concurrently. When the number of nodes increases, the throughput of transactions has a chance to increase. Currently, most DAG projects use some kinds of proof of work (PoW) to produce blocks or transactions.

Proof of stake (PoS) is a more energy saving method to qualify a node to produce blocks or transactions. PoS projects usually divide time into slots and some slots form an epoch. In each epoch, one node or some nodes are selected according to their stakes and other parameters. If some nodes are selected, the nodes form a committee. The committee may run some kinds of Byzantine Fault Tolerant (BFT) algorithms or some voting based algorithms to reach a consensus about blocks or transactions.

If we put PoS and DAG together, we could use PoS to form a committee. Each member in the committee then produces transactions or blocks to form a DAG. On the DAG side, this combination avoids the situation where some witness nodes or some coordinator servers are needed. On the PoS side, it is unnecessary to select a leader among a committee. This paper gives such a combination design.

1.1 Related Works

PoS is a promising consensus method to build a blockchain. We briefly survey four works in this direction.

- PPCoin project [20] is an earlier project of PoS. The amount of coins and their holding time are taken as parameters to decrease the mining difficulty.
- Algorand project [9] proposes to use the hash value of a node's signature to replace the hash value of a block header. The signature hash value of a leader should be less than a target. If the target could be changed according to the proportion of stakes, it is a PoS based chain.
- Snow white [6] is a provable secure PoS protocol. The snow white project selects leaders for an epoch mainly by the consensus algorithm in [15]. In the consensus algorithm [15], a node computes a hash value of their identity and a time stamp. If the value is less than a target, the node is eligible. In the snow white project, the node who can compute the hash value is limited to a committee. Each member in the committee has stakes recently.
- Cardano project [21] is supported by serial Ouroboros proposals [4,7,10]. The Ouroboros protocol [10] selects a committee for an epoch where members of the committee are stakeholders in recent slots. Then a leader is selected from the committee with a probability that is determined by their stake proportion.

The Ouroboros Praos protocol [7] uses a verifiable random function (VRF) to select leaders. If the VRF output of a node is less than a target that is determined by their stake proportion, the node is eligible. The Ouroboros Genesis protocol [4] proposes a chain selection rule when multiple leaders exist for a slot.

All these projects introduce randomness in the selection of leaders to improve fairness. However, if a node with fewer stakes has been selected as a slot leader luckly, an adversary could corrupt the node with fewer costs and launch a long range attack [22]. We try to avoid the problem by a committee governance policy and a stake lock rule.

DAG is a possible structure of a blockchain ledger. Some typical proposals are as follows.

- IOTA project [17] is an earlier project where transactions form a DAG. A tip selection algorithm helps a node to order transactions.
- Byteball project [3] proposes a main chain extraction method from a DAG. Transactions are ordered in the main chain. The method mainly relies on some nodes with good reputation.
- The Conflux system [12] chooses the GHOST rule in Ethereum [23] to select a main chain from a DAG of blocks. When the order of blocks could not be determined by their topological information, the system uses the identities of blocks to break a tie.
- The SPECTRE proposal [18] shows a voting algorithm to order each pair of blocks in a DAG. The vote of each block is interpreted according to the topological information of the DAG. They expect that the majority's aggregate vote should grow fast so that a possible tie could be solved in a short time.
- Sompolinsky and Zohar [19] propose to find a maximal k-cluster subgraph of a DAG and to order blocks according to the topological information of the subgraph. The parameter k determines the maximal new blocks within a time interval defined as a maximal network delay. They believe that the number of new blocks produced by honest players should be different to that of an adversary.
- The Avalanche protocol [16] proposes to only order dependent transactions. If there are conflict transactions, they ask random peers the preferred transaction. If the number of positive answers for a transaction is greater than a threshold value, the transaction is deemed good.

Note that the proposals in [12,16,17] are tied to PoW or the UTXO model of Bitcoin. The proposals in [18,19] totally rely on the topology of a DAG, which may suffer from the splitting attack in [17]. When we use PoS, an adversary may produce a DAG with any required topological information due to the nothing at stake attack [2].

1.2   Contributions

From the related works, we know that there are challenges to design a PoS chain or a DAG chain. The difficulties simply increase when we try to design a PoS based DAG chain. We explain the typical problems as follows.

- The PoS method is challenged by a long range attack. If an adversary tries to forge a chain from a block far from the current block, it is usually called as a long range attack. Buterin [22] proposes the attack mainly for their motivation to make the proof of work involve executing random contracts from the blockchain. An adversary could fill the blockchain with special contracts within a few days to falsify the proof of work method. The PoS in [22] is taken as a method to work around the problem. Bentov et al. [5] propose a bribe attack where an adversary could get the private keys of stakeholders who propose a block in the past. Literatures [2,13] show that it is reasonable for a stakeholder to sell their private key to an adversary. So it is practical for an adversary to sign a fork in the past when the corrupted parties were the majority. Gaži et al. [8] propose a stake bleeding attack where an adversary could build a private chain to get more stakes from transaction fees and make the private chain public when it is more longer than the public chain. AlMallohi et al. [1] propose a checkpoint method to mitigate the long range attack.
- The PoS method is also challenged by a nothing at stake attack. In the Bitcoin PoW, if a party proposes two conflicting blocks, the party has to pay roughly double works. However, in the PoS, if there are conflicting blocks, a party could sign both for profit. Poelstra[2] takes this attack as the root causes for long range attacks. Bentov et al. [5] propose a rational fork attack where rational stakeholders should sign blocks on the multiple forked chains to increase their expected reward. Li et al. [13] analyze some PoS projects against the attack. The main strategy against the attack is to make rules for stakeholders so that they may behave honestly.
- The DAG method is challenged by a splitting attack. An attacker can try to split a DAG into two branches and maintain the balance between them. This would allow both branches of the DAG to continue to grow. Although this attack could be alleviated in the PoW context, it is not easy to defend in the PoS context due to the nothing at stake attack.

We design a new framework and a simple chain building process to alleviate the above problems.

- Our chain building process includes three steps: a committee step, an extending step and a sorting step. The committee step mainly includes a protocol to select a committee with fixed size. The committee members are active chain nodes with higher stakes. Long range attacks are alleviated if the size of the committee is moderate. We enhance this point by permanently locked stakes and an initiative abdication policy.
- The extending step builds a DAG by CTs. Then from the topological information of a DAG, we could judge whether an NNT is witnessed by the majority

of the active chain nodes. If an NNT is witnessed by the majority, it is confirmed. Only confirmed NNTs could be ordered. This strategy defends against the splitting attack and other attacks in the DAG context, which is similar to the witness policy in the Byteball project [3].

– The sorting step orders NNTs mainly according to their timestamps. We assume a bounded delay network. Active chain nodes only receive NNTs within a time interval according to the timestamps. So a timestamp in an NNT has to be in a reasonable time interval accepted by the current active chain nodes, which is then used to order NNTs. Ordered NNTs are executed after several slots. Client nodes could check the state of their account to make sure whether their expected NNT is executed. There are no forks in the sorting step so that the nothing at stake problem is alleviated.

Finally, we pay more attention to exploit the DAG information to confirm transactions parallelled. In our framework, we mainly design two kinds of transactions, normal net transactions (NNTs) and chain transactions (CTs). NNTs are the objects to be confirmed and ordered. And CTs are the vertexes of a DAG. Basically, the information of an NNT may be wrapped in more CTs so that an NNT could be confirmed as soon as possible.

2   The Framework

2.1   Time

A basic time unit is a slot. An initial time and a time slot length are written in the initial chain transaction (ICT) of the chain. The first slot is denoted by slot 0. An example is shown in Fig. 1. A time anchor defines the reference time of the chain such as the Unix time "1970-01-01 00:00:00 UTC".

Fig. 1. Time slots of a chain in a node

Our framework assumes a bounded delay network. That is, if an honest node sends a transaction, other honest nodes will receive the transaction within a bounded delay Δ_1. Different nodes may have time drifts and different execution speeds. The maximal tolerable time for time drifts and time differences of node execution is denoted by Δ_2. Suppose that a node sends a transaction at its local time t_1, and the last node receives the transaction at its local time t_2. Then $t_2 \leq t_1 + \Delta_1 + \Delta_2$. Let $\Delta = \Delta_1 + \Delta_2$. Then if a node sends a transaction at its local time t_1, other nodes could receive the transaction before their local time $t_1 + \Delta$ and after their local time $t_1 - \Delta_2 + \Delta_1$.

The parameter Δ_1 could be measured in a network for each slot. It may be set according to the timeout value of the TCP. The parameter Δ_2 could be written in the code as a constant. At any local time t_3 of a node, if a transaction with a timestamp t_4 arrives at the node and $|t_3 - t_4| > \Delta$, the node will reject the transaction. That is why the timestamp in an NNT has to be in a reasonable time interval.

Another time unit in our framework is an epoch. An epoch includes e slots where e is a system parameter. We define a parameter D such that there are D slots to initialize the chain. Then we define epoch 0 be the slots from the slot $D-e$ to slot $D-1$, epoch i is the slots from the slot $D+(i-1)\times e$ to $D+i\times e-1$.

2.2 Parties

The parties in our framework are divided into four categories according to their logical functions. They are client nodes, active chain nodes, candidate chain nodes and silent chain nodes. A client node mainly produces NNTs. These transactions are used to change the global state of the chain such as token values or stake values of an account. An active chain node produces CTs to maintain the chain. A candidate chain node produces management net transactions (MNTs) to participate in a competition of selecting active chain nodes. A silent chain node produces nothing. It may listen and verify transactions or synchronize their transaction database. In Fig. 2, we show three client nodes, two silent chain nodes, two candidate chain nodes and two active chain nodes. Note that a physical node could be a client node, a chain node or both.

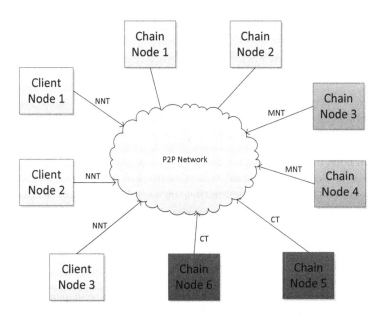

Fig. 2. An example of nodes and their transactions.

A client node mainly consists of three modules. As shown in Fig. 3, the underlying module is the network, through which NNTs are sent. The middle module is the NNT. It receives application messages, encapsulates them to NNTs and sends the NNTs to the network module. The top module is the distributed application (DAPP). It provides user interface, produces application messages and sends the messages to the NNT module.

The core function of a client node is to form NNTs. An NNT contains four fields. They are an application message m, a timestamp t, a counter c and a public key recoverable signature σ as in the Ethereum [23] for the previous fields. The message m may include a smart contract address, a function name and function arguments. Specially, transaction fees of the NNT may be included as a parameter in the function arguments. The counter c is used to authenticate the client. An example NNT is shown in Eq. (1) where $||$ denotes the concatenation of bit strings of the fields.

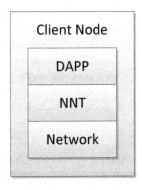

Fig. 3. Modules in a client node

$$NNT := m||t||c||\sigma \tag{1}$$

A chain node mainly consists of nine modules as shown in Fig. 4. The left side modules are to deal with different transactions. The right side modules are to store transactions and states. We describe the modules in the left side as follows.

- The underlying module is the network, through which NNT, MNT or CT transactions are received and MNT or CT transactions are sent.
- The NNT module receives NNT transactions, transfers their information to the CT module, and waits for enough confirmations to forward the confirmed NNTs to the smart contract module.
- The MNT module receives node management messages, encapsulates the messages to MNTs and sends MNTs to the network module. It also receives MNTs from the network module or the CT module, parses the MNTs to extract node management messages and submits the messages to the node management module.

- The CT module receives MNTs or NNTs, encapsulates them to CTs and sends the CTs to the network module. It also parses a CT to extract an NNT hash or an MNT and submits them to their module.
- The smart contracts module includes server side programs of DAPPs. It receives fully confirmed NNTs, and executes the NNTs to change the state database.
- The node management module provides a user interface to change the status of a node, creates node management messages and sends them to the MNT module. It also receives messages from the MNT module and parses node management messages.

In the right side, the transaction pool is a temporal storage for unordered CTs and NNTs. The transaction database is a persistent storage for CTs, MNTs and NNTs. The state database stores states for all the nodes and smart contracts. A state of a node includes token values, stake values, counter numbers and so on.

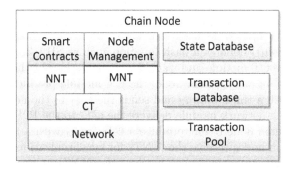

Fig. 4. Modules in a chain node

A core function of a chain node is to form CTs. A CT contains six fields. They are a payload field M which is an NNT hash value or an MNT, a reference field $\{n, H_1, \ldots H_n\}$ which typically contains two hash values of referred CTs, a timestamp T, a state root R of the stable state at the current slot, a counter C and a public key recoverable signature Σ for the previous fields. An example CT is shown in Eq. (2).

$$CT := M||n, H_1, \ldots, H_n||T||R||C||\Sigma \tag{2}$$

A CT includes the state root of a stable state. There are S slots between the current state and the stable state. Suppose that T in a CT is in slot i. If $i \leq S$, R is defined in the ICT. Otherwise, R is the root of the state at the beginning time of the slot $i - S$. Figure 5 shows the stable states of some slots.

2.3 Actions

We briefly describe the process of an NNT from creation to confirmation. The process sketches how parties in Fig. 2 play.

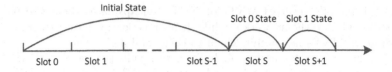

Fig. 5. Stable state of some slots

1. Suppose the client node 1 produces a NNT NNT_1 with a timestamp t_1 and sends it out through a P2P network.
2. Chain nodes receive the NNT_1.
   - Active chain nodes produce CTs for the NNT_1.
     - Suppose the chain node 5 receives the NNT_1 at its local time t_2. It is expected $t_2 + \Delta_2 - \Delta_1 > t_1 \geq t_2 - \Delta$.
       (a) The network module delivers the NNT_1 to the NNT module.
       (b) The NNT module checks whether NNT_1 is a new transaction for the node. If it is, it is stored in the transaction pool.
       (c) It computes the hash value of NNT_1 as $h_1 = hash(NNT_1)$ where $hash(\cdot)$ denotes a hash function such as SHA-3, and sends h_1 to the CT module and waits for confirmations of the NNT_1.
       (d) As an active chain node, the CT module produces a CT_1 for h_1 with a timestamp t_3 and sends the CT_1 to the network module.
       (e) The network module delivers the CT_1 to the P2P network.
     - The chain node 6 may produce a CT_2 for h_1 with a timestamp t_4.
   - Other chain nodes receive the NNT_1 for synchronization.
     - Suppose the chain node 1 receives the NNT_1 at its local time t_5. It is expected $t_5 + \Delta_2 - \Delta_1 > t_1 \geq t_5 - \Delta$. The chain node 1 executes the first three steps as an active chain node.
3. Chain nodes receive CTs to confirm NNTs.
   - Suppose the chain node 1 receives CT_1 at its local time t_6. It is expected $t_6 + \Delta_2 - \Delta_1 > t_3 \geq t_6 - \Delta$.
     (a) The CT module parses CT_1, sends confirmation information about h_1 to the NNT module. The NNT module counts the confirmations of the h_1. Here if the number of confirmations is 2, the NNT module delivers NNT_1 to the smart contract module.
     (b) The smart contract module executes the application message in the NNT_1 and puts the NNT_1 to the transaction database.

3   The Chain

CTs in the framework form a DAG. There are roughly three steps to build a DAG chain.

1. Committee Step: Given an epoch index i, output a committee for the epoch $i + 1$.

2. Extending Step: Given a DAG G and the members of a committee in an epoch, produce new transactions or blocks to output a new DAG G' where G is a subgraph of G'.
3. Sorting Step: Given a transaction list T and a subgraph G'/G, each chain node outputs a new transaction list T' where T is a sublist of T'.

3.1   Committee Step

One may use a VRF with a target to select a committee. However, for a given target, it is possible to select too much or too few nodes. Many nodes in a committee may slow the efficiency of an epoch, and several nodes in a committee may bring security issues. Instead, we use a simple protocol to select a committee with a fixed size.

Suppose the ICT of the chain defines active nodes for the initial D slots. Suppose the nodes are $\{N_0, ..., N_{l-1}\}$. For an epoch $i \geq 1$, a new committee is set up. Consider the epoch 1 as an example where the slot D is the first slot of the epoch.

1. If a silent node wants to be an active chain node in the epoch 1, it should prepare an account with stakes before the beginning time of the slot $D - e - S$. The amount of the stakes is defined by the node manager. Once an account has stakes, the node manager could only increase the amount of stakes in the account. It could not be withdrawn or transferred to other accounts. This simulates a physical miner where one has to add funds to increase computation power. To avoid the lost of the account private key, a hardware token is recommended. The node also needs to change its local status to a candidate node status so that the node management module could work correctly.
2. At the beginning time of the epoch 0, the node management module checks its local status. If it is now a candidate node, it creates a candidate request message as $CRM := 1||R$ where 1 is the epoch number and R is the root of the stable state of the slot $D-e$. The message is then sent to the MNT module which wraps it as an MNT and sends the MNT to the network module. The MNT is defined as $MNT := CRM||T||\Sigma$. For honest nodes, the timestamp T in their MNT should be at least Δ less than the end time of the slot $D-2$. Σ is still a signature for the previous fields.
3. Active chain nodes of the epoch 0 create a hash confirmation list. When an active chain node receives an MNT before the end time of the slot $D-2$, the MNT module checks the timestamp and signature. If they are correct, the MNT module recovers a public key pk from the signature and a slot number $D-e$ from the timestamp. It sends $(CRM, pk, D-e)$ to the node management module. The node management module checks R in the CMR with respect to the slot $D-e$. If R is correct, it computes an account address from the public key pk. The node management module then checks the amount of stakes $stake$ in the stable state of the slot $D-e$. Then a pair $(stake, pk)$ is inserted into a finite ordered list that is ordered by the value of stakes from

big to small. A limitation is that the node referenced by the pk is not an active node at the epoch 0. The size of the list is at least l. At the beginning time of the slot $D-1$, the node management module calculates the hash values of each element in the ordered list to form a hash confirmation list as an MNT message. The node then creates a CT message which includes the MNT and sends the CT message to the P2P network.

4. Chain nodes set the active nodes for epoch 1. When a chain node receives a CT message with an MNT message including a hash conformation list from one of the current active nodes, their node management module calculates the votes of each hash value in the list. At the end time of the slot $D-1$, if a hash value is confirmed by not less than 2/3 active nodes, the value is confirmed in the chain. The first l confirmed hash values are the image of active nodes in the next epoch. If the size of the confirmed hash value set is smaller than l, nodes $(N_0, ..., N_{l-1})$ are filled into the list. The first filled node should be N_{l*} where $l^* = 1 \mod l$ where 1 is the next epoch number. For a candidate chain node, if the hash value of its $(stake, pk)$ is not in the confirmed hash value set, the node management module changes its status to a silent chain node. Otherwise, it changes its status to an active chain node.

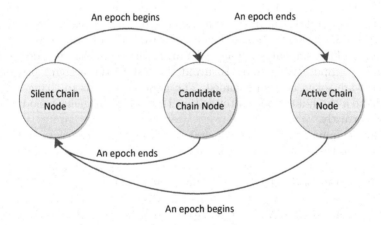

Fig. 6. A chain node status graph

The protocol could be described as free registration, stake priority and initiative abdication. As shown in Fig. 6, any silent node could make itself as a candidate node when a new epoch begins, which means free registration. For an honest node, the free registration is to show their enthusiasm to be an active chain node. So that we could avoid to select sleeping nodes. The sorting rules of the ordered list show the policy of stake priority. The limitation makes sure that an active chain node could not continue in two continuous epoches except they are initially trusted nodes.

3.2   Extending Step

When a committee for an epoch is fixed, the DAG ledger could be extended. We use the CTs as the vertexes in a DAG. A CT may contain an MNT or a hash of an NNT. So we describe this step from the creation of an NNT which follows the formats in the Eq. (1).

CT Creation. When a chain node receives a NNT, its NNT module verifies the signature, creation time and counter number. If these parameters are valid, the hash value of the NNT is computed as $h = hash(NNT)$, and (h, NNT) are stored in the transaction pool if the transaction is new. The counter number of the client node is updated by the chain node as the current state. If the chain node is active, the hash value is sent to the CT module with a probability ϵ.

The CT module wraps a received hash value as a message M. Suppose a CT contains two hash references of other CTs. Then $n = 2$. Let H_1 and H_2 be the two hash references. The creation time T is the local time. The field R is the root of the stable state at the slot of T. The field C is the current counter number of the node. Then a CT is created. The CT module increases the counter of the node by 1 and stores the CT to its transaction database. Then it sends the CT to the network module.

CT Reception. When a chain node receives a CT from one of the current active chain nodes, its CT module verifies the signature, creation time, root of stable state and counter number. If all checks are passed, the CT module updates the counter number of the sending node. If the reference hashes of the CT are in the transaction database, the CT is put into the transaction database. Otherwise, the CT is put into the transaction pool.

When a new CT is put into the transaction database, the transaction pool is updated. If the new CT is the last referenced CT of a CT in the transaction pool, the CT in the pool is put into the transaction database.

3.3   Sorting Step

A DAG contains CTs. CTs contain hashes of NNTs. NNTs could change the global state by smart contracts. To obtain a stable global state, NNTs are sorted after they are confirmed. NNTs are mainly confirmed by topological information of a DAG.

NNT Confirmation. When a new CT is put into the transaction database, the confirmation information of the NNT in the CT is delivered to the NNT module. The confirmation information is (h, H_0, H_1, H_2, pk), where h is the hash of the NNT, H_0 is the hash of the CT, (H_1, H_2) are the two hashes of the referenced CTs, and pk is the public key of the sender.

The NNT module may maintain three data structures to confirm NNTs.

1. A dynamic array A_D. The i-th element includes a CT hash H_0^i, an NNT hash h^i, the weight of the NNT w^i, the sender public key of the CT pk^i, the two references (H_1^i, H_2^i) and a list of CT hashes L_{CT} which refer to CTs with the same h^i. Initially, the weight w^i is 1 and the list L_{CT} is empty.
2. A scan array A_S. The i-th element includes a CT hash H_0^i, the sender public key of the CT pk^i and a counter. For each input, the pair (H_0^i, pk^i) are initially copied from the A_D and the counter is initialized by zero.
3. An update list L_U. The i-th element includes a CT hash H_0^i and the two references (H_1^i, H_2^i). It is initially empty for a new input.

The NNT module takes the confirmation information as an input vector (h, H_0, H_1, H_2, pk) and executes as follows.

- If H_0 is in A_D or h is in the transaction database, the module stops. Otherwise, the input is added to A_D, A_S and L_U. The new element in A_D is $(H_0, h, 1, pk, H_1, H_2, L_{CT})$. The NNT module scans A_D to initialize L_{CT}. The new element in A_S is $(H_0, pk, 0)$. The new elements in L_U is (H_0, H_1, pk) and (H_0, H_2, pk).
- For an element (H_0^*, H^*, pk^*) in L_U, the module scans A_S by (H^*, pk^*). If the i-th element in A_S satisfies $H_0^i = H^*$ and $pk^i \neq pk^*$, some events are triggered.
  1. The i-th element of A_D is updated. The module sets $w^i = w^i + 1$.
  2. The L_U is updated. The module adds (H_0^i, H_1^i, pk^i) and (H_0^i, H_2^i, pk^i) from A_D to the L_U. The module removes the element (H_0^*, H^*, pk^*) from L_U.
  3. The element H_0^* in the A_S is updated. The module increases the counter field by 1. If the counter equals $n = 2$, the element is removed from A_S.
  If all elements in L_U could not find matching elements in A_S, the procedure stops.
- The module updates A_D. For the i-th element in A_D, if $w^i + \sum_{H_0^x \in L_{CT}} w^x \geq \beta l$, the NNT with h^i is confirmed and sent to the smart contract module, where β is a system parameter. The elements containing h^i are removed from A_D.

There is a subtle problem when a new epoch begins. Suppose $\beta = 2/3$. Within an epoch, an invalid NNT may have a weight at most $l/3$. If an invalid NNT spans two epoches, it may have a weight at most $2l/3$ which makes it valid. To avoid the problem, when a new epoch begins, a chain node should clear the weights to zero in their dynamic array.

NNT Sorting. When the smart contract module receives an NNT hash, the module gets the NNT from the transaction pool and puts it to an ordered NNT list. Suppose the current slot is the slot i. The NNT may be put into the ordered list for the slot i or $i \pm 1$ according to the creation time of the NNT. If the creation time of the NNT shows that the NNT is created in a slot before the beginning time of the slot $i - 1$ or after the beginning time of the slot $i + 1$, the

NNT is dropped. The smart contract module should execute ordered NNTs at the slot $i - 2$. Transaction fees in an NNT may be shared by the active chain nodes of the slot $i - 2$.

We define the following rules to order NNTs.

- The list is mainly ordered by the creation time of NNTs. If a new NNT has an earlier creation time than an NNT in the list, the new NNT is inserted before the NNT.
- If two NNTs have the same creator, they should have different creation time and the NNT with a smaller creation time should have a smaller counter value. If the rules are violated, the two NNTs are dropped and the tokens of the creator are shared by the active chain nodes of the epoch.
- If two NNTs are created by different creators with the same creation time, the smart contract module computes two hash values. The inputs of the hash function are the epoch number, the public key of the NNT and the public keys of the active chain nodes in their epoch. Then the NNT whose hash value is smaller should be at the front.

4 Analysis

4.1 Double Spending Attack

We consider the following scenario as a double spending in the account model.

- Suppose Alice wants to buy some assets from Bob. Alice transfers her tokens to a new address $addr_f$ from $addr_a$. Then Alice creates two NNTs. The first NNT transfers all tokens of $addr_f$ back to $addr_a$. The second NNT transfers all tokens of $addr_f$ to Bob's address. Alice pays Bob with the second NNT. Then Alice sends the first NNT to the network.

According to our sorting rules, if the first NNT in the attack has a smaller creation time and counter number than the second one, the first NNT will be executed at first. Then Bob gets nothing since $addr_f$ has no tokens when the second NNT is executed.

To defend against the attack, suppose Bob runs a silent chain node. Then he has two choices.

- At first, Bob could wait S slots. At that time, no new NNTs will affect the state before S slots. Then Bob could check his account to make sure that he has received tokens from Alice.
- Secondly, Bob could check the NNT of Alice by the counter numbers. If the counter number is correct, Bob could receive Alice's tokens with a high probability.

4.2 Overall Performance

Suppose a client node sends an NNT at the time t_1. Before the time $t_1 + \Delta$, the NNT is received by active chain nodes and some CTs including the NNT information are sent. Before the time $t_1 + 2\Delta$, active chain nodes enter the extending step for the NNT. Before the time $t_1 + 5\Delta$, the NNT is confirmed. So if we omit the node executing time, an NNT should be in the NNT list of an node within 5Δ.

Suppose we have an unlimited bandwidth network and our chain nodes execute algorithms with zero delay. The expected transactions per second (TPS) is just the number of NNTs per second. So the TPS of the system is simply limited by node computation time and communication bandwidth of the underlying network.

References

1. AlMallohi, I.A.I., Alotaibi, A.S.M., Alghafees, R., Azam, F., Khan, Z.S.: Multivariable based checkpoints to mitigate the long range attack in proof-of-stake based blockchains. In: Proceedings of the 3rd International Conference on High Performance Compilation, Computing and Communications, HP3C 2019, pp. 118–122. Association for Computing Machinery, New York (2019). https://doi.org/10.1145/3318265.3318289
2. Andrew, P.: A treatise on altcoins (2016). https://download.wpsoftware.net/bitcoin/alts.pdf. Accessed 1 Feb 2020
3. Anton, C.: Byteball: a decentralized system for storage and transfer of value (2016). https://obyte.org/Byteball.pdf. Accessed 1 Feb 2020
4. Badertscher, C., Gai, P., Kiayias, A., Russell, A., Zikas, V.: Ouroboros genesis: composable proof-of-stake blockchains with dynamic availability. In: Proceedings of the ACM Conference on Computer and Communications Security, Toronto, ON, Canada, pp. 913–930 (2018). https://doi.org/10.1145/3243734.3243848
5. Bentov, I., Gabizon, A., Mizrahi, A.: Cryptocurrencies without proof of work. In: Clark, J., Meiklejohn, S., Ryan, P.Y.A., Wallach, D., Brenner, M., Rohloff, K. (eds.) FC 2016. LNCS, vol. 9604, pp. 142–157. Springer, Heidelberg (2016). https://doi.org/10.1007/978-3-662-53357-4_10
6. Daian, P., Pass, R., Shi, E.: Snow White: robustly reconfigurable consensus and applications to provably secure proof of stake. In: Goldberg, I., Moore, T. (eds.) FC 2019. LNCS, vol. 11598, pp. 23–41. Springer, Cham (2019). https://doi.org/10.1007/978-3-030-32101-7_2
7. David, B., Gaži, P., Kiayias, A., Russell, A.: Ouroboros praos: an adaptively-secure, semi-synchronous proof-of-stake blockchain. In: Nielsen, J.B., Rijmen, V. (eds.) EUROCRYPT 2018. LNCS, vol. 10821, pp. 66–98. Springer, Cham (2018). https://doi.org/10.1007/978-3-319-78375-8_3
8. Gaži, P., Kiayias, A., Russell, A.: Stake-bleeding attacks on proof-of-stake blockchains. In: 2018 Crypto Valley Conference on Blockchain Technology (CVCBT), pp. 85–92, June 2018. https://doi.org/10.1109/CVCBT.2018.00015
9. Jing, C., Silvio, M.: Algorand (2017). https://arxiv.org/abs/1607.01341. Accessed 1 Feb 2020

10. Kiayias, A., Russell, A., David, B., Oliynykov, R.: Ouroboros: a provably secure proof-of-stake blockchain protocol. In: Katz, J., Shacham, H. (eds.) CRYPTO 2017. LNCS, vol. 10401, pp. 357–388. Springer, Cham (2017). https://doi.org/10.1007/978-3-319-63688-7_12
11. Lewenberg, Y., Sompolinsky, Y., Zohar, A.: Inclusive block chain protocols. In: Böhme, R., Okamoto, T. (eds.) FC 2015. LNCS, vol. 8975, pp. 528–547. Springer, Heidelberg (2015). https://doi.org/10.1007/978-3-662-47854-7_33
12. Li, C., Li, P., Zhou, D., Xu, W., Long, F., Yao, A.: Scaling Nakamoto consensus to thousands of transactions per second. arXiv, 1805.03870 (2018). https://arxiv.org/abs/1805.03870
13. Li, W., Andreina, S., Bohli, J.-M., Karame, G.: Securing proof-of-stake blockchain protocols. In: Garcia-Alfaro, J., Navarro-Arribas, G., Hartenstein, H., Herrera-Joancomartí, J. (eds.) ESORICS/DPM/CBT -2017. LNCS, vol. 10436, pp. 297–315. Springer, Cham (2017). https://doi.org/10.1007/978-3-319-67816-0_17
14. Nakamoto, S.: Bitcoin: a peer-to-peer electronic cash system (2008). https://bitcoin.org/bitcoin.pdf. Accessed 4 Aug 2017
15. Pass, R., Shi, E.: The sleepy model of consensus. In: Takagi, T., Peyrin, T. (eds.) ASIACRYPT 2017. LNCS, vol. 10625, pp. 380–409. Springer, Cham (2017). https://doi.org/10.1007/978-3-319-70697-9_14
16. Rocket, T.: Snowflake to avalanche: a novel metastable consensus protocol family for cryptocurrencies (2018). https://ipfs.io/ipfs/QmUy4jh5mGNZvLkjies1RWM4YuvJh5o2FYopNPVYwrRVGV
17. Serguei, P.: The tangle (2015). https://www.semanticscholar.org/. Accessed 1 Feb 2020
18. Sompolinsky, Y., Lewenberg, Y., Zohar, A.: SPECTRE: serialization of proof-of-work events: confirming transactions via recursive elections. Cryptology ePrint Archive, Report 2016/1159 (2016). https://eprint.iacr.org/2016/1159
19. Sompolinsky, Y., Wyborski, S., Zohar, A.: PHANTOM and GHOSTDAG: a scalable generalization of Nakamoto consensus. Cryptology ePrint Archive, Report 2018/104 (2018). https://eprint.iacr.org/2018/104
20. Sunny, K., Scott, N.: PPCoin: peer-to-peer crypto-currency with proof-of-stake (2012). https://www.peercoin.net/. Accessed 1 Feb 2020
21. Cardano Team: Cardano settlement layer documentation (2015). https://cardanodocs.com/introduction/. Accessed 1 Feb 2020
22. Vitalik, B.: Long-range attacks: the serious problem with adaptive proof of work (2014). https://blog.ethereum.org/. Accessed 1 Feb 2020
23. Wood, D.G.: Ethereum: a secure decentralised generalised transaction ledger homestead (2014). http://gavwood.com/paper.pdf. Accessed 4 Aug 2017

Design of Personal Credit Information Sharing Platform Based on Consortium Blockchain

Jing Zhang[1,2(✉)], Rong Tan[1,2], and Yu-dong Li[1]

[1] Shanghai Business School, Shanghai 201400, People's Republic of China
zhangjing25@163.com, tanrong529@gmail.com, lydmm_2002@163.com
[2] Tehua Postdoctoral Programme, Beijing 100029, People's Republic of China

Abstract. The technical features of blockchain, including decentralization, data transparency, tamper-proofing, traceability, privacy protection and open-sourcing, make it a suitable technology for solving the information asymmetry problem in personal credit reporting transactions. Appling blockchain technology to credit reporting meets the needs of social credit system construction and may become an important technical direction in the future. This paper analyzed the problems faced by China's personal credit reporting market, designed the framework of personal credit information sharing platform based on blockchain 3.0 architecture, and studied the technical details of the platform and the technical advantages. The in-depth integration of blockchain technology and personal credit reporting helps to realize the safe sharing of credit data and reduce the cost of credit data collection, thereby helping the technological and efficiency transformation of the personal credit reporting industry and promoting the overall development of the social credit system.

Keywords: Consortium blockchain · Personal credit reporting · Credit information sharing

1 Introduction

With the continuous improvement of China's social credit system, personal credit has become an important credit indicator for natural persons in modern economic society. By the end of 2019, China's Central Bank's personal credit reporting system has collected credit information of 1.02 billion natural persons. While playing the leading role of the government, the marketization process of personal credit reporting in China is also accelerating. In May 2018, Baihang Credit was officially established, it mainly focuses on the credit business of Internet finance, which is an important complement to the Central Bank's personal credit reporting system.

The biggest development bottleneck of China's personal credit reporting industry is the integration and sharing of credit information. The Central Bank's personal credit reporting system is only open to enquiries from individuals, commercial banks, and financial institutions that conduct credit services. It is basically closed to the market, and is still far away from sharing data with Baihang Credit. The original intention of the establishment of Baihang Credit is to create a melting pot of market credit information. Its shareholders are all industry giants, covering massive Internet user data of group companies such as Ali, Tencent, and Ping An. However, the majority of shareholders did not share credit data with Baihang Credit.

1.1 Credit Data Ownership Confirmation

Data resource has the feature of being easy to copy, its confidentiality is difficult to maintain, and the credit data of the same information subject can always be collected by multiple financial institutions. Credit data is the core interest of credit reporting agencies. In the case where data ownership cannot be clearly defined, sharing data externally may lead to the leakage of commercial information and cause losses to the institution's own interests. In addition, there is currently no clear method for measuring the market value of credit data and the benefits brought by data exchanges, which also leads to the lack of incentives for institutions to share data externally.

At present, the ownership of personal information is still controversial in law. Theoretically speaking, personal information comes from individuals, and the information subject should enjoy priority data ownership. However, the information subject does not have the actual processing, use, sharing and other control capabilities of personal information [1]. The current unspoken rule in the credit reporting industry is that with the authorization of the information subject, the ownership of the personal credit information, the actual control rights, and the benefits of data transactions all belong to the information collector [2]. This mechanism obviously does not give personal information subjects the reasonable protection of the economic interest, but how to price fragmented personal information is a difficult point.

1.2 Credit Data Integration

Credit reporting is part of the financial infrastructure, and the quality of credit data has priority over the size of the data. With the deepening of Internet financial remediation, China has officially promoted the P2P online lending institutions to access the Central Bank's credit reporting system and Baihang Credit. The access of Internet financial data has brought greater challenges to the data quality management of credit bureaus. Unlike traditional financial institutions with a high degree of data normalization, Internet data sources are multi-source, diverse, and multi-domain [3], and the data integration is difficult with high cost. The data access institutions of Baihang Credit cover many fields such as online small loans, P2P platforms, consumer finance, and Internet bank. Their businesses, customer groups, and data formats are different, and their business levels are uneven [4]. Once the business operations of some institutions are not standardized, or the data is not strictly submitted in accordance with uniform standards, or even false data is submitted, the credibility of the entire credit reporting system will be reduced, which will have a great negative impact on credit management.

1.3 Credit Data Security

Data security incidents have occurred frequently in the credit reporting industry. In September 2017, Equifax, one of the three largest personal credit bureaus in the United

States, suffered the most serious cyber-attack since its establishment, resulting in the disclosure of personal key information of approximately 150 million customers. According to the data released by the National Internet Emergency Center (CNCERT) in China, in the year of 2019, a total of more than 3,000 important data breach risks and incidents were discovered in China. Mainstream databases such as MongoDB, Elasticsearch, SQL Server, MySQL, and Redis have been exposed to have serious security vulnerabilities that may lead to the risk of data leakage.

While promoting the integration and sharing of credit data between institutions, it is necessary to technically guarantee the security of the system and data. The credit reporting system should implement strict access mechanism, identity verification and permission control for data access institutions, set up database access security settings, and minimize potential data security risks such as vulnerability utilization, DDoS attacks, and brute force cracking.

1.4 Personal Information Protection

The risk of personal information leakage in China's credit service industry is severe. In 2019, many big-data risk-control companies were investigated and prosecuted for using web crawlers to illegally crawl personal data. Some online loan Apps excessively claim user authorization, and collect personal information beyond the scope, resulting in rampant phenomena such as "routine loans" and violent collection. In the era of big data, personal information protection has become the focus of global attention. Both the EU's General Data Protection Regulation (GDPR) and the US California Consumer Privacy Act (CCPA) have been promulgated, giving detailed descriptions of the rights enjoyed by information subjects and the obligations of data controllers [5]. China's big data industry has entered a period of rectification, and the "Personal Information Protection Law", "Data Security Law" and other related laws will be introduced in the near future, placing stricter requirements on privacy protection in the credit reporting industry.

In order to maintain the standardized development of the credit reporting industry, the credit reporting agencies need to implement strict and complete compliance authorization management. When collecting and using personal information, they must ensure that they have obtained explicit authorization from the information subject and use it within the scope of authorization. At the same time, the credit reporting agencies should strengthen the privacy protection, anonymize personally identifiable information, eliminate the identity attributes and sensitive data in personal information, and fully protect the legitimate rights and interests of the information subject.

1.5 Data Acquisition Cost

The credit reporting agency's own data resources are relatively limited, and usually need to obtain external data from other data service providers through purchase, exchange and cooperation [6]. The construction cost of traditional centralized database is relatively high, the authorization mechanism is complex, and the data security is difficult to guarantee, which is not conducive to mutual trust and collaboration between institutions. There is often a competitive relationship between agencies, so it is inevitable that data service providers will stop providing data or raise the price of data. The fierce data source competition has caused credit reporting agencies to spend a lot of time and economic costs in the data collection process, resulting in waste of resources, which is not conducive to the improvement of the overall efficiency of the credit reporting industry.

2 Related Work

As a disruptive technology, blockchain is leading a new round of technological and industrial changes worldwide. In January 2016, the United Kingdom took the lead in listing blockchain as a national strategy, and believed that blockchain could construct an honest society. China's "Thirteenth Five-Year Plan for National Informatization" raises blockchain as a key frontier technology at the national strategic level. Blockchain has technical characteristics such as distributed storage, point-to-point transmission, quasi-anonymity, security, trustworthiness, and programmable. It is a natural fit for personal credit reporting, and can solve the problem of credit information sharing in a targeted manner.

Many Chinese well-known scholars have recognized the advantages of applying blockchain technology to credit reporting. Liao believed that blockchain technology could be applied to the collection, transmission, processing and inspection of information, bringing new opportunities for the credit reporting industry [7]. Ba pointed out that the characteristics of blockchains such as tamper-proofing, traceability, and privacy protection made it a good way to solve the problems in the field of credit data sharing [8]. Zhu pointed out that the functional attributes of the consortium blockchain such as access mechanism, distributed database, multi-center, smart contract and incentive mechanism are suitable for credit data collection, storage, transmission, verification and supervision [9]. Liu pointed out that blockchain could provide technical architecture support for traditional credit reporting systems and solve the current pain points of the credit reporting system [10].

The application of blockchain technology to credit information sharing is a hot issue in academic research in recent years. Ju et al. designed a big-data credit reporting platform for multi-source heterogeneous data fusion based on blockchain technology and developed a prototype system [11]. Wang et al. proposed a blockchain-based information sharing and secure multi-party computing framework, and designed the detailed storage model, the consensus algorithm and the computing model [12]. Chen et al. designed and implemented a decentralized credit reporting system model, and the experimental results showed that the model could guarantee high data security [13].

Some research literature paid attention to the constraints of blockchain applied to credit information sharing. Lemieux used the land registration system of a developing country as the implementation environment of the blockchain, and studied the performance of the blockchain in the creation and preservation of trusted digital records [14]. Hofman et al. discussed the contradiction between the immutable nature of blockchain data and the de-identification of personal information specified in the EU's "General Data Protection Regulation" [15]. Franks analyzed the potential risks of blockchain's distributed ledger technology applied to information management [16].

In terms of industry applications, financial institutions have successively made preliminary attempts to combine blockchain technology with credit reporting, such as GXChain, CTRChain, LinkEye, Trust Union, JD Vientiane, etc. But in general, blockchain as a cutting-edge technology has some bottlenecks, and its application in credit information sharing is still in the exploratory stage. Existing research literature is mostly based on conceptual exploration, and its practical applications in the industry is far from being mature. In the future, it still needs a lot of technical investment and industry practice to prove its application effect.

3   Materials and Methods

3.1   The Platform Infrastructure Design

Depending on the scope, blockchain can be divided into three types: public blockchain, consortium blockchain and private blockchain. As an important part of the financial infrastructure, data security and data quality in the credit reporting business are extremely important. Therefore, when the blockchain is applied to the credit reporting field, the public blockchain mode in which nodes can freely enter and exit the network is inappropriate, and the consortium blockchain mode with strong controllability should be adopted. The consortium blockchain uses a real-name entry mechanism. Nodes can join and exit the network after being authorized. Access institutions include credit bureaus, regulatory authorities, Internet financial companies, and data service providers. The institutions form a stakeholder alliance to jointly maintain the healthy operation of the blockchain. The access mechanism of the consortium blockchain makes it more advantageous in terms of operating efficiency, cost and supervision, and it is also easier to implement applications.

As a cutting-edge technology, the basic architecture and application scenarios of the blockchain have been expanding. The blockchain 1.0 architecture is represented by bitcoin and uses blockchain as a support platform for digital currencies. The blockchain 2.0 architecture technically introduces Ethereum smart contracts, using the blockchain as a programmable distributed credit infrastructure. The application scenarios are extended to broader financial sectors such as payment, credit financing, financial transaction, securities, insurance and leasing. Blockchain 3.0 architecture has stricter access mechanism and permission control, and is oriented to enterprise-level application scenarios beyond the scope of currency and finance [17], represented by Hyperledger. The credit information service has high requirements for data security, and is more suitable for using a partially decentralized hybrid architecture. Strict access mechanisms should be implemented, and the alliance members read and write blockchain data based on authorization. Taking the blockchain 3.0 architecture as a framework, the basic architecture of the blockchain-based personal credit information sharing platform can be designed (see Fig. 1).

3.2   Detailed Design of the Platform and the Technical Advantages

Blockchain is a combination of multiple mature computer technologies including P2P network, encryption algorithm, timestamp, consensus mechanism, and smart contract. It has technical characteristics such as distributed storage, partial decentralization, quasi-anonymity, security, open source and programmable, which can solve the difficult problems in credit information sharing in a targeted manner.

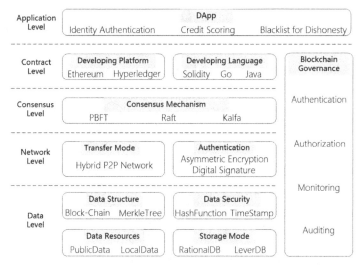

Fig. 1. Infrastructure diagram of the blockchain-based personal credit information sharing platform.

Hybrid P2P Network to Achieve Distributed Storage of Credit Data. The blockchain uses a peer-to-peer (P2P) network structure to organize all network nodes. It does not have a centralized node, but uses distributed storage technology. Each node stores a copy of the complete data. In the field of personal credit reporting, a centralized credit bureau is indispensable, so a "partially decentralized" hybrid P2P network (see Fig. 2) can be used to ensure the controllability of the system. Credit bureaus, regulatory authorities, and data service providers serve as super nodes to form a distributed network. Each super node and several ordinary nodes (users) form a local centralized network. Data does not need to be shared globally, only the super nodes have the authorities to read and write data.

The P2P structure can effectively use the large and scattered storage resources in the network to achieve distributed storage of credit data. Each node maintains a complete database, which means that all business data is open, transparent, and completely consistent. There is no need for data integration later, which reduces the cost of mutual trust between nodes. Data can be directly transmitted between nodes without going through a third party, reducing the risk of data leakage. And the reliability of the system is better. The damage of any node database will not affect the normal operation of the entire blockchain system.

Hash Function to Achieve Anonymization of Personal Information. Each piece of business data in the blockchain can be mapped into a series of hash values similar to garbled characters composed of numbers and letters through a hash encryption function, thereby hiding specific information. For example, the SHA256 hash function can convert business data of any length into a string of hash values composed of 64 numbers or letters. The hash function is unidirectional, and there is no way to reverse and decrypt. It can

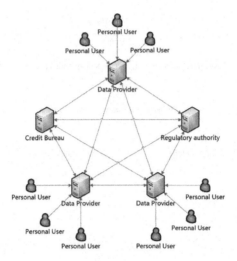

Fig. 2. Hybrid P2P network structure diagram

be used to encrypt personal identity data and sensitive data, and strengthen the privacy protection of the information subject.

Blockchain Structure to Ensure the Credit Data Cannot Be Tampered With. The blockchain adopts a block-chain data structure. The system creates a block at regular intervals. All credit business data is stored in the block, and each block is connected into a chain in the order of creation time. The block identifier in the block header is used to uniquely identify the hash value of the block. The blocks are linked by the hash value of the previous block (also known as the parent hash) and can be traced back to the first block (see Fig. 3). Credit business data is stored in the Merkle tree structure in the block body, and the leaf nodes are paired up to perform a hash operation up to the root of the Merkle tree in the block header.

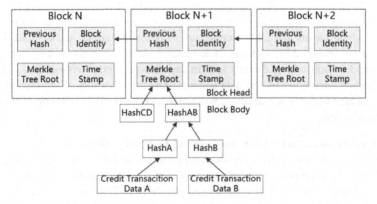

Fig. 3. Schematic diagram of blockchain data structure

The blockchain data structure can ensure that the credit business data cannot be tampered with, because once a certain piece of business data in the block is modified, the Merkle tree of the block needs to be recalculated, so that the Merkle tree root and block identification in the block header change, and no longer match the parent hash saved in the next block. The immutable nature of blockchain makes it a natural "trust machine".

Time Stamp to Ensure the Traceability of Credit Data. The timestamp is a valid proof of the order in the blockchain. It records the generation time of each block and the entry time of each piece of business data to the nearest millisecond. The timestamp adds a time dimension to the data in the block-chain, making the data easier to trace. At the same time, it also provides proof of existence for the data, ensuring the authenticity and unforgeability of the data, further increasing the difficulty of tampering with the data, and improving the credibility of the credit data.

Asymmetric Encryption Algorithm to Strengthen Credit Data Security.
The asymmetric encryption algorithm means that each node in the blockchain has a unique pair of keys, where the public key is public and indicates the identity of the node, and the private key is not public, indicating the control of information. Information encrypted using one of the keys can only be decrypted by the corresponding other key. Elliptic curve cryptography (ECC) is a classic asymmetric encryption algorithm, the equation can be written as:

$$y^2 = x^3 + ax + b(mod\ p) \tag{1}$$

In the above formula, a and b are coefficients, p is a prime number greater than 3, and $G(x, y)$ is a discrete point on the finite field F_p.

The elliptic curve has the following properties: given a certain point G of the elliptic curve, it is easy to find the points $2G, 3G, \ldots, kG$; on the contrary, if the point G and the point kG are known, it is very difficult to find k. Using this characteristic of the elliptic curve, using k as the private key and kG as the public key, asymmetric encryption can be achieved.

The information transmission process under asymmetric encryption mechanism is shown in Fig. 4. Suppose the receiver's private key is k, and the public key is $K = kG$. The sender selects a random number r, encrypts the information M with the public key K, and generates the ciphertext $C = \{rG, M + rK\}$. The information is transmitted on the network in the form of ciphertext C. After receiving the information, the receiver can decrypt the information with the private key k, that is, $M + rK - k(rG) = M$, and other nodes that receive the information cannot decrypt it. During information transmission, the private key k is not exposed on the network, which can reduce the risk of data leakage.

Digital Signature for User Identity Verification. Hash functions and asymmetric encryption algorithms can be used for digital signatures (see Fig. 5). Suppose the sender's private key is k, and the public key is $K = kG$. The specific process of digital signature is:

a. The sender uses the hash function to map the information M into a hash value h;
b. Select a random number r and calculate the point $rG(x, y)$;

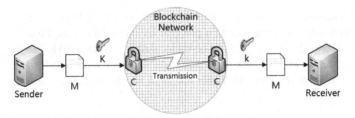

Fig. 4. Schematic diagram of asymmetric encryption mechanism

c. Encrypt the hash value h with the private key k, calculate $s = (h + kx)/r$, and get the digital signature $\{rG, s\}$;
d. Send the information M and the signature $\{rG, s\}$ together to the receiver;
e. After receiving the information and signature, the receiver first obtains the hash value h according to the information M;
f. Use the public key K to decrypt the signature, calculate $hG/s + xK/s$, and compare to rG, thereby verifying whether the information comes from the sender.

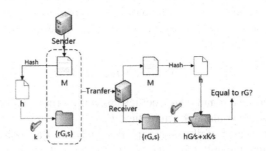

Fig. 5. Schematic diagram of digital signature principle

Consensus Mechanism to Ensure the Consistency of Credit Data. The consensus mechanism is a mechanism that uses mathematical algorithms to create trust between nodes without central control. The consortium blockchain has higher requirements for consistency, and the consensus mechanism usually uses the Practical Byzantine Fault Tolerance (PBFT) algorithm. The PBFT algorithm divides nodes into two categories: a master node and several slave nodes. The master node is responsible for sorting the requests issued by each node, and the slave nodes execute the requests in this order. After a certain node broadcasts the information to the net-work, each node uses the pairwise interaction to make the consistency judgment. When two-thirds of the nodes in the network reach a consensus on storing this information, the information can be stored in the block, thus ensuring the consistency of data storage.

The basic process of applying the PBFT algorithm in the platform is as follows:

a. Select R_0 as the master node, and the other 3n alliance members as slave nodes, and the new block is generated by the master node;

b. The alliance member R_1 sends a credit data write REQUEST to the blockchain network with private key signature and time stamp;

c. After receiving the REQUEST, the master node R_0 determines its order in the multiple credit data to be written into the new block, synthesizes the sequence number M and the REQUEST into a PRE-PREPARE message, and broadcasts it to all alliance members;

d. Each alliance member receives the PRE-PREPARE message, generates a PREPARE message, and broadcasts it to other alliance members;

e. Each alliance member receives the PREPARE message from other alliance members. When it receives 2n identical messages, it will confirm the PREPARE message, generate a confirmation message COMMIT, and broadcast to other alliance members;

f. After any alliance members in the network receives (2n + 1) COMMIT messages, it means that a consensus can be reached and the credit data can be written into a new block.

Token and Smart Contract to Achieve Credit Data Pricing. Token is a value transmission carrier in the blockchain network. By issuing tokens, the blockchain can quantify the data contribution of each node and give corresponding token rewards to realize the increase of value in the information sharing platform. A smart contract is a computer program deployed on the blockchain, which triggers automatic execution once the conditions are met. In order to clarify the benefits of data transactions and ensure a more orderly operation of the platform, tokens and smart contracts can be combined to issue a certain number of tokens on the plat-form. In the smart contract, economic factors and token incentive rules are written in the form of computer programs to realize automated and rational incentives to ensure the compensation and fairness of data transactions.

Unlike the public blockchain, the purpose of the consortium blockchain platform to issue tokens is not to seek the appreciation of tokens through secondary market transactions, but to replace the circulation of currencies and improve the efficiency of data transactions. When querying external data, the alliance agency needs to pay tokens to the data provider and access the data only after being authorized, thereby ensuring the economic interests of the data provider and encouraging institutions to actively share data.

4 Conclusion

Blockchain has many technical advantages such as distributed storage, security, reliable, quasi-anonymity, tamper proofing, open source and programmable, by applying it to the field of credit reporting, credit agencies can achieve higher efficiency to share personal credit information at a lower cost. For example, the P2P network structure of the blockchain can realize the distributed storage of massive credit information, and the system has better security, reliability and scalability; the blockchain data structure, hash algorithm and timestamp can ensure the integrity, the immutability and traceability of the credit data, improving the quality of credit data; asymmetric encryption algorithm helps to strengthen user identity verification and personal information protection in the credit reporting transaction, and improve data security; the consensus mechanism uses mathematical algorithms instead of third-party intermediaries to create trust, which can solve the problem of data ownership and ensure the consistency of data storage; smart contract can build an automated and fair incentive mechanism to guide data service providers to actively participate in data sharing.

The decentralized, tamper proofing, and self-incentive features of the blockchain pose new problems for current laws and regulations, and profoundly affect the economy, finance, society, organizational form and governance. There are still inconsistencies between the technical characteristics of the blockchain and the existing regulatory systems and methods of the credit reporting industry, which are mainly manifested in: the decentralized nature leads to the dispersion of supervision and weakens the control of the regulatory authority; the tamper-proof feature of blockchain conflicts with the "Credit Management Regulations" in China which stipulates that "credit information over 5 years should be deleted", and the archiving function can be considered to delete part of the cold data to reduce storage burden; the legal validity and compliance of smart contracts and token issuance are subject to discussion, etc. These need to be followed and explored in theoretical research and industry practice.

Blockchain research is not only a technical issue, but more importantly, it should effectively play the role of blockchain technology in reducing costs, improving efficiency, and optimizing the integrity environment in specific applications. The research on blockchain-based credit reporting should focus on the precise needs and real application scenarios of the personal credit industry, reasonably take advantage of the technical features of blockchain, rationally study the value of blockchain in traditional industries, and develop practical solutions with broad application prospects and potential value, thus giving full play to the role and positive influence of blockchain on personal credit reporting and effectively promoting the coordinated development of the social credit system.

References

1. An, X., et al.: Electron. Libr. **33**(6), 1047–1064 (2015). https://doi.org/10.1108/EL-04-2014-0059
2. Onay, C., Öztürk, E.: J. Finan. Regul. Compliance **26**(3), 382–405 (2018). https://doi.org/10.1108/JFRC-06-2017-0054
3. Zhang, J.: New trend for personal credit scoring in big data era. Credit Ref. **35**(12), 7–12 (2017)
4. Zhang, J., Li, Y.: Study on the market-oriented process of china's personal credit reporting industry from the perspective of Baihang Credit Co. Ltd. Credit Ref. **37**(12), 54–60 (2019)
5. Poritskiy, N., Oliveira, F., Almeida, F.: The benefits and challenges of general data protection regulation for the information technology sector. Digit. Policy Regul. Gov. **21**(5), 510–524 (2019). https://doi.org/10.1108/DPRG-05-2019-0039
6. Lee, C.S.: Datafication, dataveillance, and the social credit system as China's new normal. Online Inf. Rev. **43**(6), 952–970 (2019). https://doi.org/10.1108/OIR-08-2018-0231
7. Liao, L.: The developing situation and thinking of personal credit industry in China. People's Tribune **20**, 76–77 (2019)
8. Ba, S.S.: Blockchain is a good solution to solve the problem of credit reporting market. China Security News 2019–06–22(A07)

9. Zhu, H.Q.: The application prospect of financial technology in the field of market-oriented personal credit reporting. Finan. Comput. **12**, 41–44 (2018)
10. Liu, X.H., Jia, H.Y., Han, X.L.: Blockchain: a new perspective and technical architecture for credit reporting. Credit Ref. **38**(04), 13–21 (2020)
11. Ju, C.H., Zou, J.B., Fu, X.K.: Design and application of big data credit reporting platform integrating blockchain technology. Comput. Sci. **45**(S2), 522–526+552 (2018)
12. Wang, T., Ma, W.P., Luo, W.: Information sharing and secure multi-party computing model based on blockchain. Comput. Sci. **46**(09), 162–168 (2019)
13. Chen, C.L., Shen, Y., Yu, H.: Research on decentralized model for credit information system. Comput. Technol. Dev. **29**(03), 122–126 (2019)
14. Lemieux, V.L.: Trusting records: is Blockchain technology the answer. Rec. Manag. J. **26**(2), 110–139 (2016)
15. Hofman, D., Lemieux, V.L., Joo, A., Batista, D.A.: The margin between the edge of the world and infinite possibility-Blockchain, GDPR and information governance. Rec. Manag. J. **29**(1), 240–257 (2019)
16. Franks, P.C.: Implications of blockchain distributed ledger technology for records management and information governance programs. Rec. Manag. J. (2020). https://doi.org/10.1108/RMJ-08-2019-0047
17. Maesa, D.D.F., Mori, P.: Blockchain 3.0 applications survey. J. Parallel Distrib. Comput. **138**, 99–114 (2020)

Evil Chaincode: APT Attacks Based on Smart Contract

Zhenyu Li[1]📷, Yujue Wang[1]📷, Sheng Wen[2], and Yong Ding[1,2(✉)]📷

[1] School of Computer Science and Information Security,
Guilin University of Electronic Technology, Guilin 541004, China
stone_dingy@126.com
[2] Cyberspace Security Research Center, Peng Cheng Laboratory,
Shenzhen 518055, China

Abstract. In this paper, we discuss methods of stealing data via advanced persistent threat (APT) attacks on blockchains. Blockchain technology is generally used for storing data and digital coins and counts more than 562 organizations among its users. Smart contracts, as a key part of blockchain technology, are used for blockchain programmability. APT attacks are usually launched by government-backed hackers to steal data. APT attacks build hidden Command and Control (C&C) channels to steal resources remotely. Smart contracts represent a vulnerability of blockchain technology to APT attacks because of their sandbox-style open execution environment. Therefore, we performed several attack experiments to test methods of abusing smart contracts, including the remote execution of commands, and the stealing of large amounts of data. These experiments demonstrated that APT attacks could be successfully executed on a blockchain platform. In the large-scale data-stealing experiments, we found that the transmission rate for a maximum target data size of 100 MB can reach 27.771 MB/s, faster than the average rate of approximately 100 kB/s of a three-layer network proxy. We also investigated APT attacks based on public APT events, which use hidden techniques to steal data as critical APT attack actions. We propose several attack algorithms that can be applied for APT attacks.

Keywords: Blockchain · Hyperledger Fabric · Smart contracts · APT

1 Introduction

A blockchain is essentially a distributed database; each participant keeps a complete copy of the database, or at least a record of a large number of recent

This document is supported in part by the National Natural Science Foundation of China under projects 61772150, 61862012, and 61962012, the Guangxi Key R&D Program under project AB17195025, the Guangxi Natural Science Foundation under grants 2018GXNSFDA281054, 2018GXNSFAA281232, 2019GXNSFFA245015, 2019GXNSFGA245004 and AD19245048, the National Cryptography Development Fund of China under project MMJJ20170217, and the Peng Cheng Laboratory Project of Guangdong Province PCL2018KP004.

© Springer Nature Singapore Pte Ltd. 2020
G. Xu et al. (Eds.): FCS 2020, CCIS 1286, pp. 178–196, 2020.
https://doi.org/10.1007/978-981-15-9739-8_15

transactions [1]. With the development of blockchain, smart contract technology has emerged. Many large banks, internationally notable companies, and governments use blockchains to store data and use blockchain smart contracts to process business data [2].

Advanced persistent threat (APT) attacks are characterized by slow and small movements of a group of attackers to accomplish a particular goal, which is usually to steal data from a target without being caught. APT attackers might use familiar methods to break into their target entity's network, but the tools they utilize for penetration may not be familiar [3]. Large banks, internationally notable companies, and governments are often attacked by APT attackers because of the high value of their data [4].

Blockchain technology is still under development, and security researchers who study blockchain typically focus only on transaction security; however, this type of security is less relevant to APT attacks.

In this paper, we attempt to address the above problems by proposing three algorithms for APT attacks to provide a concrete illustration of the security threats faced by blockchain users, including the malicious chaincode installation, the remote execution of commands, and the stealing of large amounts of data.

In our related work, we have found that the smart contracts used in blockchain frameworks can run any code in the corresponding sandbox environment. The ability to run arbitrary code in the sandbox is extremely useful for facilitating APT attacks. We have found that APT attacks can take advantage of the unique features of smart contracts, including their native encryption for communication and their unrestricted sandbox environment. This makes smart-contract-based APT attacks on blockchain technology difficult to distinguish from legitimate activity. These novel features of smart-contract-based attacks, which can be used to hide such attacks more effectively, are therefore worthy of further study.

We design algorithms to demonstrate APT attacks based on smart contracts. Through these algorithms, we can abuse blockchain technology to quickly break the security-related restrictions of internal network area boundaries, rapidly expand the influence of an attack, and construct long-term communication channels to steal valuable data.

All experiments have succeeded in demonstrating our proposed attack techniques. In large-scale data transfer experiments, we have shown that the transmission rate for a maximum target data size of 100 MB can reach 27.771 MB/s, faster than the average rate of approximately 100 kB/s for an APT attack via a three-layer network proxy.

The contributions of this paper are summarized as follows: 1) We propose a means of launching hidden APT attacks against blockchains. 2) We demonstrate that the unrestricted smart contract environment of blockchain platforms is extremely dangerous. 3) We illustrate the security threats faced by blockchain users through experiments.

2   Related Works

2.1   Vulnerabilities and Attack Detection in Blockchain Systems

In a review of the related research, we have found that blockchain platforms have many vulnerabilities.

Yamashita et al. [5] reviewed the potential security risks posed by the smart contracts used in Hyperledger Fabric, a particular blockchain framework. These security risks can be divided into four types and 16 subtypes. There are four types of security risks caused by access from outside of the blockchain: web services, system command execution, external file access, and external library calls. Furthermore, that paper proposed a method of detecting malicious code in a smart contract based on an abstract syntax tree detection tool. However, this detection tool cannot detect smart contracts that are used only to establish Command and Control (C&C) communication channels. Nicola et al. [6] reviewed the methods of attack related to the smart contracts in Ethereum, another blockchain framework, and discussed external calls for blockchain transaction-related attacks. Alexander et al. [7] proposed a detection tool for the security vulnerabilities of Ethereum smart contracts. These authors designed a detection tool that analyzes smart contracts for malicious code. However, this detection tool is still in beta, and there are many ways it can be bypassed. Liu et al. [8] proposed the ReGuard tool to detect bugs in smart contracts. However, only smart contracts established in the C++ programming environment were discussed. There are also many ways to bypass detection by this tool. For example, we can execute the attack code after it has split into multiple smart contracts.

2.2   APT Attacks on Blockchains

In a review of APT attacks, we did not find any discussion of APT attacks against blockchains.

The construction of a C&C communication channel is a crucial research problem related to the lateral movement stage of the APT attack cycle. An attacker can use C&C tools to obtain persistent and covert access to valuable data. Furthermore, attackers can abuse various protocols for C&C communications, such as the Hypertext Transport Protocol (HTTP), HTTP Secure (HTTPS), Internet Relay Chat (IRC), and peer-to-peer (P2P). Alshamrani et al. summarized the C&C tools that can be used to abuse various protocols by generating malicious traffic that will be confused with general traffic to bypass security infrastructures [3]. However, these authors did not discuss the APT-attack-based abuse of blockchain technology. Marchetti et al. [9] proposed a detection framework that can detect a large number of suspicious host activities at high speed. This detection framework can identify abnormal encrypted communications without decrypting them. However, this framework cannot separate abnormal traffic from encrypted communications involving smart contracts, which are widely used in typical production environments. McCusker et al. [10] proposed a group-based method of detecting abnormal traffic. However, an APT attacker typically constructs a C&C communication channel through an ordinary communication traffic device using a smart contract. Consequently, the group-based method of detecting abnormal traffic is not an effective solution for detecting abnormal C&C communication.

3   Background Knowledge

This section describes some background knowledge relevant to our research, including an introduction of the Hyperledger Fabric platform, network management techniques, network protection techniques, and APT attack techniques.

3.1   Hyperledger Fabric

Hyperledger Fabric is an open-source project launched by the Linux Foundation in 2015 to promote digital technology and transaction validation for blockchains. Hyperledger Fabric uses Docker technology to host smart contracts. The smart contract applications used in this blockchain system are also known as chaincodes. In a blockchain, each peer node stores snapshots of the most recent system state in the form of key-value pairs [11].

Smart Contract: A smart contract is a computer protocol designed to disseminate, validate, or execute a contract. Smart contracts allow the execution of trusted transactions without supervision by a third party. In general, a smart contract is a segment of executable code that can deploy unalterable code without any third-party guarantee of trust. The use of smart contracts can significantly reduce manual participation, guarantee system security and efficiency, and significantly reduce transaction costs [12].

Chaincode: Chaincodes are the smart contracts of Hyperledger Fabric, which are instantiated in Docker containers [13]. However, because chaincodes run on Docker, they provide a highly convenient vector for APT attacks. APT attackers can enhance the effectiveness of their attacks by embedding malicious code in smart contracts. This malicious code can be used to execute any arbitrary operation.

Security Policy: A security policy is an essential function for smart contracts in a consortium chain. Through a suitably configured security policy, it is possible to mitigate attacks and avoid the direct execution of malicious code in smart contracts. Administrators must configure their security policies in accordance with the principle of permission minimization. If a security policy is misconfigured, a user can execute code with administrator permission, which can lead to serious security issues. We have studied the access control list (ACL) method used to divide user permissions in Hyperledger Fabric. The architecture of the Hyperledger Fabric security policy is shown in Fig. 1.

MSP: An MSP is a Membership Service Provider. The MSPs in Hyperledger Fabric provide the definitions for member operation permissions. An MSP

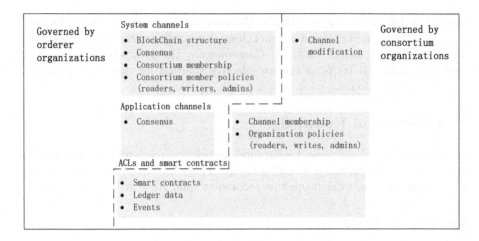

Fig. 1. Hyperledger fabric policy hierarchy [14]

abstracts the encryption mechanisms and protocols used to issue certificates, authenticate certificates, and authenticate users. An MSP manages the identities of members, the rules that govern those identities (including authentication), and authentication functionalities (including signature generation and authentication). One or more MSPs can simultaneously manage a Hyperledger Fabric network. The MSPs provide modularity of member operations and interoperability across different members [15]. Each MSP maintains cacert, keystore, signcert, tlscacert, and organization profiles.

3.2   Network Management and Protection Technology

Network management is a necessary responsibility of large enterprises. The security of an enterprise network can be enhanced by appropriate network management technology and security settings. At the same time, suitable network management technologies can make the network environment itself more hostile to attacks.

ACL: An ACL is an access control list. An ACL can be used to provide essential security control for a network. A device queries the ACL to match a received Internet Protocol (IP) packet in accordance with specified rules. If a match is found, the device will either allow or block packet transmission in a rule-based manner [16].

VLAN: A virtual local area network (VLAN) is formed by logically combining several physical subnets in different locations to function as a local area network. VLAN technology can be used to subdivide a network to limit the potential range of an attack [17].

Firewall/IDS: A firewall or intrusion detection system (IDS) is a device that APT attackers need to bypass to execute an APT attack successfully. However, the communication of smart contracts relies on Transport Layer Security (TLS), which means that firewall or IDS devices cannot be used to check such communication. Therefore, there is no inherent requirement to encrypt the contents of smart contract communication for APT attacks. However, when the victim device has a built-in IDS installed, encryption and code confusion are required [18].

3.3 APT Attack Technology

Lateral movement is a critical stage of an APT attack. Figure 2 shows the various stages of the APT attack life cycle as analyzed by FireEye, the world's leading anti-APT company. FireEye divides an APT attack into five main stages: initial reconnaissance, initial compromise, establishment of a foothold, escalation of privileges, and internal reconnaissance. Lateral movement and maintenance of presence are necessary when the initial internal reconnaissance does not acquire the necessary data.

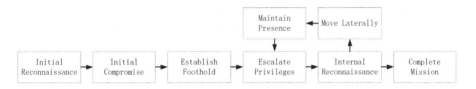

Fig. 2. APT attack life cycle [19]

Lateral Movement: Lateral movement is defined as logging onto other servers using existing credentials. Lateral movement provides communication channel support for subsequent attacks by means of remote services on a remote server [20].

Remote Command Execution: Carefully constructed code can force a victim node to execute system commands. The Docker container of the victim node can be made to execute these commands by means of code for remote command execution, which allows the attacker to control the victim Docker container [21].

4 Theory of APT Attacks Using Smart Contracts

This section describes the theory of how to abuse the smart contracts of Hyperledger Fabric to execute APT attacks. Hyperledger Fabric is a typical blockchain framework, which means that this attack theory for Hyperledger Fabric can also be extended to other blockchain systems with similar structures.

4.1   Preparation for Smart Contracts

Various programming languages can be used for coding in smart contracts. Hyperledger Fabric supports Go, Java, Node.js, and Python. For other blockchain frameworks, it would be necessary to use the corresponding software development kits (SDKs) for smart contract coding.

The coding of a smart contract includes the Init and Invoke functions. The Init function is used to initialize the smart contract, and the Invoke function is used for subsequent calls to the smart contract. The Init function is less convenient than the Invoke function for repeated calls. Therefore, we suggest that the attack code should be introduced into the Invoke method for subsequent query calls. Moreover, proper debugging and exception handling should be performed to avoid the remote smart contract container exiting due to abnormal input.

An MSP is required to certify and authenticate an installation in Hyperledger Fabric. We can use a smart contract management application to install a smart contract with the MSP. In Hyperledger Fabric, smart contracts are installed via the "peer chaincode" command. Next, "peer instantiate" or "peer upgrade" is used to start the container of a remote smart contract.

A smart contract can be called by means of a query command in the blockchain system. The blockchain system distributes smart contract operations via the communication system.

Hyperledger Fabric's official development documentation shows that the command "peer chaincode query -n mycc -c'{ "Args":["query", "a"]}' -C myc" can be used to execute a smart contract. After the smart contract runs, we can see that the result is 20 [22].

4.2   Using Smart Contracts for APT Attacks

The official query example clearly illustrates the input and output structure of a smart contract, which can be widely abused in APT attacks. An APT attacker will attempt to exploit a target system, which has a controlled input and output. After the target system is exploited, the attacker will attempt to escalate his or her privileges to the highest level, which is usually the kernel privilege level for the operating system. If this privilege escalation fails, the attacker will use the victim node as a network proxy, meaning that no code is required to be written to the drive and the attack code can be executed dynamically in the memory only.

To construct a network proxy, it is necessary to place repeated, high-frequency calls to the Invoke function. At the same time, another common APT attack function can be introduced into the Invoke function.

Depending on the attack requirements, malicious code can be embedded into a smart contract to avoid disruption by the security infrastructure to the greatest possible extent.

5   Using Smart Contracts for APT Attacks

In this section, we propose three attack algorithms that abuse smart contracts to support the postpenetration stage of an APT attack. Specifically, the algorithm for malicious chaincode installation is a prerequisite for all subsequent attacks, and the remaining two algorithms will be installed on-demand as modules in the victim nodes. These two algorithms enable lateral movement or communication channel construction for subsequent attacks.

5.1   Attack Topology

The attack topology is similar to the typical topology for APT attacks [23–26]. APT attackers commonly select valuable targets, which are usually large and contain multiple network areas. Regarding the topology design, each network area should allow the passage of traffic based on certain business requirements. Additionally, each network area should include one or more network devices and be related to a defined network security boundary area. Either direct or indirect communication between the attacker and the victim should be possible through the network; they should not be entirely physically isolated. Moreover, the network should contain valuable targets or data. The attacker must be able to steal either control permission for the victim system or valuable data through appropriate attack methods.

Crucially, for the scenario of interest in this paper, the network must contain a blockchain system that can use smart contracts. The blockchain system should be spread across multiple networks and indirectly allow an attacker to access multiple networks through the blockchain system.

5.2   Attack Framework Based on Smart Contracts

According to FireEye's 2019 APT report, the attack group known as APT37 uses lateral movement methods such as the use of compromised user credentials, among others. APT38 uses lateral movement methods such as HOT-WAX, NACHOCHEESE, REDSHAWL, WORMHOLE, Remote Desktop Protocol (RDP), ReDuh, TCP Gender Change Daemon, the use of compromised user and domain credentials, and Windows Group Policy. APT39 uses lateral movement methods such as BLUETRIP/REDTRIP/PINKTRIP, various publicly available tools (PsExec, RemCom, xCmd, and others), RDP, Server Message Block (SMB), and Secure Shell (SSH). Furthermore, the report also lists a large number of other lateral movement methods for APT attacks [27]. In addition, the papers of Li et al. [27] and Lu et al. [28] address methods of lateral movement in APT attacks. Overall, lateral movement is an important stage of the APT attack cycle.

There are many specific methods of lateral movement to support subsequent APT attacks for stealing data from other networks. The attacker does not need the highest level of privilege on the victim device to steal data. Instead, the attacker can use the victim device to access additional network resources, execute a lateral movement, find valuable resources, and steal data. In practice, if a lateral movement can provide access to more resources, then that lateral movement is meaningful.

In this section, we propose an algorithm for the remote execution of commands on a victim device that uses a remote service by means of a malicious chaincode in Hyperledger Fabric. Additionally, we review various APT events in which APT organizations such as Group 72, Unit42, APT39, APT40, and Triton have used remote service methods to attack target networks and steal data [29].

The construction of a stable communication channel is a crucial problem for lateral movement. We propose the chaincode attack execution flow chart shown in Fig. 3, which is divided into eight steps:

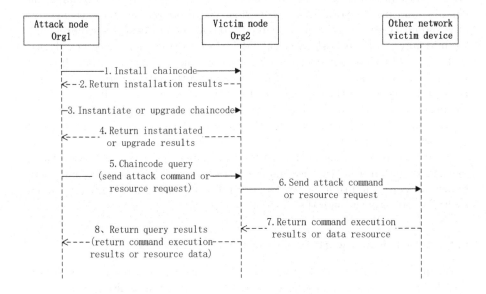

Fig. 3. Chaincode attack execution flow chart

Step 1: An attacker sends a request to install a chaincode via a controlled node. In this way, the attacker can construct an attack environment for subsequent lateral movement or other attacks.

Step 2: The results of the chaincode installation are returned.

Step 3: This step will be executed only if the returned result indicates successful chaincode installation. In this step, the attacker sends the chaincode "instantiate" or "upgrade" command to the victim node. If the chaincode is the first version, the chaincode needs to be instantiated. If the chaincode is not the first version, the chaincode needs to be upgraded. The victim node will start the Docker container of this chaincode for chaincode execution.

Step 4: The victim node returns the result of the "instantiate" or "upgrade" command.

Step 5: This step will be executed only if the returned result indicates that the chaincode on the victim node has been instantiated or upgraded successfully. In this step, the attacker executes a chaincode query command to execute system commands on the victim node through Docker remotely. Additionally, the attacker can resend attack commands or request resources from the victim node to access another victim node until the final victim node is reached. Through this step, the attacker can access multiple networks, representing lateral movement.
Step 6: This step will be executed if the attacker indirectly requests resources to access an intermediate victim node. In this step, the attacker sends a command from the current victim node to the next victim node, a process that is repeated until the final victim node is reached. Moreover, the attack payload has a multilevel embedded structure, which enables data embedding during lateral movement.
Step 7: If the final victim node is successfully accessed, the desired data will be recursively returned from the final victim node to the initial victim node. This step is complete when the initial victim node receives the data.
Step 8: The initial victim node encapsulates the data to ensure the complete transmission of the desired data to the attack node.

5.3   Attacks Based on Smart Contracts

The attacker needs to prepare a chaincode to execute remote commands or request remote resources. In this section, we propose two algorithms for

---

Algorithm 1. Malicious Chaincode Installation

Input: Victim Organization Administrator MSP f, Victim Peer Address a, Chaincode d, Chaincode Name n, Version v
Output: Installation Result s
1: **function** MALICIOUSCHAINCODEINSTALLATION(f,a,d,n,v)
2:      $isConnected :=$ Connect(f,a)
3:      **if** $isConnected$ **then**
4:          $CurrentVersion:=$ChaincodeVersion(f,a,n)
5:          **if** $v > CurrentVersion$ **then**
6:              $chaincodeInstallVersion:=$ ChaincodeInstall(f,a,d,n,v)
7:              **if** $chaincodeInstallVersion ==$ FirstVersion **then**
8:                  $s :=$ ChaincodeInstantiate(f,a,d,n,v)
9:              **else**
10:                 $s :=$ ChaincodeUpgrade(f,a,d,n,v)
11:             **end if**
12:         **end if**
13:     **else**
14:         $s :=$ ErrorMessage
15:     **end if**
16:     **return** s
17: **end function**

---

implementing commonly used attack types, namely, remote command execution, and large-scale resource transfer.

Preparation for Attack. The attacker must first prepare the attack environment for subsequent attacks, which requires several steps. The installation of malicious chaincode requires the MSP of the victim organization's administrator, the peer node address of the victim, the malicious chaincode itself, the chaincode name, and the chaincode version number. The algorithm for malicious chaincode installation is shown in Algorithm 1.

First, the attacker needs to establish a connection to the victim's peer node, for which the MSP of the victim organization's administrator and the peer node address of the victim must be provided. Second, if the connection is successfully established, the attacker should check the latest chaincode version in the blockchain system. Third, if the version number of the malicious chaincode to be installed is higher than the version number in the blockchain system, the chaincode in the blockchain system needs to be instantiated or updated. Then, once the chaincode installation is completed, the attacker will obtain the latest version of the current chaincode in the blockchain system. Fourth, if the latest version number is the first version, the chaincode should be instantiated. If the latest version number is not the first version, the chaincode should be upgraded. Finally, the result of malicious chaincode installation is returned.

Time complexity analysis of Algorithm 1: There is no loop and nested execution in the malicious code installation algorithm. Therefore, the time complexity of the malicious code installation algorithm is $O(1)$.

Remote Command Execution. The attacker achieves Remote command execution (RCE) via abuse or exploitation of a vulnerability of the victim system. The chaincode for RCE requires the MSP of the victim organization's administrator, the peer node address of the victim, the command that needs to be

---

Algorithm 2. Remote Command Execution

Input: Victim Organization Administrator MSP f, Victim Peer Address a, Command to be Executed c, Chaincode Name n
Output: Execution Result s
 1: **function** RUNREMOTECOMMAND(f,a,n,d)
 2:     $isConnected$:= Connect(f,a)
 3:     **if** $isConnected$ **then**
 4:         Request(a,n,c)
 5:         a.return :=a.RunCommand(c)
 6:         s :=a.Response(a.return)
 7:     **else**
 8:         s := ErrorMessage
 9:     **end if**
10:     **return** s
11: **end function**

---

executed remotely, and the chaincode name. The smart-contract-based RCE algorithm is shown in Algorithm 2.

Once malicious chaincode installation is complete, the RCE algorithm can be executed. For RCE, the MSP of the victim organization's administrator is needed to connect to the victim peer node. Once the connection is established, the attacker sends the chaincode name and the command to be remotely executed to the victim peer node. Once the victim peer node receives the request, it will execute the command and return the execution results to the attacker. If an error occurs during the RCE operation, the error message will be thrown back to the attacker.

Time complexity analysis of Algorithm 2: The RCE algorithm can call the RCE algorithm again for recursive execution. Therefore, the time complexity of the RCE algorithm is O(n).

Large-Scale Resource Transfer. In Hyperledger Fabric, the maximum length of the information that can be sent in response to a single request is 104857600 bytes (100 MB) by default. We propose a large-scale resource request algorithm to solve the problem of large-scale resource transfer. The data block length for a single transport is defined here as 50,000,000 by default. In practice, we have found that the data length tends to be doubled; therefore, we select 104857600/2 $\approx$ 50000000. The large-scale resource transfer algorithm is shown in Algorithm 3.

Algorithm 3. Large-Scale Resource Transfer

Input: Request URI u
Output: URI Data s
1: **function** REQUEST(u)
2:     $dataLength$:= GetDataLength(u)
3:     $splitBlockLength$:=50000000
4:     s:=InitReturn()
5:     **if** $dataLength >= splitBlockLength$ **then**
6:         **for** $startIndex=0$; $startIndex<dateLength$; $startIndex+ =splitBlockLength$ **do**
7:             $getLength$:=$splitBlockLength$
8:             **if** $getLength>dateLength-splitBlockLength$ **then**
9:                 $getLength=dateLength-splitBlockLength$
10:            **end if**
11:            $s+=$ GetDataByChunk($u,startIndex,getLength$)
12:        **end for**
13:    **else**
14:        s:= GetData(u)
15:    **end if**
16:    **return** s
17: **end function**

First, the attacker needs to obtain the length of the file to be transferred. If the length of the file is less than the chunk length, the file will be returned directly. If the length of the file exceeds the chunk length, then the chunking step will be executed. In the algorithm for data block chunking, each data read operation requires the current length of the data to be transferred and the current transfer offset. Then, the data will be transferred to the attacker, who will cyclically execute the transfer operation until the end of the transferred data block is read.

6   Experiments

APT attackers typically use a multilevel network proxy for their attacks. In practice, the data rates of multilevel network proxies are extremely low, and network performance generally does not need to be considered. Additionally, the transfer rate can be varied by modifying the code. This section presents experiments performed from two perspectives, namely, remote command execution, and large-scale data transfer, to experimentally demonstrate the requirements for attacks using smart contracts. By default, we first executed the attack preparation algorithm in all of the following experiments.

In the following experiments, we used Hyperledger Fabric version 1.4.4 for testing. To simulate real-world APT attacks, we designed an experimental environment consisting of two organizations (Org1 and Org2) and one orderer, with two peer nodes per organization and a Web server in the Org2 region to enable lateral movement experiments. The Web server can be accessed only from an Org2 device. We added settings for the router's ACL and for server access control to block the Org1 region from accessing the Org2-Server region and the Internet region. Our design goal in these experiments was to construct a stable communication channel by abusing a smart contract. We used a peer node of Org1 to initiate the attack. The graph presented in Fig. 4 shows the experimental topology diagram for an attack.

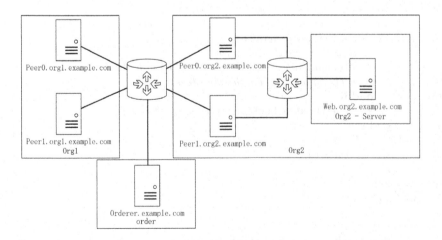

Fig. 4. Experimental topology

The configuration used for the experimental equipment is summarized in Table 1. The laboratory environment was built using the VMware ESXi virtualization platform.

Table 1. Experimental platform

Host name	CPU	RAM	NIC	Operating system
Orderer.example.com	Intel Xeon 6128 @ 3.40 GHz x4	8G	vmnic ne1000 100 Mbps	Ubuntu 18.04.3 LTS
Peer0.org1.example.com	Intel Xeon 6128 @ 3.40 GHz x4	8G	vmnic ne1000 100 Mbps	Ubuntu 18.04.3 LTS
Peer1.org1.example.com	Intel Xeon 6128 @ 3.40 GHz x4	8G	vmnic ne1000 100 Mbps	Ubuntu 18.04.3 LTS
Peer0.org2.example.com	Intel Xeon 6128 @ 3.40 GHz x4	8G	vmnic ne1000 100 Mbps	Ubuntu 18.04.3 LTS
Peer1.org2.example.com	Intel Xeon 6128 @ 3.40 GHz x4	8G	vmnic ne1000 100 Mbps	Ubuntu 18.04.3 LTS
Web.org2.example.com	Intel Xeon 6128 @ 3.40 GHz x4	4G	vmnic ne1000 100 Mbps	Windows Server 2019

6.1 Remote Command Execution (RCE)

RCE operations require the MSP of the victim organization's administrator and the peer node address of the victim.

Fig. 5. Direct access is forbidden by server access control

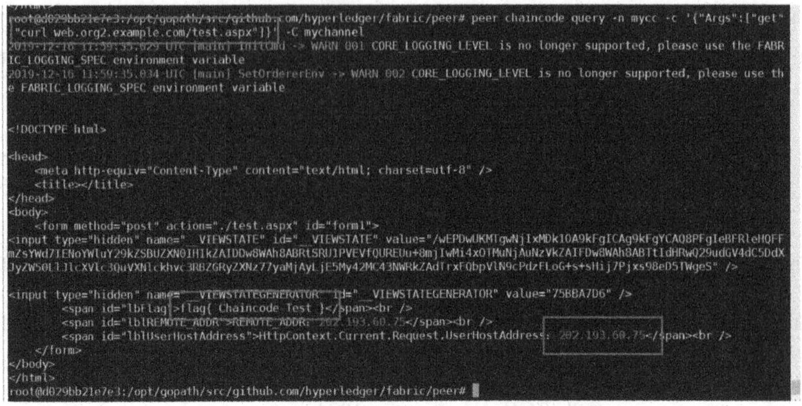

Fig. 6. Access target data via chaincode RCE

We used Hyperledger Fabric's peer application for the RCE operation. We used malicious chaincode to read out the result of a remote command executed in accordance with an input command. In this experiment, we controlled the Docker container with ID "d029bb21e7e3". Initially, we sought direct access to web.org2.example.com/test.aspx, which the flag returned by the page indicated was forbidden, as shown in Fig. 5. However, when we used RCE with the "curl" remotely command via a peer node of Org2, access to the page was granted, as shown in Fig. 6. This experiment shows that the RCE algorithm is workable. We can do the lateral movement via the RCE algorithm.

6.2 Large-Scale Data Transfer

An APT attacker usually steals data that are not fixed in size. We have proposed an algorithm for large-scale data transfer that can transfer data with no fixed size. A performance graph for the proposed large-scale data transfer algorithm is shown in Fig. 7. We used a maximum data length of 100 MB for performance testing and executed the test 1000 times with data transfer lengths varying from small to large.

We used Base64 to encode the data to ensure the correct transmission of the binary data, which increased the data length by approximately 33.3%. We defined a data limit of 50 MB for a single transfer, which should include the increase in length caused by Base64 encoding. Therefore, we chose a data length limit of 37 MB.

We found that the transmission time jitter increases as the data length increases, which indicates that larger-scale transmission has a greater effect on node performance. The proposed large-scale data transfer algorithm uses a cache to prepare the next data block for transmission, which will cost some time. We found the cache cost time to be approximately 150 ms, depending on the node performance.

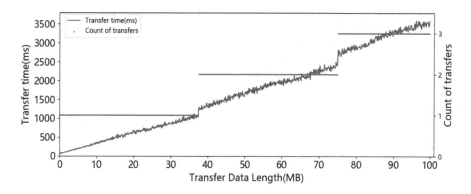

Fig. 7. Large-scale data transfer performance testing

7   Discussion

7.1   Mitigation Suggestions

Here, we propose some guidelines for attack mitigation to increase the difficulty of APT attacks and reduce the security risk posed by using blockchain smart contracts.

Keep the MSP Secure: An attacker can use the MSP of the victim organization to cause a victim node to perform any arbitrary tasks. The administrator may incorrectly certify network management actions, including copying the MSP to another computer, which would allow the administrator certificate to be stolen. An APT attacker who has stolen the MSP of a victim organization's administrator can control all nodes of the victim organization. We propose that administrators should avoid copying the MSP to any other device and should ensure that the MSP is used only on necessary nodes.

Split Large Organizations into Smaller Organizations: If the MSP of a large organization's administrator is stolen, this will place many nodes under the control of hackers. We propose splitting large organizations into smaller organizations to reduce the potential scope of the damage.

Check Smart Contract Code for Safety: Endpoint protection software can be used to monitor smart contracts in real-time, thus enabling the prompt detection of attack behavior.

Restrict the Node Communication Range: The access range of each node should be minimized, and nonessential access should be blocked.

Update the Blockchain System Version: If a new version fixes vulnerabilities, the blockchain system version should be updated.

7.2   Attack Supported Platforms

The key element of using smart contracts for APT attacks is that smart contracts can interact with outside the blockchain system for network transmission, system command execution, and other attack operation. For the programming language and remote deployment of smart contracts, we compared smart contracts in well-known blockchains, which shown in Table 2.

Table 2. Comparison of smart contracts in well-known blockchains

Platform	Hyperledger Fabric	Corda	Ethereum
Programming Language	Go, Java, etc. [30]	Kotlin, Java, etc. [31]	Solidity [32]
Remote Deployment	Yes [34]	Limited [35]	Yes [36]
Possibility to APT attack	High	Middle	Low

According to the survey, Hyperledger Fabric and Corda support general programming languages such as Java. Therefore, we can use general programming languages to call the operating system to implement APT attacks.

However, Ethereum uses its custom language, namely, Solidity. We can compile the Solidity program through a private compiler of Ethereum to generate Ethereum-based special machine code, which runs on the Ethereum Virtual Machine (EVM) [33]. Therefore, it is almost impossible for us to use Ethereum for APT attacks. At most, we can only use Ethereum's smart contracts to transfer data.

7.3   Next Research Plan

In the next research plan, we will try to use Corda's smart contract for APT attacks. Moreover, we will try to find an exploit to the machine code of Ethereum's smart contract, which can be further used to implement more kinds of APT attacks.

APT attacks have a variety of attack methods. We not only use smart contracts for the APT attack, but we can also insert malicious code into the source code of open-source blockchain to achieve APT attacks. According to Murphy's law, all of this is possible, and this is our motivation for further research.

8   Conclusion

APT attacks are a major concern in global cybersecurity, and corresponding advances in both attack theory and defense theory are urgently needed. Existing APT attack and defense mechanisms focus on typical protocols and services, whereas security against blockchain-related APT attacks is less often discussed. Moreover, most research on blockchain-related attacks and protection has focused on transactions.

This paper proposes ways to abuse blind spots in research on the smart contracts used in blockchains, addressing both attack and defense. We implemented remote command execution and large-scale data transfer by abusing a smart contract. We tested whether the data transmission rate for 100 MB of data can reach the average speed of three-level network proxies across multiple continents [37], which can fully support the maximum link rate required for an attack. The results demonstrate the necessity of defining a strict security policy for attack mitigation to reduce the associated losses.

References

1. Averin, A., Averina, O.: Review of blockchain technology vulnerabilities and blockchain-system attacks. In: 2019 International Multi-conference on Industrial Engineering and Modern Technologies, FarEastCon 2019, pp. 1–6 (2019)
2. Hyperledger: Hyperledger Supporting Members (2020). https://www.hyperledger. org/members
3. Alshamrani, A., Myneni, S., Chowdhary, A., Huang, D.: A survey on advanced persistent threats: techniques, solutions, challenges, and research opportunities. IEEE Commun. Surv. Tutor. **21**(2), 1851–1877 (2019)
4. Emm, D.: APT review: what the world's threat actors got up to in 2019 (2019). https://securelist.com/ksb-2019-review-of-the-year/95394/
5. Yamashita, K., Nomura, Y., Zhou, E., Pi, B., Jun, S.: Potential risks of hyperledger fabric smart contracts. In: 2019 IEEE 2nd International Workshop on Blockchain Oriented Software Engineering, IWBOSE 2019, pp. 1–10 (2019)
6. Atzei, N., Bartoletti, M., Cimoli, T.: A survey of attacks on Ethereum smart contracts. In: International Conference on Principles of Security and Trust, pp. 1–24, no. July (2015)
7. Mense, A., Flatscher, M.: Security Vulnerabilities in Ethereum Smart Contracts (2018)
8. Liu, C., Chen, Z., Chen, B., Roscoe, B.: ReGuard: finding reentrancy bugs in smart contracts, pp. 3–6 (2018)
9. Marchetti, M., Pierazzi, F., Colajanni, M., Guido, A.: Analysis of high volumes of network traffic for advanced persistent threat detection. Comput. Netw. **109**, 127–141 (2016)
10. McCusker, O., Brunza, S., Dasgupta, D.: Deriving behavior primitives from aggregate network features using support vector machines. In: 2013 5th International Cyber Conflict (CyCon) (2013)
11. Zhou, B., Man, Y., Liu, N., Zhang, Y., Zhang, C.: Biological data security management based on Hyperledger Fabric. Cyberspace Secur. **10**(4), 55–60 (2019)
12. Pu, H., Ge, Y., Yan-feng, Z., Yu-bin, B.: Survey on blockchain technology and its application prospect. Comput. Sci. **44**(4), 1–7 (2017)
13. Hyperledger: Hyperledger Fabric Chaincode (2020). https://github.com/hyperledger/fabric/blob/master/docs/source/chaincode.rst
14. Hyperledger: Hyperledger Fabric Policy Hierarchy (2020). https://github.com/hyperledger/fabric/blob/master/docs/source/policies/Fabric_Policy_Hierarchy.pptx
15. Hyperledger: Hyperledger Fabric Membership Service Providers (MSP) (2020). https://github.com/hyperledger/fabric/blob/master/docs/source/msp.rst
16. Fang, W., Guodong, H., Xin, L.: Access control list of router and research of realization. Comput. Eng. Des. **28**(23), 5638–5640 (2007)

17. Wei, W., Jie, D., Yin, L.: Network security and LAN security solutions. Tech. Autom. Appl. **2**, 41–44 (2001)
18. Wang, X., He, J., Xie, Z., Zhao, G., Cheung, S.C.: ContractGuard: defend ethereum smart contracts with embedded intrusion detection. IEEE Trans. Serv. Comput. 1–14 (2019)
19. FireEye: Red Team Cyber Security Assessments (2020). https://www.fireeye.com/services/red-team-assessments.html
20. Bohara, A., Noureddine, M.A., Fawaz, A., Sanders, W.H.: An unsupervised multi-detector approach for identifying malicious lateral movement. In: Proceedings of the IEEE Symposium on Reliable Distributed Systems 2017-Septe(Lm), pp. 224–233 (2017)
21. MITRE: Command and control (2020). https://attack.mitre.org/tactics/TA0011/
22. Hyperledger: Chaincode for Developers (2018). https://hyperledger-fabric.readthedocs.io/en/release-1.4/chaincode4ade.html
23. Mandiant: The Advanced Persistent Threat. FireEye (2010). https://content.fireeye.com/m-trends/rpt-m-trends-2010
24. MANDIANT: 2013 threat report. FireEye (2013). https://content.fireeye.com/m-trends/rpt-m-trends-2013
25. FireEye: M-Trends 2015: A View from the Front Lines Threa. FireEye (2015). https://content.fireeye.com/m-trends/rpt-m-trends-2015
26. FireEye: Mandiant consulting 2016. FireEye (2016). https://content.fireeye.com/m-trends/rpt-m-trends-2016
27. Li, M., Huang, W., Wang, Y., Fan, W.: The optimized attribute attack graph based on APT attack stage model. In: Proceedings of the 2016 2nd IEEE International Conference on Computer and Communications, ICCC 2016, pp. 2781–2785 (2017)
28. Lu, G., Guo, R., Wang, J.: An analysis of the behavior of APT attack in the Ngay campaign. In: 2018 18th IEEE International Conference on Communication Technology 2019-Octob, pp. 1115–1122 (2019)
29. MITRE: MITRE ATT&CK^{TM} Remote Services - Enterprise (2020). https://attack.mitre.org/techniques/T1021/
30. Hyperledger: Hyperledger Fabric application SDKs (2020). https://hyperledger-fabric.readthedocs.io/en/latest/getting_started.html#hyperledger-fabric-application-sdks
31. R3: Getting set up for CorDapp development (2020). https://docs.corda.net/docs/corda-os/4.5/getting-set-up.html
32. Ethereum: The Solidity Contract-Oriented Programming Language (2020). https://github.com/ethereum/solidity
33. Ethereum: A Python implementation of the Ethereum Virtual Machine (2020). https://github.com/ethereum/py-evm
34. Hyperledger: peer chaincode (2020). https://hyperledger-fabric.readthedocs.io/en/latest/commands/peerchaincode.html
35. R3: Building and installing a CorDapp (2020). https://docs.corda.net/docs/corda-os/4.5/cordapp-build-systems.html
36. Yohanes.gultom: Compiling, deploying and calling Ethereum smartcontract using Python (2020). https://yohanes.gultom.me/2018/11/28/compiling-deploying-and-calling-ethereum-smartcontract-using-python/
37. Yi, Y., Han, G., Yi-jun, W., Zhi, X.: Darknet resource exploring based on tor. Commun. Technol. **50**(10), 2304–2309 (2017)

NoPKI - a Point-to-Point Trusted Third Party Service Based on Blockchain Consensus Algorithm

Wei-Yang Chiu, Weizhi Meng$^{(\boxtimes)}$, and Christian D. Jensen

Department of Applied Mathematics and Computer Science,
Technical University of Denmark, Lyngby, Denmark
{weich,weme,cdje}@dtu.dk

Abstract. The increasingly interconnected network results in the change of information flow between users and service providers, hence there is an emerging need for building a secure channel for connections. Currently, Public Key Infrastructure System (shortly PKI), the hierarchical trust relationship system, is the most widely used cornerstone technology to help secure the communication channels. However, PKI recently concerns the users due to various security breaches, i.e., the compromised PKI allows attackers to issue any valid keys to the victim and decrypt any secure connections within the system. In this paper, we design a decentralized PKI system, called NoPKI, by leveraging the blockchain technology. The system has multiple small and trusted groups called the neighborhood, which can be formed dynamically. These neighbors are the players in each neighborhood, and each transaction in the PKI system (including registration, revocation, and validation) requires witnesses of neighbors. In the evaluation, we implement our system and validate that our system ensures not only long-term accessibility but also the certificate security and public audit-ability.

Keywords: Blockchain · Decentralized PKI · Neighborhood · Network security · Certificate authority · System trust

1 Introduction

The development of Internet brings the convenience of connecting with two or more parties in seconds, without the distance constrains. With the support of advanced technology, connection bandwidth keeps increasing dramatically, which boosts the growth of many online applications (transactions). Due to the sensitivity and privacy of transactions, there is a great demand for securing communication connections among participants. For this purpose, asymmetric encryption cryptography plays a crucial role. Public key infrastructure (PKI) is thus proposed to manage the legitimacy and integrity of each participant's public key, including registration, revocation, and verification of public keys.

© Springer Nature Singapore Pte Ltd. 2020
G. Xu et al. (Eds.): FCS 2020, CCIS 1286, pp. 197–214, 2020.
https://doi.org/10.1007/978-981-15-9739-8_16

Nowadays, secure connections among individuals are mostly mandatory. Google, in 2014, announced that websites without HTTPS would result in lowering its ranking results in its search engine [1], and announced that any contents with insecure connections in a secure connection webpage would be blocked in late 2019 [3]. These make traditional package eavesdropping no longer an option to obtain sensitive information from individuals. Then man-in-the-middle attack (MiTM) becomes a popular option, especially through web browsers. To defeat such attack, it requires to generate a legitimate, validatable certificate. Certificate authorities (CA), as a part of PKI, thus become a major target, in which cyber-attackers can issue any certificate if they compromise a CA.

CA, as a part of PKI, becomes too large to fail. The characteristic of centralizing the decision of trust provides the focused protection and easy management, but also concentrate the risk of security threat, resulting in the difficulties to maintain the integrity and legitimacy of system operations. Any breaches by exploiting either the system vulnerability or mis-operation of the workflow can lead to a long or permanent trust damage, like Diginotar [4]. The existing solution, X.509 Certificate Revocation List (a.k.a. CRL), may solve the issue. CRL provides a list of revoked certificates before those certificates reach their expiration date [5]. Although CRL enabled software to reject the certificate as soon as the CA issued the list, however, it requires intensive labor to find out fraudulent certificates and put them into the CRL, a time-taking process, and cannot protect end-users in real-time. Google provides another approach by providing a public log of CAs' activities, named as Certificate Transparency (CT) [6].

However, to separate the risk of the existing architecture, it is not easy to escape from the Zooko's triangle [7]. Zooko's triangle describes a trilemma of three desired properties in a network protocol, which is distributed, secure, and human-readable. Zooko's stated that there is no such a network protocol can combine more than two properties. Domain Name System Security Extension (DNSSEC) provides cryptographic authentication of domain name data on top of the current DNS Server. The service provides the properties of secure and human readability, however, centralized. It cannot tolerate failures directly from the root. The dot onion domain, a domain name service runs on top of the TOR network, provides both secure and decentralized; however, provided names are not human-readable, and end-users cannot specify names they desired.

The advent of blockchain technology becomes a potential solution at present [12]. Although this kind of solution is currently not universal, it sheds some light on how Blockchain can provide benefits to the PKI System. Namecoin [8], a domain name and PKI system combined, provides the service that meets all requirements in Zooko's triangle. However, these blockchain-based systems have some serious flaws. In the short term, contributors find it difficult to introduce new functionality to the existing blockchain network rather than perform a hard fork, which forced all nodes to participate in another blockchain network. In the long term, end-users can find the bottleneck of the system, causing inaccessibility.

Contributions. Though blockchain technology can provide many benefits, it is found that the existing blockchain-based PKI system cannot combine the characteristics of having integrity from the blockchains and the speedy performance in the current PKI. Motivated by this challenge, in this work, we design a new decentralized PKI system by leveraging the blockchain technology. **The contributions can be summarized as follows. 1) We introduce the concept of neighborhood into our designed PKI system and each neighborhood can have its own permissioned blockchain. 2) The system creates these internal networks between different sets of nodes not only temporarily but also dynamically and unpredictably. 3) In our evaluation, we show that our proposed system can ensure not only long-term accessibility but also the certificate security and public audit-ability.**

The remainder of this work is structured as follows: Sect. 2 introduces NoPKI - our proposed blockchain-based PKI system in detail. Section 3 investigates the viability of our system, and its performance under some adversarial scenarios (malicious nodes and malicious DNS). Section 4 describes the background on PKI and related studies on centralized and decentralized PKI systems. We conclude our work in Sect. 5.

2   Our Proposed System

This section first introduces our designed blockchain-based PKI system (called NoPKI) with new concept of neighborhood, and then details how it works.

2.1   System Structure Overview

The system consists of multiple nodes from various trusted networks called neighborhoods. Each neighborhood has its permissioned neighborhood chain, contains the witnesses from one neighbor to another neighbor. A node can join numerous neighborhoods, and each of them has three storage lists for different operations. The *key storage* contains the key pair of the node. The *history list* contains the information of encountered nodes, including their IP addresses, domain names, last addressed public keys, last given certificates, current neighborhood ID, and the reputation scores. The *query list* contains the query request from local or remote, as shown in Fig. 1.

2.2   The New User

The boot-up process requires a node to have at least one known node to start the process. However, for a new user, there may be no any known nodes in its storage. Thus, our system allows two methods to perform node discovery:

- Auto-discovery.
- Using a file contains the information of known nodes.

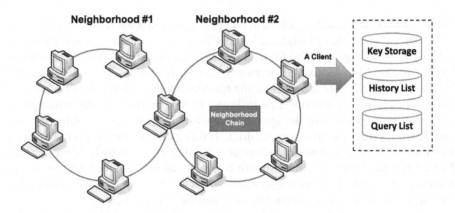

Fig. 1. The high-level overview of NoPKI system.

Auto-discovery collects the alive hosts by querying the IPv4 ARP table and the IPv6 neighbor table. Based on the list, the auto-discovery then performs the protocol discovery on the listed host. The discovered clients then can be added into the history list. If the system cannot perform auto-discovery successfully (e.g., empty ARP table or neighbor table), then the system should require the user to provide a file that contains the information of known nodes. When the history list is about to become empty, the system can re-trigger the process of node discovery.

2.3   Boot-Up Process, the Initial Step

The node needs to randomly choose from 5 to 150 live hosts in the History List that have a trustworthiness score higher than the 60th percentile. If the list cannot provide a list of nodes that meet the criteria, it needs to choose the Top 5 most upper scored nodes. The group of nodes can generate three random numbers via the random numbering protocol including Blockchain ID, Network ID, and Nonce Value, and then create the permissioned private blockchain network. If any participant already has the same Blockchain ID, Network ID, or nonce value, then they can send out overlap warning to restart the random numbering protocol to generate a new random number. If all participants make an agreement on the random number, they can form a permissioned private blockchain network, called *neighborhood chain*, and start the registration process.

The Design of the Random Numbering Protocol. This protocol consists of a group of nodes that are ready to form a neighborhood. A node with a random number generated from the protocol has to provide the following information to other nodes in the same random numbering:

- Determined digits(a minimum of 3 digits and a maximum of 5 digits).
- A list of nodes that are engaged in the random numbering.

Algorithm 1. Random Numbering Protocol

Input: d, n
Output: *answer*
   Initialisation :
 1: $freqCounter[10]$
 2: $rndStore[n][d \times 2 \times 10^{n+1}]$
 3: $answer$
   LOOP Process
 4: **for** $i = 0$ to $n - 1$ **do**
 5:    **for** $j = 0$ to $2 \times 10^{n+1} - 1$ **do**
 6:      $rndStore[n][j] = secureRand(0 \text{ to } 9)$
 7:    **end for**
 8: **end for**
 9: **for** $eachNodes$ **do**
10:   $rndStore \leftarrow randSetsFromOtherNodes$
11: **end for**
12: **for** $i = 0$ to $n - 1$ **do**
13:   $numMaxFreq = 0$
14:   $maxFreq = 0$
15:   **for** $j = 0$ to $d \times 2 \times 10^{n+1}$ **do**
16:     $freqCounter[rndStore[i][j]]++$
17:   **end for**
18:   **for** $i = 0$ to 9 **do**
19:     **if** $(maxFreq < freqCounter[i])$ **then**
20:       $maxFreq = freqCounter[i]$
21:       $numMaxFreq = i$
22:     **end if**
23:   **end for**
24:   $freqCounter \leftarrow 0$
25:   $answer+ = numMaxFreq \times 10^{n-i+1}$
26: **end for**
27: **return** *answer*

The node that either sends or receives the message can perform the following steps, as shown in Algorithm 1. We denoted d as the number of digits that the group would like to determine, and n is the number of nodes.

To limit the possibility of being sabotaged by malicious nodes, the system has the following measures:

- If a node provides a different answer, restart the random number negotiation.
- During the frequency calculating, a specific number in the set has to be 20% or more as compared with other numbers.

2.4 The Registration Process

All nodes are required to upload a self-signed X.509 certificate to the neighborhood chain with a smart contract that includes the following information.

- The X.509 Certificate in Binary Format
- Upload TimeStamp
- Revoke Status

After uploading their self-signed public keys and certificates, each neighbor in the neighborhood should validate others' public keys and certificates, and then generate a validation report. Every validation report will connect to others' validation reports. In particular, the validation report contains the validation records of each node in the neighborhood. A single validation record includes the following information.

- Originated IP of the node
- Proposed Domain Name of the node
- The node's DNS Server
- Validation TimeStamp
- The node's certificate address on the neighborhood chain.
- The addresses of other reference reports

There are many criteria for a node to determine the validation result. If the node provides the information that meets the following criteria, the validation result should be malicious (or false).

- The same public key or certificate appears in neighbor's (other) neighborhood, and the validation reports do not match.
- Either the proposed DNS of the node or the DNS used by the validator resolves an IP that is different from the originated IP of the node.
- DNSSEC validation failed.

The following information will affect the validation result by calculating the trustworthiness score from history list to determine the validity.

- The score of the node, denoted S^n
- The score of the node's DNS, denoted S^d

The system should obtain the score of the 60th, denoted S^{std}. We denote S^r as the calculation result of both score of the node and the node's DNS, where it can be calculated by Eq. (1) as below.

$$S^r = S^n \times 40\% + S^d \times 60\% \tag{1}$$

If $S^r > S^{std}$, the node passed and can continue the registration.

To defend against malicious nodes, our system use the following condition to trigger the system and make a severe penalty on the entity or node.

- A DNS provides an answer that is different from the most results from other DNSes. If the DNS is in the History List, it will be updated with a new score of 0. Otherwise, it should be added with a score of 0.

In addition, the following condition will not only trigger the system to put a severe penalty on the node, but also require to reform the neighborhood.

- Assume 40% of all validation reports in the neighborhood point out that a particular node fails the validation. If the node is already in the history list, it will be updated with a new score of 0. Otherwise, it should be added with a score of 0.
- After forming the neighborhood, if a node, which changes its certificate, causes the certificate to be not matched with others' validation reports, then the node will be applied with a new score of 0.
- If a node adds another node to the neighborhood after the neighborhood is formed, then the node will be updated with a new score of 0.

2.5 Query Process

A node can receive many certificate verification requests. It not only handles the request from itself but also helps neighbors verify their requests. A node can perform the following operations to verify a certificate.

- Check the neighborhood chain, if there is a match between the certificate and the node, it can return a verified certificate signal. If only the certificate is matched, it can return a tampered certificate signal.
- If the certificate does not match any certificate in the neighborhood chain, it then has to check its history list, and return a result, if any.
- If the certificate is neither on the neighborhood chain nor in the history list, it then has to check its query list. If the query is already on its way, it has to return 'still-in-operation'.
- If the certificate cannot be found in any storage list, it then has to put this query into the query list.

The query processor can send the query to all its neighbors, except for the neighbor who sends the query, in the neighborhood. It is worth noting that the query should be encrypted with the public key of the destination neighbor, in order to prevent possible eavesdropping and privacy leakage. Each participated node in the query chain can collect the answers from the nodes that receives the query. After receiving the answers from other nodes, it can count the result frequency. If 60% of the results show the certificate is verified, then it can return the answer as verified. If the result fails to reach a percent of 60%, then it can return the answer as questionable.

The query conclusion should add into the history list as well. The neighbors that provide the answer as most of others will have a raise in the trustworthiness score. For neighbors that provide the answer that is different from most of others will have a decrease in the trustworthiness score. In addition, to eliminate the system from causing broadcast storm and loops, each query has a serial number and a pass-along counter. 1) The serial number consists of a 64-bit Unix time integer and 6 random digits. This aims to ensure that every query is unique and identifiable, without knowing where it is originated. If a query reaches the node and the node has the same serial number as the query, then it will return the unreachable signal. 2) The pass-along counter ensures that any query should not be delivered more than 30 hops. Every time when a node passes the query, the counter will increase. If a query reaches 30 hops, then the node will return the unreachable signal.

2.6   The Neighborhood Timeout

A neighborhood without malicious nodes is good, but it does not mean that the neighborhood should exist without any time limit. This is because some nodes or a particular group of nodes may control others in practice. The use of a timeout can help reduce this risk. In this work, the timeout should be a time slot between 100 and 10000 min. Algorithm 2 shows how to compute the timeout, where we denote S as the set of scores from the neighbors of the newly formed neighborhood.

Algorithm 2. Determine neighborhood timeout

Input: S
Output: *timeout*
 1: $S^m = mode(S)$
 2: $timeout = 100 \times S^m$
 3: **return** *timeout*

2.7   Scoring a Node

The scoring system plays a crucial role in our designed system and enforces the system security. A node plays nicely has a better chance to help others. By contrast, the node that plays maliciously can still use the system to perform queries, but it has a smaller chance to be invited into another neighborhood. There are different ways for the scoring system to treat a node, but it can solely be divided as the following.

– New Node From Discovery
– New Node From Query
– Existing Nodes Play in the Network

In practice, most nodes have few chances to add a new node form discovery, as the node discovery is made by the query pass along. If a node is added into the history list via discovery, its trustworthiness score is 0. For a newly added node from the query, the score is the mode of all scores in the history list. For an existing node in the history list, the score can be calculated according to Eq. (2). Let S^o denote the original score of a node, S^n denote the new score,

$Q_h^{N(c)}$ denote the count of the node that answers the queries correctly in an hour, Q_h^A denote all occurred queries in an hour.

$$S^n = S^o \times 0.4 + \frac{Q_h^{N(c)}}{Q_h^A} \times 60 \tag{2}$$

For the existing nodes in the network, their scores should maintain updating continuously. When a query is assigned to the node and the answer is reached, the score should be updated.

2.8 The Revoke Process

For revoke process, the node has to change its certificate revoke status on the neighborhood chain. Then the neighbors that identify the revocation status can broadcast such information to its neighborhoods. It is similar to the query process, while the pass-along information is used for revocation rather than verification. After broadcasting the information, the neighbors can decide whether to leave the specific neighborhood chain. All nodes that receive the information have to perform a lookup in its history list and remove the certificate. For an on-going query, it will reply 'unreachable'.

2.9 The Update Process

The update process includes performing a revoke process once, generating another self-signed key, and performing another round of registration process.

2.10 History List Maintenance

To maintain the history list, there is a need to keep checking the node's status and performing the following:

– Check node status. If a node is disconnected or unreachable, then it can be removed.
– If a node is online but is not in the current neighborhood, then it needs to query their public keys, in order to ensure the integrity of the history list.

3 Performance Evaluation

In this section, our main goal is to evaluate the viability of our system, and its performance under some adversarial scenarios. For this purpose, we construct our system with 7 nodes using Ethereum (a decentralized open source blockchain). As shown in Table 1, the processor has the capability of Intel Core i7-8565U 1.90 GHz, with 1.5 GB memory and 16 GB storage. As there are only 7 nodes in the system, we thus randomly classify them into two neighborhoods. The network configuration including router, DNS information and node attributes can refer to Table 2.

Table 1. The configuration of nodes

Item	Attributes	
	Configuration	
VM Platform	Oracle VirtualBox 6.1.4	
Processor	2 × Intel Core i7-8565U @ 1.90 GHz	
Memory	1.5 GB	
Hard drive	16 GB	
Network	100 Mbps Virtual Switch	
OS	CentOS 8.1-1911	
Platform	OpenJDK 11, Ethereum	

Table 2. The node attributes in the network

Node Name	Attributes	
	Character in the Network	NH ID
RT.CNET	The main router and the main DNS	59810
NS1.CNET	The 2nd DNS	39605
NS2.CNET	The 3rd DNS	39605, 59810
N1	The participant	39605, 59810
N2	The participant	39605
N3	The participant	59810
N4	The participant	39605, 59810

3.1 System Performance

The first step of boot-up process in the neighborhood requires to run the random numbering protocol. Table 3 depicts the system performance in the aspect of time consumption.

Table 3. Time consumption of random numbering protocol

Number of nodes	Number of digits		
	3	4	5
5	59 ms	326 ms	1,546 ms
6	61 ms	338 ms	1,658 ms
7	63 ms	350 ms	1,770 ms

As show in Table 1, our system relies on Ethereum. Thus, if a node needs to boot up Ethereum for the first time, it has a process of generating etHashes.

This process requires to be triggered again approximately after every 30000 blocks (even if the chain belongs to a different network or chain ID). This takes around 11 min to finish the etHashes generation. After the generation process, the average time of booting up a neighborhood with 7 neighbors is 15 s 782 ms.

3.2   Under Malicious Node Scenario

In this experiment, we aim to explore our system under malicious node scenario. We denote $P_k^{(Name)}$ as the genuine public key of each node and pre-configure their history list for the test. We assume $N2$ is malicious to $RT.CNET$, which attempts to impersonate as other nodes. The public key of $RT.CNET$ is $P_k^{(N2)}$. In order to validate the performance of query process and neighborhood mechanism, we temporarily disable the history list maintainer of all nodes; otherwise, the impersonation information will be overridden by the maintainer.

In the network, when $NS1.CNET$ sends a query about public key of $RT.CNET$, the expected answer should be $P_k^{(RT)}$. If we assume that $N2$ successfully impersonates $RT.CNET$, then the public key of $RT.CNET$ is $P_k^{(N2)}$. As $NS1.CNET$ does not belong to the neighborhood with NH ID 59810, there is a need to verify whether $P_k^{(N2)}$ is the public key of $RT.CNET$. We traced the record from $NS1.CNET$ and the query graph is shown in Fig. 2.

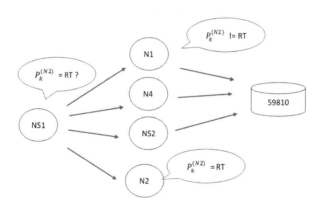

Fig. 2. The query graph of NS1.CNET.

When $NS1.CNET$ sends the query, $N2$ would directly return that $P_k^{(N2)}$ belongs to $RT.CNET$. However, $N1$ and $NS2$, which are in the same neighborhood with NH ID 59810, could directly check the neighborhood chain and identify that $P_k^{(N2)}$ does not belong to $RT.CNET$. Then $NS1.CNET$ collected all answers and found that two out of three answers indicated it is a tamp. Thus, $NS1.CNET$ would reject this certificate. This experiment indicate that our proposed system can defeat malicious nodes.

3.3 Under Malicious DNS Scenario

In this experiment, we aim to investigate our system performance under malicious DNS scenario. We can judge whether a DNS is malicious based on the status of resolve table. As shown in Table 4, we consider a normal DNS should have a correct resolve table, whereas a malicious DNS should have an incorrect resolve table. In this experiment, as a study, we set $RT.CNET$ and $NS1.CNET$ as normal while $NS2.CNET$ is malicious (with an incorrect revolve table). Table 5 shows the configuration of each node, including the DNS usage. For example, $NS1.CNET$ with IP 192.168.1.101 and DNS - $RT.CNET$, and $NS2.CNET$ with IP 192.168.1.102 and DNS - $RT.CNET$. Regarding nodes, $N1$ and $N3$ have the same DNS - $NS1.CNET$, $N2$ has the DNS - $NS2.CNET$, and $N4$ has the DNS - $RT.CNET$.

Table 4. The correct and incorrect DNS resolve table

Node name	Attributes	
	Correct resolve	Incorrect resolve
RT.CNET	192.168.1.1	192.168.1.102
NS1.CNET	192.168.1.101	
NS2.CNET	192.168.1.102	
N1	192.168.1.201	
N2	192.168.1.202	
N3	192.168.1.203	
N4	192.168.1.204	

Table 5. The network configuration of each node

Node name	Attributes	
	IP Address	DNS
RT.CNET	192.168.1.1	N/A
NS1.CNET	192.168.1.101	RT.CNET
NS2.CNET	192.168.1.102	RT.CNET
N1	192.168.1.201	NS1.CNET
N2	192.168.1.202	NS2.CNET
N3	192.168.1.203	NS1.CNET
N4	192.168.1.204	RT.CNET

In this experiment, we assume that $NS2.CNET$ tries to intercept all DNS traffic from its users (i.e., it can affect $N2$), and mainly consider the following two cases according to neighborhood formation:

- **Case-1.** The DNS pollution that happens after the neighborhood is formed.
- **Case-2.** The DNS pollution that happens before the neighborhood is formed.

Case-1. To setup the environment, we form a neighborhood including $N1$, $N2$, $N3$, $N4$ and $NS1.CNET$, while $NS2.CNET$ acts maliciously to $NS1.CNET$. Thus $NS1.CNET$ needs to ask each node to resolve the IP.

As shown in Fig. 3, suppose that $N2$ joined the neighborhood, and started the pollution. Thus, when $N2$ tries to connect to $RT.CNET$ by broadcasting a public key of $P_k^{(NS2)}$, $N2$ will send a query to all nodes that are in the same neighborhood as $RT.CNET$.

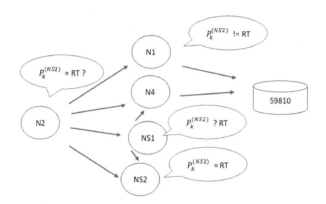

Fig. 3. The query graph of N2.

Case-2. Before the neighborhood formation, $NS2$ can directly inform $N2$ that the public key of $RT.CNET$ is $P_k^{(NS2)}$. However, $N2$ can send a query to $N1$ and $N4$, who have direct access to the same neighborhood as $RT.CNET$ (see Table 6), and then confirm that $P_k^{(NS2)}$ does not belong to $RT.CNET$. As shown in Fig. 3, even if $NS1.CNET$ may be not sure about the query, with the help from $N1$ and $N4$, $N2$ can still reject that $P_k^{(NS2)}$ belongs to $RT.CNET$.

Table 6. The resolve result of NS1.CNET

Node name	Attributes	
	Applied DNS	The resolve of NS1.CNET
N1	NS1.CNET	192.168.1.101
N3		
N4	RT.CNET	
NS1.CNET		
N2	NS2.CNET	192.168.1.102

For these nodes to form a neighborhood, it might run into a problem, as $NS1.CNET$ resolves differently from $N2$. However, most nodes' DNS server complies with $NS1.CNET$ using the correct IP 192.168.1.101. Hence the self-claimed $NS1.CNET$ is the right one that owns the domain name $NS1.CNET$, and the registration is complete.

3.4 Discussion

As described above, the main purpose of our work is to propose a new decentralized PKI system by leveraging the blockchain technology. We particularly develop the concept of neighborhood, which can be used to enhance the security. In the evaluation, we aim to investigate its feasibility and performance under some adversarial scenarios like malicious nodes and malicious DNS. The results demonstrate that our system can be robust against these attacks. As our work is at its early stage, there are many interesting topics in our future work, i.e., we plan to conduct a more thorough evaluation.

4   Related Work

In the early 2000s, transport information over the Internet is not mandatory in most sites. At the time, most web services provide information, without user interaction. Thus information flow is unidirectional.

The speedy evolution of wire and wireless connection broadband technology brings the dramatic increase of individual bandwidth, which provided the environment and inspired Web 2.0, known as participative web or social web. Unlike the Internet before, the information flow became bilateral rather than unidirectional. While users have more participation in providing content and involvement in the network, companies started to offer online services (e.g., online banking), which requires privacy-aware information. Eavesdropping connections to obtain useful details started to bring privacy threats to users. Moreover, a man-in-the-middle (e.g., an evil proxy, ARP spoofing) can easily alter the connection and create fraudulent and malicious requests, which are not users' intentions. The threats of privacy-leakage may affect the user both physically and virtually (e.g., physical damages of property, identity theft). Without encrypting these connections and create secure tunnels, users cannot immune from the threat, which leads to the demands for secure connections between sites.

4.1   Centralized PKI

Although there are many different methods for creating different secured tunnels for different protocols, these protocols mostly adopt asymmetric encryption. However, to ensure the bounding of public key or certificate is valid, certificate authorities (CAs) step in, which can perform the validation and registration process and are the only organizations that can add public keys and certificates under the root certificate trust chain. Operating environments (e.g., software,

Operating Systems) usually come with these root certificates of different CAs pre-installed in their trusted store. End users then validate others' certificates or public keys by tracing the trust chain and check the trusted store.

Disadvantages of Centralized PKI. Certificate authorities, usually under controls of specific organizations (e.g., companies, government agencies), play crucial roles in keeping the integrity of the whole PKI. Being the guards of trusted and untrusted public keys and certificates, CAs must highly value their operational integrity and system security. Breaches in the system, errors in operations, and malicious intents, by the designed structure, are not preventable for end-users, a very critical issue. According to Mozilla Telemetry, 86.01% of pages loaded by Mozilla web browsers are going through HTTPS [9]. A tampered CA or a CA with malicious intent can easily decrypt all traffic by using the root certificate to sign the unauthorized public key and certificate of the target. The signed public key and certificate then used in the man-in-the-middle attack. The end-users usually trust the public key or certificate without issue, since a valid root certificate in the trust store signs either of them.

4.2 Decentralized PKI

As centralized PKI may pose some challenges, whether the decentralization can bring desired properties to the existing PKI? Zooko's triangle [7], a trilemma, describes the incapability of having more than two of the desired properties in human-meaningful, decentralized, and secure at the same time. Our existing PKI structure provides both human-meaningful names in the certificate, collision-free in naming, and secure in operation, under the circumstances of untampered CA. The question is whether a decentralized system can provide these properties to the existing PKI.

The Web-of-Trust Based PKI. Pretty Good Privacy is the first implementation of the decentralized PKI system. The direct trusted relationship is the basis of the PGP network, relies heavily on manual verification of the individuals [15]. The indirect trusted relationship relies on the direct trusted relationship of every individual. Assume party A has direct trusted relationships with parties B and C, and party B can create an indirect trusted relationship with party C based on the network of party A. With time goes on, the whole trusted network expands and connects [13]. However, such a system has some issues. For example, a new node may find it difficult to join the network since it requires the new user to trust at least one existing user in the network as an introducer. Without an introducer, the trust cannot extend and weave into the network. The most secure and tricky way for the new node to join the existing network should be: the user meet in person with another current user in the network. The lack of flexibility is another significant issue. The certificate or public key does not expire; hence, it does not require to reauthenticate the node. That means a compromised user may find it hard to regain the trust of others or rejoin the network. The lack of revoke mechanism may cause the potential and existing compromise last long.

For example, a highly-trusted compromise key can affect the network dearly. Without the key owner personally issues the untrust notice to the other users, the compromise may continue. Applying Zooko's trilemma, PGP is decentralized and human-meaningful, but not secure. Later implemented PGP-based software, such as OpenPGP and GnuPGP, support the X.509 certificate, yet, again, the trust issues of centralization plague still exist.

The Blockchain-Based PKI. Currently, some studies move to developing blockchain-based PKI, which applies a different strategy of decentralizing the network. On a blockchain network, everything that happened in the network is a single transaction. The consensus algorithm that runs on every node describes and determines how to seal the next storage block. If all the nodes reach the consensus states, every transaction that happened in the time duration will be sealed cryptographically into the storage block, with an iterator pointed to the previous block. The sealed block then distributed to every node in the network. In a Blockchain-based system, consensus algorithm and cryptography that applies to play essential roles of the platform. Any flaw or failure in these practices can compromise from the root. Blockchain provides a secure way to distribute the information and allows all participants to audit the chain. The new characteristic of secure information distribution and preservation with the public audibility breaks the Zooko's trilemma, allowing the deployed PKI to have the capability of being human-meaningful, decentralized and secured. There are multiple different consensus algorithms apply on various platforms. Some existing studies on blockchain-based PKI system can refer but not limit to [2,16,17,19,25].

Consensus Algorithms. The blockchain-based decentralized system requires all states to reach a consensus state (e.g., chain in sync, decide the block seal hash). The consensus algorithms underlying these platforms provide the mechanism for all nodes to reach in a deal, offer rewards to the workers (miners), punish and prevent those who sabotage the system. The survey of current proposed Blockchain-based PKIs shows most of the platforms in favor of Proof-of-Work, with a minor that favor in Proof-of-Stake.

1) Proof-of-work is a mechanism that requires all nodes in the network who would like to seal the next block of the chain to solve a hard problem [24]. The answer to the problem acts as the confirmation of the added block and the transaction. The answer is easily verifiable, however, challenging to perform reverse deduction. The difficulty of the problem is an essential key in the Proof-of-Work system. *2) Proof-of-Stake* takes a different approach from that usually proposed PoW, a set of validators take turns proposing and voting on the next block. Validators are required to lock up a specific amount of coins as their stake to participate in the proposing and voting [27].

5   Conclusion

The existing PKI system is vulnerable to cyber-attacks, in which an attacker can use a compromised PKI to decrypt any secure connections. With the advent of blockchain technology, we design a decentralized blockchain-based PKI system, called NoPKI, which involves a new concept of neighborhood by leveraging the witnesses from one neighbor to another neighbor. Each neighborhood can have its own permissioned neighborhood chain. In the evaluation, we investigate the viability of our system (e.g., time consumption) and its performance under some adversarial scenarios (e.g., malicious nodes and DNS). Our results indicate that our system can be robust against these attacks. More generally, it shows that our proposed system can ensure not only long-term accessibility but also the certificate security and public audit-ability.

References

1. Bahajji, Z.A., Illyes, G.: HTTPS as a ranking signal, Google Webmaster Central Blog, 6 August 2014. https://webmasters.googleblog.com/2014/08/https-as-ranking-signal.html. Accessed 1 Jan 2020
2. Axon, L., Goldsmith, M.: PB-PKI: a privacy-aware blockchain-based PKI. In: SECRYPT 2017, pp. 311–318 (2017)
3. Stark, E., Lopez, C.: No more mixed messages about HTTPS, Chromium Blog, 3 October 2019. https://blog.chromium.org/2019/10/no-more-mixed-messages-about-https.html. Accessed 1 Jan 2020
4. Prins, J.R.: Interim Report - DigiNotar Certificate Authority breach - Operation Black Tulip," Fox-IT BV, 5 September 2011. https://www.rijksoverheid.nl/binaries/rijksoverheid/documenten/rapporten/2011/09/05/diginotar-public-report-version-1/rapport-fox-it-operation-black-tulip-v1-0.pdf. Accessed 1 Jan 2020
5. Cooper, D., Santesson, S., Farrell, S., Boeyen, S., Housley, R., Polk, W.: Internet X.509 Public Key Infrastructure Certificate and Certificate Revocation List (CRL) Profile, RFC 5280, May 2008. http://www.ietf.org/rfc/rfc5280.txt
6. Laurie, B., Langley, A., Kasper, E.: Certificate Transparency, RFC 6962, June 2013. http://www.ietf.org/rfc/rfc6962.txt
7. O'Hearn, Z.W.: Names: Distributed, Secure, Human-Readable: Choose Two. Zooko.com, 12 October 2001. https://web.archive.org/web/20011020191610/http://zooko.com/distnames.html. Accessed 15 Jan 2020
8. "Namecoin," Namecoin. https://namecoin.org. Accessed 15 Jan 2020
9. "Telemetry Measurement Dashboard," Mozilla. https://telemetry.mozilla.org. Accessed 24 Feb 2020
10. Chung, T., et al.: Is the web ready for OCSP must-staple? In: Internet Measurement Conference 2018, pp. 105–118, Boston (2018)
11. Matsumoto, S., Reischuk, R.M.: IKP: turning PKI around with decentralized automated incentives. In: 2017 IEEE Symposium on Security and Privacy, pp. 410–426, San Jose (2017)
12. Li, W., Tug, S., Meng, W., Wang, Y.: Designing collaborative blockchained signature-based intrusion detection in IoT environments. Future Gener. Comput. Syst. 96, 481–489 (2019)
13. Abdul-Rahman, A.: The PGP trust model. EFI-Forum: J. Electron. Commer. 10(3), 27–31 (1997)
14. Appelbaum J., Muffett A.: The onion Special-Use Domain Name, RFC 7686, October 2015. http://www.ietf.org/rfc/rfc7686.txt

15. Ryabitsev, K.: PGP Web of Trust: Core Concepts Behind Trusted Communication, The Linux Foundation, 7 February 2014. https://www.linux.com/tutorials/pgp-web-trust-core-concepts-behind-trusted-communication/. Accessed 27 Feb 2020
16. Karaarslan, E., Adiguzel, E.: Blockchain based DNS and PKI solutions. IEEE Commun. Stand. Mag. **2**(3), 52–57 (2018)
17. Kubilay, M.Y., Kiraz, M.S., Mantar, H.A.: CertLedger: a new PKI model with certificate transparency based on blockchain. Comput. Secur. **85**, 333–352 (2019)
18. NameID - Your Crypto-OpenID, NameID. https://nameid.org. Accessed 28 Feb 2020
19. Orman, H.: Blockchain: the emperors new PKI? IEEE Internet Comput. **22**(2), 23–28 (2018)
20. Tewari, H., et al.: X509Cloud - framework for a ubiquitous PKI. In: MILCOM 2017–2017 IEEE Military Communications Conference (MILCOM), pp. 225–230, Baltimore (2017)
21. Ethereum Network Status: Ethereum Network Status. https://ethstats.net. Accessed 28 Feb 2020
22. Bitcoin Stats: Blockchain.com. https://www.blockchain.com/stats. Accessed 28 Feb 2020
23. Namecoin (NMC) price stats and information, BitInfoCharts. https://bitinfocharts.com/namecoin/. Accessed 28 Feb 2020
24. Jakobsson, M., Juels, A.: Proofs of work and bread pudding protocols (extended abstract). In: Preneel, B. (ed.) Secure Information Networks. ITIFIP, vol. 23, pp. 258–272. Springer, Boston, MA (1999). https://doi.org/10.1007/978-0-387-35568-9_18
25. Jiang, W., Li, H., Xu, G., Wen, M., Dong, G., Lin, X.: PTAS: privacy-preserving thin-client authentication scheme in blockchain-based PKI. Future Gener. Comput. Syst. **96**, 185–195 (2019)
26. Ye, C., Li, G., Cai, H., Gu, Y., Fukuda, A.: Analysis of security in blockchain: case study in 51%- attack detecting. In Proceedings of the 5th International Conference on Dependable Systems and Their Applications (DSA), pp. 15–24, Dalian (2018)
27. Li, W., Meng, W., Liu, Z., Au, M.H.: Towards blockchain-based software-defined networking: security challenges and solutions. IEICE Trans. Inf. Syst. **E103CD**(2), 196–203 (2020)

The Research on Covert Communication Model Based on Blockchain: A Case Study of Ethereum's Whisper Protocol

Zhijie Zhang[1] (ID), Lejun Zhang[1,2] (ID), Waqas Rasheed[1] (ID), Zilong Jin[3] (ID), Tinghuai Ma[3] (ID), Huiling Chen[4] (ID), and Guangquan Xu[5(✉)] (ID)

[1] College of Information Engineering, Yangzhou University, Yangzhou 225127, China
[2] School Math and Computer Science, Quanzhou Normal University, Quanzhou 362000, China
[3] School of Computer and Software, Nanjing University of Information Science and Technology, Nanjing 21004, China
[4] Department of Computer Science and Artificial Intelligence, Wenzhou University, Wenzhou 325035, China
[5] Tianjin Key Laboratory of Advanced Networking (TANK), College of Intelligence and Computing, Tianjin University, Tianjin 300350, China
losin@tju.edu.cn

Abstract. Covert communication is an extension of the traditional encryption technology, which hides information through carriers such as text and images. Traditional covert communication relies on a third-party central node, which is easy to be detected and attacked. As a new type of decentralized technology, blockchain has been widely developed in recent years. Its anti-interference, anti-tampering and other characteristics can effectively alleviate the problems faced by traditional covert communications. Combining with blockchain technology to design an effective and feasible hidden communication model and method becomes the focus of research. To this end, this paper designs a new covert communication model suitable for Ethereum based on the whisper protocol. First, we introduce the covert communication model under the blockchain, as well as the whisper protocol in Ethereum. Then, based on the characteristics and structure of the whisper protocol, a new type of covert communication method was designed. Finally, the anti-jamming, anti-tampering and anti-detection of the model are proved, and its information embedding and transmission efficiency are also evaluated by comparing with the time-based covert communication.

Keywords: Covert communication · Blockchain · Ethereum

1 Introduction

In order to effectively protect the communication content from being leaked, information hiding has been applied to the communication field and formed the covert communication technology. Encryption, which is often used to protect information, focuses on reducing the readability of information, while covert communication reduces the existence of information [1]. Traditional covert communication uses centralized channel,

© Springer Nature Singapore Pte Ltd. 2020
G. Xu et al. (Eds.): FCS 2020, CCIS 1286, pp. 215–230, 2020.
https://doi.org/10.1007/978-981-15-9739-8_17

which makes the communication process vulnerable to interference and attack [2, 3]. Blockchain is the underlying technology of bitcoin [4], it has the characteristics of decentralization, anti-interference, and anti-tampering [5] which can solve the defects of traditional covert communication. In addition, blockchain stores information in each node in a distributed way, and relies on zero knowledge proof, smart contract, consensus mechanism and other technologies to realize point-to-point trusted transactions or data transmission between unfamiliar nodes without trusted third-party organizations. Therefore, at this stage, how to combine blockchain and covert communication to make communication more robust has become the focus of research in related fields.

Ethereum is an open-source public blockchain platform with smart contract function [6]. It provides a decentralized Ethernet virtual machine to handle point-to-point contracts through the dedicated encryption currency Ether (ETH). In addition, Ethereum provides various modules for users to develop and build applications in it, which has better scalability than bitcoin. Therefore, Ethereum is more regarded as an open application development platform with great potential. More and more users choose to use Ethereum to obtain application services and conduct transactions and communications. As with blockchain, once the operation and transaction information in Ethereum is determined, it will leave a permanent and immutable record [7]. Although this ensures the security of communication process, it makes the privacy of users easy to leak. Therefore, this paper designs a covert communication method to effectively protect the communication content of Ethereum.

In this paper, the covert communication model of blockchain is firstly introduced. Based on this, a new hidden communication model suitable for Ethereum is designed for the first time in combination with Ethereum whisper protocol. Finally, the proposed model is analyzed and evaluated, and compared with covert communication using time interval.

2 Related Work

In the early development of information hiding, it is mainly used in the military field. The military uses image audio and other media to secretly transmit military information and intelligence to resist enemy eavesdropping and interception. Literature [8] proposed an image steganography technology specifically for military covert communication, which uses parallel beam projection of images to reduce payload dimensionality. Paruchuri [9] designed a new architecture for flexible and secure networking in battlefields that enables stealthy and covert communication in the presence of node mobility. It can carry on undeterred communication without the attack/eavesdropping nodes being able to detect the presence of any communication. Moreover, the information hiding method based on digital watermarking can help the military to safely transmit geographic information [10] or optimize the navigation method of the UAV [11].

In addition to military applications, digital watermarking is a very important method for copyrights of various electronic documents and media [12]. Most watermarking algorithms transform the host image and embed the watermark information in a robust manner. Uncompressed digital images require large storage capacity and bandwidth. The digital watermarking algorithm based on DCT-DWT transformation can alleviate this phenomenon, transmit images in an efficient form and ensure the security of transmission [13]. Literature [14] proposes a robust blind watermarking scheme for 2D-vector data used in Geographical Information Systems (GIS) which is resistant to common attacks such as translations, scaling, rotation, generalization, cropping, adding objects, and noise attacks.

Depending on the medium used, covert communication can be divided into two types: time and space. Time-based covert communication often uses the timestamp of the data packet or the sending interval [15] to convey information, while the spatial type uses error correction code [16], the least significant bit (LSB) of data [17], or voice [18] as a carrier for information embedding. In addition, biological information has also been increasingly used in covert communications, such as simulating the communication mode of dolphins to achieve underwater covert communication [19, 20]. Despite the rapid development of covert communication in recent years, there are few achievements in its combination with blockchain. At this stage, blockchain development focuses on privacy protection, application development and attack resistance [21], and most of the researches on Ethereum focus on smart contracts [22]. There is no feasible solution to address the need to implement covert communication in Ethereum.

3   Research Basis

3.1   Covert Communication Model in Blockchain Environment

The traditional covert communication model is mainly composed of three parts: sender, receiver, and communication channel. According to the function of each step, the communication process can be divided into information processing, information embedding, information transmission, information extraction and restoration.

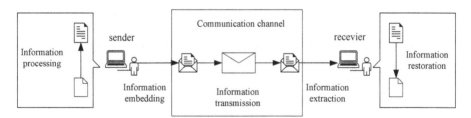

Fig. 1. Traditional covert communication model

Figure 1 shows the traditional system model of covert communication. First, the information sender performs preliminary processing on the information, such as using encryption to improve information security or encoding to better implement information embedding. Then the message is embedded into the carrier information and transmitted through the channel. After receiving the carrier information, the receiver extracts the processed message from it, decodes and decrypts the acquired information to obtain the original message.

In the above model, the communication channel often adopts centralized server and is relatively single, which makes the communication process easy to be monitored and attacked. However, in the decentralized blockchain, each node acts as a server and keeps an independent account and record. When the information is uploaded to the blockchain, it will spread among nodes in the form of broadcast. Each node is a potential information receiver, which makes communication difficult to be targeted and the identity of the receiver can be well protected. Since the blockchain network does not rely on centralized servers, it has strong anti-interference and anti-attack capabilities. Only when the attacker owns more than half of the nodes in the network can he have the chance to tamper with the information. In addition, the communication channel of the blockchain is no longer single, and multiple receivers can obtain information at the same time. Therefore, group communication is easy to achieve in blockchain. Combined with the above characteristics, the following processes can be made for blockchain based covert communication: [23].

(1) Information processing. Similar to the traditional hidden communication, the hidden communication under the blockchain still needs to process the original information. It requires the sender to encrypt the original information T with encryption algorithm E, and encode it with coding rule C to better integrate with the carrier information. The obtained processed information is recorded as T'.

(2) Information embedding. Generally speaking, the processed information cannot be transmitted directly in the channel, and the concealment of direct information transmission is poor. Therefore, the message T' to be delivered needs to be embedded in the carrier information M for delivery. In blockchain, there are many information carriers. For example, time-based covert communication can use the time stamp, transaction sending time or time interval to embed information, while space-based covert communication can use address, hash value of address, number of transactions or coins, redundancy or remark information, etc. The carrier information embedded with secret information is recorded as M'.

(3) Information transmission. In the blockchain, this process is also the process of storing information on the chain. The sender node sends M' in the form of broadcast to each node using methods like initiating transactions. Blockchain introduces a consensus mechanism to ensure the synchronization of account books. For example, in bitcoin, the proof of work (PoW) mechanism is often used to determine the accounting right. Each node calculates the hash value of the block header to make it meet the target difficulty. The node that meets the requirements earliest obtains the accounting right and gets reward. After accounting, transactions during this period will be permanently recorded in the blockchain.

(4) Information extraction. The information recorded on the blockchain can be viewed and obtained by all nodes, so the receiver node can filter out the secret information M' with specific information, such as querying the transaction initiated by the sender. After that, using the information extraction rules corresponding to the embedding rules can extract the encrypted and encoded information T' from M'.

(5) Information restoration. After obtaining T', the receiver decodes it with the decoding rule C' and decrypts it with the decryption rule E' to obtain the original information T.

According to the above steps, the covert communication model under the blockchain is expressed in Fig. 2:

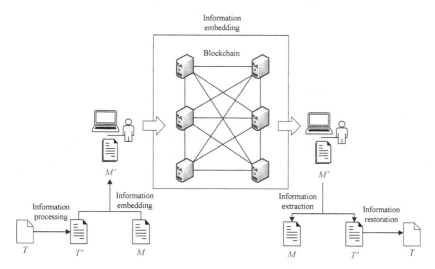

Fig. 2. Covert communication model under the blockchain

3.2 The Whisper Protocol of Ethereum

As a blockchain ecosystem, Ethereum provides a rich environment for the distributed applications (DAPP). Different from the traditional internet applications, DAPP hosts the front-end code in the distributed storage service, and uses the smart contract to replace the back-end server. Whisper, a concept derived from DAPP, is a communication protocol for synchronous information of distributed platforms. It allows nodes to interact with each other in a secure way, and hides the relevant information from the unrelated parties.

The whisper protocol exposes a set of API model similar to subscription-publishing to the upper layer. Nodes can apply for topics of interest to them. Then they will only receive messages with these topics, and messages of unrelated topics will be discarded.

Envelope is the basic form of data transmission in whisper network nodes. It contains encrypted data body and plaintext metadata which is mainly used for basic message verification and message body decryption. Envelope is transmitted in RLP encoded format, and its structure is shown in Fig. 3:

Version	Expiry	TTL
Topic	AESNonce	
Data	EnvNonce	

Fig. 3. Structure of envelope

In the above structure, the version of the current letter encryption method is up to 4 bytes (currently one byte containing zero). If the version of the letter is higher than the current value of the node, the node cannot decrypt the letter. Expiry time and TTL (time to live) are 4 bytes Unix time in seconds. The envelope will survive the time specified by TTL in the system and expire after reaching the expiry time. AESNonce is a 12-byte random data, which only presents in case of symmetric encryption, and EnvNonce is used for PoW calculation.

Trying to decrypt all incoming envelopes may not be feasible because it requires nodes to spend a lot of resources. In order to facilitate filtering, topics were introduced to the whisper protocol. Each envelope contains only one topic, and each topic corresponds to a key used for encryption and decryption. When a node receives an envelope containing a known topic, it decrypts the envelope with the corresponding key to obtain the contents. If the node fails to decrypt the envelope successfully, it should consider that there is a topic conflict has occurred, that is, other nodes set the same topic for the envelope but encrypt it with different keys. At this time, the current node only forwards the envelope further.

Data in the envelope, which is mainly composed of payload and padding, is mainly used to store message. The actual information to be transmitted is stored in the payload and is often encrypted symmetrically or asymmetrically. The padding is introduced to reduce the risk of message size exposing meta information. The default augmentation rule in version 5 is to keep the message size at a multiple of 256 bytes. These two parts can store a large number of arbitrary information, so it creates conditions for the embedding of secret information and the realization of covert communication.

The purpose of setting up PoW is to reduce the amount of spam and the network burden. If the node wants the network to store messages for a specific time (TTL), the cost of calculating PoW can be regarded as the price it pays for the allocated resources. In version 5, PoW is defined as Eq. 1. It is the average number of iterations required to find the number of leading zero bits in the hash (*BestBit*), which is divided by message size and TTL:

$$PoW = \frac{2^{BestBit}}{size \times TTL} \tag{1}$$

If the receiver node fails to receive the required envelope within its lifetime due to network failure and other reasons. It can submit identity information such as authorization information or payment information to the mail server. After the server verifies the validity of the node, it will send the expired envelope to the node in the form of P2P. At this time, the node does not need to forward this envelope.

In a complete communication process of whisper, each node of communication first interacts with the topic and the corresponding key. Then, the sending node sets the payload and padding to build the envelope's data and encrypt it symmetrically or asymmetrically using the interacted key. After that, the node sets the topic of the envelope corresponding to the key, and combines it with attributes such as TTL to build the envelope. Finally, after the envelope broadcast, the receiving node can filter out the specific envelope through the topic, and decrypt it with the corresponding key to obtain the communication content.

4 Covert Communication Method Based on Ethereum Whisper Protocol

4.1 System Model and Information Transmission Method

Combined with the characteristics of whisper protocol, the hidden communication model of blockchain can be further specified and a new model suitable for Ethereum can be obtained. The following definitions can be made for the new covert communication model:

Definition 1: Topic-key pair interaction. In whisper protocol, the successful interaction of topic and key is the premise of communication. There are three main types of current topic-key pair interactions:

(1) Other channel interaction. The communication sender transmits the topics and corresponding keys needed for communication to each receiver in other channels completely unrelated to the current communication.
(2) Interaction under asymmetric encryption. The sender node exposes its public key together with the topics to be used, while the receiver node only exposes its public key. After that, both parties use the public key of the other party to encrypt the information and use their own private key to decrypt it.
(3) Asymmetric interaction without topics. Each communication node first exposes its public key. Then the sender node encrypts the topic-key pairs with the receiver's public key, and broadcasts the envelope without setting any topic. The receiver decrypts all envelopes without topic using its own private key until the topic-key pair is successfully obtained. In order to minimize the cost of decryption by the receiver, the PoW required for the construction of the non-topic envelope is much higher than that of the normal one, so it can effectively reduce the number of malicious non-topic letters.

Definition 2: Data construction. The sender forms envelope data by concatenating related flag bytes, padding, payloads (randomly generated or provided by the user) and optional signatures.

Definition 3: Envelope construction and sending. The sender builds the envelope in combination with Fig. 3, and broadcasts the envelope after calculating the PoW successfully. Similar to the process of storing information on the blockchain, the envelope will be saved in the whisper network after being broadcast.

Definition 4: Envelope screening and content acquisition. Each node has multiple filters, and each filter contains a specific topic-key pair. When the node receives an envelope, it determines whether its topic is the same as that in its filters. A filter with the same topic will decrypt the envelope. If the decryption is successful, the content will be saved in the filter, or it will be ignored.

Combined with the above definitions, the covert communication model for Ethereum is shown in Fig. 4:

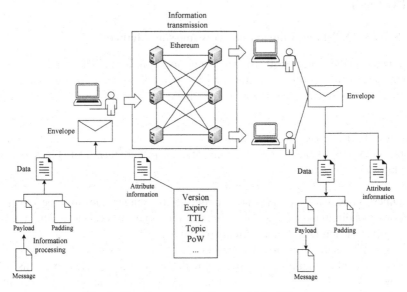

Fig. 4. Covert communication model for Ethereum

The sender first takes the processed message as the payload of the data, and randomly generates or customizes padding according to the size of the payload $L_{payload}$. The length of padding $L_{padding}$ is calculated according to Eq. 2, which ensures that the data size is a multiple of 256.

$$L_{padding} = \left(L_{payload}/256 + 1\right) \times 256 - L_{payload} \tag{2}$$

After that, the node calculates the PoW and builds the envelope with data and attribute information such as version. After the envelope is broadcast to each node of Ethereum, multiple receivers can filter out the envelope through the interacted topic. They use the key corresponding to the topic to decrypt the envelope and obtain the data, which includes payload and padding. Finally, the receiver node decodes and decrypts the payload to get the message.

4.2 Information Embedding and Extraction Method

After introducing the system model and information transmission method of the new covert communication model, in order to improve the concealment of messages, information hiding technology is used in the creation of data. Although the message in whisper protocol is encrypted to reduce readability, our method can further reduce the existence of information. Even if the content of the envelope is cracked by the attacker node, it cannot get the real information.

Specifically, the construction of data is divided into the following steps:

(1) The sender encrypts the message to ensure the unreadability of it.
(2) Payload is generated. It can be a completely random string or a user specified meaningful statement.
(3) The node matches the encrypted message with the generated payload and records the index of the same character in both. The matched characters in the message will be replaced with "*". When the message contains only "*" or the payload no longer contains the characters in the message, two index arrays are generated.
(4) When index arrays are generated, they are spliced into a string and encrypted to P_1 as part of the padding.
(5) The node sets a splitter of length L_R after P_1 and generates a random redundant field P_2 of length L_{P_2} as another part of padding, where L_{P_2} can be obtained by Eq. 3:

$$L_{P_2} = \left(\left(L_{P_1} + L_R + L_{payload} \right)/256 + 1 \right) \times 256 - \left(L_{P_1} + L_R + L_{payload} \right) \quad (3)$$

Where L_{P_1} is the length of P_1.

(6) After P_2 is generated, it is spliced after P_1 together with the separator to get padding. Finally, data can be obtained by combining payload and padding.

Assuming the encrypted message is "ayoulher" and the user specifies the payload content as "HelloHowareYou", the above processes can be summarized as Fig. 5:

After character matching, the index arrays of carrier and message are generated, which are encrypted to P_1. Unmatched characters will wait for the next round of information embedding. Data can be obtained by combining payload with padding, where padding includes P_1, splitter R and P_2. Even if the envelope is cracked and the content of data is leaked, all the things the attacker can see are the payload whose content is "HelloHowareYou", and the messy padding. Therefore, information can be well protected.

When the receiver node receives the envelope and decrypts it successfully, it deletes the R and P_2 in the padding to get P_1, and decrypts P_1 to get the index arrays. After that, the node can use the following algorithm to restore the original information by combining index arrays and payload.

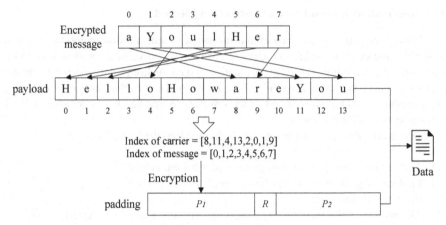

Fig. 5. Information embedding example

Algorithm name: Message restoration algorithm
Input: Index of carrier I_T, index of message I_C and payload $T_{payload}$
Output: Encrypted message T'
1) int $i = 0$;   //Parameter for cyclic control
2) for ($i=0$; $i<L_{I_C}$; $i++$) {   //L_{I_C} is the length of I_C
3) $T'[I_C[i]] = T_{payload}[I_T[i]];$}
4) return T';

5   System Evaluation and Testing

5.1   System Evaluation

Anti-jamming. For traditional covert communication, network interference is one of the most important factors that affect information transmission. Especially for time-based covert communication, network fluctuation is easy to cause information error. Assuming that the transmission time interval 1 s and 2 s correspond to binary 0 and 1 respectively, the network fluctuation of 1 s will cause information error.

In the proposed model, the information contained in the envelope can be simplified into time attribute part t and message part m, where t includes TTL and expiration time t_E as shown in Eq. 4:

$$Envelope = (t, m) = ((TTL, t_E), m) \tag{4}$$

The expiration time is calculated by the system according to Eq. 5, and its value is equal to the sum of TTL and the Unix time t_U when envelope was sent.

$$t_E = TTL + t_U \tag{5}$$

If the sender delays the broadcast time of envelope by Δt due to network fluctuation, then t_E will change accordingly as Eq. 6.

$$t_E' = TTL + t_U' = TTL + t_U + \Delta t \tag{6}$$

At this time, the envelope is constructed as Eq. 7:

$$Envelope' = (t', m) = \left(\left(TTL, t_E'\right), m\right) \tag{7}$$

Even if the network fluctuation occurs at the sender, the part m mainly used for storing information is not change. Assuming that the receiver node can successfully receive the envelope within $\Delta t'$ after it is sent, the latest effective receiving time t_r is as shown in Eq. 8:

$$t_r = \Delta t' + t_U \tag{8}$$

Because of the network fluctuation, the sender delayed the sending time of the envelope by Δt, and informed the receiver that the communication had been delayed. In this case, the receiver also delayed the receiving time by Δt. The new latest effective monitoring time t_r' is expressed as Eq. 9:

$$t_r' = \Delta t + t_r = \Delta t + \Delta t' + t_U = t_U' + \Delta t' \tag{9}$$

This equation can be deformed to obtain Eq. 10:

$$t_r' - t_U' = \Delta t' \tag{10}$$

Therefore, even if the communication is delayed due to the network fluctuation of the sender, the receiver can still receive the envelope successfully. If the network fluctuation of the receiver causes the node not to receive the envelope within its lifetime, it can be solved by the mail server mentioned before.

Tamper Resistance. The premise of information tampering is that the attacker intercepts the packets sent by the sender, otherwise the receiver will receive the real message and fake message at the same time, which will cause the suspicion of the normal node. In the proposed model, it is assumed that there are n nodes in the network, and the envelope sent by the sender only passes to m nodes in the first round of broadcast. The probability of an attacker with k nodes successfully intercepting the envelope is:

$$P_{n,m}^k = \frac{C_k^m}{C_n^m} = \frac{k(k-1)(k-2)\ldots(k-m+1)}{n \times (n-1) \times (n-2) \ldots \times (n-m+1)} \tag{11}$$

If there are 1000 nodes in the network and 50 nodes are selected as the receiver in the first round of broadcast, the probability of attackers with up to 500 nodes successfully intercepting the envelope and making it unable to transmit to the normal node is only 2×10^{-6}. In fact, it is difficult for attackers to have so many nodes, and with the continuous expansion of the network scale, the number of normal nodes is increasing, so it is almost impossible for attackers to successfully intercept the envelope.

Resistance to Detection. In the time-based covert communication, data packet transmission interval or the number of packets sent per unit time are often used to transmit information [22]. For example, packet sending interval {5 s, 10 s, 25 s, 30 s} or the number of packets sent every five minutes {5, 10, 15, 20} corresponds to information {00, 01, 10, 11}. In order to reduce the error, neither the sending intervals nor the number of packets can be too small and close. This will lead to a significant change in channel traffic once covert communication occurs, which will increase the risk of covert communication being detected.

In the proposed model, spatial carriers are used to embed information instead of time attributes. After analyzing the normal sending interval of packets in the network, once the PoW is calculated, the user can set the sending time of the packet. As long as the sending time interval of the covert communication envelope is kept at the level of normal communication, the fluctuation of the number of packets can be reduced. In addition, whisper protocol encourages users to send noisy letters at regular intervals to make it more difficult for attackers to crack envelopes. Therefore, when in normal communication, the sender node sends many noisy letters every few minutes, and reduces the number of noisy letters in the process of covert communication to ensure that the total number of envelopes sent over a period of time is stable. This can help covert communication avoid detection effectively.

5.2 Comparative Test of Information Embedding and Transmission Efficiency

For covert communication methods that use data packet transmission time intervals, the content of the information transmitted each time is actually a binary segment corresponding to the time interval. Suppose that the interval sequence {5 s, 10 s, 15 s, 20 s} corresponds to the binary sequence {00, 01, 10, 11}. The sender sends a data packet with an interval of 5 s to pass the 2-bit information "00". Therefore, the efficiency of information embedding in this way is 1 bit per character.

In the proposed method, if the payload is a completely random character string and contains only lowercase English letters, the amount of information can be calculated by Eq. 12 as $\log_2 26$ bits per character.

$$H(x) = \sum_{i=0}^{n} p(x_i) \log_2 \frac{1}{p(x_i)} \tag{12}$$

Where H is the amount of information contained in each symbol of the source, $p(x_i)$ is the probability of the i-th character appearing in the carrier, and n is the type of character in the effective carrier. Therefore, the relationship between the amount of information and the number of characters in the hidden communication method based on the time interval and the proposed method is shown in Fig. 6:

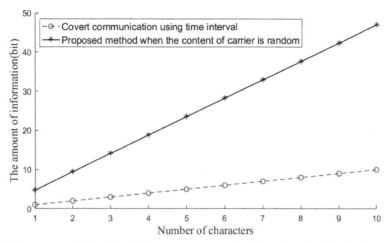

Fig. 6. The amount of information in the covert communication method based on the time interval and the proposed method

It can be seen that the amount of information in the proposed method is almost five times that of the covert communication method using time interval. In the covert communication method using time interval, 2^{α} time series are needed to map binary segments of α bits. For example, 2^2 time series are needed to correspond to binary fragments $\{00, 01, 10, 11\}$. In order to reduce the time required, the time series is assumed to start from 1 s. In this case, if α bits binary is transmitted each time, the time T_{α} required to transmit information with a length of 10 bytes is calculated by Eq. 13:

$$T\alpha = \frac{2^{\alpha} + 1}{2} \times \frac{8 \times 10}{\alpha} = 40\frac{2^{\alpha} + 1}{\alpha} \tag{13}$$

To facilitate comparison, the average time of each communication in the proposed method is set to the same as the time-interval based method which is equal to $\frac{2^{\alpha}+1}{2}$, and the time T_{α}' required for the proposed method to transmit 10 bytes of message is:

$$T_{\alpha}' = \frac{2^{\alpha} + 1}{2} \times \frac{10}{\alpha / \log_2 26} \tag{14}$$

In this case, the relationship between the time required for the two methods to transmit 10 bytes of information and the length of information transmitted each time is shown in Fig. 7:

It can be clearly seen from the above figure that the proposed method requires less time to transmit information than the time-based method, and the gap between the two methods is increasing. In fact, the carrier information of the proposed method has a larger information capacity, which is not limited to lowercase English letters. The payload often contains dozens or even hundreds of bytes of information, which can be used to embed messages. When the information in the payload is long enough, the sender can even send all the information in one envelope. The proposed method at this time only requires the time for one communication to finish the covert communication. In this case,

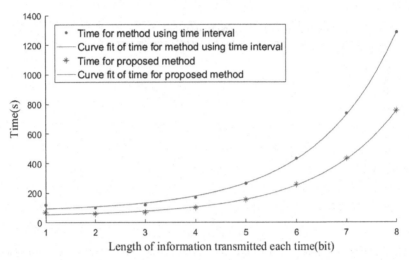

Fig. 7. Time for the covert communication method based on the time interval and the proposed method to transfer 10-byte information

assuming that the average time for one communication is β, the time required for the covert communication method using time interval which transmits α bits of information each time to transfer γ bytes of message is $\frac{8\gamma\beta}{\alpha}$ times the time required by the proposed method. Therefore, the proposed method has higher information transmission efficiency.

6   Conclusion

Based on the covert communication model under blockchain, this paper designs a new covert communication model suitable for Ethereum. It combines the whisper protocol and transmits information in the form of envelope. First, the parties of communication interact with each other on the topics and keys required for covert communication. Second, the sender encrypts the information to be transferred with interacted key and generates a payload as a carrier of the message. Thirdly, the node matches the encrypted message with the payload, encrypts and expands the generated index arrays as padding, and forms data together with the payload. Fourth, the sender forms an envelope with data and other augmentations such as topic and broadcasts the envelope to Ethereum. After filtering out the envelope by topic, the receiver node decrypts it using the corresponding key. Finally, the receiver obtains the index from the decrypted padding and restores the original message in combination with the payload.

This paper proposes a new type of covert communication model for Ethereum, and proves that it has the characteristics of anti-interference, anti-tampering, anti-detection and has higher information embedding and transmission efficiency than time-based covert communication. In the future, how to apply this model to smart contracts and deploy it to DAPP is our research focus.

Acknowledgements. This work is sponsored by the Natural Science Foundation of Heilongjiang Province of China under Grant No. LC2016024. Natural Science Foundation of the Jiangsu Higher

Education Institutions Grant No. 17KJB520044 and Six Talent Peaks Project in Jiangsu Province No. XYDXX-108.

References

1. Krutz, E.C.R.D.: Hiding in plain sight: steganography and the art of covert communication. Indiana, Canada (2016)
2. Archibald, R., Ghosal, D.: A covert timing channel based on fountain codes. In: 2012 IEEE 11th International Conference on Trust, Security and Privacy in Computing and Communications, pp. 970–977 (2012)
3. Backs, P., Wendzel, S., Keller, J.: Dynamic routing in covert channel overlays based on control protocols. In: 2012 International Conference for Internet Technology and Secured Transactions, pp. 32–39 (2012)
4. Nakamoto S.: Bitcoin: A Peer-to-Peer Electronic Cash System. Manubot (2019)
5. Swan, M.: Blockchain: blueprint for a new economy (2015)
6. Wood, G.: Ethereum: a secure decentralised generalised transaction ledger. Ethereum Proj. Yellow Pap. 151(2014), 1–32 (2014)
7. Pilkington, M.: Blockchain technology: principles and applications. In: Research Handbook on Digital Transformations. Edward Elgar Publishing (2016)
8. Roy, R., Changder, S.: Steganography with projection aided payload dimension reduction and reconstruction for military covert communication. Int. J. Comput. Appl. 139(3), 32–37 (2016)
9. Paruchuri, V., Durresi, A., Chellappan, S.: Secure communications over hybrid military networks (2008)
10. Rhoads, G.B., Lofgren, N.E., Patterson, P.R.: Geographic information systems using digital watermarks, US (2007)
11. Stach, J., Brundage, T.J.: Digital watermarks for unmanned vehicle navigation, US (2008)
12. Keshav, S.R., Dheerendra, S.T.: Digital watermarking schemes for authorization against copying or piracy of color images. Indian J. Comput. Sci. Eng. 1(4), 295–300 (2010)
13. Raval, K., Zafar, S.: Digital watermarking with copyright authentication for image communication. In: 2013 International Conference on Intelligent Systems and Signal Processing (ISSP). IEEE (2013)
14. Kim, J., Won, S., Zeng, W., Park, S.: Copyright protection of vector map using digital watermarking in the spatial domain. In: International Conference on Digital Content. IEEE (2011)
15. Berk, V., Giani, A., Cybenko, G., Hanover, N.: Detection of covert channel encoding in network packet delays. Rapport technique TR536, de lUniversité de Dartmouth, 19 (2005)
16. Chen, Q.Y., Liu, Z.H., et al.: Application of error-correction code in steganographic arithmetic. Commun. Technol. 81(4), 78–79 (2003)
17. Tian, H., Zhou, K., Huang, Y., Feng, D., Liu, J.: A covert communication model based on least significant bits steganography in voice over IP. In: International Conference for Young Computer Scientists. IEEE Computer Society (2008)
18. Wu, Z.J.: Covert communication based on the voip system. In: Information Hiding in Speech Signals for Secure Communication, vol. 13, no. 2, pp. 127–142 (2015)
19. Ahn, J., Lee, H., Kim, Y., Chung, J., Lee, S. K.: Machine learning based dolphin whistle transceiver for bio-inspired underwater covert communication. Oceans MTS/IEEE Seattle. IEEE (2019)
20. Liu, S., Qiao, G., Ismail, A.: Covert underwater acoustic communication using dolphin sounds. J. Acoust. Soc. Am. 133(4), EL300 (2013)

21. Xu, G., et al.: Am i eclipsed? A smart detector of eclipse attacks for Ethereum. Comput. Secur. **88**, 101604 (2019)
22. Tikhomirov, S., Voskresenskaya, E., Ivanitskiy, I., Takhaviev, R., Alexandrov, Y.: SmartCheck: static analysis of Ethereum smart contracts. In: The 1st International Workshop. IEEE Computer Society (2018)
23. Sellke, S.H., Wang, C.C., Bagchi, S., Shroff, N.B.: TCP/IP timing channels: theory to implementation. In: 28th IEEE International Conference on Computer Communications, Joint Conference of the IEEE Computer and Communications Societies, INFOCOM 2009, 19–25 April 2009. IEEE, Rio de Janeiro (2009)

Cyber-Physical Systems Security

A New Face Detection Framework Based on Adaptive Cascaded Network

Gangting Liu[1], Jianhong Lin[2(✉)], Yifan Ding[2], Shihong Yang[2], and Yunhua Xu[2]

[1] China Mobile Communications Guangdong Co., Ltd., Guangzhou 510623, China
[2] Zhejiang Ponshine Information Technology Co., Ltd., Hangzhou 311100, China
linjianhong@ponshine.com

Abstract. In recent years, face detection and face recognition were widely used in fields like identity-verification system, security system and financial system. However, some of the real-time face detection tasks are still challenging due to the overflowed computational cost of a discriminative system. To resolve this issue, we propose a cascaded network based on CNN, which has simple architecture and light-weighted parameters. The network consists of three stages and operates with a image pyramid (same image with different resolutions), the first stage quickly discriminates faces (proposals) from background, and the other two stage specifically evaluate those proposals to determinate whether a proposal contains face or not. We also address an adaptive method that dynamically drops those redundant proposal regions generated in first stage to avoid prohibitive computation. The model we trained runs at 180 ms for processing a single image on CPU, and keeps an accuracy around 98.4%.

Keywords: Face detection · Multi-resolution · Adaptive · Cascade architecture · Convolutional neural network

1 Introduction

Face recognition is an important research field in computer vision and has become increasingly important due to its wide use in commercial and security applications. Like protecting mobile or computers from unauthorized access for instance. Usually, face recognition goes through two stages. The first stage is locating, including face detection and face alignment. The second stage is face classification. Face detection, in first stage, is of great significance in practical use [1]. and has achieved lots of mile-stones so far [2]. However, there are still challenges we facing: (1) Human face has strong variability due to factors as face shape, expression, skin color, lighting, occlusion, unconstrained environment, etc. (2) The face can be anywhere or any size in a detection space. The first challenge expects the detection algorithm being robust under complex circumstances;the second challenge requests the algorithm being capable to find as many faces as possible in a single image or video scene.

This work was supported by 2019 Industrial Internet Innovation Development Project-Industrial Internet Network Security Public Service Platform Project (TC190H3WN).

© Springer Nature Singapore Pte Ltd. 2020
G. Xu et al. (Eds.): FCS 2020, CCIS 1286, pp. 233–242, 2020.
https://doi.org/10.1007/978-981-15-9739-8_18

In recent face detection algorithms, Bianhang [3] improved Adaboost to effectively reduce the number of weak classifiers, and promote the computational efficiency. Kalinovskii et al. [4] proposed a compact convolutional neural network being able to handle real-time detection of ultra-high-definition video streams on mobile platforms. In addition to the cascade structure, Mathias et al. [5–7] introduced the deformable part model (DPM) for face detection, and achieved remarkable performance. However, the they often require high computational costs and expensive annotations for preparing the training data set. Sun et al. [8] improved fast RCNN by combining multiple strategies, and was ranked as one of the best models in terms of ROC curves of the published methods on the FDDB benchmark. Shi et al. [9] proposed a novel rotation-invariant face detector, that is, a progressive calibration network (PCN) to better distinguish faces from non-faces. Liu et al. [10] proposed a single-shot detector for multiple categories, which is faster and more accurate than YOLO.

In past few years, ways of extracting facial features have evolved from those artificial methods like Haar-Like, Viola and Jones [11], SURF [12] to automatic ones like deep convolution neural network. The cascade CNN is one of the deep convolution neural network based methods. The cascade cnn network normally consists of three light-weighted modules, means less BFLOPs in a single forward pass, and is able to distinguish those frames with faces from non-face frames in very early stage [13, 14], so that the detection speed is relatively fast. Dong et al. [15] used normal distribution to track the difference between current and previous network and dynamically choose the most relevant image blocks for training, which reduced the model complexity and enhanced robustness; the detector proposed by Zhou et al. [16] can process UHD video streams in real time. The cascade cnn framework of Chen et al. [17] can reliably estimate the apparent age of faces in images; Diba et al. [18] introduced a model consists of two cascade stages and three end-to-end pipeline, which improved the performance of the model in target detection, classification and positioning. Zhang et al. [19] introduced a dual-stream context CNN architecture, using a data routing mechanism to optimize layer parameters, reduce computation, and improve detection accuracy; Ranjan et al. [20] proposed HyperFace, which can perform face detection, key point positioning, pose estimation and gender recognition in the mean-time.

To reduce computational burden, [21] performs face detection directly on the complete feature maps. [22] detects abnormally distributed samples based on uncertainty prediction and the L2-normed features. To promote robustness of face detection, [23] builds deep learning network by cascading multiple features, from edge features, contour features, local features to semantic features, and advances layer by layer. A global detector and several local detectors are trained simultaneously, and are suitable for dense face detection [24]. [25] proposes a face detector (DSFD) based on Faster R-CNN being capable of detecting different scaled faces. [26] devises an efficient anchor-based cascade framework greatly improves the detection accuracy while it still runs in comparable speed. In terms of distance calculation, [27] proves that Euclidean-L3P is more efficient than Manhattan-L3P and Chebyshev-L3P in terms of computational overhead through performance analysis.

In order to get a faster face detection system, we proposed a modified cascade CNN network. Like mentioned above, the network consists of three stages. And we made some significant adaptions including adding an adaptive selection mechanism to eliminate redundant proposals. The details will be described in Sect. 3.1.

2 Related Parameters

2.1 Intersection Over Union

Intersection over Union (IoU) calculates the ratio of the intersection and union of "predicted border" and "true border". IoU = (A ∩ B)/(A ∪ B) (Fig. 1).

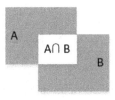

Fig. 1. Schematic diagram of IoU.

2.2 Non-maximum Suppression

In the cascade cnn network, we use the first stage to generate proposals for face detection. We applying sliding windows on input image and processing it through convolution neural network to get a confidence score map. Each pixel in the score map indicates whether the corresponding receptive field of the pixel in the original image contains a face or not. But usually, the neighborhood windows would have very similar scores, and will leads to redundant proposal regions. And it will be cumbersome if all those proposals were evaluated by the rest of the network. Thus we use a Non-maximum Suppression (NMS) strategy to filter the candidate boxes (proposals) based on some criteria: assume we have a proposal boxes list A, and a list of filtered proposals B, 1) figure out the proposal T with the highest confidence score in A 2) calculate the IOU of this proposal T with all the others in A, If IoU is greater than a threshold, the proposal compared with T will be removed from A. 3) move the proposal T from A to B. 3) Then select the one with the highest score from the remaining proposals in A, 4) repeat the process until all the proposal boxes in A were transported to B.

2.3 Classifier and Loss Function

In this paper, we use confidence map and bounding regression map to train our CNN network.

(a) We use cross entropy as the loss function,

$$H(y) = -\sum_i y_i' * \log(y_i) \tag{1}$$

where y_i represents the predicted label and $y_i^{'}$ represents the true classification corresponding to the image.

Using the cross entropy function as the loss function to find the deviation between the predicted value and the true value, the smaller the cross entropy value, the closer the two probability distributions are. Reverse derivation of $H(y)$ to obtain partial differentiation of the weights of each layer to update the weights.

(b) For the regression problem of detection boxes, Euclidean Loss is used as the loss function of border regression. The Euclidean distance loss function refers to the mean squared distance between the predicted value and the true value of the sample, that is, the root mean square error. The formula for this loss function is shown in Eq. 2 as

$$L = \frac{1}{2n} \sum_{n=1}^{N} \left\| \hat{y}_n - y_n \right\|_2^2 \tag{2}$$

where $\hat{y}_n$ represents the predicted value, and the meaning is shown in Eq. 3 as,

$$\hat{y} = (x_1^{det}, y_1^{det}, w^{det}, h^{det}) \tag{3}$$

where y_n represents the true value and its formula is shown in Eq. 4 as,

$$y = (x_1^{gt}, y_1^{gt}, w^{gt}, h^{gt}) \tag{4}$$

where $(x_1^{det}, y_1^{det}, w^{det}, h^{det})$ represents the coordinates, height and width of the upper left corner of the predicted face detection box. $(x_1^{gt}, y_1^{gt}, w^{gt}, h^{gt})$ represents the coordinates, height and width of the upper left corner of the true face detection box.

3 Cascade CNN

3.1 Adaptive Scale Selection Mechanism

In order to accurately differentiate all the possible faces from background in an given image P with resolution $(H \times W)$, we usually zoomed the original image in/out with as many scales as possible to compose an image pyramid, which is the input of the cascade cnn network. However, too many zoom in/out scales may also cause problem like redundant proposals for unnecessary NMS calculation, Sect. 2.2. To address this problem, an adaptive online scale selection mechanism was designed. Let the zooming scales be S, $S = [S_1, S_2 \dots S_n]$. Using scale S_i in that set, we can turn the original image P into a image P_i with resolution $(H_i \times W_i)$, where $H_i = H * S_i$, $W_i = W * S_i$. The P_i is then evaluated by 12-Net, described in 3.2, to get a confidence score map C_i. We count all the scores greater than threshold 0.9 in C_i to get a number N_i, which is the number of proposals found in current image P_i. A ratio T_i can be measured as $T_i = N_i/\sqrt{H_i \times W_i}$. We calculate the n images in sequence to get all the T_i, $i \in [1, \dots, n]$, and use them to form a sorted list from high value to low value. The only top N elements in list and the proposals found in correlated P_i will be concerned. All the other proposals that are not generated by top N P_i will be dropped.

To find the most appropriate top number N, we make experiment to figure out the relation between top number, time consumption and detection coverage shown in Table 1. To make a balance between detection speed and coverage percentage, we choose N to be 3.

Table 1. Relation of top number and coverage of found face.

# of top selected	Time consumption (ms)	Face detection coverage
1	30	92.1%
3	70	98.9%
5	150	98.9%
7	430	99.0%

3.2 12-Net

Figure 2 shows brief structure of 12-Net, which is the first stage of cascade cnn network. The sliding window size is $12 \times 12 \times 3(HEIGHT \times WIDTH \times CHANNEL)$. After processing the sliding window through three convolution blocks, each consists of a convolution layer, a relu layer and a max pool layer, we can get a feature map with size $1 \times 1 \times 32$. Using that feature map and two different convolution kernels with size 1×1. The final outputs of a sliding window are $1 \times 1 \times 2$ confidence map and $1 \times 1 \times 4$ bounding regression map, the former indicates whether there was a face in the a sliding window, the latter shows how the window should be adjusted in size and orientation to obtain a proposal region if it contains face. More generally, when the input image size is $H \times W$, we can get a bounding regression map with size $H_o \times W_o \times 4$ and confidence map with size $H_o \times W_o \times 2$, where $H_o = (H - 2)/2 - 4, W_o = (W - 2)/2 - 4$. Once confidence maps and regression maps are known, we will use adaptive scale selection mechanism discussed in 3.1 and NMS described in 2.2 to get all the possible proposals, which will be analyzed by 24-Net to get more specified classification results and accurate bounding boxes. The purpose of the 12-Net is scanning the image pyramid, to rapidly locate as many proposal regions as possible.

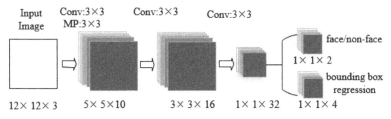

Fig. 2. 12-net structure.

3.3 24-Net

All possible proposal regions calculated in 3.2 will be processed through 24-net, which has structure shown in Fig. 3 and is the second stage of cascade CNN network. Before computation, the size of every single proposal is re-sized to $24 \times 24 \times 3$. By passing through 24-net we will get a 1×2D confidence array indicates whether there is a face in candidate and a 1×4D bounding info array used to restrain the margin of a bounding box for every candidate. In this stage, those candidates with confidence score greater than 0.9 and have NMS less than 0.7 with all the other candidates will be retained as list of candidates L_s for calculation of the finally stage.

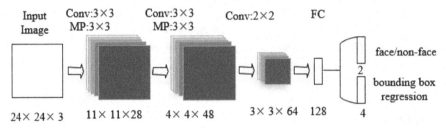

Fig. 3. 24-net structure.

3.4 48-Net

The third stage of the cascade cnn net work is a 48-net, which has structure shown in Fig. 4. The size of the candidate in L_s will be re-sized to $48 \times 48 \times 3$. Similarly, the output of 48 net consists of a 1×2D confidence array and a 1×4D bounding info array. In this stage NMS and confidence threshold have been set to 0.7 and 0.95. Only the candidates satisfy both of the conditions will be taken into account as final outputs.

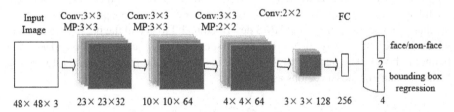

Fig. 4. 48-net structure.

4 Experiments

4.1 Dataset

Custom dataset: we collected 12880 images from the Internet, and generated 159230 candidate boxes, of which the ratio of face boxes to non-face boxes is 1:4, the ratio of training samples to valid samples is 8:2. 40%, 30% and 30% of the training samples were used to train 12-net, 24-net and 48-net. The data set distribution is shown in Table 2.

Table 2. Data set category distribution.

	Training set	Test set	Total
Face box	25477	6369	31846
Non-face box	101907	25477	127384
Total	127384	31846	159230

4.2 Experimental Results and Analysis

The experiment is based on CPU Intel(R) Core (TM) i5-7200U 2.50 GHz + memory 8 GB + graphics card NVIDIA GeForce 920MX for training and test data. Training on a custom data set, the cascade classification accuracy rate is 99.7%, and the cascade regression r-square is 0.94. Figure 5 shows part of the detection results on the custom data set.

Fig. 5. Part of the detection results of the cascade network.

4.3 Runtime Efficiency

Under the premise of all calculations processed by a CPU, tests are carried out by taking Fig. 6 as an example. It was found experimentally, the detection time of the model with the adaptive image scale selection mechanism introduced is 180 ms while the detection time of a cascade network without adaptive selection mechanism is 570 ms. we can get better performance with less runtime and high accuracy (the result is shown in Table 3. For fair comparison, we use the same data for both methods).

Table 3. Comparison of speed and accuracy.

Model	# of Top selected	Time consumption (ms)	Accuracy
Cascade network	–	570	93.2%
SIFT	–	360	95.1%
Our model	1	30	94.4%
	3	70	96.9%
	5	150	98.4%

Fig. 6. Detection image after adaptive adjustment.

5　Conclusions

This paper proposes an adaptive scale selection in cascaded CNN network for fast and accurate face detection. Firstly, evaluate the input image pyramid at a low resolution and adaptively choose the appropriate proposal areas. Secondly, process those proposal areas with higher resolution for more accurate detection. The algorithm is very robust against complex backgrounds. Our follow-up research object will be promoting the performance of face detection on low-quality images.

References

1. Wang, Y.M.: Research on Face Detection Matching and Recognition Algorithm. Harbin Institute of Technology, Harbin (2018). (in Chinese)
2. Wang, C.J.: Research on Face Detection Method Based on Fully Convolutional Neural Network. Xiamen University, Xiamen (2018). (in Chinese)
3. Bian, H.: Research on Face Detection and Recognition Algorithm. Beijing University Of Technology, Beijing (2017). (in Chinese)
4. Kalinovskii, I., Spitsyn, V.: Compact convolutional neural network cascade for face detection. Comput. Sci. **2**(2), 110 (2015)
5. Mathias, M., Benenson, R., Pedersoli, M., Van Gool, L.: Face detection without bells and whistles. In: Fleet, D., Pajdla, T., Schiele, B., Tuytelaars, T. (eds.) ECCV 2014. LNCS, vol. 8692, pp. 720–735. Springer, Cham (2014). https://doi.org/10.1007/978-3-319-10593-2_47
6. Yan, J., Lei, Z., Wen, L., Li, S.: The fastest deformable part model for object detection. In: IEEE Conference on Computer Vision and Pattern Recognition, pp. 2497–2504 (2014)
7. Zhu, X., Ramanan, D.: Face detection, pose estimation, and landmark localization in the wild. In: IEEE Conference on Computer Vision and Pattern Recognition, pp. 2879–2886 (2012)
8. Sun, X., Wu, P., Hoi, S.C.H.: Face detection using deep learning: an improved faster RCNN approach. Neurocomputing **299**, 42–50 (2018)
9. Shi, X., Shan, S., Kan, M., et al.: Real-time rotation-invariant face detection with progressive calibration networks (2018)
10. Liu, W., et al.: SSD: single shot multibox detector. In: Leibe, B., Matas, J., Sebe, N., Welling, M. (eds.) ECCV 2016. LNCS, vol. 9905, pp. 21–37. Springer, Cham (2016). https://doi.org/10.1007/978-3-319-46448-0_2
11. Viola, P., Jones, M.J.: Robust real-time face detection. Int. J. Comput. Vis. **57**(2), 137–154 (2004)
12. Li, J., Wang, T., Zhang, Y.: Face detection using surf cascade. In: 2011 IEEE International Conference on Computer Vision Workshops (ICCV Workshops), pp. 2183–2190. IEEE (2011)
13. Li, H., Lin, Z., Shen, X., et al.: A convolutional neural network cascade for face detection. In: 2015 IEEE Conference on Computer Vision and Pattern Recognition (CVPR). IEEE (2015)
14. Yang, Z,. Nevatia, R.: A multi-scale cascade fully convolutional network face detector (2016)
15. Dong, Y., Wu, Y.: Adaptive cascade deep convolutional neural networks for face alignment. Comput. Stand. Interfaces **42**, 105–112 (2015)
16. Zhou, E., Fan, H., Cao, Z., et al.: Extensive facial landmark localization with coarse-to-fine convolutional network cascade. In: Proceedings of the 2013 IEEE International Conference on Computer Vision Workshops. IEEE (2013)
17. Chen, J.C., Kumar, A., Ranjan, R., et al.: A cascaded convolutional neural network for age estimation of unconstrained faces. In: 2016 IEEE 8th International Conference on Biometrics Theory, Applications and Systems (BTAS). IEEE (2016)
18. Diba, A., Sharma, V., Pazandeh, A., et al.: Weakly supervised cascaded convolutional networks (2017)
19. Zhang, K., Zhang, Z., Wang, H., et al.: Detecting faces using inside cascaded contextual CNN. In: 2017 IEEE International Conference on Computer Vision (ICCV). IEEE (2017)
20. Ranjan, R., Patel, V.M., Chellappa, R.: HyperFace: a deep multi-task learning framework for face detection, landmark localization, pose estimation, and gender recognition (2019)
21. Guo, G., Wang, H., Yan, Y., et al.: A fast face detection method via convolutional neural network (2018)
22. Yu, C., Zhu, X., Lei, Z., et al.: Out-of-distribution detection for reliable face recognition. IEEE Signal Process. Lett. **PP**(99), 1 (2020)

23. Dong, Z., et al.: Face detection in security monitoring based on artificial intelligence video retrieval technology. IEEE Access **8**, 62433–63421 (2020)
24. Ke, X., Li, J., Guo, W.: Dense small face detection based on regional cascade multi-scale method. IET Image Proc. **13**(14), 2796–2804 (2019)
25. Face detection with different scales based on faster R-CNN. IEEE Trans. Cybern. 1–12 (2019)
26. Yu, B., Tao, D.: Anchor cascade for efficient face detection. IEEE Trans. Image Process. **28**(5), 2490–2501 (2019)
27. Han, S., et al.: Location privacy-preserving distance computation for spatial crowdsourcing. IEEE Internet Things J. **7**, 1 (2020)

Atomic Cross-Chain Swap-Based Decentralized Management System in Vehicular Networks

Chenkai Tan[1(✉)], Zhengjun Jing[1,2], and Shaoyi Bei[1]

[1] School of Vehicle and Traffic Engineering, Jiangsu University of Technology,
Changzhou 213001, China
tanchenkai@163.com
[2] School of Computer Engineering, Jiangsu University of Technology,
Changzhou 213001, China

Abstract. Blockchain-based applications in VANETs could improve traffic safety and efficiency by dynamic key management and distributed trust management. However, the limited performance of a single blockchain cannot meet the needs of large-scale applications in VANETs. In this paper, to enhance the scalability of blockchain-based applications in VANETs, we design a decentralized management system based on an atomic cross-chain swap. Furthermore, we introduce public-key encryption with keyword search in the system to protect user privacy and increase cross-chain efficiency. Analysis and simulations are conducted to evaluate the scheme in terms of security and performance, and the results show that the scheme can realize cross-chain swap while protecting vehicle privacy.

Keywords: VANETs · Blockchain · Cross-chain protocol · Value transfer

1 Introduction

In recent years, the technology of connected autonomous vehicles (CAVs) has increased rapidly. Vehicle ad hoc networks (VANETs), which improve road safety and transport efficiency for CAVs, can provide internet access services for CAVs. For example, safety VANETs applications warn CAVs of an imminent collision; dissemination of emergency messages gives additional time for a driver to respond and avoid accidents [1]. Traffic-responsive VANETs applications adaptively control traffic lights (flow) to improve traffic efficiency [11].

Sjöberg et al. [20] based on the initial deployment strategy IEEE 802.11p, created a four-stage deployment strategy in VANETs. In the initial phase, CAVs receive status information of neighbouring CAVs (by VANETs). In the sensing driving phase, CAVs gain additional information from the various on-board sensors in neighbouring CAVs. In the cooperative driving phase, trajectories

© Springer Nature Singapore Pte Ltd. 2020
G. Xu et al. (Eds.): FCS 2020, CCIS 1286, pp. 243–253, 2020.
https://doi.org/10.1007/978-981-15-9739-8_19

or planned manoeuvres are shared by CAVs, in which neighbour CAVs optimize their decisions and procedures. In the last phase, VANETs can exchange and synchronize driving trajectories to achieve optimal driving patterns. With the increased phase of VANETs, CAVs need to evaluate the trustworthiness of other CAVs to determine the reliability of received messages. Additionally, how to safely and efficiently communicate between CAVs is also a critical problem. Blockchain-based VANETs schemes not only provide security and privacy of key transfers [10] but also realize decentralized trust management [24].

Blockchain is a synchronized and distributed ledger formed by distributed data storage, P2Ps, encryption algorithms, consensus mechanisms, and smart contracts. The deployment of VANETs has led researchers to address many attacks and challenges [4,21], which may be solved through blockchain. However, the throughput of blockchain is limited by network bandwidth and consensus algorithms. For example, the current maximum throughput of EOS [9] is approximately 4,000 transactions per second (TPS), and transaction throughput on Ethereum [22] is 10–30 TPS. CAVs will reach 2 billion within the next 10–20 years [7]. The limited performance of a single blockchain cannot meet the needs of large-scale CAVs applications. Therefore, hybrid blockchain based on geographical location is a scalable method in VANETs.

In this paper, we introduce blockchain-based dynamic key management [10] and blockchain-based trust management [24] in VANETs. We developed an atomic cross-chain swap-based management system (ACSMS) to enhance the scalability of these schemes. Furthermore, we introduce public-key encryption with keyword search (PKES) in the system. By PKES, only the keyword is encrypted and provided in the blockchain, and encrypted documents are saved in the cloud. Thus, in PKES, a malicious searcher cannot learn CAVs' real identity by analyzing blockchain data. On the other hand, cross-chain transmission encrypted keyword is efficient than transmission encrypted documents. Therefore, ACSMS can enhance interoperability between chains and increase blockchain-based applications scalability.

The rest of the paper is organized as follows. In Sect. 2, we introduce related works and their deficiencies. Section 3 describes the ACSMS in detail. Section 4 shows the analysis and simulation of this scheme. Then, we conclude the paper and identify future directions in Sect. 5.

2   Related Work

2.1   Blockchain-Based Key Management in VANETs

Blockchain-based key management(BKM) is a precondition and guarantee of other blockchain-based applications in VANETs. Lei et al. [10] proposed BKM to simplify the distributed key management in heterogeneous VANET security domains. To support key updates and revocation in VANETs, Ma et al. [13] proposed a lightweight BKM protocol that can resist collusion attacks, public-key tampering attacks, DoS attacks, and internal attacks. Shrestha et al. [19] also used BKM to disseminate information in VANETs. Besides, they partitioned maps into regions based on the density of CAVs in a country, and each region manages and maintains independent blockchains. However, [19] does not support cross-chain technology for BKM.

BKM store and transmit user keys using a peer-to-peer decentralized system, which does not rely on Trust Authority (TA) and resists a single point of failure. Figure 1 shows the basic structure of the blockchain [16]. The block header includes the version, hash of the previous block (PreHash), Merkle root, timestamp (TS), difficulty target, and nonce. The Merkle root is the root hash of the Merkle hash tree (MHT). If the blockchain uses the proof of work (PoW) consensus protocol, the difficulty target is calculated by the miners as Hash (PreHash | TS | MerkleRoot | nonce) < difficulty target. After a miner finds a nonce and broadcast block in the network, if this block belongs to the parent blockchain, other nodes acknowledge the validity of this block.

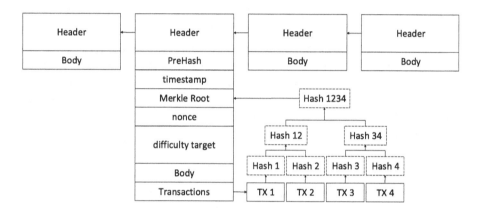

Fig. 1. Blockchain structure

2.2 Blockchain-Based Trust Management in VANETs

Blockchain-based trust management (BTM) in VANETs maintains a consistent database in the roadside unit (RSU). BTM can evaluate the trustworthiness of CAVs by generating a rating for CAVs. Yang et al. [24] proposed a decentralized BTM to determine the trustworthiness of received messages. Lu et al. [12] offered an anonymous BTM to break the linkability between public keys and real identities. Unlike Yang et al., they used TA to issue public-key certificates and record messages transparently in blockchains that were provided by RSUs. Furthermore, Zhao et al. [25] used software-defined vehicular networks (SDVNs) to associate resource allocation with the trust value of CAVs. Zhao et al. adopted a PBFT&PoS based BTM, which can support cross-chain technology. However, [25] cannot support cross-chain technology for PoW-based BKM and BTM. Thus, this paper uses atomic cross-chain swap and PKES to realize cross-chain technology for PoW-based BKM and BTM.

CAVs upload the rating to the nearest RSU periodically. The RSU calculates the trust value of the CAVs and adds the corresponding blocks into the distributed blockchain. Zhao et al. classifies CAVs into three roles to calculate trust value: privilege vehicles(C_1), enterprise vehicles(C_2), and individual vehicles(C_3). The initial credibility of CAVs are $\gamma_1(C_1)$, $\gamma_2(C_2)$, and $\gamma_3(C_3)$. CAVs separate received messages into M groups $\{g_1, g_2, ..., g_M\}$. Therefore, the tuple of specific messages [12,24,25] (W_k^j) is defined as

$$W_k^j = (d_k^j, t_k^j, OC_P), P \in (C_1, C_2, C_3) \tag{1}$$

The receiver CAVs obtain message k from CAV j. d_k^j is the distance between CAV j and the event location. t_k^j is the message received time of CAV j, and OC_P is the confidence value that CAV j hold. By W_k^j, the credibility of specific messages (c_k^j [25]) is calculated as

$$c_k^j = \eta e^{-\alpha d_k^j} + (1 - \eta)m_k^j + OC_p \tag{2}$$

η is the balance coefficient between timeliness and distance. α is a parameter to control the bound, and m_k^j is used to judge the message from the same CAVs at different times. CAVs obtain message credibility set $C = \{C_1, C_2, ..., C_M\}$, where vector C_M represents the credibility for event e_M and contains $\{C_1^M, C_2^M, ..., C_j^M\}$. After the CAVs calculate credibility of event e_M using Bayesian Inference [18] as (3), the receiver CAVs upload the calculation results to the RSU.

$$P(e|C_M) = \frac{P(e) \cdot P(C_M|e)}{P(C_M)} = \frac{P(e) \cdot \prod_{k=1}^{j} P(C_k^M|e)}{P(e) \cdot \prod_{k=1}^{j} P(C_k^M|e) + P(\bar{e}) \cdot \prod_{k=1}^{j} P(C_k^M|\bar{e})} \tag{3}$$

$\bar{e}$ is the complementary event of e. $P(e) \in [0,1]$ is the prior probability of event e. Compared $P(e|C_M)$ with a threshold(Thr), the receiver regards this event as true or false and generates ratings (i.e., +1 or −1) on messages. Once RSUs get conflicting ratings about event e_M, RSUs use weighted aggregation (3) to obtain the offset of trust value $\in [0, 1]$. m and n are the numbers of positive(+1) and negative(−1) rating. $F(\cdot)$ controls the sensitivity to the minority group of ratings.

$$o_M = \frac{F(m) \cdot m + F(n) \cdot n}{m + n} \tag{4}$$

3   Atomic Cross-Chain Swap in VANETs

3.1   System Model

As shown in Fig. 2, ACSMS includes three types of entities: CAVs, RSU and TA.

CAVs: Each CAV is equipped with an on-board unit (OBU) and a hardware security module (HSM) that provide wireless communication and security storage. Additionally, every CAV has a blockchain account that contains keywords

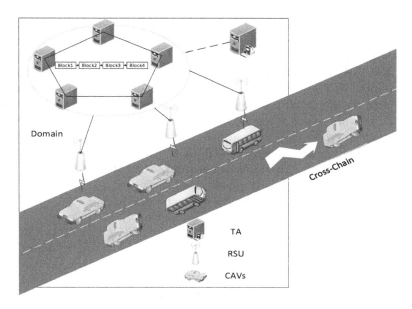

Fig. 2. System model

and a trust value. CAVs can realize cross-chain token transfer between different accounts through atomic cross-chain swaps.

RSU: The RSU, as a node in the blockchain, creates new blocks to maintain the ACSMS. The RSU constructs a P2P network and PoW-based blockchain in different regions, which is partitioned based on the density of CAVs in a country.

TA: The TA's main task includes an identity review of new CAVs and the recovery identity of CAVs. The TA constructs a blockchain to record the identity of new CAVs. After the initial registration, CAVs can transfer tokens into the nearby blockchain, and use blockchain-based Apps.

3.2   ACSMS Overview

The ACSMS consists of two subsystems: BTM [10,13,19] and BKM [12,24]. We classify ACSMS into three stages: system setup stage, blockchain stage, and cross-chain stage.

System Setup Stage. First, the TA and the RSU generate the algorithms and parameters. Second, country maps are partitioned into regions based on the CAV density. Third, the TAs and the RSUs in different regions create a new blockchain and initialize a smart contract. Finally, administrators apply blockchain-based trust management and blockchain-based key management to these blockchains.

Blockchain Stage. The TA registers users into the blockchain to ensure user legitimacy, which is described as follows:

(1) The TA registers CAVs through relevant CAV information such as licence plate, driver's licence, phone number, and driver's ID. The TA has public-private key pairs (Pub_{TA}, Pri_{TA}).

(2) CAVs create a public-private key pair (Pub_k, Pri_k) through elliptic curve cryptography [8]. Then, CAVs encrypt relevant CAV information and outsource the data to the cloud. The TA and the CAVs can use the public-key encryption with keyword search scheme (PKES) [6] to find encrypted data. PKES are realized as follow:

$$\text{Encryption}_{data} = \text{Encrypt}(Pub_k, \text{data}),$$
$$\text{Trapdoor}_{data} = \text{Trapdoor}(\text{Keyword, AES, SHA256}),$$
$$\text{Encryption}_{data} = \text{Trapdoor}_{data} + \text{Encryption}_{data}$$
$$b = \text{test}(\text{Keyword, Encryption}_{data}) = \{0,1\}.$$

If b is true, users find encrypted data in the cloud.

(3) The TA, according to the roles of CAVs, transfer token into the original blockchain account. Blockchain transactions require parties to have public-private key pairs to sign signatures [3]. $C_T = \text{Encrypt}(Pub_k, \text{Sig}(\text{keyword}+\text{index}, TA))$ is recorded in this account. The relevant CAV information can be found by decrypting C_T. Important evidence of CAVs can be outsourced to the cloud in the same way. After TA registers the user, the user can use blockchain applications [10,12,13,19,24] to authenticate other CAVs and calculate the trust value of other CAVs.

Cross-Chain Stage. Atomic cross-chain swaps [5,14,15,17] are considered to be a trust-free, Byzantine-hardened form of distributed coordination task without involving any centralized intermediary. The atomicity property refers to all-or-nothing. There mainly including 4 categories cross-chain technologies [23] include multi-center witness, side chain, hash locking and distributed private key control. Hash locking has an important advantage: realize fair cross-chain exchange in original blockchain without the participation of trusted third parties. In our scheme, an atomic cross-chain swap between two homogeneous blockchains is known as a hash locking atomic swap. The ACSMS exchange encrypted keyword(C_T) and confidence value(OC_P) cross multiple blockchains by atomic cross-chain swaps. The atomic swap protocol guarantees cross-chain swaps, protocol punishment of malicious parties, and no coalition has an incentive to deviate from the contract. Figure 3 illustrates the cross-chain model as an asset transfer.

The atomic swaps protocol problem in ACSMS is as follows. Assume Alice has an account (Pub_k, Pri_k) and holds an asset $Z(\{ C_{T_1}, C_{T_2},...,C_{T_n} \}, OC_p)$ in blockchain A. $\{ C_{T_1}, C_{T_2},...,C_{T_n} \}$ is a special message. OC_p is specification ethereum token [2] that ensures different types of tokens will uniformly perform in any place. Alice creates a new account (Pub_{k_1}, Pri_{k_1}) in blockchain B that does not hold assets. Alice wants to trade asset Z to blockchain B. Therefore,

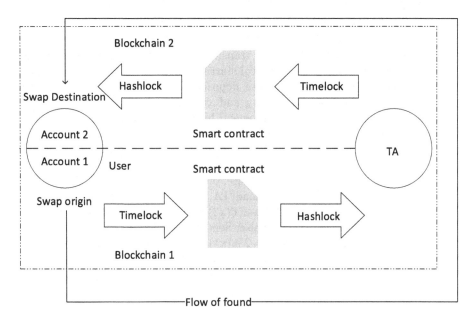

Fig. 3. Atomic cross-chain swap

Alice, blockchain A, and blockchain B need to arrange a three-way swap: Alice transfers asset Z to blockchain A, blockchain A transfers asset Z to blockchain B, and blockchain B transfers asset Z to Alice's new account (Pub_{k_1}, Pri_{k_1}). Based on transfer necessary conditions, assets are transferred through irrevocable smart contracts, which are published on the blockchain. Alice places her asset in escrow by publishing a smart contract with hash-lock(h) and time-lock(t, hashed time-lock contract(HDFS) [15]). Nodes in blockchain B send the secret(s); if cartographic hash function $H(s) = h$, then the smart contract transfers assets from blockchain A to blockchain B. If secret(s) is incorrect or fails to produce before t, then the escrowed assets are sent back to Alice.

If RSU node has token in two blockchains, CAVs can deal with RSU as the above problem. Another option is matched cross-chain token from different CAVs. Compared with the RSU and other CAVs, CAVs deal with the TA more securely [13] and efficient, which can resist man-in-the-middle attacks. Therefore, the three-way swap becomes a two-way swap: Alice transfers asset Z to the TA account (Blockchain A), and the TA account (Blockchain B) transfers asset Z to Alice's new account. The steps of the atomic swap can be referenced as escrow agent [14,15,17]. Smart contract technology realizes the atomic cross-chain swap by a computer program. The following algorithm causes an atomic cross-chain swap to occur for ACSMS.

Atomic swap for ACSMS {
        depositA, depositB : bool ; hash1, hash2 : int256;
    //the deposit function allows user transfer of the asset to the smart contract
        uint startA, startB; // protocol starting time
        initialize {deposited A := False; deposited B := False; hash1=hash2=0;}
        depositA{if sender = $account_A$ and asset=Z:
                Then depositA:=True and hash = h1 and startA = time()}
        depositB{if sender = TA and asset=Z :
                Then depositB:=True and hash = h2 and startB = time()}
        Finalise{if depositA and depositB and now < startA + $time_{set}$:
                Then { depositA:= False; depositB:= False
                send($account_B$,Z), send(TA,Z)}}
        cancelA{if (depositA and sha-256(x2) = h2) or now > startA + $time_{set}$
                then {depositA:=False; Send($account_A$,Z)}}
        cancelB{if (depositB and sha-256(x1) = h1) or now > startB + $time_{set}$
                then {depositB:=False; Send(TA,Z)}}
    }

4   Analysis and Simulations

4.1   Security Analysis

Blockchain stage security: The user can use blockchain applications [10, 12, 13, 19, 24] to authenticate other CAVs and calculate the trust value of other CAVs. These researches ensure the blockchain stage security, including certificate security, broadcast message security, CAVs privacy, RSU node decentralization, tamper-proofing blockchain records, and a consistent trust database. By comparing with the above blockchain-based schemes, as shown in the Table 1, we can see that the proposed system can provide cross-chain function, which enhances the scalability of blockchain-based applications in vehicular networks. Compared with [25], ACSMS support cross-chain stage security and compatible with PoW-based applications in VANETs.

    Cross-chain stage security:

    CAVs privacy: CAVs' relevant information and CAVs' evidence are encrypted and outsourced to the cloud. Then, the encrypted keyword in the blockchain will not reveal identifying information. Additionally, TA cooperation with the user can decrypt keyword to find relevant information and CAVs evidence.

4.2   Performance Evaluation

We use an Intel Core 2.6 GHz processor to evaluate the computational cost. The distance between CAVs is a uniform distribution between 5 and 100 m. One CAVs we assume send 1–2 transactions to blockchain per unit minute. We create two PoW-based blockchains in truffle and ganache with Solidity language to test the ACSMS. Z({ C_{T_1}, C_{T_2},...,C_{T_n}), OC_p }) is calculated in the setup stage and blockchain stage, which have no impact on cross-chain efficiency. There are two

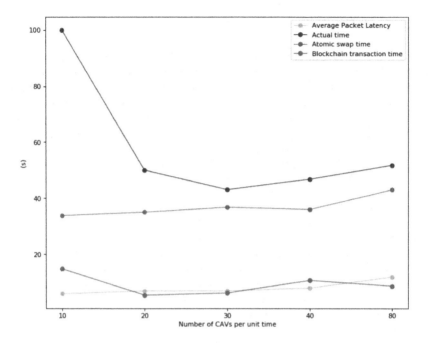

Fig. 4. Average delay over different number of CAVs

Table 1. Comparison of Related Work.

Feature	[10]	[19]	[13]	[24]	[25]	[12]	ACSMS
Work Introduction	BKM	BKM	BKM	BTM	BTM	BKM&BTM	BKM&BTM
Consensus algorithm	PoW	PoW	PoW	PoW	PBFT&PoS	PoW	PoW
Smart Contract	No	No	Yes	No	Yes	No	Yes
No TA	Yes	Yes	No	Yes	No	No	No
Authentication	Yes	Yes	Yes	Yes	Yes	Yes	Yes
Key agreement	Yes	Yes	Yes	No	Yes	No	Yes
Cross-Chain	No	No	No	No	Yes	No	Yes
Cross-Chain Privacy	No	No	No	No	No	No	Yes

end-to-end packet transmission latencies in the atomic swap. The specification ERC-20 token defines a set of rules that allow different tokens to interact seamlessly. We use ERC20 to represent OC_p, which allows other CAVs to find a user's balance and transfer funds from one user to another with proper authorization.

Considering the block generation rate PoW-based blockchain, the throughput of each blockchain is limited (adjustment through difficulty target). The latency increases with the increase in CAVs [13] per unit time. We simulate 1,000 cross-chain swaps with different latencies. Figure 4 shows the average delay over the different number of CAVs per unit time.

5 Conclusion

Aiming at enhancing interoperability between chains and increasing blockchain-based application scalability, this paper proposes the atomic cross-chain swap-based decentralized management system (ACSMS). ACSMS is proposed for key management and trust management for VANETs. ACSMS ensures the security of the cross-chain stage through PKES-based cloud storage and atomic cross-chain swap. Finally, we analyze scheme's security and evaluate the performance, showing that the system has good security and efficiency. Our future work aims at permissioned blockchain-based (Hyperledger Fabric) application in VANETs.

References

1. Fadilah, S.I., Shariff, A.R.M., Hilmi, M.N.M.: Crash avoidance based periodic safety message dissemination protocol for vehicular ad hoc network. In: 2019 IEEE 89th Vehicular Technology Conference (VTC2019-Spring), pp. 1–7. IEEE (2019)
2. Fenu, G., Marchesi, L., Marchesi, M., Tonelli, R.: The ICO phenomenon and its relationships with Ethereum smart contract environment. In: 2018 International Workshop on Blockchain Oriented Software Engineering (IWBOSE), pp. 26–32. IEEE (2018)
3. Gura, N., Patel, A., Wander, A., Eberle, H., Shantz, S.C.: Comparing elliptic curve cryptography and RSA on 8-bit CPUs. In: Joye, M., Quisquater, J.-J. (eds.) CHES 2004. LNCS, vol. 3156, pp. 119–132. Springer, Heidelberg (2004). https://doi.org/10.1007/978-3-540-28632-5_9
4. Hasrouny, H., Samhat, A.E., Bassil, C., Laouiti, A.: VANet security challenges and solutions: a survey. Veh. Commun. **7**, 7–20 (2017)
5. Herlihy, M.: Atomic cross-chain swaps. In: Proceedings of the 2018 ACM Symposium on Principles of Distributed Computing, pp. 245–254 (2018)
6. Jeong, I.R., Kwon, J.O., Hong, D., Lee, D.H.: Constructing PEKS schemes secure against keyword guessing attacks is possible? Comput. Commun. **32**(2), 394–396 (2009)
7. Jia, D., et al.: A survey on platoon-based vehicular cyber-physical systems. IEEE commun. Surv. Tutor. **18**(1), 263–284 (2015)
8. Johnson, D., Menezes, A., Vanstone, S.: The elliptic curve digital signature algorithm (ECDSA). Int. J. Inf. Secur. **1**(1), 36–63 (2001)
9. Larimer, D.: DPOS consensus algorithm-the missing white paper (2017)
10. Lei, A., Cruickshank, H., Cao, Y., Asuquo, P., Ogah, C.P.A., Sun, Z.: Blockchain-based dynamic key management for heterogeneous intelligent transportation systems. IEEE Internet Things J. **4**(6), 1832–1843 (2017)
11. Liu, J., Li, J., Zhang, L., Dai, F., Zhang, Y., Meng, X., Shen, J.: Secure intelligent traffic light control using fog computing. Future Gener. Comput. Syst. **78**, 817–824 (2018)
12. Lu, Z., Wang, Q., Qu, G., Liu, Z.: BARS: a blockchain-based anonymous reputation system for trust management in VANETs. In: 2018 17th IEEE International Conference On Trust, Security And Privacy In Computing And Communications/12th IEEE International Conference On Big Data Science And Engineering (TrustCom/BigDataSE), pp. 98–103. IEEE (2018)

13. Ma, Z., Zhang, J., Guo, Y., Liu, Y., Liu, X., He, W.: An efficient decentralized key management mechanism for VANET with blockchain. IEEE Trans. Veh. Technol. (2020)
14. van der Meyden, R.: On the specification and verification of atomic swap smart contracts. In: 2019 IEEE International Conference on Blockchain and Cryptocurrency (ICBC), pp. 176–179. IEEE (2019)
15. Miraz, M.H., Donald, D.C.: Atomic cross-chain swaps: development, trajectory and potential of non-monetary digital token swap facilities. Ann. Emerg. Technol. Comput. (AETiC) **3** (2019)
16. Nakamoto, S.: Bitcoin: A peer-to-peer electronic cash system. Technical report, Manubot (2019)
17. Nolan, T.: Alt chains and atomic transfers. In: Bitcoin Forum, May 2013
18. Raya, M., Papadimitratos, P., Gligor, V.D., Hubaux, J.P.: On data-centric trust establishment in ephemeral ad hoc networks. In: IEEE INFOCOM 2008-The 27th Conference on Computer Communications, pp. 1238–1246. IEEE (2008)
19. Shrestha, R., Bajracharya, R., Nam, S.Y.: Blockchain-based message dissemination in VANET. In: 2018 IEEE 3rd International Conference on Computing, Communication and Security (ICCCS), pp. 161–166. IEEE (2018)
20. Sjoberg, K., Andres, P., Buburuzan, T., Brakemeier, A.: Cooperative intelligent transport systems in Europe: current deployment status and outlook. IEEE Veh. Technol. Mag. **12**(2), 89–97 (2017)
21. Vaibhav, A., Shukla, D., Das, S., Sahana, S., Johri, P.: Security challenges, authentication, application and trust models for vehicular ad hoc network-a survey. IJ Wirel. Microw. Technol. **3**, 36–48 (2017)
22. Wood, G., et al.: Ethereum: a secure decentralised generalised transaction ledger. Ethereum Proj. Yellow Pap. **151**(2014), 1–32 (2014)
23. Yang, D., Long, C., Xu, H., Peng, S.: A review on scalability of blockchain. In: Proceedings of the 2020 The 2nd International Conference on Blockchain Technology, pp. 1–6 (2020)
24. Yang, Z., Yang, K., Lei, L., Zheng, K., Leung, V.C.: Blockchain-based decentralized trust management in vehicular networks. IEEE Internet Things J. **6**(2), 1495–1505 (2018)
25. Zhao, N., Wu, H., Zhao, X.: Consortium blockchain-based secure software defined vehicular network. Mob. Netw. Appl. **25**(1), 314–327 (2020)

Detecting Intrusions in Railway Signal Safety Data Networks with DBSCAN-ARIMA

Yuming Fan[1], Kaiyuan Tian[2], Xuyu Wang[3], Zhuo Lv[4], and Jian Wang[2(✉)]

[1] CRRC ACADEMY, Beijing 100039, China
fanyuming@crrcgc.cc
[2] School of Electronics and Information Engineering, Beijing Jiaotong University,
Beijing 100044, China
{17120273,wangj}@bjtu.edu.cn
[3] Signal & Communication Research Institute, China Academy of Railway Sciences
Corporation Limited, Beijing 100081, China
wang2710@126.com
[4] State Grid Henan Electric Power Research Institute, Zhengzhou 450052, China
zhuanzhuan2325@sina.com

Abstract. Railway Signal Safety Data Network (SSDN) is an important part of railway signal system, and its security directly affects the safety of passengers. However, with the continuous improvement of information and automation level of Chinese Train Control System Level 3 (CTCS-3), there are more and more interfaces between SSDN and other systems. The data sharing among the equipment has become increasingly frequent, the content has become increasingly abundant, and the data volume has become increasingly larger. While the operation efficiency of SSDN is improved, its information security risk increased too. In order to secure SSDN, the intrusions should be detected accurately. In this work, we proposed an intrusion detection method based on DBSCAN-ARIMA. In the algorithm, K-Average Nearest Neighbor (KANN) algorithm is used to determine the parameters of Density-Based Spatial Clustering of Applications with Noise (DBSCAN) clustering algorithm, calibrate the clustering results, and then improve the TPR by Multiple Seasonal Autoregressive Integrated Moving Average (ARIMA) model. The experimental results show that our method outperforms other existing methods, with an average TPR of 98.9501%.

Keywords: Signal Safety Data Network · IDS · DBSCAN · KANN · ARIMA

1 Introduction

Railway signal system is an important infrastructure in China. Its security is directly related to the safety of the lives of the majority of passengers. Therefore, it has a very high safety requirements [22]. China's high-speed railway signal

© Springer Nature Singapore Pte Ltd. 2020
G. Xu et al. (Eds.): FCS 2020, CCIS 1286, pp. 254–270, 2020.
https://doi.org/10.1007/978-981-15-9739-8_20

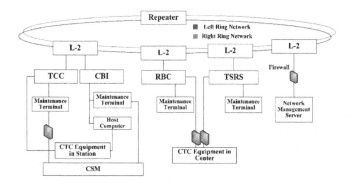

Fig. 1. Basic structure of SSDN.

system (CTCS-3) is mainly composed of four parts [6], which are Centralized Traffic control (CTC), Signal Safety Data Network (SSDN), signal centralized monitoring network and Global System for Mobile Communications for Railway (GSM-R). Among them, SSDN is the "control nerve center" of the railway signal system, aiming to ensure the reliable transmission of information between the station and relay station equipment and between the station and the central signal equipment, and its safety will directly affect the traffic safety [5]. The basic structure of SSDN is shown in Fig. 1.

SSDN is composed of redundant double ring network through the industrial Ethernet switch equipment of each station and relay station, which is physically isolated. The connection between switches adopts special single-mode optical fiber [8], which is used for information transmission of computer-based interlocking (CBI), train control center (TCC), temporary speed restriction server (TSRS), raid block center (RBC) and network management system. A large number of them adopt special operating system and hardware, and follow the fail-safe principle. The key equipment is redundant structure. If the current system fails, it will switch to another system immediately.

In 2003, the railway signal system in the eastern part of the United States was attacked by Sobig virus, which infected the computer system of CSX headquarters, shut down the signal and dispatching systems, resulting in the shutdown of the high-speed loop line in the District of Columbia. On January 14, 2008, a hacker attacked the tram system in Lodz City, Poland, resulting in derailment of four carriages and injury of 12 passengers. On January 17, 2011, the screen of the integrated management system at the headquarters in Tokyo was displayed, and the management system controlling the timetable, signal and line switch machine was abnormal. For safety reasons, the five Shinkansen lines took shutdown measures. In 2016, the ticket price system of San Francisco Metro suffered blackmail virus, which affected the normal operation of the billing system.

Intrusion detection based on clustering method is one of the main research directions of Intrusion Detection System (IDS) at present. Clustering method establishes a normal behavior pattern, when the behavior to be detected does not meet the pattern, it will be judged as an attack behavior, so its advantage is that it can detect unknown attacks through outliers. Leonid et al. put forward two hypotheses of clustering method applied to intrusion detection [11]: (1) normal data occupies the vast majority of all data; (2) abnormal data has obvious features, and the value deviates from the normal range greatly. The traffic in SSDN has the features of relatively fixed communication content and strong periodicity, and the majority of normal traffic occurs when the intrusion occurs. Therefore, to meet the above assumptions, clustering method can be used for intrusion detection.

However, because the traditional clustering method may fall into the local optimal solution, only using the clustering method will produce problems such as low true positive rate (TPR) and high false positive rate (FPR). Therefore, Wang et al. proposed a clustering time series detection model. Using the K-means average time series method, it is verified that the model can obtain higher TPR and lower FPR compared with the single clustering model [13].

Wang et al. [15] propose a novel framework of autonomic intrusion detection that fulfills online and adaptive intrusion detection over unlabeled HTTP traffic streams in computer networks. The test results show that the autonomic model achieves better results compared to adaptive Sequential Karhunen-Loeve method and static AP as well as three other static anomaly detection methods, namely k-NN, PCA and SVM. In addition, there are also network based intrusion detection [14,17], botnet detection [18], mobile malicious application detection and analysis [9,16,19–21].

In the industrial control network, communication between equipments often have strong periodicity. Therefore, Ramin Sadre proposed a method to detect abnormal traffic by using the periodicity of traffic [1]. This method uses the periodicity of traffic in SCADA to detect abnormal traffic, including DoS attacks, vulnerability scanning, etc. Zare et al. proposed to use ARIMA model in network traffic prediction and anomaly detection, and decompose the traffic into two parts: following certain rules and predictable changes and unpredictable anomalies composed of mutations [10]. Through ARIMA analysis and modeling, traffic anomalies can be detected and identified. Therefore, based on the idea of clustering and periodic detection of time series, this paper proposes an intrusion detection method of SSDN based on DBSCAN-ARIMA.

In this paper, we make the following contributions: (1) DBSCAN is used to cluster intrusion flow and calibrate the categories. (2) Using ARIMA to compensate for low TPR of single DBSCAN algorithm. (3) DBSCAN-ARIMA intrusion detection method is designed.

2   Flow Features of SSDN

2.1   Representation of Flow Feature

It is important to extract appropriate flow features in SSDN. KDD99 data set [12] is the IDS test data set established by Lincon Laboratory of MIT, and it is an authoritative data set in IDS field at present. Based on KDD99 data set, this paper classifies the flow features into four types, including basic data features, data content features, traffic sliding window features and time sliding window features, with a total of 4 types and 28 features, as shown in Table 1.

If there are n flow types may appear in SSDN (B is the type of network congestion flow, with $n - 1$ types in total, normal communication type is defined as N). For the j-th flow of the i-th flow type $FLOW_{i,j}$, we define its flow feature value as $S_{i,j(1)}$, $S_{i,j(2)}$, ..., $S_{i,j(m)}$, class FLAG is 1, 2, ..., $n - 1$, n. Then the final flow feature vector is shown in Table 2.

2.2 Feature Standardization

There are four types in features S_1 to S_{28}: string type, integer type, floating point type and Boolean type, so it is necessary to standardize the feature. Among them, the MAC address and IP address of the equipment in SSDN are continuous, so the feature MAC address and IP address take the last two decimal digits, which are converted into integer type and used as the features S_1 to S_4; UDP protocol record 0, TCP protocol record 1, ICMP protocol record 2 give the features S_7; SF is normal mark 0, and 10 error types give the features S_8 in turn. Then the non-Boolean feature in features S_1 to S_{28} are normalized:

$$S_{m_{normal}} = \frac{S_m - S_{m_{normal}}}{S_{m_{max}} - S_{m_{min}}} \tag{1}$$

2.3 Feature Dimension Reduction

In this paper, 28 features are selected for the flow of SSDN, but manual feature selection may cause poor independence between features, and even reduce the accuracy of classification in some cases. Therefore, in this section, principal component analysis (PCA) will be used to reduce the dimension of flow features of SSDN, and select the features suitable for DBSCAN method.

PCA method is a more commonly used dimension reduction method in machine learning at present. Through linear mapping, high-dimensional features are mapped to low-dimensional space and replaced by fewer features, while the mapped features have weak correlation and most of the knowledge of the original high-dimensional features [4].

2.4 Feature Case Analysis

In this paper, the real flow data of two-way communication (UDP) between TSRS and TCC, two-way communication (TCP) between TSRS and adjacent TSRS in the northern part of China are used as two kinds of normal traffic data. The vulnerability scanning flow, virus propagation flow, password dictionary attack flow and special signal device operating system vulnerability attack flow are used as four kinds of intrusion flow data. Intrusion training data set as shown in Table 3.

Table 1. Flow features types of SSDN

	No	Lists	Types	Meaning
Basic Data	S_1	SMAC	STR	Source MAC address
	S_2	DMAC	STR	Destination MAC
	S_3	SIP	STR	Source IP address
	S_4	DIP	STR	Destination IP address
	S_5	SPORT	INT	Source port
	S_6	DPORT	INT	Destination port
	S_7	PTYPE	STR	Protocol type
	S_8	FLAG	STR	Connection OK or wrong status
	S_9	SBYTE	INT	Bytes from source
	S_{10}	DBYTE	INT	Bytes received from source
Data Content	S_{11}	HOT	INT	Access sensitive files
	S_{12}	NFL	INT	Failed logins
	S_{13}	LOGIN	BOOL	Login success or not
	S_{14}	ROOT	BOOL	Get root permission or not
Flow Sliding Window	S_{15}	FC	INT	Number of same source and destination IP packets
	S_{16}	FCSSIP	INT	Number of IP packets of the same origin
	S_{17}	FCSDIP	INT	Number of IP packets of the same destination
	S_{18}	FCSDP	INT	Number of same destination port packets of same origin IP
	S_{19}	FCSSP	INT	Number of same destination IP same origin port packets
	S_{20}	FSIZE	INT	Data size
	S_{21}	FTIME	FLO	Time spent in traffic window
Time Sliding Window	S_{22}	TC	INT	Number of same source and destination IP packets
	S_{23}	TCSSIP	INT	Number of IP packets of the same origin
	S_{24}	TCSDIP	INT	Number of IP packets of the same destination
	S_{25}	TCSDP	INT	Number of same destination port packets of same origin IP
	S_{26}	TCSSP	INT	Number of same destination IP same origin port packets
	S_{27}	TSIZE	INT	Data size
	S_{28}	TFLOW	FLO	Time window traffic size

Table 2. Flow feature vector

	S_1	S_2	...	S_m	Flag
B_1	$S_{1,j}(1)$	$S_{1,j}(2)$	...	$S_{1,j}(m)$	1
B_2	$S_{2,j}(1)$	$S_{2,j}(2)$	...	$S_{2,j}(m)$	2
...	...	...	...	...	...
B_{n-1}	$S_{n-1,j}(1)$	$S_{n-1,j}(2)$	...	$S_{n-1,j}(m)$	$n-1$
N	$S_{n,j}(1)$	$S_{n,j}(2)$	...	$S_{n,j}(m)$	n

The format of the original flow data is PCAP file, which needs to extract features according to the format mentioned above, and standardize and normalize the features. Among them, M = 50, i.e. the first 50 packets of traffic sliding

Table 3. Intrusion training data set

No	Type	Amount	Proportion	Description
1	Normal (UDP)	3761	74.8%	Two-way traffic data between TSRS and TCC in field environment
2	Normal (TCP)	628	12.5%	Two-way traffic data between TSRS and adjacent TSRS in field environment
3	Scanning	223	4.4%	Vulnerability scanning traffic data
4	Virus	95	1.9%	Propagation traffic data of a virus in the test environment
5	Password	235	4.7%	Slow password dictionary attack traffic data
6	Vulnerability	87	1.7%	Special signal device operating system vulnerability attack traffic data

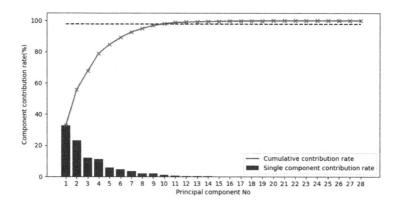

Fig. 2. PCA principal component contribution rate.

window; $t = 0.1$ s, i.e. the first 0.1 s of time sliding window. According to the data preprocessing process described above, after data feature extraction and standardization, PCA method is used to reduce the dimension of features.

As shown in Fig. 2, the value of the black dotted line is 98%, so the feature of the first 10 dimensions can meet 98% of the reconstruction requirements after dimension reduction by PCA.

3   DBSCAN Intrusion Detection Method

3.1   DBSCAN

Density based spatial clustering of applications with noise (DBSCAN) algorithm is a density based clustering algorithm [2]. DBSCAN is defined as a cluster based on the maximum set of certain density points, so it has a great advantage in discovering outliers. At the same time, it can also form clusters of any shape according to the density in the data space. DBSCAN algorithm sets a selected core point as the initial cluster, and the cluster can be expanded by the density around the point. Finally, the cluster can be represented as the largest area including the core point and the boundary point. All the core points and the boundary points in the cluster are connected with each other in density.

If the dataset $X = \{x^{(1)}, x^{(2)}, ..., x^{(N)}\}$, we introduce cluster tag array:

$$m_j = \begin{cases} j(j > 0), & if\ x^{(i)}\ belongs\ to\ the\ j-th\ cluster \\ -1, & if\ x^{(i)}\ is\ an\ outlier \end{cases} \tag{2}$$

By cluster marking array $m_i(i = 1, 2, ..., N)$, DBSCAN algorithm divides data set X into K clusters. Where k is the number of different positive integers in $\{m_i\}_{i=1}^{N}$.

DBSCAN clustering training is applied to the data after dimension reduction of network attack training data set. As shown in Fig. 3(a), the Z-axis coordinates are the number of clusters, and the X and Y-axis coordinates are eps and MinPts respectively. It can be seen that the parameters have a greater impact on the clustering results.

Figure 3(b) shows the contour coefficients corresponding to different parameters. The z-axis coordinates are the contour coefficients after DBSCAN model clustering. The X and Y-axis coordinates are eps and MinPts respectively. It can be seen that the larger the neighborhood radius is, the smaller the core threshold of the neighborhood point is, and the larger the contour coefficient is.

In addition, the noise ratio is also one of the evaluation indexes to measure the clustering effect of DBSCAN. It is defined as the percentage of the noise samples after clustering to the total samples, and the value range is [0, 1]. The closer to 1, the less the noise proportion, the better the clustering effect. As shown in Fig. 3(c), the noise ratio corresponding to different parameters is shown. The z-axis coordinate is the noise ratio, and the X and Y-axis coordinates are eps and MinPts respectively. From the trend, it can be seen that the larger the neighborhood radius is, the greater the core threshold of the neighborhood point is, the smaller the noise ratio is.

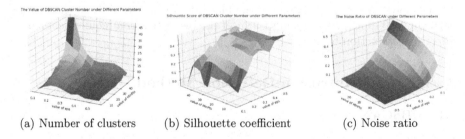

(a) Number of clusters   (b) Silhouette coefficient   (c) Noise ratio

Fig. 3. DBSCAN clustering results

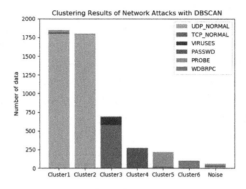

Fig. 4. DBSCAN detection results.

It can be seen that the defects of DBSCAN algorithm is that the final performance of the algorithm is highly dependent on eps and MinPts parameters, and the selection of the two parameters is set when the algorithm is initialized, which has a strong subjectivity. Inappropriate parameter selection will directly affect the final clustering results. Therefore, in this paper, KANN parameter adaptive optimization method is introduced to generate parameter candidate sets of eps and MinPts through data sets, and then select the optimal parameters adaptively. By using the algorithm steps of reference [7], the final cluster number converges to 6. At this time, the maximum value is k = 12, corresponding eps = 0.11439, MinPts = 51.

3.2   Intrusion Detection Instance Based on DBSCAN

The parameters determined by KANN adaptively are input to DBSCAN algorithm, and the final clustering results are shown in Fig. 4. The cluster after DBSCAN clustering is calibrated, the detection threshold θ is set, and the cluster whose data point proportion is greater than θ is defined as normal flow cluster, and the cluster whose data point proportion is less than θ is defined as abnormal cluster. Mark the data before clustering, and compare the calibration after clustering with that before clustering. As θ increases, TPR, FPR and FNR of clustering are shown in Fig. 5. It can be seen that when the detection threshold is higher than 13%, the TPR reaches the highest level, while the FPR and FNR at a low level. At this time, TPR = 93.91%, FPR = 14.74%, FNR = 6.09%. It can be seen that only the calibration clustering method is used for detection, there is a large FPR. This is because it is difficult to distinguish virus and normal TCP flow under DBSCAN algorithm.

Therefore, this paper improves the detection method of homopolymer, and improves the detection threshold to normal threshold θ_{normal} and abnormal threshold $\theta_{abnormal}$. The cluster whose data point ratio is more than θ_{normal} is calibrated as normal cluster, the cluster whose data point ratio is less than $\theta_{abnormal}$ is calibrated as abnormal cluster, and the cluster between them is calibrated as undetermined cluster. In the detection, according to the relationship

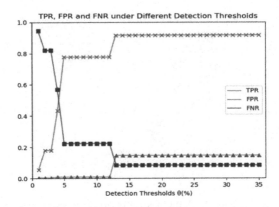

Fig. 5. Accuracy under different detection thresholds.

between the points to be detected and each cluster, the points are divided into a cluster. If the points are divided into the undetermined clusters, they are input into Multiple Seasonal ARIMA.

4   Multiple Seasonal ARIMA

4.1   Model Overview

Multiple Seasonal ARIMA is suitable for the modeling of time series when it is seasonal and there are complex relationships among the periodicity, volatility and trend of time series. If the time series $X_t = \{x_t\}$ is a non-stationary series, the mathematical expression of Multiple Seasonal ARIMA model ARIMA(p, d, q)(P, D, Q)^s is [3]:

$$\phi_p(B)\Phi_p(B^s)\nabla^d\nabla_s^D x_t = \theta_q(B)\Theta_Q(B^s)\varepsilon_t \tag{3}$$

where ∇^n is the n-th order difference calculation, d is the trend difference order, D is the seasonal difference order, s is the seasonal cycle of the sequence, $B^s x_t = x_{t-s}$ is the s-order backward calculation of x_t, $\nabla_s = 1 - B^s$, $\phi_p(B)$ is the p-order polynomial expression of B, $\theta_q(B)$ is the q-order polynomial expression of B, $\Phi_P(B^s)$ is the p-order polynomial expression of B^s, $\Theta_Q(B^s)$ is the q-order polynomial expression of B^s, as shown in the following formula:

$$\begin{aligned}
\phi_p(B) &= 1 - \varphi_1 B - \ldots - \varphi_p B^p \\
\theta_q(B) &= 1 - \theta_1 B - \ldots - \theta_q B^q \\
\Phi_P(B^s) &= 1 - \varphi_1 B^s - \ldots - \varphi_P B^{sP} \\
\Theta_Q(B^s) &= 1 - \theta_1 B^s - \ldots - \theta_Q B^{sQ}
\end{aligned} \tag{4}$$

4.2   Modeling Instance

The data set used in this section is composed of the field data of SSDN from a certain line in the north of China. The feature S_{22}–S_{28} is extracted, in which

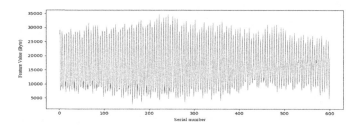

Fig. 6. Time series of feature S_{28}.

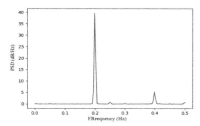

Fig. 7. PSD of TFLOW.

the time sliding window t $= 0.1$ s. The model construction process is described by taking the traffic volume of the feature S_{28} time window (in bytes) as an example. After processing the PCAP traffic file, the feature time series within 60s is obtained, with a total of 600 sequence values, as shown in Fig. 6.

We can see that if the byte is taken as the unit, the sequence value will appear a large order of magnitude, so the natural logarithm is taken for the sequence value, and the newly generated logarithm sequence is recorded as TFLOW. Under the process of building Multiple Seasonal ARIMA:

a. Periodic Test

Power spectral density (PSD) was used to test TFLOW periodically. For the time series TFLOW described above, its power spectral density is shown in Fig. 7. It can be seen that the power spectral density of the sequence has a higher peak value at 0.2 Hz, so it can be considered that the time sequence has a period of 5, which is also consistent with the polling mechanism among the devices of SSDN.

b. Stationarity Test

Because the sequence TFLOW has periodicity and does not have stationarity, it needs to be treated as stationarity. Specifically, it needs to carry out the first-order seasonal difference, taking the period as the difference step, and the step size is taken as 5, but the original sequence obviously does not have the trend, so there is no need to carry out the trend difference, and the sequence after the seasonal difference is recorded as STFLOW. The stability of STFLOW sequence was tested by ADF test. The original hypothesis is that there is unit root, if the value of t statistic is significantly less than the critical statistic value of 1%, 5%

and 10% confidence, and the p value of t statistic (P_Value) is very close to 0, the original hypothesis is rejected, that is, there is no unit root, and the original sequence is stable. Call the adfuller function of stattools module in Python, and the result is as follows:

.adf $= -7.883109046788815$

.pvalue $= 4.6457782953604625e-12$

.critical values: '1%': -3.4378627516320006, '5%': -2.8648563831383322, '10%': -2.568535885040459

Obviously, the operation results meet the conditions of rejecting the original hypothesis, so the sequence STFLOW does not have unit root, and the sequence is stable. At the same time, the parameters $d=0$, $D=1$, $s=5$ of Multiple Seasonal ARIMA can be obtained.

c. Model Order Determination

Considering the combination of parameters (p, q) (P, Q), four combinations of white noise fitting residuals are selected here, and AIC criterion functions are calculated respectively. The results are shown in Table 4. Through the comparison of AIC functions, it can be concluded that the least value of AIC function is the combination of parameters $p=3$, $q=1$, $P=0$, $Q=0$, which is the optimal parameter. Combined with the 1 order 5 step seasonal difference, the final model is $ARIMA(3, 0, 1)(0, 1, 0)^5$.

Table 4. AIC value under different parameters

(P,Q)	P$=0$, Q$=0$	P$=0$, Q$=0$	P$=1$, Q$=0$	P$=1$, Q$=1$
(p,q)	p$=3$, q$=0$	p$=3$, q$=1$	p$=3$, q$=1$	p$=2$, q$=1$
AIC	-1412.10	-1426.06	-1419.53	-1419.79

d. Parameter Estimation

The parameters of the sequence are obtained from the least square estimation. The expression of the final model is as follows:

$$(1 + 0.2064B + 0.1384B^2 + 0.1151B^3)\nabla_5^1 x_t = (1 + 0.3034B)\varepsilon_t \qquad (5)$$

Where $\nabla_s = 1 - B^s$, B is the backward operator, x_t is the TFLOW sequence value, ε_t is the expected white noise sequence of 0.

e. Prediction and Evaluation

TFLOW is obtained from the logarithm of the original sequence value, so if the original sequence is predicted, TFLOW needs to be restored. After exponential reduction, the feature values of time window traffic in the last 2 periods (i.e. 10 future time series) are predicted (the results are rounded), as shown in Fig. 8. The residual and error rate of the predicted value and the true value are shown in Table 5. The residual value is the difference between the predicted value and the

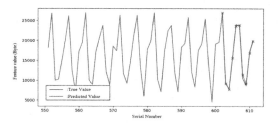

Fig. 8. Prediction results.

Table 5. Comparison between predicted value and true value

No	1	2	3	4	5	6	7	8	9	10
Ture Value	26876	9468	7764	15708	24024	23768	10524	8700	17148	20064
Predicted Value	26931	9233	7716	15718	23696	23920	11509	9229	16884	19801
Residual	55	235	48	10	328	152	985	529	264	263
Error Rate	0.33%	1.42%	0.29%	0.00%	1.98%	0.92%	5.96%	3.20%	1.60%	1.59%

true value, and the error rate is the ratio of the residual absolute value and the sample mean value. The average error rate of the prediction is only 1.73%, which proves that the Multiple Seasonal ARIMA has a good effect on the prediction of the original series.

5 DBSCAN-ARIMA Intrusion Detection Method

5.1 Theory of Detection Method

When a single DBSCAN is used for intrusion detection, the feature distribution of some kind of intrusion data is very similar to that of normal data, and the FPR and FNR of DBSCAN algorithm will be significantly increased. Therefore, based on the above algorithms, this section proposes an intrusion detection method based on DBSCAN-ARIMA. Its core idea is to give full play to the advantages of DBSCAN clustering algorithm in outlier detection, train in unmarked data sets, label clusters as normal, abnormal or pending clusters by setting the threshold values of normal and abnormal clusters. On the other hand, input the feature history of data into ARIMA to get the prediction features. If the current data is classified as the pending cluster by DBSCAN detection, further detection will be carried out according to the error between ARIMA's feature prediction value and the real value of the current feature. If the error exceeds the threshold value of the feature, it will be determined as abnormal. The overall flow of the method is shown in Fig. 9.

a. Data Preprocessing

The input is the original flow collected in SSDN. The purpose is to get the feature information, including feature extraction, feature standardization and feature normalization.

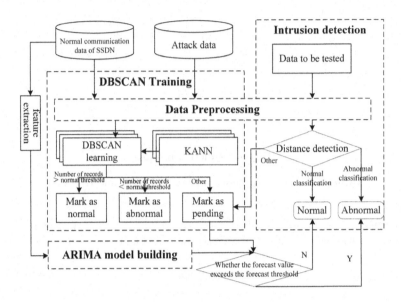

Fig. 9. Prediction results.

b. DBSCAN Training
The optimal parameters are adaptively obtained by KANN and input to DBSCAN algorithm to obtain K clusters. Set θ_{normal} threshold, $\theta_{abnormal}$ as the abnormal threshold, the function $num(C_i)$ represents the number of points in the cluster C_i, and n is the total amount of data, then the steps of cluster calibration can be described as: Traverse K clusters, if $num(C_i) > n \times \theta_{normal}$, C_i is calibrated as normal flow cluster, if $num(C_i) < n \times \theta_{abnormal}$, C_i is calibrated as abnormal cluster, otherwise, Ci is calibrated as undetermined cluster.

c. ARIMA Model Building
Input the features of data points arranged in time order, train each feature sequence from S_{22} to S_{28} for a single time, and finally output the fitting model of each feature sequence.

d. Intrusion Detection

- Extract the features of flow x_{n+1}, and standardize the features.
- Determine the ownership of this point. If there is a point x_j in the original data set, making $dist(x_j, x_{n+1}) < eps$, then the ownership of the calibration point x_{n+1} is the cluster C_{x_j} of the point x_j; if there is no point satisfying the conditions, then the calibration point x_{n+1} is the outlier.
- The standard class of cluster C_{x_j} in DBSCAN learning module, x_{n+1} is normal traffic if it is normal traffic cluster, x_{n+1} is abnormal if it is abnormal cluster or x_{n+1} is outlier, x_{n+1} is pending if it is undetermined cluster, then the feature $w_{n+1,22}, w_{n+1,23}, ..., w_{n+1,28}$ of x_{n+1} is taken as the real value and compared with the predicted value of each matching model in ARIMA model

building module. The condition of normal flow determined by comparison is that all features meet the following requirements:

$$\frac{w_{n+1,i} - w_i^{'}}{ave_i} < \theta_{predict} \tag{6}$$

Otherwise, x_{n+1} is judged as normal. Among them, $w_i^{'}$ is the prediction value of the i-th Multiple Seasonal ARIMA for the current time, ave_i is the sample mean value of the i-th feature, and $\theta_{predict}$ is the prediction threshold.

5.2 Performance of Detection Method

In this paper, according to the analysis of the previous calculation example, the parameter $\theta_{normal} = 25\%$, $\theta_{abnormal} = 8\%$, $\theta_{predict} = 10\%$ is set, and the DBSCAN model and ARIMA model adopt the parameters obtained from the previous calculation example. The data in the test data set is sorted by time series, and each data is marked to determine whether it is an intrusion. The composition of the test data set is shown in Table 6. The detection results of the three data sets are shown in Fig. 10, where the value of the ordinate, 1 indicates that the point is marked as normal, −1 indicates that the point is marked as abnormal, the vertical black dotted line indicates that the data of the point is judged incorrectly, the blue point indicates that only DBSCAN division is used

Table 6. Composition of testing data set

Data set	Composition	Number
1	Normal	1421
	Vulnerability	127
2	Normal	1421
	Virus	127
3	Normal	1421
	DoS	127

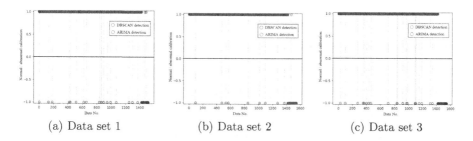

(a) Data set 1   (b) Data set 2   (c) Data set 3

Fig. 10. Data set calibration category (Color figure online)

Table 7. Performance of DBSCAN-ARIMA detection

Data set	TPR	FPR	FNR
1	97.6378%	1.2667%	2.3622%
2	99.2126%	0.6334%	0.7874%
3	100%	1.4778%	0
Ave.	98.9501%	1.1260%	1.0499%

to draw the conclusion, the red point indicates that the current point is divided into pending clusters by DBSCAN.

Based on the detection data of three data sets, the detection performance of DBSCAN-ARIMA method can be calculated, as shown in Table 7. Finally, the average TPR of the three data sets reached 98.9501%. Therefore, in the face of different kinds of network attacks, intrusion detection based on DBSCAN-ARIMA shows high TPR and low FPR and FNR, which proves the effectiveness of this method.

5.3   Comparison with Existing Methods

In reference [11], clustering and time series model are used to detect network attacks, and the method is verified by the DoS attack and probe attack data in KDD99 data set. Among them, K-means algorithm is used in clustering method, and mean prediction is used in time series model. When the clustering radius is $R = 7$, the TPR of DoS attack is the highest, 94.3%; when $R = 10$, the TPR of probe attack is the highest, 94.5%. The comparison of the detection performance between the DBSCAN-ARIMA model proposed in this paper and the existing detection methods is shown in Table 8. It can be seen that in the study of clustering time series detection model, the TPR of existing methods is 0.49% higher than that of single DBSCAN method, but the average TPR of DBSCAN-ARIMA method proposed in this paper for network attacks is 98.95%, which is greatly improved compared with the existing K-means average time series method, with the average TPR increased by 4.55%. FPR and FNR is greatly reduced, so the effectiveness of the intrusion detection method proposed in this paper is proved.

Table 8. Comparison between proposed method and existing method

Detection method	Average TPR	Average FPR	Average FNR
DBSCAN	93.91%	14.74%	6.09%
Kmeans- mean time serier	94.4%	3.3%	5.6%
DBSCAN-ARIMA	98.95%	1.13%	1.05%

6   Conclusion

This paper proposes an intrusion detection method based on DBSCAN-ARIMA. Firstly, this paper defines the features of network traffic of SSDN, then expounds the principle and process of DBSCAN algorithm. Based on the defect that DBSCAN parameters can not be selected automatically, we introduces KANN method to optimize parameters, then expounds the principle of Multiple Seasonal ARIMA, and puts forward DBSCAN-ARIMA intrusion detection method for SSDN. After performance analysis, the average TPR of the proposed method is 98.9501%, which is 4.55% higher than the existing method, and the FPR is 1.13%. It can well detect the intrusion originated from SSDN, and make contribution to the information security of SSDN.

Acknowledgements. The work reported in this paper was supported by China State Railway Group Co., Ltd., under Grant 2016X008-B. Thanks for the equipment and data provided by the China Academy of Railway Sciences.

References

1. Barbosa, R., Sadre, R., Pras, A.: Towards periodicity based anomaly detection in SCADA networks, pp. 1–4, September 2012
2. Chakraborty, S.: Analysis and study of incremental DBSCAN clustering algorithm. Int. J. Enterp. Comput. Bus. Syst. **1** (2011)
3. Chen, C., Pei, Q., Ning, L.: Forecasting 802.11 traffic using seasonal ARIMA model. Comput. Sci. Technol. Appl. Int. Forum **2**, 347–350 (2009)
4. Chen, P.: Principal component analysis and its application in feature extraction. Ph.D. thesis, Shanxi Normal University (2014)
5. Li, S., Yan, L., Guo, W., Chen, J.: SD-SSDN: software-defined signal safety data network for high-speed railway systems. Tiedao Xuebao/J. Chin. Railway Soc. **40**, 81–92 (2018)
6. Li, S., Yan, L., Guo, W., Guo, J., Chen, J., Pan, W., Fang, X.: Analysis of network security for Chinese high-speed railway signal systems and proposal of unified security control. Xinan Jiaotong Daxue Xuebao/J. Southwest Jiaotong Univ. **50**, 478–484, 503 (2015)
7. Li, W., Yan, S., Jiang, Y.: Research on method of self-adaptive determination of DBSCAN algorithm parameters. Comput. Eng. Appl. **55**(5), 1–7, 148 (2019)
8. Liu, D.: Analysis of CTCS-3 safety data network. Railway Signal. Commun. Eng. **26**, 1057–1063 (2010)
9. Liu, X., Liu, J., Zhu, S., Wang, W., Zhang, X.: Privacy risk analysis and mitigation of analytics libraries in the android ecosystem. IEEE Trans. Mob. Comput. **19**(5), 1184–1199 (2020)
10. Moayedi, H., Masnadi-Shirazi, M.: Arima model for network traffic prediction and anomaly detection, vol. 4, pp. 1–6, September 2008
11. Portnoy, L., Eskin, E., Stolfo, S.: Intrusion detection with unlabeled data using clustering, November 2001
12. Tavallaee, M., Bagheri, E., Lu, W., Ghorbani, A.: A detailed analysis of the KDD cup 99 data set. In: IEEE Symposium on Computational Intelligence for Security and Defense Applications, CISDA, vol. 2, July 2009

13. Wang, L., Teng, S.: Application of clustering and time-based sequence analysis in intrusion detection: application of clustering and time-based sequence analysis in intrusion detection. J. Comput. Appl. **30**, 699–701 (2010)

14. Wang, W., Guan, X., Zhang, X., Yang, L.: Profiling program behavior for anomaly intrusion detection based on the transition and frequency property of computer audit data. Comput. Secur. **25**(7), 539–550 (2006)

15. Wang, W., Guyet, T., Quiniou, R., Cordier, M., Masseglia, F., Zhang, X.: Autonomic intrusion detection: adaptively detecting anomalies over unlabeled audit data streams in computer networks. Knowl.-Based Syst. **70**, 103–117 (2014)

16. Wang, W., Li, Y., Wang, X., Liu, J., Zhang, X.: Detecting android malicious apps and categorizing benign apps with ensemble of classifiers. Future Gener. Comput. Syst. **78**, 987–994 (2018)

17. Wang, W., Liu, J., Pitsilis, G., Zhang, X.: Abstracting massive data for lightweight intrusion detection in computer networks. Inf. Sci. **433–434**, 417–430 (2018)

18. Wang, W., Shang, Y., He, Y., Li, Y., Liu, J.: BotMark: automated botnet detection with hybrid analysis of flow-based and graph-based traffic behaviors. Inf. Sci. **511**, 284–296 (2020)

19. Wang, W., Wang, X., Feng, D., Liu, J., Han, Z., Zhang, X.: Exploring permission-induced risk in android applications for malicious application detection. IEEE Trans. Inf. Forensics Secur. **9**(11), 1869–1882 (2014)

20. Wang, W., et al.: Constructing features for detecting android malicious applications: issues, taxonomy and directions. IEEE Access **7**, 67602–67631 (2019)

21. Wang, X., Wang, W., He, Y., Liu, J., Han, Z., Zhang, X.: Characterizing android apps' behavior for effective detection of malapps at large scale. Future Gener. Comput. Syst. **75**, 30–45 (2017)

22. Yan, F., Tang, T.: Research and development of safety technology in signaling system of rail transit. Chin. Saf. Sci. J. **15**, 94–99 (2005)

Dynamic Trajectory for Visual Perception of Abnormal Behavior

Changqi Zhang, Jiang Yu, Yudong Li, and Wen Si[✉]

Faculty of Business Information, Shanghai Business
School, Shanghai 201400, People's Republic of China
zhangcq@sbs.edu.cn, heroyujiang@163.com, lydmm_2002@163.com,
siwen@fudan.edu.cn

Abstract. Computer vision and intelligent analysis technology has been extensively applied to video surveillance and security system. Motion trajectory feature is used to detect abnormal motion behavior. Because the trajectory mainly reflects the spatial change of the moving object in the foreground, there are some limitations to reflect the time information. In this paper, a time encoding method for particle trajectory is proposed, which is based on the information of temporal and spatial changes of particle motion. Based on the trajectory of motion, it describes how the object moves and its position changes in space, reflecting the spatial distribution of motion mode and energy. Based on the dynamic particle trajectory, the video motion evolution pattern is presented in the form of visual behavior template, and the performance of visual features is enhanced by pseudo color coding. Compared with the spatial motion trajectory, the proposed time encoding trajectory method can effectively improve the recognition performance.

Keywords: Intelligent video surveillance · Abnormal behavior recognition · Motion trajectory

1 Introduction

Video surveillance and security systems are receiving wide attention as one of the most common security and protection measures with the continuous development of network and computer related technologies and the increasing demand of public security. The development of intelligent surveillance has been gotten more and more attentions. It is very pivotal to recognize some abnormal behaviors from surveillance videos in visual-based behavior understanding technology.

Because the motion behavior is a complex dynamic process, and is affected by many factors. It is a very challenging work to extract high-level abstract features from the original video stream to accurately describe the motion behavior. Universal and effective behavior representation is the key and difficulty of behavior understanding. In recent years, with the rapid development of deep learning technology and the improvement of computing power, a lot of achievements have been made in the research and application of computer vision [1].

© Springer Nature Singapore Pte Ltd. 2020
G. Xu et al. (Eds.): FCS 2020, CCIS 1286, pp. 271–282, 2020.
https://doi.org/10.1007/978-981-15-9739-8_21

The deep learning method represented by the deep convolution network (CNN) provides an effective solution for the task of automatic extraction of visual features. In the research of visual motion behavior analysis, simonyan and zisserman [2] proposed a dual stream CNN method for video motion recognition. In this method, video stream and optical stream are used as two independent data sources to extract spatial motion information from video. Each data stream uses the deep convolution network to extract features and fuse the softmax output of each network. However, due to its convolution network architecture can not make full use of time information, the performance is often affected by space information and appearance information. At the same time, although the deep learning method can be used to extract the apparent features that are helpful for classification and recognition from the image, compared with the traditional manual features, it is not enough to analyze the motion behavior simply by using the image apparent information. The main reason is the lack of the time information description of the dynamic evolution of the motion behavior. Therefore, it is still insufficient to apply the deep learning method to analyze the abnormal behavior in the intelligent vision monitoring system.

In this paper, the dynamic trajectory map is proposed by encoding the time information into the particle trajectory, and further enhance the dynamic characteristics of motion trajectory by pseudo color coding. Among them, the dynamic trajectory map can be regarded as a time series signal, which can reflect the time-space information of motion and capture the characteristics of dynamic time evolution of motion behavior patterns in video. In order to ensure the smoothness of video signal and eliminate the jitter of feature, a time-varying mean vector method of video frame feature smoothing is proposed. Combined with the deep learning method, the video frame image and the dynamic trajectory image are treated as two independent information sources through the double flow convolution network. After the convolution layer, the appearance information and the motion information are fused to realize the detection of abnormal motion behavior. This method combines the appearance information of moving object and the temporal and spatial evolution of moving behavior, and combines 3D convolution and pooling strategy to integrate the appearance change and dynamic trajectory evolution into effective behavior feature description. The dynamic trajectory map is used to guide the deep convolution network to learn the feature representation of motion behavior and realize the detection of abnormal motion behavior.

2   Motion Trajectory Temporal Encoding

Particle dynamic trajectory image can effectively represent the dynamic evolution process of motion behavior in space-time by encoding the latest motion. Let $P(x, y, t)$ be the particle distribution map, where $P(x, y, t) = 1$ indicates that there are moving particles at the time t and image position (x, y). The function $M(x, y, t)$ calculates the particle dynamic trajectory at time t:

$$M(x, y, t) = \begin{cases} \tau & , \quad if \ P(x, y, t) = 1 \\ \max(0, M(x, y, t - 1)), & else \end{cases} \tag{1}$$

where τ represents the movement time, and δ is the decay parameter, which is used to suppress the influence of historical movement on current movement.

The evolution information of motion behavior pattern in a period of time can be recorded by continuously calculating the dynamic trajectory map. Compared with the traditional trajectory, particle dynamic trajectory map has the following advantages: it effectively integrates the spatial and temporal information of motion, records the evolution process of motion trajectory, and reflects the dynamic evolution mode of motion behavior in a period of time. As shown in Fig. 1, by comparing the motion trajectory in typical indoor and outdoor monitoring environment, it shows that the dynamic motion trajectory by time coding can well reflect the time correlation of movement behavior and how the movement evolves. The motion trajectory is transformed into a visual motion pattern. In Fig. 1, it shows that the moving object walks in the video, while the traditional trajectory only shows the walking path of the moving object, which cannot reflect the walking process. The dynamic trajectory with temporal encoding can reflect the dynamic walking process of the moving object.

3 Motion Trajectory Map Enhancement

Compared with gray image, color image can express more image information. Multiple channels of the image can describe the visual information in more detail. Relevant research shows that [3], color is beneficial to reveal more information in the image, and for some applications, some types of color scales are better than other color scales [4]. Through pseudo color encoding, we can get more significant information from gray-scale texture, and it can improve the algorithm's perception of visual information. Therefore, on the basis of dynamic trajectory map, we can transform the gray-scale trajectory map into three-channel color trajectory map to enhance the performance of action patterns, and non-linear color transformation can improve the gray-scale contrast of image [5].

The improved rainbow color coding method is used, which is a variant of optical spectrum mapping method. This method has uniform color distribution, which is very beneficial to enhance the visual significance of the image. The color coding method adopts (2):

$$C_i = \{sin[2\pi \cdot (-I + \varphi_i)] \cdot \frac{1}{2} + \frac{1}{2}\}^\alpha \cdot f(I) \tag{2}$$

where $C_{i=1,2,3}$ represent BGR channel, I is the normalized gray value, φ_i represents the phase of three channels, and $f(I)$ is the amplitude modulation function.

The power exponent α can control the smoothness of color mapping and suppress a specific gray range. In this application, the channel phase value $\varphi_i = 1, 2, 3$ and the amplitude modulation function $f(I)$ are set to (3):

$$\varphi_{i=1,2,3} = \frac{1}{5} - \frac{1}{2}\pi \ , \ \frac{1}{5} - \frac{1}{2}\pi - \frac{3}{14} \ , \ \frac{1}{5} - \frac{1}{2}\pi - \frac{6}{14}$$

$$f(I) = \frac{1}{4} + \frac{3}{4}I \tag{3}$$

In order to encode the motion trajectory map, it is necessary to normalize the gray value of the motion trajectory map to $I \in [0, 1]$. Figure 2 shows the color coding curves with different values of $\alpha = 1, 5, 10$ and 20. Through observation, it can be found that

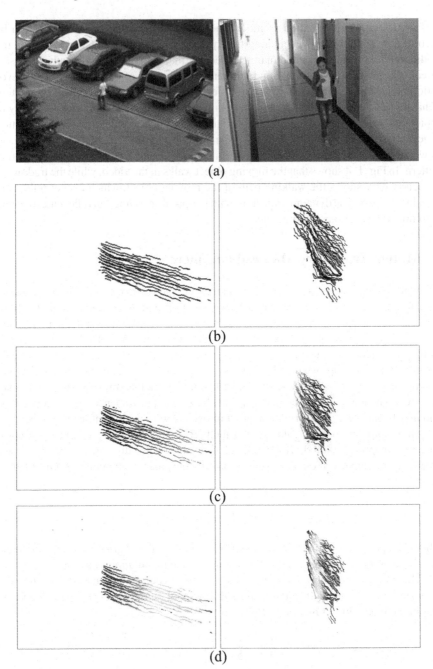

Fig. 1. Comparison of traditional trajectorys and dynamic trajectorys in different scenes. (a) original image frame, (b) motion trajectory, (c) temporal encoding dynamic trajectory, (d) color enhanced trajectory (Color figure online)

the smaller a value color changes relatively smoothly, and with the increase of α value, RGB color will gather in a specific gray range, the color change gradient will become larger, and there will be a dark color area between the high gray value and the low gray value, which will suppress part of the gray range. The gray-scale change of motion trajectory in dynamic trajectory map reflects the time correlation of motion, and the motion always evolves from light gray to dark gray. Therefore, in order to maintain the smooth transition of gray level in the process of color coding, the value of α is not easy to be too large, and the trajectory with smooth gray level can better reflect the whole process of motion evolution. It can be noted from Figs. 4, 5, 6 and 7 that the closer the motion trajectory is to the starting end, the closer it is to the end of the motion trajectory, the closer it is to the red, and the color transition in the middle is smoother. Compared with the gray-scale trajectory, the dynamic evolution process of motion is significantly enhanced.

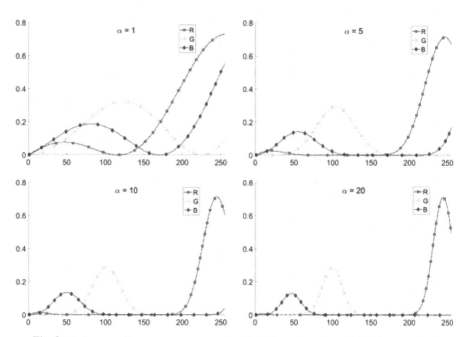

Fig. 2. Color encoding curves corresponding to different α values (Color figure online)

4 Video Signal Smoothing

For video data, even in the ideal environment without noise, there is still a large degree of data fluctuation. In order to reduce the influence of noise and data fluctuation, the original video signal needs to be smoothed. In this section, we will discuss the methods to obtain smooth and robust signal from video frame data x_t.

In order to capture the dynamic evolution of video, the most direct description is to use a frame of continuous image, which is also the most common way. But there are two obvious shortcomings in this way. First of all, the original signal may have significant fluctuations, as shown in Fig. 3(a), which usually causes the learning algorithm to pay too much attention to irrelevant time evolution mode in the feature extraction stage. Single frame image may lead to higher learning error in the training stage; secondly, independent image frame description will lack the correlation between v_t and time t, and that will make the learning algorithm unable to accurately capture the time evolution information of the motion.

For time series data, moving average is usually used to eliminate short-term fluctuations and highlight longer-term trends or periodic changes. The threshold between the short and long term depends on the application. Moving average is a one-dimensional

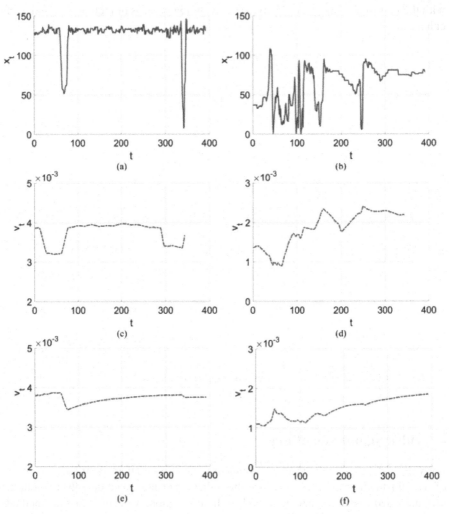

Fig. 3. Video signal smoothing, (a), (b) original video signal, (c), (d) moving average processing, (e), (f) time-varying cumulative average (Color figure online)

convolution operation, which has the characteristics of low-pass filter. It can filter out the components of higher frequency and obtain smooth data. Inspired by the method of time series analysis, we consider to calculate the moving average value of video signal with window size T at time t, and hope to transform video signal into local smooth signal. The moving average usually selects the data in the fixed window to calculate the simple weighted average.

There is time series data $\{x_1, x_2, \ldots, x_t\}$ at time t, the sliding average with window size T is calculated as follows:

$$v_t = \bar{x}_t = \frac{x_t + x_{t-1} + \cdots + x_{t-(T-1)}}{T} = \frac{1}{t} \sum_{i=0}^{T-1} x_{t-i} \qquad (4)$$

With the sliding average, the signal will have the following two characteristics. First, the video signal will be smoother. In addition, it can be ensured that the smooth signal v_t is locally dependent on the video frame $[T, t + T]$ near time t. Different from using independent video frame to describe the video, the correlation between the smooth signal v_t and time t is established by moving average processing. Figure 3 shows a relatively smooth relationship between signal v_t and video frame index (time variable), where window $t = 50$.

Although the moving average representation can reflect the time evolution of video information, we can still find that the signal is unstable to some extent. In addition, the sliding average representation also introduces uncertain empirical parameters. For example, the selection of window size T, the appropriate t value is difficult to choose, because the motion behavior often occurs in different time segments. In addition, due to the boundary effect, the smooth signal v_t is undefined for the video at the end of the time t.

In order to solve the limitation of independent image frame and moving average representation, a time-varying cumulative mean vector is proposed. For time series data $\{x_1, x_2, \ldots, x_t\}$, the signal mean at time t is expressed as $m_t = 1/t \sum_{\tau=1}^{t} x_\tau$, and v_t represents the unit cumulative mean vector at time t, such as (5) and (6).

$$m_t = \frac{x_1 + x_2 + \cdots + x_t}{t} = \frac{1}{t} \sum_{\tau=1}^{t} x_\tau \qquad (5)$$

$$v_t = \frac{m_t}{\|m_t\|} \qquad (6)$$

In Fig. 3, the relationship between the smooth signal v_t and the time variable t is plotted respectively. It shows that the signal v_t is smooth, which is similar to the monotone increasing function. Different from the representation of independent image frame, the time-varying cumulative mean vector v_t has better time variable dependence, so the encoding function can learn the dynamic evolution of normalized time-varying mean vector with time t.

However, it needs to store all the historical data in order to calculate the time-varying cumulative mean. In order to improve the calculation efficiency, when the new data x_{t+1} is obtained at time $t + 1$, the following incremental calculation method is applied:

$$x_1 + \cdots + x_t = t \cdot m_t \qquad (7)$$

The incremental formula for calculating m_{t+1} can be obtained:

$$
\begin{aligned}
m_{t+1} &= \frac{(x_1 + x_2 + \cdots + x_t) + x_{t+1}}{t+1} \\
&= \frac{x_{t+1} + t \cdot m_t}{t+1} \\
&= \frac{x_{t+1} + (t+1-1) \cdot m_t}{t+1} \\
&= \frac{(t+1) \cdot m_t + x_{t+1} - m_t}{t+1} \\
&= m_t + \frac{x_{t+1} - m_t}{t+1}
\end{aligned}
\tag{8}
$$

5 Experimental Results

In order to verify the effectiveness of the algorithm, three public video libraries are selected for testing, respectively from UMN [6] (video frame size: 320×240 pixels), Caviar [7] (384×288 pixels) and Web [8] (320×240 pixels). Among them, some sequence examples and their corresponding dynamic trajectory are shown in Fig. 4.

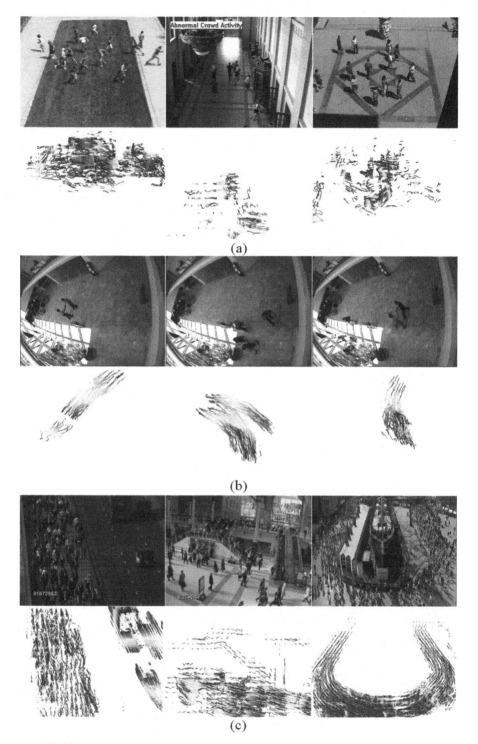

Fig. 4. Examples of video sequences and dynamic trajectorys (Color figure online)

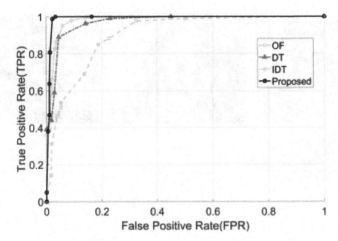

Fig. 5. ROC for UMN video sequence (Color figure online)

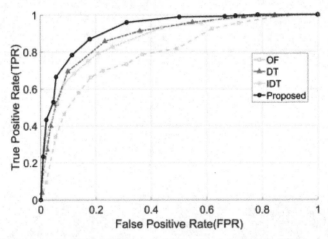

Fig. 6. ROC for Caviar video sequence (Color figure online)

In the experiment, the foreground segmentation method proposed in reference [9] is used to remove the background area. LK sparse optical flow is calculated in the moving foreground area, and moving particles are extracted. After obtaining the effective moving particles, the time information is encoded by calculating the dynamic motion trajectory. In the dual stream deep convolution network, we use two vgg-16 network models which are pre trained by ImageNet [10]. For quantitative evaluation of algorithm performance, ROC curve is used to compare the proposed algorithm with optical flow feature (OF) [2], dense trajectory based (DT) [11] and improved dense trajectory (IDT) [12]. The experimental results are shown in Fig. 5, Fig. 6 and Fig. 7. The proposed algorithm has better performance.

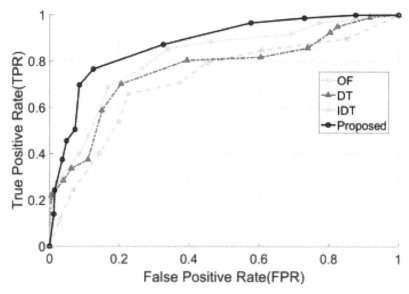

Fig. 7. ROC for Web video sequence (Color figure online)

6 Conclusions

In this paper, a time encoding method for motion trajectory has been developed to integrate both spatial and domain change information of particle motion. The motion trajectory is employed to describe how the object moves and changes its position in space, which reflects the motion pattern and energy spatial distribution. The motion temporal encoding is performed based on the motion trajectory of dynamic particles. The motion evolution model has been presented in a form of visual behavior template. The visual features are enhanced by pseudo-color coding. Compared with space motion trajectories, the proposed method can improve the recognition performance.

References

1. Guo, Y., Yu, L., Oerlemans, A., et al.: Deep learning for visual understanding: a review [J]. Neurocomputing **187**, 27–48 (2016)
2. Simonyan, K., Zisserman, A.: Two-stream convolutional networks for action recognition in videos. In: Proceedings of IEEE Conference on Neural Information Processing Systems, pp. 1–11 (2014)
3. Abidi, B.R., Zheng, Y., Gribok, A.V., et al.: Improving weapon detection in single energy X-ray images through pseudocoloring. IEEE Trans. Syst. Man Cybern. Part C Appl. Rev. **36**(6), 784–796 (2006)
4. Wang, P., Li, W., Gao, Z., et al.: Action recognition from depth maps using deep convolutional neural networks. IEEE Trans. Hum.-Mach. Syst. **46**(4), 498–509 (2016)
5. Johnson, J.: Not seeing is not believing: improving the visibility of your fluorescence images. Mol. Biol. Cell **23**(5), 754–757 (2012)

6. Unusual Crowd Activity Dataset of University of Minnesota. http://mha.cs.umn.edu/Movies/CrowdActivity-All.avi
7. The EC Funded CAVIAR project. http://homepages.inf.ed.ac.uk/rbf/CAVIAR/
8. The Web Datasets. http://www.vision.eecs.ucf.edu/projects/rmehran/cvpr2009/Abnormal_Crowd.html
9. Chen, Z., Ellis, T.: A self-adaptive gaussian mixture model. Comput. Vis. Image Underst. **122**(5), 35–46 (2014)
10. Russakovsky, O., Deng, J., Su, H., et al.: ImageNet large scale visual recognition challenge. Int. J. Comput. Vis. **115**(3), 211–252 (2015)
11. Wang, H., Kläser, A., Schmid, C., et al.: Dense trajectories and motion boundary descriptors for action recognition. Int. J. Comput. Vis. **103**(1), 60–79 (2013)
12. Wang, H., Schmid, C.: Action recognition with improved trajectories. In: Proceedings of IEEE International Conference on Computer Vision, pp. 3551–3558 (2014)

Fuzzy Petri Nets Based Information System Security Situation Assessment Model

Hongyu Yang[1][✉] [iD], Yuhao Feng[1], Guangquan Xu[2] [iD], and Jiyong Zhang[3]

[1] Civil Aviation University of China, Tianjin 300300, China
yhyxlx@hotmail.com
[2] Tianjin University, Tianjin 300350, China
[3] Swiss Federal Institute of Technology in Lausanne, 1015 Lausanne, Switzerland

Abstract. Existing assessment models have inconvenient statistics of fuzzy factors and lack of intuitive graphical implementation methods. This paper proposes an information system security situation assessment model based on fuzzy Petri nets (ISSSAF). Firstly, a general hierarchical assessment index system is established. According to the assessment system, a fuzzy Petri net (FPN) model is built and a fuzzy inference algorithm is designed. Secondly, the credibility of each proposition is calculated by inference, and the security situation of the system is graded by grey assessment and inference algorithm. Finally, an assessment experiment of a domestic departure control system (DCS) is carried out. The experimental results verify the effectiveness of ISSSAF. Compared with the traditional methods, it is more objective and accurate, which can help the relevant personnel to formulate effective security protection strategies for the information system.

Keywords: Security situation · Index system · Fuzzy petri nets · Quantitative method

1 Introduction

With the rapid development of information technology, the demand of various industries for the information system is increasing rapidly. It has become an indispensable part of information construction. At present, the main problem that restricts the information system to play a role has changed from the technical problem to the information system security supervision problem. As an important step of information system security supervision, it is the information system security situation assessment and risk control [1].

In recent years, the research of information system security situation assessment has become a hot subject, and the model-based methods have made some achievements. Zhao et al. [2] obtained the index comprehensive weight through a G-ANP method and determined the system risk level by using the grey statistical theory, but there was no intuitive graphical expression in the process of realizing the model. Fu et al. [3] proposed an information system security risk assessment model, which uses an entropy weight coefficient method to determine the index weight vector and reduce the subjective

© Springer Nature Singapore Pte Ltd. 2020
G. Xu et al. (Eds.): FCS 2020, CCIS 1286, pp. 283–293, 2020.
https://doi.org/10.1007/978-981-15-9739-8_22

influence of expert experience. Pan et al. [4] proposed a dynamic reassessment model for mobile ad hoc networks, but the algorithm is complex and difficult to implement. Li et al. [5] proposed a quantitative assessment model of the vulnerability of civil aviation network system based on spatial local hazards, but only considered the hazard prevention level of some nodes. Wang et al. [6] evaluated the security situation of the information system through a mixed index and fuzzy method but did not consider the credibility of fuzzy language expression.

Although these methods provide a reference for information system security construction and management decision-making, they also have some problems, such as 1) there are fuzzy factors in the assessment which are inconvenient for statistics; 2) they are not suitable for modeling and inference empirical knowledge; 3) they are not easy to simulate through the model to analyze the performance of the system. In the inference and judgment of uncertainty and fuzziness of information system security situation assessment, the fuzzy Petri net (FPN) can represent logical knowledge in an intuitive and visual way [7]. So it is of wide significance to use FPN to describe and analyze the information system security situation.

2 Security Situation Model Based on FPN

In the security situation assessment, the construction of the assessment index system is the most critical link. It will directly affect the comprehensiveness, rationality, and effectiveness of the assessment. Therefore, an in-depth analysis must be carried out to determine their relative importance in the security assessment.

With reference to relevant security standards and guidelines, and information system security situation assessment hierarchical model is established based on the analytic hierarchy process [8]. The hierarchical model is shown in Table 1.

Table 1. Security situation assessment index system.

Target layer	Criterion layer	Scheme layer
Comprehensive security situation (A)	Host system security (B_1)	User identification (C_{11})
		Disk utilization (C_{12})
		CPU utilization (C_{13})
		Memory usage (C_{14})
	Network security (B_2)	Network access control (C_{21})
		Network topology (C_{22})
		Network security audit (C_{23})
		Network traffic (C_{24})
	Data security (B_3)	Data integrity (C_{31})
		Data confidentiality (C_{32})
		Data availability (C_{33})
		Backup and recovery (C_{34})

And the method of information system security situation assessment based on the FPN is illustrated in Fig. 1.

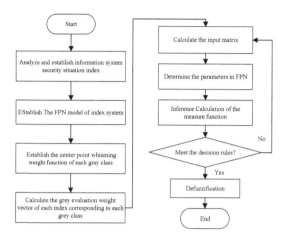

Fig. 1. Process of information system security situation assessment based on fuzzy Petri net.

3 Fuzzy Petri Nets

3.1 Production Rules for FPN

In the information system security situation assessment, it is often difficult to obtain data in an accurate digital form. Therefore, fuzzy production rules are widely used in fuzzy, imprecise, and uncertain knowledge in the field of expert systems. Each fuzzy production rule is usually coded in the form of IF-THEN rules [9]. If the preceding or following part of the fuzzy production rule contains the "AND" or "OR" connector, it is called a compound fuzzy production rule. In the front and back, fuzzy items represented by fuzzy sets are allowed.

FPN is a rule-based system. Each fuzzy production rule can be represented by a corresponding FPN. Different fuzzy production rules and corresponding FPN structures can be divided into the following five types.

Type 1: IF P_1, THEN P_g (refer to Fig. 2).
Type 2: IF P_1 AND P_2 AND … AND P_n, THEN P_g (refer to Fig. 3).
Type 3: IF P_1 OR P_2 OR … OR P_n, THEN P_g (refer to Fig. 4).
Type 4: IF P_g, THEN P_1 AND P_2 AND … AND P_n (refer to Fig. 5).
Type 5: IF P_g, THEN P_1 OR P_2 OR … OR P_n (refer to Fig. 6).

All the above five rule types can be represented by FPN, as shown in Fig. 2, 3, 4, 5 and 6. This paper will not discuss type 4 and type 5 rules because they can be generated by multiple rule conversions of type 1.

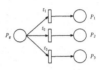

Fig. 2. FPN representation of type 1 rule.

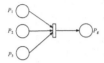

Fig. 3. FPN representation of type 2 rule.

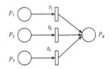

Fig. 4. FPN representation of type 3 rule.

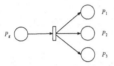

Fig. 5. FPN representation of type 4 rule.

Fig. 6. FPN representation of type 5 rule.

3.2 Definition of FPN

FPN is an extension of the classic Petri Net (PN), used to deal with inaccurate, and fuzzy information in knowledge-based systems [10]. It has been widely used to model fuzzy production rules (FPR) and automatic inference based on fuzzy rules. FPN is a marked graphics system that contains a place and a transition, expresses logical knowledge intuitively. Where, the circle graph represents the place, the bar graph represents the transition, and the directed arc represents the relationship from the place to the transition or from the transition to the place. The main feature of FPN is that it supports the structure of information organization, provides visualization of knowledge inference, and helps design effective fuzzy inference algorithms.

A fuzzy Petri net model is established based on the information system security situation assessment system (refer to Fig. 7).

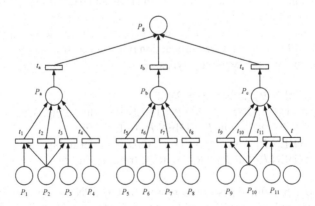

Fig. 7. FPN model of information system security situation assessment system.

A FPN model of information system security situation assessment system can be defined as a 10-tuple: FPN = $(P, T, D, I, O, \beta, W, U, Th, M)$.

1. $P = \{p_1, p_2, ...,p_n\}$ denotes a finite nonempty set of places;
2. $T = \{t_1, t_2,...,t_m\}$ denotes a finite nonempty set of transitions;
3. $D = \{d_1, d_2,...,d_n\}$ denotes a finite set of propositions;
4. $I: P \times T \rightarrow \{0,1\}$ is an $m \times n$ input incidence matrix defining the directed arcs from places to transitions;
5. $O: T \times P \rightarrow \{0,1\}$ is an $m \times n$ input incidence matrix defining the directed arcs from places to transitions;
6. $\beta: P \rightarrow D$ is an association function representing a bijective mapping from places to propositions;
7. $W: P \times T$ is an input function and can be expressed as an $m \times n$ dimensional matrix, which indicates the influence degree of p_i on transition t_j;
8. $U: T \times P$ is a vector $U = (\mu_1, \mu_2, ..., \mu_m)^T$, and μ_i is the certainty factor of transition t_i, n is the number of transitions;
9. $Th = (\lambda_1, \lambda_2, ..., \lambda_n)^T$ is an output function which assigns a certainty value between 0 and 1 to each output place of a transition;
10. M is a marking of the FPN. The initial marking is denoted by M_0. Its determination should be based on actual status. Hence, its value could be understood as the dynamic input and directly influence the dynamic behavior of the FPN.

4   Initial State Matrix Processing

Prior knowledge can be evaluated by numbers or language, and these two methods are widely used in the knowledge system. However, the acquisition of expert knowledge is based on the subjective judgment of experts, and there are certain uncertainties. Therefore, this paper chooses to use the center point triangle whitening weight function [11] to deal with the expert score.

Step 1: Determine the grey class.

Set the index value as 4 gray categories, namely "low", "medium", "high", "higher". Select the center point $\lambda_1, \lambda_2, \lambda_3, \lambda_4$ closest to gray class 1, 2, 3, 4, and the values are 2.0, 4.0, 6.0 and 8.0 respectively. Then extend the gray value of the index to the left and right to $\lambda_0 = 0$, $\lambda_5 = 10$, which are "very low" and "very high" respectively. Therefore, the value of each index can be divided into 5 gray-class intervals $[\lambda_0, \lambda_1]$, $[\lambda_1, \lambda_2]$, $[\lambda_2, \lambda_3]$, $[\lambda_3, \lambda_4]$, $[\lambda_4, \lambda_5]$, namely [0.0, 2.0], [2.0, 4.0], [4.0, 6.0], [6.0, 8.0], [8.0, 10.0].

Step 2: Determine the value of indexes.

According to prior experience, the index value is determined by scoring the index, and each index is scored n times. Referring to the information security situation index system, the index is investigated independently, and each assessment index is evaluated and scored, based on which the assessment sample matrix D is obtained.

Step 3: Establish the center point whitening weight function of each gray class.

An observed value x of index j belongs to the center whitening function $f_j^k(x)$ of gray class k ($k = 0, 1, 2, 3, 4, 5$).

$$f_j^k(x) = \begin{cases} 0, x \notin [\lambda_{k-1}, \lambda_{k+1}] \\ \frac{x-\lambda_{k-1}}{\lambda_k - \lambda_{k-1}}, x \in (\lambda_{k-1}, \lambda_k] \\ \frac{\lambda_{k+1}-x}{\lambda_{k+1}-\lambda_k}, x \in (\lambda_k, \lambda_{k+1}) \end{cases} \tag{1}$$

Step 4: Calculate the grey assessment weight vector of each index corresponding to each grey class.

For example, the grey assessment coefficient of the M-th assessment gray class of P_i in the place is denoted as M_m and defined

$$M_{im} = \sum_{h=1}^{n} f_i^m(p_{ih}) \tag{2}$$

Where n is the rating times, P_{ih} is the rating of place P_i for the h-th time and is recorded

$$M_i = \sum_{m=1}^{6} M_{im} \tag{3}$$

5 Security Situation Fuzzy Inference Algorithm

According to the characteristics of fuzzy Petri, the following two algorithms are used to calculate the security situation values.

5.1 Propositional Credibility Inference Algorithm

According to the prior experience, the credibility of places corresponding to the scheme layer proposition $d(c_{ij})$ is summarized. Based on the sps set, tcs set, and wcs set, the credibility of all places corresponding to the reachable set of sps set is iteratively deduced.

Definition 1: The wcs is the set of place and place credibility, whose elements are P, $W(P)$.

Definition 2: The tcs is the set of transition and transition credibility, whose elements are t, $W(t)$ respectively.

Definition 3: The tis and tos are respectively the transition input place and the transition output place. Their elements are $tis(t)$, $tos(t)$.

Definition 4: The sps is a set of initial place.

Step 1: Set $u = 1$, initialize the credibility of the place, and set the unknown credibility to 0;

Step 2: Find the u-th place in the initial place set sps, and delete it after taking it out;

Step 3: If the sps set is empty, stop the calculation;

Step 4: Traverses set tis. If the place P belongs to tis, take out the corresponding transition T;

Step 5: Take out other places under the same transition and put them into the temporary place set tps;

Step 6: Determine the weights of the places in the set tps, and perform weighted calculation on the credibility of the places in the set to obtain the weight w_s, let $w_s = w(t) \times w_s$;

Step 7: Traverse the set tos, take out the location p_o of the transition output, if $w(p_o) < w_s$, then set $w(p_o) = w_s$, set u++, return Step 2.

5.2 Security Situation Fuzzy Inference Algorithm

After establishing the FPN model of information system security situation, an inference algorithm is proposed to calculate the value of the information system comprehensive security situation.

Define the following rules:

$$\mathbf{A} \oplus \mathbf{B} = \mathbf{C}, \ c_{ij} = \max\{a_{ij}, b_{ij}\} \tag{4}$$

$$\mathbf{A} \otimes \mathbf{B} = \mathbf{C}, \ c_{ij} = \max_{1 \leq k \leq n} (a_{ik} \cdot b_{kj}) \tag{5}$$

$$\mathbf{A} \circ \mathbf{B} = \mathbf{C}, \ c_{ij} = a_{ij} \times b_{ij} \tag{6}$$

$$\mathbf{A} \triangleright \mathbf{B} = \mathbf{C}, \ c_{ij} = 1, \text{ if } \sum_{i=n/2}^{n} a_{ij} \geq b_i, \sum_{i=1}^{n/2} a_{ij} \leq b_i; \text{ else } c_{ij} = 0 \tag{7}$$

Step 1: Let $k = 1$, k is the time of iterations.

Step 2: Calculate the input matrix $S^{(k)} = I \circ W$.

Step 3: Calculate the equivalent input $\Theta^{(k)} = OWA_{(S^{(k)})^{\mathrm{T}}}(M_{k-1}(1), M_{k-1}(2), \cdots, M_{k-1}(m))$. This step calculates the input weight of the change of the place according to the impact degree matrix and state matrix M of the place on the change.

Step 4: Calculate the support vector $H^{(k)}(i) = \Theta^{(k)}(i) \triangleright Th(i)$, the output of this step is a 0,1 matrix, indicating whether the transition is triggered.

Step 5: Calculate the output credibility vector $Z^{(k)} = H^{(k)} \circ U$.

Step 6: Calculate the new state matrix $M_k = M_{k-1} \oplus \left((O \otimes Z^{(k)}) \Theta^{(k)} \right)$.

Step 7: If $M_k = M_{k-1}$, stop the calculation, otherwise return step 2.

Step 8: The state matrix is de-fuzzed to obtain qualitative and quantitative security situation assessment values.

In this algorithm, the comprehensive security situation assessment value of the system is determined by the credibility W of the place and its corresponding assessment index. The matrix operation is adopted in the inference algorithm, and the parallel processing ability of the fuzzy Petri net is fully utilized. The inference process is simpler and easier to implement.

6 Experiment and Analysis

To verify the feasibility of the model and inference algorithm, it was applied to the departure control system of a civil aviation airport, and the historical data of each Thursday during October and November 2019 was extracted for security situation assessment.

6.1 Initial State Matrix Processing

The eight sub-indexes subordinate to network security B_2 and data security B_3 were scored five times according to prior experience. The index scoring results are shown in Table 2.

Table 2. Index scoring table.

Times	C_{21}	C_{22}	C_{23}	C_{24}	C_{31}	C_{32}	C_{33}	C_{34}
1	9.7	8.6	9.0	8.9	7.6	8.2	8.1	7.2
2	9.5	8.2	8.5	8.7	7.8	8.6	8.6	7.3
3	9.6	8.3	8.7	8.9	7.2	8.1	8.2	7.8
4	9.2	9.0	8.2	8.0	7.9	8.3	8.4	7.1
5	9.4	8.5	8.4	9.0	7.5	8.4	8.2	7.4

Table 3. Grey assessment weight of each index belonging to each grey class.

Index	Class 0	Class 1	Class 2	Class 3	Class 4	Class 5
C_{21}	0	0	0	0	0.26	0.74
C_{22}	0	0	0	0	0.74	0.26
C_{23}	0	0	0	0	0.72	0.28
C_{24}	0	0	0	0	0.65	0.35
C_{31}	0	0	0	0.2	0.8	0
C_{32}	0	0	0	0	0.84	0.16
C_{33}	0	0	0	0	0.85	0.15
C_{34}	0	0	0	0.32	0.68	0

According to the above scoring results, the grey assessment weight matrix was calculated by using central point triangular whitenization weight function. The grey assessment weight is shown in Table 3.

6.2 Inference Calculation

According to prior experience, the credibility of propositions in the scheme layer index can be set as $w_1 = 0.6$, $w_2 = 0.5$, $w_3 = 0.7$, $w_4 = 0.5$, $w_4 = 0.8$, $w_5 = 0.9$, $w_6 = 0.7$, $w_7 = 0.7$, $w_8 = 0.8$, $w_9 = 0.9$, $w_{10} = 0.7$, $w_{11} = 0.6$, $w_{12} = 0.8$. The credibility of transitions can be set as $U = \{\mu_j\} = \{0.3, 0.5, 0.4, 0.6, 0.8, 0.6, 0.7, 0.6, 0.8, 0.5, 0.5, 0.6, 0.9, 0.8, 0.8\}$.

Using the above data in the inference algorithm, the credibility of propositions is shown below. $w_a = 0.76$, which indicates that there are vulnerabilities in the security of the host system, and the credibility is 0.76. $w_b = 0.85$, which indicates that there are hidden dangers in network security, and the credibility is 0.85. $w_c = 0.87$, which indicates that data security is at risk, and the credibility is 0.87. $w_g = 0.84$, which indicates that the credibility of the overall security situation of the system is 0.84.

For Security situation fuzzy inference algorithm, state matrixes can be obtained.

$$M(0) = \begin{bmatrix} 0 & 0 & 0 & 0.36 & 0.64 & 0 \\ 0 & 0 & 0 & 0.2 & 0.8 & 0 \\ 0 & 0 & 0 & 0 & 0.64 & 0.36 \\ 0 & 0 & 0 & 0.2 & 0.8 & 0 \\ 0 & 0 & 0 & 0 & 0.26 & 0.74 \\ 0 & 0 & 0 & 0 & 0.74 & 0.26 \\ 0 & 0 & 0 & 0 & 0.72 & 0.28 \\ 0 & 0 & 0 & 0 & 0.65 & 0.35 \\ 0 & 0 & 0 & 0.2 & 0.8 & 0 \\ 0 & 0 & 0 & 0 & 0.84 & 0.16 \\ 0 & 0 & 0 & 0 & 0.85 & 0.15 \\ 0 & 0 & 0 & 0.32 & 0.68 & 0 \\ 0 & 0 & 0 & 0 & 0 & 0 \\ 0 & 0 & 0 & 0 & 0 & 0 \\ 0 & 0 & 0 & 0 & 0 & 0 \\ 0 & 0 & 0 & 0 & 0 & 0 \end{bmatrix}, \ M(2) = M(3) = \begin{bmatrix} 0 & 0 & 0 & 0.36 & 0.64 & 0 \\ 0 & 0 & 0 & 0.2 & 0.8 & 0 \\ 0 & 0 & 0 & 0 & 0.64 & 0.36 \\ 0 & 0 & 0 & 0.2 & 0.8 & 0 \\ 0 & 0 & 0 & 0 & 0.26 & 0.74 \\ 0 & 0 & 0 & 0 & 0.74 & 0.26 \\ 0 & 0 & 0 & 0 & 0.72 & 0.28 \\ 0 & 0 & 0 & 0 & 0.65 & 0.35 \\ 0 & 0 & 0 & 0.2 & 0.8 & 0 \\ 0 & 0 & 0 & 0 & 0.84 & 0.16 \\ 0 & 0 & 0 & 0 & 0.85 & 0.15 \\ 0 & 0 & 0 & 0.32 & 0.68 & 0 \\ 0.126 & 0.340 & 0.253 & 0.132 & 0.072 & 0.078 \\ 0.020 & 0.084 & 0.091 & 0.264 & 0.274 & 0.250 \\ 0.075 & 0.088 & 0.282 & 0.256 & 0.173 & 0.107 \\ 0.081 & 0.097 & 0.126 & 0.251 & 0.230 & 0.281 \end{bmatrix}.$$

When k equals 3, $M(3)$ equals $M(2)$. Thus, the algorithm process ends. It can be seen from the results that the information system security situation vector is $(0.081 \ 0.097 \ 0.126 \ 0.251 \ 0.230 \ 0.281)$.

The score of the target index through the weighted average is 6.854.

Multiply the above index score and the credibility of the index w_g to obtain the system's comprehensive situation assessment value: 5.757. According to this value, the system's security situation level is judged to be between medium and high. The result is consistent with the actual security situation.

6.3   Comparative Experiments and Results

To further verify the effectiveness of ISSSAF, two typical method Analytic Hierarchy Process (AHP) and Entropy-Weight method (EWM) applied DCS were tested.

The test results of AHP, EWM, and ISSSAF are compared as shown in Fig. 8.

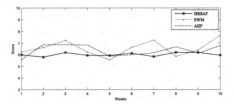

Fig. 8. The comprehensive security posture of the information system.

According to the expert feedback, the security situation value obtained by the model in this paper is more in line with the actual situation. It can be seen from Fig. 8 that the fluctuation of the security situation value obtained by model evaluation in this paper is less than that obtained by traditional methods.

7   Conclusions

This paper presents a security situation assessment model for information systems based on fuzzy Petri nets. The model quantifies the security situation by constructing the FPN model and iteratively inferring the place credibility and state matrix. And the feasibility and effectiveness of the model in this paper are verified by the security situation assessment experiment of an airport departure control system. By comparing the traditional methods with the model evaluation results in this paper, it is found that the model inference calculation method in this paper has better adaptability and stability.

References

1. Yang, H.: Wireless network intrusion detection based on improved convolutional neural network. IEEE Access **7**, 64366–64374 (2019)
2. Zhao, G.: Information security risk assessment base on G-ANP. J. Tsinghua Univ. (Sci. Technol.) **53**(12), 1761–1767 (2013)
3. Fu, Y.: An approach for information systems security risk assessment on fuzzy set and entropy-weight. Acta Electronica Sinica **38**(07), 1489–1494 (2010)
4. Pan, L.: Dynamic information security evaluation model in mobile Ad Hoc network. Comput. Appl. **7**(3), 245–256 (2015)
5. Li, H.: A new quantitative method for studying the vulnerability of civil aviation network system to spatially localized hazards. Int. J. Disaster Risk Sci. **7**(3), 245–256 (2016)
6. Wang, D.: Mixed-index information system security evaluation. J. Tsinghua Univ. (Sci. Technol.) **56**(05), 517–521+529 (2016)
7. Liu, F.: Dynamic adaptive fuzzy petri nets for knowledge representation and inference. IEEE Trans. Syst. Man Cybern. Syst. **43**(6), 1399–1410 (2013)

8. Li, M.: Study on fuzzy evaluation of the quality of MOOC teaching based on AHP. In: 13th International Conference on Computer Science & Education (ICCSE), Colombo, pp. 1–4. IEEE (2018)
9. Zakharov, S.: The analysis and monitoring of ecological risks on the basis of fuzzy Petri nets. In: 3rd Russian-Pacific Conference on Computer Technology and Applications (RPC), Vladivostok, pp. 1–5. IEEE (2018)
10. Liu, H.: Knowledge acquisition and representation using fuzzy evidential inference and dynamic adaptive fuzzy Petri nets. IEEE Trans. Cybern. **43**(3), 1059–1072 (2013)
11. Liu, S.: Two stages decision model with grey synthetic measure and a betterment of triangular whitenization weight function. Control Decis. **29**(07), 1232–1238 (2014)

Invulnerability of Heterogeneous CPFS Under Different Intranal Border-adding Strategies

Hao Peng[1,2], Can Liu[1], Dandan Zhao[1(✉)], Zhaolong Hu[1], and Jianmin Han[1]

[1] College of Mathematics and Computer Science, Zhejiang Normal University,
Jinhua 321004, Zhejiang, China
ddzhao@zjnu.edu.cn
[2] Shanghai Key Laboratory of Integrated Administration Technologies
for Information Security, Shanghai 200240, China

Abstract. With the development of the Industrial Internet, the invulnerability of the cyber-physical fusion system (CPFS) has received extensive attention and in-depth research in recent years. In this paper, based on the theory of network cascading failure and facing the heterogeneous information physics fusion system environment, we propose a system enhancement reliability strategy based on the intranal edge of the network. By calculating the size of the most significant functional component in the entire system, we compared and analyzed the heterogeneous information physical fusion system's invulnerability under random attack.

Keywords: Cyber-Physics Fusion System · Border-adding strategies · Cascading failure · Robustness

1 Introduction

Cyber-Physical Fusion Systems (CPFS) is a highly integrated system of cyber processes and physical components [4,15]. Computers are used to control and monitor physical processes [7]. CPFS plays an important role in our daily life; it gets a fast-growing research [4]. We regard the power grid system as a typical representative of the CPFS [4,15]. It is particularly important to maintain the robustness of CPFS.

For improving the robustness of CPFS, scholars have proposed many theories. Based on the differences of equipment, scholars explore the approaches to CPFS's reliability from hardware adjustment [10,12]. The cyber network controls physical components. Thus, holding on the robustness of the cyber network by software controls is an effective method [1,18]. Abstracting CPFS into interdependent networks is another approach to reach the reliability of CPFS [6,14].

© Springer Nature Singapore Pte Ltd. 2020
G. Xu et al. (Eds.): FCS 2020, CCIS 1286, pp. 294–304, 2020.
https://doi.org/10.1007/978-981-15-9739-8_23

1.1   Interdependent Networks

Buldyrev et al. [2] proposed a 'one-to-one correspondence' model to connect nodes from different networks. In this model, two interdependent networks A and B have the same number of nodes, and each node on network A has function depending on exactly only one node in the network B, and vice versa.

'Multiple-to-multiple correspondence' [3] is a model that a single node in the network A operates depending on more than one node in the network B, and vice versa. This complicated coupling relationship is more closed to the real world.

'One-to-multiple correspondence' model [3,5] is different to 'one-to-one correspondence' and 'multiple-to-multiple correspondence' model. Firstly, it increases the singularity of the 'one-to-one correspondence' model inter-links connection. Then, it improves the overcomplexity of the 'multiple-to multiple correspondence' model.

1.2   Contribution

Our main contributions in this paper are:

i). Propose new adding intra-links strategies which have better effects in improving CPFS reliability.

ii). The maximum value of each node degree is restricted. One node cannot have intra-links without limit.

iii). Use extensive simulations to give insightful views on cascading failure in interdependent networks under different interdependence models and network topologies. We have reached more general conclusions.

1.3   Organization

The outline of this work is as follows: we introduce the model of CPFS in Sect. 2. In Sect. 3, we analyze the different adding strategies. Section 4 performs the results of the simulations and analysis points. Conclusions and future works in Sect. 5.

2   The Model

In this section, we describe the CPFS models we will simulate in Sect. 4. Then we propose the 'one-to-multiple' model cascading failure's theoretical formulas based on the Buldyrev et al. studies [2]. Finally, the cascading failure of our model is given by a simple model.

2.1   Interdependent Model

We consider the CPFS is composed of two interdependent networks. To merely the model and two networks, we denote these networks are A and network B,

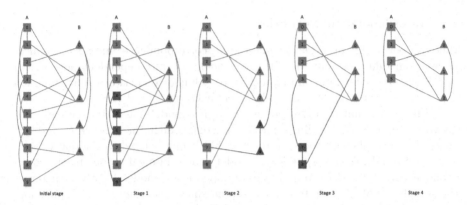

Fig. 1. The cascading failure in interdependent networks. Initially, there are ten nodes and five nodes in the network A and B. In the final stage, the remaining nodes of this interdependent network reach one stable situation without further cascading failures. There are four nodes in the network A and three nodes in the network B. (Color figure online)

respectively. The links connect nodes within the individual networks as intra-links and connect the nodes from different networks as inter-relationships [9]. We assume that all intra-links and inter-links are unidirectional in our models.

To meet the requirements of real-network connection and maintain the generality of the network model, we apply the 'one-to-multiple correspondence' model in our paper. The inter-links are the random connection between network A and B. In the following simulation models, we set the coupling ratio is 3:1. This means that node u in the network A depends on one node v in the network B while node v has three inter-links from network A. If node v fails, node u will fail. Nevertheless, the failure of node u may not cause the node v to fail. Only all interlinks within node v are removed, node v is failed.

2.2 Cascading Failure in Model

Buldyrev et al. derive the theoretical formulas of final nodes number after cascading failure [2]. In the next, they test the correctness of formulas through experimental simulation. The main notations of formulas sre shown in Table 1. In the 'one-to-one correspondence' model, the nodes number of the stablestate is:

$$
\begin{cases}
x = g_A(y)p \\
y = g_B(x)p
\end{cases}
\tag{1}
$$

where p is the fraction of nodes which is not failed after initial attack.

In this paper, we remain at the previous studies of cascading failure. The theoretical formulas must be changed due to the relationship of inter-links. Cascading failure is triggered by a minor failure. We assume that the initial random attack occurs in the network A and a $1 - p$ fraction nodes are attacked. In this

Table 1. Key notations in the analysis of cascading failures functions

Symbol	Meaning
N_{Ai}, N_{Bi}	The fraction of nodes in the giant component of network A, B in stage i
N'_{Ai}, N'_{Bi}	The number of nodes is remaining in the network A, B in stage i
μ_i	The fraction of remaining in network nodes
μ'_i	The fraction of normal operation nodes in network
g_A, g_B	The generating functions of network A, B

way, we randomly removing a $1 - p$ fraction of the nodes of network A and removing all the links connected to these removed nodes. The fraction of nodes in the giant component in N'_{A1} is:

$$N_{A1} = g_A(\mu'_1)N'_{A1} = \mu'_1 g_A(\mu'_1)N_{A1} = \mu_1 \cdot N_A \tag{2}$$

Since failed nodes and intra-links connected within them are removed, network B fragment into several components. The fraction of normal operation nodes in the network B is:

$$N_{B2} = g_B(\mu'_2) \cdot N'_{B2} = \mu'_2 \cdot g_B(\mu'_2) \cdot N_B = \mu_2 \cdot N_B \tag{3}$$

$$\mu_2 = \mu'_2 \cdot g_B(\mu'_2) \tag{4}$$

$$\mu'_2 = 1 - (1 - \mu_1)^3 = \mu_1^3 - 3\mu_1^2 + 3\mu_1 = (\mu_1^2 - 3\mu_1 + 3)\mu'_1 g_A(\mu'_1) \tag{5}$$

Failure in the network B might lead to further failure in the network A. When failure stops, the network must obey:

$$\begin{cases} \mu'_{2i} = \mu'_{2i-2} = \mu'_{2i+2} \\ \mu'_{2i+1} = \mu'_{2i-1} = \mu'_{2i+3} \end{cases} \tag{6}$$

From the above equations, we derive the final fraction of remain functional nodes in the network A and B are [17]:

$$\mu_{A_\infty} = x g_A(x) \tag{7}$$

$$\mu_{B_\infty} = y g_B(y) \tag{8}$$

where

$$\begin{cases} x = p g_B(y) \\ y = p[(x g_A(x))^2 - 3x g_A(x) + 3]g_A(x) \end{cases} \tag{9}$$

The Eq. 9 can be written as:

$$x = p \cdot g_B \left\{ p[(x \cdot g_A(x))^2 - 3x g_A(x) + 3] \cdot g_A(x) \right\} \tag{10}$$

To describe the cascading failure processes in detail, we give the graph of a part of our model in Fig. 1. In the initial stage, there are ten nodes in the network A and five nodes in the network B. The initial attack occurs in-network A and causes A_5 node fails (shown in Fig. 1 stage 1 red circle). When the cascading failure stops, there are four nodes in the network A, and three nodes in the network B can operate normally.

3   The Method

In this section, we give seven kinds of adding intra-links strategies to improve the robustness of the CPFS. Ji et al. show different adding intra-links strategies (such as low degree strategy and low betweenness strategy) in improving robustness in 'one-to-one correspondence' models [11]. We propose seven adding strategies based on three centralities that play a major role in measuring nodes' importance in networks.

I. Startegy 1: Random adding strategy (RA)
The random adding strategy is as follows: random choosing two nodes and adding an intra-link between them. This process repeats until a demanding number of intra-links are added in A and B network, respectively. Parallel intra-links and self-loop intra-links are not allowed to exist.

II. Startegy 2: Low degree adding strategy (LD)
In an undirected graph, one node degree value is equal to the number of intra-links with it [16]. Low degree adding strategy is described as calculating all nodes degree values and adding an intra-link between a pair of nodes with the most moderate degree values. This process repeats until the number of intra-links is added in-network A and B, respectively. Parallel intra-links and self-loop intra-links are not permitted to exist.

III. Strategy 3: High degree adding strategy (HD)
A high degree-adding strategy is described as calculating all node degree values, ranking nodes in decreasing order, and adding an intra-link between a pair of nodes with the highest degree. This process repeats until a demanding number of intra-links are added in-network A and B, respectively. Parallel intra-links and self-loop intra-links are not allowed to exist.

IV. Strategy 4: Low betweenness adding strategy (LB)
Betweenness centrality is the metric to evaluate nodes' importance by paths [11, 13]. The betweenness centrality value of a node can be calculated by:

$$B(v) = \sum_{i \neq j} \frac{\sigma_{ij}(v)}{\sigma_{ij}} \tag{11}$$

where σ_{ij} is the number of the shortest paths going from node i to node j and $\sigma_{ij}(v)$ is the number of shortest paths going from node i to node j through node v [11,16].

Low betweenness adding strategy is as follows: First, calculating all nodes betweenness centrality values; In the next, ranking nodes in increasing order; In the end, adding an intra-link between a pair of nodes with the lowest betweenness centrality values. This process repeats until the number of intra-links is added in-network A and B, respectively. Parallel intra-links and self-loop intra-links are not allowed to exist.

V. Strategy 5: High betweenness adding strategy (HB)
A high betweenness-adding strategy is described as calculating all node between-ness centrality values, ranking nodes in decreasing order, and adding an intra-link between a pair of nodes with the highest betweenness centrality values. This process repeats until a demanding number of intra-links is added in-network A and B, respectively. Parallel intra-links and self-loop intra-links are not allowed to exist.

VI. Strategy 6: Low eigenvector centrality adding strategy (LEC)
On account of the nodes' eigenvector centrality value is considering all its neigh-bors, we need to construct an all nodes' adjacency matrix A and A_{ij} is an element of this matrix. A_{ij} reflects the link between node i and node j. If there is one intra-link between node i and node j, A_{ij} is 1; otherwise, A_{ij} is 0. Each x_i is the eigenvector centrality value of node i and the initial value of x_i is setting to 1. Through adding consideration of neighbors' importance, x_i will change into x_i' [16]:

$$x_i' = \kappa_1^{-1} \sum_j A_{ij} x_j \tag{12}$$

where κ_1 is the largest eigenvector value of A.

Low eigenvector centrality adding strategy is as following: i. Calculating all nodes' eigenvector centrality values; ii. Ranking nodes in increasing order; iii. They are adding an intra-link between a pair of nodes with the lowest eigenvector centrality values. This process repeats until the number of intra-links is added in-network A and B, respectively. Parallel intra-links and self-loop intra-links are not allowed to exist.

VII. Strategy 7: High eigenvector centrality adding strategy (HEC)
High eigenvector centrality adding strategy is presented as calculating all nodes eigenvector centrality values, ranking one network's nodes in decreasing order, and adding an intra-link between a pair of nodes with the highest eigenvector centrality values. This process repeats until a demanding number of intra-links are added in-network A and B, respectively. Parallel intra-links and self-loop intra-links are not allowed to exist.

4   Simulations and Analysis

In this section, we briefly introduce all parameters of our models. Then we sim-ulate CPFS models and apply cascading failure in our models to obtain the best strategy for enhancing interdependent network reliability.

4.1   Model Parameters

We build the interdependent network by 'one-to-multiple correspondence' model and set the ratio of interlinks is 3:1 without loss generality. According to the

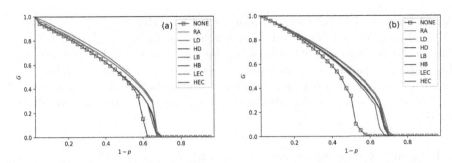

Fig. 2. The fraction of function nodes in systems when $f_L = 15\%$ in ER-ER and SF-SF system which is shown in Fig. (a) and (b), respectively. Seven swapping strategies are compared with original independent networks (NONE) in different system structures.

above settings, the nodes number of network A is $N_A = 9000$ and network B is $N_B = 3000$. The average degree of ER network and SF network is $\langle k \rangle = 4$. The parameter of SF degree distribution is $\gamma = 3$. We assume that all links in our models are unidirectional.

We are required to ensure the number of adding intra-links in both network A and B. f_L defines as the fraction of adding links by different adding strategies:

$$f_L = \frac{L'}{L_A + L_B} \tag{13}$$

where L_A and L_B represent the number of intra-links in-network A and B, respectively. L' is the number of adding links. Based on the actual situation and economic cost considerations, we can't add intra-links in one node indefinitely. The high degree value of social interaction is greater than 6 [8]. We set 8 as the upper limit of one node degree value in our simulation. If one node degree is greater than 8, this node will not add intra-links. Under these settings, the maximum value of f_L is 50%.

4.2   System Robustness Metric

We simulate random attack as the types of attacks in our models. To measure the robustness of a CPFS to tolerate random attacks, we introduce G, which means the fraction of nodes that can normally work at a stable state. G can be described as:

$$G = \frac{N'_A + N'_B}{N_A + N_B} \tag{14}$$

where $N'_A(N'_B)$ represents the number of nodes that remain functioning in-network $A(B)$ after the cascading failure. To measure the maximum of the CPFS's tolerant ability against random failure, we will observe the values of p_c.

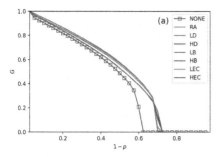
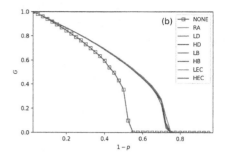

Fig. 3. The fraction of function nodes in systems when $f_L = 25\%$ in ER-ER and SF-SF system which is shown in Fig. (a) and (b), respectively. LD is the best effect in enhancing G in (a) and LEC shows the best performance in improving p_c values in subfigures.

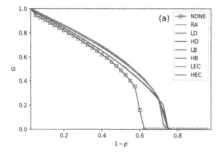
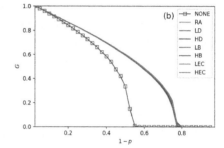

Fig. 4. The fraction of function nodes in systems when $f_L = 35\%$ in ER-ER and SF-SF system which is shown in Fig. (a) and (b), respectively. LD is the best effect in enhancing G in (a), and LEC shows the best performance in improving p_c values in subfigures.

4.3   Impact of Network Size and p_c

We conduct performance comparisons among the seven adding strategies mentioned in Sect. 3. The values of f_L in Fig. 2, Fig. 3, Fig. 4 and Fig. 5 are 15%, 25% and 35% and 45%. In all figures, we plot the relationship among G, p_c and $1 - p$ under seven adding strategies. From Fig. 2, Fig. 3, Fig. 4 and Fig. 5, we can observe the following situations and conclusions:

   I. Adding intra-links in a CPFS can enhance its reliability against cascading failure and higher robustness can be obtained when f_L increases. The values of G and p_c are increasing as f_L increases. In Fig. 2(b), the p_c value of LEC is closed to 0.7. When f_L increases into 45%, the value of p_c in LEC is more than 0.8 (shown in Fig. 5). This finding is to obey the conclusion of [11].

  II. Under the same number of adding links, adding intra-links with low centrality values always perform better in improving G than by high centrality values. This phenomenon is more clear when f_L is small (such as Fig. 2). This finding is similar to the conclusion of [12]. This phenomenon is due

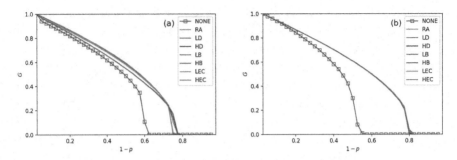

Fig. 5. The fraction of function nodes in systems when $f_L = 45\%$ in ER-ER and SF-SF system which is shown in Fig. (a) and (b), respectively. Adding intra-links with low centrality values can get better G values than other strategies.

to that adding intra-links with high centrality values will make the nodes' number of the giant component of networks bigger. Then cascading failure will provoke a large number of nodes cannot perform a normal operation. The result of adding intra-links of low centrality values is the opposite. The probability of the giant component in the networks being attacked will be smaller.

III. The LD strategy is the best choice in enhancing reliability under ER-ER interdependent networks (shown in Fig. 2(a), Fig. 3(a), Fig. 4(a) and Fig. 5(a)). In the other subgraphs, LEC performs the best influence in improving G and p_c. In Fig. 3(b), Fig. 4(b) and Fig. 5(b), seven adding strategies can be regarded as approximately equivalent in improving G and p_c. Adding intra-links with high centrality values is some adding intra-links coincide with by low centrality values when $f_L > 25\%$. The overlapping links will get bigger and bigger when f_L increases. Because of the upper limit of adding intra-links is 50%, the topology of intra-links is more similar among our models.

5   Conclusion

In this paper, we add intra-links in networks to enhance the reliability of interdependent networks. The approach with low centrality values can get better system robustness. The above simulation results show that the low degree adding method performs the best effect in enhancing G under the ER network couples ER network model and the low eigenvector centrality strategy is the best choice in improving robustness in other models.

In the future, we will use more evaluation metrics to describe network reliability more comprehensively and accurately. We are trying to study new strategies to maximize the number of nodes in the giant component.

References

1. Banerjee, S., Balas, V.E., Pandey, A., Bouzefrane, S.: Towards intelligent optimization of design strategies of cyber-physical systems: measuring efficacy through evolutionary computations. In: Llanes Santiago, O., Cruz Corona, C., Silva Neto, A.J., Verdegay, J.L. (eds.) Computational Intelligence in Emerging Technologies for Engineering Applications. SCI, vol. 872, pp. 73–101. Springer, Cham (2020). https://doi.org/10.1007/978-3-030-34409-2_5
2. Buldyrev, S.V., Parshani, R., Paul, G., Stanley, H.E., Havlin, S.: Catastrophic cascade of failures in interdependent networks. Nature **464**(7291), 1025–1028 (2010)
3. Chen, L., Yue, D., Dou, C., Cheng, Z., Chen, J.: Robustness of cyber-physical power systems in cascading failure: survival of interdependent clusters. Int. J. Electr. Power Ener. Syst. **114**, 105374 (2020)
4. Ding, D., Han, Q.L., Wang, Z., Ge, X.: A survey on model-based distributed control and filtering for industrial cyber-physical systems. IEEE Trans. Ind. Inf. **15**(5), 2483–2499 (2019)
5. Dong, G., Chen, Y., Wang, F., Du, R., Tian, L., Stanley, H.E.: Robustness on interdependent networks with a multiple-to-multiple dependent relationship. Chaos Interdisc. J. Nonlinear Sci. **29**(7), 073107 (2019)
6. Gazafroudi, A.S., Shafie-khah, M., Fitiwi, D.Z., Santos, S.F., Corchado, J.M., Catalão, J.P.S.: impact of strategic behaviors of the electricity consumers on power system reliability. In: Amini, M.H., Boroojeni, K.G., Iyengar, S.S., Pardalos, P.M., Blaabjerg, F., Madni, A.M. (eds.) Sustainable Interdependent Networks II. SSDC, vol. 186, pp. 193–215. Springer, Cham (2019). https://doi.org/10.1007/978-3-319-98923-5_11
7. Hassan, M.U., Rehmani, M.H., Chen, J.: Differential privacy techniques for cyber physical systems: a survey. IEEE Commun. Surv. Tutorials **22**, 746–789 (2019)
8. Hesse, M., Dann, D., Braesemann, F., Teubner, T.: Understanding the platform economy: signals, trust, and social interaction. In: HICSS 2020 Proceedings, Maui, pp. 1–10 (2020)
9. Huang, Z., Wang, C., Stojmenovic, M., Nayak, A.: Characterization of cascading failures in interdependent cyber-physical systems. IEEE Trans. Comput. **64**(8), 2158–2168 (2015)
10. Jerraya, A.A.: Hardware/software interface codesign for cyber physical systems. In: Bhattacharyya, S.S., Potkonjak, M., Velipasalar, S. (eds.) Embedded, Cyber-Physical, and IoT Systems, pp. 73–77. Springer, Cham (2020). https://doi.org/10.1007/978-3-030-16949-7_3
11. Ji, X., et al.: Improving interdependent networks robustness by adding connectivity links. Physica A Stat. Mech. Appl. **444**, 9–19 (2016)
12. Kandah, F., Cancelleri, J., Reising, D., Altarawneh, A., Skjellum, A.: A hardware-software codesign approach to identity, trust, and resilience for IoT/CPS at scale. In: 2019 International Conference on Internet of Things (iThings) and IEEE Green Computing and Communications (GreenCom) and IEEE Cyber, Physical and Social Computing (CPSCom) and IEEE Smart Data (SmartData), pp. 1125–1134. IEEE (2019)
13. Kumari, P., Singh, A.: Approximation and updation of betweenness centrality in dynamic complex networks. In: Verma, N.K., Ghosh, A.K. (eds.) Computational Intelligence: Theories, Applications and Future Directions - Volume I. AISC, vol. 798, pp. 25–37. Springer, Singapore (2019). https://doi.org/10.1007/978-981-13-1132-1_3

14. Lai, R., Qiu, X., Wu, J.: Robustness of asymmetric cyber-physical power systems against cyber attacks. IEEE Access **7**, 61342–61352 (2019)
15. Li, S., Zhao, S., Yang, P., Andriotis, P., Xu, L., Sun, Q.: Distributed consensus algorithm for events detection in cyber-physical systems. IEEE Internet Things J. **6**(2), 2299–2308 (2019)
16. Newman, M.: Networks. Oxford University Press, Oxford (2018)
17. Peng, H., Kan, Z., Zhao, D., Han, J.: Security assessment for interdependent heterogeneous cyber physical systems. Mob. Netw. Appl. **12**(1), 1–11 (2019)
18. Yamagata, Y., Liu, S., Akazaki, T., Duan, Y., Hao, J.: Falsification of cyber-physical systems using deep reinforcement learning. IEEE Trans. Softw. Eng. (2020). https://doi.org/10.1109/TSE.2020.2969178

Robustness Enhancement Analysis of CPS Systems Under the Swapping Strategies Between Different Networks

Hao Peng[1,2], Can Liu[1], Dandan Zhao[1(✉)], Jianmin Han[1], and Zhonglong Zheng[1]

[1] College of Mathematics and Computer Science, Zhejiang Normal University, Jinhua 321004, Zhejiang, China
ddzhao@zjnu.edu.cn

[2] Shanghai Key Laboratory of Integrated Administration Technologies for Information Security, Shanghai 200240, China

Abstract. With the advent of the Internet of Everything, the robustness of cyber physics system (CPS) has received more attention and research. In this paper, for the heterogeneous CPS network environment, based on the exchange edge enhancement strategy between the neutron networks of the system, we study the robustness of CPS. Based on the performance analysis of the most significant functional component in the system, we comparatively analyze the robustness of CPS under random attacks. Our simulation results show that the system's heterogeneity will affect the system reliability under the exchange-side strategy. Besides, we have drawn a graph of node central values after different approaches to explain and supplement the above analysis conclusions.

Keywords: Cyber physics system (CPS) · Swapping strategy · Cascading failure · Reliability

1 Introduction

Cyber-physical system (CPS) is an integrated system which coupled with computer components and physical components [14,16,30]. Computer components process the acquired data and issue corresponding control instructions to make the physical components operate normally. The physical components provide power or sources which are needed by computer components, and obtain real-time data. A large number of infrastructure systems can be considered CPS. Such as, the power grid system is usually regarded as a typical representative of the cyber-physical system [17,26]. To ensure our daily life, these infrasture systems must be in a safty state. Maintaining the reliability of CPS is an important research direction of CPS.

Depending on CPS's characteristics, existing enhancements of CPS's reliability can be divided into several research directions. The first direction is hardware

© Springer Nature Singapore Pte Ltd. 2020
G. Xu et al. (Eds.): FCS 2020, CCIS 1286, pp. 305–314, 2020.
https://doi.org/10.1007/978-981-15-9739-8_24

adjustment [15, 20]. Computer components and physical components have a lot of equipment. The safety of these devices is essential for maintaining the reliability of the CPS. The second direction is software [1, 20, 30]. Computer components and physical components are controlled by many software. Softwares can ensure that these components are in a safe state. The another direction is abstracting networks into graphics [10, 18]. Disregard the differences of the components between computer and physical components and treat them as identical nodes. In addition, machine learning and reinforcement learning are increasingly being applied to the research of interdependent networks [13, 21, 23].

1.1   Interdependent Networks

To simplify the simulation model's complexity and not lose the generality of the model, scholars usually think that the CPS is composed of two networks, which are named network A and B [3, 9].

The simplest coupling relationship is 'one-to-one correspondence' model [3, 12]. This model means that two interdependent networks A and B have the same number of nodes, and each node on network A has to function depending on exactly only one node in the network B, and vice versa. This one-to-one supply relationship is very rare in reality except for some special application scenarios.

In the real world networks, many components have a coupling relationship with more than one other component. With this background, 'multiple-to-multiple correspondence' model has been proposed [8, 19, 29]. This model means that one node in the network A operates depending on more than one node in the network B, and vice versa. Although this model is more closer to social networks, this multiple-to-multiple supply relationship is too complicated in the experimentit and it has a few limitations that are not solved [11, 32].

'One-to-multiple correspondence' model [6, 7, 9] means that one node in the network A has the dependent relationship of some nodes in the network B and a node in the network B only has one depending node in the network A. This model well shows some of the characteristics of the above two models and its supply relationship has relatively wide applications in reality. 'One-to-multiple correspondence' model is well simulating the dependent relationship of the power grid. One power station provides power for various devices, but one control device only controls one power station [17, 26]. 'One-to-multiple correspondence' model is commonly used in researching of the power grid.

1.2   Contribution

Our main contributions in this paper are:

- i). Propose new swapping inter-links strategies which have better effects in improving CPS reliability than existing approaches.
- ii). Indirectly prove the relationship between node centrality values.

1.3 Organization

The outline of this work is as follows: we introduce the model of CPS in Sect. 2. In Sect. 3, we describe different swapping strategies in detail. Section 4 performs the results of the simulation and analysis points. Conclusions and future work in Sect. 5.

2 The Models

In this section, we will describe our simulation CPS models in detail. After that, we derive the 'one-to-multiple' model cascading failure's theoretical formulas.

2.1 Complex Networks

Erdös-Rényi network (ER network) and scale-free network (SF network) are researched to reflect features of real-world systems [22,31]. Node degree distribution follows binomial distribution in ER networks. The degree distribution in SF networks follows power-law as $P(k) \propto k^{-\gamma}$ where $P(k)$ is the degree distribution, and γ is the power-law exponent [22,28]. All intra-links are randomly connecting in both network A and B.

2.2 Interdependent Models

In this paper, we still follow the characteristics of the previously studied network model and believe that the interdependent networks are formed by the coupling of two systems. We denote these two networks are network A and network B, respectively. The links connect nodes in a single network as intra-links and connect them from different systems as inter-links [11]. All intra-links and inter-links in our models are unweighted and unidirectional.

We apply the 'one-to-multiple correspondence' model in our paper to represent the relationship of nodes. All inter-links are the random connection between network A and B. In our simulation models, the coupling ratio of inter-links is 3:1. This means that node u in the network A depends on only one node v in the network B while node v has three inter-links from network A. If node v fails, node u will fail. However, the failure of node u may not cause the node v to fail. Only all inter-links of node v are failed, node v will be failed.

2.3 Cascading Failure

In [3], Buldyrev et al. propose the theoretical formulas of cascading failure in the 'one-to-one correspondence' model. The number of nodes in the state stage is:

$$\begin{cases} x = g_A(y)p \\ y = g_B(x)p \end{cases} \tag{1}$$

where $g_A(y)(g_B(x))$ means the fraction of normal working nodes of network $A(B)$ and p is the fraction of nodes which are not failed in the initial stage.

We assume that the initial random attack occurs in the network A and a $1 - p$ fraction nodes are attacked in our models. At first, we randomly removing a $1-p$ fraction of the node in the network A as random attacks. Then, we remove all links of these removed nodes. The fraction of normal working nodes in the network A is:

$$N_{A1} = g_A(\mu_1')N_{A1}' = \mu_1' g_A(\mu_1')N_{A1} = \mu_1 \cdot N_A \qquad (2)$$

where μ' is the fraction of nonde that remaining nodes and N_{A1}' is the number of nodes is remaining in the network A.

The cascading failure occurs in the network B since some nodes of network B lose depending inter-links from network A. In 'one-to-one coorespondencce' model, the number of the normal working noes in network B is [3]:

$$N_{B2} = \mu_2 N_B = g_B(\mu_1)\mu_1 N_B = pg_A(p)g_B(\mu_1)N_B \qquad (3)$$

and

$$\mu_2 = \mu_1' \cdot g_B(\mu_1') \qquad (4)$$
$$\mu_2' = pg_B(\mu_1') \qquad (5)$$

In our 'one-to-multiple correspondence' model, when failure stops in the network B, the normal working nodes in the network B is:

$$N_{B2} = g_B(\mu_2') \cdot N_{B2}' = \mu_2' \cdot g_B(\mu_2') \cdot N_B = \mu_2 \cdot N_B \qquad (6)$$

and

$$\mu_2 = \mu_2' \cdot g_B(\mu_2') \qquad (7)$$

$$\mu_2' = 1 - (1 - \mu_1)^3 = \mu_1^3 - 3\mu_1^2 + 3\mu_1 = (\mu_1^2 - 3\mu_1 + 3)\mu_1' g_A(\mu_1') \qquad (8)$$

According to the above derive formulas, the number of nodes in the network when failure stops must obey:

$$\begin{cases} \mu_{2i}' = \mu_{2i-2}' = \mu_{2i+2}' \\ \mu_{2i+1}' = \mu_{2i-1}' = \mu_{2i+3}' \end{cases} \qquad (9)$$

And the final fraction of remain functional nodes in the network A and B are [24]:

$$\mu_{A_\infty} = xg_A(x) \qquad (10)$$

$$\mu_{B_\infty} = yg_B(y) \qquad (11)$$

where

$$\begin{cases} x = pg_B(y) \\ y = p[(xg_A(x))^2 - 3xg_A(x) + 3]g_A(x) \end{cases} \qquad (12)$$

The Eq. 12 can be written as:

$$x = p \cdot g_B \left\{ p[(x \cdot g_A(x))^2 - 3xg_A(x) + 3] \cdot g_A(x) \right\} \qquad (13)$$

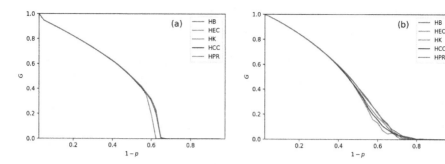

Fig. 1. The fraction of function nodes in systems when $f_N = 20\%$. Fig(a) and (b) are the systems that are are combined with ER-ER and SF-SF, respectively. HCC has the best effect in improving the reliability of ER-ER CPS. HPR and HB get better G than others strategies in SF-SF model.

3   The Method

In Sect. 3, three new swapping inter-links strategies will be described in detail. We have known that connecting nodes with high centrality values by inter-links could enhance CPS reliability [5]. Thus, we follow this finding to propose new strategies.

3.1   Strategy 1: High K-Shell(HK)

K-Shell decomposition is used to partition the network into hierarchically ordered sub-structures, by decomposing the system iteratively removing all the nodes with the order until no removing is possible [4]. HK swapping strategy is as following: calculating all nodes K-Shell values and ranking nodes in decreasing order. An inter-link is exchanged between two nodes, which have the highest Shell values.

3.2   Strategy 2: High Closeness Centrality(HCC)

Closeness centrality is the reciprocal of the path length needed to reach another node. If the path length to reach another node is small, the closeness centrality of the node is large [2]. The node closeness centrality can be calculated by the following equation:

$$C(i) = \frac{1}{\sum_j d(i,j)} \tag{14}$$

where $d(j,i)$ means the distance between node j and node i.

HCC swapping strategy is as following: calculating all nodes closeness centrality values and ranking nodes in descending order. An inter-link is exchanged between two nodes, which have the highest closeness centrality values.

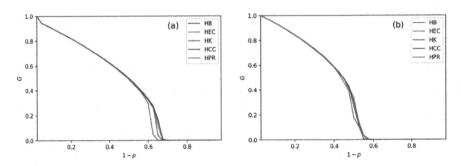

Fig. 2. The fraction of function nodes in systems when $f_N = 40\%$. Fig(a) and (b) are the systems that are are combined with ER-ER and SF-SF, respectively. HCC gets best G values in ER-ER. In SF-SF, all srtategies have a similar performance in improving G.

3.3   Strategy 3: High Page Rank(HPR)

One node gets greater importance to the opinion of a high Page Rank probability neighbor as compared to the view of a low Page Rank probability neighbor [27]. One node PageRank value is:

$$PR(u) = \sum_{v \in B_u} \frac{PR(v)}{L(v)} \tag{15}$$

In this equation, B_u is the collection of all node linked to the ndoe u and $L(v)$ is the number of links of node v.

HPR swapping strategy is as following: calculating all nodes Page Rank values and ranking nodes in descending order. An inter-link is exchanged between two nodes, which have the highest Page Rank values.

4   Simulation Results and Analysis

In Sect. 4, we simulate CPS models and the cascading failure to obtain the best strategy to enhance CPS's reliability. In [25], we have got that high betweenness centrality strategy and high eigenvector centrality strategy gets the best enhancement in different models. In this paper, we use the above two strategies as control experiments to test the enhancement effect of new strategies.

4.1   Model Parameters

We build two kinds of CPS models by ER networks and SF networks. They are ER network couples ER network(ER-ER) and SF network couples SF network(SF-SF). The average degree is $\langle k \rangle = 4$ on both of ER networks and SF networks. The parameter $\lambda = 3$ in the SF network. 'One-to-multiple correspondence' is the dependent relationship of two systems in our CPS models. We

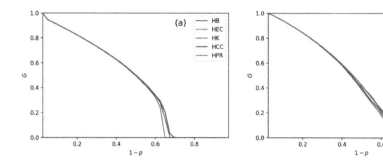

Fig. 3. The fraction of function nodes in systems when $f_N = 60\%$. Fig(a) and (b) are the systems that are are combined with ER-ER and SF-SF, respectively. HCC gets best G values in ER-ER. In SF-SF, all srtategies have a similar performance in improving G.

set N_A, and N_B are 15000 and 5000, and the connection ratio of inter-links is 3:1.

We define the nodes' fraction of swapping inter-links f_N as:

$$f_N = \frac{N_S}{N_A} \tag{16}$$

where N_S means the number of nodes' which are swapped inter-links by strategies.

We randomly remove $(1 - p)$ fraction of the network A node as the failed node. This will result in the cascading failure to iterate in CPS. To reduce the error of the experimental results, we simulate 20 times for each $1 - p$ under one specific swapping strategy and take the average of these results. G means the proportion of normal working nodes of the entire system.

$$G = \frac{N'_A + N'_B}{N_A + N_B} \tag{17}$$

Where $N'_A(N'_B)$ is the number of normal working nodes at steady state after cascading failure. After that, we observe the values of p_c to measure maximum tolerant ability against random failure. When G gets 0, the value of $1 - p$ is the p_c value.

4.2   Impact of Network Size G and p_c

We simulate the entire cascading failure in two certain CPS models under $f_N = 20\%$, $f_N = 40\%$, $f_N = 60\%$ and $f_N = 80\%$. From Figs. 1, 2, 3 and 4, we can observe the following situations and conclusions:

I. HCC strategy has the best effect on improving the reliability of the ER-ER model. HPR and HB get better G than other strategies in the SF-SF model. The differences between these two strategies can be ignored.

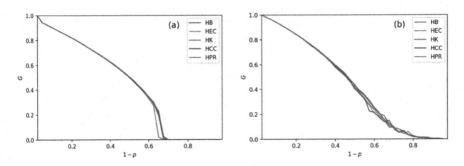

Fig. 4. The fraction of function nodes in systems when $f_N = 80\%$. Fig(a) and (b) are the systems that are are combined with ER-ER and SF-SF, respectively. HCC gets best G values in ER-ER. In SF-SF, all srtategies have a similar performance in improving G. HPR and HB get better G than others strategies in SF-SF model.

II. HK strategy shows the worst effect in enhancing ER-ER CPS reliability. However, it shows different performances in SF-SF CPS model. In Fig. 1(b), Fig. 3(b) and Fig. 4(b), HK performs a similar effect in improving G as other strategies.

III. With the increase of f_N, the gaps between different strategies performances a phenomenon of first increasing and then decreasing. This shows that nodes with higher different centrality values in the network are the same, and the nodes with lower centrality values are the same. The nodes in the middle of the centrality values sorting are quite different.

IV. The values of p_c in all figures become larger as the value of f_N become larger in ER-ER. In SF-SF, when $f_N = 40\%$, the value of p_c is decreasing from $f_N = 20\%$. As $f_N > 40\%$, the value of p_c is increasing. In Fig. 1(b), the value of p_c is less than 0.6. In Fig. 2(b), p_c becomes 0.58. When f_N is 80% in Fig. 4, p_c is more than 0.8.

5   Conclusion and Future Work

We build two kinds of interdependent network models with the coupled ratio at 3:1 to explore the reliability enhancement approach. We find that swapping inter-links with high closeness centrality values can get better system robustness in ER-ER CPS. High Page Rank values strategy and high betweenness strategy get better G than other strategies in SF-SF CPS. With the number of swapping inter-links increasing, the reliabilty of SF-SF is reduced at first and then stronger.

In the future, we will build new complex interdependent systems to better simulating realistic networks. We are trying to find different strategies to maximize the number of normal working nodes after cascading failure.

Acknowledgments. This work was supported in part by the National Natural Science Foundation of China (Grant No.61902359, No.61672467 and No.61672468), in part by Zhejiang Provincial Natural Science Foundation of China (Grant No.LQ19F030010), and in part by the Opening Project of Shanghai Key Laboratory of Integrated Administration Technologies for Information Security (Grant No.AGK2018001).

References

1. Banerjee, S., Balas, V.E., Pandey, A., Bouzefrane, S.: Towards intelligent optimization of design strategies of cyber-physical systems: measuring efficacy through evolutionary computations. In: Llanes Santiago, O., Cruz Corona, C., Silva Neto, A.J., Verdegay, J.L. (eds.) Computational Intelligence in Emerging Technologies for Engineering Applications. SCI, vol. 872, pp. 73–101. Springer, Cham (2020). https://doi.org/10.1007/978-3-030-34409-2_5
2. Bergamini, E., Borassi, M., Crescenzi, P., Marino, A., Meyerhenke, H.: Computing top-k closeness centrality faster in unweighted graphs. ACM Trans. Knowl. Discov. Data (TKDD) **13**(5), 1–40 (2019)
3. Buldyrev, S.V., Parshani, R., Paul, G., Stanley, H.E., Havlin, S.: Catastrophic cascade of failures in interdependent networks. Nature **464**(7291), 1025–1028 (2010)
4. Burleson-Lesser, K., Morone, F., Tomassone, M.S., Makse, H.A.: K-core robustness in ecological and financial networks. Sci. Rep. **10**(1), 1–14 (2020)
5. Chattopadhyay, S., Dai, H., Hosseinalipour, S., et al.: Designing optimal interlink patterns to maximize robustness of interdependent networks against cascading failures. IEEE Trans. Commun. **65**(9), 3847–3862 (2017)
6. Chen, L., Yue, D., Dou, C.: Optimization on vulnerability analysis and redundancy protection in interdependent networks. Phys. A: Stat. Mech. Appl. **523**, 1216–1226 (2019)
7. Chen, L., Yue, D., Dou, C., Chen, J., Cheng, Z.: Study on attack paths of cyber attack in cyber-physical power systems. IET Gener. Transm. Distrib. **14**(12), 2352–2360 (2020)
8. Chen, L., Yue, D., Dou, C., Cheng, Z., Chen, J.: Robustness of cyber-physical power systems in cascading failure: survival of interdependent clusters. Int. J. Electr. Power Energy Syst. **114**, 105374 (2020)
9. Dong, G., Chen, Y., Wang, F., Du, R., Tian, L., Stanley, H.E.: Robustness on interdependent networks with a multiple-to-multiple dependent relationship. Chaos: Interdisc. J. Nonlinear Sci. **29**(7), 073107 (2019)
10. Gazafroudi, A.S., Shafie-khah, M., Fitiwi, D.Z., Santos, S.F., Corchado, J.M., Catalão, J.P.S.: Impact of strategic behaviors of the electricity consumers on power system reliability. In: Amini, M.H., Boroojeni, K.G., Iyengar, S.S., Pardalos, P.M., Blaabjerg, F., Madni, A.M. (eds.) Sustainable Interdependent Networks II. SSDC, vol. 186, pp. 193–215. Springer, Cham (2019). https://doi.org/10.1007/978-3-319-98923-5_11
11. Huang, Z., Wang, C., Stojmenovic, M., Nayak, A.: Characterization of cascading failures in interdependent cyber-physical systems. IEEE Trans. Comput. **64**(8), 2158–2168 (2015)
12. Iri, N., Kosut, O.: Fine asymptotics for universal one-to-one compression of parametric sources. IEEE Trans. Inf. Theory **65**(4), 2442–2458 (2019)
13. Ishigaki, G., Devic, S., Gour, R., Jue, J.P.: Deeppr: progressive recovery for interdependent VNFs with deep reinforcement learning. IEEE J. Sel. Commun. (2020)
14. Javed, Y., Felemban, M., Shawly, T., Kobes, J., Ghafoor, A.: A partition-driven integrated security architecture for cyberphysical systems. Computer **53**(3), 47–56 (2020)

15. Jerraya, A.A.: Hardware/software interface codesign for cyber physical systems. In: Bhattacharyya, S.S., Potkonjak, M., Velipasalar, S. (eds.) Embedded, Cyber-Physical, and IoT Systems, pp. 73–77. Springer, Cham (2020). https://doi.org/10.1007/978-3-030-16949-7_3

16. Jiang, J., Xia, Y., Xu, S., Shen, H.L., Wu, J.: An asymmetric interdependent networks model for cyber-physical systems. Chaos: Interdisc. J. Nonlinear Sci. **30**(5), 053135 (2020)

17. Kong, P.Y.: Optimal configuration of interdependence between communication network and power grid. IEEE Trans. Ind. Inform. **15**(7), 4054–4065 (2019)

18. Lai, R., Qiu, X., Wu, J.: Robustness of asymmetric cyber-physical power systems against cyber attacks. IEEE Access **7**, 61342–61352 (2019)

19. Lee, L., Hu, P.: Vulnerability analysis of cascading dynamics in smart grids under load redistribution attacks. Int. J. Electr. Power Energy Syst. **111**, 182–190 (2019)

20. Majchrzak, T.A., Kaindl, H., Grønli, T.M.: Introduction to the minitrack on software development for mobile devices, the internet-of-things, and cyber-physical systems. In: Proceedings of the 53rd Hawaii International Conference on System Sciences (2020)

21. Mekonnen, Y., Namuduri, S., Burton, L., Sarwat, A., Bhansali, S.: Machine learning techniques in wireless sensor network based precision agriculture. J. Electrochem. Soc. **167**(3), 037522 (2019)

22. Newman, M.: Networks. Oxford University Press, United Kingdom (2018)

23. Ni, Z., Paul, S.: A multistage game in smart grid security: a reinforcement learning solution. IEEE Trans. Neural Netw. Learn. Syst. **30**(9), 2684–2695 (2019)

24. Peng, H., Kan, Z., Zhao, D., Han, J.: Security assessment for interdependent heterogeneous cyber physical systems. Mob. Netw. Appl. **12**(1), 1–11 (2019)

25. Peng, H., Liu, C., Zhao, D., Ye, H., Fang, Z., Wang, W.: Security analysis of CPS systems under different swapping strategies in IoT environments. IEEE Access **8**, 63567–63576 (2020)

26. Sen, A., Basu, K.: On connectivity of interdependent networks. In: 2019 IEEE Global Communications Conference (GLOBECOM), pp. 1–6. IEEE (2019)

27. Singh, A., Cherifi, H., et al.: Centrality-based opinion modeling on temporal networks. IEEE Access **8**, 1945–1961 (2019)

28. Xie, J., Yuan, Y., Fan, Z., Wang, J., Wu, J., Hu, Y.: Eradicating abrupt collapse on single network with dependency groups. Chaos: Interdisc. J. Nonlinear Sci. **29**(8), 083111 (2019)

29. Xing, J., Wei, Z., Zhang, G.: A line matching method based on multiple intensity ordering with uniformly spaced sampling. Sensors **20**(6), 1639 (2020)

30. Yamagata, Y., Liu, S., Akazaki, T., Duan, Y., Hao, J.: Falsification of cyber-physical systems using deep reinforcement learning. IEEE Trans. Softw. Eng. (2020)

31. Zhong, J., Zhang, F., Yang, S., Li, D.: Restoration of interdependent network against cascading overload failure. Phys. A: Stat. Mech. Appl. **514**, 884–891 (2019)

32. Zhou, Y., Lutz, P.E., Ibrahim, E.C., Courtet, P., Tzavara, E., Turecki, G., Belzeaux, R.: Suicide and suicide behaviors: a review of transcriptomics and multiomics studies in psychiatric disorders. J. Neurosci. Res. **98**(4), 601–615 (2020)

Security Assessment for Cascading Failures of Cyber-Physical Systems Under Target Attack Strategy

Hao Peng[1,2], Zhen Qian[1], Zhe Kan[1], Hongxia Ye[1], Zian Fang[1], and Dandan Zhao[1(✉)]

[1] Zhejiang Normal University, Jinhua 321004, Zhejiang, China
ddzhao@zjnu.edu.cn
[2] Shanghai Key Laboratory of Integrated Administration Technologies for Information Security,
Shanghai 200240, China

Abstract. This paper focuses on the reliability of the cyber-physical system under the targeted attack strategy. The cyber-physical system is composed of interdependent physical resources and computing resources. Attackers can attack physical space based on information space, resulting in cascading failure. We first build a model by introducing the interdependent network. Based on this model, we theoretically analyze the cascading failure process of networks under targeted attack. Secondly, we use simulation experiments to verify the results of theoretical analysis and give the main factors that affect the security of the cyber-physical information system. Finally, we discuss the shortcomings of this paper and put forward the direction of the next work.

Keywords: Cyber-physical systems · Target attack · Cascading failures · Security assessment

1 Introduction

In recent years, the cyber-physical system (CPS) has been a new and vital field in surgical technology and academia. CPS is the product of close combination and coordination of computing resources and physical resources. With the increasing integration of the communication network and physical equipment, CPS's security has become the focus of attention [1]. CPS is usually modeled as two interdependent networks [2–4], communication network and physical network. In the interconnected network, the nodes of a system are destroyed, which has a significant impact. The failure of a node will not only affect the structure of the network itself but also affect the nodes of another system due to the interdependence of network, which will lead to iterative network failure [5]. We call this failure cascading failure. Therefore, it is essential for CPS to evaluate the risk of the coupled network.

Early research mainly focused on a single network, but with the progress and development of society, the research direction gradually changed to an interactive system [6–8]. Erdos and RéNYI et al. [9, 10] proposed a random network with a degree distribution of Poisson distribution. For each node pair, the probability that one node has a

© Springer Nature Singapore Pte Ltd. 2020
G. Xu et al. (Eds.): FCS 2020, CCIS 1286, pp. 315–327, 2020.
https://doi.org/10.1007/978-981-15-9739-8_25

link with another node is the same. With the deepening of research, scholars found that the distance between any two nodes in the actual network is minimal [11]. So, watts and Strogatz put forward the classic small-world network model, namely the WS model [12]. However, in real life, the network is not a random connection, nor is it a single invariable. Therefore, Barab á Si, and Albert proposed the famous BA model in 1999 [13]. In their network model, there are a few nodes with a large degree in the network, and most of the nodes have a small degree. This is a milestone in the study of complex systems. Many scholars have proposed more network growth models according to the actual situation [14, 15].

This paper aims to establish an appropriate interdependent network model and analyze the robustness of CPS in the face of deliberate attacks. In this paper, the cascading failure process of the coupled system under intentional attack is explained in detail. The theoretical solution of the seepage threshold is obtained through theoretical analysis, and simulation results verify the correctness of the academic answer. This work can help us to analyze better the characteristics of CPS in the face of deliberate attacks, and then help other aspects of research.

2   Model and Concepts

This chapter mainly introduces the network model and analyzes the process of cascading failure based on the model. We build an information physical network model with a coupled network based on the cyber-physical system in real life. If the communication network is deliberately attacked, the combined system will fail in cascade. We analyze the process of cascading failure and show when the network will collapse and no longer fail.

2.1   Model

In today's world, cyber-physical system exists in many fields. To facilitate the research, we abstract the cyber-physical system into a communication network and a physical network. The communication network and physical network are represented by X and Y, respectively, and their number of nodes is NX and NY. Through observation and data research, we can find that the number of nodes in a communication network is higher than that in physical systems. In this paper, we assume that the node ratio of the communication network and the physical network is 3:1, and the connection between nodes is random, and the relationship between nodes of network X and Y is also casual. In this paper, we assume that the networks X and Y are scale-free networks.

2.2   Concepts

In reality, the failure of network nodes is usually not random but targeted to attack nodes. Assuming that some nodes of communication network X are deliberately destroyed, since X and Y are coupled networks, the failure of one node in X will affect the nodes in Y, failing the nodes in Y. Node failure in Y will, in turn, affect nodes in X, resulting in node failure in X, and so on. We call this process cascading failure, as shown in Fig. 1.

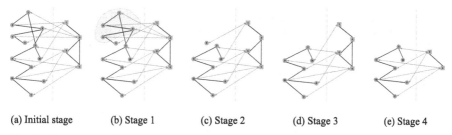

(a) Initial stage   (b) Stage 1   (c) Stage 2   (d) Stage 3   (e) Stage 4

Fig. 1. The process of cascading failure. The network node fails until it reaches a stable state.

The cascading failure process is clear, and we need to determine when it will stop. When two networks collapse, or the remaining nodes in the system no longer fail, and the network reaches a stable state, the cascading failure stops. Therefore, when the cascading failure no longer occurs, the network reaches a steady-state, and only functional nodes remain in the network. In the next section, we will use mathematical methods to analyze the cascading failure process in detail.

3 Theoretical Analysis of Cascading Failures Process

In this section, we build a theoretical framework to analyze the cascading failure process of X and Y networks. Firstly, the process of intentional attack is transformed to investigate an intentional attack by analyzing random attacks directly. Then, the process of cascading failure is analyzed by mathematical methods. Finally, the expression of cascading failure at a steady state is obtained.

3.1 Stage 1: Target Attack in Cyber Network

Different nodes in the network have different importance. Some nodes play a key role in the connectivity of the network. There are many methods to evaluate the importance of nodes. Gallos [16] proposed the influence of vertex degree on network robustness. According to this, deliberate attacks can be analyzed by transforming them into random attacks. In Ref. [16], a family of functions is defined:

$$W_\alpha(k_i) = \frac{(k_i + 1)^\alpha}{\sum_{i=0}^{N}(k_i + 1)^\alpha} \tag{1}$$

$W_\alpha(k_i)$ is assigned to each node, indicating the probability that node i with degree k is attacked and fails.

When $\alpha < 0$, the nodes with low degree are more likely to be attacked, and the nodes with high degree are protected. When $\alpha > 0$, the nodes with high degree are more likely to be attacked, and the nodes with low degree are protected. When $\alpha = 0$, W0 = 1/N, all nodes have the same probability of failure, which is equivalent to random attack.

The main idea of our method is to find an equivalent network X', so the targeted attack problem on the interdependent network X and Y can be transformed into the random attack problem on the interdependent network X' and Y'. We use the method framework proposed in [17] to map targeted attacks to random attacks, and then analyze the network percolation under targeted attacks. First of all, according to Eq. (1), we remove the nodes with a scale of $(1-p)$ from the network, but do not remove the connection between the remaining nodes and the removed nodes. Then the degree distribution $P_p(k)$ of the remaining nodes is:

$$P_p(k) = \frac{A_p(k)}{pN_A} \tag{2}$$

We assume $A_p(k)$ represent the number of nodes with degrees k in the remaining nodes.

When another nodes is deleted, $A_p(k)$ will become:

$$A_{(p-1/N)}(k) = A_p(k) - \frac{P_p(k)(k+1)^\alpha}{\sum_k P_p(k)(k+1)^\alpha} \tag{3}$$

In the limit of $N \to \infty$, the Eq. (3) can be showed as derivative of $A_p(k)$ with respect to p:

$$\frac{dA_p(k)}{dp} = N \frac{P_p(k)(k+1)^\alpha}{\sum_k P_p(k)(k+1)^\alpha} \tag{4}$$

When $N \to \infty$ combining Eq. (2) with Eq. (4) we can get

$$-p \frac{dA_p(k)}{dp} = P_p(k) - N \frac{P_p(k)(k+1)^\alpha}{\sum_k P_p(k)(k+1)^\alpha} \tag{5}$$

In order to solve the Eq. (5), we define a new function $G_\alpha(x) = \sum_k P(k)x^{(k+1)^\alpha}$ and $t = G_\alpha^{-1}(p)$ [18], then we can solve Eq. (5) to get

$$P_p(k) = \frac{1}{p}P(k)t^{(k+1)^\alpha} \tag{6}$$

$$\sum_k P_p(k)(k+1)^\alpha = \frac{tG_\alpha'(t)}{G_\alpha(t)} \tag{7}$$

Thus, the generating function of $P_p(k)$ is

$$G_{Xb}(x) \equiv \sum_k P_p(k)x^k = \sum_k P_p(k)t^{(k+1)^\alpha}x^k \tag{8}$$

Since the connections in network X are randomly connected, the probability of deleting the edges in the remaining nodes is equal to the ratio of the number of edges in the remaining nodes to the number of edges in the original network:

$$\tilde{p} \equiv \frac{pN\langle k(p)\rangle}{N\langle k\rangle} = \frac{\sum_k P(k)kt^{(k+1)^\alpha}}{\sum_k P(k)k} \tag{9}$$

Where $\langle k \rangle$ is the average degree of the original network, and $\langle k(p) \rangle$ is the average degree of the remaining nodes in the network after targeted attack. Using the method in reference [19], we can get the generating function of the remaining nodes as follows:

$$G_{Xc}(x) \equiv G_{Xb}(1 - \tilde{p} + \tilde{p}x) \tag{10}$$

Equation (10) is the generating function of the remaining nodes after network X is targeted attacked. The cascading failure of targeted attacks and random attacks are only different in the first step. If we find a network X' and its generating function $\tilde{G}_{X0}(x)$, satisfying the condition that the generation function of the remaining nodes after deleting the $(1-p)$ scale nodes under random attack is $G_{Xc}(x)$, we can solve the problem of targeted attack. Therefore, we can turn the targeted attack in the coupled network X and Y into the random attack in the cyber-physical system X' and Y' From reference [19], we use the equation $\tilde{G}_{X0}(1 - p + px) = G_{Xc}(x)$ gives:

$$\tilde{G}_{X0}(x) = G_{Xb}\left(1 + \frac{\tilde{p}}{p}(x - 1)\right) \tag{11}$$

When the network X' is randomly attacked to delete $(1-p)$ proportion of nodes, the degree distribution of the remaining nodes in the network will change, and the generating function of the corresponding degree distribution will also change. The number of remaining nodes in the network is $N_{X1} = p * N_X$ after X' is removed due to random attack. The ratio of the number of functional nodes, that is, the number of nodes in the largest connected cluster to the number of nodes in the original network is:

$$g_X(p) = 1 - \tilde{G}_{X0}\left[1 - p(1 - f_X)\right] \tag{12}$$

Where f_X is the function of p, satisfies the transcendental equation

$$f_X = \tilde{G}_{X1}\left[1 - p(1 - f_X)\right] \tag{13}$$

In network Y, we can get a similar theory. Using the above theory, we can analyze the cascading failure of each step in detail. Using the method of generating function, we can get the iterative equation of cascading failure. In the next section, we will list the specific analysis process (Table 1).

3.2 Stage 2: Equivalent Random Failure in Network X'

According to the previous analysis, we have transformed targeted attacks into random attacks.

In the initial attack, the network X' has a random failure. We assume that there are $(1-p)$ proportion of nodes that fail due to the attack. We can get the number of remaining nodes as follows:

$$N'_{X1} = p \cdot N_X = \mu'_1 \cdot N_X \tag{14}$$

Where μ'_1 is the ratio of the number of remaining nodes after deleting $(1-p)$ scale nodes to the number of nodes in the original network. From Eq. (16), we can get $\mu'_1 = p$.

Table 1. Symbol Definition

Symbol	Explanation
N_X, N_Y	The quantity of nodes in the network X and network Y
N_{X_i}, N_{Y_j}	The quantity of nodes that remain functional in the network X and network Y after the i or j failure
N'_{X_i}, N'_{Y_i}	Number of nodes which have supporting inter link in the network X and network Y after the i or j failure
μ'_i, μ'_j	After the i or j failure, there is a ratio of the number of nodes that have supporting inter link in the network X and network Y
λ_A, λ_B	Parameters of the degree distribution of network X and network Y
μ_i, μ_j	The fraction of the number of nodes that remain functional in the network X and network Y after the i or j failures

According to the previous analysis, we can know that the number of nodes belonging to the giant component in N'_{X1} is:

$$N_{X1} = g_X\left(\mu'_1\right) \cdot N'_{X1} = \mu'_1 \cdot g_X\left(\mu'_1\right) \cdot N_X = \mu_1 \cdot N_X \qquad (15)$$

3.3 Stage 3: Cascading Failures in Network Y Due to X-Node Failures

Due to the coupling of cyber-physical system, the function of nodes in network Y depends on nodes in network Y', so nodes in network Y will fail due to the failure of nodes in network X'. Because each node in network Y is connected to three nodes in network X', and the connections between networks are random, we can get the number of nodes with dependency in network Y:

$$N'_{Y2} = \left[1 - (1 - \mu_1)^3\right] \cdot N_Y = \left(\mu_1^3 - 3 \cdot \mu_1^2 + 3 \cdot \mu_1\right) \cdot N_Y = \mu'_2 \cdot N_Y \qquad (16)$$

Similar to the analysis in the previous section, we can find that the number of nodes belonging to the giant component in N'_{Y2} is:

$$N_{Y2} = g_Y\left(\mu'_2\right) \cdot N'_{Y2} = \mu'_2 \cdot g_Y\left(\mu'_2\right) \cdot N_Y = \mu_2 \cdot N_Y \qquad (17)$$

3.4 Stage 4: More Fragment in Network X'

After the analysis of cascading failures in the above two sections, we can get the number of nodes with dependency in the remaining nodes of network X'. According to the random failure in the first step, we can know that a node in network Y may be connected to one, two or three nodes in network X'. In Table 2, we list the proportion of various connections in the original network.

Table 2. The proportion of the number of nodes in the network A to which the nodes in the network B are connected.

0	1	2	3
$(1 - \mu_1)^3$	$C_3^1 \cdot \mu_1 \cdot (1 - \mu_1)^2$	$C_3^2 \cdot (1 - \mu_1) \cdot \mu_1^2$	μ_1^3

According to our modeling of the coupling system, we can know that there is no relationship between the intra-network connection and the inter-network connection, which is completely random. Therefore, the number of nodes with dependencies in the network X' is

$$N_{X3}' = \mu_2 \cdot N_Y \cdot \frac{[C_3^1 \cdot \mu_1 \cdot (1 - \mu_1)^2 \cdot 1 +}{C_3^1 \cdot (1 - \mu_1) \cdot 2 + \mu_1^3 \cdot 3]} \Big/ \left[1 - (1 - \mu_1)^3\right] \tag{18}$$

From N_{X1} to N_{X3}', we know that

$$N_{X1} - N_{X3}' = \left(1 - g_Y\left(\mu_2'\right)\right) \cdot N_{X1} = \left(1 - g_Y\left(\mu_2'\right)\right) \cdot N_{X1}' \tag{19}$$

The fraction of the total removed nodes to the original network X′ is

$$1 - \mu_1' + \left(1 - g_Y\left(\mu_2'\right)\right) \cdot \mu_1' = 1 - \mu_1' \cdot g_Y\left(\mu_2'\right) \tag{20}$$

So, the number of nodes belonging to the giant component in N_{X3}' is,

$$N_{X3} = \mu_3' \cdot g_Y\left(\mu_3'\right) \cdot N_X = \mu_3 \cdot N_X \tag{21}$$

3.5 Stage 5: Further Cascading Failures on Network Y Once Again

Since the coupling of the cyber-physical system, the nodes in the network Y will fail due to the failure of the nodes in the network X' in the previous step. Similar to the second step, we can find the number of dependent nodes in the remaining nodes in network Y

$$N_{Y4}' = \left[1 - (1 - \mu_3)^3\right] \cdot N_Y = \left(\mu_3^3 - 3 \cdot \mu_3^2 + 3 \cdot \mu_3\right) \cdot N_Y \tag{22}$$

From N_{Y2} to N_{Y4}', we can obtain

$$N_{Y2} - N_{Y4}' = \left[1 - \left(\mu_3^3 - 3 \cdot \mu_3^2 + 3 \cdot \mu_3\right)/\mu_2\right] \cdot N_{Y2}' \tag{23}$$

Therefore, the fraction of the total failed nodes in network Y is

$$1 - \mu_2' + \mu_2' \cdot \left[1 - \left(\mu_3^3 - 3 \cdot \mu_3^2 + 3 \cdot \mu_3\right)/\mu_2\right]$$
$$= 1 - \mu_1' \cdot \left(\mu_3^2 - 3 \cdot \mu_3 + 3\right) \cdot g_X\left(\mu_3'\right) \tag{24}$$

We can find that the number of nodes belonging to the giant component in N'_{Y4} is

$$N_{Y_4} = \mu'_4 \cdot g_Y\left(\mu'_4\right) \cdot N_Y \tag{25}$$

According to the previous analysis of cascading failure process method, we can know the number of nodes in the network after each cascading failure. We can use the following equations to express:

$$\begin{cases} \mu'_{2i} = \mu'_1 \cdot \left(\mu^2_{2i-1} - 3 \cdot \mu_{2i-1} + 3\right) \cdot g_X\left(\mu'_{2i-1}\right) \\ \mu'_{2i+1} = \mu'_1 \cdot g_Y\left(\mu'_{2i}\right) \end{cases} \tag{26}$$

In the next section, we will find a method to analyze the Eq. (26) in detail, and then obtain the critical threshold.

4 Calculate the Equation

From the previous analysis, we can know that when the cascading failure stops, there is no node failure in the network, and the cascading failure stops. Therefore, we can get the following equations when the cascading failure stops in the coupling system:

$$\begin{cases} \mu'_{2i} = \mu'_{2i-2} = \mu'_{2i+2} \\ \mu'_{2i+1} = \mu'_{2i-1} = \mu'_{2i+3} \end{cases} \tag{27}$$

In order to solve the iterative formula of cascading failure conveniently, variables x, y satisfying the following equations are defined:

$$\begin{cases} y = \mu'_{2i} = \mu'_{2i-2} = \mu'_{2i+2} \\ x = \mu'_{2i+1} = \mu'_{2i-1} = \mu'_{2i+3} \end{cases} \quad (0 \le x, y \le 1) \tag{28}$$

Therefore, Eq. (28) can be shown as:

$$\begin{cases} y = p \cdot \left((x \cdot g_X(x))^2 - 3 \cdot x \cdot g_X(x) + 3\right) \cdot g_X(x) \\ x = p \cdot g_Y(y) \end{cases} \tag{29}$$

For the elimination of Eq. (29), we can obtain:

$$x = p \cdot g_Y\left[p \cdot \left((x \cdot g_X(x))^2 - 3 \cdot x \cdot g_X(x) + 3\right) \cdot g_X(x)\right] \tag{30}$$

In the process of practical solution, we find it is difficult to directly substitute the degree distribution function into scale-free networks. So, we rewrite the equation into two equations, and make the two functions approach infinitely by drawing, then we can get the percolation threshold of the network. Therefore, Eq. (30) is changed to the following equations:

$$\begin{cases} z = x \\ z = p \cdot g_Y\left[p \cdot \left((x \cdot g_X(x))^2 - 3 \cdot x \cdot g_X(x) + 3\right) \cdot g_X(x)\right] \end{cases} \tag{31}$$

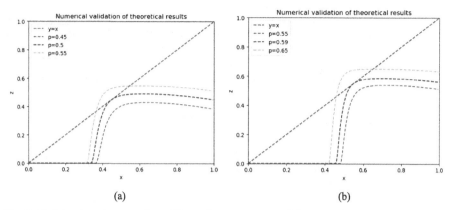

Fig. 2. Solving iterative equations. We set the parameter λ of the network to 2.8 and change the value of α.

According to Eq. (31), the two lines are drawn in the graph. When the two lines are tangent, the intersection point is the solution of Eq. (26). As shown in the two figures in Fig. 2.

In Fig. 2, we can see that when α is 1, the percolation threshold of the network is 0.5, and when α is 2, the percolation threshold of the network is 0.59. So far, we have obtained the theoretical results of the coupled system when the cascading failure stops. To verify the accuracy of the results, we will carry out the numerical simulation.

5   Simulation Results and Analysis

In this section, the correctness of the theoretical value is verified by simulation experiments. First of all, we compare the critical values of coupled network collapse under different conditions through several groups of experimental data. Secondly, we focus on the points near the critical value and compare the changes of the number of nodes in different networks near the critical value. Finally, we analyzed the influence of different α and λ on the critical value.

5.1   Simulation and Analysis

We use the experimental data to verify the accuracy of the theoretical results. First of all, we build two scale-free networks. The nodes of two networks are set to 9000 and 3000, respectively. Then, according to the previous model, three nodes of network X are randomly connected with one node of network Y. The connection between nodes in the network itself is also random. Finally, when the node of network X is removed, it will also lead to node failure in network Y, and vice versa. After each step of failure, we save the remaining nodes of the network from facilitating the analysis of data. When there is no further failure of the nodes in both networks, we think that the cascading failure has stopped. We save the remaining network nodes when the cascading failure stops.

In Fig. 3, we can observe that the value of the abscissa corresponding to the phase transition of the remaining nodes of the network corresponds to the theoretical value, which verifies the theoretical value obtained by the formula before.

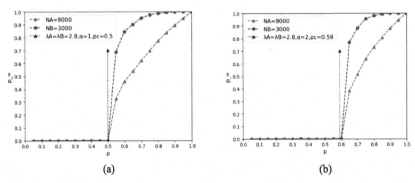

(a)   (b)

Fig. 3. The fraction of survival nodes in both networks. Abscissa p represents the proportion of nodes that are not attacked in the process of target attack. Ordinate p_∞ represents the proportion of remaining nodes when cascading failure stops after the coupled network receives target attack.

From Fig. 3, we can also find that when one network in the coupled system has nodes, the other network also has nodes. When one network completely collapses, the other network must even collapse altogether. When p is close to the critical threshold pc, the value of the ordinate increases in a straight line. This shows that when p is greater than the critical threshold, the coupling system may collapse, or some nodes may exist. This is consistent with our previous analysis.

In Fig. 2(a) and Fig. 2(b), we set the power-law index of scale-free network to be the same, both of which are 2.8, and change the attack parameter α. We can find that the larger the attack function α is, the larger the percolation threshold pc is, and the lower the network's reliability. The increase of α indicates that the nodes with medium size in the network have a higher probability of being attacked, so the robustness of the networks decreases. This is consistent with our expected results and once again verifies the accuracy of the theoretical results.

In Fig. 4, we select multiple values of p in the range [0.485, 0.545] near the critical threshold $pc = 0.5$, and conduct 50 experiments at each point to count the number of times that the coupled system has not entirely collapsed. By observing it, we can see that the curve is getting closer to the critical importance as the number of nodes increases. When the scale of network nodes reaches a specific value, the first-order phase transition occurs near the critical threshold, which is different from the second-order phase transition of single networks.

In Fig. 5, we specify that the other parameters of the network remain unchanged under different values of λ, and the attack parameter α is set to 1. The changing trend is shown in Fig. 5. We can see that when the power-law index λ increases, the essential decreases of the threshold. The magnitude of this reduction is not apparent. This shows that in the scale-free network of interaction, merely changing the power-law property of

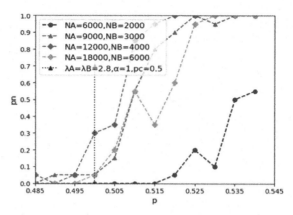

Fig. 4. The probability of having a giant component. we select several groups of values near the critical threshold for comparative analysis. The vertical coordinate *pn* represents the probability of the largest connected cluster's existence when the cascading failure stops, and the horizontal parallel *p* represents the number of the nodes in the network that are not attacked.

scale-free network cannot provide great help to increase the robustness of the network. It also tells us that cascading failures have different effects on different network structures.

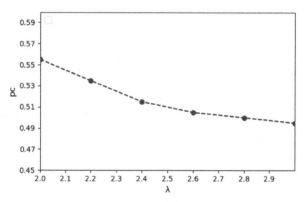

Fig. 5. The relationship between pc and λ. We compare the change of the critical threshold pc in the case of different power-law indexes λ.

6   Conclusion and Future Work

In this paper, the analysis model and security evaluation index of cyber-physical system are proposed. Under the deliberate attack strategy, the cascading failure process of cyber-physical system is considered. However, our proposed model still has some limitations, which is also the consideration of our future work direction. We think that the communication network and physical network of CPS are scale-free networks, which is not accurate. There have been relevant literature and data that a scale-free system cannot summarize CPS. For future work, we are trying to find a more practical network model. Another possible practice is to analyze the situation of more nodes with different proportions.

Acknowledgements. This work was supported in part by the National Natural Science Foundation of China (Grant No. 61902359), in part by Zhejiang Provincial Natural Science Foundation of China (Grant No. LQ19F030010), and in part by the Opening Project of Shanghai Key Laboratory of Integrated Administration Technologies for Information Security(Grant No. AGK2018001).

References

1. Lalropuia, K.C., Gupta, V.: Modeling cyber-physical attacks based on stochastic game and Markov processes. Reliab. Eng. Syst. Saf. **181**, 28–37 (2019)
2. Saad, E.: A colonel blotto game for interdependence-aware cyber-physical systems security in smart cities. In: International Workshop on Science of Smart City Operations & Platforms Engineering. ACM (2017)
3. Zeng, X., Xu, G., Zheng, X., Xiang, Y., Zhou, W.: E-AUA: an efficient anonymous user authentication protocol for mobile IoT. IEEE Internet Things J. **6**(2), 1506–1519 (2019)
4. Xu, G., Liu, J., Lu, Y., Zeng, X., Zhang, Y., Li, X.: A novel efficient MAKA protocol with desynchronization for anonymous roaming service in Global Mobility Networks. J. Netw. Comput. Appl. **107**, 83–92 (2018)
5. Lin, D., Tan, M.: Robustness of random scale-free networks against cascading failure under edge attacks. J. Commun. **11**(12), 1088–1094 (2016)
6. Kotzanikolaou, P., Theoharidou, M., Gritzalis, D.: Interdependencies between critical infrastructures: analyzing the risk of cascading effects. In: Bologna, S., Hämmerli, B., Gritzalis, Dimitris, Wolthusen, S. (eds.) CRITIS 2011. LNCS, vol. 6983, pp. 104–115. Springer, Heidelberg (2013). https://doi.org/10.1007/978-3-642-41476-3_9
7. Laprie, J.-C., Kanoun, K., Kaaniche, M.: Modelling interdependencies between the electricity and information infrastructures (2008)
8. Panzieri, S., Setola, R.: Failures propagation in critical interdependent infrastructures. Int. J. Model. Ident. Control **3**(1), 69–78 (2008)
9. Renyi, E.: On random graph. Publ. Math. **6** (1959)
10. Erdős, P., Rényi, A.: On the evolution of random graphs (1961)
11. Guare, J.: Six Degrees of Separation: A Play (1990)
12. Watts, D.J., Strogatz, S.H.: Collective dynamics of small world networks. Nature **393**(6684), 440–442 (1998)
13. Barabasi, A.L., Albert, R.: Emergence of scaling in random networks. Science **286**(5439), 509–512 (1999)
14. Barabási, A.-L., Albert, R., Jeong, H.: Mean-field theory for scale-free random networks. Phys. A: Stat. Mech. Appl. **272**(1-2), 17–187 (2000)
15. Dorogovtsev, S.N., Mendes, J.F.F.: Scaling properties of scale-free evolving networks: continuous approach. Phys. Rev. E **63**(5), 056125 (2001)
16. Gallos, L.K., Cohen, R., Argyrakis, P., Bunde, A., Havlin, S.: Stability and topology of scale-free networks under attack and defense strategies. Phys. Rev. Lett. **94**(18), 188701 (2005)
17. Huang, X., Gao, J., Buldyrev, S.V., Havlin, S., Stanley, H.E.: Robustness of interdependent networks under targeted attack. Phys. Rev. E **83**(6), 065101 (2011)

18. Yagan, O., Qian, D., Zhang, J., Cochran, D.: Optimal allocation of interconnecting links in cyber-physical systems: interdependence, cascading failures, and robustness. IEEE Trans. Parallel Distrib. Syst. **23**(9), 1708–1720 (2012)
19. Buldyrev, S.V., Parshani, R., Paul, G., Stanley, H.E., Havlin, S.: Catastrophic cascade of failures in interdependent networks. Nature **463**(7291), 1025–1028 (2010)

Cryptography

Heterogeneous Deniable Authenticated Encryption Protocol

Chunhua Jin$^{(\boxtimes)}$ ⓘ, Ge Kan ⓘ, Guanhua Chen ⓘ, Changhui Yu ⓘ,
and Chengjie Xu ⓘ

Faculty of Computer and Software Engineering,
Huaiyin Institute of Technology, Huai'an 233003, China
`xajch0206@163.com`

Abstract. Deniable authenticated encryption can achieve confidentiality and deniable authentication in a logical single step. Such a cryptographic primitive simplifies the design of cryptographic scheme and reduces the cost of computation and communication. In this paper, we propose a heterogeneous deniable authenticated encryption scheme called HDAE. The proposed scheme permits a sender in a public key infrastructure environment to transmit a message to a receiver in an identity-based environment. Our design utilizes tag-key encapsulation mechanism (tag-KEM) and data encapsulation mechanism (DEM) hybrid encryption methods, which is especially applicable in some privacy protection occasions. In addition, we give how to design an HDAE scheme utilizing a heterogeneous deniable authenticated tag-KEM (HDATK) and a DEM. We also construct an HDATK scheme and provide security proof in the random oracle model. Comprehensive analysis shows that our scheme is efficient and secure.

Keywords: Deniable authenticated encryption (DAE) · Privacy · Heterogeneous systems · Random oracle model

1 Introduction

Authentication plays a very important role in true applications. It means that only authorized users can access the system. Typically, we utilize digital signature technology to achieve authentication. However, there is also non-repudiation in digital signature. That is, the sender cannot deny the message he/she signed. To resolve this issue, deniable authentication [1] is proposed which has two characteristics: (1) the receiver has the capability of identifying a given message is from the sender; (2) any third party is incapable of determining the given message is from the sender or the receiver even though the third party colludes with

Supported by the Industry University Research of Jiansu Province (grant no. BY2019161), the Natural Science Research in Colleges and Universities of Jiansu Province (grant no. 19KJB510020).

© Springer Nature Singapore Pte Ltd. 2020
G. Xu et al. (Eds.): FCS 2020, CCIS 1286, pp. 331–346, 2020.
https://doi.org/10.1007/978-981-15-9739-8_26

the receiver since the receiver is able to generate a probabilistically indistinguishable transcript from the sender. However, in privacy-preserving scenario, the transmitted message needs to be encrypted to achieve confidentiality. Wu and Li [2] first presented an identity-based DAE scheme to achieve confidentiality as well as deniable authentication in an efficient approach.

In order to make the designed scheme more practical, we require the sender and receiver to be in different cryptographic environments. In this paper, we design a heterogeneous deniable authenticated encryption (HDAE) scheme which permits a sender in a public key infrastructure (PKI) setting to deliver a message to a receiver in an identity-based cryptography (IBC) setting. The proposed scheme can achieve confidentiality and deniable authentication in a logical single step. Such a cryptographic primitive simplifies the design of cryptographic scheme and reduces the cost of computation and communication. In addition, this design utilizes tag-KEM and DEM hybrid encryption methods which is especially suitable for actual application scenarios. We construct an HDAE scheme utilizing a heterogeneous deniable authenticated tag-KEM (HDATK) and a DEM. We also design an HDATK scheme and give security proof in the random oracle model (ROM) under DBDH and BDH assumptions. Our experimental analysis displays that our HDATK scheme has a high efficiency and security.

Organization. The rest of this paper is arranged below. Section 2, Related work is presented. We design a formal model for HDAE in Sect. 3. Section 4, a security model for HDATK is depicted. An HDAE design is presented in Sect. 5, and we design an HDATK scheme in Sect. 6. Performance analysis is discussed in Sect. 7. Conclusion is drawn in Sect. 8.

2   Related Work

Three related notions including hybrid encryption, deniable authenticated encryption, and heterogeneous deniable authentication are introduced.

Hybrid encryption constitutes a key encapsulation mechanism (KEM) and a data encapsulation mechanism (DEM). The KEM encrypts a session key by public key, whereas the DEM encrypts the real data by session key. For large messages, hybrid encryption is the best choice. Cramer and Shoup [3] designed practical and provably secure hybrid KEM/DEM schemes. Abe et al. [4] put forward a more efficient tag-KEM/DEM scheme. Then, many KEM/DEM schemes [5–12] have been proposed. These design support both components modular design. Sahai et al. [13] put forward a tag-KEM/DEM scheme by a non-interactive proof method. The proposed scheme can encrypt message with arbitrary length. Baek et al. [14] presented a stateful KEM-DEM scheme. It is highly effective by utilizing a state to produce the random parameters.

Deniable authentication encryption (DAE) is a cryptographic primitive which can accomplish concurrently public key encryption and deniable authentication. Its cost is lower than that needed by deniable authentication-then-encryption manner. DAE can achieve deniable authentication and confidentiality simultaneously which is well adopted for privacy-protecting scenarios.

Li et al. [15] constructed a DAE scheme with formal security proof. They also constructed an email system scheme based on the designed DAE scheme. Jin et al. [16] constructed a DAE scheme which can realize simultaneously deniable authentication, confidentiality, and ciphertext anonymity. Rasmussen and Gasti [17] proposed a DAE based on two encryption scheme with strong and weak properties. Recently, Huang et al. [18] constructed a DAE scheme for privacy protection with formal security proof. The above mentioned schemes are all in PKI environment which has public key management problems, including distribution, storage, and revocation. To resolve this issue, lots of identity-based deniable authenticated encryption (IBDAE) schemes have been constructed. Wu and Li [2] constructed an IBDAE scheme which provides formal security proof. Li et al. [19] (denoted by LZJ) proposed an IBDAE scheme for e-mail system. In their scheme, they utilize tag-KEM/DEM hybrid encryption technology which is more suitable for actual applications. Jin and Zhao [20] designed an IBDAE scheme which admits formal security proof. The aforementioned schemes have key escrow problems, i.e., a third party called private key generator (PKG) knows all user's private key. To avoid this problem, a certificateless deniable authenticated encryption (CLDAE) scheme [21] has been designed. Recently, Chen et al. [22] proposed a certificateless hybrid KEM/DEM scheme. It separates two parts to provide better security and efficiency.

The aforementioned DAE schemes have a common feature, i.e., the entities of these schemes are all in the same cryptosystem. Such characteristic makes these schemes are not well suitable for LBS system. Li et al. [23] (denoted by LHO) designed two heterogeneous deniable authentication (HDA) schemes. Their designed schemes allow batch verification to accelerate the authenticators' verification. Jin et al. [24] constructed an HDA scheme. In their scheme, a sender in a CLC setting to deliver a message to a receiver in an IBC setting. However, these schemes does not achieve confidentiality.

3   PI-HDAE

We describe security notions for HDAE in this section. In the designed HDAE scheme, a sender in a PKI environment, while a receiver in an IBC environment. PI-HDAE is denoted by this kind of DAE as follows.

3.1   Syntax

A PI-HDAE scheme comprises five algorithms below:

Setup: Given system parameter 1^k, the PKG obtains the *params* and a master private key s. In other algorithms, we neglect *params* due to they are public.

PKI-KG: A user belongs to the PKI setting elects a secret key sk and calculates its public key pk.

IBC-KE: A user in the IBC setting transmits its identity ID to the PKG who computes its private key S_{ID} and securely passes it to the user. Here, let the user's public key be its identity ID.

Deniable-Authenticated-Encrypt(DAE): Given a message m, a sender's secret key sk_s, public key pk_s, and a receiver's identity ID_r, the sender obtains a ciphertext σ.

Deniable-Authenticated-Decrypt(DAD): Given a ciphertext σ, a sender's public key pk_s, a receiver's identity ID_r, and its private key S_{ID_r}, the receiver obtains a message m or a symbol $\perp$.

If $\sigma = DAE(m,sk_s,pk_s, ID_r)$, then $m = DAD(\sigma,pk_s,ID_r, S_{ID_r})$.

3.2   Security Notions

We rewrite the notions [19] to meet our scheme. For confidentiality, the standard security concept, indistinguishability against adaptive chosen ciphertext attacks (IND-CCA2) is employed in our construction.

For IND-CCA2 security in a PI-HDAE scheme, it is assumed that this game below is between an adversary $\mathcal{F}$ with its challenger $\mathcal{C}$.

"IND-CCA2" game (Game-I):

Setup: $\mathcal{C}$ performs *Setup* algorithm to get *params*, releases it to $\mathcal{F}$ and saves s. $\mathcal{C}$ also executes PKI-KG algorithm to obtain a sender's private/public key pair (sk_s^*, pk_s^*). Then it passes pk_s^* to $\mathcal{F}$.

Phase 1: $\mathcal{F}$ adaptively issues the queries below.

- Key extraction queries: $\mathcal{F}$ picks an identity ID. $\mathcal{C}$ obtains the private key S_{ID} by running an IBC-KE algorithm and transmits it to $\mathcal{F}$.
- DAE queries: $\mathcal{F}$ selects a receiver's identity ID_r, and a message m. Then $\mathcal{C}$ executes DAE$(m, sk_s^*, pk_s^*, ID_r)$ and transmits the result σ to $\mathcal{F}$.
- DAD queries: $\mathcal{F}$ selects a ciphertext σ, and a receiver's identity ID_r. $\mathcal{C}$ obtains S_{ID_r} by implementing key extraction algorithm. It then transmits $\sigma = $ DAD$(\sigma, pk_s^*, ID_r, S_{ID_r})$ to $\mathcal{F}$ (the resulting $\perp$ indicates σ is invalid).

Challenge: $\mathcal{F}$ determines when Phase 1 ends. $\mathcal{F}$ creates a challenge identity ID_r^* and two messages (m_0, m_1). In phase 1, it does not support to request a key extraction query on ID_r^*. $\mathcal{C}$ randomly picks $b \in \{0,1\}$, computes $\sigma^* = $ DAE$(m_b, sk_s^*, pk_s^*, ID_r)$ and outputs σ^* to $\mathcal{F}$.

Phase 2: $\mathcal{F}$ makes queries as in Phase 1 except it neither requests a key extraction query on identity ID_r^* nor executes a DAD query on $(\sigma^*, pk_s^*, ID_r^*)$.

Guess: $\mathcal{F}$ returns b', and it wins the game if $b' = b$.

$\mathcal{F}$'s advantage is

$$Adv_{PI-HDAE}^{IND-CCA2}(\mathcal{F}) = |2Pr[b' = b] - 1|,$$

where $Pr[b' = b]$ expresses the probability.

Definition 1. A PI-HDAE scheme is IND-CCA2 secure if there is a probabilistic polynomial time (PPT) adversary $\mathcal{F}$ wins "IND-CCA2" game with negligible advantage.

In the aforementioned definition, $\mathcal{F}$ is permitted to gain the sender's private key S_{ID_s} [25]. Namely, the confidentiality is retained if S_{ID_s} is compromised.

For deniable authentication, the security concept, deniable authentication against adaptive chosen message attacks (DA-CMA) is employed in our construction.

For DA-CMA in a PI-HDAE scheme, this game below is between $\mathcal{F}$ and $\mathcal{C}$. "DA-CMA" game (Game-II):

Setup: This is identical to Game-I.

Attack: This is identical to Game-I.

Forgery: $\mathcal{F}$ creates a pair (σ^*, ID_r^*). $\mathcal{F}$ succeeds if the conditions below are satisfied:

1. $DAD(\sigma^*, pk_s^*, ID_r^*, S_{ID_r}) = m^*$.
2. $\mathcal{F}$ has not issued a key extraction query on ID_r^*.
3. $\mathcal{F}$ has not issued a DAE query on (m^*, ID_r^*).

$\mathcal{F}$'s advantage is defined as the probability that it will win.

Definition 2. A PI-HDAE scheme is DA-CMA secure if there is a PPT adversary $\mathcal{F}$ wins the "DA-CMA" game with a negligible advantage.

In the aforementioned definition, $\mathcal{F}$ does not issue a key extraction query on ID_r^*. This is for deniability. In other words, the two parties involved communication are able to produce a transcript with indistinguishable probability.

3.3   Data Encapsulation Mechanism (DEM)

Two algorithms are included in a DEM.

- Enc: Given 1^k, a message m, and a key K, this algorithm outputs a ciphertext c. It is denoted as $c = Enc(K, m)$.
- Dec: Given a key K, and a ciphertext c, this algorithm outputs a message m or $\perp$.

For a DEM, the security concept, indistinguishability against passive attackers (IND-PA) is employed in our construction. The game below is between $\mathcal{A}$ and $\mathcal{C}$.

IND-PA game (Game-III):

Setup: $\mathcal{A}$ transmits two messages (m_0, m_1).

Challenge: $\mathcal{C}$ picks K, $\beta \in \{0, 1\}$, and outputs a challenge ciphertext $c^* = Enc(K, m_\beta)$ to $\mathcal{A}$.

Guess: $\mathcal{A}$ returns β', and it will win the game if $\beta' = \beta$.
$\mathcal{A}$'s advantage is

$$Adv_{DEM}^{IND-PA}(\mathcal{A}) = |2Pr[\beta' = \beta] - 1|,$$

where $Pr[\beta' = \beta]$ expresses the probability.

Definition 3. A DEM is DA-CPA secure if there is a PPT adversary $\mathcal{A}$ wins "DA-CPA" game with a negligible advantage.

4   PI-HDATK

The security notions for heterogeneous deniable authenticated tag-KEM (HDATK) are given in this section. In the designed HDATK scheme, a sender belongs to a PKI setting, while a receiver belongs to an IBC setting. PI-HDATK is denoted by this kind of DATK scheme as follows.

4.1   Syntax

A PI-HDATK scheme comprises six algorithms below:

Setup: Given 1^k, the PKG obtains the *params* and a master private key s. Due to *params* are public, we neglect them in other algorithms.

PKI-KG: A user in the PKI setting calculates a secret/public key pair (sk, pk).

IBC-KE: A user in the IBC setting transmits its identity ID to the PKG who computes its private key S_{ID} and securely transmits it to the user. Here, we assume that the user's public key is its identity ID.

Sym: Given a sender's secret key sk_s, public key pk_s, and a receiver's identity ID_r, the sender produces an encryption key K and state information ω.

Encap: Given a tag τ and the state information ω, the sender creates an encapsulation ϕ.

Decap: Given a sender's public key pk_s, a receiver's identity ID_r, private key S_{ID_r}, a tag τ, and an encapsulation ϕ, the receiver outputs K or $\perp$.
    If $(k, \omega) = Sym(sk_s, pk_s, ID_r)$ and $\phi = Encap(\omega, \tau)$, then $K = Decap(\phi, \tau, pk_s, ID_r, S_{ID_r})$.

4.2   Security Notions

The confidentiality and deniable authentication should be satisfied for the PI-HDATK scheme. For IND-CCA2 security in a PI-HDATK scheme, it is assumed that this game below is between $\mathcal{F}$ and $\mathcal{C}$.
    "IND-CCA2" game (Game-IV):

Setup: $\mathcal{C}$ performs *Setup* algorithm, delivers *params* to $\mathcal{F}$ and saves s. $\mathcal{C}$ also executes PKI-KG algorithm to obtain a sender's private/public key pair (sk_s^*, pk_s^*). Then it delivers pk_s^* to $\mathcal{F}$.

Phase 1: $\mathcal{F}$ adaptively issues queries below:

- Key extraction queries: This is identical to Game-I.
- Symmetric key generation queries: $\mathcal{F}$ submits a receiver's identity ID_r to $\mathcal{C}$. $\mathcal{C}$ then performs $(K, \omega) = Sym(sk_s^*, pk_s^*, ID_r)$, stores the state information ω, and sends the key K to $\mathcal{F}$.
- Encapsulation queries: $\mathcal{F}$ picks a tag τ. If ω is not matched, $\mathcal{C}$ outputs $\perp$. If matched, $\mathcal{C}$ deletes the exist one and produces $\phi = Encap(\omega, \tau)$
- Decapsulation queries: $\mathcal{F}$ picks an encapsulation ϕ, a receiver's identity ID_r, and a tag τ. $\mathcal{C}$ produces S_{ID_r} by performing key extraction algorithm. It outputs the result of $Decap(\phi, \tau, pk_s^*, ID_r, S_{ID_r})$ to $\mathcal{F}$.

Challenge: $\mathcal{F}$ determines when Phase 1 is over. $\mathcal{F}$ then outputs a challenge identity ID_r^*. In phase 1, it does not support to request a key extraction query on ID_r^*. $\mathcal{C}$ executes $(K_1, \omega^*) = Sym(sk_s^*, pk_s^*, ID_r^*)$, picks $b \in \{0,1\}$, $K_0 \in \mathcal{K}_{\mathcal{PI}-\mathcal{HDATK}}$, and passes K_b to $\mathcal{F}$. when $\mathcal{F}$ obtains K_b, it will issue the identical queries as before. $\mathcal{F}$ then returns a tag τ^*. $\mathcal{C}$ calculates a challenge encapsulation $\phi^* = Encap(\omega^*, \tau^*)$ and outputs it to $\mathcal{F}$.

Phase 2: $\mathcal{F}$ makes queries as in Phase 1 except it neither requests a key extraction query on identity ID_r^* nor executes a decapsulation query on $(\phi^*, \tau^*, pk_s^*, ID_r^*)$.

Guess: $\mathcal{F}$ returns b', and it wins the game if $b' = b$, .
$\mathcal{F}$'s advantage is

$$Adv_{PI-HDATK}^{IND-CCA2}(\mathcal{F}) = |2Pr[b' = b] - 1|,$$

where $Pr[b' = b]$ expresses the probability.

Definition 4. A PI-HDATK scheme is IND-CCA2 secure if a PPT adversary $\mathcal{F}$ wins "IND-CCA2" game with negligible advantage.

In the above definition, it is allowed that $\mathcal{F}$ gets the sender's secret key S_{ID_s}. Namely, the confidentiality is maintained if S_{ID_s} is compromised.

For deniable authentication, the security concept, deniable authentication against adaptive chosen message attacks (DA-CMA) is employed in our design.

For DA-CMA security in a PI-HDATK scheme, it is assumed that this game below is played between $\mathcal{F}$ with $\mathcal{C}$.

"DA-CMA" game(Game-V):

Setup: This is identical to Game-III.

Attack: This is identical to Game-III.

Forgery: $\mathcal{F}$ creates an element (ϕ^*, τ^*, ID_r^*). $\mathcal{F}$ succeeds if the contexts below are met:

1. $DAD(\sigma^*, pk_s^*, ID_r^*) = m^*$.
2. $\mathcal{F}$ has not issued a key extraction query on ID_r^*.
3. $\mathcal{F}$ has not issued a DAE query on (m^*, ID_r^*).

$\mathcal{F}$'s advantage is defined as the probability that it will win.

Definition 5. A PI-HDATK scheme is DA-CMA secure if a PPT adversary $\mathcal{F}$ wins the "DA-CMA" game with a negligible advantage.

In the aforementioned definition, $\mathcal{F}$ does not issue a key extraction query on ID_r^*. This is for deniability. That is, the two parties involved communication are able to produce an indistinguishable transcript.

5   A Hybrid PI-HDAE Scheme

Figure 1 depicts a hybrid PI-HDAE scheme that constitutes a PI-HDATK and a DEM. In DEM part, the ciphertext is a tag. This construction provides simple description. Theorems 1 and 2 present the security consequences.

PI-HDAE.Setup: Inputting a security parameter k:
1. $(params,s)=$**PI-HDATK.Setup** (k)
2. Return the system parameters $param$ and the master private key s

PI-HDAE.PKI-KG: Inputting a random value x_s as the private key sk_s:
1. $PK_s=$**PI-HDATK.PKI-KG**(x_s)
2. Returns the private key sk_s and the corresponding public key PK_s

PI-HDAE.Extract: Inputting the master private key s and an identity $ID \in \{0,1\}^*$:
1. $S_{ID}=$**PI-HDATK.IBC-KE**(ID,s)
2. Return the private key S_{ID}

PI-HDAE.Deniable-Authenticated-Encrypt: Inputting a message $m \in \{0,1\}^*$, a sender's private key sk_s, public key pk_s, and a receiver's identity ID_r:
1. $(K,\omega)=$**PI-HDATK.Sym**(pk_s,sk_s,ID_r)
2. $c=$**DEM.Enc**(K,m)
3. $\Phi=$**PI-HDATK.Encap**(ω,c)
4. Return the ciphertext $\sigma=(\Phi,c)$

PI-HDAE.Deniable-Authenticated-Decrypt: Inputting a ciphertext σ, the sender's public key pk_s, the receiver's identity ID_r, and private key S_{IDr}:
1. $K=$**PI-HDATK.Decap**$(\Phi,c,pk_s,ID_r,S_{IDr})$
2. If $K=\perp$, then return $\perp$ and stop
3. $m=$**DEM.Dec**(K,c)
4. Return the message m

Fig. 1. Construction of PI-HDAE from PI-HDATK and DEM.

Theorem 1: Let a hybrid PI-HDAE scheme constitute a PI-HDATK and a DEM which are IND-CCA2 and IND-CPA secure, respectively, PI-HDAE is IND-CCA2 secure. to be specific, we receive

$$Adv_{PI-HDAE}^{IND-CCA2}(\mathcal{F}) = Adv_{PI-HDATK}^{IND-CCA2}(\mathcal{C}_1)+$$

$$Adv_{DEM}^{IND-PA}(\mathcal{C}_2),$$

Proof: Due to space limitations, please contact the corresponding author to see the full proof.

Theorem 2: Let a PI-HDAE constitutes a PI-HDATK and a DEM. If PI-HDATK is DA-CMA secure, PI-HDAE is also DA-CMA secure. to be specific, we receive

$$Adv_{PI-HDAE}^{DA-CMA}(\mathcal{F}) \leq Adv_{PI-HDATK}^{DA-CMA}(\mathcal{C}),$$

Proof: Due to space limitations, please contact the corresponding author to see the full proof.

6   A PI-HDATK Scheme

There are six algorithms to describe our proposed scheme. Figure 2 shows the main description. In DEM part, a tag is the ciphertext. This construction provides simple description and realizes better universal security.

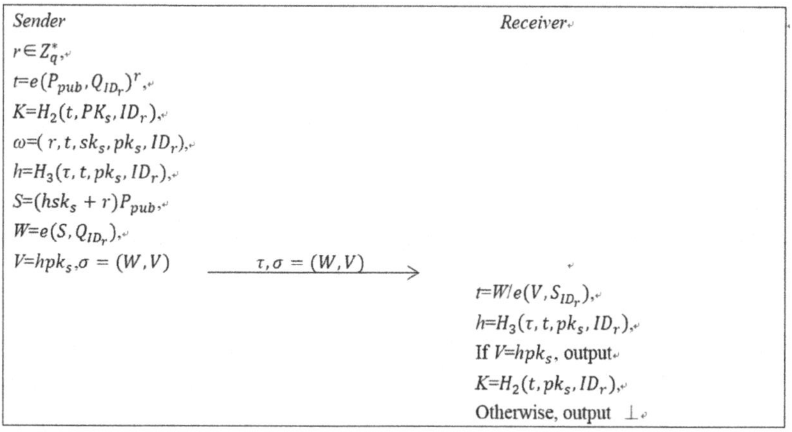

Sender	Receiver
$r \in Z_q^*$,	
$t=e(P_{pub}, Q_{ID_r})^r$,	
$K=H_2(t, PK_s, ID_r)$,	
$\omega=(r, t, sk_s, pk_s, ID_r)$,	
$h=H_3(\tau, t, pk_s, ID_r)$,	
$S=(hsk_s+r)P_{pub}$,	
$W=e(S, Q_{ID_r})$,	
$V=hpk_s, \sigma=(W,V)$ $\xrightarrow{\quad \tau,\sigma=(W,V)\quad}$	$t=W/e(V, S_{ID_r})$,
	$h=H_3(\tau, t, pk_s, ID_r)$,
	If $V=hpk_s$, output
	$K=H_2(t, pk_s, ID_r)$,
	Otherwise, output $\perp$

Fig. 2. The main contribution of PI-HDATK.

6.1   Basic Knowledge

In this section, we provide bilinear pairings properties, decisonal bilinear Diffie-Hellman problem (DBDHP), and bilinear Diffie-Hellman problem (BDHP).

Let G_1, G_2 be an additive group and a multiplicative group, respectively. P is a generator of G_1, and G_1 as well as G_2 have the same prime order q. A bilinear pairing is a map $e : G_1 \times G_1 \to G_2$ with the following properties:

1. Bilinearity: $e(aP, bQ) = e(P, Q)^{ab}$ for all $P, Q \in G_1, a, b \in Z_q^*$.

2. Non-degeneracy: There exists $P, Q \in G_1$ such that $e(P, Q) \neq 1$.
3. Computability: There is an efficient algorithm to compute $e(P, Q)$ for all $P, Q \in G_1$

The modified Weil and Tate pairings are the admissible maps ([26] offers more information). This scheme's security depends on the difficulty of dealing with the following problems.

Definition 1. Decisional Bilinear Diffie-Hellman Problem (DBDHP): In the light of bilinear pairing's basic definition as above mentioned, DBDHP is to determine $\theta = e(P, P)^{abc}$ given (P, aP, bP, cP) with $a, b, c, \theta \in Z_q^*$.

Definition 2. Bilinear Diffie-Hellman Problem (BDHP): In the light of bilinear pairing's basic definition as above mentioned, BDHP is to calculate $e(P, P)^{abc}$ given (P, aP, bP, cP) with $a, b, c \in Z_q^*$.

6.2   Our Scheme

Setup: Given G_1, G_2, P, and e as in Subsection A of Section VII. Let k be a security parameter ($q \geq 2^k$) and n be a a DEM's key length. H_1, H_2, H_3 are three cryptographic hash functions, where $H_1: \{0,1\}^* \to G_1$, $H_2: \{0,1\}^* \times G_1 \times G_2 \to \{0,1\}^n$ and $H_3: \{0,1\}^* \times G_1 \times G_2 \to Z_q^*$. The KGC randomly selects a master key $s \in Z_q^*$ and calculates $P_{pub} = sP$. The public *params* are $(G_1, G_2, e, q, n, k, P, P_{pub}, H_1, H_2, H_3)$ and a master private key is s.

PKI-KG: A user belongs to a PKI setting elecets $x_i \in Z_q^*$ randomly as its secret key sk_i, and calculates $pk_i = sk_iP$ as its public key. Here, $i = s$ denotes the sender, and $pk_s = x_sP, sk_s = x_s$ denotes the sender's public/private key pair.

IBC-KE: A user belongs to an IBC setting gives its identity ID to the PKG. The PKG calculates its private key $SK_{ID} = sQ_{ID}(Q_{ID} = H_1(ID))$ and securely transmits it to the user. Here, ID_r denotes the receiver, and $pk_r = ID_r, sk_r = S_{ID_r}$ denote the receiver's public and private key.

Sym: Given a sender's private/public key pair (sk_s, pk_s), and a receiver's identity ID_r, the algorithm below is done.

1. Pick $r \in Z_q^*$.
2. Compute $t = e(P_{pub}, Q_{ID_r})^r$.
3. Calculate $K = H_2(t, pk_s, ID_r)$.
4. Return K and $\omega = (r, t, sk_s, pk_s, ID_r)$.

Encap: Given a tag τ and the state information ω, the algorithm below is done.

1. Compute $h = H_3(\tau, t, pk_s, ID_r)$.
2. Compute $S = (hsk_s + r)P_{pub}$.
3. Compute $W = e(S, Q_{ID_r})$.

4. Compute $V = hpk_s$.
5. Compute $\sigma = (W, V)$.

Decap: Given a tag τ, an encapsulation σ, a sender's public key pk_s, a receiver's private key S_{ID_r}, identity ID_r, the algorithm below is executed.

1. Compute $t = W/e(V, S_{ID_r})$.
2. Compute $h = H_3(\tau, t, pk_s, ID_r)$.
3. If $V = hpk_s$, output $K = H_2(t, pk_s, ID_r)$; if not, return the symbol $\perp$.

The consistency of the designed HDATK scheme can be verified. Because $W = e(S, Q_{ID_r})$, $V = hpk_s$, we can get

$$
\begin{aligned}
t = W/e(V, S_{ID_r}) &= e(S, Q_{ID_r})/e(hpk_s, S_{ID_r}) \\
&= e((hx_s + r)P_{pub}, Q_{ID_r})/e(hpk_s, sQ_{ID_r}) \\
&= e(hx_s P_{pub}, Q_{ID_r})e(rP_{pub}, Q_{ID_r})/e(hx_s sP, Q_{ID_r}) \\
&= e(hx_s sP, Q_{ID_r})e(rP_{pub}, Q_{ID_r})/e(hx_s sP, Q_{ID_r}) \\
&= e(P_{pub}, Q_{ID_r})^r
\end{aligned}
$$

6.3 Security

Theorems 3 and 4 offer the security consequences for PI-HDATK.

Theorem 3: Under DBDH assumption, in ROM, $\mathcal{F}$ wins the IND-CCA2 game with a non-negligible advantage ϵ_{datk} when issuing q_{H_i} queries to H_i ($i = 1, 2, 3$), q_{ke} key extraction queries, q_{gsk} generation symmetric key queries, q_{ke} key encapsulation queries, and q_{kd} key decapsulation queries in a time t, $\mathcal{C}$ resolves DBDH problem with probability

$$
\epsilon_{datk} \geq \frac{\epsilon - q_{kd}/2^{k-1}}{2q_{H_1}}
$$

within $t' \leq t + O(q_{gsk} + q_{ke} + q_{kd})t_p$, in which t_p is one paring computation.

Proof: Due to space limitations, please contact the corresponding author to see the full proof.

Theorem 4: Under BDH assumption, in ROM, $\mathcal{F}$ has a non-negligible advantage $\epsilon_{datk} \geq 10(q_{ke} + 1)(q_{ke} + q_{H_3})q_{H_1}/(2^k - 1)$ winning the DA-CMA game when issuing q_{H_i} queries to H_i ($i = 1, 2, 3$), q_{ke} key extraction queries, q_{gsk} generation symmetric key queries, q_{ke} key encapsulation queries, and q_{kd} key decapsulation queries in a time t, $\mathcal{C}$ resolves BDH problem in expected time $t \leq 120686q_{H_3}q_{H_1}2^k/\epsilon_{datk}(2^k - 1)$.

Proof: Due to space limitations, please contact the corresponding author to see the full proof.

7   Performance

We conduct a main computational cost comparison of the construction with existing schemes LZJ [19] and HDA-I of LHO [23] listed in Table 1. The point multiplication in G_1, the exponentiation calculation in G_2, the addition calculations in G_1, and the pairing calculation in G_2 are denoted by PM, EC, AD, and PC, respectively. We ingore XOR, and hash function since they are trival. In all computational cost, the PC evaluation is the most time-consuming. From Table 1, it shows that the computation overhead of our scheme is less than that of LZJ [19], but more than that of the HDA-I of LHO [23]. It is noted that LZJ [19] is not a heterogeneous DAE scheme which is not catered for LBS and HDA-I of LHO [23] cannot achieve confidentiality.

Table 1. Performance comparison

Schemes	Computational cost				Security		Heterogeneity
	PM	BP	AD	EP	DA-CMA	IND-CCA2	
LZJ [19]	4	3	1	1	√	√	×
HDA-I of LHO [23]	3	2	1	0	×	√	√
Ours	3	3	0	1	√	√	√

An experiment is conducted on the PBC library with A pairing [27]. The A pairing is designed on an elliptic curve $y^2 = x^3 + x \bmod p$ for some prime $p \equiv 3 \bmod 4$. As needed, we set the order of G_1 is q and the library's embedding degree to 2. Here, 80-bit, 112-bit, and 128-bit denotes three kinds of AES [28] key size security level, respectively. Table 2 shows the description for different security level.

Table 2. Description for different security level

Security level	Size of P	Size of q
80-bit	512	160
112-bit	1024	224
128-bit	1536	256

We implement the experiment on an Intel Pentium(R) with 2,048 MB of RAM (2,007.04 MB available) and Dual-Core processor running at 2.69 GHz. On this machine, a PM takes 15.927 ms, and an AD requires 0.065ms employing an ECC with q of 160 bits. A PC and an EC take 26.68 ms and 3.126 ms, respectively. LZJ [19] takes 146.939 ms, HDA-I of LHO [23] takes 101.206 ms, and our scheme takes 130.947 ms. Figure 3 depicts the comparison computational

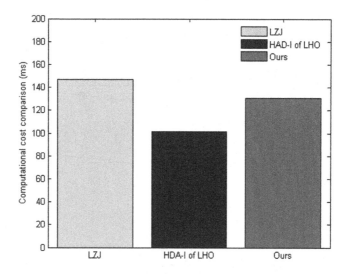

Fig. 3. Computational cost comparison.

cost for LZJ [19], HDA-I of LHO [23], and our scheme. From Fig. 3, we can see that the implementation results are consistent with the theoretical analysis.

For the communication cost, LZJ [19], HDA-I of LHO [23], and our scheme are $|m| + |G_1| + |G_2|$. They possess the identical communication cost. $|x|$ is the size of x. For 80-bit security level, $|p| = 512$ bits, $|G_1| = 1024$ bits, $|q| = 160$ bits. If the standard compression techniques are used, G_1 can be reduced to 65 bytes. $G_2 = 1024$ bits $= 128$ bytes. Therefore, the communication cost of three scheme is $|m| + |G_1| + |G_2| = |m| + 65 + 128 = |m| + 193$ bytes. For 112-bit security level, $|p| = 1024$ bits, $|G_1| = 2048$ bits, $|q| = 224$ bits. Using the standard compression technique, G_1 can be reduced to 129 bytes. $G_2 = 2048$ bits $= 256$ bytes. Therefore, the communication cost of three scheme is $|m| + |G_1| + |G_2| = |m| + 129 + 256 = |m| + 385$ bytes. For 128-bit security level, $|p| = 1536$ bits, $|G_1| = 3072$ bits, $|q| = 256$ bits. Using the standard compression technique, G_1 can be reduced to 193 bytes. $G_2 = 3072$ bits $= 384$ bytes. Therefore, the communication cost of three scheme is $|m| + |G_1| + |G_2| = |m| + 193 + 384 = |m| + 577$ bytes. Figure 3 shows the communication cost at different security level. It shows that from Fig. 4 the 80-bit security level is our best choice for the current computing condition.

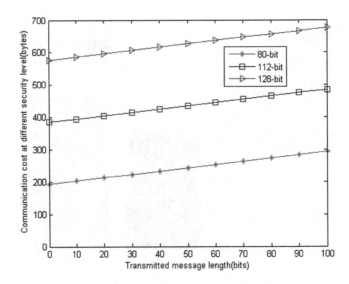

Fig. 4. Communication cost at different security level.

8   Conclusion

In this paper, we designed a hybrid DAE scheme which comprises a PI-HDAE scheme and a DEM scheme. The entities are in a heterogeneous system where the sender belongs to the PKI environment, while the receiver belongs to the IBC environment. Our construction can achieve confidentiality and deniable authentication in a single logic step. We give a formal security proof in the ROM. Our performance results show that this construction is secure and efficient.

References

1. Aumann, Y., Rabin, M.O.: Authentication, enhanced security and error correcting codes. In: Krawczyk, H. (ed.) CRYPTO 1998. LNCS, vol. 1462, pp. 299–303. Springer, Heidelberg (1998). https://doi.org/10.1007/BFb0055736
2. Wu, W., Li, F.: An efficient identity-based deniable authenticated encryption scheme. KSII Trans. Internet Inf. Syst. **9**(5), 1904–1919 (2015)
3. Cramer, R., Shoup, V.: Design and analysis of practical public-key encryption schemes secure against adaptive chosen ciphertext attack. SIAM J. Comput. **33**(1), 167–226 (2003)
4. Abe, M., Gennaro, R., Kurosawa, K.: Tag-KEM/DEM: a new framework for hybrid encryption. J. Cryptol. **21**(1), 97–130 (2007). https://doi.org/10.1007/s00145-007-9010-x
5. Choi, K.Y., Cho, J., Hwang, J.Y., Kwon, T.: Constructing efficient PAKE protocols from identity-based KEM/DEM. In: Kim, H., Choi, D. (eds.) WISA 2015. LNCS, vol. 9503, pp. 411–422. Springer, Cham (2016). https://doi.org/10.1007/978-3-319-31875-2_34

6. Emura, K., et al.: A KEM/DEM-based construction for secure and anonymous communication. In: Ahamed, S.I. (ed.) proceedings of IEEE 39th Annual Computer Software and Applications Conference, COMPSAC Workshops 2015, Taichung, Taiwan. IEEE, pp. 1–5 (2015)

7. Xu, J., Wen, Q., Li, W., et al.: Circuit ciphertext-policy attribute-based hybrid encryption with verifiable delegation in cloud computing. IEEE Trans. Parallel Distrib. Syst. **27**(1), 119–129 (2015)

8. Bansal, T.K., Chang, D., Sanadhya, S.K.: Sponge based CCA2 secure asymmetric encryption for arbitrary length message. In: Foo, E., Stebila, D. (eds.) ACISP 2015. LNCS, vol. 9144, pp. 93–106. Springer, Cham (2015). https://doi.org/10.1007/978-3-319-19962-7_6

9. Ishida, Y., Shikata, J., Watanabe, Y.: CCA-secure revocable identity-based encryption schemes with decryption key exposure resistance. Int. J. of App. Cryptol. **3**(3), 288–311 (2017)

10. Wu, X., Han, Y., Zhang, M., Zhu, S.: Parallel long messages encryption scheme based on certificateless cryptosystem for big data. In: Chen, X., Lin, D., Yung, M. (eds.) Inscrypt 2017. LNCS, vol. 10726, pp. 211–222. Springer, Cham (2018). https://doi.org/10.1007/978-3-319-75160-3_14

11. Giacon, F., Kiltz, E., Poettering, B.: Hybrid encryption in a multi-user setting, revisited. In: Abdalla, M., Dahab, R. (eds.) PKC 2018. LNCS, vol. 10769, pp. 159–189. Springer, Cham (2018). https://doi.org/10.1007/978-3-319-76578-5_6

12. Ge, A., Wei, P.: Identity-based broadcast encryption with efficient revocation. In: Lin, D., Sako, K. (eds.) PKC 2019. LNCS, vol. 11442, pp. 405–435. Springer, Cham (2019). https://doi.org/10.1007/978-3-030-17253-4_14

13. Sakai, Y., Hanaoka, G.: A remark on an identity-based encryption scheme with non-interactive opening. In: proceedings of 2018 International Symposium on Infor. Theory and Its Apps (ISITA), pp. 703–706. Springer, Singapore (2018)

14. Baek, J., Susilo, W., Salah, K., Ha, J.S., Damiani, E., You, I.: Stateful public-key encryption: a security solution for resource-constrained environment. In: Li, K.-C., Chen, X., Susilo, W. (eds.) Advances in Cyber Security: Principles, Techniques, and Applications, pp. 1–22. Springer, Singapore (2019). https://doi.org/10.1007/978-981-13-1483-4_1

15. Li, F., Zhong, D., Takagi, T.: Efficient deniably authenticated encryption and its application to e-mail. IEEE Trans. Inf. Forensics Secur. **11**(11), 2477–2486 (2016)

16. Jin, C., et al.: Deniable authenticated encryption for e-mail applications. Int. J. Comput. Appl. **42**(5), 429–438 (2020)

17. Rasmussen, K., Gasti, P.: Weak and strong deniable authenticated encryption: on their relationship and applications. In: Kieran, M. (ed.) proceedings of 16th Annual Conference on Privacy, Security and Trust (PST), pp. 1–10. Springer, Belfast (2018)

18. Huang, W., Liao, Y., Zhou, S., et al.: An efficient deniable authenticated encryption scheme for privacy protection. IEEE Access **7**, 43453–43461 (2019)

19. Li, F., Zheng, Z., Jin, C.: Identity-based deniable authenticated encryption and its application to e-mail system. Telecommun. Syst. **62**(4), 625–639 (2016)

20. Jin, C., Zhao, J.: Efficient and short identity-based deniable authenticated encryption. In: Sun, X., Chao, H.-C., You, X., Bertino, E. (eds.) ICCCS 2017. LNCS, vol. 10603, pp. 244–255. Springer, Cham (2017). https://doi.org/10.1007/978-3-319-68542-7_20

21. Ahene, E., Jin, C., Li, F.: Certificateless deniably authenticated encryption and its application to e-voting system. Telecommun. Syst. **70**(3), 417–434 (2019)

22. Chen, G., Zhao, J., Jin, Y., et al.: Certificateless deniable authenticated encryption for location-based privacy protection. IEEE Access **7**, 101704–101717 (2019)
23. Li, F., Hong, J., Omala, A.A.: Practical deniable authentication for pervasive computing environment. Wireless Netw. **24**(1), 139–149 (2018)
24. Jin, C., Chen, G., Yu, C., et al.: Heterogeneous deniable authentication and its application to e-voting systems. J. Inf. Secur. Appl. **47**, 104–111 (2019)
25. An, J.H., Dodis, Y., Rabin, T.: On the security of joint signature and encryption. In: Knudsen, L.R. (ed.) EUROCRYPT 2002. LNCS, vol. 2332, pp. 83–107. Springer, Heidelberg (2002). https://doi.org/10.1007/3-540-46035-7_6
26. Boneh, D., Franklin, M.: Identity-based encryption from the weil pairing. SIAM J. Comput. **32**(3), 586–615 (2003)
27. PBC Library. http://crypto.stanford.edu/pbc/
28. Daemen, J., Rijmen, V.: The design of Rijndael: AES-The Advanced Encryption Standard. Springer, Heidelberg (2013)

Identify-Based Outsourcing Data Auditing Scheme with Lattice

Han Wang[1,2], Xu An Wang[1,2], Jiasen Liu[2], and Chuan Lin[1(✉)]

[1] Guizhou Provincial Key Laboratory of Public Big Data, GuiZhou University,
Guiyang 550025, Guizhou, China
aca_wang@163.com, wangxazjd@163.com
[2] Key Laboratory of Network and Information Security under PAP, Engineering,
University of PAP, Xi'an 710086, China

Abstract. To reduce the burden and overhead of local storage, more and more organizations and individuals chosen to outsourcing data to cloud servers. Cloud users can access cloud data through any network. At the same time, as users lose actual control over the data, the data security in the cloud server is exposed to great risks. Therefore, how to ensure the integrity and security of cloud data has become an open issue. Around this problem, researchers have put forward many plans. However, these schemes are based on traditional cryptography, they cannot resist quantum attacks and have high computational complexity. It cannot meet the needs of interconnection of everything in the future. To solve this problem, we propose an identity-based outsourcing data integrity auditing scheme with lattice, which has forward security. Our proposed scheme is based on lattice cryptosystem, which not only has higher security and computational efficiency, but also has forward security. In the proposed scheme, the data owner can designate a proxy to outsource the data, thus reducing the local computing burden. In addition, we analyze the security of the scheme through the assumption of ISIS problem, which shows the theoretical security of the scheme. Theoretical analysis and comparison indicate that our proposed scheme is more secure and practical.

Keywords: Cloud storage · Identity-based · Public auditing · Lattice-based cryptography

1 Introduction

In the past few years, data outsourcing system has attracted the attention of researchers and developers. The key issue is how to verify the integrity of the data on a semi-trusted cloud. To solve this problem, Antienese et al. [1] proposed data integrity verification (DIV) technology in 2007, and first proposed the provable data transmission protocol (PDP), which changed the previous point-to-point transmission of large amounts of data authentication mode.

© Springer Nature Singapore Pte Ltd. 2020
G. Xu et al. (Eds.): FCS 2020, CCIS 1286, pp. 347–358, 2020.
https://doi.org/10.1007/978-981-15-9739-8_27

Now, more and more organizations and companies are using the online collaborative office service provided by Internet companies, and people in different regions can edit and modify files at the same time, such as Google Docs [3], Office 365 [4], and Quip [5]. We can foresee the development and progress will greatly change the way people work in this area.

In traditional model, DIV technology is generally composed of three entities [6]: User, Third Party Auditor and Cloud Service Providers. When the data owner uploads a file to the cloud server, the data label of the file is computed to upload it to the cloud server as well. During the data integrity review, the user sends a TPA audit request, and the TPA randomly generates a challenge sequence to send to the cloud server. Then the cloud server generates the corresponding audit certificate according to the challenge sequence and sends it to the TPA. If the auditing verification is successful, the data is reported to the user as Ture; otherwise, the data verification fails.

Although cloud storage technology has greatly improved people's work efficiency, it also brought various aspects of the problem such as data integrity, confidentiality and user account privacy. Recently, great achievements have been made on the basis of PDP protocol [9,11,12], but most of them have some problems in one way or another. Such as TPA and CSP contract attacks [8], TPA disclosure of user privacy [13], and key exposure. In order to solve these problems, researchers have put forward lots of scheme. However, these schemes are based on traditional cryptographic systems, such as bilinear mapping, RSA. These schemes are often accompanied by huge computational overhead and do not have resistance to quantum attacks.

In this paper, in order to solve these problems, we propose an identity-based public auditing scheme for data outsourcing. Our scheme uses lattice cryptography technology to realize forward security, with lower computational load and higher security. Our contribution can be summarized as follows:

1. We propose a new identity-based data outsourcing audit protocol. The protocol realizes privacy protection and forward security. These functions use random replacement technology and lattice walking technology.
2. Our proposed scheme allows the data owner to designate a specific agent to process outsourced data. The data has proxy information generated by personal private key and signed, and the proxy generates proxy key pairs according to the information. And every time a data outsourcing operation is carried out, the key pair is upgraded to ensure forward security. In addition, we have proved the safety of the scheme. Security analysis shows that our plan can resist the forgery attack.

2   Related Work

With the change of business structure and work style, the auditing of cloud data storage has become an indispensable development direction. At the same time, the security and privacy of data stored in the cloud are also threatened unprecedentedly, such as integrity, confidentiality, availability. To solve these problems, many new cryptographic technologies and schemes have been proposed. In 2007, Ateniese et al. [1] was the first to propose a PDP protocol that verifies data integrity using TPA. In this paper, a homomorphic tag scheme based on RSA is implemented and the audit efficiency is improved by random checking. Then Ateniese et al. [2] proposed a scheme using symmetric encryption technique to solve the problem that the PDP scheme does not support data dynamics. After that, many excellent plans were put forward one after another.

Wang et al. [13] proposed the first privacy-preserving public auditing scheme based on ring signature. This scheme allows members of the user group to share data and will not disclose any private information of members to TPA during the audit. In [13], Wang et al. proposed a new public data audit scheme using random mask technology. Fu et al. [21] proposed a data sharing public audit scheme based on HVT group signature, realizing multi-level privacy-preserving capability. However, when the group members change, the key must be regenerated. Luo et al. [10] improved the original privacy-preserving model and proposed a data integrity auditing scheme based on BLS signature, which supports batch audit operations. In 2019, Tian et al. [7] proposed a cloud storage audit scheme based on zero knowledge proof, which realized the privacy protection of data and identity.

While protecting users' privacy, the disclosure of keys in cloud storage is also a high-risk area. Yu et al. proposed the problem of user key leak in cloud environment for the first time [15], and proposed a key evolution algorithm to solve the problem. In [14], Yu et al. reduced the computational burden on the client by using authorized third parties to update the key. Subsequently, Ding et al. [16] proposed a public audit scheme with intrusion flexibility. The protocol divides the lifetime of data stored on the cloud server into lots of time periods and update time periods. The audit private key and its corresponding secret value are updated in each time period and update period respectively.

In the above integrity auditing schemes, PKI and complex certificate management system are needed. This method greatly increases the computational cost of TPA, so Yu et al. [19] first proposed an identity-based uncertified public cloud audit protocol in 2013, eliminating the burden of certificate management that is repeated in traditional schemes. Recently, many excellent scheme have been proposed. Peng et al. [17] proposed an identity-based multi-copy data audit protocol, but the scheme does not support data dynamics. Zhang et al. [18] proposed an effective user revocation scheme, which is based on identity cryptosystem and improves efficiency.

Although the efficiency of the protocol is improved by introducing a new authentication mechanism, it still cannot cover up the limitations of the underlying cryptographic scheme. The above schemes all adopt bilinear pairing and modular exponentiation. TPA and users often need to spend a lot of computing costs. In addition, the traditional cryptosystem cannot resist the threat brought by quantum computation [20]. Recently, some schemes based on lattice signature have been proposed one after another [22–26]. There are some problems in these schemes, for example they cannot resist forgery attacks and cannot protect users' privacy.

3   Preliminaries

3.1   System Model and Formal Definition

In the section, we will show the system model of the identity-based data outsourcing public auditing scheme. As illustrated in Fig. 1, the system model is consisted of five entities: CSP, Data Owner, Proxy singer, TPA, KGC.

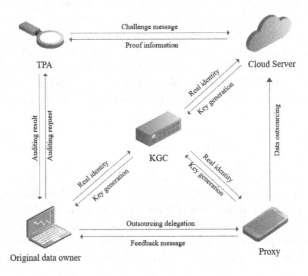

Fig. 1. System model

1. **Data Owner (DO).** The original owner of the data can designate an agent to outsource a large number of books to a remote server. And the data can be remotely verified through TPA.
2. **Proxy (Po).** Specified by the data owner to operate on the data through the permissions granted.
3. **Cloud Service Provider (CSP).** Cloud service providers have a large amount of data storage space and computing power. Ensure the safety of user data.
4. **Third Party Auditor (TPA).** According to the user's command, an audit sequence is generated, the integrity of cloud data is checked, and the audit sequence is responsible to the data owner.
5. **key generation center (KGC).** A key pair is generated according to the user's information by using the master key.

3.2   Lattice

A m-dimensional full-rank lattice is $\Lambda = \{BC = \sum c_i b_i, c_i \in Z^m\}$, where the basis B are linearly independent consists of the m columns vectors $b_1, \cdots, b_m \in R^m$.

For a matrix $A \in Z^{n \times m}$, prime q, the q-modular integer lattices can be defines as follows:

$$\begin{aligned}
\Lambda_q(A) &= \{z \in Z_q^m : \exists x \in Z_q^n, z = A^T y \bmod q\} \\
\Lambda_q^{\perp}(A) &= \{z \in Z_q^m : Az = 0 \bmod q\} \\
\Lambda_\sigma^{\perp}(A) &= \{z \in Z_q^m : Az = y \bmod q\}
\end{aligned} \tag{1}$$

Definition 1: A probabilistic polynomial-time algorithm $TrapGen(q, n)$ generates $(A \in Z_q^{n \times m}, T_A \in Z_q^{m \times m})$, where A is uniformly randomly distributed in $Z_q^{n \times m}$, and T_A is a basis of $\Lambda_q^{\perp}(A)$.

Definition 2: A probabilistic polynomial-time algorithm $SamplePre(A, T_A, y, \sigma)$ generates $b \in Z_q^m$, that satisfies $Ab = y$, where $y \in Z_q^n$ and $b \leftarrow D_{\Lambda_q^u(A), \sigma}$.

Definition 3: A probabilistic polynomial-time algorithm $NewBasisDel()$ generates a short lattice T_B of $\Lambda_q^{\top}(A)$, where $Q = AR^{-1}$.

3.3   Hardness Assumption

Definition 4: The Small Integer Solution (SIS) Problem: For a prime q, a real number $\varsigma > 0$ and choose a matrix $A \in Z^{n \times m}$, to solve a nonzero integer vector $e \in Z^m$ such that $Ae = 0$ and $\| e \| \leq \varsigma$.

Definition 5: The Inhomogeneous Small Integer Solution (ISIS) Problem: For a prime q, a real number $\varsigma > 0$ and choose a matrix $A \in Z^{n \times m}$, to solve a nonzero integer vector $e \in Z^m$ such that $Ae = y$ and $\| e \| \leq \varsigma$.

3.4   Security Model

Here we will give the security model of proxy signature, and the security of the scheme will be discussed in the later security analysis.

Setup: The challenger $\mathcal{C}$ generates system public parameters pp and return it to the adversary $\mathcal{A}$. The adversary $\mathcal{A}$ choose a identity ID_P^* to $\mathcal{C}$, which will be challenged as following four queries:

KeyExtract Query: $\mathcal{A}$ could query for any private key T_{ID} of ID, and the challenger $\mathcal{C}$ will return a corresponding T_{ID} to $\mathcal{A}$.

Proxy Signer Private Key Query: $\mathcal{A}$ receives (w, θ_w, i) from data owner, where θ_w is a signature of w and i is the time period. $\mathcal{A}$ send it to $\mathcal{C}$ for querying the private key. $\mathcal{C}$ generates a corresponding private key T_{pro} and return it to $\mathcal{A}$.

Proxy TagGen Query: $\mathcal{A}$ query data file $F = (F_1, F_2, \cdots, F_l)$ to $\mathcal{C}$. Then, $\mathcal{C}$ will return a set of signatures for F_i and send it to $\mathcal{A}$.

Challenge: $\mathcal{C}$ chooses a specific challenge message *chal* and sends it to $\mathcal{A}$.

Forgery Phase: the adversary $\mathcal{A}$ forges a response information *Proof* for the audit request *chal*. The adversary $\mathcal{A}$ wins the game if $ProofVerify(ID_p^*, i^*, chal, Proof^*) = 1$.

4   The Concrete Our Scheme

4.1   Overview

In this chapter, we will propose a public audit protocol scheme for identity-based data outsourcing. Our scheme consists of six parts: Setup, Extract, Proxy KeyGen, Proxy TagGen, Challenge, Auditing.

1) Setup and TrapGen: In this phase, PKG is responsible for initializing the security parameters of q-modular lattices and ensuring that the size of public and private key pairs is unchanged by using lattice basis delegation technology for corresponding secret key pairs of other entities in the system.
2) Proxy KeyGen: At this stage, the data owner generates an authorization $w \in \{0, 1\}^*$ and sends it to the proxy signer.
3) TagGen: The proxy generates a new key pair based on the authorization information w and the time parameter t. Outsourcing the data according to the data owner's instructions.
4) Data auditing: After the TPA receives the audit request from the data owner, the TPA randomly generates a set of audit sequences and sends them to the CSP. The CSP performs calculations based on the data stored in the cloud, and generates corresponding verification information proof. Finally CSP returns it to the TPA.

4.2   The Construction of Our Scheme

In this section, we will give a specific description of the identity-based public audit protocol for outsourced data.

Setup(k): First input a security parameter k, and then the system initializes through the following steps:

1. Determine a prime number r, the discrete Gaussian distribution χ and secure Gaussian parameters $\delta = \{\delta_0, \cdots, \delta_r\}, \sigma = \{\sigma_0, \cdots, \sigma_r\}$.
2. Run $TrapGen(q, n)$ generates a matrix $A \in Z_p^{n \times m}$, $T_q \in Z_p^{m \times m}$, then calculates $T_A = pT_q$, and we get $T_A \in \Lambda = pZ^m \cap \Lambda_q^{\perp}(A)$, and we get the master key pair $(pk, sk) = (A, T_A)$.

3. The system defines six hash functions: $H_1 = \{0,1\}^* \to Z_q^{m \times m}, H_2 = \{0,1\}^* \times \{0,1\}^* \times \{0,1\}^* \times \{0,1\}^* \times Z_q^n \to Z_q^n$, $H_3 = \{0,1\}^* \times \{0,1\}^* \times \{0,1\}^* \times \{0,1\}^* \times Z_q^m \to z_q^{m \times m}$, $H_4 = \{0,1\}^* \times \{0,1\} \to Z_Q^n$, $H_5 = \{0,1\}^* \times \{0,1\} \to Z_Q^n$, $H_6 = \{0,1\}^{k_2} \times Z_q^n \times Z_q^m \times Z_q^m \to Z_q$,

finally, system output $pp = \{pZ^m, A, H_1, \cdots, H_6, \delta, \sigma\}$ as the public parameters, and the KGC keep the master key $Msk = T_A$.

$KeyExtract(T_A, ID)$: Input a unique $ID \in \{0,1\}^{k_1}$ and public parameter pp, and then KCG generates the corresponding private key for user:

1. Compute $R_{ID} = H_1(ID)$, and compute $Q_{ID} = A(R_{ID})^{-1}$ as the public key of ID.
2. Then run $NewBasisDel(A, R_{ID}, T_A, \delta)$ to get a short lattice basis $T_{ID} \in Z_q^{m \times m}$ as the secret key of ID.

In this phase, the KGC will generate corresponding secret keys for Data Owner, Proxy signer and CSP respectively.

ProxyKeyGen. After the data owner selects the corresponding proxy signer, the data owner and the proxy generate the proxy private key through the following steps.

1. Data Owner creates a warrant sequence $w \in \{0,1\}^{k_2}$. Then Date Owner signs w to generate a signature $v_w = Sample(A_{ID_o}, T_{ID_o}, u_w, \sigma_0)$ where $u_w = H_2(ID_o\|ID_p\|w\|v_w)$ and $v_w \in Z_q^n$.
2. Once receiving (w, v_w, θ_w), the proxy signer verifies it by computing $A_{ID_o}\theta_w = u_w$. If the verification equation does hold, ID_p computes $R_{w\|1} = H_3(ID_o\|ID_p\|w\|\theta_w\|1)$, and computes $T_{pro} = NewBasisDel(Q_P, R_w, T_{ID_p}, \delta)$, together with the proxy signing private key $A_{pro\|1} = A_{ID_p}(R_{w\|1})^{-1}$.

$KeyUpdate(pp)$: After the proxy signer generates a key pair, when a new signature is made each time, a new secret key needs to be generated according to the parameter τ, in which the real-time parameter $\tau < t < r$. The proxy signer run $NewBasisDel(A_{ID_{pro\|\tau}\|\tau}, R_{ID_{pro\|\tau \to t}}, T_{ID_{pro\|\tau}}, \sigma_t)$ to get $T_{pro\|t}$. Here,

$$
\begin{aligned}
R_{pro\|\tau \to i} &= H_1(ID_p\|i) \cdots H_1(ID_p\|\tau+1) \\
R_{pro\|\tau} &= H_1(ID_p\|\tau) \cdots H_1(ID_p\|1) \\
A_{pro\|\tau} &= A(R_{pro}\tau)^{-1} \\
A_{pro\|i} &= A(R_{pro\|i})^{-1} = A(R_{pro\|\tau \to i}R_{pro\|\tau})^{-1}
\end{aligned}
\tag{2}
$$

Proxy TagGen: ID_p divides the file F into l blocks $\{m_1, m_2, \cdots, m_l\}$. and selects a name N_i for each m_i. Then, ID_p generates the signature as follows:

1. Compute $A_{ID_c} = AR_{ID_c}^{-1} \in Z_q^{n \times m}$ and $\eta_i = H_4(N_i\|i) + A_{ID_c}m_i \in Z_q^n$.
2. Compute $\rho_{i,j} = \langle \eta_i, \lambda_j \rangle, 1 \leq j \leq n$, $\lambda_j = H_5(ID_p\|j)$, then set $\rho_i = (\rho_{i,1}, \cdots, \rho_{i,n})^T \in Z_q^n$.
3. Run $SamplePre(A_{pro\|t}, T_{pro\|t}, \rho_i, \sigma_t)$ to get $e_i \in Z_q^m$

Finally, ID_p outsourcing $((F_i, N_i, e_i)_{1 \leq i \leq l}, w, v_w, \theta_w, t)$ to the CSP.

Challenge: TPA generates a challenge information $chal = \{L, \beta\}$, where $L = (l_1, L_2, \cdots, l_c)$ is a subset of $(1, 2, \cdots, l)$, and selects a random value β_i for each l_i. Finally, the TPA sends $chal$ to the CSP.

ProofGen: Once CSP receive $chal$ from TPA, CSP computes $f = f' + hH_6(w\|v_w\|\theta_w\|\xi)$ and $e = \sum_{i=l_1}^{i=l_c} \beta_i e_i \in Z_q^m$, where $\xi \in Z_q^m$ is a random vector and $h = Sample(A_{ID_c}, T_{ID_c}, \xi, \sigma_0)$. Then, CSP sends $Proof = (f, e, \xi, w, v_w, \theta_w, t)$ to TPA.

ProofVerify: When TPA receives $Proof$, TPA first checks whether ID_p has warrant. Then, verify the proof as following:

1. Compute $\lambda_j = H_5(ID_p\|j), 1 \leq j \leq n$, set $B = (\lambda_1, \cdots, \lambda_n)^T$, and compute $\mu = B(\sum_1^{l_c} \beta_i H_4(N_i\|i) + R_{ID} f - \xi H_6(w\|v_w\|\theta_w\|\xi)$.
2. Check $A_{pro\|t} e = \mu \bmod q$ and $0 < \|e\| \leq c\sigma_t \sqrt{m}$.

5   Analysis of the Proposed Scheme

5.1   Security Analysis

In this section, we will give the proof of our scheme that is secure.

Theorem 1. *The proposed proxy scheme achieves the storage correctness, provided that the hardness assumption of ISIS problem is intractable.*

Proof. We will We assume that the adversary A can pass the verification with a non-negligible probability of ε, and the challenger C can solve the ISIS problem through A as a subroutine.

Given a challenge matrix $U \in Z_q^m$, the challenger C tries to solve the vector $e^* \in Z_q^m$. A determines the challenge identity ID_p^* and the time period i^* and the challenger C maintains three empty lists L_1, L_2, L_3. C samples a random set $R_*^2, \cdots, R_*^{i^*} \leftarrow D_{m \times m}$ by running $SampleRwithBasis$, then calculates $A = BR_*^{i^*} R_*^{i^*-1} \cdots R_*^0$. Finally, C return the system parameter $(A, spk, \delta, \theta, H_1, H_2, H_3, H_4, H_5, H_6)$, and send it to A.

$A_{ID_p^*\|1} = A_1(R_*^1)^{-1}$ and $A_{ID_p^*\|j} = A_{ID_p^*\|j-1}(R_*^j)$ for $1 < j < i^*$ and recode those into L_1.

Hash Queries: The adversary A can run H_1, H_2, H_3, H_4, H_5 and H_6 queries as follows:

$H_1(ID)$ **query:** Giving an identify ID, C return R_{ID}, if there exists $(ID, R_{ID}, Q_{ID}, T_{ID})$ in L_1. Otherwise, C performs $SampleRwithBasis(A)$ to get $R_{ID} \leftarrow D_{m \times m}$ and a short basis T_{ID}, then add $(ID, R_{ID}, A_{ID}, \perp)$ to L_1, and return it to A.

$H_2(ID_O\|ID_P\|w\|v_w)$ **query:** Given an hash value u_w, C checks if the value exist in L_2. if it was, C return the value. Otherwise, C randomly choose a vector $v_w \leftarrow Z_q^n$ to add it to L_2. Then, C returns it to A.

$H_3(ID_O\|ID_P\|w\|\theta_w\|t)$ **query:** Given an indentity ID_p and a time period t, if (ID_p, i) exist in L_3, C returns R_{pro_i}. Otherwise, C will calculate as following:

(a) If $ID_p = ID_*$ and $t = t^* + 1$, C run $SampleRwithBasis()$to get a matrix $R_{i^*+1} \leftarrow D_{m \times m}$ and a random short basis $T_{ID_* \| t}$. Then, the challenger C add $(ID_o, ID_p, t^* + 1, A_{ID_* \| t^* + 1}, R_{t^* + 1}, T_{ID_* \| t^* + 1})$ to L_3 and return $R_{i^* + 1}$ to $\mathcal{A}$.

(b) If $ID_P = ID_*$ and $t > t^* + 1$, the challenger $\mathcal{C}$ first to get $T_{ID^* \| t + 1}$ by H_3 query. Then, the challenger $\mathcal{C}$ selects a random matrix $R_{w \| t} \leftarrow D_{m \times m}$, and runs $NewBasisDel(A_{ID_p \| t - 1}, R_{w \| t}, T_{ID_p \| t - 1}, \sigma_0)$ to get $T_{pro \| t}$. Finally, $\mathcal{C}$ add $(ID_o, ID_p, t, w, v_w, \theta_w, R_{w \| t}, A_{pro \| t}, T_{pro \| t})$ to L_3 and return $R_{w \| t}$ to $\mathcal{A}$.

(c) If $ID_P \neq ID_*$ and $i = 1$, the challenger $\mathcal{C}$ can search L_1 to find out T_{ID_p}, randomly chooses $R_{w \| 1} \leftarrow D_{m \times m}$, and gets $T_{pro \| 1}$ by running $NewBasisDel$ $(A_{ID_p}, R_{w \| 1}, T_{ID_p}, \delta_1)$. Finally, $\mathcal{C}$ puts $(ID_o, ID_p, 1, w, v_w, \theta_w, R_{w \| 1}, A_{pro \| 1}, T_{pro \| 1})$ to L_3, and return $R_{w \| 1}$ to $\mathcal{A}$.

(d) If $ID_P \neq ID_*$ and $t > 1$, the challenger $\mathcal{C}$ perform $H_3(ID_o, ID_p, w, \theta_w, t)$ to get $T_{pro \| t - 1}$. Then, $\mathcal{C}$ selects a random matrix $R_{w \| t} \leftarrow D_{m \times m}$, and gets $T_{pro \| 1}$ by running $NewBasisDel(A_{ID_p}, R_{w \| t}, T_{ID_p}, \delta_t)$. Finally, $\mathcal{C}$ adds $(ID_o, ID_p, t, w, v_w, \theta_w, R_{w \| t}, A_{pro \| t}, T_{pro \| t})$ to L_3, and return $R_{w \| t}$ to $\mathcal{A}$.

The adversary $\mathcal{A}$ performs queries for other hash functions to the advanser $\mathcal{C}$. $\mathcal{C}$ can also return result to $\mathcal{A}$, and $\mathcal{C}$ adds results to list $L4, L5, L6$, respectively.

KeyExtract Query: For the query on ID, the challenger $\mathcal{C}$ first searches ID in list L_1. If it exists, $\mathcal{C}$ returns $T_I D$ to $\mathcal{A}$. Otherwise, $\mathcal{C}$ do as $H_1(ID)$ query.

Proxy Signing Private Key Query: $\mathcal{A}$ submit a request $(ID_O, ID_P, w, \theta_w, t)$ to $\mathcal{C}$ for private key $T_{pro \| i}$. $\mathcal{C}$ confirm whether the value exist in L_3. If it was not in L_3, $\mathcal{C}$ do as $H_3(ID_o \| ID_p \| w \| \theta_w \| t)$ query.

Proxy TagGen Query: $\mathcal{A}$ submit a set $(F', ID_c, , ID_p)$ to $\mathcal{C}$. Then, $\mathcal{C}$ look into L_3, L_4, L_5 to find out $(ID_c, R_{ID_c}, Q_{ID_c}, T_{ID_c})$, $(ID_O, ID_P, w, \theta_w, i, R_w, Q_{pro \| i}, T_{pro \| i})$, $(N'_i, i, H_4(N'_i \| i))_{i = 1, \cdots, l}$ and $(ID_p, j, H_5(ID_p \| j))_{j = 1, \cdots, n}$. finally, $\mathcal{C}$ performs the process in section to generates $chal = \{i, \beta_i\}_{i \in \Omega}$.

Forgery Query: We assume the adversary $\mathcal{A}$ can temper with the data and signature as (F_k^*, e_k^*). With the private key $T_{pro \| i}$, $\mathcal{A}$ can forge $Proof^* = \{f^*, e^*, \xi\}$ through the process in section.

5.2 Performance Evaluation

The Computation cost of our scheme is given in Table 1, where T_{mul}, T_{hash} denotes multiplication operation and hash operation, respectively.

Table 1. The Computation cost of our scheme

Delegation	AuthGen
$T_{hash} + nm \cdot T_{mul}$	$2n \cdot T_{hash} + (n + 2nm)T_{mul}$
ProofGen	Proofverify
$(2cm + 1)T_{hash}$	$(n + c + 1)T_{hash} + (n^2 + 2nm + n)T_{mul}$

6   Conclusion

In this paper, we propose a novel identity-based forward-secure outsourcing with public auditing scheme from lattice, which realizes privacy-preserving and post-quantum security. Our scheme allows the data owner to designate a proxy to outsource the data instead, and can conduct integrity audit of cloud data through TPA. In the scheme, the proxy's key will be changed periodically. We formalize the identify-based public auditing scheme system design and security model. After that, we described in detail the identity-based forward security data outsourcing audit scheme. Theoretical analysis shows that our scheme can resist forge data from malicious cloud and has higher computational efficiency.

Acknowledgement. This work was supported by the National Cryptography Development Fund of China (No. MMJJ20170112), Natural Science Basic Research Plan in Shaanxi Province of China (No. 2018JM6028), National Natural Science Foundation of China (No. 61772550, U1636114 and 61572521), the Foundation of Guizhou Provincial Key Laboratory of Public Big Data (No. 2019BDKFJJ008), and National Key Research and Development Program of China (No. 2017YFB0802000). This work is also supported by Engineering University of PAP's Funding for Scientific Research Innovation Team (No. KYTD201805).

References

1. Ateniese, G., et al.: Provable data possession at untrusted stores. In: Proceedings of the 14th ACM Conference on Computer and Communications Security, pp. 598–609. ACM, New York (2007). https://doi.org/10.1145/1315245.1315318
2. Ateniese, G., et al.: Scalable and efficient provable data possession. In: Proceedings of the 4th International Conference on Security and Privacy in Communication Networks, SecureComm 2008, p. 1. ACM Press, Istanbul (2008). https://doi.org/10.1145/1460877.1460889
3. Google Docs. https://www.google.com
4. Office 365. https://www.office.com/
5. Quip. https://quip.com/
6. Liu, C.-W., et al.: A survey of public auditing for shared data storage with user revocation in cloud computing. IJ Netw. Secur. **18**, 650–666 (2016)
7. Tian, H., et al.: Privacy-preserving public auditing for secure data storage in fog-to-cloud computing. J. Netw. Comput. Appl. **127**, 59–69 (2019). https://doi.org/10.1016/j.jnca.2018.12.004

8. Zhou, L., Fu, A., Yu, S., Su, M., Kuang, B.: Data integrity verification of the outsourced big data in the cloud environment: a survey. J. Netw. Comput. Appl. **122**, 1–15 (2018)
9. Shen, J., Zhou, T., Chen, X., et al.: Anonymous and traceable group data sharing in cloud computing. IEEE Trans. Inf. Forensics Secur. (2017). https://doi.org/10.1109/TIFS.2017.2774439
10. Luo, X., et al.: An Effective Integrity Verification Scheme of Cloud Data Based on BLS Signature (2020). https://www.hindawi.com/journals/scn/2018/2615249/. https://doi.org/10.1155/2018/2615249
11. Curtmola, R., Khan, O., Burns, R., et al.: MR-PDP: multiple-replica provable data possession. In: The 28th International Conference on Distributed Computing Systems, pp. 411–420. IEEE (2008)
12. Wang, B., Li, B., Li, H.: Knox: privacy-preserving auditing for shared data with large groups in the cloud. In: Bao, F., Samarati, P., Zhou, J. (eds.) ACNS 2012. LNCS, vol. 7341, pp. 507–525. Springer, Heidelberg (2012). https://doi.org/10.1007/978-3-642-31284-7_30
13. Wang, B., Li, B., Li, H.: Oruta: privacy-preserving public auditing for shared data in the cloud. In: Proceedings of the 5th IEEE International Conference on Cloud Computing, pp. 295–302. IEEE (2012)
14. Yu, J., Ren, K., Wang, C.: Enabling cloud storage auditing with verifiable outsourcing of key updates. IEEE Trans. Inf. Forensics Secur. **11**(6), 1362–1375 (2016)
15. Yu, J., Ren, K., Wang, C., Varadharajan, V.: Enabling cloud storage auditing with key-exposure resistance. IEEE Trans. Inf. Forensics Secur. **10**(6), 1167–1179 (2015)
16. Ding, R., Xu, Y., Cui, J., Zhong, H.: A public auditing protocol for cloud storage system with intrusion resilience. IEEE Syst. J. (2019). https://doi.org/10.1109/JSYST.2019.2923238
17. Peng, S., Zhou, F., Wang, Q.: Identity-based public multi-replica provable data possession. IEEE Access **5**, 26990–27001 (2017)
18. Zhang, Y., Yu, J., Hao, R., et al.: Enabling efficient user revocation in identity-based cloud storage auditing for shared big data. IEEE Trans. Dependable Secure Comput. (2018). https://doi.org/10.1109/TDSC.2018.2829880
19. Yu, Y., Xue, L., Au, M.H., et al.: Cloud data integrity checking with an identity-based auditing mechanism from RSA. Future Gener. Comput. Syst. **62**, 85–91 (2016)
20. Shor, P.W.: Polynomial-time algorithms for prime factorization and discrete logarithms on a quantum computer. SIAM J. Comput. **26**(5), 1484–1509 (1997)
21. Fu, A., et al.: NPP: a new privacy-aware public auditing scheme for cloud data sharing with group users. IEEE Trans. Big Data. 1 (2017). https://doi.org/10.1109/TBDATA.2017.2701347
22. Liu, Z., et al.: Identity-based remote data integrity checking of cloud storage from lattices. In: 2017 3rd International Conference on Big Data Computing and Communications (BIGCOM), Chengdu, pp. 128–135. IEEE (2017). https://doi.org/10.1109/BIGCOM.2017.29
23. Yang, Y., et al.: Secure cloud storage based on RLWE problem. IEEE Access **7**, 27604–27614 (2019). https://doi.org/10.1109/ACCESS.2018.2887135
24. Zhang, X., et al.: Identity-based key-exposure resilient cloud storage public auditing scheme from lattices. Inf. Sci. **472**, 223–234 (2019). https://doi.org/10.1016/j.ins.2018.09.013

25. Zhang, X., et al.: LDVAS: lattice-based designated verifier auditing scheme for electronic medical data in cloud-assisted WBANs. IEEE Access **8**, 54402–54414 (2020). https://doi.org/10.1109/ACCESS.2020.2981503
26. Zhang, X., Xu, C.: Efficient identity-based public auditing scheme for cloud storage from lattice assumption. In: 2014 IEEE 17th International Conference on Computational Science and Engineering, Chengdu, China, pp. 1819–1826. IEEE (2014). https://doi.org/10.1109/CSE.2014.334

Database Security

A Security Problem Caused by the State Database in Hyperledger Fabric

Zhen Gao$^{(\boxtimes)}$, Dongbin Zhang, and Jiuzhi Zhang

School of Electrical and Information Engineering, Tianjin University, Tianjin 300072, China
zgao@tju.edu.cn

Abstract. Blockchain technology has been widely used in many applications, but its tamper proof capability is still a problem. Hyperledger Fabric is a typical alliance chain platform for reliable data sharing among multiple enterprises. To facilitate data query and transaction verification, Fabric introduces the concept of state data. However, the state data is not stored on the chain but in the local database. Through analysis of the Fabric source code, we found that the queried data from local data base will not be verified by comparing with the data on the chain, so it would be easy to modify the state data and issue 'valid' transactions based on the tampered data. This problem is confirmed by laboratory experiments. In the test, we modified the state data on the endorsing peers through the data base interface, and the transactions based on the tampered data were successfully synchronized to all the nodes in the same channel. This work reveals that the off-chain data could be a big security threat for small scale Fabric networks.

Keywords: Fabric · State database · Query · Security

1 Introduction

Fabric is one of the Hyperledger projects hosted by the Linux Foundation [1]. It is designed to provide blockchain technology for enterprise alliances to achieve trustworthy data sharing, which can effectively reduce the cost of trust caused by complex interactions between enterprises. Hyperledger Fabric is actually a modular and extensible open source system. Unlike public blockchain networks (such as Bitcoin and Ethereum) that anyone can join, Fabric is a blockchain network that only permissioned members can participate [2]. Based on such a permissioned chain, the data sharing between organizations could be realized without explicit incentive. Moreover, Fabric supports users to deploy chaincode for access of the on-chain data [3], which greatly improves the practicality and scalability of the system. Currently, Fabric has quite a wide range of application scenarios. Walmart built a food trace system based on Fabric [4], and then reduced the trace time from 7 days to 2.2 s. Change Healthcare applied Fabric to improve efficiency and transparency in the medical insurance claims process [5]. Dltledgers is a blockchain-based commodity trade financing platform that digitizes trade and financing processes, greatly reducing the transaction time [6]. Based on Fabric, Ian Zhou et al. proposed a blockchain-based paper review system, which not only protects the anonymity of authors and reviewers,

© Springer Nature Singapore Pte Ltd. 2020
G. Xu et al. (Eds.): FCS 2020, CCIS 1286, pp. 361–372, 2020.
https://doi.org/10.1007/978-981-15-9739-8_28

but also solves the problems of inconsistent review indicators and review bias [7]. Tomas Mikula proposed an identity and access management system that applied Fabric for the authentication and authorization of entities in digital systems [8]. Christopher Harris used ordered transactions in Fabric to improve back-end tasks in the telecom industry, such as roaming and inter-carrier settlements [9].

In Fabric system, the shared data is stored on the chain and is difficult to tamper with due to the cryptography protected chain structure and the mutual restriction among organizations. However, to improve the efficiency of data query and transaction verification, each node in the network would store the latest state information of all accounts (called the World State) in a local database. The World State is actually out of the tamper proof capability of the blockchain, and could be modified being discovered. This defect seriously threatens the security of the Fabric system. This paper will discuss this issue in depth.

The remainder of this paper is organized as follows. Section 2 describes Fabric's network architecture and storage structure. Section 3 analyzes the state-data's query process based on source code. Section 4 discusses the feasibility of modifying the state data. In Sect. 5, we performed experiments to demonstrate the security problem by modifying the state data and confirming the transactions based on the modified data. The paper is concluded in Sect. 6.

2   Brief Introduction of Fabric

2.1   Network Architecture and Transaction Flow

As shown in Fig. 1, the Fabric system is composed of an alliance with multiple *Organizations*, an *Orderer* cluster, the certificate authorities (*CA*) and clients. The client is operated by the system users to issue transactions. Each *Organization* is composed of several nodes. A node must be a committing peer (committer) for ledger storage, and it can also play as an endorsing peer (endorser) for transaction endorsement, a leader peer for broadcasting of new block within the organization, or an anchor peer for communications among the organizations. The *CA* provides registration services for the system maintainers to implement access control over all the participating peers. The *Orderers* are responsible to collect the endorsed transactions from clients, to packet them into blocks, and to send the blocks to each organization. In addition, Fabric introduces a concept of *Channel*. Organizations in the same channel maintain the same ledger, and the ledgers in different channels are isolated.

In Fabric, the transaction flow involving all above parts are listed as follows.

(1) User initiates transactions on the client via command "*peer chaincode invoke...*";
(2) Client sends transactions to the endorsing peers in each organization;
(3) Endorsing peers simulate and execute the transactions, and return it with digital signatures;
(4) Client sends the endorsed transactions to the orderer;
(5) Orderer packets the endorsed transactions into a new block, and send it to each organization;
(6) Committing peers verify and execute the transactions, and store the block on chain.

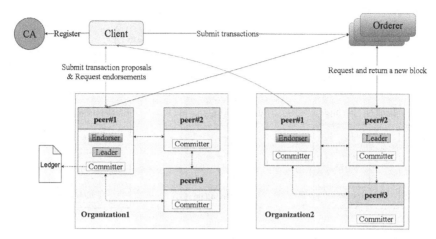

Fig. 1. Fabric network architecture

2.2 Storage Structure

As shown in Fig. 2, Fabric's block is composed of three parts: *Header*, *Data*, and *Metadata*. The *Header* stores the hash and height of the current block and the hash of the previous block. The hash is the identifier of a block, and can be used to prove the completeness of the data packed in the block. The *Data* part contains a list of ordered transactions, and each transaction contains the read-write set of the World State before and after the transaction. The *Metadata* contains additional information about the block, such as the time when the block was written, the writer's certificate, and so on. In such a structure, all blocks are linked through their hash value, so any modification of the data in a block could be easily detected by the mismatch of the "hash of the previous block" stored in the next block. Therefore, the modification of on chain data would be successful only when the all the following blocks are regenerated on all the committing peers, which would be very difficult and thus achieve the tamper proof capability for on chain data.

In addition to the blockchain data that is stored in blockfiles, there are other data storage on each node in the Fabric system, including the World State, the block index database and the historical database. The World State stores the latest state information of each account, and are updated by each transaction that is stored in the blockchain. In Fabric, Word State is stored in a database named *VersionedDB*, which is based on *LevelDB* by default and can be replaced to *CouchDB* for richer query methods. *LevelDB* is an efficient *key-value* database. The key of each item in the database is "channel name + chaincode name + account address", and the *value* is the specific state information.

3 Query Process of State Data in Fabric

For a blockchain system, the most common operations include writing new data on the chain and reading data from the chain, which are both related to the World State. As we introduced in Sect. 2.1, a new transaction needs to be verified by the endorsing peers

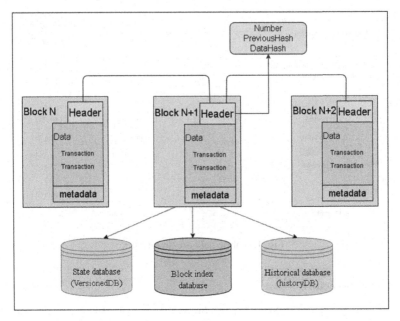

Fig. 2. Data storage structure of Fabric

and the committing peers. To speed up the verification process, the process is based on the state data that is stored in the local database, e.g. whether the balance of an account is enough for a new transaction, instead of recovering the balance based on the data on the chain. On the other hand, the most common query request is the balance of an account, which is usually not read from the blockchain but from the World State in the local database for higher efficiency. In this section, we will introduce the complete query process of state data based on the Fabric source code, and analyze the detail execution process on the peers.

3.1 General Process of State Inquiry in Fabric

In the implemented Fabric system, a client is connected to a peer node through the initial configuration of *"CORE_PEER_ADDRESS"*, and can query the state data on the peer through command *"peer chaincode query..."*. As shown in Fig. 3, the query process involves the client, the chaincode container, and the peer, and the detail process is introduced as follows.

(1) The client will first parse the query request, and apply the results as parameters to call the method *chaincodeQuery()→chaincodeInvokeOrQuery()* to construct a specification object. Then the encapsulated signed proposal message is sent to the peer.

(2) The peer sends a *ChaincodeMessage_TRANSACTION* message to the chaincode Docker container. After receiving the message, the chaincode container will hand

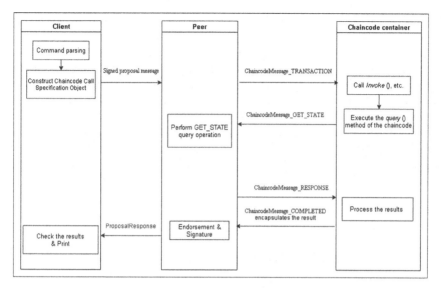

Fig. 3. The general execution process of the "query" command

it to the *Handler* and the Finite State Machine (FSM), and call the method *handler.handleTransaction()→handler.cc.Invoke()*.

(3) Based on the input parameters, the *query()* method in the chaincode and the *stub.Getstate()* method in the state query API will be executed. And a *ChaincodeMessage_GET_STATE* message will be constructed and sent to the peer, requesting to query the account state data.

(4) After receiving the request, the peer will query the state data from the local database (more details in Sect. 3.2), and the result will be encapsulated into a *ChaincodeMessage_RESPONSE* message and sent to the chaincode container.

(5) After processing the query results, the chaincode container will send a *ChaincodeMessage_COMPLETED* message to the peer, which indicates the completion of the *Invoke()* method on the chaincode container.

(6) After the endorsement of the message, the peer will send a *ProposalResponse* message to the client.

(7) Finally, the client will check the returned query results.

3.2   Specific Query Process on the Peer

As shown in Fig. 4, after receiving the *ChaincodeMessage_GET_STATE* message from the chaincode container, the peer calls the method *handleMessage()→ handleMessageReadyState()* that is defined in *fabric/core/chaincode/handler.go* for processing. Then the system calls the method *HandleGetState()* and its sub-method *QueryExecutor. GetState()*. *QueryExecutor* is a query executor interface that supports multiple query methods, and supports inquiry and modification of *LevelDB* and *CouchDB*. The *lockBasedQueryExecutor* structure implements the *QueryExecutor* interface and contains a *helper* field of *queryHelper* type. Therefore, what is actually executed in the *QueryExecutor* is *lockBasedQueryExecutor. GetState()→queryHelper. GetState()*. The *queryHelper* encapsulates a transaction manager (*LockBasedTxMgr* type) that holds a state database (*VersionedDB*) object. Next, the *txmgr.db.GetState()* method in the transaction manager combines the incoming parameters, channel name, chaincode name, and account address into a key to obtain the state data from *VersionedDB*. The underlying *VersionedDB* also has objects such as *DBHandle*, which are used to read/write data from *LevelDB*. When reading the state data, *LevelDB* will call the method *Get()* to query the value corresponding to the key, and return the result. Then the query process on the peer is complete.

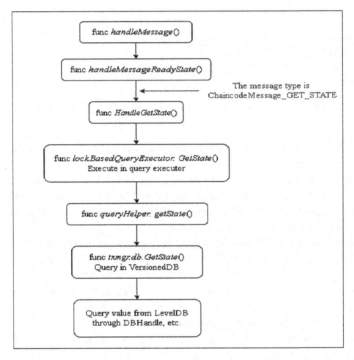

Fig. 4. Detail query process of state data on the peer

4   Feasibility of Modification of State Data in Fabric

The immutability of the blockchain is premised on effective verification. According to the analysis in Sect. 3, state data is read directly from *VersionedDB*, and there is no verification mechanism to check whether the returned data has been modified. First, the system could check the correctness of the queried state data by comparing with that recovered by the data on the chain. Second, the query results on a node could also be verified by comparing with that queried on other nodes. But both these two schemes are not supported in current Fabric project. In this case, the modification of the state information in the database will not be identified until a new transaction is verified to be invalid based on the modified state data.

With *LevelDB* as the default database for *VersionedDB*, the *DBHandle* object in *Versioned* can be used to read and write data in *LevelDB* through the method *Get()* and *Put()*, respectively. So we can simply use *DBHandle* to modify the state data.

5 Experiments and Analysis for Data Modification

To validate the security problem introduced in Sect. 3, we built a small scale Fabric network. In the experiments, we modified the database of state data on single and all peers, respectively, and analyzed the system status for each case. In addition, the effect of the state data modification is analyzed under different endorsement policies.

5.1 Testing Platform and System Initialization

The experiments were carried out in VMware virtual machines created on a Windows-10 PC. The configuration of virtual machine and test environment are shown in Table 1. The information of Fabric images we used in the experiment are shown in Table 2. During the tests, we ran a small-scale network in the official sample set, *first-network* [12]. As shown in Fig. 5, the *first-network* is composed of two organizations (Org), a client and an Orderer. Each organization contains one endorsing peer and one committing peer. The peers in both organizations belong to one channel named "mychannel", and we deployed a chaincode named "mycc" in this channel. Each peer maintains the blockchain that contains the transactions between two accounts "a" and "b" and keeps their balance in the local database. The initialized account information of the ledger is shown in Table 3. The default endorsement policy is that a transaction is valid only when all endorsing peers return the same simulation results.

Table 1. Virtual machine configuration

Item	Descriptions
Operating system	ubuntu-18.04.1-desktop-amd64
Docker version	v19.03.8
Docker-compose version	v 1.25.4
Golang version	go1.13.7 linux/amd64
Git version	v 2.26.0

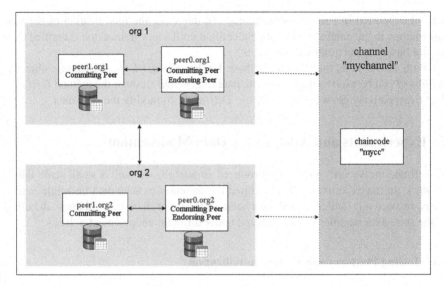

Fig. 5. Structure of the *first-network*

Table 2. Fabric images

Image	Version	Image ID
Fabric-peer	1.3.0	f3ea63abddaa
Fabric-javaenv	1.3.0	2476cefaf833
Fabric-ca	1.3.0	5c6b20ba944f
Fabric-tools	1.3.0	c056cd9890e7
Fabric-ccenv	1.3.0	953124d80237
Fabric-orderer	1.3.0	f430f581b46b
Fabric-zookeeper	0.4.13	e62e0af39193
Fabric-kafka	0.4.13	4121ea662c47
Fabric-couchdb	0.4.13	1d3266e01e64
Fabric-baseimage	amd64-0.4.13	27240288889f
Fabric-baseos	amd64-0.4.13	f0fe49196c40

Table 3. Initial ledger information of first-network

Item	Descriptions
"a" balance	60
"b" balance	240
Block number	7

5.2 Modification of State Data on Single Endorsing Peer

According to the analysis of the feasibility of tampering the database in Sect. 4, we modified the database of the peer0.org1 (endorsing peer). As shown in Fig. 6, the balance of the account "a" is successfully changed from 60 to 100. Then the client initiated a transaction that "a" transfers 90 digital currency to "b". As shown in Fig. 7, the client reported an error as "could not assemble transaction: ProposalResponse Payloads do not match...". At this moment, we checked the log file of peer1.org1 and peer1.org2 (committing peers) as shown in Fig. 8, and did not find any information about synchronization of a new block, which could be explained as follows.

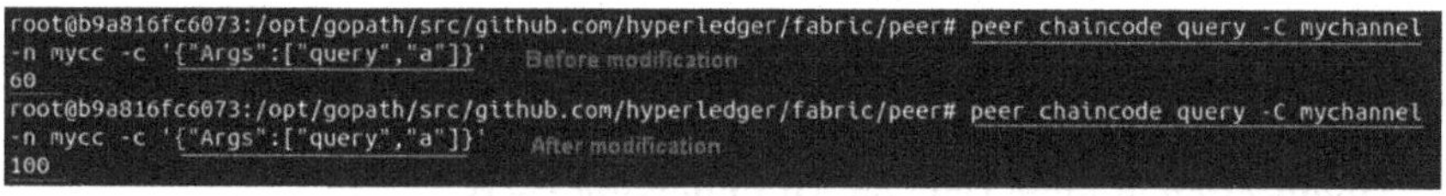

Fig. 6. Query the balance of "a" before and after the modification

Fig. 7. Transaction issuing and error report on the client

Fig. 8. The logs of Endorsing Peer: the transaction wasn't written to the ledger

In Fabric, after simulating the transaction, the endorsing peer will encapsulate the execution result, endorsement signature, and chaincode execution message into a *ProposalResponse* and send it to the client. The client will compare the responses when enough endorsements are collected, and send it to the Orderer if the endorsement policy is satisfied. This process is implemented in the *CreateSignedTx()* function defined in fabric/protos/utils/txutils.go, as shown in Fig. 9. In our case, the responses from two endorsing peers were different, which did not meet the endorsement policy, so we got the error report "ProposalResponsePayloads do not match".

```
// CreateSignedTx assembles an Envelope message from proposal, endorsements,
// and a signer. This function should be called by a client when it has
// collected enough endorsements for a proposal to create a transaction and
// submit it to peers for ordering
func CreateSignedTx(proposal *peer.Proposal, signer msp.SigningIdentity, resps ...*peer.ProposalResponse) (*common.Envelope, error) {
    if len(resps) == 0 {
        return nil, errors.New("at least one proposal response is required")
    }
              ......

    // ensure that all actions are bitwise equal and that they are successful
    var a1 []byte
    for n, r := range resps {
        if n == 0 {
            a1 = r.Payload
            if r.Response.Status < 200 || r.Response.Status >= 400 {
                return nil, errors.Errorf("proposal response was not successful, error code %d, msg %s", r.Response.Status, r.Response.Messa
            }
            continue
        }

        if bytes.Compare(a1, r.Payload) != 0 {
            return nil, errors.New("ProposalResponsePayloads do not match")
        }
    }
              ......
}
```

Fig. 9. Part of func *CreateSignedTx*()

5.3 Modification of State Data on All Endorsing Peers

This time, we did the same state data modification on peer0.org2, so that the balance of "a" becomes 100 on both of the endorsing peers. Then the same transaction was issued by the client. As shown in Fig. 10, the transaction was successfully executed, and the balance of "a" became 10 after the transaction. At this moment, we checked the log file of the endorsing peers and that of the committing peers. As we can see from Fig. 11, a new block was generated and successfully synchronized on all peers, which implied that the modification of the balance in the state database is not detected by all peers and the transaction based on the modified balance could be accepted by the system.

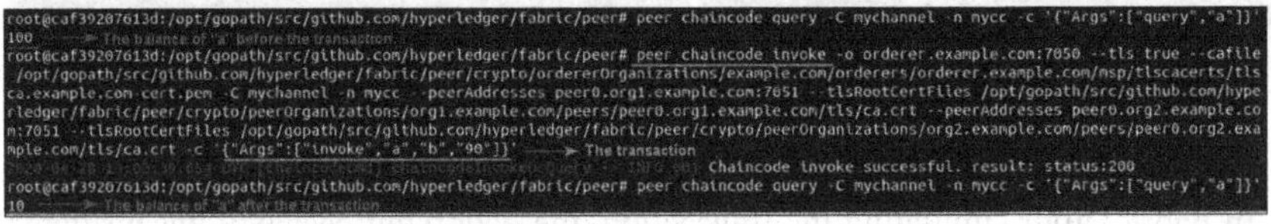

Fig. 10. Transaction issued on client and successfully executed

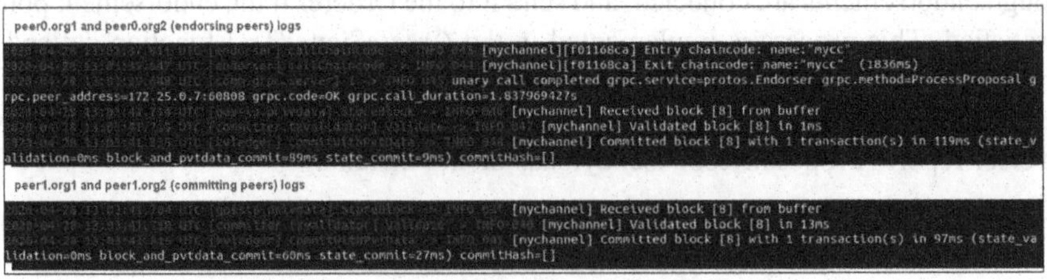

Fig. 11. The logs of Endorsing Peers and Committing Peers

It should be noted that we did not modify the state database on the committing peers, but they did not identify the invalid transaction. This means that the committing peers will not verify the transactions in the block from the Orderer based on the local state information. Actually, we had also repeated the experiments by modifying the balance of "a" on all the endorsing peers and committing peers, and got exactly the same results, which means the modification of the state data on endorsing peers is enough to issue invalid transactions.

5.4 Revise the Endorsement Policy

In Fabric, the endorsement policy specifies which endorsing peers' simulation execution results and endorsement are required for a new transaction [13]. In the above experiments, the endorsement from all endorsing peers are required to verify a transaction. In this experiment, we modified the endorsement policy to that only one endorsing peer is required to verify a transaction. Then we modified the balance of the account "a" from 60 to 100 only on peer0.org1, issued the same transaction, and sent it only to peer0.org1 for endorsement. As expected, the endorsed transaction by peer0.org1 met the new endorsement policy, and the new block containing the invalid transaction was successfully accepted by all the committing peers. These results mean that a less restrict endorsement policy may further lower the difficulty for an attacker to issue invalid transactions in Fabric.

6 Conclusions

This paper reports a potential security problem in the Fabric network. By analyzing the query process of the state data based on the source code, we found that the returned result is read from the local database, and would not be verified by the on-chain data. Then we performed experiments on a small-scale Fabric network (first-network), and got two important conclusions: 1) the state information of any account can be easily modified through the database interface; 2) if the balance of an account is modified on all the endorsing peers, the transaction based on the modified balance could be successfully executed and then recorded on the chain. These results reveal that although the on-chain data are trustable in Fabric, the off-chain data are not well protected, which may bring security risks to the whole system, especially for small scale networks or the ones with loose endorsement policy.

A possible solution to this problem is to improve the transaction verification process by confirming the off-chain balance with the on-chain data. But this will introduce much computation for each trasaction, so that the transaction throughput would be decreased. Optimization of the transaction verification process will be the focus of our future work.

Acknowledgments. This work is supported by the Tianjin Natural Science Foundation (19JCY-BJC15700).

References

1. Hyperledger Fabric project. http://github.com/hyperledger/fabric
2. Dinh, T.T.A., Liu, R., Zhang, M., Chen, G., Ooi, B.C., Wang, J.: Untangling blockchain: a data processing view of blockchain systems. IEEE Trans. Knowl. Data Eng. **30**(7), 1366–1385 (2018)
3. Szabo, N.: Smart contracts: building blocks for digital markets. EXTROPY: J. Transhumanist Thought, (16) (1996)
4. How Walmart brought unprecedented transparency to the food supply chain with Hyperledger Fabric. https://www.hyperledger.org/learn/publications/walmart-case-study
5. Change Healthcare using Hyperledger Fabric to improve claims lifecycle throughput and transparency. https://www.hyperledger.org/learn/publications/changehealthcare-case-study
6. Dltledgers. https://www.dlt.sg
7. Zhou, I., Makhdoom, I., Abolhasan, M., Lipman, J., Shariati, N.: A blockchain-based file-sharing system for academic paper review. In: 2019 13th International Conference on Signal Processing and Communication Systems (ICSPCS), Gold Coast, Australia, pp. 1–10 (2019)
8. Mikula, T., Jacobsen, R.H.: Identity and access management with blockchain in electronic healthcare records. In: 2018 21st Euromicro Conference on Digital System Design (DSD), Prague, pp. 699–706 (2018)
9. Harris, C.: Improving telecom industry processes using ordered transactions in hyperledger fabric. In: 2019 IEEE Globecom Workshops (GC Wkshps), Waikoloa, HI, USA, pp. 1–6 (2019)
10. Lee Kuo Chuen, D.: Handbook of Digital Currency, Elsevier (2015)
11. Nakamoto, S.: Bitcoin: a peer-to-peer electronic cash system (2009). http://bitcoin.org/bitcoin.pdf
12. Fabric-samples. https://github.com/hyperledger/fabric-samples/tree/release-1.3
13. Baliga, A., Solanki, N., Verekar, S., Pednekar, A., Kamat, P., Chatterjee, S.: Performance characterization of hyperledger fabric. In: 2018 Crypto Valley Conference on Blockchain Technology (CVCBT), Zug, pp. 65–74 (2018). https://doi.org/10.1109/cvcbt.2018.00013

Efficient Boolean SSE: A Novel Encrypted Database (*EDB*)

Xueling Zhu, Huaping Hu, Shaojing Fu, Qing Wu, and Bo Liu(✉)

College of Computer, National University of Defense Technology, Changsha, China
kyle.liu@nudt.edu.cn

Abstract. Searchable symmetric encryption (SSE) with increasing expressiveness was proposed to acquire optimal communication complexity, but it has poor efficiency compared to the single-word query. Many of the existing expressive SSE mechanisms use the inverted index to build the encrypted database (EDB) for the sub-linear search complexity. However, this inevitably brings about the problems of repeated storage and low efficiency of set operations. To this end, we introduced a new approach, using the boolean vectors (BV) instead of the inverted indexes to build EDB, which dramatically improves the search efficiency and reduces the storage space. While boolean operation must run on the closed space, we divided the full queried space into several disjoint closed sub-spaces and proved its correctness theoretically. Our construction supports arbitrary conjunctive, disjunctive, and boolean queries. The experiments prove that our system is more efficient in storage and search complexity than existing methods.

Keywords: Searchable encryption · Boolean query · Structured encryption · Boolean vector structure

1 Introduction

Searchable Symmetric Encryption (SSE) was first proposed by Song et al. in 2000 [22]. In this scheme, they used the symmetric encryption to realize the retrieval of a single keyword. Later, a series of research [5,6,8,13,18] gives SSE practical constructions that support single keyword queries. For efficiency and privacy, all of these SSE schemes are severely limited in their expressiveness during the search: a client can only specify a single keyword to search on, but it receives all of the documents containing that keyword. Like remotely-stored email or large databases, a single-keyword search will often return many records in practical settings. This process often results in inefficient searches (e.g., half the database size if one of the conjunctive terms is "gender = male") and significant leakage (e.g., it reveals the set of documents matching each keyword) [4].

Supported by the National Natural Science Foundation of China under grant No. 61572513.

ⓒ Springer Nature Singapore Pte Ltd. 2020
G. Xu et al. (Eds.): FCS 2020, CCIS 1286, pp. 373–387, 2020.
https://doi.org/10.1007/978-981-15-9739-8_29

Recent works focus on increasing expressiveness, such as conjunctive queries and boolean queries. Golle firstly proposed the conjunctive equality queries in [15]. Another example is the BlindSeer project from Pappas et al. [19] and Fisch et al. [11], which present a solution that supports boolean and range queries as well as stemming in sub-linear time. L. Ballard [1] and J. W. Byun [2] show how to build for each conjunctive query a set of tokens that can be tested against each document in the database to identify matching documents. Cash et al. [4] proposed OXT, the first optimal-time conjunctive keyword search scheme. However, none of the above solutions extend to general boolean queries.

Kamara et al. [16] first propose non-interactive highly efficient SSE schemes, which handles arbitrary disjunctive and boolean queries with worst-case sublinear search and optimal communication complexity. However, it forces queries to be in Conjunctive Normal Form and not supporting negations. Bernardo's [10] efficient boolean searchable encryption mechanism, BISEN, supports arbitrarily complex boolean queries, verifiability to malicious users, and achieves minimal leakage. However, it is based on the principle of trusted regions and requires new commodity trusted hardware on the server-side, which not only leads to an increase in cost and makes its security closely related to trusted hardware.

There is also some researches dedicated to increasing functionality. Some researches [9,20,24] added dynamic update and multi-user functions based on the OXT algorithm, [21] introduced attribute-based encryption (ABE) technology to realize fine-grained access control, thus realizing multi-user extension functions supporting boolean queries. In these mechanisms, there is no substantial improvement in algorithm efficiency.

Actually, in many of the existing schemes, inverted indexes [3,4,6,8,17,18] are used to build *EDBs* in the light of its sub-linear search time. However, when used for expressive queries, it brings some shortcomings. First, constructing *EDB* for expressive queries brings about a significant problem of repeated storage, where the complexity of storage is $O(n^2)$, n is the number of id/keyword pairs, the efficiency decreases significantly with the increase of file set. Second, the searching process needs many set operations, such as intersection, union, and complement of sets. For two sets of order k, the set operation's complexity is $O(k^2)$.

We propose a novel method to construct *EDB*, which avoids the problems caused by the inverted index. Our construction's security is controlled disclosure [6], which can be viewed as a compromise between full security [7,12,14,23] and efficiency. Our main contributions are as follows:

(1) We propose a novel boolean vector(BV) data structure, which is used to convert set operations into logical computer operations. For sets of order n and m, the set operation's complexity is $n \times m$, while our algorithm is only $c \times min(n, m)$, where c is a constant.
(2) We managed to cut the full queried space to several closed and disjoint subspaces, generating *EDB* according to these sub-spaces, which minimize the storage space.

(3) Using *BVs*, we propose a novel boolean query scheme *BBVX* with optimal storage complexity and better search complexity than Kamara's *IEX-2Lev*. As in *BVX*, we strived to divide the full queried space into several sub-spaces supporting the boolean operations and successfully proving its correctness theoretically.

We analyze the properties of *BVX* and *BBVX*, then compare it with Kamara's scheme [16]. Table 1 shows the details.

Table 1. Property comparison.

scheme	mode	Storage	search time	Token
IEX[16]	*Conj and Disj.*	$\sum_w strg(S_w)$	$O(q^2 \cdot M)$	$O(q^2/2)$
BIEX[16]	*Arbitrarily Boolean.*	same as IEX	$O(q^2 \cdot (M_1 + l \cdot M_2))$	$O(q^3/2)$
BVX	*Conj and Disj.*	$\sum_w C_w \cdot \#co(w)$	$O(q^2 \cdot C_M)$	$O(q^2/2)$
BBVX	*Arbitrarily Boolean.*	Same as BVX	$O(q^2 \cdot (c_1 + l \cdot c_2))$	$O(q^2/2 + q^2 \cdot l)$
Remarks	c_1, c_2,C_M,C_w are all close to constant; M_i is much larger than c_i.			

$$M = max\{\#DB(w_i)\}_{i \in [q]}$$
$$M_1 = max\{\#DB(w)\}$$
$$S_w = \sum_{v \in co(w)} \#\{DB(v) \cap DB(w)\}$$
$$M_2 = \#DB(\Delta_1)$$

2   Preliminaries

Notation. The set of all binary strings of length n is denoted as $\{0,1\}^n$, and the set of all finite binary strings as $\{0,1\}^*$. $[n]$ is the set of integers $\{1, \cdots, n\}$, and $2^{[n]}$ is the corresponding power set. We write $x \leftarrow \chi$ to represent an element x being sampled from a distribution X, The output x of an algorithm A is denoted by $x \leftarrow \mathcal{A}$. Given a sequence v of n elements, we refer to its ith element as v_i or $v[i]$. If S is a set then $\#S$ refers to its cardinality. If s is a string then $|s|$ refers to its bit length and s_i to its ith bit. Given strings s and r, we refer to their concatenation as either $\langle s,r \rangle$ or $s\|r$.

Basic Data Type. A multimap MM with capacity n is a collection of n label/tuple pairs $(l_i, V_i)_{i \leq n}$ that supports Get and Put operations. We write $V_i = MM[l_i]$ to denote getting the tuple associated with label l_i and $MM[l_i] = V_i$ to denote operation of associating the tuple V_i to label l_i. Multi-maps are the abstract data type instantiated by an inverted index.

Collections. A document collection is a set of documents $D = (D_1, \cdots, D_n)$, each document consisting of a set of keywords from some universe W. We denote by $W[i]$ the ith keyword in W, denote by $id(D_i)$ the document identifier. we refer to any multi-map derived from a document collection as a database and denote it DB. Given a keyword w, we denote by $coDB(w) \subseteq W$ the set of keywords in W that co-occur with w; that is, the keywords that are contained in documents that contain w. When DB is clear from the context, we omit DB and write only $co(w)$.

Definition 1 (Adaptive security) [6,8]: Let $\sum_T = (Setup, Token, Query)$ be a structured encryption scheme for type T and consider the following probabilistic experiments where A is a stateful adversary, S is a stateful simulator, $\mathcal{L}_S$ and $\mathcal{L}_Q$ are leakage profiles and $z \in \{0,1\}^*$:

- $Real_{\sum,A}(k)$: given z the adversary A outputs a structure DS of type T and receives EDS from the challenger, where $(K, EDS) \leftarrow Setup(1^k, DS)$. The adversary then adaptively chooses a polynomial number of queries $q_1, \cdots, q_m$. For all $i \in [m]$, the adversary receives $tk_i \leftarrow Token(K, q_i)$. Finally, A outputs a bit b that is output by the experiment.
- $Ideal_{\sum,A,S}(k)$: given z the adversary A generates a structure DS of type T which it sends to the challenger. Given z and leakage $\mathcal{L}_S(DS)$ from the challenger, the simulator S returns an encrypted data structure EDS to A. The adversary then adaptively chooses a polynomial number of operations $q_1, \cdots, q_m$. For all $i \in [m]$, the simulator receives query leakage $\mathcal{L}_Q(DS, q_i)$ and returns a token tk_i to A. Finally, A outputs a bit b that is output by the experiment.

We say that $\sum$ is adaptively $(\mathcal{L}_S, \mathcal{L}_Q)$-secure if for all PPT adversaries A, there exists a PPT simulator S such that for all $z \in \{0,1\}^*$,

$$| Pr[\mathbf{Real}_{\sum,A}(k) = 1] - Pr[Ideal_{\sum,A,S}(k) = 1]| \leq l(k)$$

3   Boolean Vector Structure Encryption

A boolean vector bv with length n is an array of n binary bits, which is a member of the universe $\{0,1\}^n$. We denote the universe space of boolean vector with length n as B^n. A boolean vector structure BV of capacity N is a collection of N label/value pairs $\{(l_i, bv_i)\}_{i \leq N}$. We write $bv_i = BV[l_i]$ to denote getting the value associated with label l_i and $BV[l_i] = bv_i$ to denote the operation of associating the value bv_i in BV with label l_i.

The existing structured encryption scheme(STE) commonly used to encrypt matrix, dictionary, multi-map and graph structure [6]. We now present a encryption scheme for BV data structure. Given $BV = \{l_i, bv_i\}_{i \in [n]}$, the encryption details are in Table 2.

4   BVX: A Disjunctive SSE Scheme

4.1   Main Construction

For two boolean vector $bv_1, bv_2 \in B^n$, we define three operations $'|'$, $'\&'$ and $'!'$ in B^n equal to computer logic operations *or*, *and* and *not*. In this section we study the disjunctive queries, which is a vector of keywords $w_1 \vee w_2 \vee \cdots \vee w_q, w_i \in$

Table 2. *BV* encryption scheme.

Let $F : \{0,1\}^k \times W \to \{0,1\}^*$, and $P : \{0,1\}^k \times W \to \{0,1\}^k$ be pseudo random functions, the *BV* encryption scheme $\sum_{BV} = (Setup, Token, Get)$ is defined as follows:

   $-Setup(1^k)$:

      1.sample two random k-bit keys K_1, K_2, Set $K = (K_1, K_2)$.

      2.initiate a boolean structure EBV, for $i = 1, \cdots, n$,

         (a)compute $k_i \leftarrow P_{K_1}(l_i)$

         (b)append $bv_i \bigoplus F_{K_2}(l_i)$ with search key k_i to EBV.

   $-Token(K, l)$:

      compute $tk = (F_{K_2}(l), P_{K_1}(l))$.

   $-Get(EBV, tk)$:

      1.parse tk as (α, β).

      2.compute $bv \leftarrow EBV(\beta) \bigoplus \alpha$, where $EBV(\beta)$ refers to the value stored in EBV with search key β.

      3. If β is not in EBV, output $J = \emptyset$. Otherwise output bv.

$W, i = 1, \cdots, q$. Suppose database $DB(w_1)$ contains n file tags $(id_1, \cdots, id_n)$, the collection of boolean vector related to w_1 is B_1^n. For each $i = 1, \cdots, q$, we can get a boolean vector bv_i from database $DB(w_1) \cap DB(w_i)$ as in Table 3, then we acquire the boolean data structure $BV = \{(w_1, bv_1), \cdots, (w_q, bv_q)\}$. Obviously, $bv_i \in B_1^n$. If we want to compute

$$T_1 = DB(w_1) \setminus \bigcup_{i=2}^{q} (w_1 \cap w_i),$$

then do the boolean operations

$$bv = bv_1 \& (!(bv_2 \mid \cdots \mid bv_q)).$$

If $(bv[i] == 1)$, then the ith tag of $DB(w_1)$ is in the T_1.

Table 3. Boolean vector for 3 keywords

$DB(w_1)$	id_1	id_2	id_3	id_4	id_5	id_6	id_7
$bv1 : DB(w_1) \bigcap DB(w_1)$	1	1	1	1	1	1	1
$bv2 : DB(w_1) \bigcap DB(w_2)$	0	1	1	0	1	1	1
$bv3 : DB(w_1) \bigcap DB(w_3)$	1	0	1	0	1	0	1

At a high-level, our main construction, *BVX*, makes use of a *BV* encryption scheme $\sum_{BV} = (Setup, Token, Get)$, a multi-map encryption scheme $\sum_{MM} = (Setup, Token, Search)$, a pseudo-random function F, a *RCPA-secure* private-key encryption scheme $SKE = (Gen, Enc, Dec)$, and a funtion $GetTag\{\cdot\}$ to get tags from boolean vector and document database. The scheme is dipicted as follows, and the details are provided in Table 4.

Setup. The *Setup* algorithm takes as input a security parameter k and an index database(DB). It makes use of a data structure BV and a multi-map MM. MM maps every keyword $w \in W$ to an encryption of the identifiers in $DB(w)$. We refer to these encryptions as *Tags*. The MM is then encrypted using $\sum_{MM}$, resulting in encrypted multi-map(EMM). For each keyword pair $(w, v \in W)$, if $DB(w) \bigcap DB(v) \neq \emptyset$, suppose $\#DB(w) = n$, the algorithm creates a collection of boolean data structure BV that maps the keywords $v \in W$ to a n bits boolean vector bv. Intuitively, the purpose of the BV is to quickly find out which documents contain both w and v. The BV are then encrypted with $\sum_{BV}$. This results in encrypted boolean structure EBV, which are appended to EMM referred before. The output of *Setup* includes the encrypted structures(EMM, EBV) as well as their keys.

Token. The *Token* algorithm takes as input a key and a vector of keywords $w = (w_1, \cdots, w_q)$, and output token $TK = (tk_1, \cdots, tk_{q-1}, tk_q)$. That is for all $i \in [q]$, it creates a sub-token $tk_i = (gtk_i, btk_i, \cdots, btk_q)$ composed of a multi-map global token gtk_i for w_i, a vector of boolean tokens btk_j for w_j, with $j = i, \cdots, q$.

Search. The Search algorithm takes as input $EDB = (EMM, EBV)$ and a token $TK = (tk_1, \cdots, tk_{q-1}, tk_q)$. For each sub-token $tk_i = (gtk_i, btk_i, \cdots, btk_q)$, the server does the following. It first uses gtk_i to query the global multi-map EMM and recover a set of identifier tags for $DB(w_i)$. Then for $j = i, \cdots, q$, it uses btk_j to query the encrypted boolean vectors EBV to recover the boolean vector related to w_j. Once it finishes processing all boolean tokens in tk_i, it get $q - i + 1$ boolean vector $bv_i, \cdots, bv_q$. Let b^i is a boolean vector related to w_i, we do the following operations

$$b^i = bv_i \& (!(bv_{i+1} \mid \cdots \mid bv_q)).$$

Using $GetTag(b^i, DB(w_i))$ funtion, we can acquire

$$T_i = DB(w_i) \setminus (\bigcup_{j=i+1}^{q} (DB(w_i) \cap DB(w_j))) \tag{1}$$

Once it finishes processing all the sub-tokens $tk_i, i = 1, \cdots, q-1$, the server holds tags T_1 through T_{q-1}. For gtk_q, the server just queries the global multi-map to recover T_q. Finally, it outputs the set

$$T = \bigcup_{i=1}^{q} T_i$$

4.2   Correctness and Efficiency

We now analyze the correctness and efficiency. The correctness of BVX follows from operations in the collection of the boolean vectors. Given a disjunctive query $w = (w_1, \cdots, w_q)$, $BVX.Search(EDB, Token(K, w))$ will output

Table 4. A disjunctive SSE scheme

Let F be a pseudo-random function, $SKE = (Gen, Enc, Dec)$ be a private-key encryption scheme, $\sum_{BV} = (Setup, Token, Get)$ be a boolean vector encryption scheme, $\sum_{MM} = (Setup, Token, Get)$ be a multi-map encryption scheme. Consider the disjunctive SSE scheme $BVX = (Setup, Token, Search)$ defined as follows:

  $-Setup(1^k, DB)$:

    1.sample $K_1, K_2 \leftarrow \{0,1\}^k$;

    2.initialize a multi-map MM;

    3.for all $w \in W$,

      (a) for all $id \in DB(w)$, let $tag_{id} := SKE.Enc_{K_1}(id; F_{K_2}(id \| w))$;

      (b) set $MM[w] := (tag_{id})_{id \in DB(w)}$;

      (c) for all $v \in W$, if$(DB(v) \bigcap DB(w) \neq \emptyset)$, initialize a boolean vector b_v, the size of b_v is $\#DB(w)$;

      (d)for $i = 1, \cdots, \#DB(w)$, if $id_i \in (DB(v) \bigcap DB(w))$, let $b_v[i] = 1$, else, let $b_v[i] = 0$.

    4.compute $(K_g, EMM) \leftarrow \sum_{MM}.Setup(1^k, MM)$;

    5.compute $(K_b, EBV) \leftarrow \sum_{BV}.Setup(1^k, BV)$;;

    6.set $K = (K_g, K_b)$ and $EDB = (EMM, EBV)$;

    7.output (K, EDB).

  $Token(K, w)$:

    1.parse w as $(w_1, \cdots, w_q)$;

    2.for all $i \in [q-1]$,

      (a) compute $gtk_i \leftarrow \sum_{MM}.Token(K_g, w_i)$;

      (b) for all $j = i, i+1, \cdots, q$,

        compute $btk_j \leftarrow \sum_{BV}.Token(K_b, w_j)$;

      (c) set $tk_i = (gtk_i, btk_{i+1}, \cdots, btk_q)$;

    3.compute $tk_q \leftarrow \sum_{MM}.Token(K_g, w_q)$;

    4.output $tk = (tk_1, \cdots, tk_{q-1}, tk_q)$.

  $-Search(EDB, tk)$:

    1.parse EDB as (EMM, EBV);

    2.parse tk as $(tk_1, \cdots, tk_{q-1}, tk_q)$;

    3.for all $i = 1, i+1, \cdots, q-1$,

      (a)parse tk_i as $(gtk_i, btk_i, \cdots, btk_q)$

      (b)compute $T' \leftarrow \sum_{MM}.Get(EMM, gtk_i)$;

      (c)for all $j = i, i+1, \cdots, q$,compute $b^j \leftarrow \sum_{BV}.Get(EBV, btk_j)$;

      (d)compute $b = b^i \& (!(b^{i+1} \mid \cdots \mid b^q))$;

      (e)compute $T_i = GetTag(b, T')$;

    4. compute $T^q \leftarrow \sum_{MM}.Get(EMM, gtk_q)$;

    5. output $\bigcup_{i \in [q]} T_i$;

$$T = \bigcup_{i=1}^{q} T_i,$$

we can know from [16] that

$$T = \bigcup_{i=1}^{q} T_i = \bigcup_{i=1}^{q} DB(w_i).$$

Now we need to prove the boolean operation is valid. Take T_1 for example, according to Morgan's law, suppose $DB(w_1) \cap DB(w_j) = A_j$, obviously, $A_j \subset DB(w_1)$, then we have the following equation:

$$T_1 = DB(w_1) \setminus \left(\bigcup_{j=2}^{q} (DB(w_1 \cap DB(w_j))) \right)$$

$$= (DB(w_1) \cap DB(w_1)) \setminus \left(\bigcup_{j=2}^{q} (DB(w_1) \cap DB(w_j)) \right)$$

$$= A_1 \setminus \left(\bigcup_{j=2}^{q} A_j \right)$$

$$= A_1 \cap \overline{\left(\bigcup_{j=2}^{q} A_j \right)}$$

For $j = 1, \cdots, q$, given A_j, we can acquire a boolean vector b_j, let $\#DB(w_1) = n$, the universe of boolean vectors related to $DB(w_1)$ is B_1^n, because $A_j \subset DB(w_1)$, then $b_j \in B_1^n$. As the set operations are concurrent to the boolean operations, we can acquire the same results as Eq. (1) using boolean operations in equation $BVX.Search.3.d$.

Efficiency. The search complexity of BVX contains $O(q^2)$ search operations and an equal number of boolean operations, q is the number of terms in the disjunction. Tokens are of size $O(q^2)$. The community complexity is optimal, because for $i, j \in [q], i \neq j, T_i \cap T_j = \emptyset$, so the final set T don't have reduntant identifiers. The storage complexity is

$$O\left(strg\left(\sum_{w} \#DB(w) \right) \right) + \sum_{w} (C_w \times (\#co(w))),$$

where C_w is a constant related to w, $strg$ is the storage complexity of the underlying encrypted multi-map encryption scheme $\sum_{MM}$.

4.3   Security

The security of BVX is controlled disclosure [6], which includes the *setup* leakage and *query* leakage. We now give a precise description of BVX leakage profile and show that it is adaptively-secure to it. Its *setup* leakage is

$$\mathcal{L}_S^{bvx}(DB) = \left(\mathcal{L}_S^{mm}(MM), \mathcal{L}_S^{bvx}(BV)\right),$$

where $\mathcal{L}_S^{mm}(MM)$ and $\mathcal{L}_S^{bvx}(BV)$ are the *setup* leakages of the underlying multi-map encryption schemes and boolean vector, respectively. Its query leakage is

$$\mathcal{L}_Q^{bvx}(DB, w) = ((\mathcal{L}_S^{mm}(MM_i), \mathcal{L}_Q^{mm}(MM_g, w_i),$$
$$\mathcal{L}_Q^{bv}(BV, w_i), \cdots, \mathcal{L}_Q^{bv}(BV, w_q), TagPat_i(DB, w))_{i \in [q-1]},$$
$$\mathcal{L}_Q^{mm}(MM_g, w_q), TagPat_q(DB, w))$$

where for all $i \in [q]$,

$$TagPat_q(DB, w) = \left((f_i(id))_{id \in DB(w_i) \cap DB(w_{i+1})}, \cdots, \right.$$
$$\left. (f_i(id))_{id \in DB(w_i) \cap DB(w_q)}\right),$$

and f_i is a random function from $\{0,1\}^{|id| + log\#W}$ to $\{0,1\}^k$.

Theorem 1. If $\sum_{MM}$ is adaptively $\left(\mathcal{L}_S^{mm}, \mathcal{L}_Q^{mm}\right)$-secure, *SKE* is *RCPA*-secure and F is pseudo-random, then *BVX* is $\left(\mathcal{L}_S^{bvx}, \mathcal{L}_Q^{bvx}\right)$-secure.

Proof. We give the proof of Theorem 1 in the extended version.

5   BBVX: Boolean Queries with BVX

5.1   Main Construction

The boolean queries are similar to *BVX* in that it uses the same encrypted structures but different *Token* and *Search* algorithms. We refer to the boolean queries as *BBVX*. We now provide an overview of how *BBVX* works.

According to Kamara's *IEX-2lev* [16], any boolean query can be written in conjunctive normal form(CNF) $\triangle_1 \wedge \cdots \wedge \triangle_l$, such that $\triangle_i = w_{i,1} \vee \cdots \vee w_{i,q}$. We want to get the set T_b, where:

$$T^b = \bigcap_{i \in [l]} \bigcup_{j \in [q]} DB(w_{i,j}).$$

For simplicity, we assume that for $i = 1, 2, \cdots, l$, the disjunctions in $\triangle_i$ have q terms.

In consideration of efficiency, we tried to perform the queries using boolean operations. Because the bool operations must run on the closed space, we managed to divide the full query space into several disjoint closed sub-spaces $(B_1, \cdots, B_q)$. In each B_i, we ran arbitrary bool operations independently and get T_i^b, and finally we get $T^b = \bigcup_{i=1,\cdots,q} T_i^b$. We gave the method of dividing and proof of correctness in Subsect. 5.2, and dipicted the details of *BBVX* in Table 5.

Table 5. A Boolean SSE scheme

Let $BVX = (Setup, Token, Search)$ be the BVX scheme described in Table 4
and let $\sum_{BV} = (Setup, Token, Get)$ and $\sum_{MM} = (Setup, Token, Get)$ be its
underlying boolean-vector and multi-map encryption schemes, respectively.
The boolean SSE encryption scheme $BBVX = (Setup, Token, Search)$ is
defined as follows:

$-Setup(1^k, DB)$:output$(K, EDB) \leftarrow BVX.Setup(1^k, DB)$.

$-Token(K, w)$:

  1.parse K as $(K_g, \{K_{w_i}\}_{w_i \in W})$;

  2.parse w as $\triangle_1 \wedge \cdots \wedge \triangle_l$ where for all $i \in [l]$, $\triangle_i = (w_{i,1} \vee \cdots \vee w_{i,q})$;

  3.compute $tk_1 \leftarrow BVX.Token_K(\triangle_1)$, as in 4.1 we know

    $tk_1 = tk_{1,1}, \cdots, tk_{1,q-1}, gtk_{1,q}$;

  4.for all $k = 1, \cdots, q$,

    a.for all $i = 2, \ldots, l$, $j = 1, \cdots, q$,

      compute $btk_{k,i,j} = \sum_{BV}.Token(w_{1,k}, w_{i,j})$

    b.let $subtk_k = \{btk_{k,i,j}\}_{i=2,\cdots,l, j \in [q]}$

  5.output $tk = (tk_1, subtk_1, \cdots, subtk_q)$;

$-Search(EDB, tk)$:

  1.parse EDB as (EMM, EBV);

  2.parse tk as $(tk_1, subtk_1, \cdots, subtk_q)$;

  3.for $i = 1, \cdots, q$,

    i.compute $b_i' \leftarrow BVX.Search(EDB, tk_1)$;

    ii.compute $DB(w_{1,i}) \leftarrow BVX.Search(EDB, tk)$;

  4.for all $k = 1, \cdots, q$,

    (a)initial a boolean vector b_k, parse

      $subtk_k = \{btk_{k,i,j}\}_{i=2,\cdots,l, j \in [q]}$;

    (b)for $i = 2, \cdots, l$,

      i.initial a boolean vector $bv_{k,i}$

      ii.for $j \in [q]$,

        initial a boolean vector $bv_{k,i,j}$,

        compute $bv_{k,i,j} \leftarrow \sum_{BV}.Search(EBV, btk_{k,i,j})$

        compute $bv_{k,i} = bv_{k,i} \mid btk_{k,i,j}$;

      iii.compute $bv_k = bv_k \& bv_{k,i}$;

    (c)compute $bv_k = bv_k \& b_k'$;

    (d).for all $k = 1, \cdots, q$, compute $I_k = BVX.GetTag(bv_k, DB(w_{1,k}))$;

  5.output $I = I_1 \cup \cdots \cup I_l$.

5.2   Correctness and Efficiency

Correctness. To show the correctness of *BBVX*, we need to show that, given a boolean query in CNF $\triangle_1 \wedge \cdots \wedge \triangle_l$ such that $\triangle_i = w_{i,1} \vee \cdots \vee w_{i,q}$, BIEX.Search outputs T^b:

$$T^b = \bigcap_{i \in [l]} \bigcup_{j \in [q]} DB(w_{i,j})$$

Proof. We give the proof of the correctness in the extended version.

Efficiency. The storage complexity of *BBVX* is the same as *BVX*. Its search complexity contains $O(q^2) + O(q \cdot n)$ search operation and $O(q^2)$ boolean operation, where $O(q^2)$ is the complexity of the disjunction of $\triangle_1$, $O(q \cdot n)$ is the search complexity of $(\triangle_i)_{i=2,\cdots,l}$. The communication complexity of *BBVX* is optimal since for $i, j \in [q], i \neq j, T_i^b \cap T_j^b = \emptyset$, so the final set T^b does not contain any redundant identifiers. Finally, note that it is non-interactive and token size is independent of the query selectivity.

Security. The *BBVX* is adaptive-secure under controlled disclosure. *BBVX*'s leakage contains *setup* leakage and *query* leakage. We now give a precise description of *BBVX* leakage profile and show that it is adaptively-secure concerning it. Its *setup* leakage is

$$\mathcal{L}_S^{BBVX}(DB) = \left(\mathcal{L}_S^{bvx}(DB) \right),$$

where $\left(\mathcal{L}_S^{bvx}(DB) \right)$ is the *setup* leakages of *BVX*. Given a *CNF* query $\triangle_1 \wedge \cdots \wedge \triangle_l$, the query leakage is

$$\mathcal{L}_Q^{bbvx}(DB, \bigwedge_{i=1}^{\ell} \triangle_i) = \left(\mathcal{L}_Q^{bvx}(DB, \triangle_1), \left(\mathcal{L}_Q^{mm}(MMi, w_{l,1}), \cdots, \mathcal{L}_Q^{mm}(MM_i, w_{l,q}), \right. \right.$$

$$TagPat_{i,l}(DB, \bigwedge_{i=1}^{\ell} \triangle_i)_{i \in [q], l \in [2, \cdots, l]}),$$

where, for all $i \in [q]$,

$$TagPat_q(DB, w) = \left((f_i(id))_{id \in DB(w_i) \cap DB(w_{i+1})}, \cdots, \right.$$

$$\left. (f_i(id))_{id \in DB(w_i) \cap DB(w_q)} \right),$$

and f_i is a random function from $\{0,1\}^{|id|+log\#W}$ to $\{0,1\}^k$.

Theorem 2. *If $\sum_{MM}$ is adaptively $(\mathcal{L}_S^{bv}, \mathcal{L}_Q^{bv})$ secure, SKE is RCPA-secure and F is pseudo-random, then BBVX is $(\mathcal{L}_S^{bvx}, \mathcal{L}_Q^{bvx})$-secure.*

Proof. The proof of Theorem 5.1 is similar to the proof of Theorem 4.1.

6   Empirical Evaluation

All experiments were run on Intel(R) Core(TM) i5-8400 CPU@2.80 GHz processor with 8 Gi-RAM attached to a commodity win10 system, we implement our
work in C++. To show the practical viability of our solution we run tests on *NSF*
email data set which generate 7.28 MB distinct (keyword,docId) pairs. The *Tag*
algorithm is *HMAC-SHA1*, the encryption for *BV* is *AES-CBC*. We perform the
Setup, *Search* and *Token* algorithm of *BVX* and *BBVX* respectively.

First, *BVX Setup* algorithm is the same as *BBVX*. We tested the storage
sizes and the time to generate *EDB*. We ran experiments with the number of
keyword/id pairs ranging from 31034 to 7655799. Figure 1 shows the results,
both time and space show exponential growth, consistent with the theoretical
model of $O(n^2)$.

In *Setup* experiment, our scheme requires 9.3 min to process 7.28 MB pairs,
which is approximately 73 µs per pair, while IEX-2Lev requires 1.17 h to process
61.5M pairs, approximately 68 µs per pair. Considering our experiment environment is *PC*, it would be improved using the cloud server like Kamara. In
storage experiment, our scheme get 0.65 GB, 1.2 GB, 2.6 GB *EDBs* respectively
to process 1.2 MB, 2.5 MB, 7.28 MB keyword/id pairs, while Kamara get 1.6 GB
for 1.5M keyword/id pairs.

The experiment results are shown in Fig. 1-a and Fig. 1-b. The number of
words in the dictionary is 30799, the abscissa is the number of pairs (w, id),
in Fig. 1-a, the ordinate is the *Setup* time, in Fig. 1-b, the ordinate is the *Setup*
storage. The Figure gives the *Setup* time in seconds and *Setup* storage in *GBs*
as a function of the number of keyword/id pairs in the dataset.

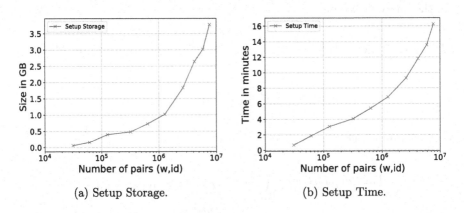

(a) Setup Storage.   (b) Setup Time.

Fig. 1. Setup.

Second, we focused on test the retrieval process's time efficiency, which
includes two steps: one is the generation of a token; the other is the keyword
searching. We consider disjunctive and boolean queries all on an *EDB* with
7.6 MB keyword/id pairs generated from a subset of the *NSF* dataset, Kamara

ran the experiment with $2M$ keyword/id pairs. We use 100000 experimental results as the test standard.

We first tested how the different search keywords affected the running time of the *Token* algorithm. We choose the number of search keywords as $3/6/9/12/15/18$. The experiments show that for *BBVX*, the *Token* running time is linear with the search keywords number, while *BVX*, the *Token* running time rises exponentially.

Then, we test the time complexity of the *Search* algorithm. For *BVX*, when the number of keywords is 3, we carried out 100000 retrieval experiments, and the average retrieval time is about 0.137 ms, while in Kamara's *IEX-2Lev* when the number of keywords is 2, the retrieval time reaches up to 1.2 ms. For *BBVX*, when the number of keywords is 18, the average retrieval time is about 0.337 ms for 100000 retrieval experiments, while for Kamara'*IEX-2Lev*, when 4 keywords are combined, the retrieval time reaches up to 2.4 ms.

Figure 2-a shows the experiment results, the abscissa is the number of search keywords, and the ordinate is the *Token* time. Figure 2-b, the abscissa is the number of search keywords, and the ordinate is the *Search* time. Because *Search* time is directly proportional to the number of sub-tokens queried, search time and *Token* time show the same rule.

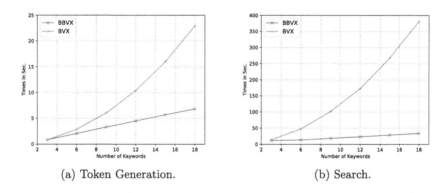

(a) Token Generation.   (b) Search.

Fig. 2. Time of retrieval.

7   Conclusion

In this paper, we proposed two efficient searchable encryption mechanisms *BVX*, and *BBVX* for expressive queries, among which we used *BVX* for conjunctive queries and *BBVX* for boolean queries. These two mechanisms' core idea is to transform the set operations with high computational complexity into efficient computer logic operations. For this reason, We abandon the classic inverted index method and build a new type of *BV*(boolean vector) data structure when generating *EDB*. To further reduce the storage and computing redundancy, we managed to divide the full queried space into several disjoint closed sub-spaces, thus dramatically improving the calculation and storage efficiency. Because the set segmentation in $BBVX$ is harder than BVX, we strived to achieve it and gave the theoretical proof. Through analysis and demonstration, the security of BVX and $BBVX$ has reached *adaptive-security*. The experimental results show that the complexity of storage and computation is much lower than the Kamara's.

References

1. Ballard, L., Kamara, S., Monrose, F.: Achieving efficient conjunctive keyword searches over encrypted data. In: Qing, S., Mao, W., López, J., Wang, G. (eds.) ICICS 2005. LNCS, vol. 3783, pp. 414–426. Springer, Heidelberg (2005). https://doi.org/10.1007/11602897_35
2. Byun, J.W., Lee, D.H., Lim, J.: Efficient conjunctive keyword search on encrypted data storage system. In: Atzeni, A.S., Lioy, A. (eds.) EuroPKI 2006. LNCS, vol. 4043, pp. 184–196. Springer, Heidelberg (2006). https://doi.org/10.1007/11774716_15
3. Cash, D., et al.: Dynamic searchable encryption in very-large databases: data structures and implementation. In: 21st Annual Network and Distributed System Security Symposium, NDSS 2014, San Diego, California, USA, 23–26 February 2014. The Internet Society (2014). https://www.ndss-symposium.org/ndss2014/dynamic-searchable-encryption-very-large-databases-data-structures-and-implementation
4. Cash, D., Jarecki, S., Jutla, C., Krawczyk, H., Roşu, M.-C., Steiner, M.: Highly-scalable searchable symmetric encryption with support for boolean queries. In: Canetti, R., Garay, J.A. (eds.) CRYPTO 2013. LNCS, vol. 8042, pp. 353–373. Springer, Heidelberg (2013). https://doi.org/10.1007/978-3-642-40041-4_20
5. Chang, Y.-C., Mitzenmacher, M.: Privacy preserving keyword searches on remote encrypted data. In: Ioannidis, J., Keromytis, A., Yung, M. (eds.) ACNS 2005. LNCS, vol. 3531, pp. 442–455. Springer, Heidelberg (2005). https://doi.org/10.1007/11496137_30
6. Chase, M., Kamara, S.: Structured encryption and controlled disclosure. In: Abe, M. (ed.) ASIACRYPT 2010. LNCS, vol. 6477, pp. 577–594. Springer, Heidelberg (2010). https://doi.org/10.1007/978-3-642-17373-8_33
7. Chaum, D., Crépeau, C., Damgård, I.: Multiparty unconditionally secure protocols (Abstract). In: Pomerance, C. (ed.) CRYPTO 1987. LNCS, vol. 293, pp. 462–462. Springer, Heidelberg (1988). https://doi.org/10.1007/3-540-48184-2_43
8. Curtmola, R., Garay, J.A., Kamara, S., Ostrovsky, R.: Searchable symmetric encryption: improved definitions and efficient constructions. In: Juels, A., Wright, R.N., di Vimercati, S.D.C. (eds.) Proceedings of the 13th ACM Conference on Computer and Communications Security, CCS 2006, Alexandria, VA, USA, 30 October–3 November 2006, pp. 79–88. ACM (2006). https://doi.org/10.1145/1180405.1180417
9. Du, L., Li, K., Liu, Q., Wu, Z., Zhang, S.: Dynamic multi-client searchable symmetric encryption with support for boolean queries. Inf. Sci. **506**, 234–257 (2020). https://doi.org/10.1016/j.ins.2019.08.014
10. Ferreira, B., Portela, B., Oliveira, T., Borges, G., Domingos, H., Leitão, J.: BISEN: efficient boolean searchable symmetric encryption with verifiability and minimal leakage. In: 38th Symposium on Reliable Distributed Systems, SRDS 2019, Lyon, France, 1–4 October 2019, pp. 103–112. IEEE (2019). https://doi.org/10.1109/SRDS47363.2019.00021

11. Fisch, B.A., et al.: Malicious-client security in blind seer: a scalable private DBMS. In: 2015 IEEE Symposium on Security and Privacy, SP 2015, San Jose, CA, USA, 17–21 May 2015, pp. 395–410. IEEE Computer Society (2015). https://doi.org/10.1109/SP.2015.31

12. Gentry, C.: Fully homomorphic encryption using ideal lattices. In: Mitzenmacher, M. (ed.) Proceedings of the 41st Annual ACM Symposium on Theory of Computing, STOC 2009, Bethesda, MD, USA, 31 May–2 June 200, pp. 169–178. ACM (2009). https://doi.org/10.1145/1536414.1536440

13. Goh, E.: Secure indexes. IACR Cryptol. ePrint Arch. **2003**, 216 (2003). http://eprint.iacr.org/2003/216

14. Goldreich, O., Micali, S., Wigderson, A.: How to play any mental game or a completeness theorem for protocols with honest majority. In: Aho, A.V. (ed.) Proceedings of the 19th Annual ACM Symposium on Theory of Computing, 1987, New York, USA, pp. 218–229. ACM (1987). https://doi.org/10.1145/28395.28420

15. Golle, P., Staddon, J., Waters, B.: Secure conjunctive keyword search over encrypted data. In: Jakobsson, M., Yung, M., Zhou, J. (eds.) ACNS 2004. LNCS, vol. 3089, pp. 31–45. Springer, Heidelberg (2004). https://doi.org/10.1007/978-3-540-24852-1_3

16. Kamara, S., Moataz, T.: Boolean searchable symmetric encryption with worst-case sub-linear complexity. In: Coron, J.-S., Nielsen, J.B. (eds.) EUROCRYPT 2017. LNCS, vol. 10212, pp. 94–124. Springer, Cham (2017). https://doi.org/10.1007/978-3-319-56617-7_4

17. Kamara, S., Papamanthou, C.: Parallel and dynamic searchable symmetric encryption. In: Sadeghi, A.-R. (ed.) FC 2013. LNCS, vol. 7859, pp. 258–274. Springer, Heidelberg (2013). https://doi.org/10.1007/978-3-642-39884-1_22

18. Kamara, S., Papamanthou, C., Roeder, T.: Dynamic searchable symmetric encryption. In: Yu, T., Danezis, G., Gligor, V.D. (eds.) the ACM Conference on Computer and Communications Security, CCS 2012, Raleigh, NC, USA, 16–18 October 2012, pp. 965–976. ACM (2012). https://doi.org/10.1145/2382196.2382298

19. Pappas, V., et al.: Blind seer: a scalable private DBMS. In: 2014 IEEE Symposium on Security and Privacy, SP 2014, Berkeley, CA, USA, 18–21 May 2014, pp. 359–374. IEEE Computer Society (2014). https://doi.org/10.1109/SP.2014.30

20. Sun, L., Xu, C., Zhang, Y.: A dynamic and non-interactive boolean searchable symmetric encryption in multi-client setting. J. Inf. Secur. Appl. **40**, 145–155 (2018). https://doi.org/10.1016/j.jisa.2018.03.002, https://doi.org/10.1016/j.jisa.2018.03.002

21. Wang, Y., et al.: Towards multi-user searchable encryption supporting boolean query and fast decryption. J. UCS **25**(3), 222–244 (2019). http://www.jucs.org/jucs_25_3/towards_multi_user_searchable

22. Xiaodong, D., Song, D., Perrig, W.A.: Practical techniques for searches on encrypted data (2002)

23. Yao, A.C.: Protocols for secure computations. In: Proceedings of IEEE Symposium on Foundations of Computer Science (1982)

24. Zeng, M., Zhang, K., Qian, H., Chen, X., Chen, J.: A searchable asymmetric encryption scheme with support for boolean queries for cloud applications. Comput. J. **62**(4), 563–578 (2019). https://doi.org/10.1093/comjnl/bxy134

Research on Database Anomaly Access Detection Based on User Profile Construction

Xuren Wang[1,4](✉), Zhou Fang[2], Dong Wang[3], Anran Feng[1](✉), and Qiuyun Wang[4]

[1] Information Engineering College, Capital Normal University, Beijing 100048, China
wangxuren@cnu.edu.cn
[2] State Grid Zhejiang Electric Power Co., Ltd., Information and Communication Branch,
Hangzhou 310013, Zhejiang, China
[3] State Grid Electronic Commerce Co., LTD. (State Grid Xiong'an Financial Technology Group
Co., LTD.), Beijing 100053, China
[4] Key Laboratory of Network Assessment Technology, Institute of Information Engineering,
Chinese Academy of Sciences, Beijing 100093, China

Abstract. As a platform for data storage and administration, database contains private and large information, which makes it a target of malicious personnel attacks. To prevent attacks from outsiders, database administrators can limit unauthorized user access through role-based access control system, while masquerade attacks from insiders are often less noticeable. Therefore, the research on database anomaly detection based on user behavior has important practical application value. In this paper, we proposed the anomaly detection system for securing database. We took advantage of a user profile construction method to describe database user query statements without user grouping. Then k-means and random tree were applied to the user profile. With the specified user profile constructed according to the characteristics of the query submitted by the user, the k-means is used to group the users. Then random tree algorithm is used to train anomaly detector. The experimental results show that this method proposed is fast and effective for detecting anomaly of database user behaviors.

Keywords: Anomaly detection · Database · User behavior · k-Means · Random tree algorithm

1 Introduction

As data occupies an increasingly important position in modern life, data security issues are becoming more prominent. The average cost of global data breaches in 2018 was $3.86 million, 6.4% higher than that in 2017 [1]. The reasons for data leakage are diverse. Verizon released the 11th data breach investigation report in 2018 by analyzing 53,000 security incidents and 2,216 data breaches in 65 countries [2]. The report shows that

This work is supported by the science and technology project of State Grid Corporation of China "Research on Key Technologies of dynamic identity security authentication and risk control in power business " (Grand No. 5700-201972227A-0-0-00).

about 28% of security breaches come from the internal of enterprise or organization. Among them, the internal leakage of medical treatment exceeded the data leakage caused by external attacks, accounting for 56% of the total leakage incident. Data leakage caused by internal personnel's interests or improper operation is generally difficult to detect, which will cause serious economic losses. The report shows that about 68% of data breaches are still undetected within a few months of the occurrence.

As a "warehouse" for storing data, the database is often the attacking focus of malicious personnel. Traditional database security protection mainly relies on the blocking mechanism of firewalls facing abnormal network communication at the network layer [3–5]. However, internal personnel have reasonable access rights, then no abnormal communication alarms will be triggered during their operation to the database, and the data leakage will not be noticed. Therefore, in the access process of the database, there must be a strict anomaly detection mechanism, which can monitor the behavior of the visitors and determine whether it matches to the normal user's behavior pattern, thereby achieving the purpose of preventing internal and external attacks. Based on this, this paper proposes a database user access behavior anomaly detection method based on k-means and random tree.

The main contributions of this paper are as follows:

1) Specified the representation of user profile, reducing the training and testing time of the model;
2) Proposed a user behavior anomaly detection method based on k-means and random tree, which can evaluate the user behavior of the database without user grouping;
3) Experimental results show that the user behavior anomaly detection method proposed in this paper can detect abnormal users quickly and effectively.

The structure of this paper is as follows: Sect. 1 mainly introduces related work; Sect. 2 introduces the algorithm used in this paper; Sect. 3 describes the system structure constructed in this paper and the specific steps of system training and testing; Sect. 4 analyzes the results of the experiment, and Sect. 5 summarizes the full text.

2 Related Work

In order to manage users accessing the database, some scholars improved the access control method of the database, so that the permission control strategy can solve more complex practical application problems [6–10]. However, this method of privilege control can only prevent malicious attacks from unauthorized external users, which didn't work for internal authorized users and masquerade attacks. Since Lee [11] introduced data mining technology into the field of intrusion detection, scholars began to use data mining technology to build an anomaly detection system for database. A lightweight database with simple query syntax or single user type generally does not have a role-based access control system. The user role cannot be used as a classification label to discriminate the abnormal behavior from the user behavior during the anomaly detector training. Therefore, lightweight database without user groups cannot directly use classifiers, in which case it is often necessary to construct classifiers using unsupervised machine learning algorithms.

Geng [12] used a density-based clustering algorithm by combining the idea of k-means clustering with a density-based clustering algorithm to overcome the limitations of k-means that need to be selected for k-values. The algorithm reduced the effect of the randomly selected initial cluster center on the final clustering effect; at the same time, the pre-sampling method reduced the computation time. In the anomaly detection phase, the newly submitted user behavior feature is compared with the priority feature mode, the central point feature of each cluster, if it is inconsistent, then it would be determined to be abnormal. When outlier detection algorithms are used, benign outliers (long-term independent points that are not in the 90% confidence interval) are often ignored or mis-judged as abnormal points, and Karami [13] treat benign outliers as a new class, then new classes are trained using the Self Organizing Map (SOM) method to improve the accuracy of detection. J. ROH [14] analyzed the user's access pattern stored in database log and detecting the anomalous access event. Bossi [15] build application profiles, instead of users', to create a succinct representation of its interaction with the database. Chen [16] constructed a community anomaly detection system for shared information systems using k-nearest neighbor (KNN) algorithm, which can detect user behavior anomalies under dynamic grouping. Markus [17] uses the method of incremental clustering on the system log to detect anomaly, and separates the intensive computational training module from the fast detection module, which can be used to detect online data. Sun [18] obtained user behavior data, including role attribute and behavior habit attribute, by the Web log and click stream to realize the timely discovery of illegal operations and illegal users and to realize real-time early warning. Ashish [19] proposed an anomaly detection model for databases without user grouping based on the structure of the enterprise database management system, in which clustering algorithms such as k-center and k-means are used to cluster users as user groups, and then anomaly detection models are constructed using naive Bayesian classification and outlier detection. Asmaa [20] uses the clustering algorithms such as k-means, expectation-maximization (EM) and simple incremental concept clustering (COBWEB) to classify users and map the clustering results to the user's query. The user-cluster mapping table is used as an anomaly detection model.

The database anomaly access detection method based on k-means and random tree proposed in this paper constructs the user profile by using the simplified user profile construction method, which reduces the training and test time. Then the k-means clustering algorithm is used to group the users. Finally, the random tree algorithm is used to train the anomaly detection model, which effectively improves the anomaly detection rate.

2.1 K-Means Algorithm

K-means clustering is a partitioning clustering algorithm and is the most widely used algorithm in clustering algorithms. From a geometric point of view, the main idea of the k-means algorithm is to divide a data set into several clusters according to the spatial distribution of data points, so that the distances of the data points in the cluster are close and the distance among clusters are far apart. The practical significance of the k-means algorithm is to group data according to the similarity of its attributes. The specific algorithm steps are as follows.

Algorithm 1 - k-means

Input: dataset of samples $D = \{x_1, x_2, ..., x_m\}$, number of clusters k, and the maximum number of iterations N

Output: Cluster set $C = \{C_1, C_2, ..., C_k\}$

1. Randomly select k samples from dataset D as the initial cluster center: $\{\mu_1, \mu_2, ..., \mu_k\}$
2. Initialize cluster set $C_t = \varnothing$, $t = 1, 2, ..., k$
3. For $n = 1, 2, ..., N$
4.   For $i = 1, 2, ..., m$
5.   Calculate the distance between the sample x_i and each cluster center:
6. μ_j $(j=1, 2, ..., k)$: $d_{ij} = \left\| x_i - \mu_j \right\|_2^2$
7.   select the smallest d_{ij} as the category λ_i corresponding to x_i
8.   update $C_{\lambda i} = C_{\lambda i} \cup \{x_i\}$
9.   For $j = 1, 2, ..., k$
10.   recalculate new cluster centers for all sample points in C_j:
11. $\mu_j = \frac{1}{|c_j|} \sum_{x \in c_j} x$
12.   If all k cluster center vectors have not changed, go to step 13
13. Output Cluster set $C = \{C_1, C_2, ..., C_k\}$

The k-means clustering algorithm has certain limitations. The selection of the cluster number k and the initial cluster centers at the beginning of the algorithm will affect the final clustering effect.

For the limitations of k-means algorithm, this paper sets k according to the actual application scenario of the database. When selecting the initial clustering center, to ensure the accuracy of the clustering results, the optimal clustering is selected according to the squared error smallest principle in multiple experiments.

2.2 Radom Tree Algorithm

Random tree is an improved algorithm of decision tree algorithm [21]. The decision tree algorithm model is a nonparametric classifier and one of the most widely used algorithms in the classification model. The construction of decision tree algorithm model generally includes three steps, attribute selection, decision tree generation and pruning. The key of decision tree algorithm is how to choose the optimal partitioning attribute as a child node in the process of spanning tree. According to different attribute selection criteria, the decision tree algorithm is divided into ID3, C4.5, CART, etc. Among them, ID3, C4.5, and CART algorithms use information gain, information gain ratio, and Gini index as the attribute selection criteria.

Training dataset D has n classes C_k, $k = 1, 2, ..., n$. Among them, feature A has m different values $\{a_1, a_2, ..., a_m\}$. According to the value of the feature A, the dataset D can be divided into m subsets $\{D_1, D_2, ..., D_m\}$. The information gain G (D, A) of feature A is defined as

$$G(D, A) = H(D) - H(D|A) \tag{1}$$

H(D) represents the entropy of the dataset D, which is used to measure the uncertainty of the value of the attribute. H(D) is defined as

$$H(D) = -\sum_{k=1}^{n} \frac{|C_k|}{|D|} \log_2 \frac{|C_k|}{|D|} \qquad (2)$$

H(D|A) represents the conditional entropy of attribute A on dataset D, which is defined as

$$H(D|A) = \sum_{i=1}^{m} \frac{|D_i|}{|D|} H(D_i) \qquad (3)$$

The decision tree algorithm is fast and accurate, but it is prone to over-fitting in the classification process. The random tree algorithm improves the attribute selection method in the decision tree construction process. Instead of the traversal of all attribute features, the k attributes are randomly selected to calculate the information gain. Compared with the decision tree, the random tree algorithm has lower computational time and is less prone to overfitting.

3   Anomaly Access Detection System Based on K-means and Random Tree

3.1   Model Frame

The model architecture is shown in Fig. 1. The system's workflow is divided into two phases, the training phase and testing phase.

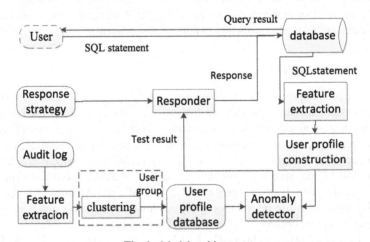

Fig. 1. Model architecture.

The steps in the training phase are as follows:

- Pre-process the historical audit log, and remove the system log to obtain the user query data;

- extract the characteristics of the query data to obtain a feature vector, that is, the behavior profile of the user;
- Use the k-means algorithm to cluster the user's profile to obtain the user's group;
- train the user's behavior profile labeled user's group using a random tree algorithm to obtain an anomaly detection model.

The testing phase steps are as follows:

- Pre-process the query submitted by the user;
- extract the characteristics of the query data to obtain a user contour vector;
- input the user behavior vector into the anomaly detection model to obtain the detection result;
- Input the detection result into the responder and send a response according to the preset response policies.

3.2 User Profile Construction

The construction method of the user behavior profile not only determines the detection efficiency of the anomaly detection module, but also affects the final detection result. Fine-grained construction methods may increase the training and testing time of the anomaly detector; while the coarse-grained construction method constructs a user profile that is not sufficient to describe the user's behavioral characteristics, resulting in poor detection results. This paper uses a user profile construction method that combines mapping and statistics to describe database user query statements without user grouping.

The vector V (C, T, A, R) is used to represent the attribute features extracted from the query log. The vector V is the user profile, where C is the command type of the statement, T is the table for the query retrieval, and is represented by $1 - N$, where N is the number of data tables included in the database. If the database contains only a small number of cross-queries, in order to reduce the storage space of the vector, the attributes in the tables retrieved by several cross-queries are re-integrated into several new tables, starting from $N + 1$. A is the attribute information retrieved by the query statement, represented by a vector. The length of the vector A is the maximum value of all the table lengths. The mapping between the attribute and the vector is: when the query contains an attribute in the table, set the bit of the attribute in the vector to 1, otherwise 0. R is the proportion of the query result, calculated by the ratio of the number of rows of the query result to the total number of rows in the retrieved table.

4 Experiment and Discussion

4.1 Evaluation Method

In order to evaluate the anomaly detection effect of the system, the following three evaluation methods are used:

Precision: the proportion of the true normal sample in the normal sample determined by the classifier, which is defined as follows:

$$P = \frac{TP}{TP + FP} \tag{4}$$

Recall: Also known as True Positive Rate, it reflects the proportion of the normal sample that is correctly determined to the total normal sample, as defined below:

$$R = \frac{TP}{TP + FN} \qquad (5)$$

F-measure: a weighted average of precision and recall rates, defined as follows:

$$F = \frac{2PR}{P + R} \qquad (6)$$

TP means the percent of correctly classified normal samples; FN is the percent of classify normal samples as abnormal samples; FP is the percent of classify abnormal samples as normal samples; TN is the percent of correctly classified abnormal samples.

4.2 Dataset

Since the background audit log of the real database is not easy to obtain, this experiment uses the TPC-C database as the experimental data set. TPC (Transaction Processing Performance Council) is a non-profit organization that evaluates the performance of hardware and software in large database systems. The specifications developed by TPC have been applied in the field of database anomaly detection [20, 22, 23]. TPC-C [24] is a specification developed by the TPC Association for online transaction processing systems (OLTP systems). The model used in the TPC-C test is a large sales company that has several warehouses of goods distributed in different regions. The trading transactions that the system needs to deal with are mainly divided into the following five types: new orders, payment, delivery, order-status, and stock-level.

In the Linux system, the script provided by TPC is used to build the TPC-C database, tables, and five kinds of transactions. Tables 1, 2 and 3 are examples of V vectors representing user profiles of database constructed according to TPC-C. Table 1 is the client table, Table 2 is the product table, Table 3 is example of Q vector [20] and V vector.

Table 1. Clients' table.

'	c_name
1	c1
2	c2
3	c3
4	c4

The Q vector contains four attributes: command type (Cm), table vector (Pr), attribute vector (Pa), and the ratio of retrieved information (Sr). Take the first Q vector ['SELECT', [1,0], [[1,0], [0,0]], ['s', null]] as an example: the command Cm of the statement is

Table 2. Products' table.

p_ID	p_price
1	1
2	2
3	5
4	8

Table 3. Vector $V(C, T, A, R)$ representation as an example.

Query	$Q(Cm, Pr, Pa, Sr)$	$V (C, T, A, R)$
SELECT * FROM Clients WHERE c_ID = 3;	['SELECT', [1,0], [[1,0], [0,0]], ['s',null]]	['SELECT', 1, [1,0], 0.25]
SELECT * FROM Products WHERE p_price < 5;	['SELECT', [0,1], [[0,0], [0,1]], [null,'m']]	['SELECT', 2, [0,1], 0.5]

SELECT; the table vector Pr is [1, 0], that is, the first table client; the attribute vector Pa is [[1, 0], [0, 0]], that is, the first attribute c_ID in the Table 1 (client) is retrieved, and product information in the Table 2 is not retrieved; the ratio Sr of the retrieved information is ['s', null], that is, information was retrieved from Table 1. If the ratio is greater than 1/3 and less than 2/3, then it will be recorded as m; and if it is greater than 2/3, it will be recorded as l, which mean that.

The V vector ['SELECT', 1, [1, 0], 0.25] indicates that the command C of the statement is SELECT; the retrieved table T is the Table 1 or the client table; the retrieved attribute A is [1, 0], that is, the first attribute c_ID in the Table 1; the proportion R of the query result is 0.25, that is, the number of records satisfying the condition c_ID = 3 occupies 25% of the entire data table.

Using the V vector to represent user queries with fewer cross-queries saves half of the storage space compared to the vector Q, which can effectively reduce the training time of the anomaly detection model.

4.3 Data Preprocessing

The TPC-C raw dataset contains a large number of system commands and other data that are not related to user transactions. Remove these data and leave relevant information for user queries. In order to fully verify the validity of the model and method, five different scale TPC-C datasets are collected as experimental datasets in Table 4. 80% of the five datasets are used as training datasets, and the remaining 20% are used as test sets. The data distribution of the datasets is shown in Table 4.

Table 4. Data distribution of five datasets of TPC-C.

(in the number of records)	Dataset1	Dataset2	Dataset3	Dataset4	Dataset5
Training data	83339	160641	242339	322657	401554
Testing data	20835	40160	60585	80664	100388
toTal	104174	200801	302924	403321	501942

4.4 Experiments and Results

After pre-processing, the user profile is clustered using the k-means algorithm, and k is set to 2 according to the scenario simulated by the TPC-C database, representing two groups in the database: customer and staff. Due to the limitations of the k-means algorithm, the initial cluster centers are changed to perform multiple experiments on the k-means algorithm. As shown in Fig. 2, different random seed numbers will result in different initial cluster centers, making a change in the final clustering result. Since the slight change in the number of random seeds does not affect the final clustering result, the magnitude of the random seed number change would be set to 50, and the change of the squared error of five data sets in clustering would be recorded, when the number of random seeds changes from 50 to 1000.

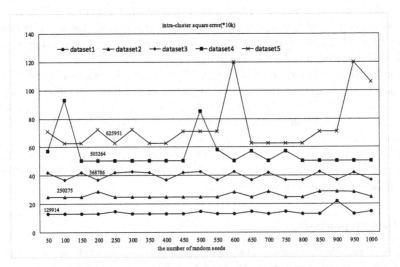

Fig. 2. Influence of initial cluster center point on clustering effect.

As an index for evaluating the result of k-means clustering, the smaller the value of the squared error in the cluster, the better the clustering effect. It can be seen from Fig. 2 that the five data sets obtain the minimum intra-cluster square error of 129914, 250275, 368786, 503264, and 625951 respectively when the number of random seeds is 50, 100, 200, 200, and 250. Therefore, the random seed numbers 50, 100, 200, 200,

250 are taken as the clustering parameters of the five data sets respectively, and the user group clustering model is constructed.

After k-means clustering, the random tree algorithm is used to train the anomaly detector, and the detection effect is compared with the common four classification algorithms. The four algorithms are: Back Propagation Neural Network (BP), C4.5 decision tree, Random Forest and Support Vector Machine (SVM). In [20], the same dataset was used to train the anomaly detection model, and the average detection results of the five experiments are compared with the model, as shown in Table 5.

Table 5. Comparison of detection results of different classification algorithms.

Classifiers	P (%)	R (%)	F (%)	Training time (ms/record)	Testing time (ms/record)
MLC [20]	94.6	99.7	97.1	11.453	890
COBWEB [20]	100	99.1	99.5	10.236	17
BP	100	100	0	2.772	0.003
C4.5	100	100	0	0.021	0.001
Random forest	100	100	0	0.25	0.005
SVM	100	100	0	0.029	0.01
Random tree	**100**	**100**	**0**	**0.007**	**0.001**

Compared with the multi-label classification (MLC) and the incremental clusterer (COBWEB), in which the user grouping is defined by the experimenters in paper [20], this paper uses k-means clustering as the label to train classifiers. All indicators have improved. The accuracy rate was increased by 0~5.4%, the recall rate was increased by 0.3%~0.9%, and the F value was increased by 0.5%~2.9%. For the training time, this paper adopts a more specified user profile construction method, which greatly reduced the training and detection time of each record. The training speed was increased by about 3.7 times to 1600 times, and the testing speed was increased by about 1700 times to 890,000 times. According to the test results in Table 5, the random tree algorithm has the best comprehensive detection effect, which has high detection rate and the highest training and testing speed.

5   Conclusions

This paper proposed a database user behavior anomaly detection method based on k-means and random tree algorithm. Firstly, a simplified user profile construction method is proposed. Then the k-means clustering algorithm is used to group the users. Finally, the random tree algorithm is used to train the anomaly detection model. In the simulation experiment, compared with the anomaly detection model using the same dataset [20], the accuracy and recall rate of the five algorithms used in this experiment are improved, and the training and testing speed is improved obviously, among which the random tree has the best comprehensive detection effect. The detection rate and the training and testing speed of random tree algorithm are all higher than other algorithms in the experiments.

References

1. IBM: Ponemon Institute: 2018 Cost of a data breach study: a global overview. https://www.ibm.com/security/data-breach. Accessed 15 Aug 2019
2. Verizon RISK Team: Data breach investigations report. https://enterprise.verizon.com/resources/reports/DBIR_2018_Report_execsummary.pdf. Accessed 25 Dec 2019
3. Na, W.: Anomaly detection and assessment of user behavior for database access. M.S. thesis, Southeast Univ., Jiangsu, China (2017)
4. Dapeng, C.: Intrusion detection system of database based on user behavior of analysis and identification. M.S. thesis, Univ. of Electronic Science and Technology, Sichuan, China (2015)
5. Xiqiang, D.: Research on database intrusion detection based on data mining. M.S. thesis, Jiangsu Univ., Jiangsu, China (2009)
6. Li, N., Tripunitara, M.V.: Security analysis in role-based access control. In: Proceedings of ACM SACMAT, New York, YK, USA, pp. 126–135 (2004)
7. Ni, Q., et al.: Privacy-aware role-based access control. In: Proceedings of ACM SACMAT, New York, YK, USA, pp. 41–50 (2007)
8. Haddad, M., et al.: Access control for data integration in presence of data dependencies. In: Proceedings of DASFAA, Switzerland, pp. 203–217 (2014)
9. Abiteboul, S., Bourhis, P., Vianu, V.: A formal study of collaborative access control in distributed datalog. In: Proceedings of 11th International Conference on Digital Telecommunications, pp. 1–17. Xpert Publishing Services, Lisbon, Portugal (2016)
10. Bossi, L., Bertino, E., Hussain, S.R.: A system for profiling and monitoring database access patterns by application programs for anomaly detection. IEEE Trans. Softw. Eng. **43**(5), 415–431 (2017)
11. Lee, W., Stolfo, S.J.: Data mining approaches for intrusion detection. In: 7th Conference on USENIX Security Symposium, San Antonio, Texas, USA, pp. 26–29. USENIX Association, Berkeley (1998)
12. Geng, J., et al.: A novel clustering algorithm for database anomaly detection. In: Proceedings on Security and Privacy in Communication Networks, Dallas, USA, pp. 682–696 (2015)
13. Karami, A.: An anomaly-based intrusion detection system in presence of benign outliers with visualization capabilities. Exp. Syst. Appl. **108**, 36–60 (2018)
14. Roh, J., Lee, S., Kim, S.: Anomaly detection of access patterns in database. In: Proceedings on Information and Communication Technology Convergence (ICTC), Jeju, South Korea, pp. 1112–1115 (2015)
15. Bossi, L., Bertino, E., Hussain, S.R.: A system for profiling and monitoring database access patterns by application programs for anomaly detection. IEEE Trans. Softw. Eng. **43**, 415–431 (2016)
16. Chen, Y., Nyemba, S., Malin, B.: Detecting anomalous insiders in collaborative information systems. IEEE Trans. Depend. Secure Comput. **9**(3), 332–344 (2012)
17. Wurzenberger, M., et al.: Incremental clustering for semi-supervised anomaly detection applied on log data. In: Proceedings of the 12th International Conference on Availability, Reliability and Security, pp. 1–6. ACM, Reggio Calabria Italy (2017)
18. Sun, X., Yang, G., Zhang, J.: A Real-time detection scheme of user behavior anomaly for management information system. In: Proceedings of IEEE 4th Information Technology, Networking, Electronic and Automation Control Conference (ITNEC), Chongqing, China, pp. 1054–1058. (2020)

19. Karami, A., Terzi, E., Bertino, E.: Detecting anomalous access patterns in relational databases. J. Very Large Data Base **17**(5), 1063–1077 (2008)
20. Sallam, A., Fadolalkarim, D., Bertino, E., et al.: Data and syntax centric anomaly detection for relational databases. J. Data Mining Knowl. Disc. **6**(6), 231–239 (2016)
21. Java Code Examples for weka.classifiers.trees.RandomTree. https://www.programcreek.com/java-api-examples/index.php?api=weka.classifiers.trees.RandomTree. Accessed 01 mar 2019
22. Ronao, C.A., Cho, SB.: Mining SQL queries to detect anomalous database access using random forest and PCA. In: Proceedings of the 28th International Conference on Current Approaches in Applied Artificial Intelligence, Seoul, South Korea, pp. 151–160 (2015)
23. Islam, S.M., Kuzu, M., Kantarcioglu, M.: A dynamic approach to detect anomalous queries on relational databases. In: Proceedings of the 5th ACM Conference on Data and Application Security and Privacy, San Antonio, Texas, USA, pp. 245–252 (2015)
24. TPC Benchmark C Standard Specification Revision 5.11. http://www.tpc.org/tpc_documents_current_versions/pdf/tpc-c_v5.11.0.pdf. 15 Sep 2018

Depth Estimation

An Effective Occlusion Edge Prediction Method in Light Field Depth Estimation

Chao Zhou[1], Qian Zhang[1]([⊠]), Bin Wang[1], Yunzhang Du[1], Tao Yan[2], and Wen Si[3,4,5]

[1] College of Information, Mechanical and Electrical Engineering, Shanghai Normal University, Shanghai 200234, China
qianzhang@shnu.edu.cn
[2] School of Information Engineering, Putian University, Putian 351100, Fujian, China
[3] College of Information and Computer Science, Shanghai Business School, Shanghai 201400, People's Republic of China
[4] Department of Rehabilitation, Huashan Hospital, Fudan University, Shanghai 200040, People's Republic of China
[5] College of Engineering, University of South Florida, Tampa, USA
http://xxjd.shnu.edu.cn/

Abstract. Occlusion is one of the most complicated and difficult problem to deal with in light field depth estimation. Previous methods usually use edge detection of central view as the basis for subsequent depth estimation. However, few algorithms take the correlation between light field sub-aperture images into consideration, which makes the incorrect depth estimation in the occlusion areas and object boundaries. In this paper, based on the refocusing theory, we explore three occlusion prediction methods and derive model to make full use of the correlation between different sub-aperture to handle the occlusions in depth estimation, the obtained occlusion map is used as a guidance for the depth estimation. Markov Random Field is built to regularize the depth map and smoothing filtering, which is used at the background area of the non-occlusion area to process noise in order to improve estimation results. Experimental results on the real light-field data sets show that the proposed algorithm can greatly improve the depth estimation results compared with state-of-the-art algorithms, especially in complex occlusion areas.

Keywords: Occlusion prediction · Depth estimation · Light field · Occlusion model

1 Introduction

Nowadays, depth estimation has become one of the important research tasks in the field of computational vision. Since the depth information reflects the

This work was jointly supported by Natural Science Foundation of China (No. 61741111), Program for New Century Excellent Talentsin Fujian Province University; in part by Natural Science Foundation of Jiangxi (No. 20161BAB212031, 20181BAB202011).

© Springer Nature Singapore Pte Ltd. 2020
G. Xu et al. (Eds.): FCS 2020, CCIS 1286, pp. 403–416, 2020.
https://doi.org/10.1007/978-981-15-9739-8_31

three-dimensional spatial information of the target, accurate depth information can provide positive effects in computer vision tasks such as target localization [6], target recognition [13], 3D reconstruction [19], semantic segmentation [16], and saliency detection [26].

Recently, many methods have been proposed for depth estimation using Light Field Image (LFI) captured by a Light field camera such as a Lytro-Illum camera. Wanner et al. [23] redefine the stereo matching problem as a constrained label problem on a polar plane image. In the total variational framework, the structural tensor is used to calculate the main direction of the pixel of the polar plane image to obtain the local depth map. Jeon et al. [9] proposed a multi-view stereo correspondence using sub-pixel precision to estimate the depth of the lenslet light field camera, and the cost and error correction method were used to refine the local depth map. Inspired by Wanner and Jeon's idea a large number of depth estimation algorithms [5,7,11,17,22,25] based on the EPI framework have emerged. Chen [12] uses the polar plane image to obtain the depth consistency curve, obtains the initial depth value by calculating the minimum value of the curve, and designs a bilateral consistency measurement method to measure the unoccluded area. Recently, Wang [21] use reliability guided disparity propagation (RGDP) to global optimize the local disparity. Zhu [24] proposed an anti-occlusion model for occlusion problems for depth estimation. Wisarut Chantara [4] use adaptive window matching on initial depth estimation. Xihao Pan [14] use the Lucas-Kanade optical flow algorithm to extract occlusion edges.

But all of these methods can not accurately estimate the depth of the complex occlusion light field. Wang [21] used the global optimization method but ignored the local occlusion situation, so the depth estimation result will be very fuzzy, and the confidence of the estimation result at the occlusion is very low. Chen [5], wang [20] only considered simple occlusion situations which occlusion size and occlusion range need to be set in advance, which is not suitable for multiple-occlusion scenes. Zhu [24] did not fully consider the correlation between sub-apertures, and there were a lot of noise and even depth reversal in the depth map. These algorithms based on their assumptions and premises, can obtain good depth estimates in scenes with low complexity and no occlusion. In this paper, we propose different algorithms to make full use of the correlation between light field sub-aperture images to predict the occlusion area. The depth estimation at the occlusion boundary is more discriminative and the accuracy of the depth estimation is improved.

The rest of this paper is organized as follows: In Sect. 2, we focus on the details of the three occlusion prediction methods proposed. In Sect. 3, we introduce optimization of occlusion maps and depth regularization to get final depth estimation. The experimental process and comparison with other algorithms are shown in Sect. 4 and the conclusions are drawn in Sect. 5.

2   Occlusion Prediction

Common depth estimation methods are based on the principle of imaging consistency [1]. Under the rough Lambertian plane, the color of the same spatial

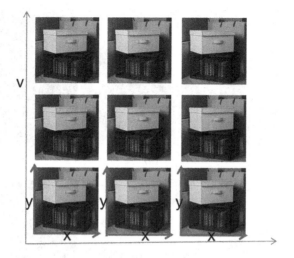

Fig. 1. Subaperture multi-view.

point observed from different directions are similar (or the same), which explains when the light field 5D data is converted into a large picture of the original light field data of $(u * x,\ v * y,\ 3)$, it has a great similarity to the magnified light field sub-aperture image.

This property can also be understood as color consistency, but this principle does not hold when there is occlusion, and algorithms based on the above principles naturally have errors. Taking the HCL [8] dataset "Boxes" as an example, Fig. 1 shows the multi-view of the sub-aperture, and the angle of view is 9*9(81 pictures). It can be concluded from Fig. 2 that the greater the distance between viewpoints, the greater the difference in viewpoint images, and the occlusion area is the place where the difference is greatest. Based on this analysis, firstly, we propose three occlusion point detection methods. Each algorithm represents a mathematical model for evaluating the correlation of sub-apertures. The model accurately describes the difference of pixels at each position in each angle, so as to accurately classify the occlusion and un-occlusion area. Secondly, we compare the three models. Finally, we select the best model as the standard algorithm for occlusion prediction.

2.1 Three Occlusion Point Detection Methods Description

Method A

$$O_{cc}(x, y) = \left(\sum_{u,v \in \Omega_a} abs\left(I_{u,v}(x, y) - I_{u_o, v_o}(x, y) \right) \times k > \theta_{occ} \right) \tag{1}$$

where $O_{cc}(x, y)$ is the final calculation of the occlusion prediction map, the value of the point (x, y) should be 0 or 1 (logical value), u, v is the angular resolution.

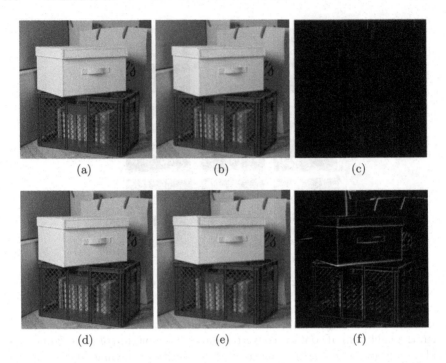

Fig. 2. Subaperture image difference map. (a), (b) are viewpoint views of two adjacent viewing angles, (c) is the difference between (a) and (b). (d) and (e) are the 1st and 81st angle views of scenes respectively, and (f) is the difference of (d) and (e).

With the "Boxes" sequence as an example, the angular resolution is 9*9, x, y is the spatial resolution, and the "Boxes" is 512*512. $I_{u,v}(x,y)$ is the grayscale value(In order to reduce the computational overhead, we convert the RGB value into a gray value) at the point (x,y) in the determined angle (u,v), $I_{u_o,v_o}(x,y)$ is the grayscale value of the central viewpoint point (x,y), $abs(\cdot)$ is an absolute value function. k is the magnification factor to increase discrimination. θ_{occ} is the threshold, greater than the threshold means that there is a large difference at this pixel. The difference and color consistency cause the two portions to be separated by the threshold.

Method B

$$O_{cc}(x,y) = \left(\sum_{(u,v)\in\Omega} \left[(I(x,y)/I(x_0,y_0) - \bar{v}_{(x,y)}) \right]^2 \times k_1 > \theta_{occ1} \right) \quad (2)$$

$$\bar{v}_{(x,y)} = \frac{\sum_{(u,v)\in\Omega_a} (I(x,y)/I(x_0,y_0))}{u \times v} \quad (3)$$

where $O_{cc}(x,y)$ is the occlusion prediction map of method B. There are only two choices: 0 or 1. u, v for angular resolution. For example, the "boxes" has an angular resolution of 9*9, x, y is the spatial resolution, and the "Boxes" is 512*512, $I(x,y)$ is the grayscale value at the point (x,y) in the sub-aperture image at the determined angle, $I(x,y)$ is the grayscale value of the central viewpoint point (x,y), $I(x,y)/I(x_0,y_0)$ is a normalization operation, divide the same position pixel value from the center view to get a value close to 1. $\bar{v}(x,y)$ is the average of each point after normalization, then find the variance at each pixel. k_1 and θ_{occl} are the same meaning as in formula (1), but the value is different.

Method C

Using the refocusing theory [18], the Initial disparity estimation formula is expressed as:

$$\overline{L}(x,y,s_i) = \frac{1}{M} \sum_{u,v} (u,v,x - s_iu,y - s_iv), \quad i = 1,2\cdots,N \tag{4}$$

where u, v is the angular resolution, x, y is the spatial resolution, S_i is the focus depth of refocusing (we get from data sets), and M is the number of light field sub-apertures. We calculate the variance of the light field at each refocusing angle and take the refocusing angle with the smallest variance as the initial depth. Equation 5 is the variance at depth s_i, Eq. 6 is the optimal depth.

$$V(x,y,s_i) = \frac{1}{M} \sum_{u,v} \left[L(u,v,x - s_iu,y - s_iv) - \overline{L}(x,y,s_i) \right]^2 \tag{5}$$

$$D(s) = \arg\min_{s_i} \{V(x,y,s_i)\}, \quad i = 1,2,\cdots,N \tag{6}$$

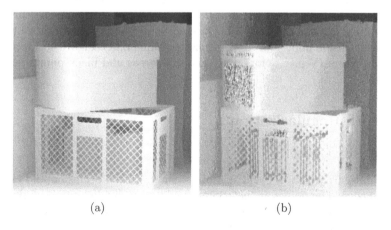

(a)   (b)

Fig. 3. (a) Gt depth, (b) initial depth estimation

Figure 3(a) is the real disparity map, Fig. 3(b) is the initial disparity estimation, in Fig. 3(b), we can see that there is a lot of noise in the disparity map, and the other areas except the book box are basically consistent with the real picture, but the disparity estimation at the linear occlusion texture on the frame surface is very unsatisfactory and does not reflect the true linear frame(shown in the red rectangles of Fig. 3(a) and Fig. 3(b)). It can be concluded from Fig. 3 that depth estimation based on refocusing works poorly at occlusion but can be used as a clue for occlusion prediction.

$$O_{cc} = (HX > \theta_{occ}) \tag{7}$$

X is the initial disparity matrix, and HX represents an judging criteria as shown in Algorithm 1.

Algorithm 1. $O_{cc} = (HX > \theta_{occ})$

Input: Initial disparity map X, Threshold θ_{occ}
Output: Occlusion map
 1: A window with a size of 3*3 centered on each point (i, j) of the disparity map X;
 2: Calculate window variance;
 3: Compare the variance with the threshold and assign the result to $O_{cc}(i, j)$;

2.2 Edge Detection Algorithm

Traditional edge detection methods such as Candy edge detection. Readers are referred to [28] for more details of Candy edge detection.

Figure 4 shows the results of each method. In the Fig. 4(b), 4(c), 4(c) show the comparison of the fluctuation of the sub-aperture image and the threshold, and a white dot means there is a big difference at that point (which we think it may be a occlusion point and black for unocclusion point). Figure 4(e) is result of candy algorithm (White points represent edge areas and black points represent flat areas).

3 Depth Regularization

3.1 Density Clustering

The optimized prediction result is more sensitive to the occlusion and the non-occluded edge. The points at the occlusion edges are divided into occluded areas and non-occluded areas by density clustering. A window with size of 3*3 at the center of each point is used to optimize the result, and the RGB value of each sub-aperture image is used as a classification basis, and the center point is used as a classification reference, finally occlusion and non-occluded parts are generated.

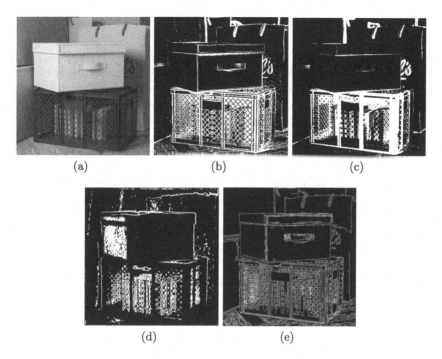

(a)   (b)   (c)

(d)   (e)

Fig. 4. Comparison of different occlusion prediction results. (a) Central view, (b) Method A: Difference from central view, (c) Method B: variance after normalization, (d) Method C: Continuity of initial disparity map values, (e) Candy edge detection.

3.2 Final Depth Regularization

In this section, inspired by Williem [15], we use Markov Random Field (MRF) to regularize the depth.

$$E = \sum_m E_{uocc}(m, s(m)) + \lambda_s \sum_{m,n} E_{smooth}(m, n, s(m), s(n)) \tag{8}$$

$$E = \sum_m E_{uocc}(m, s(m)) + \lambda_s \sum_{m,n} E_{smooth}(m, n, s(m), s(n)) \tag{9}$$

Where, $s(m)$ represents the depth value of the pixel point m. m, n are adjacent pixels, λ, is the factor that controls the smoothing term, which is set as 0.32 in the experiment. Data item E_{uocc} is a measure of the imaging consistency of the non-occluded view.

$$E_{uocc}(m, s(m)) = 1 - e^{-\frac{V(x,y,s(m))^2}{2\sigma_{uocc}^2}} \tag{10}$$

σ_{uocc} (Set as 3.1) controls the effect on sensitivity of the function caused by large disparity. The definition of $V(x, y, s(m))$ can be found in formula (5). Smoothing item E_{smooth} smoothes constraints on adjacent pixels.

$$E_{smooth}(m, n, s(m), s(n)) = \omega_{mn}|s(m) - s(n)| \tag{11}$$

$$\omega_{m,n} = e^{-\frac{(O_{cc}(m)-O_{cc}(n))^2}{2\eta_{occ}^2} - \frac{(I(m)-I(n))^2}{2\eta_c^2}} \tag{12}$$

I is the central viewpoint image of the light field sub-aperture, $O_{cc}(p)$ is the value of the occlusion point p after clustering (value is 0 or 1), η_{occ}, η_c is two weighting factors (1.6 and 0.08), using $\omega_{m,n}$ to sharpen the occlusion boundary and maintain the similarity of depth in the same property region. The final depth map is obtained by minimizing the formula (13).

$$s^* = \arg\min_s E \tag{13}$$

By using the GCO package to perform operations [2,3,10]. The complete experimental procedure is expressed as follows: firstly, the initial occlusion prediction result is obtain by using the proposed occlusion prediction method, which is proposed in Sect. 2, then optimize and using density clustering to re-divide the occlusion points, the initial depth map is obtained by the refocusing theory. Finally, the occlusion map, the sub-aperture center view and the initial depth are regularized by the Markov energy function to obtain the final depth estimation.

4   Experimental Results

In this section, the "Boxes" scenes is used as a benchmark to evaluate the proposed method, and get the most accurate depth estimation results.

4.1   Occlusion Prediction Benchmark Algorithm

Final depth maps of the four prediction algorithms are shown in Fig. 5(b), 5(c), 5(d), 5(e), where Fig. 5b, 5(c), 5(d) are our proposed occlusion prediction methods, and 5(e) is the traditional candy edge detection algorithm. Figure 5(f), 5(g), 5(h), 5(i) are the inner part of red rectangle. Figure 5(j), 5(k), 5(l), 5(m) are the inner part of blue rectangle. From Fig. 6(c), 6(h), 6(j), it can be seen that the method B has the best depth estimation effect both in the overall and in the details. So the method B (variance after normalization)is selected as the final occlusion prediction method.

4.2   Comparative Experiment

In order to show the superiority of our algorithm for occlusion, we will compare with some other algorithms, including spo [27], Wang [21], Ting-Chun Wang [27].

4.3   Experiment Apparatus

All experimental code run on Matlab 2018a (inter i5 2.6 GHz) and the experimental parameters were consistent or use the default parameters in the open source code.

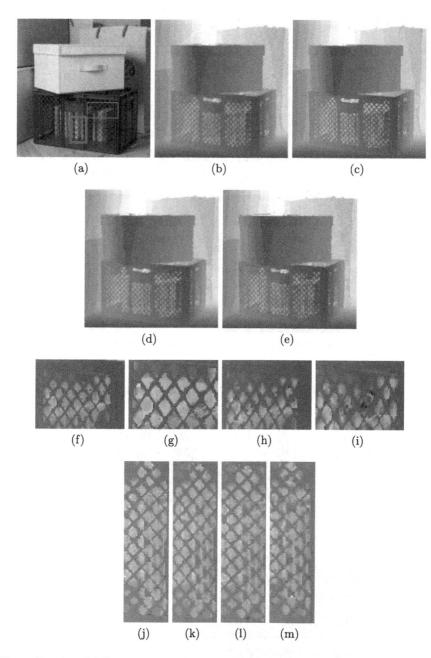

Fig. 5. Results of different occlusion prediction depth estimation. (a) is a central perspective picture, (b) is the result of Method A (Difference from central view), (c) is Method B (variance after normalization), (d) is Method C (Continuity of initial disparity map values), (e) is Method D (Candy Edge Detection), (f~m) are the results of each depth estimation algorithm in details.

(a) Cotton   (b) Occlusion   (c) Initial depth

(d) Optimization   (e) Final depth

(f) Rosemary   (g) Occlusion   (h) Initial depth

(i) Optimization   (j) Final depth

Fig. 6. The result of our algorithm on different sequence.

4.4   Performance on the Data Set

The various algorithms run on the HCL [8,24] data set, which is a 9*9 sub-aperture image array published by HCL Labs. Using real depth maps to evaluate depth estimation algorithms. In Fig. 6, two light field scenes in HCL data set are used to show the whole depth estimation process.

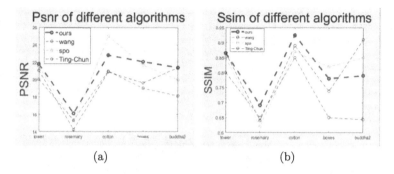

(a)   (b)

Fig. 7. Objective quality of different algorithms. (a) and (b) are the PSNR and SSIM of different algorithms respectively. The red line is our proposed algorithm, black represents wang, green is spo algorithm, blue is Tingchun algorithm. (Color figure online)

Table 1. RMSE of different algorithms

Scene	Ting-Chun	spo	wang	ours
Boxes	0.24	0.21	0.26	0.20
Cotton	0.23	0.14	0.229	0.204
Buddha2	0.3	0.25	0.144	0.14
Tower	0.214	0.21	0.22	0.207
Rosemary	0.44	0.45	0.49	0.39

We use PSNR ,SSIM and RMSE as evaluation criteria, Fig. 7 and Table 1 show the comparison of these results.Depth estimation results of different algorithms on the data set which tested on "Boxes", "Herbs", "buddha2" are shown in Fig. 8. It can be concluded that each algorithm in different scenes has the same trend. Our algorithm achieves leading results on most scenes, but our performance on "Cotton" is inferior to the spo algorithm. In this cotton scene, there are not too many occlusion areas, so our occlusion prediction algorithm does not perform very well.

Fig. 8. Experiment on HCL data set.

5 Conclusion

In this paper, we propose a light field depth estimation algorithm based on occlusion prediction, which can achieve an accurate estimation on the occlusion light field, and achieves the state-of-art results. But there are also some challenging problems such as highlights and reflection of mirror. These require our further research and optimization. Furthermore, since the using of a classification algorithm at each occlusion prediction point increased time consumption for depth estimation. So future work shall be devoted to optimize the algorithm and improve algorithm efficiency.

References

1. Bowen, A.: Photo-consistency and multiresolution methods for light field disparity estimation. In: IEE International Conference on Visual Information Engineering (2008)
2. Boykov, Y., Kolmogorov, V.: An experimental comparison of min-cut/max-flow algorithms for energy minimization in vision. IEEE Trans. Pattern Analysis Mach. Intell. **26**(9), 1124–1137 (2004)
3. Boykov, Y., Veksler, O., Zabih, R.: Fast approximate energy minimization via graph cuts. IEEE Trans. Pattern Anal. Mach. Intell. **23**(11), 1222–1239 (2001)
4. Chantara, W., Ho, Y.S.: Initial depth estimation using adaptive window size with light field image. In: 2018 International Workshop on Advanced Image Technology (IWAIT), pp. 1–3. IEEE (2018)
5. Chen, C., Lin, H., Yu, Z., Bing Kang, S., Yu, J.: Light field stereo matching using bilateral statistics of surface cameras. In: Proceedings of the IEEE Conference on Computer Vision and Pattern Recognition, pp. 1518–1525 (2014)
6. Fujimura, K., Zhu, Y.: Target orientation estimation using depth sensing (Nov 17 2009), uS Patent 7,620,202
7. Heber, S., Ranftl, R., Pock, T.: Variational shape from light field. In: International Workshop on Energy Minimization Methods in Computer Vision & Pattern Recognition (2013)
8. Honauer, K., Johannsen, O., Kondermann, D., Goldluecke, B.: A dataset and evaluation methodology for depth estimation on 4D light fields. In: Lai, S.-H., Lepetit, V., Nishino, K., Sato, Y. (eds.) ACCV 2016. LNCS, vol. 10113, pp. 19–34. Springer, Cham (2017). https://doi.org/10.1007/978-3-319-54187-7_2
9. Jeon, H.G., Park, J., Choe, G., Park, J., Bok, Y., Tai, Y.W., Kweon, I.S.: Accurate depth map estimation from a lenslet light field camera. In: Computer Vision & Pattern Recognition (2015)
10. Kolmogorov, V., Zabin, R.: What energy functions can be minimized via graph cuts? IEEE Trans. Pattern Anal. Mach. Intell. **26**(2), 147–159 (2004)
11. Li, J., Lu, M., Li, Z.N.: Continuous depth map reconstruction from light fields. IEEE Trans. Image Process. **24**(11), 3257–3265 (2015)
12. Lin, H., Chen, C., Kang, S.B., Yu, J.: Depth recovery from light field using focal stack symmetry. In: IEEE International Conference on Computer Vision (2015)
13. Maeno, K., Nagahara, H., Shimada, A., Taniguchi, R.I.: Light field distortion feature for transparent object recognition, pp. 2786–2793 (2013). https://doi.org/10.1109/CVPR.2013.359

14. Pan, X., Zhang, T., Wang, H.: A method for handling multi-occlusion in depth estimation of light field. In: 2019 IEEE International Conference on Image Processing (ICIP) (2019)

15. Park, I.K., Lee, K.M., et al.: Robust light field depth estimation using occlusion-noise aware data costs. IEEE Trans. Pattern Anal. Mach. Intell. 40(10), 2484–2497 (2017)

16. Qi, X., Liao, R., Jia, J., Fidler, S., Urtasun, R.: 3D graph neural networks for RGBD semantic segmentation. In: 2017 IEEE International Conference on Computer Vision (ICCV) (2017)

17. Tao, M.W., Hadap, S., Malik, J., Ramamoorthi, R.: Depth from combining defocus and correspondence using light-field cameras. In: Proceedings of the 2013 IEEE International Conference on Computer Vision (2013)

18. Tao, M.W., Hadap, S., Malik, J., Ramamoorthi, R.: Depth from combining defocus and correspondence using light-field cameras. In: Proceedings of the IEEE International Conference on Computer Vision, pp. 673–680 (2013)

19. Tian, L., Waller, L.: 3D intensity and phase imaging from light field measurements in an led array microscope. Optica 2(2), 104 (2015)

20. Wang, T.C., Efros, A.A., Ramamoorthi, R.: Occlusion-aware depth estimation using light-field cameras. In: IEEE International Conference on Computer Vision (2016)

21. Wang, Y., Yang, J., Mo, Y., Xiao, C., An, W.: Disparity estimation for camera arrays using reliability guided disparity propagation. IEEE Access 6, 21840–21849 (2018)

22. Wanner, S., Goldluecke, B.: Globally consistent depth labeling of 4D light fields. In: 2012 IEEE Conference on Computer Vision and Pattern Recognition, pp. 41–48. IEEE (2012)

23. Wanner, S., Goldluecke, B.: Variational light field analysis for disparity estimation and super-resolution. IEEE Trans. Pattern Anal. Mach. Intell. 36(3), 1 (2013)

24. Wanner, S., Meister, S., Goldluecke, B.: Datasets and benchmarks for densely sampled 4D light fields. In: VMV, vol. 13, pp. 225–226. Citeseer (2013)

25. Yu, Z., Guo, X., Lin, H., Lumsdaine, A., Yu, J.: Line assisted light field triangulation and stereo matching. In: Proceedings of the IEEE International Conference on Computer Vision, pp. 2792–2799 (2013)

26. Zhang, J., Wang, M., Gao, J., Wang, Y., Wu, X.: Saliency detection with a deeper investigation of light field. In: International Conference on Artificial Intelligence (2015)

27. Zhang, S., Sheng, H., Li, C., Zhang, J., Xiong, Z.: Robust depth estimation for light field via spinning parallelogram operator. Comput. Vis. Image Understand. 145(145), 148–159 (2016)

28. Zhu, H., Wang, Q., Yu, J.: Occlusion-model guided antiocclusion depth estimation in light field. IEEE J. Sel. Topics Sig. Process. 11(7), 965–978 (2017)

Mobile Security

DexFus: An Android Obfuscation Technique Based on Dalvik Bytecode Translation

Naitian Hu, Xingkong Ma, Fuqiang Lin, Bo Liu$^{(\boxtimes)}$, and Tong Lu

National University of Defense Technology, Changsha, Hunan Province, China
kyle.liu@nudt.edu.cn

Abstract. Cracking and repackaging is a severe threat to Android applications. Obfuscation increases the difficulty of reverse analysis without changing the semantics of the original code. However, current Android obfuscation techniques primarily concentrate on Dalvik bytecode obfuscation, as Dalvik bytecode contains much semantic information, obfuscation does not hinder the attacker much. We propose a new technique named DexFus for protecting Android code based on Dalvik bytecode translation. DexFus applies obfuscation on translated C code instead of the original Dalvik code, which provides a higher level protection for applications. A prototype deployment on the Android platform demonstrates that DexFus is able to protect target applications with reasonable storage and memory overhead and high stability.

Keywords: Android obfuscation · Repackage · Code translation · Encryption

1 Introduction

Android has become the most popular mobile OS in recent years [1]. The number of available apps in the Google Play Store was most recently placed at 2.87 million apps [3]. In 2019, 84.3 billion downloads were made through Google Play [4]. Accordingly, the security problem of Android applications is becoming more and more dangerous. Android app codes are able to be easily disassembled back into the Java language via existing tools such as JEB [25], JADX [26], Androguard [17], which may result in cracking and repackaging.

As a mainstream security technology, obfuscation increases the difficulty of code analysis without changing the original code's semantics. Existing Android obfuscation tools mainly focus on Dalvik bytecode obfuscation, including encrypting the original DEX file and migrating x86 Arch obfuscation techniques. However, they are inadequate to achieve high security. On the one hand, the decrypted DEX file will be loaded into memory at runtime and thus

This paper is supported by the National Natural Science Foundation of China under grant No. 61572513.

© Springer Nature Singapore Pte Ltd. 2020
G. Xu et al. (Eds.): FCS 2020, CCIS 1286, pp. 419–431, 2020.
https://doi.org/10.1007/978-981-15-9739-8_32

can be obtained by attackers via memory dumping attack. On the other hand, the Dalvik bytecode contains too much analytical data, which makes it much easier to analyze than the assembly code.

To this end, we present a new obfuscation tool based on Dalvik bytecode translation to native C code. As native code carries less semantical information, it is harder to analyze than Dalvik bytecode, especially after obfuscation. Also, as the protected methods are marked as native functions in Dalvik bytecode, attackers cannot get useful information via memory dumping attack.

We make the following contributions:

- We propose a new technique, named DexFus, which works on APK files so that developers can apply the tool without modifying the code of their application.
- We implement the prototype, including plain-text encryption, loading and linking native methods, reducing JNI calls, and oLLVM compilation.
- We test it on 400 real-world Android applications. Our experimental results show that DexFus effectively protects the target code with modest storage overhead and high stability.

2   Related Work

The most common techniques applied by existing Android obfuscation systems include the following.

Proguard. ProGuard is the most popular optimizer for Java bytecode and is integrated into Android Studio [5]. It provides minimal protection against reverse engineering by obfuscating the names of classes, fields, and methods. Proguard also reduces the compiled APK file size and makes applications faster. Since Proguard does not modify the control flow, the obfuscated code may be easily recovered by existing tools [2,6]. However, Proguard acts at compiling time so that it can be applied together with DexFus, making the protected application harder to analyze.

Android Shelling. Currently, mature commercial Android packers mainly work at the DEX obfuscation level, such as 360 [21], Tencent [22], iJiami [20]. These tools replace the origin Dex file with a stub Dex file, they encrypt the origin Dex file and hide the encrypted Dex file to assets directory. The stub dex file will decrypt and load the encrypted Dex file when execution. Shelling prevents protected applications from being analyzed by static reverse tools such as JEB [25], JADX [26], and IDA Pro [27]. However, the decrypted Dex file will appear in memory or flash once the corresponding encrypted Dex file is loaded. Thus it is possible to obtain the DEX file by hooking DEX loading functions or memory dumping [7–9,23,24].

Compile-Time Code Virtualization. Automatic tools to transfer code virtualization from DEX level to native level at compile time were proposed [19]. The project contains two components, the pre-compilation component for improving the performance, and the compile-time virtualization component that automatically translates Dalvik bytecode to LLVMIR. After that, it applies a unified code virtualization pass for the translated code. This work translates Dalvik bytecode into VM instructions instead of raw native code and split the method into small ones, which sacrifices few efficiencies. Moreover, it does not consider plain-text string encryption, which may leak valuable information to attackers.

Migrate x86 Obfuscation Techniques. Migrate traditional obfuscation techniques like control flow flattening, instructions substitution, and junk instruction insertion to Dalvik byte code. Wang *et al.* [13] use switch statement to flatten the control flow. Balachandran *et al.* [14] propose packed-switch and try-catch obfuscation to make the Control Flow Graph (CFG) more complicated. Their work increases the cost of reverse engineering. However, Dalvik bytecode, which can be disassembled back into .smali file, is easier to read than assembly language. Attackers may not spend too much time to understand the obfuscated Dalvik bytecode.

To overcome the weaknesses of traditional obfuscation techniques mentioned above, we propose a new technique named DexFus. DexFus works on APK files directly, and thus it can be applied together with compile-time obfuscation techniques such as field name renaming. DexFus translates Dalvik bytecode to native code and obfuscates it, which means the original method body in Dalvik bytecode is stripped. Hence the attackers will never get valuable information via memory dump tools like DexExtractor. Moreover, native code carries less semantic information such as symbols than Dalvik bytecode, which means it is harder to analyze.

3   DexFus

3.1   Overview

Our proposed system translates essential methods in the origin Dalvik bytecode to C code and obfuscates it to perform an expressive obfuscation. The structure of DexFus is illustrated in Fig. 1, and the key components are described as follows.

Step 1. Dalvik bytecode translation. We use Apktool [10] to decompile Dex files in Android applications. For each method in decompiled Dalvik bytecode, if it is essential and needs to be protected, we perform the Dalvik bytecode to C code translator (DCC) [11] on the method. DexFus will mark the translated methods as native methods, and register these methods to JNI methods dynamically.

Step 2. DexFus obfuscation. To hide JNI call strings and UTF8 strings in the methods, DexFus encrypts and replaces these strings with function calls that decrypt strings when execution. DexFus replaces Hot DVM methods with C methods if it can be translated, to reduce JNI call consumption. The C methods can be compiled with compilation suites applied sophisticated obfuscation techniques, such as oLLVM.

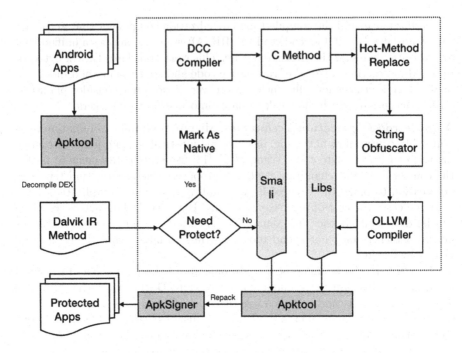

Fig. 1. Overview of DexFus

Step 3. Compile and repackage. DexFus aims to obfuscate the compiled APK files of Android apps without the needs of developers modifying their source code. Thus it will insert the code of loading compiled native libraries automatically. In this step, we use apktool to repack the modified Dex files and compiled native libraries together to an obfuscated APK file.

Figure 2 shows the structures of the APK files before and after applying Dex-Fus. To achieve better obfuscation, we firstly proposed plain-text string encryption, which effectively protects this essential information from being located by attackers statically. We then implemented a dynamical method linking to strip the significant function names. We considered reducing JNI call consumption by replacing them with native function calls. Finally, we applied the oLLVM compilation to provide essential functions more protection.

3.2 Plain-Text String Encryption

After translating from Dalvik bytecode to C via DCC, the code still contains plain-text strings such as JNI methods signatures and UTF8 Java strings. Plain-text strings are useful information for the attackers to locate the essential function while reversing applications. Encrypting and protecting the strings can effectively increase the difficulty for the attacker to statically crack and analyze. Dex-Fus mainly protects two types of strings, including strings for JNI function calls and plain-text strings of Java type String.

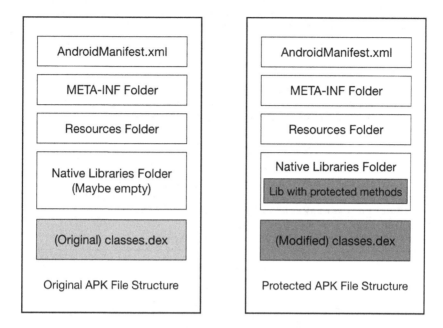

Fig. 2. APK Structures before and after applying DexFus

After encryption, the original plain text string will not appear in the dynamic link library and will be replaced by a function call in the form of GetResource (StringId). DexFus indexes the strings and decrypts the references through independent functions. Figure 3 shows the difference between the DCC translated C code and the DexFus encrypted C code.

In this example, the Java code decrypts some assets file with a plain-text key. The key and the significant method name are also exposed in the Dalvik code, and the original DCC translated C code. DexFus encrypts the plain-text strings, which makes it more challenging to do reverse engineering.

3.3   Loading and Linking Native Methods

DexFus marks obfuscated methods as native methods in Dalvik bytecode. The compiled dynamic library, which contains the native functions, is loaded with the System.loadLibrary method [12]. According to the Java JNI doc, we can call this method in the static block of the class that contains the native functions. In Dalvik bytecode, these static blocks translate into a special method called ⟨clinit⟩, which stands for "class init". DexFus locates the ⟨clinit⟩ methods of all modified classes automatically and inserts the Dalvik bytecode block of loading the library. If the original class does not contain a ⟨clinit⟩ method, DexFus will generate one that carries the code of loading the library.

```
1  DecryptAssetsWithKey("PlainTextKey");
```

(a) Java Code

```
1  const-string v0, 'PlainTextKey'
2  invoke-direct v1, v0, Ldexfus/test/MainActivity;->
      DecryptAssetsWithKey(Ljava/lang/String;)V
```

(b) Dalvik Code

```
1  v1 = (jstring) env->NewStringUTF("PlainTextKey");
2  D2C_RESOLVE_METHOD(clz, mid, "dexfus/test/MainActivity", "
      DecryptAssetsWithKey", "(Ljava/lang/String;)V");
3  jvalue args[] = {{.l = v1}};
4  env->CallVoidMethodA(v0, mid, args);
```

(c) DCC Translation

```
1  v1 = (jstring) env->NewStringUTF(getResource(0));
2  D2C_RESOLVE_METHOD(clz, mid, getResource(1), getResource
      (2), getResource(3));
3  jvalue args[] = {{.l = v1}};
4  env->CallVoidMethodA(v0, mid, args);
```

(d) DexFus Encryption

Fig. 3. Difference between the DCC translated C code and the DexFus encrypted C code

To call the methods correctly, DCC practices JNI static registration that establishes a one-to-one correspondence between the Java method and the JNI function according to the function name. However, the JNI method must follow the rules [12]. Its name is very long and contains a fully-qualified class and method name, which can help reverse engineers locate the method in disassembler tools fast. DexFus uses the RegisterNatives method to register JNI functions, and the name can be random and meaningless. Moreover, the class and method name string, which passed to the RegisterNatives method, can be encrypted through the same method described in subsection B.

3.4 Reduce JNI Calls

Translated native code methods will call Java functions via JNI calls, which consumes CPU cycles and may impact the application performance [29, p.102]. To lessen JNI consumption, we considered reducing JNI function calls.

We have analyzed hundreds of Android Apps from ApkPure Leaderboard to collect the most frequently called Java functions. For each function, if its parameters and return values and the function process do not involve non-JNI basic type variables. Then the function implementation can be completely converted into C code (such as most functions in the java.lang.Math class). Furthermore, the call to this function can be directly converted to a C function call without passing through JNI, which can save a considerable portion of JNI function call time. Calls to translated C functions also replace calls to JNI, reducing JNI call consumption.

3.5 oLLVM Compilation

The existing mature obfuscation compiler oLLVM [28] can compile functions that need to be specially protected. It works on the LLVM Intermediate Representation (IR) code and provides code transformation to increase software resistance. oLLVM mainly offers three obfuscating methods, including Bogus Control Flow, Instruction Substitution, and Control Flow Flattening. The first two techniques are semantic obfuscations that work at the instruction level, while the last one reconstructs the entire control flow. oLLVM is used to make the compiled dynamic link library binary files more difficult to analyze.

4 Experiments and Evaluation

In this section, we first describe the environment of the experiment, then evaluate DexFus in terms of resilience, size overhead, and stability.

4.1 Environment Setup

We performed our evaluation on Huawei Mate 30 running Android 10, Linux Kernel 4.14.116 version. We compiled the protected code with NDK version 20.1.5948944 and oLLVM version 8.0 [16]. The backend tools we used are Apktool version 2.4.1 [10] and Androguard version 3.3.5 [17]. The following tested apps are different kinds of real-world apps downloaded from ApkPure [18].

4.2 Resilience

After obfuscation, the protected methods are marked as native functions in Dalvik bytecode. Therefore, attackers cannot get the body of the methods via Java/Dalvik disassemblers such as JEB, JADX. As Fig. 4 and Fig. 5 shows, the body of the method is stripped and stored in native libs.

To compare with the Android shelling techniques mentioned above, we tested DexFus and different shelling tools with unpackers based on memory dumping. These tools, including DexHunter [23], FDex2 [31], Youpk [30], FART [32], are widely used by attackers to dump original Dex files at runtime. Table 1 shows the result of the test. As DexFus translated the Dalvik bytecode and obfuscated

```
1   protected void onCreate(Bundle bundle) {
2       super.onCreate(bundle);
3       setContentView((int) R.layout.activity_main);
4       this.textView = (TextView) findViewById(R.id.textView)
        ;
5       this.button = (Button) findViewById(R.id.button);
6       this.button.setOnClickListener(new OnClickListener() {
7           public void onClick(View view) {
8               MainActivity.this.buttonCall();
9           }
10      });
11  }
```

Fig. 4. Java code decompiled from the original code using JADX.

```
1   protected native void onCreate(Bundle bundle);
2
3   static {
4       try {
5           System.loadLibrary("dexfus");
6       } catch (UnsatisfiedLinkError e) {
7           e.printStackTrace();
8       }
9   }
```

Fig. 5. Java code decompiled from the protected code using JADX.

the C code, the body of the methods stay empty at runtime. Thus attackers cannot retrieve the method body via memory dumping tools.

Table 1. Test result with memory dumping tools

Tools	Shelling on dex	Shelling on methods	DexFus
DexHunter	✓	✓	✗
FDex2	✓	✗	✗
Youpk	✓	✗	✗
FART	✓	✓	✗

With the help of native binary disassemblers like IDA Pro or radare2, attackers may find the implementation of the protected methods ideally. However, the name of the methods are stripped, and the plain-text strings are encrypted. Moreover, as Fig. 6 shows, the control flow graph of one logically simple method becomes much more complicated after translated and obfuscated, which means attackers will take immense time to locate the method and get the raw logic.

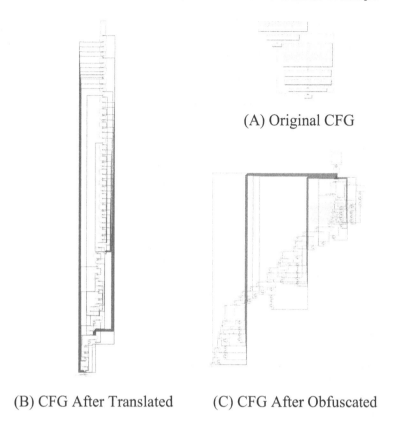

(A) Original CFG

(B) CFG After Translated   (C) CFG After Obfuscated

Fig. 6. CFG before and after applying DexFus

4.3 Size and Memory Overhead

We choose eight different apps from ApkPure "The most popular" ranking page. They are representative of real-world apps from varied kinds. For each app, we apply obfuscation on 10% of methods, closer to the real needs of protecting important methods than obfuscating all methods. We then scaled the size of the original app and the obfuscated app. We installed the original and the obfuscated app separately, after they are completely launched, we measured the memory cost of them with the dumpsys command.

Table 2 shows the result of the size measurement, and Table 3 reveals the memory measurement. On average, the size overhead of DexFus obfuscation is about 531 bytes per method, and the growth rate of memory cost is around 5%, which are both sustainable.

Table 2. Size overhead on test apps

App name	10% methods	Original bytes	Obfuscated bytes	Average bytes per method
Canva	7080	29888392	33538332	515
Whatsapp	3160	28082147	31462384	1069
Google Earth	1801	10383000	11292390	504
MX Player	7738	32365222	34361380	257
Google Meet	3177	12212964	13599507	436
Gmail	7231	27151389	30216130	423
Opera Mini	6168	12470953	15881646	552
FaceApp	5284	20272565	22868300	491
Average	5204	21603329	24152508	531

Table 3. Memory overhead on test apps

App name	Original memory cost (KiB)	Obfuscated memory cost (KiB)	Memory cost growth rate (%)
Canva	101725	111613	9.72
Whatsapp	68434	72262	5.60
Google Earth	105297	109869	4.34
MX Player	63234	64658	2.25
Google Meet	42729	45053	5.44
Gmail	82253	86838	5.58
Opera Mini	89450	92166	3.04
FaceApp	59790	62023	3.74
Average	76614	80560	4.96

4.4   Stability

We tested the stability of DexFus on 400 different real-world apps downloaded from the ApkPure ranking page. We executed testings as follows.

Step 1: Apply DexFus on original APK files, and make sure the onCreate methods of each Activity are protected.

Step 2: Install all protected APK files from Step 1, test each app with monkey [15] to observe whether it crashes or responds correctly.

Step 3: Check the APK files of apps that failed at Step 2, repackage them by Apktool without any modification. Next, install and test them with monkey the same as Step 2.

Step 4: Check the APK files of apps that failed at Step 1, try to repackage them by Apktool without any modification.

Table 4. Stability test result of Dexfus

	Count	Percentage
Total Test Apps	400	1
Succeeded at Step 1	367	0.9175
Failed at Step 1	33	0.0825
Failed at Step 2	35	0.0875
Failed at Step 3	32	0.08
Failed at Step 4	6	0.015
Succeeded in Step 1&2	332	0.83

Table 4 shows the result of the stability test. Dexfus successfully repackaged 367 apps in Step 1. Among them, 332 apps can be installed and worked well, which means Dexfus successfully protected about 83% of apps. For the 35 apps that failed at Step 2, we repackaged them without any modification to check whether Dexfus or Apktool causes it. Thirty-two of them also failed in Step 3, which means that they may have mechanisms like APK signature checking to shield them from repackaging. Among the 33 apps that failed at Step 1, 6 of them cannot be repackaged by Apktool. According to the log files, the rest 27 of them failed because the backend analyzer DexFus used, Androguard, cannot recognize several field types of the methods to be protected.

5   Conclusions

Android applications are facing severe threats like cracking and repackaging. In this paper, we propose a new technique named DexFus for protecting Android code based on Dalvik bytecode to native code translation. DexFus applies obfuscation on translated C code, which provides a higher level protection than obfuscating the original Dalvik bytecode. This paper introduces the architecture and basics of DexFus. Moreover, we implemented and evaluated DexFus in real-world applications. The experimental results show that DexFus can protect target applications at good stealthiness with reasonable storage and memory overhead and high stability.

References

1. Mobile operating system market share worldwide. https://gs.statcounter.com/os-market-share/mobile/worldwide. Accessed 15 Mar 2020
2. Cimato, S., De Santis, A., Petrillo, U.F.: Overcoming the obfuscation of Java programs by identifier renaming. J. Syst. Softw. **78**(1), 60–72 (2005)
3. Number of available applications in the Google Play Store. https://www.statista.com/statistics/266210/number-of-available-applications-in-the-google-play-store/. Accessed 15 Mar 2020

4. The top mobile apps, games, and publishers of 2019. https://sensortower.com/blog/top-apps-games-publishers-2019. Accessed 15 Mar 2020

5. Shrink, obfuscate, and optimize your app. https://developer.android.com/studio/build/shrink-code. Accessed 15 Mar 2020

6. Baumann, R., Protsenko, M., Müller, T.: Anti-proguard: towards automated deobfuscation of Android apps. In: Proceedings of the 4th Workshop on Security in Highly Connected IT Systems, pp. 7–12 (2017)

7. Dextra. http://newandroidbook.com/tools/dextra.html. Accessed 15 Mar 2020

8. Yang, W., et al.: AppSpear: bytecode decrypting and DEX reassembling for packed Android malware. In: Bos, H., Monrose, F., Blanc, G. (eds.) RAID 2015. LNCS, vol. 9404, pp. 359–381. Springer, Cham (2015). https://doi.org/10.1007/978-3-319-26362-5_17

9. Kim, N.Y., Shim, J., Cho, S.-J., Park, M., Han, S.: Android application protection against static reverse engineering based on multidexing. J. Internet Serv. Inf. Secur. **6**(4), 54–64 (2016)

10. APKtool: a tool for reverse engineering Android APK files. https://ibotpeaches.github.io/Apktool/. Accessed 15 Mar 2020

11. Dcc. https://github.com/amimo/dcc. Accessed 15 Mar 2020

12. JNI design overview. https://docs.oracle.com/javase/6/docs/technotes/guides/jni/spec/design.html. Accessed 15 Mar 2020

13. Wang, C., Hill, J., Knight, J., Davidson, J.: Software tamper resistance: obstructing static analysis of programs. Technical Report CS-2000-12, University of Virginia, 12 2000, Technical report (2000)

14. Balachandran, V., Tan, D.J., Thing, V.L., et al.: Control flow obfuscation for Android applications. Comput. Secur. **61**, 72–93 (2016)

15. UI/Application exerciser monkey. https://developer.android.com/studio/test/monkey. Accessed 15 Mar 2020

16. oLLVM-8.0. https://github.com/heroims/obfuscator/tree/llvm-8.0. Accessed 15 Mar 2020

17. Desnos, A., et al.: Androguard (2011)

18. Apkpure.com: Download APK free online downloader. https://www.apkpure.com. Accessed 15 Mar 2020

19. Zhao, Y., et al.: Compile-time code virtualization for Android applications. Comput. Secur. 101821 (2020)

20. iJiami: Sharing IoE and guarding the smart world. https://www.ijiami.cn/. Accessed 15 Mar 2020

21. https://jiagu.360.cn/. Accessed 15 Mar 2020

22. https://cloud.tencent.com/product/ms. Accessed 15 Mar 2020

23. Zhang, Y., Luo, X., Yin, H.: DexHunter: toward extracting hidden code from packed Android applications. In: Pernul, G., Ryan, P.Y.A., Weippl, E. (eds.) ESORICS 2015. LNCS, vol. 9327, pp. 293–311. Springer, Cham (2015). https://doi.org/10.1007/978-3-319-24177-7_15

24. Sun, C., Zhang, H., Qin, S., He, N., Qin, J., Pan, H.: DexX: a double layer unpacking framework for Android. IEEE Access **6**, 61 267–61 276 (2018)

25. JEB decompiler by PNF software. https://www.pnfsoftware.com/. Accessed 15 Mar 2020

26. Jadx - Dex to Java decompiler. https://github.com/skylot/jadx. Accessed 15 Mar 2020

27. Eagle, C.: The IDA Pro Book. No Starch Press (2011)

28. Junod, P., Rinaldini, J., Wehrli, J., Michielin, J.: Obfuscator-LLVM-software protection for the masses. In: 2015 IEEE/ACM 1st International Workshop on Software Protection, pp. 3–9. IEEE (2015)

29. Nolan, G., Truxall, D., Cinar, O., Sood, R.: Android Best Practices. Apress (2013)

30. Youpk. https://github.com/Youlor/Youpk. Accessed 28 July 2020

31. Fdex2. https://bbs.pediy.com/thread-224105.htm. Accessed 28 July 2020

32. Fart. https://github.com/hanbinglengyue/FART. Accessed 28 July 2020

Robust Android Malware Detection Based on Attributed Heterogenous Graph Embedding

Yonghao Gu[1](✉), Liangxun Li[1], and Yong Zhang[2]

[1] Beijing Key Laboratory of Intelligent Telecommunication Software
and Multimedia, School of Computer Science, Beijing University of Posts
and Telecommunications, Beijing 100876, China
{guyonghao,lilx}@bupt.edu.cn
[2] School of Electronic Engineering, Beijing University of Posts
and Telecommunications, Beijing 100876, China
yongzhang@bupt.edu.cn

Abstract. While Machine learning is widely used in Android malware detection, it has been shown that machine learning based malware detection is vulnerable to adversarial attacks. Existing defense methods improve robustness at the cost of decrease in accuracy. In this paper, we propose a Heterogeneous Graph Embedding Malware Detection method, called HGEMD. It could improve both accuracy and robustness by making use of relations between apps. Specifically, we firstly extract API calls from the individual app as attribute and auxiliary information (i.e., permission, third-party library) from massive apps to construct relations. Then, we build an Attributed Heterogeneous Graph (AHG) to simultaneously model attribute and relations. Furthermore, we adopt graph convolution network and attention mechanism to fuse above heterogeneous information. Experimental results on large-scale dataset collected from Google Play demonstrate that the proposed method outperforms the state-of-the-art methods in the respect of accuracy and robustness.

Keywords: Android malware detection · Adversarial attacks · Heterogenous graph

1 Introduction

Android is the most popular mobile operating system with a worldwide market share of 75.16% in 2018. As Google's official app store, the number of available apps in the Google Play is placed at 2.7 million in 2019 [1]. While, due to its large market share and open source ecosystem, security threats on Android are reportedly growing exponentially. It's reported that about 0.45% of all Android devices have installed Potentially Harmful Applications, also known as malwares [2]. App store (e.g., Google Play and Huawei AppGallery) is a type of digital distribution platform for mobile applications. In order for the app to be installed and

G. Xu et al. (Eds.): FCS 2020, CCIS 1286, pp. 432–446, 2020.
https://doi.org/10.1007/978-981-15-9739-8_33

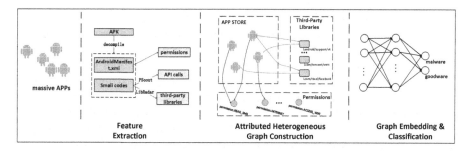

Fig. 1. Overview of the developed system HGEMD for more robust Android malware detection.

used by the consumers, developers first need to upload their apps to the app store. App store is responsible for the security and privacy check of those apps, including malware detection. In order to prevent the spread of malware, it is very important for app store operators to detect malware effectively.

Conventional malware detection methods exploit rule matching, including signature-based rules and malicious behavior-based rules. Rule matching based methods have the advantages of high-speed real-time detection and low false positive rate. However, they suffer from high false negative because of its dependency of predefined rule database which needs to be updated continuously and is costly. Machine learning is widely used in malware detection due to its flexibility [3]. Many previous works, like Drebin [4] and MamaDroid [5], focus on how to extract more effective features from app's codes. Unfortunately, with app's complexity constantly expanding, it's gradually more difficult to extract valid features directly from individuals. Even deep learning methods [6] cannot avoid feature extraction and suffer from the curse of dimensionality.

Another headache for malware detection is evasion attack which means malware camouflages itself to bypass detection. Many technologies, such as obfuscation and polymorphism, are proposed to bypass rule matching based detection. While machine learning methods are immune to above technologies, recent study [6] shows that they are vulnerable to adversarial attacks. Adversarial samples [7] are derived from regular inputs by minor yet carefully selected perturbations that deceive models into desired misclassification. Chen, et al. [8] successfully bypasses Drebin and MamaDroid through adversarial attack algorithm. Given the high security requirements, robustness is the necessary condition for the deployment of malware detection model.

In fact, there are rich auxiliary data(a.k.a., side information) yet not exploited if we treat specific app as a member of thousands of apps in app store instead of individual. For example, it's common that app uses third-party libraries to enrich its content, and apps containing the same third-party library usually share similar functionality. Those auxiliary data always be ignored by existing Android malware detection methods which focus on extracting features from individual app. There are lots of successful cases of using auxiliary data in recommender system [9] and text classification [10] by modeling it from relational perspective. Motivated by these works, we think of massive apps as an ecosystem where exists lots of relations between apps constructed via auxiliary data (i.e., permission, third-party library). For example, two apps are neighbors if they contain the same third-party library. Auxiliary data alleviates the extremely demand of traditional feature extraction. While there are relations between apps, model's prediction for a specific app is not only decided by itself, but also influenced by its neighbors in ecosystem. Neighbors contribute to model's robustness since evasion attacks are dedicated to make perturbation in regular input (i.e., API calls) of individual app.

In this paper, we propose a novel Android malware detection method which fuses attribute and relation information to boost both robustness and accuracy. As API calls are the most common used features by existing detection methods [4,11], we extract API calls from the individual app as attribute. Then we further extract auxiliary data, like third-party libraries and permissions (Sect. 3.1 for details), to construct relations between apps. This paper defines two kinds of semantic relations, whether apps contain the same third-party library and whether apps use the same permission. Since there are attribute and multiple relations simultaneously, we build an Attributed Heterogeneous Graph (AHG) which consists of multiple types of edges and nodes to model multiple relations, where attribute is attached to node. Each app corresponds to a node in the AHG and therefore we can regard Android malware detection as node classification. In order to make effective use of heterogeneous information, we embed all of them into the same low-dimensional vector space to fuse both attribute and multiple relations. In particular, we decompose AHG to several views according to different relations. Then we adopt graph convolution network to fuse attribute and single relation for each view, and an attention layer is followed to fuse outputs of all views. The final learned embeddings, encoding all heterogeneous information, are fed to a classifier. Figure 1 shows the system overview of our proposed model.

In summary, our work has the following contributions.

- We think of massive apps as an ecosystem and use auxiliary data to construct relations between apps. As far as we know, it is the first attempt which considers third-party libraries for Android malware detection.
- We propose a novel malware detection model HGEMD. We build AHG to simultaneously model attribute and relations, and adopt graph convolution network and attention mechanism to fuse heterogeneous information for detection. Prediction of HGEMD depends not only by the given app, but also by its neighbors. HGEMD show strong robustness to adversarial attacks.
- Experimental results on real-world dataset show that HGEMD is more robust to a variety of adversarial attacks compared to state-of-the-art methods whilst is slightly better in accuracy.

The remainder of this paper is organized as follows. Section 2 present preliminaries about Android app. Section 3 describes the proposed malware detection method. Then, experiments are reported in Sect. 4. Section 5 introduces the related works. Finally, we conclude the paper in Sect. 6.

2   Preliminary

Android app is compiled and packaged in a single *jar*-like archive file named android application package (abbreviated as apk), apk packs the application's codes(*classes.dex* files), resources, assets and manifest(*AndroidManifest.xml*). Static analysis of apk focuses on analyzing *classes.dex* and *AndroidManifest.xml*.

classes.dex contains all precompiled application's code. *.dex* is binary format that can be interpreted by Dalvik (Android's Java VM implementation). While *classes.dex* is unreadable, we decompile it to smali codes using baksmali[1]. Smali can be seen as an assembly language and we can extract features, such as API calls, from smali codes.

AndroidManifest.xml is the manifest of app, which is in *.xml* format. It's designed to store meta-data, such as app's name, version ID, permissions, hardwares, etc.

3   Proposed Method

In this section, We present the proposed Heterogeneous Graph Embedding based Android malware detection model, called HGEMD shortly. Firstly, we extract features from apps by static analysis and then we use Attributed Heterogeneous Graph to simultaneously model them. Finally, we adopt graph convolution network and attention mechanism to fuse above heterogeneous information for classification.

3.1   Feature Extraction

We first decompile *classes.dex* to smali codes and extract API calls, third-party libraries from codes, then permissions will be parsed from *AndroidManifest.xml*. Although there're many kinds of meta-data in manifest, we only extract permissions, which is proven to be useful features in Android malware detection [13].

API Calls. API calls are the most common used features in scenarios of malware detection because each API implicitly contains specific semantic information. We use APIs listed in PScout [14] to construct our initial feature dictionary. There are more than 20,000 APIs with detail information, and in this paper 5000 APIs with highest discrimination are selected through Chi-square test.

Permission. Android security management mechanism adheres to the principle of least privilege, and app can only access limited system resources by

---

[1] smali/baksmali is an assembler/disassembler for the dex format used by Dalvik. https://github.com/JesusFreke/smali.

default. In order to gain access to more resources, app must declare the corresponding permissions in the *AndroidManifest.xml* file and the permissions are authorized by user during the installation phase (some low-level permissions are automatically authorized by Android OS). For example, if the app wants to read and send SMS content, it needs to explicitly declare in manifest by *android.permission.READ_SMS* and *android.permission.WRITE_SMS* to gain authorization. It's appropriate to model permission from relational perspective as it belongs to meta-data install of running codes.

Third-Party Libraries. One particular feature of Android apps is that most of them use third-party libraries (abbreviated as TPLs), such as advertising service libraries. Wang, et al. [15] reports that about 57% of sensitive API calls invoked by app come from third-party libraries. Previous work [11] removes API calls that exclusively invoked by third-party libraries since they may reduce the difference between apps. Considering the fact that apps containing the same third-party library usually share similar functionality and the quantity of third-party libraries could be countless as they are constantly created day by day, we believe that making use of third-party libraries from relational perspective is a suitable way. Specifically, we can construct relation between apps subject to whether they contain the same third-party library. We resort to LibRadar [16], which is a third-party libraries detecting tool for Android app, to extract third-party libraries from *classes.dex*. As far as we know, it is the first attempt which makes use of third-party libraries for Android malware detection.

3.2 AHG Construction

We discribe in this section how to model heterogeneous features extracted in previous section. We construct binary feature vector using API calls as app's attribute information in consistent with classic malware detection methods [4,11]. Inspire by social network analysis in recommender system [9], we think of massive apps as an ecosystem where exists lots of relations between apps constructed via auxiliary data (i.e., permission, third-party library). Following [18], we build an Attributed Heterogeneous Graph, formalized as following, to simultaneously model attribute and relation information.

Definition 1 *Attributed Heterogeneous Graph (AHG).* *An Attributed Heterogeneous Graph, denoted as $\mathcal{G} = \{\mathcal{V}, \mathcal{E}, \boldsymbol{X}\}$, encodes the relations between different objects, where $\mathcal{V}$ is a set of objects and $\mathcal{E}$ is a set of edges between the objects. $\boldsymbol{X} \in \mathbb{R}^{|\mathcal{V}| \times d}$ represents objects' attribute vectors, d is the dimension of vector space. An AHG is associated with a object type mapping $\phi : \mathcal{V} \to \mathcal{A}$ and a edge type mapping $\psi : \mathcal{E} \to \mathcal{R}$, where $\mathcal{A}$ and $\mathcal{R}$ denote the sets of object and edge types, where $|\mathcal{A}| + |\mathcal{R}| > 2$.*

We model the scenario of Android malware detection using an AHG, where there are three type of objects (i.e., app, third-party library, permission) and two type of edges(app-permission, app-tpl). Each app takes its API calls as attribute, we ignore the attribute of permissions and TPLs cause those two type objects are only used to build composite relations between apps. Figure 2(a) demonstrates the AHG instance used in out paper.

Definition 2 Meta-path *[19]. A meta-path ρ is defined as a path in the form of $A_1 \xrightarrow{R_1} A_2 \xrightarrow{R_2} \cdots \xrightarrow{R_l} A_{l+1}$ (abbreviated as $A_1 A_2 \cdots A_{l+1}$), which describes a composite relation $R = R_1 \circ R_2 \circ \cdots \circ R_l$ between object A_1 and A_{l+1}, where $\circ$ denotes the composition operator on relations.*

Meta-path describing a composite relation between two objects is a powerful tool for analyzing heterogeneous graph. For example, two apps can be connected via meta-path $app \xrightarrow{use} permission \xrightarrow{use^{-1}} app(APA)$. Particularly, if two objects connected via a meta-path belong to the same type, we can decompose heterogeneous graph into homogeneous graph, called **view**, according to the meta-path. Each view contains single type of objects and single type of edges. We define two meta-paths, APA and ATA, in Fig. 2(b). Two views are obtained through the above meta-paths respectively.

Here we model the scenario of Android malware detection with an AHG which can simultaneously model attribute and rich relations. Now, each app corresponds to an object(node) in the AGH so that we can regard Android malware detection as node classification.

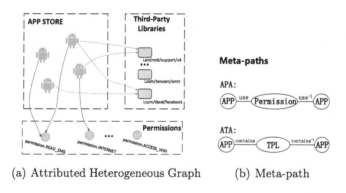

(a) Attributed Heterogeneous Graph   (b) Meta-path

Fig. 2. Scenario of Android malware detection.

3.3 Graph Embedding and Classification

We adopt graph embedding [17] to fusing heterogeneous information in AHG. The basic idea of graph embedding is to embed each node in graph into a low-dimensional vector space, graph structure information is encoded in embedding vectors. Embedding provides a natural way to fusion as we can embed different information into the same vector space. Following [21], we first decompose AHG into several views according to meta-paths and learn node's embeddings for each view, then the final node's embeddings are gained by weighted summing all embeddings from views. The final embeddings are fed to subsequent classifier.

For each view, there are single type edge and single type node and our goal is to learn node's embeddings that encode both attribute and relations. We initialize the hidden states of nodes through thier attributes, then update those hidden states for K iterations, the last hidden states are read out as embeddings. For the k_{th} iteration, the input to graph convolution layer is nodes' hidden states, $h^k = \{h_1^k, h_2^k, ..., h_N^k\}, h_i^k \in \mathbb{R}^d$, where N is the number of nodes, and d is the dimension of hidden state vectors. The layer outputs a new set of node hidden states, $h^{k+1} = \{h_1^{k+1}, h_2^{k+1}, ..., h_N^{k+1}\}, h_i^{k+1} \in \mathbb{R}^{d'}$. We update nodes' hidden states as following [20]:

$$h_v^{k+1} = \sigma(concat(Wh_v^k, \sum_{u \in N(v)} \frac{Wh_u^k}{|N(v)|})) \tag{1}$$

where $W \in \mathbb{R}^{d' \times d}$ is the weight matrix to perform linear transformation. $N(v)$ represents the neighbors of node v. $concat$ represents concatenation operation and σ is the nonlinearity. The final hidden states h^K will be read out as the embeddings which encode both attribute and K-order neighbors' structure (relation) information.

In the above steps, we could obtain multiple embeddings based on different views, which are expected to collaborate with each other for better classification. Following [21], we adopt co-attention mechanism to fuse multiple embeddings. The input embeddings are denoted as $z_{view} = \{z_1, z_2, \cdots, z_p\}$ where p is the number of views(meta-path), z_i represent the embedding learned from view i. The weight of each view, denoted as α_i, is automatically learned by co-attention mechanism. With the learned weights as coefficients, we fuse all view embeddings by weighted sum to obtain the final embedding z.

$$z = \sum_{i=1}^{p} \alpha_i \cdot z_i \tag{2}$$

The embedding vector z encoding attribute and multiple relations, and we feed z into binary classifier to obtain probability vector p_z. The loss function is negative log likelihood which can be formulated as follows:

$$\mathcal{L}(\theta) = -\mathbb{E}_{z, y \sim p_{data}} log p_z + \lambda ||\theta||^2 \tag{3}$$

where p_{data} represents the true distribution of dataset, y is the ground truth for the give app, 1 for malware and 0 for goodware. θ is the parameter set of the proposed model and λ is the regularizer parameter. The optimization algorithm Adam [27] is adopted for model learning.

4   Experiments

In this section, we will demonstrate the effectiveness of HGEMD by performing experiments on large-scale dataset collected from Google Play. The performance of malware detection is evaluated from two aspects, namely accuracy and robustness. Accuracy refers to model's performance in normal environment while robustness refers to model's performance in adversarial environment.

4.1   Experimental Setup

Dataset. For all experiments, we consider a real-world dataset collected from Google Play during 2014 to 2017. To determine malicious and good apps, we upload all the apps to VirusTotal[2], a popular online malware analysis service that aggregates more than 60 anti-virus engines. To reduce false positives, we flag app as malware at least 10 engines identify it as malware, as suggested by previous studies [4,28]. While malware is the minority class in Google Play, we use subset of goodwares to avoid data imbalance. The final dataset contains 9995 goodwares and 9929 malwares. We randomly split dataset into training, validation and testing at the rate of 60%, 20% and 20%.

Metrics. We evaluate the accuracy performance using the measures shown in Table 1, which are widely adopted in previous malware detection works [4,23].

Table 1. Accuracy metrics of Android malware detection.

Metrics	Description
TP	# of apps correctly classified as malware
TN	# of apps correctly classified as goodware
FP	# of apps mistakenly classified as malware
FN	# of apps mistakenly classified as goodware
Precision	$TP/(TP + FP)$
Recall	$TP/(TP + FN)$
F1	$(2 \times Precision \times Recall)/(Precision + Recall)$

For robustness performance, we attack models through adversarial attacks and using *Recall* and *Foolingrate* to evaluate their robustness. Since we only craft adversarial samples for malwares to bypass detection, *Recall* is intuitive in such case. To eliminate the performance difference between models caused not by adversarial attacks (e.g., Recalls of MLP and HGEMD are different in normal environment), we also evaluate robustness in terms of the *Foolingrate*, defined as the ratio of examples for which the model predicts a different label as the result of the perturbation [26]. There are three possible situations:

(1) Malware is misclassified as goodware even no attack and we don't bother to craft adversarial sample for it. The frequency of such cases is denoted as x.

---

[2] https://www.virustotal.com.

(2) Malware is misclassified as goodware after perturbation, which means a successful attack and we denote the frequency of such cases as y.

(3) Malware is still classified as malware after perturbation, which means a failed attack and we use z to denote frequency of such cases.

Recall and *Foolingrate* can be formulated as follows:

$$Recall = \frac{z}{x + y + z} \tag{4}$$

$$Foolingrate = \frac{y}{y + z} \tag{5}$$

4.2   Accuracy Evaluation

In this section, we evaluate the accuracy of HGEMD model without considering attacks. We compare the following methods.

- **Drebin** [4]: It is the classic Android malware detection method by extracting extensive features to construct binary vectors and SVM are used as classifier. We reimplement Drebin using the released code[3].
- **MLP** [6]: It is a deep learning-based approach which uses Multi-Layer Perceptrons. We feed attribute vectors constructed by API calls to this model and denote it as MLP.
- **AiDroid** [23]: It models all obtainable information as relations between apps and uses a biased random walk method to classification. We use all extracted data (API calls, third-party libraries, permissions) to construct relations, and reimplement AiDroid as described in the original paper.
- **HGEMD$_t$**: It represents the view of AHG corresponding to meta-path ATA, where API calls are used as app's attribute and construct relation between apps only by third-party libraries. Node-level fusion is used to fuse above two heterogeneous information.
- **HGEMD$_p$**: It represents the view of AHG corresponding to meta-path APA, where API calls are used as app's attribute and construct relation between apps only by permissions. Node-level fusion is used to fuse above two heterogeneous information.
- **HGEMD**: It is the proposed Android malware detection based on AHG. which contains attribute (API calls) and multiple relations (APA, ATA). View-level fusion is used to integrate HGEMD$_t$ and HGEMD$_p$.

We report the comparison results of the proposed method and baselines in Table 2. The major findings from Experimental results can be summarized as follows:

(1) Our model outperforms all baselines in F1 score, which indicates that our model adopts a more principled way to leverage heterogeneous information for improving accuracy.

---

[3] https://github.com/MLDroid/drebin.

Table 2. Results of accuracy evaluation.

Methods	F1-score	Precision	Recall
Drebin	0.9938	0.9928	0.9949
MLP	0.9932	0.9935	0.9930
AiDroid	0.9928	0.9958	0.9911
HGEMD$_p$	0.9939	**0.9970**	0.9909
HGEMD$_t$	0.9942	**0.9970**	0.9914
HGEMD	**0.9947**	0.9940	**0.9955**

(2) Comparing with MLP which uses only attribute, we can find that HGEMD significantly outperforms MLP in all metrics. Results demonstrate relation information exploited in out paper is really helpful for detection performance. However, modeling all type of information as relations is not a suitable practice as AiDroid's F1 is slightly lower than MLP. It's sensible to distinguish attribute and relation information.

(3) Although HGEMD$_p$ and HGEMD$_t$ achieve high F1, their Recalls are lower than baselines. As combination of different views through attention mechanism, HGEMD shows highest Recall. Results indicate that better performance can be achieved by fusing more relations.

4.3   Robustness Evaluation

In this section, we evaluate HGEMD's robustness against adversarial attacks. We only consider classic adversarial attacks which arm to modify regular input in this paper. Specifically, we only modify app's attribute (API calls). We use MLP as the baseline since it shows competitive accuracy and attacking Drebin can actually be converted as attacking a MLP model [8]. While adversarial attacks for graph is an emerging research field [29], we will study attacks from relational perspective and make robustness comparison with AiDroid in future work.

Attack Algorithms. Crafting an adversarial sample $\hat{x}$, misclassified by model $f(\cdot)$, from legitimate sample x can be formalized as following [7]:

$$\hat{x} = x + \delta_x = x + min\|z\|$$
$$s.t. \quad f(\hat{x}) \neq f(x) \tag{6}$$

where δ_x is the minimal perturbation yielding misclassification, according to a norm $\| \cdot \|$ appropriate for the input domain. We use the L_1 normal to bound perturbation distance (number of modified bits). There is a special restriction on crafting adversarial examples for Android malwares that perturbation cannot destroy app's functionality. We only add API calls to app to avoid affecting its original functionality, as suggested in [8]. Specifically, we only allow $0 \rightarrow 1$

operator as the input is binary attribute vector where 1 indicates usage of a specific API.

We attack models through two widely used adversarial attack algorithms.

FGSM Fast Gradient Sign Method(FGSM) [12] generates an adversarial example $\hat{x}$ for and input x with label y as follows:

$$\hat{x} \leftarrow x + \epsilon sign(\nabla_x J(f(x), y)) \tag{7}$$

where $J(f(x), y)$ is the loss function, and ϵ controls the magnitude of perturbation. We set $\epsilon = 1$ and only change d features which have largest gradient and meet above restrictions. d can be regarded as perturbation distance.

JSMA Jacobian Saliency Map Attack (JSMA) [6] is an iterative algorithm. It first (1) computes saliency score for each feature, which indicates the possibility of triggering misclassification if the corresponding feature is modified, then (2) one feature with highest saliency score is modified. The algorithm repeats (1) and (2) until either it successfully causes a misclassification or reaches the limit for maximum iteration d. d can be regarded as perturbation distance.

In the following experiments, for both FGSM and JSMA, we empirically set perturbation distance $d = 10, 20, 30, 40, 50$ where $d = 50$ counts for 1% as the dimension of input vector space is 5000 (API calls, see in Sect. 3.1).

Robustness Comparison. Robustness comparison between HGEMD and classic MLP is shown in Fig. 3. We can clearly see that HGEMD shows excellent robustness against both FGSM and JSMA attacks. Results indicate that HGEMD is a relatively general defense method. While it still can be successfully attacked, attacks have to generate much stronger perturbation in order to fool the proposed methods. HGEMD is almost immune to JSMA attack, where Recall is up to 90% even perturbation distance $d = 50$.

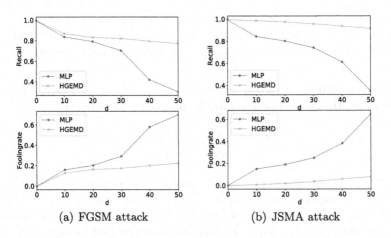

(a) FGSM attack   (b) JSMA attack

Fig. 3. Robustness comparison of HGEMD and classic MLP against FGSM and JSMA attacks.

Table 3. Results of comparison with existing defense methods against two attacks w.r.t. perturbation distance.

Metrics	Methods	FGSM					JSMA				
		d = 10	d = 20	d = 30	d = 40	d = 50	d = 10	d = 20	d = 30	d = 40	d = 50
Recall	MLP_{fgsm}	0.9491	0.9416	0.9275	**0.9124**	**0.8922**	0.8197	0.8056	0.7956	0.7840	0.7769
	MLP_{jsma}	0.9280	0.8233	0.8021	0.7815	0.7477	0.9481	0.8328	0.8082	0.7920	0.7729
	PeerNets	0.8162	0.8046	0.7835	0.7603	0.7256	0.9330	0.8454	0.8097	0.7961	0.7865
	$HGEMD_p$	0.8505	0.8162	0.7628	0.7100	0.5700	0.9350	0.8308	0.8077	0.7628	0.7069
	$HGEMD_t$	**0.9738**	**0.9562**	**0.9381**	0.8771	0.8364	0.8469	0.8429	0.8288	0.8117	0.7885
	HGEMD	0.8676	0.8318	0.8218	0.7951	0.7714	**0.9859**	**0.9748**	**0.9572**	**0.9361**	**0.9149**
Foolingrate	MLP_{fgsm}	0.0383	0.0459	0.0602	**0.0755**	**0.0959**	0.1681	0.1824	0.1926	0.2044	0.2115
	MLP_{jsma}	0.0635	0.1692	0.1905	0.2114	0.2454	0.0437	0.1600	0.1849	0.2011	0.2204
	PeerNets	0.1738	0.1855	0.2069	0.2304	0.2655	0.0546	0.1434	0.1796	0.1934	0.2031
	$HGEMD_p$	0.1409	0.1755	0.2294	0.2828	0.4242	0.0559	0.1612	0.1845	0.2298	0.2862
	$HGEMD_t$	**0.0183**	**0.0360**	**0.0543**	0.1157	0.1569	0.1475	0.1515	0.1657	0.1830	0.2063
	HGEMD	0.1276	0.1635	0.1737	0.2005	0.2243	**0.0086**	**0.0197**	**0.0375**	**0.0587**	**0.0800**

Comparison with Existing Defenses. We further compare HGEMD's robustness with existing defense methods.

Adversarial training [7] boosts model's robustness by adding adversarial examples during training. We retrain MLP model with presence of adversarial examples crafted by FGSM and JSMA separately and denote them as MLP_{fgsm} and MLP_{jsma}. Adversarial examples crafted with different perturbation distances ($d = 10, 20, 30, 40, 50$) are mixed during retraining and the rate of regular and adversarial examples is 1:1. What's more, adversarial examples for both malwares and goodwares are used to avoid decrease of Precision.

PeerNets [26] adopts graph convolutions to boost robustness. For an input image, PeerNets searches for most similar images from batch as its neighbors. Prediction depends not only by the given image, but also by its neighbors. While PeerNets is originally applied in computer vision, we develop a variant of it for malware detection. We choose PeerNets as a comparison because HGEMD shares the similar intuition that neighbors contribute to robustness.

HGEMD and PeerNets are trained using Adam without adversarial training. Actually, they can also benefit from adversarial training. Results of comparison are reported in Table 3. The major findings from the experimental results can be summarized as follows:

(1) HGEMD is the most robust against JSMA attack in all perturbation distances, while $HGEMD_t$ achieves best robustness against FGSM attack in most perturbation distances less than 40. Results indicate that our model adopts a more principled way to leverage heterogeneous information for improving robustness performance.

(2) Adversarial training is less general as model trained with examples crafted by FGSM is less robust to examples crafted by JSMA algorithm and vice versa. HGEMD is more general as it performs convincing robustness against both attack algorithms.

(3) Our method outperforms PeerNets in each case, which indicates that the neighbors defined in our paper is more effective for improving robustness.

(4) HGEMD$_t$ performs better than HGEMD$_p$ in most cases, which indicates that third-party libraries serves as a stronger relations. HGEMD's robustness is more stable to different perturbation distance.

5   Related Work

In this section, we will review the related studies in two aspects.

Android Malware Detection. Machine learning is widely used in Android malware detection. Aung. et al. [13] extract permissions from app to construct binary feature vectors which is fast and resource intensive. However, permissions are less effective for malware detection since developers tend to apply for more permissions than actually used. DroidAPIMiner [11] construct binary feature vectors using API calls. Drebin [4] extracts more information to construct feature vectors, including API calls, IP, components, etc. Despite the excellent performance, the size of feature set inflates rapidly as the amount of data expanding. MamaDroid[5] analyzes sequences of abstracted API calls to construct features. grosse, et al. [6] introduces a deep learning-based approach that takes the same input features as Drebin but uses MLP as classifier. The above classical methods treat each app as an independent individual, ignoring the relations between apps. HinDroid [22] analyzes relations between apps (e.g., two apps invoke the same API) and models all apps as a relational network. AiDroid [23] models relations between apps similar to HinDroid, but adopts a biased random walk method for node classification which is more scalable than SVM used in HinDroid. The method proposed in our paper is inspired by AiDroid. Instead of modeling everything as relations, we reserve feature vectors used in traditional methods while modeling auxiliary data as relations. Our method is naturally scalable and can be accelerated by parallelization.

Adversarial Attack and Defense. Adversarial samples [7] are derived from regular inputs by minor yet carefully selected perturbations that deceive machine learning models into desired misclassification. Many adversarial attack algorithms have been proposed in recent years, such as FGSM [12], JSMA [24], etc. Although most of those attacks' original scenario is image recognition, they can easily be applied to malware detection with some modification. Adversarial attack is a new powerful means for malware evasion. Grosse, et al. [6] successfully crafts adversarial samples for malwares to bypass a deep learning based detection through the variant of JSMA. Chen, et al. [8] shows that Drebin and MamaDroid can also be bypassed by adversarial attack. There has been significant recent effort trying to strategies against adversarial perturbations. Adversarial train [7] boosts the robustness of model by adding adversarial samples to dataset during training phase. Papernot, et al. [25] propose defensive distillation. Different from previous defense methods which keep model's structure unchanged, recently proposed PeerNets [26] adopts graph convolutions to harness information from a graph of peer samples. For an input image, PeerNets searches for similar images as its neighbors. Prediction depends not only by the given image, but also by its neighbors. Our model get inspiration from PeerNets. The difference lies in that we deliberately construct heterogeneous neighbors which are more effective than neighbors randomly sampled in PeerNets.

6 Conclusion

This paper presents a novel Android malware detection model called HGEMD, which achieves high accuracy and shows strong robustness to adversarial attacks. We use auxiliary data extracted from app ecosystem to construct relations between apps, and build AHG to simultaneously model attribute and relation information. We fuse heterogeneous information using graph convolution network and attention mechanism for Android malware detection. Experimental results on large-scale and real-world dataset prove the effectiveness of HGEMD in terms of accuracy and robustness. In the future, we plan to investigate adversarial attacks from relational perspective to further evaluate model's robustness. Besides, we also consider to improve explainability of graph-based Android malware detection.

Acknowledgment. This work is supported by the National Natural Science Foundation of China (No. 61873040, U1836108, U1936216) and the State Major Science and Technology Special Projects (No. 2014ZX03004002)

References

1. Statistics. https://www.statista.com
2. Android security & privacy review 2018. https://source.android.com/security/reports/Google_Android_Security_2018_Report_Final.pdf
3. Ye, Y., Li, T., Adjeroh, D., Iyengar, S.S.: A survey on malware detection using data mining techniques. ACM Comput. Surv. (CSUR) **50**(3), 41 (2017)
4. Arp, D., Spreitzenbarth, M., Hubner, M., Gascon, H., Rieck, K., Siemens, C.: Drebin: effective and explainable detection of android malware in your pocket. In: NDSS (2014)
5. Mariconti, E., Onwuzurike, L., Andriotis, P., De Cristofaro, E., Ross, G., Stringhini, G.: Mamadroid: detecting android malware by building markov chains of behavioral models. In: NDSS (2017)
6. Grosse, K., Papernot, N., Manoharan, P., Backes, M., McDaniel, P.: Adversarial examples for malware detection. In: Foley, S.N., Gollmann, D., Snekkenes, E. (eds.) ESORICS 2017. LNCS, vol. 10493, pp. 62–79. Springer, Cham (2017). https://doi.org/10.1007/978-3-319-66399-9_4
7. Szegedy, C., et al.: Intriguing properties of neural networks. In: ICLR (2014)
8. Chen, X., et al.: Android HIV: a study of repackaging malware for evading machine-learning detection. IEEE Trans. Inf. Forensics Secur. **15**, 987–1001 (2019)
9. Shi, C., Hu, B., Zhao, W.X., Yu, P.S.: Heterogeneous information network embedding for recommendation. IEEE Transactions on Knowledge & Data Engineering **31**(2), 357–370 (2019)
10. Tang, J., Qu, M., Mei, Q.: Pte: predictive text embedding through large-scale heterogeneous text networks. In: Proceedings of the 21th ACM SIGKDD International Conference on Knowledge Discovery and Data Mining, pp. 1165–1174. ACM (2015)

11. Aafer, Y., Du, W., Yin, H.: DroidAPIMiner: mining API-level features for robust malware detection in android. In: Zia, T., Zomaya, A., Varadharajan, V., Mao, M. (eds.) SecureComm 2013. LNICST, vol. 127, pp. 86–103. Springer, Cham (2013). https://doi.org/10.1007/978-3-319-04283-1_6

12. Goodfellow, I.J., Shlens, J., Szegedy, C.: Explaining and harnessing adversarial examples. In: ICLR (2015)

13. Aung, Z., Zaw, W.: Permission-based android malware detection. Int. J. Sci. Technol. Res. 2(3), 228–234 (2013)

14. Au, K.W.Y., Zhou, Y.F., Huang, Z., Lie, D.: Pscout: analyzing the android permission specification. In: Proceedings of the 2012 ACM Conference on Computer and Communications Security, pp. 217–228. ACM (2012)

15. Wang, H., Guo, Y., Ma, Z., Chen, X.: Wukong: a scalable and accurate two-phase approach to android app clone detection. In: Proceedings of the 2015 International Symposium on Software Testing and Analysis, pp. 71–82. ACM (2015)

16. Ma, Z., Wang, H., Guo, Y., Chen, X.: Libradar: fast and accurate detection of third-party libraries in android apps. In: Proceedings of the 38th International Conference on Software Engineering Companion, pp. 653–656. ACM (2016)

17. Hamilton, W.L., Ying, R., Leskovec, J.: Representation learning on graphs: methods and applications. IEEE Data Eng. Bull. 40, 52–74 (2017)

18. Hu, B., Zhang, Z., Shi, C., Zhou, J., Li, X., Qi, Y.: Cash-out user detection based on attributed heterogeneous information network with a hierarchical attention mechanism. In: AAAI (2019)

19. Sun, Y., Han, J., Yan, X., Yu, P.S., Wu, T.: Pathsim: meta path-based top-k similarity search in heterogeneous information networks. Proc. VLDB Endowment 4(11), 992–1003 (2011)

20. Gilmer, J., Schoenholz, S.S., Riley, P.F., Vinyals, O., Dahl, G.E.: Neural message passing for quantum chemistry. In: Proceedings of the 34th International Conference on Machine Learning-Volume 70, pp. 1263–1272. JMLR (2017)

21. Xiao, W., et al.: Heterogeneous graph attention network. In: The World Wide Web Conference, pp. 2022–2032 (2019)

22. Shou, S., Ye, Y., Song, Y., Abdulhayoglu, M.: Hindroid: an intelligent android malware detection system based on structured heterogeneous information network. In: Proceedings of the 23rd ACM SIGKDD International Conference on Knowledge Discovery and Data Mining, pp. 1507–1515. ACM (2017)

23. Ye, Y., et al.: Out-of-sample node representation learning for heterogeneous graph in real-time android malware detection. In: IJCAI (2019)

24. Papernot, N., McDaniel, P., Jha, S., Fredrikson, M., Celik, Z.B., Swami, A.: The limitations of deep learning in adversarial settings. In: 2016 IEEE European Symposium on Security and Privacy (EuroS&P), pp. 372–387. IEEE (2016)

25. Papernot, N., McDaniel, P.: On the effectiveness of defensive distillation. arXiv preprint arXiv:1607.05113 (2016)

26. Svoboda, J., Masci, J., Monti, F., Bronstein, M.M., Guibas, L.: Peernets: exploiting peer wisdom against adversarial attacks. In: ICLR (2019)

27. Kingma, D.P., Ba, J.: Adam: a method for stochastic optimization. In: International Conference on Learning Representations (ICLR) (2015)

28. Wang, H., Li, H., Guo, Y.: Understanding the evolution of mobile app ecosystems: a longitudinal measurement study of google play. In: The World Wide Web Conference, pp. 1988–1999. ACM (2019)

29. Zügner, D., Akbarnejad, A., Günnemann, S.: Adversarial attacks on neural networks for graph data. In: Proceedings of the 24th ACM SIGKDD International Conference on Knowledge Discovery & Data Mining, pp. 2847–2856. ACM (2018)

Network Security

A Network Traffic Classification Method Based on Hierarchical Clustering

Yong Ma[1]([⊠]), Yang Hu[1], and Chang Cai[2]

[1] Civil Aviation Electronic Technology Co., Ltd., Chengdu, China
{mayong,huyang}@caacetc.com
[2] Civil Aviation University of China, Tianjin, China
heimajushi@sina.com

Abstract. With the continuous expansion of civil aviation airport information system, the types and quantities of traffic carried in the network are also increasing rapidly. But during the information system construction, there was no strict sorting of the network traffic types of the information system, and network equipment could not formulate strict network access control policies, which caused the flow data of various information systems to be intertwined and increased the difficulty of information system security maintenance. At the same time, some malicious attack traffic was also mixed, which posed a great threat to the security of information systems. In order to further improve the efficiency of information security protection equipment and improve the recognition rate of abnormal traffic, this paper proposed a network traffic classification method based on hierarchical clustering, which sorts out network traffic in order to find abnormal traffic and improve the protection strategy of network security equipment, thereby improving the network security protection capability of the entire information system.

Keywords: Civil aviation information system · Network traffic classification · Clustering algorithm

1 Introduction

With the promotion of the construction of "four airports" in civil aviation, the number and types of airport information systems are increasing at an unprecedented speed, and the complexity of airport information systems is becoming more and more complex. At present, due to various reasons, the network system management is not in place, the security policy configuration is not correct, these have provided the attack surface to the opponent. The attacker can make use of these loopholes to attack the airport network, seriously affecting the safe operation of the airport business. But how to manage the huge and complex network system inside the airport and reduce the threat of network security is a huge challenge for airport network managers.

At present, in order to reduce the threat of network security and improve the operational efficiency of airports, many airports have deployed network security

© Springer Nature Singapore Pte Ltd. 2020
G. Xu et al. (Eds.): FCS 2020, CCIS 1286, pp. 449–458, 2020.
https://doi.org/10.1007/978-981-15-9739-8_34

devices such as firewalls, but because of the complex traffic in the network, network managers are often at a loss, there is no way to know what policies to deploy on a secure device are truly effective; there are also some abnormal traffic in this huge network traffic, which is likely to be malicious, the same identification of these malicious traffic, to improve the security of the airport network has an important role. Many network security companies and research teams have done a lot of research on malicious traffic identification, identifying abnormal traffic in the network through various algorithms, but rarely combing network traffic according to business content, to help Network administrator improve their network protection strategies. At present, the Network administrator mainly uses Network Traffic Analysis tools such as Wireshark and Colasoft Network Analysis System for manual Analysis and screening. This method is heavy workload and low efficiency, so the Network strategy combing is often left out intentionally or unintentionally. The main work of this paper is to sort out the traffic in the network based on the traffic analysis and using the hierarchical classification method combined with the expert experience of the airport business department, it is of great significance to enhance the network security protection ability.

For an internet-oriented intranet this work will be very complex and difficult, but for the production network within the airport, it has its own distinctive features. Because of these characteristics, it reduces the difficulty of network traffic analysis, and makes the research content of this paper feasible. Airport information systems [1] also have some characteristics in network traffic:

- **Network access is limited.** Since the airport information system mainly carries the internal business of the airport, the servers and business terminals of the information system are deployed in the internal network of the airport, and the data interaction with the external information system is limited and relatively clear. Therefore, the network access scope of all kinds of information systems in the airport is limited, and mainly limited to the airport internal network.
- **Network traffic features are quite distinct.** Since the airport information system carries the specific business, the characteristics of the network traffic of each information system are closely related to the business content. Therefore, the network traffic of each information system has distinct characteristics for easy identification, including port number, network transmission protocol, packet transmission frequency and so on.
- **The network access path is clear.** Because the airport information system carries the specific business, the network access path between the server and the business terminal of each information system is relatively fixed. Therefore, the access path for the whole network is relatively clear.

Although the airport information system has these distinct characteristics in terms of network traffic, in the actual construction process of informatization, the airport still has the situation of lax network traffic control and empty network equipment strategy, which led to malicious attacks that cannot be effectively monitored and intercepted. The main reasons for these problems are as follows:

- In order to ensure the operation of the information system, the network strategy is not strictly sorted out.
- The field implementers are not familiar with the information system under construction, and do not understand the open ports and network traffic of the system, which makes the network equipment debugging personnel unable to formulate security policies.
- During the operation of the system, multiple systems are adjusted or increased and the information system change management measures are not in place, resulting in the confusion of network equipment policies.

To solve the problem in the process of information system project implementation and operation of network traffic grooming and strategy management, further enhance the efficiency of the information security protection equipment, improving the abnormal traffic identification, this paper puts forward a method based on hierarchy clustering to classify network traffic, in order to find abnormal traffic and improve the network safety protection strategy and thus improve the network security protection ability of the whole information system.

While using machine learning method to classify network traffic research [2–4] has a lot of, and research is very thorough, but this article is mainly aimed at the airport network system of research in this particular environment, the airport for the features of information system in the aspect of network traffic is the important basis of this thesis research.

2   Hierarchical Clustering

2.1   Basic Idea of Hierarchical Clustering

The basic idea of hierarchical clustering method [5] is that hierarchical clustering is a classification method based on a posterior model, which forms a classification tree by calculating some similarity between records in the test set and sorting them according to the size of similarity. The advantage of this method is that the partition can be stopped at any time. The main steps are as follows:

- Remove all edges in the network to obtain the initial state with N isolated nodes;
- Calculate the similarity of each pair of nodes in the network;
- According to the similarity degree, the corresponding node pairs are connected from strong to weak to form a tree graph;
- According to the actual requirement, the classification results are obtained.

2.2   Hierarchical Clustering Model

Sample set:$S = \{P_1, P_2, ...P_n\}$,there are n samples.

Article i record:$P_i = \{x_i1, x_i2, ...x_im\}$ there are m features. Using Markov distance to calculate the distance between samples:

$$dist(P_i, P_j) = \sqrt[1/2]{(x_i + x_j)^T S^{-1}(x_i + x_j)} \tag{1}$$

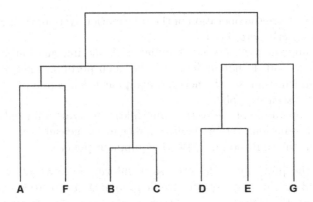

Fig. 1. Schematic diagram of hierarchical clustering.

where T is transposed matrix, x_i and x_j are vectors composed of M indicators of the i_{th} and $j_t h$ samples respectively, and S is the sample covariance matrix.

This time using the minimum distance method as an example, suppose C_1 is a set of partially clustered samples, and C_2 is a set of unclustered samples:

$$dist(C_1, C_2) = \min_{P_i \in C_1, P_j \in C_2} dist(P_i, P_j) \qquad (2)$$

Put P_j in C_1, then repeat the above steps until the number of records in C_2 is 0, and finally achieve clustering through this method.

2.3 Application of Hierarchical Clustering Algorithm in Airport Network

The airport involves a large number of equipment, especially various kinds of sensing and monitoring equipment, which not only has a large number, but also uses different technical structures. Moreover, it is difficult for these terminal equipment to install a unified authentication system, which makes it difficult for these equipment to carry out unified management in access control. The current MAC address binding method can access the internal network by forging the MAC address. In order to solve this problem, the hierarchical clustering method is proposed in this paper. Basic principle: all kinds of Internet of things devices will send back information to the "brain" in real time or at a fixed time. The ports, protocols and contents of these returned data packets are relatively fixed. By monitoring the returned data packets through network monitoring technology, analyzing the returned ports, protocols and contents in the data packets, we can determine whether the accessed devices are the expected devices. In the centralized network of intelligent devices, the open port of intelligent devices is taken as its fingerprint information (the open port of intelligent devices is relatively fixed), the device address in network traffic is monitored and analyzed, and the legality of the device is monitored by using the fingerprint information of the device, so as to realize the detection of illegal access. In order to support the implementation of the project, the project team purchased the network access management system. Use the registration system of the network access management system to obtain the fingerprint information of the device. The port information of the device is mainly used as the fingerprint information in this project. By identifying the abnormal access traffic in the network traffic, illegal network devices are detected.

3 Data Preprocessing

The test data sets used in this time are all from the airport internal network, and 10.6G traffic packets are obtained through the network packet capture tool, as shown in Fig. 2. This clustering algorithm takes 11 characteristics of network

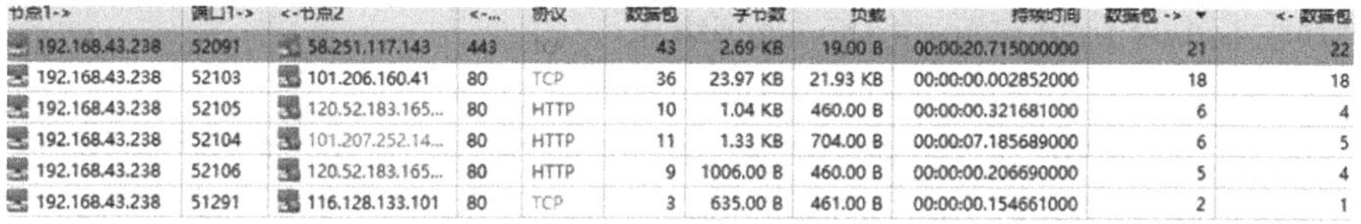

节点1->	端口1->	<-节点2	<-...	协议	数据包	子协议	负载	持续时间	数据包 -> ▾	<- 数据包
192.168.43.238	52091	58.251.117.143	443	TV	43	2.69 KB	19.00 B	00:00:20.715000000	21	22
192.168.43.238	52103	101.206.160.41	80	TCP	36	23.97 KB	21.93 KB	00:00:00.002852000	18	18
192.168.43.238	52105	120.52.183.165...	80	HTTP	10	1.04 KB	460.00 B	00:00:00.321681000	6	4
192.168.43.238	52104	101.207.252.14...	80	HTTP	11	1.33 KB	704.00 B	00:00:07.185689000	6	5
192.168.43.238	52106	120.52.183.165...	80	HTTP	9	1006.00 B	460.00 B	00:00:00.206690000	5	4
192.168.43.238	51291	116.128.133.101	80	TCP	3	635.00 B	461.00 B	00:00:00.154661000	2	1

Fig. 2. Traffic information.

packets as classification attributes, including source IP, source port, destination IP, destination port, transmission protocol, number of packets, number of bytes, total load, transmission time, the number of packets from source IP and the number of packets from destination IP.

The data set of this classification algorithm is obtained through data processing of each attribute. The specific method is as follows.

- **IP address preprocessing.** Since the IP address obtained directly is segmented, the IP address obtained is converted into decimal IP address for the convenience of data classification. For example, 192.168.0.1 converts the decimal IP address to 3232235521, and the maximum number of bits is 10 bits.
- **Port information preprocessing.** The computer port range is 0-65535. Since the commonly used ports are concentrated below 4000 and are mainly 3-digit ports, in order to prevent the annihilation of port attribute classification caused by excessive difference between IP addresses, the port data are increased by 10 times in data preprocessing.
- **Transport protocol preprocessing.** The transmission protocols in the network are mainly divided into three categories: TCP, UDP, and other protocols (such as TLS protocol). In order to number the protocol's types and prevent the IP address difference from causing the annihilation of port attribute classification, the values of these three types of protocols are 1000, 2000 and 3000 respectively.

– **Preprocessing of duration.** Duration format in hours, minutes and seconds. In order to facilitate the clustering algorithm, the time was uniformly converted to the unit of seconds, and 4 decimal places were taken after the decimal point was dropped, and the number was increased by 10,000 times.
– **Other data and processing content.** In order to ensure the normal operation of the clustering algorithm, the abnormal data in the test set are cleaned in addition to the above preprocessing methods.

4   Data Clustering

4.1   Hierarchical Clustering Code Implementation

After cleaning and processing the data set, the hierarchical clustering method is adopted to classify the data set. The hierarchical clustering algorithm in Sklearn library is used to implement the algorithm.

Algorithm 1. Hierarchical clustering algorithm pseudocode

1: **function** AGGLOMERATIVECLUSTERING
2:    $affinity$='euclidean'
3:    $compute\_full\_tree$='auto'
4:    $connectivity$=None
5:    $linkage$='word'
6:    $memory$=None
7:    $n\_clusters$=2
8:    $pooling\_func$=function mean at 0x110d8f840
9: **end function**

The constructor parameters of class AgglomerativeClustering are: $n\_clusters$, $linkage$, and $affinity$. These three parameters are described below:

– **n_clusters (number of clusters):** It is required by the user. In general, the number of clusters does not need to be specified for the aggregation level clustering. But the *sklearn* class needs to specify the number of clusters. The algorithm will judge the final merging basis according to the number of clusters, and this parameter will affect the clustering quality.
– **Linkage (Connection methods):** A measure of the distance between clusters. Specifically, it includes minimum distance, maximum distance and average distance. Corresponding to the cluster fusion method, the minimum distance between observation points is the cluster distance, the maximum distance between observation points is the cluster distance, and the average distance between observation points is the cluster distance. In general, average distance is a compromise.
– **Affinity (Connection metric option):** It is a distance calculation method between clusters, including various Distance calculation methods of Euclidean

space and non-Euclidean space. In addition, this parameter can be set to pre-computed, that is, the distance matrix computed by the user input. The generation method of distance matrix: assuming that the user has N observation points, then the distance list between pairs of n points is constructed in turn, that is, a distance list of length $n * (n - 1)/2$. The distance matrix can then be constructed using the squareform function of the dist library of scipy.spatial.distance. The advantage of this approach is that users can use their own defined methods to calculate the distance between any two observation points and then cluster them.

4.2   The Experimental Results

In order to ensure better classification effect, several adjustments were made to the parameter $n\_clusters$ during the experiment, and $n\_clusters$ were set as 5, 6, 7, 8, and 9 respectively. A better classification effect was achieved when $n\_clusters = 5$ was found through the pattern results. At the same time, the 11 attributes of source IP, source port, destination IP, destination port, transmission protocol, number of packets, number of bytes, total load, transmission time, the number of packets from source IP and the number of packets from destination IP were tested respectively. We find that in this application scenario, if the classification effect is acceptable, in order to reduce the computational intensity, only retaining the 5 tuples of network packets can achieve better classification effect. The experimental results are shown in the Fig. 3 and Fig. 4. Where each

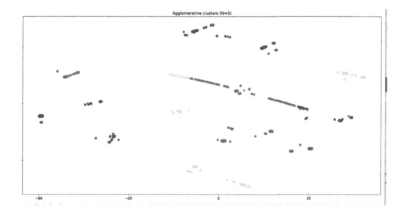

Fig. 3. Cluster renderings.

data records the next row of Numbers is the classification result. By analyzing the classification results, it is found that the Internet traffic and Intranet traffic can be quickly classified by using the above classification methods, and the traffic of different ports in the Intranet can be classified. Combined with the characteristics mentioned above, such as limited network access range, distinct network traffic

['192', '168', '2', '188'] 42268 ['192', '168', '2', '132'] 11111 TCP
3
['192', '168', '2', '188'] 58232 ['192', '168', '2', '132'] 11357 TCP
3
['192', '168', '2', '132'] 56008 ['192', '168', '2', '1'] 53 UDP
3
['192', '168', '2', '132'] 48449 ['192', '168', '2', '1'] 53 UDP
3
['192', '168', '2', '1'] 53 ['192', '168', '2', '132'] 56008 UDP
4
['111', '161', '121', '2'] 80 ['192', '168', '2', '132'] 1873 TCP
1
['27', '221', '30', '106'] 80 ['192', '168', '2', '132'] 1874 TCP
1
['80', '239', '205', '50'] 80 ['192', '168', '2', '132'] 1875 TCP
1
['192', '168', '2', '132'] 1875 ['80', '239', '205', '50'] 80 TCP
2
['192', '168', '2', '132'] 60679 ['192', '168', '2', '1'] 53 UDP
3
['192', '168', '2', '1'] 53 ['192', '168', '2', '132'] 60679 UDP
4
['80', '239', '205', '50'] 80 ['192', '168', '2', '132'] 1875 TCP
1
['192', '168', '2', '132'] 1875 ['80', '239', '205', '50'] 80 TCP
2
['192', '168', '2', '132'] 49140 ['192', '168', '2', '1'] 53 UDP
3
['192', '168', '2', '1'] 53 ['192', '168', '2', '132'] 49140 UDP
4
['192', '168', '2', '132'] 54757 ['192', '168', '2', '1'] 53 UDP
3
['192', '168', '2', '1'] 53 ['192', '168', '2', '132'] 54757 UDP
4
['192', '168', '2', '132'] 1880 ['13', '33', '169', '4'] 443 TCP
2

Fig. 4. Clustering results.

characteristics and clear network access path, they play an important role in quickly discovering abnormal traffic in the network and formulating security policies for network security equipment.

For example, in Table 1 the following strategies are sorted out against the firewall by using the above classification methods:

4.3 Expert Experience

In the airport production network, every device and every system in the network should set their own access control permissions. Once the access control permissions are exceeded, it will be judged that they are using illegally. This illegal operation is likely to come from the attacker. Therefore, this paper uses expert experience to establish an access control matrix, as shown in see Fig. 5. Access control refers to the means by which the system limits the ability of users to use data resources on their identities and their predefined policy groups. It is usually used by system administrator to control user s access to server, directory, file and other network resources. Access control is an important foundation of system confidentiality, integrity, availability and legitimate use, which is one of the key strategies of network security and resource protection. On the meanwhile, it is also the different authorization access of subject to object itself or its resources according to some control strategies or permissions. The main purpose of access control is to restrict the access of the subject to the object, so as to ensure the effective use and management of data resources within the legal scope. In order

Table 1. Strategy table for firewalls based on classification method.

Source address	Destination address	Open port number	Open protocol
192.168.2.*	*	80	TCP
192.168.3.*	*	443	TCP
192.168.4.*	172.10.10.5	9600	TCP
192.168.5.*	172.10.10.5	9600	TCP

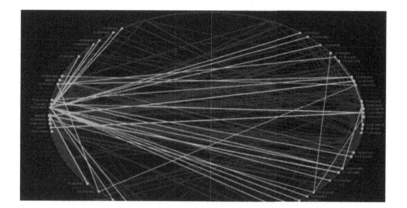

Fig. 5. Access control matrix.

to achieve the above purpose, access control needs to complete two tasks: identifying and confirming the user who accesses the system, and deciding what type of access the user can make to a system resource. By establishing the authority control matrix and combining with the hierarchical clustering method, the abnormal traffic in the network can be identified more quickly and the strategy can be sorted out.

5   Conclusion

In this paper, the hierarchical clustering method is used to classify the airport network traffic. To a certain extent, the airport network traffic can be sorted out quickly to find the abnormal traffic in the network. At the same time, this method can quickly help network administrators sort out network security policies and improve the security protection ability of airport network. But the experiment also found that this method also has some shortcomings. For example, the classification is not detailed enough, which results in the annihilation of a small amount of traffic in the process of classification, but often these small amounts of traffic are malicious traffic. To solve these problems, on the one hand, the classification algorithm is proposed to be improved and the algorithm model is further improved by combining the particularity of airport network. On the other hand, the analysis model is specially established for the relatively small traffic in the network to identify the malicious traffic in the network more accurately.

References

1. Jiang, D.: The construction of smart city information system based on the Internet of Things and cloud computing. Comput. Commun. **150**, 158–166 (2020)
2. Dovrolis, C. (ed.): PAM 2005. LNCS, vol. 3431. Springer, Heidelberg (2005). https://doi.org/10.1007/b135479
3. Williams N., et al.: A preliminary performance comparison of five machine learning algorithms for practical IP traffic flow classification. In: ACM Special Interest Group on Data Communication, vol. 36, no. 5, pp. 5–16 (2006)
4. Huang, C., Dun, J.: A distributed PSO-SVM hybrid system with feature selection and parameter optimization. Appl. Soft Comput. **8**(4), 1381–1391 (2008)
5. Galili, T.: dendextend: an R package for visualizing, adjusting and comparing trees of hierarchical clustering. Bioinformatics **31**(22), 3718–3720 (2015)
6. Arbib, C., Moghaddam, M.T., Muccini, H.: IoT flows: a network flow model application to building evacuation. In: Dell'Amico, M., Gaudioso, M., Stecca, G. (eds.) A View of Operations Research Applications in Italy, 2018. ASS, vol. 2, pp. 115–131. Springer, Cham (2019). https://doi.org/10.1007/978-3-030-25842-9_9
7. Hui-Min Z., Lin-Sheng F., Xue-Huan Q.: Network flow identification strategy based on improved hierarchy CBF. J. Acad. Armored Force Eng. (2018)
8. Sinha, A., Modiano, E.: Optimal control for generalized network-flow problems. IEEE/ACM Trans. Netw. **26**(1), 506–519 (2018)
9. Mingoti, S.A., Lima, J.O.: Comparing SOM neural network with fuzzy c-means, K-means and traditional hierarchical clustering algorithms. Eur. J. Oper. Res. **174**(3), 1742–1759 (2006)
10. Su, L., et al.: Hierarchical clustering based network traffic data reduction for improving suspicious flow detection. In: 2018 17th IEEE International Conference on Trust, Security and Privacy in Computing and Communications/12th IEEE International Conference on Big Data Science and Engineering (Trust-Com/BigDataSE) (2018)

DPC: A Delay-Driven Prioritized TCP Congestion Control Algorithm for Data Center Networks

Xianliang Jiang$^{(\boxtimes)}$, Jiahua Zhu, and Guang Jin

Ningbo University, Ningbo 315211, China
`jiangxianliang@nbu.edu.cn`

Abstract. Data centers have become one of the crucial infrastructures to support diversified internet services. Meanwhile, optimizing the TCP congestion control algorithm in data centers is still a hot research topic and faces some challenges (e.g. the high flow completion time of short flows) in recent years. To minimize the flow completion time of small flows, meet the deadline demand of time-sensitive flows, and maximize the throughput of large flows simultaneously, many customized data center TCPs have been proposed for data center networks, e.g. DCTCP and L^2DCT. They can get good performance in most network scenarios. However, most of them require the support of the well-configured explicit congestion notification from in-network switches. Different from previous schemes, we propose a delay-sensitive TCP congestion control algorithm, named DPC, for data centers based on the packet delay and the flow priority in this paper. Specifically, the congestion window adjustment of DPC is dominated by the flow priority, the packet delay and the extent of the network congestion. Different from L^2DCT, the low-priority flows of DPC release the occupied bandwidth for high-priority flows when the network is in a mild congestion state. This guarantees that DPC can achieve differentiated congestion control for flows with different priorities. Actually, DPC is close to the priority-based preemption scheduling. Through extensive simulations using a network simulator, we prove that DPC can minimize the flow completion time of short flows and the number of TCP's retransmission timeout comparing with TCP SACK, DCTCP and L^2DCT, mitigate the micro burst of short flows.

Keywords: Data center network · Congestion control · Packet delay · Flow priority

1 Introduction

The development of high-speed networking techniques makes data centers, employing the transmission control protocol (TCP) to exchange massive data,

This work is supported by the Zhejiang Provincial Natural Science Foundation of China (LY20F020008, LY18F020011), Public Technology Projects of Zhejiang Province (LGG18F020007), K. C. Wong Magna Fund in Ningbo University.

© Springer Nature Singapore Pte Ltd. 2020
G. Xu et al. (Eds.): FCS 2020, CCIS 1286, pp. 459–474, 2020.
https://doi.org/10.1007/978-981-15-9739-8_35

become a pivotal infrastructure to support vast tightly-coupled and time-constrained computing tasks, e.g. web search, social network, recommender system, *etc.*. Meanwhile, the emerging applications result in the diverse demands (e.g. high-throughput for long-term flows and low-latency for time-sensitive flows) for data transmission in data centers. However, because of the partition/aggregation and highly concurrent traffic pattern of data centers, most legacy TCPs with the improper congestion control policy is inefficient (e.g. throughput-collapse) to exchange massive data. The user-perceived quality of service and the revenue of companies are inevitable to be affected by them. Therefore, how to design and implement a high-throughput, low-latency and deadline-aware TCP congestion control algorithm is a crux to accelerate the data transmission in data centers.

To control the sending rate, some existing data center TCPs keep the increasing of the congestion window when the network is in the mild congestion state (the queue backlog without congestion signal generated by explicit congestion notification (ECN) [1] or packets dropping). This is inappropriate when high priority (short) flows coexist with low-priority (large) flows and could induce the high flow completion time (FCT). Although the switch scheduling algorithms [2,3] can guarantee the performance of high-priority flows when coexist with low-priority flows, the program of switch hardwares must be modified or configured inevitably. Note that, we only focus on the pure end-to-end TCPs with or without the support of ECN [4] and random early detection (RED [5]) algorithm from in-network switches in this paper.

Inspired by L^{2}DCT [6], we design and implement a delay and priority sensitive data center TCP, named DPC, without the support of ECN from in-network switches in this paper. When the network is in the mild congestion state, flows with high priority increase the sending rate while low priority flows decrease the sending rate. Similar to L^{2}DCT, DPC depends on the transmitted flow size to adjust the congestion window. But, different from L^{2}DCT, DPC only uses the transmitted flow size to compute the flow priority. Combining the flow priority and packet delay, DPC can achieve the differentiated TCP congestion control. As a matter of fact, the packet latency has been widely used for the design of delay-based TCPs [7,8] in other types of networks.

Note that, due to the lack of the flow information (the total flow size and flow deadline are unknown in advance) in most cases, we commonly adopt the transmitted flow size (like L^{2}DCT) to build our new TCP in this paper. If the flow information is given, our new TCP can be easily extended. In addition, considering the traffic characteristics ($\leq$200 KB: mice, $\leq$1 MB: cat, $>$1 MB: elephant) [6,9] in data centers, reducing the FCT of mice flows while keeping the high throughput of elephant flows as much as possible is crucial to meet the demands of data center transports. Hence, the key goal of DPC is to solve the high FCT of short flows ($\leq$200 KB in our experiments) caused by the competing large flows and the vast retransmission timeout of short flows.

Roughly, the **contributions** of this paper include (1) a method to compute the flow priority using the amount of transmitted data (and the remaining time to flow deadline), (2) a redesigned TCP congestion control algorithm based on the flow priority, the round trip time (RTT)-based network congestion degree, and the estimated queuing delay. To verify the performance of DPC, we implement it in a network simulator v2 (NS-2) [10] and conduct extensive experiments with different topologies and traffic workloads like [11].

The rest of this paper is organized as follows. Section 2 gives a short summary about the data transmission methods in data centers. Then, we present the detailed design and implementation of DPC in Sect. 3. In Sect. 4, we conduct extensive simulations using NS-2 to evaluate DPC. Section 5 provides concluding remarks.

2   Related Work

It has been found that TCPs for traditional networks are hard to be applied in data centers, which is featured by high bandwidth, low latency, and high concurrent data transfer. Recently, many data center TCP variants have been proposed.

In [1], Alizadeh *et al.* utilized ECN bits stream to estimate the extent of the network congestion and then proposed a datacenter TCP (DCTCP) to stabilize the queue length around a threshold K. When a packet loss occurs, DCTCP adopts the extent of the network congestion to adjust the congestion window. The experimental results show that DCTCP can enhance the performance of the standard TCP (TCP Reno) and mitigate the TCP Incast problem. However, due to the unpredictability of the flow deadline, DCTCP can not meet the demand of deadline-sensitive flows. To solve the problem, Vamanan *et al.* [12] proposed a deadline-aware TCP (D^2TCP). When the congestion event occurs, flows close to the deadline are allocated with more link bandwidths. The results show that D^2TCP can reduce the deadline missed rate of deadline-sensitive flows. In [13], Wilson *et al.* proposed a deadline-aware protocol (D^3), which allocates more bottleneck bandwidths to urgent flows on the basis of the explicit rate control mechanism in switches. The experimental results show that D^3 is better than DCTCP.

Furthermore, the amount of the transmitted data can also be used to adjust the congestion window and achieve implicit priority scheduling with least attained service (LAS). In [6], Munir *et al.* adopted the flow sizes, which are estimated based on the amount of data a flow has sent so far, and the extent of the network congestion to regulate the congestion window and proposed the L^2DCT protocol. However, L^2DCT is a deadline agnostic protocol and can't ensure the transmission performance of deadline-sensitive flows. To solve the problem, A^2DTCP [14] was proposed. It adopts the urgent degree of flows and the extent of the network congestion to adjust the congestion window. Note that the urgent degree of flows is estimated by the remaining flow size and deadline. In addition, considering the characteristic of data center networks, some receiver-based congestion control protocols, e.g. ICTCP [15], IA-TCP [16] and OFTCP [17], were also proposed. They can solve the network congestion in the last hop.

In [18], Alizadeh *et al.* presented a reserved bandwidth mechanism (named HULL) to minimize the FCT, caused by the large queuing delay, of deadline-sensitive flows in switches. However, HULL needs the support of the switch hardware and is hard to be deployed in current data centers. In [19,20], QCN and its variants were proposed. In these schemes, flows can be scheduled and controlled by the pause mechanism in switches. As an centralized scheduling scheme, PDQ [21] adopts the Earliest Deadline First (EDF) and Shortest Job First (SJF) schedulers to guarantee the transmission performance of deadline-sensitive flows. In [2], Alizadeh *et al.* proposed a clean-slate scheme, named pFabric, to provide near theoretically optimal FCTs. The scheme decouples flow scheduling from rate control and provides a priority-based scheduling/dropping mechanism. In [22], a clean-slate scheme, called TFC, based on the explicit transmission control mechanism was proposed. It adopts tokens to denote the link bandwidth resource and allocates tokens to each sender every time slot. The results show that TFC can achieve high throughput and fast convergence, as well as low queuing delay and packets loss in various scenarios. In [23], a server-based flow scheduling (SFS) scheme was proposed to minimize the FCT through traffic control and flow scheduling. Each server dispatches flows according to the flow priority. It keeps the highest-priority flow active and pauses the low-priority ones when the network congestion occurs. In [24], He *et al.* proposed a light-weight and flexible scheme, called AC/DC TCP. It enforces per-flow congestion control in Open vSwitch based on the fine-grained control over tenant TCP stacks.

In addition, Munir *et al.* proposed a transport framework, called PASE [25], which synthesizes end-host TCPs, in-network prioritization, and distributed arbitrators. In deployment, PASE is friendly and does not require changing the network fabric. In [26], Perry *et al.* proposed a data center network framework, called Fastpass, to achieve the high bandwidth utilization with zero queueing. The scheme can provide low median and tail latencies for flows, along with high data rates between machines, and flexible network resource allocation policies. In [27], a new transport framework was designed to achieve the near-optimal performance of pFabric and the commodity network design of Fastpass. Specifically, a host-based scheduling mechanism was proposed. It involves request-to-send (RTS), per-packet token assignment, and receiver-based selection of pending flows.

3   DPC Protocol

In this section, we illustrate the design and implementation of DPC. Different from previous data center TCP (e.g. L^2DCT [6]), DPC adopts a priority-aware method to regulate the size of its congestion window without knowing the flow information (including the flow size and deadline). In implementation, DPC combines the flow priority, the queuing delay and the extent of the network congestion to increase or decrease the size of its congestion window. In Sect. 3.1, we give an overview of the DPC structure. And then a detailed DPC congestion avoidance algorithm is introduced in Sect. 3.2.

3.1 DPC Overview

The goal of DPC is to achieve the differentiated congestion control for TCP flows with different priorities. It's close to the priority-based preemption scheduling. DPC has three key components including RTT Measurement Engine (RME), Flow Priority Estimator (FPE), and Congestion Control Engine (CCE) as shown in Fig. 1. The detailed descriptions on the three components will be given later. Note that, DPC relies on the packet delay (or RTT) instead of the ECN marking to indicate the network congestion. This can guarantee to achieve the pure end-to-end TCP congestion control without the support (proper configurations for ECN marking or priority queues) of in-network switches.

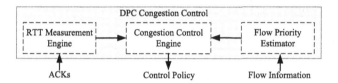

Fig. 1. An overview of DPC congestion control

To estimate the packet delay precisely, RME adopts the timestamp in the TCP header, which is a selectable feature in current network stack [28]. This method has been widely used in previous schemes (e.g. DX [29]). Note that, because of the clock synchronization problem, we adopt RTT instead of one-way delay to implement DPC in this paper. In addition, FPE computes the flow priority with the transmitted data volume. CCE regulates the congestion window of DPC according to the flow priority, the queuing delay, and the network congestion level. In Sect. 3.2, more details about FPE and CCE will be provided.

3.2 Congestion Avoidance Algorithm

In DPC, we only redesign the congestion avoidance stage of the standard TCP (Reno) while keep other features unchanged. Next, we present how to compute the flow priority with the transmitted data volume and estimate the network congestion level with packets' RTT, and an integrated congestion avoidance algorithm.

Computing Flow Priority. To compute the flow priority, p, in FPE, we only consider the transmitted flow size, f_s, because the flow information, like the flow size and deadline, for data center applications is not always available [11]. In future, if we can get more detailed information from the application layer, we want to design an enhanced congestion control algorithm to support information-agnostic and information-knowable data center applications simultaneously.

Considering the size range of mice, cat and elephant flows [6], we define two thresholds, m_c and c_e, to differentiate them. Note, there is no unified standard

---

Algorithm 1. RTT-based Congestion Level Estimation

1: **for** each ACK **do**
2:     **if** $RTT_{min} == 0 \;||\; RTT < RTT_{min}$ **then**
3:         $RTT_{min} \leftarrow RTT$;
4:     **end if**
5:     $RTT_o = RTT_o + 1$;
6:     **if** $RTT > RTT_{min} + O_{th}$ **then**
7:         $RTT_s = RTT_s + 1$;
8:     **end if**
9: **end for**
10: **for** every window **do**
11:     $f \leftarrow RTT_s/RTT_o$;
12:     $\alpha \leftarrow (1 - g) \cdot \alpha + g \cdot f$;
13:     $RTT_s \leftarrow 0$;
14:     $RTT_o \leftarrow 0$;
15: **end for**

---

to limit the size range of mice, cat and elephant flows. To map f_s, we also define the flow weight, s_c, and its upper bound, s_{max}, and lower bound, s_{min}. Note, $s_{max} = 2.5$ and $s_{min} = 0.125$ are empirical values like [6]. s_c varies in $[s_{min}, s_{max}]$ as

$$s_c = \begin{cases} s_{max}, & f_s \leq m_c \\ s_{min}, & f_s \geq c_e \\ s_{min} + (s_{max} - s_{min}) \cdot \frac{c_e - f_s}{c_e - m_c}, & \textbf{otherwise} \end{cases} \qquad (1)$$

where m_c and c_e are fixed to 200 KB and 1 MB like [6]. Using s_c, we can update p as

$$p = \frac{s_c - s_{min}}{s_{max} - s_{min}}. \qquad (2)$$

Note, we fix $p = p_c$ when $p < p_c$ (a threshold). In this paper, $p_c = 0.125$ is an empirical value to balance the responsiveness and efficiency of DPC congestion control.

Estimating Congestion Level. How to estimate the network congestion level, α, is a challenging problem. In [1], Alizadeh *et al.* propose an ECN-based method. It needs the support of in-network switches with proper configurations. To get a pure end-to-end data center TCP, we adopt a RTT-based (named **virtual ECN**) method like [30] in CCE. Note that, vECN is an emulated ECN mechanism using RTT information on end hosts. The supports from in-network switches is unnecessary. This means that vECN can be implemented in pure end-to-end manner. More details are shown in Algorithm 1. RTT_{min} is an observed minimal RTT in a fixed time period. RTT_o and RTT_s are the total number of received RTT and the number of marked RTT in every sending window, respectively. O_{th} is a virtual ECN threshold to support the estimation of network congestion level. $g = 0.0625$ is a weighted factor like [30].

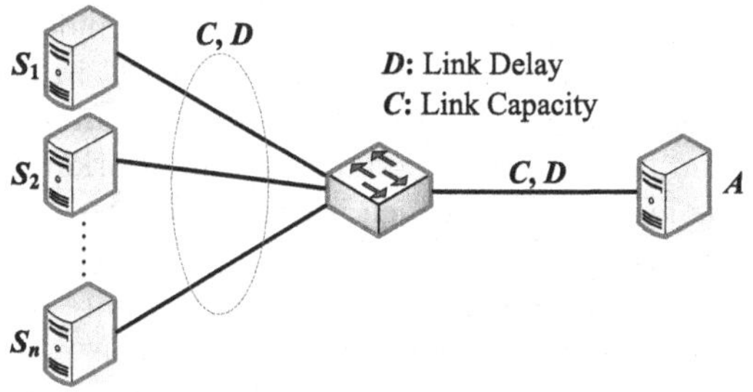

Fig. 2. The single bottleneck link topology

Congestion Control Model. On the basis of p, α and the queuing delay, Q_d, which can be calculated by $RTT - RTT_{min}$, DPC can regulate the congestion window in the CCE component as follows.

$$\textbf{Each RTT: } cwnd \leftarrow cwnd + c_{inc}$$
$$\textbf{vECN: } cwnd \leftarrow (1 - \frac{\alpha^p}{2}) \cdot cwnd \tag{3}$$

where the increment of the congestion window size, c_{inc}, is updated as following.

$$c_{inc} = (p^\alpha \cdot O_{th} - Q_d)/(O_{th}). \tag{4}$$

The goal of the congestion control model is to guarantee the data transfer of high priority flows when the queue backlog appears at in-network switches. If α is zero (no congestion), high priority flows have the identical speed to seize the bottleneck bandwidth with low priority flows. This ensures the high link utilization of the bottleneck link. If $\alpha > 0$ (mild or heavy congestion), low priority flows decrease their sending rate earlier than high priority flow. For example, suppose that two flows with different p values (high priority: 0.8 and low priority: 0.3) compete the bottleneck bandwidth and α is 0.6, the p^α is 0.87 and 0.48, respectively. Hence, the c_{inc} of the high priority flow is larger than the low priority flow. When Q_d is greater than $p^\alpha \cdot O_{th}$, the DPC sender will decrease the sending rate. In short, the two mechanisms jointly ensure the performance of DPC. To achieve the high utilization and low queue backlog, we adopt a similar method like [30] to set O_{th}. It can guarantee the performance of DPC when all flows are with the lowest priority.

4   Performance Evaluation

To evaluate DPC, we conduct extensive experiments with an event-driven network simulator (NS-2) [10], which has been extended with DPC, DCTCP [1] and L^{2}DCT [6]. Therein, DCTCP is a seminal TCP for data centers and widely used as a benchmark. The design of DPC is motivated by L^{2}DCT. Because DPC is a pure end-to-end scheme, we omit the comparison with PIAS [11] in this paper.

We first give an in-depth analysis on the congestion window, aggregated flow throughput, queuing behaviour and robustness of DPC in a single bottleneck topology, which is shown in Fig. 2. After that, we adopt an online data intensive (OLDI) traffic (including web search and data mining workload like [11]) to evaluate DPC in a spine-leaf topology which is shown in Fig. 6. All these topologies are widely used in previous works.

Considering the agnostic flow information and the pure end-to-end features, we just select TCP SACK, DCTCP and L^2DCT with ECN-enabled RED as compared schemes, which parameters are their optimal values. Without any other statements, the ECN marking threshold, K, and the upper bound of RED is 65 (widely adopted by compared schemes) and 240 packets for all queues. The link capacity and delay are 10 Gbps and 25 μs, respectively. The packet size is 1500B (1460B payload). The RTO_{min} and initial window of all protocols are fixed to 10 ms as suggested in [11] and 2 packets (10 packets in OLDI simulations), respectively. For DPC, Q_{th} is configured according to the ECN marking threshold, that is $Q_{th} = K*1500*8/10$ Gbps. And DPC use the default DropTail algorithm for all queues.

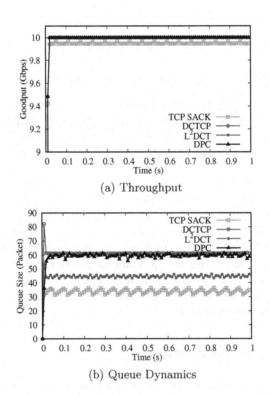

(a) Throughput

(b) Queue Dynamics

Fig. 3. Throughput and queue length dynamics of two long-lived DPC flows

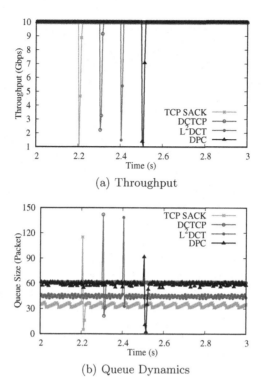

(a) Throughput

(b) Queue Dynamics

Fig. 4. Robustness of two long-lived DPC flows when a sudden burst of 100 short flows arrives at the same time

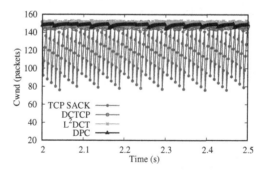

Fig. 5. The evolution of DPC's congestion window

Next, we first discuss the micro features of DPC using a single bottleneck topology, which has 100 μs base RTT. After that, we conduct several large-scale simulations using a spine-leaf topology and two real data center traffic loads to prove the realistic performance of DPC.

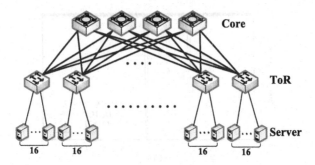

Fig. 6. The spine-leaf topology

4.1 Long-Lived Flows

Firstly, we set two long-lived DPC flows, whose traffic is generated by FTP applications to demonstrate the long-lived flows' performance of DPC in this experiment. The aggregate throughput and transient queue length of two flows are shown in Fig. 3. As can be seen from the results, all compared schemes except TCP SACK can get the similar throughput. The queue length for all schemes is close to K. These also prove that DPC has the features of the high throughput and low latency like other ECN-enabled schemes.

4.2 Robustness with Micro Burst

Secondly, we set two long-lived flows (start at 0 s) and 100 short-lived flows to evaluate the robustness of DPC with the micro burst of short flows. The block size of short-lived flows is 64 KB [15]. Also, the aggregate throughput of the long-lived flow and the transient queue length for all compared schemes are shown in Fig. 4. To facilitate the comparison, we set different start times (2.2 s for TCP SACK, 2.3 s for DCTCP, 2.4 s for L^2DCT, 2.5 s for DPC) for short-lived flows

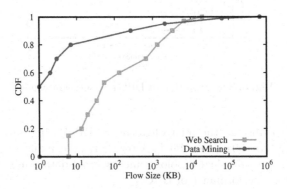

Fig. 7. The distribution of traffic workload

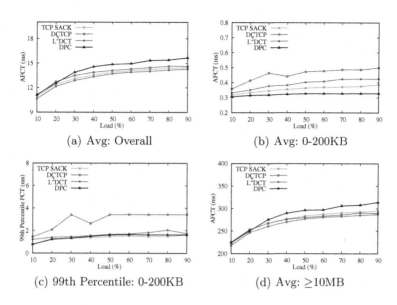

Fig. 8. The FCT statistics of different schemes with the data mining workload ($RTO_{min} = 1\,\mathrm{ms}$)

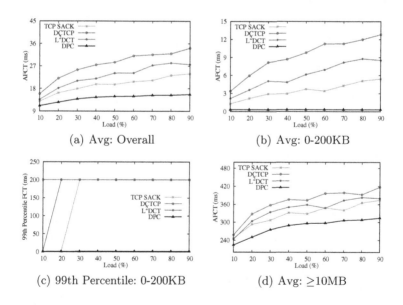

Fig. 9. The FCT statistics of different schemes with the data mining workload ($RTO_{min} = 200\,\mathrm{ms}$)

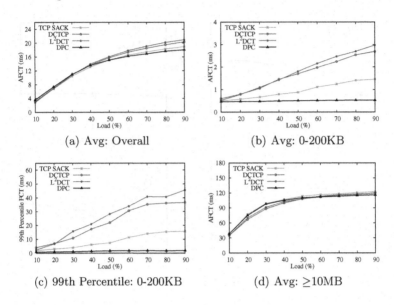

Fig. 10. The FCT statistics of different schemes with the web search workload ($RTO_{min} = 1\,\text{ms}$)

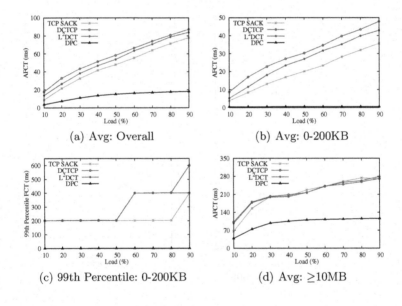

Fig. 11. The FCT statistics of different schemes with the web search workload ($RTO_{min} = 200\,\text{ms}$)

in different schemes. As can be seen from the results, all compared schemes can quickly adapt to the sudden bursts of short-lived flows. But, DPC can absorb the micro burst generated by short-lived flows with a smaller buffer.

4.3 Congestion Window Evolution

Thirdly, we set one long-lived flow (start at 0 s) to elaborate the congestion window evolution of DPC. As can be seen from Fig. 5, the congestion window of DPC is more stable than compared schemes. For TCP SACK, the congestion window is in drastic fluctuation because of the aggressive cutdown policy. This uncovers the reason why TCP SACK has worst aggregated throughput as shown in Fig. 3.

4.4 OLDI Performance

To prove the realistic performance of DPC for OLDI applications, we conduct several large-scale simulations using a spine-leaf topology and two real data center traffic loads.

Setting: In this experiment, the leaf-spine topology has 144 hosts, 9 top-of-rack(ToR) switches and 4 core switches. Each ToR switch has 16×10 Gbps downlinks with the link delay of 30 μs to hosts, and 4×40 Gbps uplinks with the link delay 5 μs to core switches. To maintain the consistency with compared schemes, we set the initial window size to 10, and employ the equal-cost multipath for the links' load balancing. For RTO_{min}, we set two different values, 1 ms and 200 ms (default configuration for operating systems), for different simulations. Furthermore, we adopt two traffic load distributions (shown in Fig. 7), which is widely used in compared schemes, to investigate DPC. All simulations last for 10000 flows.

The results in Fig. 8 and 10 show the FCT for all schemes when RTO_{min} is 1 ms. Fig. 9 and 11 present the FCT when RTO_{min} is 200 ms. To explore the root cause of the high FCT, we provide the number of the retransmission timeout in Fig. 12 and 13. Note that the number of the retransmission timeout for DPC is zero. As can be seen from the results, the FCT (including average FCT(AFCT) and 99th percentile FCT) of short flows for DPC is better than TCP SACK, DCTCP, L²DCT when RTO_{min} is 1 ms. But, when RTO_{min} is 200 ms, the FCT of DPC, <1 ms for the AFCT of short flows and <2 ms for the 99th percentile FCT of short flows, is tremendous lower than TCP SACK, DCTCP, L²DCT. We think this is caused by the large number of the retransmission timeout as shown in Fig. 12 and 13. All in all, the experimental results prove that DPC can achieve the differentiated congestion control for flows with different priorities and reduce the average and 99th percentile FCT of short flows when coexist with the large flows.

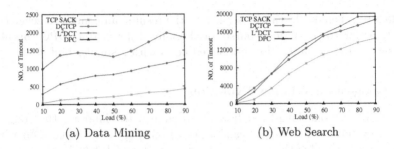

(a) Data Mining   (b) Web Search

Fig. 12. The number of timeout for different schemes in leaf-spine topology (RTO_{min} = 1 ms)

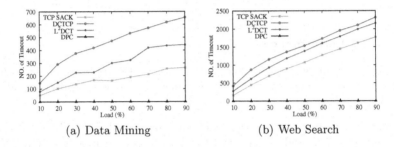

(a) Data Mining   (b) Web Search

Fig. 13. The number of timeout for different schemes in leaf-spine topology (RTO_{min} = 200 ms)

5   Conclusion

The congestion control in data centers is still a challenging problem. To meet the demand of delay-sensitive and throughput-sensitive flows, various TCP variants for data centers have been proposed in the last few years. However, most of them need the support of in-network switches. In this paper, we presented a delay-sensitive data center TCP, named DPC, based on the packet delay, the flow priority and the network congestion level. It's a pure end-to-end TCP. In DPC, High priority flows can preempt the occupied bandwidth of low priority flows when the network is in the mild congestion state. If the bottleneck link has spare bandwidth, DPC flows can occupy it rapidly and fairly.

Using NS2, we conduct extensive simulations with different network scenarios. The experimental results indicated that DPC is better than TCP SACK, DCTCP and L^{2}DCT. In future, we will implement DPC in Linux kernel and test it in a small-scale data center network.

References

1. Alizadeh, M., Greenberg, A., Maltz, D., et al.: Data center TCP (DCTCP). In: Proceedings of the SIGCOMM, New Delhi, India, August 2010 (2010)

2. Alizadeh, M., Yang, S., Sharif, M., et al.: pFabric: minimal near-optimal datacenter transport. In: Proceedings of the SIGCOMM, Hong Kong, China, August 2013 (2013)

3. Cho, I., Jang, K., Han, D.: Credit-scheduled delay-bounded congestion control for datacenters. In: Proceedings of the SIGCOMM, Los Angeles, USA, August 2017 (2017)

4. Ramakrishnan, K., Floyd, S., Black, D.: The addition of explicit congestion notification (ECN) to IP. RFC3168, September 2001. https://tools.ietf.org/html/rfc3168

5. Floyd, S., Jacobson, V.: Random early detection gateways for congestion avoidance. IEEE/ACM Trans. Netw. 1(4), 397–413 (1993)

6. Munir, A., Qazi, I.A., Uzmi, Z.A., et al.: Minimizing flow completion times in data centers. In: Proceedings of the INFOCOM, Toronto, Canada, April 2014 (2014)

7. Arun, V., Balakrishnan, H.: Copa: practical delay-based congestion control for the internet. In: Proceedings of the NSDI, Renton, USA, April 2018 (2018)

8. Dong, M., Meng, T., Zarchy, D., et al.: PCC Vivace: online-learning congestion control. In: Proceedings of the NSDI, Renton, USA, April 2018 (2018)

9. Chen, L., Chen, K., Bai, W., et al.: Scheduling mix-flows in commodity datacenters with karuna. In: Proceedings of the SIGCOMM, Florianopolis, Brazil, August 2016 (2016)

10. Chen, L., Chen, K., Bai, W., et al.: The Network Simulator NS-2 (2018). http://www.isi.edu/nsnam/ns/

11. Bai, W., Chen, L., Chen, K., et al.: PIAS: practical information-agnostic flow scheduling for commodity data centers. IEEE/ACM Trans. Netw. 25(4), 1954–1967 (2017)

12. Vamanan, B., Hasan, J., Vijaykumar, T.N.: Deadline-aware datacenter TCP (D2TCP). In: Proceedings of the SIGCOMM, Helsinki, Finland, August 2012 (2012)

13. Wilson, C., Ballani, H., Karagiannis, T., et al.: Better never than late: meeting deadlines in datacenter networks. In: Proceedings of the SIGCOMM, pp. 50–61 (2011)

14. Zhang, T., Wang, J., Huang, J., et al.: Adaptive-acceleration data center TCP. IEEE Trans. Comput. 64(6), 1522–1533 (2015)

15. Wu, H., Feng, Z., Guo, C., et al.: ICTCP: incast congestion control for TCP in data center networks. IEEE/ACM Trans. Netw. 21(2), 345–358 (2013)

16. Hwang, J., Yoo, J., Choi, N.: IA-TCP: a rate based incast-avoidance algorithm for TCP in data center networks. In: Proceedings of the ICC, pp. 1292–1296 (2012)

17. Huang, J., Li, S., Han, R., et al.: Receiver-driven fair congestion control for TCP outcast in data center networks. J. Netw. Comput. Appl. 131, 75–88 (2019)

18. Alizadeh, M., Kabbani, A., Edsall, T., et al.: Less is more: trading a little bandwidth for ultra-low latency in the data center. In: Proceedings of the NSDI, pp. 253–266 (2012)

19. Alizadeh, M., Atikoglu, B., Kabbani, A., et al.: Data center transport mechanisms: congestion control theory and IEEE standardization. In: Proceedings of Annual Allerton Conference on Communication, Control, and Computing, pp. 1270–1277 (2008)

20. Zhang, Y., Ansari, N.: Fair quantized congestion notification in data center networks. IEEE Trans. Commun. 61(11), 4690–4699 (2013)

21. Hong, C., Caesar, M., Godfrey, P.B.: Finishing flows quickly with preemptive scheduling. In: Proceedings of the SIGCOMM, pp. 127–138 (2012)

22. Zhang, J., Ren, F., Shu, R., et al.: TFC: token flow control in data center networks. In: Proceedings of the EuroSys (2016)

23. Zhang, J., Zhang, D., Huang, K., et al.: Minimizing datacenter flow completion times with server-based flow scheduling. Comput. Netw. **94**, 360–374 (2016)
24. He, K., Rozner, E., Agarwal, K., et al.: AC/DC TCP: virtual congestion control enforcement for datacenter networks. In: Proceedings of the SIGCOMM (2016)
25. Munir, A., Baig, G., Irteza, S.M., et al.: Friends, not foes: synthesizing existing transport strategies for data center networks. In: Proceedings of the SIGCOMM, pp. 491–502 (2014)
26. Perry, J., Ousterhout, A., Balakrishnan, H., et al.: Fastpass: a centralized "zero-queue" datacenter network. In: Proceedings of the SIGCOMM, pp. 307–318 (2014)
27. Gao, P.X., Narayan, A., Kumar, G., et al.: pHost: distributed near-optimal data-center transport over commodity network fabric. In: Proceedings of the CoNEXT (2015)
28. Leong, W.K., Wang, Z., Leong, B.: TCP congestion control beyond bandwidth-delay product for mobile cellular networks. In: Proceedings of the CoNEXT, Seoul, South Korea, December 2017 (2017)
29. Lee, C., Park, C., Jang, K., et al.: DX: latency-based congestion control for data-centers. IEEE/ACM Trans. Netw. **25**(1), 335–348 (2017)
30. Shewmaker, A.G., Maltzahn, C., Obraczka, K., et al.: TCP inigo: ambidextrous congestion control. In: Proceedings of the ICCCN, Hawaii, USA, August 2016 (2016)

SA Dots: A Sensitive and Self-adaptable Framework for Cross-Region DDoS Processing

Li Su$^{(\boxtimes)}$, Meiling Chen$^{(\boxtimes)}$, Wei Li, Peng Ran, and Yang Sun

China Mobile Research Institute, 32 Xuanwumen West Street, Xicheng District, Beijing, China
{suli,chenmeiling}@chinamobile.com

Abstract. This paper proposed a SA DOTS architecture and system with attack types awareness and alarm threshold self-adaptable mechanism to improve the capability of DDos mitigation which across multi-networks. Firstly, we designed an expanded Dots protocol that includes attack type extensions which enables accurate sensing of attack types. Then, the feedback receiving module are extended in Dots framework to realize the alert threshold self-learning ability which based on time slice. It can effectively establish dynamic threshold curve and intelligently match real attack distribution. Verified by actual network, SA DOTS mechanism can keep high correct rate of warning while increase the ability to detect attacks. While using SA DOTS architecture, the experiment analysis shows that the accuracy increased by 70.22% and attack detection probability increased by 19.5%.

Keywords: Dots · DDoS attack · Self-adaptable · Cooperative disposal

1 Background

Distributed Denial of Service (DDoS) is a type of resource-consuming attack, which exploits a large number of attack resources and uses standard protocols for attacking. DDoS attacks consume a large amount of target object network resources or server resources, so that the target object cannot provide network services normally. At present, DDoS attack is one of the most powerful and indefensible attacks on the Internet, and due to the extensive use of mobile devices and IoT devices in recent years, it is easier for DDoS attackers to attack with real attack sources (broilers).

In 2018, the threat of DDoS attacks is still increasing, the traffic of DDoS reflection attack using memcached server vulnerabilities reached a peak of 1.7 Tbps. The opening ceremony of Pyeongchang Winter Olympics was subjected to DDoS attacks for up to 12 h. The industries affected by DDoS attack include banks, governments and game companies.

The current anti-DDoS modes mainly include three modes: one is single-point operation, such as self-built anti-DDoS equipment in the machine room [1]; the Second is cloud protection which achieve unified protection through flow drainage; The third is joint prevention within an organization (called a domain) [2], such as anti-DDoS cooperative processing and cloud cleaning centers. However, the current attack presents a

© Springer Nature Singapore Pte Ltd. 2020
G. Xu et al. (Eds.): FCS 2020, CCIS 1286, pp. 475–488, 2020.
https://doi.org/10.1007/978-981-15-9739-8_36

distributed and large traffic trend, and the attack sources are spread all over the world. As far as the current situation is concerned, a certain range of defenses can no longer meet the anti-DDoS attack requirements, and comprehensive cross-network collaboration is required [3]. In order to shield operator differences from defending DDoS attacks across the entire network (global), the IETF working group proposed the DOTS framework [4], which is used to automate and standardize DDoS countermeasures and to shield differences in various anti-ddos solutions.

SE DOTS [5] architecture expands the mitigation request method and identifies attack type within signal channel, so mitigator [4] can deal with the attack specifically. SE DOTS adds HTTP method for mitigation request and triage strategy module in dots server, which can choose the attack mitigation method according to the attack situation, so as to improve DDoS attack defense under DOTS framework.

Based on SE DOTS, this paper proposes a SA DOTS architecture with adaptive ability of attack type sensing and warning threshold. Firstly, the mitigation request method of signal channel was extended with the target-attack-type-threshold and attack-src-ip-number which will be used for warning threshold self-learning. Secondly, feedback receiving module is added between mitigator and DOTS Server which result in dynamic warning threshold model by self learning based on time slice, in this way the flow model will much more appropriate to the actual business traffic and effectively reduce the false alarm probability of attack target. Based on the analysis of the existing network alarm data, SA DOTS can improve the alarm accuracy by 49.5% and the attack detection ability by 19.5%.

2   Existing Technologies and Shortcomings

At present, the main technologies of DDOS attack protection include single equipment protection and collaborative defense.

Single protection relies on the deployment of DDOS devices to protect, and cooperate with the router to detect attacks and traffic cleaning. It is simple to deploy in this way, but limited to the ability of a single device to deal with attacks, it is not able to deal with large traffic attacks that lead to network congestion [6].

Collaborative defense is to coordinate multiple anti-ddos devices or multiple cleaning centers to make them cooperate to mitigate DDOS attacks [7]. In recent years, DDoS attacks have presented the characteristics of super-large scale and ultra-high peak value, collaborative defense against DDoS attack has become the mainstream technology [8].

DOTS is a cross-domain (cross-organization) processing framework for DDoS attacks defined by IETF, which is an implementation of collaborative defense technology. DOTS is a general architecture, method and processing mechanism established without focusing on specific attack mitigation equipment and means [9], which is very suitable for the scenario of network operation and separation of business operations, the basic structure is shown in Fig. 1. DOTS framework consists of the following four roles: Attack Target, DOTS Client, DOTS Server, and Mitigator.

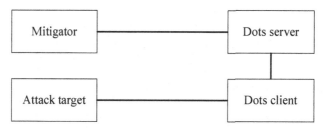

Fig. 1. DOTS logical architecture

SE DOTS architectureadd attack type and bandwidth for the improvement of mitigator scheduling, it is compatible with BGP and HTTP for mitigation signaling [10], the process of SE DOTS is shown in Fig. 2.

The process is as follows:

(1) DOTS Client sends the mitigation request after the Attack target is attacked by DDoS;
(2) DOTS Server receives DOTS Client request, and DOTS Server analyzes request packet to obtain attack details, such as IP address information;
(3) Mitigator is notified by DOTS Server by BGP or HTTP through the triage strategy module;
(4) Mitigator aims to mitigate DDoS attacks according to attack types.

At present, no matter what kind of protection mechanism is adopted, the determination of DDOS attack generally adopts the alarm mechanism of fixed threshold value, which is not matched with the model of users' dynamic business traffic and prone to generate false alarm. Although SE DOTS achieves a good scheduling function, it only realizes a one-way notification and mitigation mechanism, but lacks a two-way mitigation result feedback mechanism natively. Therefore, feedback mechanism can be added to SE DOTS architecture, and "alert-feedback" information can be continuously trained based on machine learning, so as to achieve dynamic baseline capability matching business traffic dynamic model.

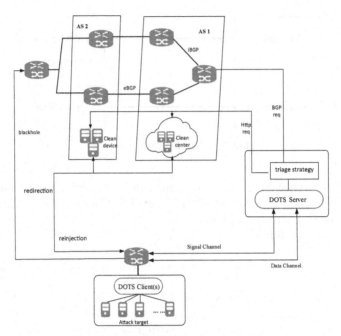

Fig. 2. SE DOTS architecture

3   SA DOTS Technical Principle

SA DOTS is based on SE DOTS framework, adding target-attack-type-threshold and attack-src-ip number in mitigation request. Mitigator feedback receiving module is added between mitigator and DOTS Server. Through periodic learning of the response results from mitigator and then form a time-slice alarm threshold fitting curve based on DDoS Attack Type. Thus, it improves the alert accuracy of DOTS linkage and effectively reduces the miss rate.

3.1   Attack Type Sensitive

In SE DOTS, when DOTS client detects a DDoS attack, it will send a mitigation request via signal channel [11], which includes the following fields: target-prefix, Target-port-range, Target-protocol, Target-fqdn, Target-uri, Alias-name, Lifetime, Attack-type, Bandwidth. Add the field of "attack type alert threshold" in SE Dots mitigation request to support the self-learning ability of alert threshold and solve the problem of imprecise attack alert threshold. Specific implementation process includes:

(1) Fields of "target-attack-type-threshold" and "attack-src-ip-number" are added when Attack Target creates mitigation request;
(2) DOTS Client responds to the request and sends the message to DOTS Server according to the existing process;
(3) DOTS Server analyzes the request, selects the notification method for Mitigator according to the triage strategy module, and generates the mitigation request;

SA DOTS adds "target-attack-type-threshold" and "attack-src-ip-number" fields in mitigation requests, which belongs to Signal channel messages, and are generated by attack target and sent to DOTS Client, added fields as shown in Fig. 3 below.

```
Header:PUT (Code=0.03)
Uri=Host: "host"
...
Content-Type:"application/cbor"
{
  "mitigation-scope":{
   "client-identifier":[
    "string"
   ],
   "scope":[
     ...
      "target-Attack-Type":[
        {
            "Attack-Name":"string"
            "Attack-Alias":"string"
            "target-Attack-Type-threshold": "string"
        }
      ],
      "target-bandwidth":[
         "string"
      ],
      "Attack-src-IP-number":[
         "string"
      ],
      ...
    }
  }
}
```

Fig. 3. SA DOTS protocol extensions

For the target-attack-type-threshold field, defined as a string and the threshold is set for each attack Type. Based on the current situation of the network, DDoS attacks are mostly distributed attacks; it is more effective to count the number of IP addresses than all IP addresses, and more helpful to determine the scale of the attack. The attack-src-ip-number field is also defined as a string, which refers to the number of attack source ip.

Based on SA DOTS, the Mitigator can be transferred by DOTS Server to obtain more detailed information about the number of attack sources and the warning standard of attack target.

3.2 Self-adaptive Extension

DOTS framework and SE DOTS framework only define one-way requests that only send mitigation requests to mitigator for DDoS attack mitigation, and easy result in false alarm of Attack Target caused by unreasonable threshold setting and waste of network handling capacity.

SA DOTS extends the feedback receiving capability of SE DOTS framework. A new feedback receiving module is added between DOTS Server and Mitigator to receive mitigation results, the SA DOTS system architecture diagram for extending the feedback mechanism is shown in Fig. 4.

The process of SA DOTS system after adding feedback mechanism is as follow:

(1) DOTS client sends mitigation request;
(2) DOTS server receives mitigation request, analyzes the request, transfers mitigation parameters to the triage strategy module, and starts mitigators selection;
(3) send the mitigation request to the corresponding cleaning device (or cleaning center). The cleaning device (or cleaning center) triggers the flow drainage and then injected normal flow back to the attack target link;
(4) Mitigator feeds back the cleaning result (including the size of attack traffic, attack type, cleaning results, etc.) to Dots Server, which will be received and stored by dots server;
(5) Dots Server analyzes whether the threshold setting of Attack Target is reasonable based on Mitigator feedback information, and proposes alert trigger threshold. Specific treatment methods includes:

   a) If the flow after cleaning is approximately equal to the flow before cleaning, it means that the mitigation request is a false alarm request, then feedback and suggest to adjust the threshold target-attached-threshold;
   b) If the flow after cleaning is less than the flow before cleaning, it means that it is an effective mitigation request at this time, and the flow that has been cleaned is fed back, and the target attached-type-threshold can be optimized according to the gap between the original flow and the feedback flow.

(6) Adjust the threshold after the Attack Target receives the adjustment suggestion from Dots Server.

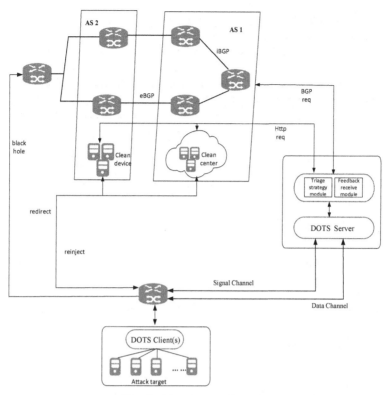

Fig. 4. SA DOTS architecture

4 Intelligent Cleaning Decision Model Based on Negative Feedback

4.1 Model Building

Based on the feedback receiving function of Dots Server and Mitigator's feedback, SA Dots achieves intelligent analysis and scheduling capability. The model consists of three parts: feature extraction, parameter calculation and model building.

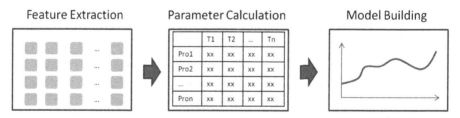

Define the following parameters:

- Attack Target: $Tar_1, Tar_2, ..., Tar_n$
- Attack Type: $Att_1, Att_2, ..., Att_n$

- Time slice (from the beginning to the end): $T_i = (T\_Start, T\_End)$
- Total Flow reported by Tar_i: Tot_Flow_i
- Total amount of Attack Type with flowsize of an attacked target: $Att\_msg\_Tar_k = \{(Att_1, F_1), (Att_2, F_2), ..., (Att_n, F_n)\}$
- Cleaning result of Tar_k(Attack Clean Flow), the flow cleaned by device: Cle_Flow_k
- The detail information of a cleaning node for Tark: $Cle\_msg\_Tar_k = \{(Att_1, CF_1), (Att_2, CF_2), ..., (Att_n, CF_n)\}$, CF represent Cleaned_Flow that residual cleaning flow.

(1) Feature Extraction

The following information can be obtained from the attack information reported by the target Tar_i:

- Tot_Flow_i
- T_k, the interval between start and end is TX
- $Attack\text{-}src\text{-}IP\text{-}number$
- $Att\_msg\_Tar_i$

If the warning is analyzed as an aggressive behavior that requires cleaning, mitigator is deployed on DOTS Server. After cleaning, the following information is obtained from the feedback results of cleaning:

- Cle_Flow_k
- $Cle\_msg\_Tar_k = \{(Att_1, CF_1), (Att_2, CF_2), ..., (Att_n, CF_n)\}$

(2) Parameter Calculation

Calculate the new parameters from the above 7 parameters once per T second, such as T = 300 s. The main calculated parameters include:

- IP_num: the number of ip during T
- $Flow\_msg\_Tar_k = \{(Type_1, F_1), (Type_2, F_2), ..., (Type_n, F_n)\} = AVG(Att\_msg\_Tar_k)$
- $Cle\_msg\_Tar_k = \{(Type_1, CF_1), (Type_2, CF_2), ..., (Type_n, CF_n)\} = AVG(Cle\_msg\_Tar_k)$
- Calculate non-attacking traffic for each protocol,

$$Valid\_Flow\_msg\_Tar_k = Flow\_msg\_Tar_k - Cle\_msg\_Tar_k \tag{1}$$

Calculate the behavior characteristics of each IP, including:

- Average Non-attacking traffic of each IP:

$$Nor\_IP\_Flow = Valid\_Flow\_msg\_Tar_k / (IP\_num - attack\text{-}src\text{-}IP\text{-}number) \tag{2}$$

- Average attacking traffic of each IP:

$$Att\_IP\_Flow = Cle\_msg\_Tar_k \ / \ attack\text{-}src\text{-}IP\text{-}number \tag{3}$$

After analysis, attack IP is variable and attack type is variable.

(3) Model Building

In time slices, Calculate the average normal flow per time slice of a single IP Nor_IP_Flow and average traffic to attack IP Att_IP_Flow. In a time slice:

$$Nor\_IP\_Flow\_T_k = (Nor\_IP\_Flow\_1, Nor\_IP\_Flow\_2, \ldots Nor\_IP\_Flow\_i),$$
$$Att\_IP\_Flow\_T_k = (Att\_IP\_Flow\_1, Att\_IP\_Flow\_2, \ldots Att\_IP\_Flow\_i),$$

and i = T/Tk, Calculate the values of the above two parameters over V time slices (V $\geq$ 1). Take the time slice as the horizontal axis, take $Nor\_IP\_Flow_{Tk}$ and $Att\_IP\_Flow_{Tk}$ as the vertical axis to fit the dynamic threshold curve function $F(x)$, finally complete the single IP modeling of normal traffic and abnormal traffic.

The modeling process is described below:

1. When the device is initially configured, all traffic is assumed to be suspected traffic and alarm is given;
2. In two attack-free cycles, $Cle\_msg\_Tar_k = 0$ in each time slice,then the following model is obtained after learning:

    - Single-parameter modeling is carried out for normal flow, get the fitting curve $F = f(T_i, Flow_i)$, f is the fitting function and i is the number of time slice ($i = 1, 2, .., n$).
    - Average fluctuation range of normal IP traffic, k is adjustment coefficient.

    $$Fluc\_nor\_t = |Nor\_IP\_Flow\_1 - Nor\_IP\_Flow\_2| * k \tag{4}$$

    - Average fluctuation range of attack IP traffic, l is adjustment coefficient

    $$Fluc\_att\_t = |Att\_IP\_Flow\_1 - Att\_IP\_Flow\_2| * l. \tag{5}$$

The final construction of the decision model:

$$Decision\_Tar_i = (F, Fluc\_nor\_t, Fluc\_Att\_t)$$

4.2 A Example of Model Building Process

Collect the current network traffic include attack traffic for parameter modeling, then obtain the fitting curve $F = f(Interval, Flow)$, f is for fitting function. The modeling method is as follows:

1. Data within a time period (such as 1 day or 1 week) are adopted and the time slice is set as T for data sampling;
2. Analyze whether the data within multiple time periods have similar waveforms;
3. If the waveform is similar, data will be superimposed;
4. According to the superimposed result of sampling, the dynamic threshold curve is formed based on machine learning.

Take the data of a point as an example, the sampling period $T = 5$ *min* is used for data sampling, and then automatic learning of dynamic threshold curve is carried out.

(1) Data within one day (0:00:00–23:59:59) are sampled according to T, and obvious deviation points are eliminated.
(2) After analyzing the data of several days, it is found that the daily statistics have good data consistency and data superposition can be carried out;
(3) Select the data by day, for example, Fig. 5 shows the data of the first day, and Fig. 6 shows the data of the second day.

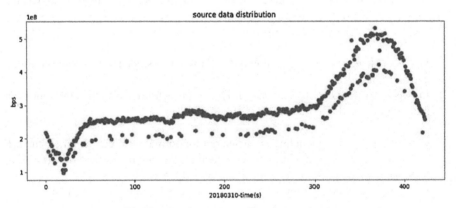

Fig. 5. Waveform of sampling data on day 1

(4) Sampling data are processed by neighborhood weighting method. Gaussian function is used to weight sampling points in this sample set, as shown in the blue curve in Fig. 7. Abnormal points may be deleted during preprocessing.
(5) Based on the experimental analysis, Savitzky-Golay smoothing filter [12] was used to construct the dynamic threshold curve of this sample set, as shown in the red curve in Fig. 7.

According to the above steps, the data collected from the current network were modeled and fitted, and the dynamic threshold curve was obtained, as shown in the red curve in Fig. 7.

Based on the above data, the normal traffic fluctuation model of a single IP (traffic unit is Mb) is calculated. The adjustment system k = 2 was adopted for time-slice analysis:

$$Fluc\_nor\_t_i = |Nor\_IP\_Flow\_1 - Nor\_IP\_Flow\_2| * k \qquad (6)$$

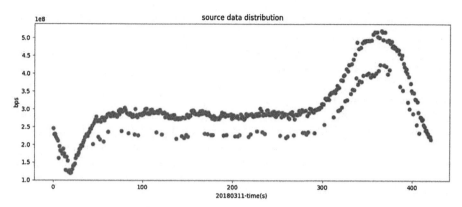

Fig. 6. Waveform of sampling data on day 2

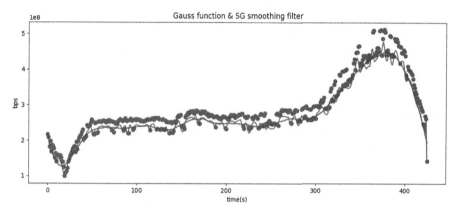

Fig. 7. Gaussian weighted and SG fitting curves

For all time slices to calculate:

$$Fluc = \frac{\sum_{i=1}^{480} |Fluc\_nor\_t_i|}{480} * k \tag{7}$$

Finally obtain the fluctuation threshold $Fluc = 236000(bps)$, Any value above $Fluc$ is a suspected warning.

5   SA DOTS Technical Advantage Analysis and Experiment

In SA DOTS, Attack Target can report all attack information to DOTS Server through one message sending, while DOTS Server can automatically form dynamic threshold baseline through feedback receiving module of mitigator, then compared with the information of attack reported by Attack Target. If the Attack Target itself has the dynamic adjustment ability of threshold baseline, it can reduce invalid alarms at the source. If the Attack Target does not have the dynamic adjustment ability of threshold baseline, DOTS

Server can deal with invalid alarms from the receiving module and effectively improve the handling ability of alarms.

In the following experimental network, the simulation experiment is carried out to simulate the existing network environment:

- The bandwidth of link where the protected object is 10G;
- Traffic model of protected objects: the average of normal access is 300M, and the maximum traffic is 500M; all are HTTP access (and generate TCP SYN traffic); the total limited bandwidth is 1G, and the alarm is performed in excess of 600M;
- Total attack traffic: the maximum is 1G and use pulse attack mode, keep attacking for 5 min and size of the attack is random from 100M to 1000M; in this attack experiment, the total attack traffic in 5 min is 5859 Mbps;
- Time distribution of attack: 24 h will be divided into 2400 time slices, Attacks occur in 5% time slices;
- Distribution of the disturbance: there is a surge of user disturbance within a slice per hour (the traffic is increased, but the behavior is normal);
- Cluster cleaning ability: attack cleaning ability is about 100%.

In the above model, continuous periodic simulation of a superposition state is shown in Fig. 8:

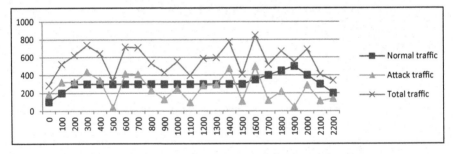

Fig. 8. A traffic diagram simulating an attack

In the above scenario, Set 3 experience thresholds: threshold of mode 1 is 400M, threshold of mode 2 is 500M, threshold of mode 3 is 600M. The simulation experiment was carried out for 100 rounds and 120 min per round, 120 min were divided into 24 time slices, including 1 reset time slices (Table 1).

The experimental results show that SA DOTS can guarantee a very high alert accuracy while reduce the false alert rate. The average correct rate of the traditional modes is When the alert accuracy is improved by 70.22%, the missed alert is reduced by 19.5%. This mechanism can effectively coordinate the protection capability of the existing network and ensure the network smoothly and healthy.

Table 1. SA DOTS attack mitigation result comparative analysis

	Total alerts (times)	False alerts (times)	Correct alerts (times)	Correct rate (%)	Missed alerts (times)	Missed alert traffic (Mbps)	Missed alert attack traffic ratio (%)
Mode 1	480	382	98	20.42	20	457.89	7.95
Mode 2	272	192	81	29.78	35	808.67	14.04
Mode 3	47	2	45	95.74	70	2356.62	40.92
Avg	266.33	192	74.33	27.91	125	3623.2	20.97
SA Dots	107	2	105	98.13	10	84.94475	1.47

6 Conclusion

In this paper, DDOS attack protection technology is comprehensively analyzed. Based on the DOTS mechanism of IETF, SA DOTS framework with attack type sensitive and intelligent dynamic threshold baseline capability is designed. The experimental result shows that: SA DOTS can better identify and mitigate DDOS attacks while ensure the success rate of user access business.

From the development perspective, SA DOTS will be further used in ISP and IDC service providers, and further promotion of the industry standardization is needed in the follow-up work to reduce the risk of DDOS attack.

References

1. Akamai: How to protect against DDoS attacks - stop denial of service (2016). https://www.akamai.com/us/en/resources/protect-against-ddos-attacks.jsp. Accessed 10 Jan 2017
2. Rodrigues, B., Bocek, T., Stiller, B.: Multi-domain DDoS mitigation based on blockchains. In: Tuncer, D., Koch, R., Badonnel, R., Stiller, B. (eds.) AIMS 2017. LNCS, vol. 10356, pp. 185–190. Springer, Cham (2017). https://doi.org/10.1007/978-3-319-60774-0_19
3. Rodrigues, B., Bocek, T., Lareida, A., Hausheer, D., Rafati, S., Stiller, B.: A blockchain-based architecture for collaborative DDoS mitigation with smart contracts. In: Tuncer, D., Koch, R., Badonnel, R., Stiller, B. (eds.) AIMS 2017. LNCS, vol. 10356, pp. 16–29. Springer, Cham (2017). https://doi.org/10.1007/978-3-319-60774-0_2
4. Mortensen, A., Andreasen, F., Reddy, T., Teague, N., Compton, R.: Draft-ietf-dots-architecture [EB/OL].https://tools.ietf.org/html/draft-ietf-dots-architecture-18
5. Su, L., Chen, M., Peng, J., Ran, P.: SE Dots: a sensitive and extensible framework for cross-region DDoS processing. In: Li, J., Liu, Z., Peng, H. (eds.) SPNCE 2019. LNICSSITE, vol. 284, pp. 509–517. Springer, Cham (2019). https://doi.org/10.1007/978-3-030-21373-2_41
6. Dobbins, R., Migault, D., Fouant, S., Moskowitz, R., Teague, N.: Draft-ietf-dots-use-cases [EB/OL].https://tools.ietf.org/html/draft-ietf-dots-use-cases-25
7. Mortensen, A., Moskowitz, R., Reddy, T.: RFC 8612 [EB/OL]. https://tools.ietf.org/html/draft-ietf-dots-requirements
8. Steinberger, J., Kuhnert, B., Sperotto, A., Baier, H., Pras, A.: Collaborative DDOS defense using flow-based security event information. In: NOMS 2016–2016 IEEE/IFIP Network Operations and Management Symposium, pp. 516–522, April 2016

9. Grady, J., Christiansen, C.A., Price, C., Richmond, C.: Worldwide DDoS prevention products and services 2013–2017 forecast. IDC #239954e, vol. 1, March 2013

10. Fayaz, S.K., Tobioka, Y., Sekar, V.: Bohatei: flexible and elastic DDoS defense. In: 24th USENIX Security Symposium, August 2015

11. Reddy, T., Boucadair, M., Patil, P., Mortensen, A., Teague, N.: RFC 8782 [EB/OL].https://tools.ietf.org/html/draft-ietf-dots-signal-channel

12. Chen, J., Jonsson, P., Tamura, M., et al.: A simple method for reconstructing a high-quality NDVI time-series data set based on the Savitzky-Golay filter. Remote Sens. Environ. Interdisc. J. **91**(3/4), 332–344 (2004)

Privacy

Characterizing the Security Threats of Disposable Phone Numbers

Yanan Cheng, Han Wang, Zhaoxin Zhang$^{(\boxtimes)}$, and Ning Li$^{(\boxtimes)}$

Faculty of Computing, Harbin Institute of Technology, Harbin, Heilongjiang, China
{zhangzhaoxin,li.ning}@hit.edu.cn

Abstract. Many organizations require users to provide a phone number for verification when registering an account. Simultaneously, because of the convenience and security of SMS-based two-factor authentication, many organizations adopt this method to enable users to log in their accounts. On the other hand, many web service platforms provide a mass of disposable phone numbers for receiving SMS messages. The original intention of these platforms is to provide user privacy protection services; however, people know very little about the threat that this service poses to the organization's security. In this paper, we collected data from 9 disposable phone platforms with high traffic in China. These data include 4,669 phone numbers and 30 million messages. These phone numbers come from 44 countries, and most of the phone number carriers are mobile virtual network operators in China. To the best of our knowledge, this is the first paper that discloses the OTA (Online Travel Agency) accounts registered by disposable phone numbers, which would leak a large number of passenger information. Furthermore, we discovered that cybercriminals use temporary OTA accounts to carry out airline seat spinning attacks. Among the organizations we surveyed, only 47% of the organizations' security mechanisms can detect accounts that registered with disposable numbers. Our findings indicate that disposable phone numbers pose potential threats to cybersecurity, and new solutions are needed to address the threat.

Keywords: Disposable phone number · Privacy leak · Airline seat spinning attack

1 Introduction

SMS (short message service) is a text messaging service component of most telephone, Internet, and mobile device systems [1]. SMS-based two-factor authentication (2FA) is a security verification procedure, which is triggered when a user logs in a website, software or application. Although SMS-based 2FA suffers

This work is supported by National Major Science and Technology Projects of China (Grant No. 2018YFB1800202, 2017YFB0803001, 2018YFB0804703) and National Natural Science Foundation of China (Grant No. 61571144, U1836117).

© Springer Nature Singapore Pte Ltd. 2020
G. Xu et al. (Eds.): FCS 2020, CCIS 1286, pp. 491–507, 2020.
https://doi.org/10.1007/978-981-15-9739-8_37

from some security concerns, it is still adopted by many organizations because it is convenient for users to log into their accounts. Simultaneously, people are often required to provide phone numbers for identity verification when registering accounts. Data security and privacy leaks occur every year, such as Facebook security breach exposes accounts of 50 million users [2]. These cases lead people to pay more attention to personal account security and privacy protection.

At the same time, there are many free SMS service platforms on the Internet. These platforms can provide people with phone numbers that can receive SMS messages. These phone numbers are called temporary phone numbers, or disposable phone numbers. People do not need a mobile phone; all they need to do is visit the platform's website and then select a phone number to receive SMS messages. These phone numbers belong to different countries and carriers. Besides, the messages received by these numbers are public to everyone, which means that everyone can view or collect these messages.

When people do not want to use their actual mobile phone numbers to receive SMS, the disposable phone number is an ideal alternative. The use of disposable numbers can reduce the risk of personal privacy leakage. However, many disposable phone numbers are misused or maliciously used, which causes security problems and privacy leakage. Cybercriminals can also use disposable phone numbers to register fake accounts for attacks, which causes losses to many organizations. Besides, how many organizations are affected by these phone numbers? Why do people choose these organizations? What are the size and characteristics of disposable phone numbers? These questions have not been investigated in the previous works and will be answered in this article.

Previous studies collected a large amount of SMS data, and analyzed the behavior of these messages, indicating that public gateways are primarily used for evading account creation policies that require verified phone numbers [3,4]. Researchers also introduced a man-in-the-middle attack, which exploits a set of vulnerabilities in password reset procedures of famous (and other) websites and applications [5]. Some work investigated SMS spam based on the collected messages [6,7]. Other researchers looked in how disposable phone numbers are used to create phone-verified fake accounts in online services. Their results highlight how blackmarket monitoring can provide an invaluable oracle into the performance of abuse safeguards [8]. In SIM (Subscriber Identification Module) swap attacks, an attacker impersonates the victim to a carrier to receive a SIM card for the victim's account, allowing the attacker to intercept security-sensitive messages [9]. At this point, they can intercept any two-factor authentication codes sent by text message. Like this type of attack, the messages received by a disposable phone number can be obtained by anyone. If this phone number is associated with an important account, it can be logged in and obtained by someone.

In this paper, we collected data from 9 disposable phone number platforms with high traffic in China from June 6, 2019 to June 1, 2020. This information includes 4,669 phone numbers and 30 million messages. Based on these data, we analyzed the size and characteristics of disposable mobile numbers and people's intentions to use disposable phone numbers. To the best of our knowledge, this is the first paper that discloses the OTA (Online Travel Agency) accounts registered by disposable phone numbers, which would leak a large number of passenger information. Besides, we disclosed that cybercriminals used OTA accounts to carry out airline seat spinning attacks, that is, temporarily holding many seats in airlines without paying.

The contributions of this paper are summarized as follows:

- **Disclosure of disposable number causing privacy leak.** We disclosed that when people use a disposable phone number to register an account, they may unintentionally leak their or others' privacy. Taking OTA as an example, more than 83% of the disposable number accounts that we tested have passenger privacy data, such as ID number, name, and vacation itinerary.
- **Exposing airline seat spinning attack.** We exposed the OTA accounts registered with the disposable phone numbers to conduct airline seat pinning attacks. Of the two OTAs, 34 of 60 accounts implemented this attack, which affects the normal purchase of 892 seats on 93 flights of 12 airlines. This attack severely damaged the interests of airlines, OTAs, and passengers.
- **Evaluation of organizations detect disposable numbers.** We carefully selected 76 organizations and 20 disposable phone numbers for each organization to verify whether these organizations have restrictions on these numbers. We found that only 47% of organizations banned disposable numbers for registration or login. Moreover, the correct rate of these organizations identifying disposable phone numbers is about 55%. Therefore, the security threats caused by disposable phone numbers have not been paid enough attention by most organizations.
- **Speculating the intention of malicious attackers.** Based on a large number of SMS messages and the intelligence evidence we collected, we try to speculate why cybercriminals use disposable phone numbers to register accounts on some organizations, i.e., to answer why attackers choose these organizations.

2 Methodology

In this section, we introduce the disposable phone number platforms, describe the techniques for obtaining and analyzing data, and discuss the methods for discovering privacy leakage caused by disposable phone numbers.

2.1 Disposable Phone Number Platforms

The disposable phone number platforms publish many phone numbers through the website for people to use. These sites are completely public and can be accessed by anyone. Given that this article focuses on the impact of disposable phone numbers in China, we employ multiple search engines such as Google, Baidu, Yahoo to search by keywords, such as *Cloud SMS*, *Free SMS*, and *Cloud*

Verification Code. In the search results, we select the top 9 websites as our data source, as shown in Table 1. Each disposable phone number is characterized by sender phone numbers, message body, and received time.

Table 1. The sources of disposable phone numbers.

Platform	Messages	Phones	Valid phones	Creation date	Country
freesmscode.com	1398508	1435	205	2017-8-29	VN
yinsiduanxin.com	6626583	697	164	2019-10-31	US
mianfeijiema.com	1931879	427	382	2019-10-4	PA
yunduanxin.net	11058325	418	393	2019-1-1	US
smsreceivefree.com	339008	67	40	2014-9-11	CA
bfkdim.com	827988	38	27	2019-10-31	CN
yunjiema.net	5635148	946	182	2019-5-13	CA
becmd.com	288651	20	20	2013-8-31	CN
us-phone-number.com	2087542	621	523	2019-9-15	PA

Although we have carefully selected nine accessible sources of temporary phone numbers, to the best of our knowledge, this paper obtained the largest disposable phone number dataset so far. However, given that the data source does not cover all disposable phone number platforms, the dataset inevitably suffers from biases. We want to clarify these biases upfront to provide a more accurate interpretation of the analysis results later. First, this study uses multiple search engines to get nine platforms with high traffic. These sources are the most frequently visited by netizens, which can alleviate the impact of our dataset not covering all disposable phone platforms. Secondly, the focus of this study is to expose the abuse caused by disposable phone numbers, such as causing privacy leaks, not just data-driven analysis based on the dataset we collected.

2.2   Crawling Phone Numbers and Messages

For the website of each disposable phone number platform, we build a crawler to obtain phone numbers and messages periodically. The main steps of the crawler are as follows.

The crawler's task is to crawl all the disposable phone numbers published by the platform and the received messages, which include the sender's number, the body of the message, and the received time. The crawlers regularly obtain disposable phone numbers and messages. Therefore, the crawler only obtains data that has not been collected each time. We combined the message and received time to generate a hash value and compare it to determine whether the data has been acquired. Besides, the message receiving time of each platform is inconsistent, and the crawler needs to convert them to standard time.

For ethical considerations, we strictly limit the frequency of data obtained by each crawler to avoid affecting the disposable phone number service. The interval between the crawler obtaining two pages is between 5 and 15 s, to ensure that we can get all the data, and not access the website too frequently, so as not to cause trouble to the platform operators.

2.3 Analyzing Phone Numbers

For disposable phone numbers, we statistically analyze their country, lifetime, valid, and carrier. We rely on Google's open-source [10] phone number database to analyze the country location of mobile phone numbers. Especially for phone numbers in China, we use the interface provided by ip138 [11] to query the province and carrier of phone numbers.

2.4 Analyzing Messages

Our dataset contains a large number of messages received by disposable phone numbers. The analysis of messages mainly answers two questions: Which organizations send messages to disposable mobile numbers, and how many of these organizations? We answer the above questions by analyzing the source of messages. In China, the business messages sent by organizations usually contain the company's full name or short name (called SMS signature). The signature is enclosed in square brackets, so we can get the organization that sent the message by extracting the keywords in the square brackets.

2.5 Analyzing Privacy Leak

The primary purpose of people using disposable mobile numbers is to protect personal privacy. Ironically, people may also inadvertently leak personal or other person's data when using these numbers in some organizations. This study designed an experiment to verify that the disposable mobile phone number used on the OTA caused a large amount of personal data leakage. We selected 5 Chinese OTAs. Their names and rankings of the transaction scale in 2019 [12] are shown in Table 2. These agencies are the most frequently used by people in China to book air tickets, hotels, and vacations.

From the data collected, we selected 30 valid disposable phone numbers for each OTA according to the number of received messages. A valid phone number can still receive messages from organizations. The reason for choosing a valid phone number is that we do not know the login password of the OTA accounts registered by disposable phone numbers, so we need the one-time verification code received by the phone number to log in. After logging in to the account, we check whether the account has the personal data.

Also, based on ethical considerations, after logging in to the account, we do not perform any operations on the account (for example, change the password) except to view the personal data contained in the account. Therefore, our actions

Table 2. Five OTAs and their transaction size rankings in 2019

Agency	Website	Ranking
Ctrip	www.ctrip.com	1
Qunar	www.qunar.com	2
Tongcheng	www.lv.com	4
eLong	www.elong.com	5
Lvmama	www.lvmama.com	8

will not affect the account owner. Besides, we will not try to use the account to book hotels or tickets, so there will be no loss or impact on the OTA. Finally, we will not disclose the personal data we obtain, but only as statistical data for our research.

3 Data Summary

In this section, we describe the disposable phone numbers and messages collected. Overall, our database covers nearly one year of data from 9 disposable phone number platforms.

3.1 Platforms

As shown in Table 1, nine platforms published 4,669 disposable phone numbers within a year and received more than 30 million messages. There are seven platforms whose website language is Chinese, which mainly serves Chinese customers, and two websites are for international users. Only two domain name registration countries are in China. By analyzing the registration time of the domain names of these platforms, most platforms only provide services in the past year. However, more than 30 million messages have been received by the platform in only one year, which shows that many people are using the services provided by these platforms.

3.2 Charactering Disposable Phone Numbers

We obtained 4,669 mobile phone numbers from 9 platforms, as shown in Table 1. The characteristics of these phone numbers are as follows.

Shared. As in previous studies, we also found that these disposable numbers are shared. After the deduplication of 4669 mobile phone numbers, only 2782 mobile phone numbers were left, and the sharing rate was 40%. We speculate that there are several reasons for this fact. First, collaborating parties operate these platforms. Second, these disposable phone numbers are assigned to the lower platform by the superior administrator, and some phone numbers are assigned repeatedly. Third, some platforms use web crawlers to obtain phone numbers and messages from other platforms in real-time.

Availability. These platforms publish many disposable phone numbers, but some of them no longer receive messages. We call the mobile phone number that has received messages in the last 24 h as a valid phone number. Table 1 shows that each platform has many disposable phone numbers to provide services every day.

Countries. Disposable phone numbers we collected belong to 44 countries. As shown in Table 3, the phone number of the top 10 countries accounted for 93.9% of the total, especially phone numbers in the United States and China accounted for 61%. On the one hand, this fact shows people's regional needs and preferences for disposable phone numbers. On the other hand, it indicates that the platforms are easier to obtain phone numbers in these countries. Besides, we found that the number of messages received by phone numbers in China accounted for nearly 80% of the total, indicating that China's phone numbers are heavily used.

Table 3. Number of disposable phones and messages owned by top 10 countries

Country	Phones#	Phones%	Messages#	Messages%
United States	1035	37.20	1730561	7.04
China	670	24.08	15996491	78.46
Canada	487	17.51	682230	2.70
United Kingdom	169	6.07	490781	1.96
Russia	102	3.67	249038	0.87
Hong Kong SAR China	48	1.73	490925	4.36
Burma	34	1.22	41279	0.15
Philippines	29	1.04	37321	0.15
Ukraine	21	0.75	68074	0.24
Sweden	20	0.72	43711	0.15
SUM	2615	93.99	19830411	96.06

Carriers. We obtained carriers of phone numbers belonging to mainland China and counted the number of phones of each carrier, as shown in Table 4. It shows that nearly 80% of the disposable phone numbers of the Chinese belong to MVNO, especially the number of mobile phones of China Telecom's virtual operators exceeds 54%. Cybercriminals often use disposable phone numbers to register a large number of fake accounts to carry out attacks, such as false comments and Internet fraud. Therefore, to manage these phone numbers from the source, some telecom operators, such as Unicom, need to pay more work. Simultaneously, the organization's security mechanisms and technologies can also conduct

Table 4. Distribution of carriers of disposable phone number collected (China)

Carrier	Number	Percent (%)
China mobile	54	8.06
China unicom	94	14.03
China telecom	2	0.30
MVNO (China mobile)	158	23.58
MVNO (China unicom)	362	54.03
MVNO (China telecom)	0	0

targeted detections for different carriers when recognizing the malicious behavior of disposable phone numbers.

Hourly Activity. We counted the number of messages received by each disposable phone number per hour in a day to evaluate the activity of numbers, as shown in Fig. 1. We found that although the disposable phone number receives more messages during the day than at night, the phone number receives a large number of messages throughout the day. The average number of messages received by a phone number per hour is 477. Besides, we noticed that by 1 AM, the number of messages received by the phone number still exceeds the average. This case indicates that many people are still frequently using these phone numbers for activities at this time.

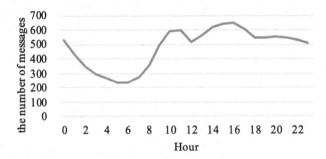

Fig. 1. Number of messages received per phone number per hour (in the 24-h clock)

Lifetime. The average lifetime for the disposable phone number is 33 days, and the median is 24 days. Figure 2 is a histogram of the number of disposable phone numbers with different lifetime days.

3.3   Charactering Messages

The collected data contains 30 million messages covering almost a year. We believe that the disposable phone number platforms receive more messages

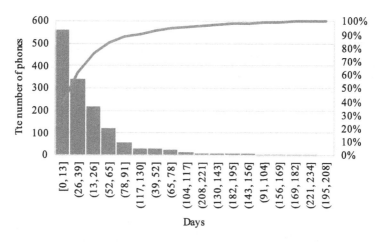

Fig. 2. Lifetime of disposable phone numbers

because some platforms only display the messages received by the phone number recently. Nevertheless, we can still analyze these collected messages to understand people's intention to use these phone numbers and which organizations these messages come from.

The signature in the SMS sent by each organization is different, so each SMS signature is regarded as an organization. In the end, we extracted 76,827 organizations from 14 million messages. We found that organizations that only sent one message accounted for 20% of all organizations, and more than 60% of organizations sent less than ten messages. This fact indicates that the primary use of disposable phone numbers is in some unimportant organizations.

We focus on 40% of organizations that send messages more than ten times. Figure 3 shows the cumulative distribution function (CDF) of the number of messages sent by each organization from high to low. As shown in Fig. 3, the number of messages sent by some organizations exceeded 100,000, and the top 500 organizations sent messages accounted for nearly 70% of all messages. This case shows that people also use disposable phone numbers coincidentally in some well-known organizations. Table 5 shows the information of the 20 organizations that send the most SMS messages.

As shown in Table 5, these 20 organizations sent 32.54% of the total messages. This fact indicates that people use many disposable phone numbers to operate on the websites or apps of these organizations, such as registering accounts and logging in. The categories of these organizations are mainly entertainment, such as games, video, live broadcast, and music, but also include technology companies, such as Apple and Google.

Why do people use many disposable phone numbers to register accounts of these well-known organizations? This behavior is contrary to the original intention of using a disposable phone number, which is to use disposable numbers in some unimportant organizations. We explain this behavior from the perspective

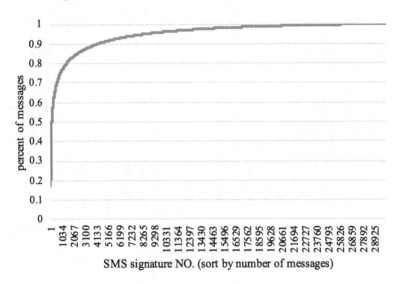

Fig. 3. The percentage of each organization sent the messages

of cybercriminals using these organizations' accounts to conduct malicious activities.

Get a Deal. People use a large number of fake accounts to obtain benefits issued by the organization to newly registered users. For example, Kugou Music released a profit-making task in April 2020, and the number of messages sent by Kugou on the disposable phone number platform increased significantly, as shown in Fig. 4.

Fake Reviews. The fake reviews are the reviews with untruthful consumption experience and evaluation of products, which may be good reviews about the products of cooperators or bad reviews about the products of competitors driven by commercial profits [13]. For example, the Apple's Chinese App Store is littered with fake reviews [14].

Ghost Followers. People register invalid accounts in some social and entertainment applications, which are used to increase the number of fans for certain users, especially celebrity ones, and get them more attention.

Porn Live. Some people perform pornographic performances in a live broadcast application. They use disposable phone numbers to register accounts for evasion tracking.

Table 5. Categories of top 20 organizations and number of messages sent

Organization	Messages (%)	Category
Apple	17.01	Technology
ZAO	2.51	Entertainment
Hago	1.27	Social
Tencent Technology	1.18	Game, social
Bilibili	1.15	Entertainment
Netease (Chinese)	0.98	Game
Pinduoduo	0.96	Shopping
SoulAPP	0.95	Social
Cute	0.80	Social
KuaiShou Technology	0.71	Social
Weibo	0.60	Social
TikTok (Chinese)	0.59	Social
Taole Network	0.55	Game
Meituan	0.53	Lifestyle
Google	0.49	Technology
Eleme	0.48	Lifestyle
22 gram	0.46	Game
Kugou Music	0.46	Entertainment
Zhihu	0.43	Social
iQiyi	0.43	Entertainment

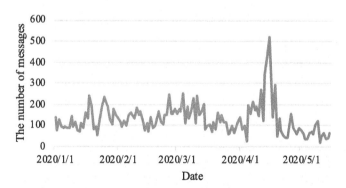

Fig. 4. The number of messages sent by Kugou Music every day

3.4   Detecting Disposable Phone Numbers

According to the above section, disposable mobile numbers have been used to register accounts in numerous organizations. So, how many of these organizations have a detection mechanism for disposable phone numbers, and what is the detection rate? We design an experiment to answer these questions.

Seventy-six organizations were selected from the top 100 organizations with the most disposable phone numbers. The websites or apps of these organizations are valid, and users can log in accounts using phone numbers. For each organization, we tried to use 20 disposable phone numbers to log in to the organization's account. If all 20 mobile phone numbers can successfully log in to the account, it means that the organization has no detection mechanism. Otherwise, we believe that there is a detection mechanism in the organization, and the detection rate is based on the proportion of phone numbers that cannot be logged in.

Of the 76 organizations tested, only 47% had a detection mechanism for disposable phone numbers. Most organizations will remind users that the account is abnormal and cannot log in. The reasons for the abnormal account include posting malicious content, spam content, and violations. The detection rate of these organizations for registering accounts with disposable phone numbers is shown in Fig. 5. It can be seen from the figure that most organizations' security mechanisms do not detect all accounts registered with disposable phone numbers. These temporary accounts may cause harm to the organizations.

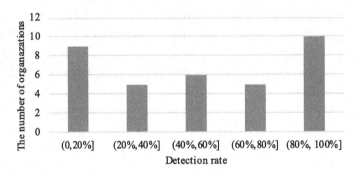

Fig. 5. Number of organizations in the detection rate range

7% of organizations prohibit users from registering accounts with phone numbers of some virtual operators. This method prevents not only disposable phone numbers but also prevents virtual phone numbers used by ordinary users. In particular, among the 77 organizations where disposable phone numbers are most widespread, nearly 46% of organizations have not guarded against these phone numbers. Therefore, accounts registered with disposable numbers may cause harm to the organization. For example, when an organization sends promotional activities to a disposable phone number, it wastes the organization's budget.

4   Analyzing Privacy Leak

In this section, we disclosed that the OTA accounts registered with the disposable phone numbers caused massive personal data leaks, such as passengers' name, ID, and journeys.

As detailed in the previous section, we selected 30 valid phone numbers that have registered accounts with 5 OTAs. We found that a large number of temporary OTA accounts contain passengers' data. These personal data can be viewed, collected, or disseminated by anyone logged into the account, causing personal privacy leakage, as shown in Table 6.

Table 6. Statistics of personal data leaked from OTAs account registered with disposable phones numbers

Company	Accounts	Number of people with privacy leaks					
		Name	Gender	Phone	Birthday	ID	Journeys
Ctrip	26	51	27	5	27	27	47
Qunar	27	55	18	14	18	7	91
Tongcheng	23	46	37	15	37	37	32
eLong	27	373	26	8	26	26	37
Lvmama	22	137	137	80	137	137	14

Number of Accounts Leaking Personal Data. Of the 150 OTA accounts registered with the disposable phone number we checked, more than 83% of the accounts contained personal data. However, the remaining accounts that do not contain passenger information may be used after a period, which may also cause personal privacy leakage. Besides, the privacy data may be unintentionally leaked by the account user, that is, the user forgets to delete the personal data after using the account. It may also be that the account user steals the identity information of others to carry out malicious acts, and does not pay attention to whether it leads to privacy leakage.

Passenger Names. Passenger names are the most leaked personal data in OTA accounts, especially in the 49 accounts of eLong and Lvmama, we collected more than 500 passenger names. The passenger names collected mainly come from a large number of canceled flight orders. We will analyze this behavior in detail in the next section.

Identity Information, Gender and Birthdate. It is well known that identity information is one of the most important personal data of people. In China, the ID number contains the individual's gender, birth date, and the province of birth. Table 6 shows that accounts are leaking personal identity information in the five OTAs, especially the Lvmama, which has 22 accounts leaking the identity information of 137 passengers. We believe that the main reason for the leakage of identity information is that OTAs do not encrypt identity information so that anyone who logins the account can view and collect it. For example, the ID information of all passengers in the Lvmama is in plain text. For another example, although Qunar encrypted the identity information of the passengers in the account, it was not encrypted in the travel contract.

Contact Information and Journeys. We found many passengers' phone numbers in accounts that leaked personal data, mainly from travel contracts or flight booking orders. Also, there is a large amount of travel information in these accounts, including scheduled attractions, hotels, and vacation itineraries.

5   Analyzing Airline Seat Spinning Attack

Airline seat spinning is an attack, which bot or human operators hold airline seats at no cost for a while to resell for a higher fee, skew flight popularity and allow for outsider monetary gain [15]. In the previous section, when analyzing the OTA account registered by the disposable phone number, which caused people privacy leakage, we found that many OTA accounts had a large number of canceled flight orders. We inquired about the status of these flights at that time and found that these flights arrived at the destination normally [16]. What is more interesting is that the information of the passengers in the orders in different accounts is the same. Therefore, we identified that this behavior is the airline seat spinning attack. Airlines or ticket agents sell air tickets through the OTAs, which creates a way for cybercriminals to use the OTA platform to carry airline seat spinning attacks.

In this section, for the first time, we analyzed the airline seat spinning attack in *eLong* and *Lvmama*. Cybercriminals use disposable phone numbers to register many temporary OTA accounts, and then use these accounts to carry out seat spinning attacks. We analyzed the behavior, scale, and damage to airlines of this attack. Table 7 shows the attacks that occurred in *Lvmama* and *eLong*.

Table 7. Airline seat spinning attacks that occurred in *Lvmama* and *eLong*

Type	Lvmama	eLong
Phone numbers	18	16
Cities (total/departure/arrival)	45/32/30	23/16/15
Flight number/airline	49/11	32/5
Seats spinning	327	565
Ticket price	0.66 million	1.23 million
Month/number of flights	12/35, 1/34, 11/12, 10/7, 4/5	
Attack time (hours)	Mean: 8, Median: 5	

Accomplices in Seat Spinning Attacks. To hide their identities, the attackers registered many temporary OTA accounts with disposable phone numbers to carry out seat spinning attacks. As shown in Table 7, more than half of the 60 temporary OTA accounts carry out seat spinning attacks. During the implementation of these attacks, the disposable phone number played an accomplice role, which was the first step in the attack.

Departure and Arrival Cities. The total number of flight departure and arrival cities is 48, which are mainly China's first-tier and second-tier cities (accounting for nearly 60% of the total number of cities) or cities featuring tourism, such as Sanya and Xishuangbanna. Therefore, OTAs should focus on flights of first-tier, second-tier, and popular tourist cities when defending against seat spinning attacks.

Flight Number and Airlines. Airline seat spinning attacks involved 80 flights, of which Lvmama and eLong were 49 and 32 flights, respectively. For example, there are 16 valid orders for flight HU7330. These flights belong to 12 Chinese airlines, of which Hainan Airlines has up to 31 flights, followed by China Southern Airlines, with 14 flights. The invalid orders of these two companies accounted for nearly 70% of the total. These attacks have severely affected the business of the two airlines.

Seat Spinning. These attacks held a total of 892 seats, which means that 892 people cannot buy these seats normally. If the attacker resells these seats, passengers would need to pay more for these seats. On the other hand, before the flight takes off, if no passengers purchased these seats, it would harm airlines' interests.

Number of Flights per Month. The seat spinning attacks mainly occurred in December 2019 and January 2020, due to the holidays such as the New Year and the Chinese New Year, and the increase in tourism and other activities. Conversely, in February and March 2020, we did not find any malicious behavior in OTA accounts. The main reason is that China bans regional activities because of the COVID-19 and cancels a large number of flights. Otherwise, these attacks should be more serious. In April 2020, due to the alleviation of the epidemic in China, many flights resumed, and the seat pinning happened again. Once again proved that these attacks are related to holidays that can increase the number of flights.

Tickets Price. The invalid orders canceled in the OTA accounts involved a total of 1.89 million yuan in airfare, and the average fee that should be paid for each order was about 7,000 yuan. If the seats are held due to seat pinning attacks, and the seats cannot be provided to the real purchasers, it will cause substantial economic losses to the airlines.

Attack Time. We found that most of the seat pinning attacks occurred 5 h before the flight took off. At that time, a large number of seats are held, which may raise the ticket price, affect the normal airfare mechanism, and damage the interests of airlines and passengers.

The attacker holds seats to block legitimate purchases, or to sell seats to the consumer at a higher price, causing economic losses to the consumers. Besides, it wastes airline bandwidth resources, consumes airline search fees, and disrupts the order of the air transport market and the normal operations of airlines. In particular, the resulting fluctuations in ticket bookings have led to misjudgments in the airline's revenue management system algorithm, giving fare adjustments that are not in line with actual conditions, damaging user rights, and the reputation of the OTAs.

6   Countermeasures

Regarding the threats of disposable phone numbers, we believe that companies should start with two aspects: how to prohibit the use of phone numbers to register fake accounts and discover accounts registered with disposable phone numbers. The following countermeasures are mainly adopted by analyzing organizations with a detection mechanism for the disposable phone number.

- When registering an account, the company requires the user to send a message to the designated phone number to obtain a verification code. Because the disposable phone number can only be used to receive messages, the user cannot use the disposable phone number to register an account.
- Some organizations remind users that the phone number entered is already associated with too many accounts and cannot continue to register for a new account.
- Because most temporary phone numbers belong to MVNOs, some organizations prohibit the use of phone numbers of MVNOs to register accounts. Therefore, this mechanism can prohibit phone numbers belonging to MVNOs from registering new accounts.
- Besides, the account registered with the temporary phone number has malicious behavior, such as publishing malicious content, which causes the account to be frozen and cannot log in.

In particular, airline seat spinning attacks, OTAs need to detect the behavior of their accounts. When a large number of fake scheduled flights are found in an account, the account's attack behavior is determined by combining other abnormal parameters of the account. On the other hand, for accounts with privacy leaks, OTAs need to encrypt passenger information in every content of their websites or apps. We will further study the countermeasures against temporary phone numbers in our future work.

7   Conclusions and Future Work

In summary, people use disposable phone numbers to register temporary accounts on some unknown organizations to protect their privacy. However, many disposable phone numbers are used to create accounts on well-known organizations, such as Apple and Google. Then, the disposable phone number becomes an accomplice of cybercriminals, causing privacy leaks and malicious attacks. In addition, among the organizations which are most affected by disposable phone numbers, more than half of the organizations' account security mechanisms fail to detect these phone numbers. Therefore, researchers should pay more attention to the security threats caused by disposable phone numbers.

Future research should consider the potential threats of disposable phone numbers in other fields, for example, social app. Besides, based on a large number of temporary mobile phone numbers and SMS data collected, a check tool can be developed and provided to companies to check fake accounts. More importantly, based on existing countermeasures, it is necessary to design more robust and complete methods to counter the threat of disposable phone numbers.

References

1. SMS. https://en.wikipedia.org/wiki/SMS. Accessed 18 June 2020
2. The New York Times, Facebook Security Breach Exposes Accounts of 50 Million Users. https://www.nytimes.com/2018/09/28/technology/facebook-hack-data-breach.html. Accessed 18 June 2020
3. Reaves, B., Scaife, N., Tian, D., Blue, L., Traynor, P., Butler, K.R.: Sending out an SMS: characterizing the security of the SMS ecosystem with public gateways. In: 2016 IEEE Symposium on Security and Privacy (SP), pp. 339–356. IEEE, May 2016
4. Reaves, B., et al.: Characterizing the security of the SMS ecosystem with public gateways. ACM Trans. Priv. Secur. (TOPS) **22**(1), 1–31 (2018)
5. Gelernter, N., Kalma, S., Magnezi, B., Porcilan, H.: The password reset MitM attack. In: 2017 IEEE Symposium on Security and Privacy (SP), pp. 251–267. IEEE, May 2017
6. Jiang, N., Jin, Y., Skudlark, A., Zhang, Z.L.: Greystar: fast and accurate detection of SMS spam numbers in large cellular networks using gray phone space. In: 22nd USENIX Security Symposium (USENIX Security 2013), pp. 1–16 (2013)
7. Murynets, I., Piqueras Jover, R.: Crime scene investigation: SMS spam data analysis. In: Proceedings of the 2012 Internet Measurement Conference, pp. 441–452, November 2012
8. Thomas, K., Iatskiv, D., Bursztein, E., Pietraszek, T., Grier, C., McCoy, D.: Dialing back abuse on phone verified accounts. In: Proceedings of the 2014 ACM SIGSAC Conference on Computer and Communications Security, pp. 465–476, November 2014
9. SIM swap fraud explained and how to help protect yourself. https://us.norton.com/internetsecurity-mobile-sim-swap-fraud.html. Accessed 4 Aug 2020
10. Google-libphonenumber. https://github.com/google/libphonenumber. Accessed 18 June 2020
11. Mobile phone number attribution. https://www.ip138.com/sj/. Accessed 18 June 2020
12. Analysys. https://boyue.analysys.cn/view/article.html?articleId=20019710&columnId=8. Accessed 18 June 2020
13. Heydari, A., ali Tavakoli, M., Salim, N., Heydari, Z.: Detection of review spam: a survey. Expert Syst. Appl. **42**(7), 3634–3642 (2015)
14. Apple called out for fake reviews on iOS App Store by Chinese state media. https://www.abacusnews.com/big-guns/apple-called-out-fake-reviews-ios-app-store-chinese-state-media/article/3017845. Accessed 20 June 2020
15. How Bots Are Disrupting Airline Ticket Sales. https://www.eweek.com/enterprise-apps/how-bots-are-disrupting-airline-ticket-sales. Accessed 20 June 2020
16. Flight status. http://www.variflight.com/ah118114/HistoryDataSearchRight.asp. Accessed 20 June 2020

Efficient Discrete Distribution Estimation Schemes Under Local Differential Privacy

Wenlong Dun[1] and Youwen Zhu[1,2(✉)]

[1] College of Computer Science and Technology,
Nanjing University of Aeronautics and Astronautics, Nanjing 211106, China
zhuyw@nuaa.edu.cn
[2] Guangxi Key Laboratory of Trusted Software,
Guilin University of Electronic Technology, Guilin 541004, China

Abstract. Recently, local differential privacy (LDP) has increasingly been leveraged to cope with privacy issues in data collection. Discrete distribution estimation schemes under LDP are the fundamental tools in the LDP setting, which enable data collector to collect discrete distribution estimation information about a population while protecting each individual's privacy, without relying on a trusted third party. Among these schemes, Ye-Barg mechanisms achieve the best utility in the medium privacy regime. Nevertheless, their communication cost between the user and data collector is $O(k)$ which is too large to be deployed in practice when the domain size k is large (or even unbounded). In this paper, we propose a family of new efficient discrete distribution estimation schemes under LDP which reduce the communication cost to less than $O(\log(2 + e^\epsilon))$ and obtain almost the same expected estimation loss as Ye-Barg mechanisms under ℓ_2^2 metric and ℓ_1 metric. Additionally, we compare our schemes with Ye-Barg mechanisms theoretically and experimentally and confirm our conclusion.

Keywords: Local differential privacy · Discrete distribution estimation · Utility · Communication cost

1 Introduction

Differential privacy [1] has increasingly become the de facto standard for data privacy in the research community. It provides a formal definition of privacy and provable privacy protection. Roughly speaking, differential privacy requires that the adversary cannot reliably infer an individual's data from public statistics regardless of the adversary's background and computational power [2]. Recently, local differential privacy (LDP) [3,4] has been proposed to protect the users' privacy without relying on a trust third data curator. In LDP, each user's raw data is perturbed before being sent to a data collector so that the perturbed data follows the requirement of LDP. After that, the data collector estimates valuable information about the whole dataset from the perturbed data submitted

© Springer Nature Singapore Pte Ltd. 2020
G. Xu et al. (Eds.): FCS 2020, CCIS 1286, pp. 508–523, 2020.
https://doi.org/10.1007/978-981-15-9739-8_38

by users. In recent years, more and more attention from academic and industrial community is focused on LDP. Google developed a LDP tool, RAPPOR [5,6], which has been employed in Chrome to collect the default homepage of the browser and the default search engine to defend the hijacking of user settings. Apple is also utilizing LDP-based mechanisms to identify popular emojis, new words, and other preferences in Safari [7]. Similar LDP techniques also have been deployed by Microsoft [8] and Alibaba [9].

The mechanisms to estimate discrete distribution under LDP are the fundamental tools in LDP. The works [10–14] present several LDP mechanisms for discrete distribution estimation in different situations. Among these works, Ye-Barg mechanisms [14] achieve the best performance in the existing discrete distribution estimation schemes in the medium privacy regime when $1 \ll e^\epsilon \ll k$, where ϵ is the privacy budget to measure the privacy level of the LDP schemes and k is the domain size of the discrete distribution. However, the communication cost of Ye-Barg mechanisms is $O(k)$ for each user which is too high to be deployed in practice when k is very large (or even unbounded). In order to reduce the communication cost between the user and data collector, we propose a family of new efficient discrete distribution estimation mechanisms based Ye-Barg mechanisms. We denote these mechanisms by EDDE. Not only the communication cost of EDDE can be reduced to less than $O(\log{(2 + e^\epsilon)})$, but also the utility of EDDE is almost the same to Ye-Barg mechanisms.

Our Main Contributions: We propose a family of new efficient discrete distribution estimation schemes under LDP whose utility is order-optimal in the medium to high privacy regime when $e^\epsilon \ll k$. We show that our schemes reduce the communication overheads between the user and data collector to less than $O(\log(2 + e^\epsilon))$ and obtain almost the same expected estimation loss as Ye-Barg mechanisms under ℓ_2^2 metric and ℓ_1 metric in the medium privacy regime when $1 \ll e^\epsilon \ll k$. Experiment results and theoretical analysis confirm that our new schemes obtain almost the same utility as Ye-Barg mechanisms in the medium privacy regime.

The rest of the paper is organized as follows. Section 2 reviews the problem model and introduce Ye-Barg mechanisms. We propose our new efficient discrete distribution estimation schemes in Sect. 3, and evaluate their performance by ℓ_2^2 metric and ℓ_1 metric. Section 4 describes the comparison between our schemes and Ye-Barg mechanisms through theoretical analysis and experimental results. Section 5 reviews related work. Finally, Sect. 6 concludes this paper.

2 Problem Model

2.1 Local Differential Privacy

Local differential privacy [3,4] is an extended version of differential privacy [1] in the local model, which is suitable for data collection without a trusted center.

Definition 1 (Local Differential Privacy). *One perturbation algorithm* A *satisfies ϵ-local differential privacy (ϵ-LDP), where $\epsilon > 0$, if and only if for any input x_1 and x_2, and any $y \in \mathrm{Range}(A)$, it has*

$$\Pr\big(A(x_1) = y\big) \leqslant e^{\epsilon}\Pr\big(A(x_2) = y\big) \tag{1}$$

where $\mathrm{Range}(A)$ *denotes the output space of* A.

2.2 Problem Definition

Let $\mathcal{X} = \{1, 2, \cdots, k\}$ and $\boldsymbol{p} = (p_1, p_2, \cdots, p_k)$ be a probability distribution on $\mathcal{X}$. The distribution $\boldsymbol{p} \in \Delta_k$, where $\Delta_k = \{\boldsymbol{p} \in \mathbb{R}^k \mid p_i \geqslant 0 \text{ for each } i = 1 \text{ to } k,$ and $\sum_{i=1}^{k} p_i = 1.0\}$. We consider the situation consisting of a data collector DC and n independent users $\{u_1, u_2, \cdots, u_n\}$. For $i = 1$ to n, user u_i has a private value $x_i \in \mathcal{X}$ which follows the probability distribution $\boldsymbol{p}$. If the privacy of private value is not considered, we are given direct access to i.i.d. samples $\{x_i\}_{i=1}^{n}$ generated from some unknown distribution $\boldsymbol{p} \in \Delta_k$ and obtain the estimation of unknown distribution $\hat{\boldsymbol{p}}$ based on the samples. In order to protect the privacy of user's private value, the user u_i perturbs its raw data x_i through a LDP mechanism locally and sends the perturbed reports $\boldsymbol{y}^{(i)}$ to the data collector. In the private distribution estimation model, we only estimate the distribution $\boldsymbol{p}$ according to the privatized samples $\{\boldsymbol{y}_i\}_{i=1}^{n}$ rather than the raw samples $\{x_i\}_{i=1}^{n}$.

We evaluate the utility of discrete distribution estimation schemes by the expected ℓ_2^2 loss and expected ℓ_1 loss between $\hat{\boldsymbol{p}}$ and $\boldsymbol{p}$. More especially,

$$\mathbb{E}\left(\ell_2^2\big(\hat{\boldsymbol{p}}(\{\boldsymbol{y}^{(i)}\}_{i=1}^{n}), \boldsymbol{p}\big)\right) = \sum_{i=1}^{k} \mathbb{E}(\hat{p}_i - p_i)^2,$$

$$\mathbb{E}\left(\ell_1\big(\hat{\boldsymbol{p}}(\{\boldsymbol{y}^{(i)}\}_{i=1}^{n}), \boldsymbol{p}\big)\right) = \sum_{i=1}^{k} \mathbb{E}|\hat{p}_i - p_i|^2.$$

2.3 Ye-Barg Mechanisms

To the best of our knowledge, Ye-Barg mechanisms [14] achieve the best performance in the existing discrete distribution schemes for k-ary alphabets under LDP, in the medium privacy regime, when $1 \ll e^{\epsilon} \ll k$. The Ye-Barg mechanisms work as follows.

Given a positive integer d where $1 \leq d < k$, each user u_i generates an k-dimensional binary vector $\boldsymbol{y}^{(i)} = (y_1^{(i)}, y_2^{(i)}, \cdots, y_k^{(i)})$ by the following method. (i) User u_i generates $y_{x_i}^{(i)}$ following the distribution in Eq. (2).

$$y_{x_i}^{(i)} = \begin{cases} 1, & \text{with probability } q_{\epsilon,k,d} \\ 0, & \text{with probability } 1 - q_{\epsilon,k,d} \end{cases} \tag{2}$$

where $q_{\epsilon,k,d} = \frac{e^\epsilon d}{e^\epsilon d+k-d}$. (ii) If $y_{x_i}^{(i)} = 1$, then user u_i uniformly randomly selects $d-1$ distinct numbers $\{i_1, i_2, \cdots, i_{d-1}\}$ from $\{1, 2, \cdots, k\}\backslash\{x_i\}$, and sets $y_j^{(i)} = 1$ if $j \in \{i_1, i_2, \cdots, i_{d-1}\}$ and $y_j^{(i)} = 0$ otherwise. If $y_{x_i}^{(i)} = 0$, user u_i uniformly randomly chooses d numbers $\{i_1, i_2, \cdots, i_d\}$ from $\{1, 2, \cdots, k\}\backslash\{x_i\}$, and sets $y_j^{(i)} = 1$ if $j \in \{i_1, i_2, \cdots, i_d\}$ and $y_j^{(i)} = 0$ otherwise.

We note that $\sum_{j=1}^k y_j^{(i)} = d$ where $y_j^{(i)}$ denotes the j-bit of $\boldsymbol{y}^{(i)}$. Obviously, all users' output alphabets can be denoted by $\mathcal{Y}_{k,d} = \{\boldsymbol{y} \in \{0,1\}^k \mid \sum_{j=1}^k y_j = d\}$. Each user u_i submits the perturbed report $\boldsymbol{y}^{(i)}$ to the data collector. Consequently, for each private value $x \in \mathcal{X}$, the probability p_x is estimated by the following Eq. (3).

$$\hat{p}_x = \frac{k \sum_{i=1}^n y_x^{(i)} - nd}{n(kq_{\epsilon,k,d} - d)}. \tag{3}$$

3 Our Proposed Mechanisms

In this section, we introduce our proposed mechanisms for discrete distribution estimation under LDP. The core idea of our mechanisms inspired by the Bloom filter of RAPPOR method is to utilize hashing to reduce the domain size of the discrete distribution. Our mechanisms reduce the communication overheads of Ye-barg mechanisms from $O(k)$ to less than $O(\log(2 + e^\epsilon))$ and at no cost of utility. In Sect. 3.1, we introduce our perturbation mechanism in the user-side. In Sect. 3.2, we introduce our aggregation and estimation mechanisms in the server-side and evaluate the performance of our mechanisms.

3.1 Perturbation Mechanism

Let $\mathbb{H}$ be a universal hash function family, in which each hash function H takes as input in $\mathcal{X}$ and outputs a value in $\{1, 2, \cdots, m\}$ with uniform distribution. Then, our proposed perturbation mechanism works as follows.

Given two positive integers m and d where $1 \leqslant d < m \leqslant k$, each user u_i selects a hash function $H_i \in \mathbb{H}$, computes $v_i = H_i(x_i)$, and then generates an m-dimensional binary vector $\boldsymbol{y}^{(i)} = (y_1^{(i)}, y_2^{(i)}, \cdots, y_m^{(i)})$ by the following method. (i) User u_i first generates $y_{v_i}^{(i)}$ according to the distribution in Eq. (4).

$$y_{v_i}^{(i)} = \begin{cases} 1, & \text{with probability } q_{\epsilon,m,d} \\ 0, & \text{with probability } 1 - q_{\epsilon,m,d} \end{cases} \tag{4}$$

where $q_{\epsilon,m,d} = \frac{e^\epsilon d}{e^\epsilon d+m-d}$. (ii) If $y_{v_i}^{(i)} = 1$, then user u_i uniformly randomly selects $d-1$ distinct numbers $\{i_1, i_2, \cdots, i_{d-1}\}$ from $\{1, 2, \cdots, m\}\backslash\{v_i\}$, and sets $y_j^{(i)} = 1$ if $j \in \{i_1, i_2, \cdots, i_{d-1}\}$ and $y_j^{(i)} = 0$ otherwise. If $y_{v_i}^{(i)} = 0$, user u_i uniformly randomly chooses d numbers $\{i_1, i_2, \cdots, i_d\}$ from $\{1, 2, \cdots, m\}\backslash\{v_i\}$, and sets $y_j^{(i)} = 1$ if $j \in \{i_1, i_2, \cdots, i_d\}$ and $y_j^{(i)} = 0$ otherwise.

Clearly, each output $\boldsymbol{y}^{(i)}$ belongs to the set $\mathcal{Y}_{m,d} = \{\boldsymbol{y} \in \{0,1\}^m \mid \sum_{j=1}^m y_j = d\}$ where y_j denotes the j-th bit of $\boldsymbol{y}$, and $\mid \mathcal{Y}_{m,d} \mid = \binom{m}{d}$. The perturbed value $\boldsymbol{y}^{(i)}$ and hash function H_i will be submitted to the data collector.

Proposition 1. *The proposed perturbation mechanism is ϵ-LDP.*

Proof. For any input $x \in \mathcal{X}$, let $\boldsymbol{y} = (y_1, y_2, \cdots, y_m)$ be its perturbed result and $v = H(x)$ be the hash value during generating $\boldsymbol{y}$. Then, if $y_v = 1$, $\Pr(\boldsymbol{y} \mid x) = \frac{e^\epsilon d}{e^\epsilon d + m - d} * \frac{1}{\binom{m-1}{d-1}} = \frac{(m-d)! * d! * e^\epsilon}{(m-1)! * (e^\epsilon d + m - d)}$; if $y_v = 0$, it is $\Pr(\boldsymbol{y} \mid x) = \frac{m-d}{e^\epsilon d + m - d} * \frac{1}{\binom{m-1}{d}} = \frac{(m-d)! * d!}{(m-1)! * (e^\epsilon d + m - d)}$.

Therefore, for any inputs x_1 and x_2, and any output $\boldsymbol{y} \in \mathcal{Y}_{m,d}$, it has

$$\Pr(\boldsymbol{y} \mid x_1) \leqslant e^\epsilon \Pr(\boldsymbol{y} \mid x_2).$$

Namely, the proposed mechanism is ϵ-LDP.

3.2 Aggregation and Estimation Mechanisms

The aggregation and estimation mechanisms in the server-side are as follows. After the data collector collects all users' perturbed results, for each $x \in \mathcal{X}$, the probability p_x is estimated by the following Eq. (5), where $q_{\epsilon,m,d} = \frac{e^\epsilon d}{e^\epsilon d + m - d}$.

$$\hat{p}_x = \frac{m \sum_{i=1}^n y_{H_i(x)}^{(i)} - nd}{n(mq_{\epsilon,m,d} - d)} \tag{5}$$

Note that the hash function H_i submitted to data collector by user u_i can be encoded using an index for the universal hash function family $\mathbb{H}$ and takes only $O(\log n)$ bits. In a real application scenario, each user u_i can utilize the hashcode of his or her unique identity information which has been shared with data collector such as IP address, Email address and so on, to denote the index of H_i so that the communication cost between each user and the data collector can be reduced to $O(m)$ by this time.

Proposition 2. *The estimate in Eq. (5) is unbiased. For all ϵ, k, m and d, the expected ℓ_2^2 loss is given by Eq. (6), and the expected ℓ_1 loss in the situation of large n is given by Eq. (7).*

$$\mathbb{E}\left(\ell_2^2\left(\hat{\boldsymbol{p}}(\{\boldsymbol{y}^{(i)}\}_{i=1}^n), \boldsymbol{p}\right)\right) = \frac{1}{n}\left(\frac{k(e^\epsilon d + m - d)^2}{(m-d)d(e^\epsilon - 1)^2} + \frac{(m-2d)(e^\epsilon d + m - d)}{(m-d)d(e^\epsilon - 1)} - \sum_{x=1}^k p_x^2\right). \tag{6}$$

$$\mathbb{E}\left(\ell_1\left(\hat{\boldsymbol{p}}(\{\boldsymbol{y}^{(i)}\}_{i=1}^n), \boldsymbol{p}\right)\right) = \sum_{x=1}^k \sqrt{\frac{2}{n\pi}\left(\frac{e^\epsilon d + m - d}{(e^\epsilon - 1)d} - p_x\right)\left(\frac{e^\epsilon d + m - d}{(e^\epsilon - 1)(m - d)} + p_x\right)} + o(\frac{1}{\sqrt{n}}). \tag{7}$$

Proposition 3. *Let $\theta_{\epsilon,k}$ denote the value $\sqrt{\frac{e^\epsilon(e^\epsilon k - e^\epsilon + 1)}{k + e^\epsilon - 1}}$. Given ϵ and k, for any d, the optimal choice of m for the expected ℓ_2^2 loss and the expected ℓ_1 loss in worst case can be achieved by either $\lfloor(1 + \theta_{\epsilon,k})d\rfloor$ or $\lceil(1 + \theta_{\epsilon,k})d\rceil$.*

Proof. (*i*) We begin with the expected ℓ_2^2 loss. Let $f(m, d)$ denote the terms that contains (m, d) in Eq. (6). That is,

$$f(m, d) = \frac{k(e^\epsilon d + m - d)^2}{(m - d)d(e^\epsilon - 1)^2} + \frac{(m - 2d)(e^\epsilon d + m - d)}{(m - d)d(e^\epsilon - 1)}. \tag{8}$$

For the optimal choice, we need to minimize the $f(m, d)$. We take the derivative with respect to m and gain

$$\frac{\partial f}{\partial m} = \frac{(m - (1 + \theta_{\epsilon,k})d)(m - (1 - \theta_{\epsilon,k})d)}{(m - d)^2 d(e^\epsilon - 1)^2}.$$

While k is large and $\epsilon > 0$, it is easy to say $\theta_{\epsilon,k} > 1$. Besides, $1 \leqslant d < m$. Then, if $d < m < (1 + \theta_{\epsilon,k})d$, it has $\frac{\partial f}{\partial m} < 0$. If $(1 + \theta_{\epsilon,k})d < m$, it will be $\frac{\partial f}{\partial m} > 0$. Then, for any d, the minimum of $f(m, d)$ occurs, when $m = (1 + \theta_{\epsilon,k})d$. Since m is an integer, the optimal choice of m is thus $\lfloor(1 + \theta_{\epsilon,k})d\rfloor$ or $\lceil(1 + \theta_{\epsilon,k})d\rceil$.
(*ii*) We further consider the expected ℓ_1 loss in the worst case. According to Cauchy-Schwarz inequality, we can gain that the expected ℓ_1 shown in Eq. (7) reaches its maximum while $\boldsymbol{p}$ is the uniform distribution $\boldsymbol{p}_U = (\frac{1}{k}, \frac{1}{k}, \cdots, \frac{1}{k})$. Meanwhile, the expected ℓ_1 loss in the worst-case distribution is given by Eq. (9).

$$\mathbb{E}\left(\ell_1(\hat{\boldsymbol{p}}(\{\boldsymbol{y}^{(i)}\}_{i=1}^n), \boldsymbol{p}_U)\right) = \sqrt{\frac{2k}{n\pi}\left(\frac{k(e^\epsilon d + m - d)^2}{(m - d)d(e^\epsilon - 1)} + \frac{(m - 2d)(e^\epsilon d + m - d)}{(m - d)d(e^\epsilon - 1)} - \frac{1}{k}\right)} + o(\frac{1}{\sqrt{n}}). \tag{9}$$

Clearly,

$$\mathbb{E}\left(\ell_1(\hat{\boldsymbol{p}}(\{\boldsymbol{y}^{(i)}\}_{i=1}^n), \boldsymbol{p}_U)\right) = \sqrt{\frac{2k}{n\pi}\left(f(m, d) - \frac{1}{k}\right)} + o(\frac{1}{\sqrt{n}}).$$

Therefore, the minimum of the worst-case ℓ_1 loss can be achieved by the same parameter setting as that of the ℓ_2^2 loss. That is, for any d, the optimal choice of m for the expected ℓ_1 loss in the worst case is also either $\lfloor(1 + \theta_{\epsilon,k})d\rfloor$ or $\lceil(1 + \theta_{\epsilon,k})d\rceil$.

The above shows the minimums of the ℓ_2^2 loss and the worst-case ℓ_1 loss both occur while $m = (1 + \theta_{\epsilon,k})d$. In this situation, we have

$$f((1 + \theta_{\epsilon,k})d, d) = \frac{k(e^\epsilon + \theta_{\epsilon,k})^2}{\theta_{\epsilon,k}(e^\epsilon - 1)^2} + \frac{(\theta_{\epsilon,k} - 1)(e^\epsilon + \theta_{\epsilon,k})}{\theta_{\epsilon,k}(e^\epsilon - 1)}$$

which is constant for any d. Let $\lambda_{\epsilon,k} = f((1 + \theta_{\epsilon,k})d, d)$. For any $d \geqslant 1$, while $m = \lfloor(1 + \theta_{\epsilon,k})d\rfloor$ or $\lceil(1 + \theta_{\epsilon,k})d\rceil$, the ℓ_2^2 loss and the worst-case ℓ_1 loss always reach their optimums nearly. To save the communication overheads, we take $d =$

1 and $m = \lceil 1 + \theta_{\epsilon,k} \rceil$. In the following, we give the upper bound of the ℓ_2^2 loss and the worst-case ℓ_1 loss while (m, d) takes the nearly optimal choice ($\lceil 1 + \theta_{\epsilon,k} \rceil, 1$). Under the circumstances, m dimensional binary vector only including one 1 is sparse, so that we can send the index of 1 in this vector to the data collector. Hence, the communication overheads between user and data collector can be reduced to $O(\log(\lceil 1 + \theta_{\epsilon,k} \rceil))$ less than $O(\log(2 + e^\epsilon))$.

Proposition 4. *While $d = 1$ and $m = \lceil 1 + \theta_{\epsilon,k} \rceil$, for all ϵ, n, k and $\boldsymbol{p} \in \Delta_k$, we have*

$$\mathbb{E}\Big(\ell_2^2(\hat{\boldsymbol{p}}(\{\boldsymbol{y}^{(i)}\}_{i=1}^n), \boldsymbol{p})\Big)$$
$$< \frac{4e^\epsilon k}{n(e^\epsilon - 1)^2}\Big(1 + \frac{2e^\epsilon - 3}{4k} + \frac{k + 2e^\epsilon}{4e^\epsilon(e^\epsilon + 1)k}\Big) - \frac{1}{nk} \tag{10}$$

for large n, we have

$$\mathbb{E}\Big(\ell_1(\hat{\boldsymbol{p}}(\{\boldsymbol{y}^{(i)}\}_{i=1}^n), \boldsymbol{p}_U)\Big)$$
$$< \sqrt{\frac{8e^\epsilon}{\pi n}}\frac{k}{e^\epsilon - 1}\sqrt{\Big(1 + \frac{2e^\epsilon - 3 + \frac{k + 2e^\epsilon}{e^\epsilon(e^\epsilon + 1)}}{4k}\Big) - \frac{(e^\epsilon - 1)^2}{4k^2 e^\epsilon}} \tag{11}$$

In the regime $e^\epsilon \ll k$, we have

$$\mathbb{E}\Big(\ell_2^2(\hat{\boldsymbol{p}}(\{\boldsymbol{y}^{(i)}\}_{i=1}^n), \boldsymbol{p})\Big) = \Theta\Big(\frac{e^\epsilon k}{n(e^\epsilon - 1)^2}\Big)$$
$$\mathbb{E}\Big(\ell_1(\hat{\boldsymbol{p}}(\{\boldsymbol{y}^{(i)}\}_{i=1}^n), \boldsymbol{p}_U)\Big) = \Theta\Big(\frac{k}{e^\epsilon - 1}\sqrt{\frac{e^\epsilon}{n}}\Big) \tag{12}$$

In the regime $1 \ll e^\epsilon \ll k$, we have

$$\mathbb{E}\Big(\ell_2^2(\hat{\boldsymbol{p}}(\{\boldsymbol{y}^{(i)}\}_{i=1}^n), \boldsymbol{p})\Big) = \Theta\Big(\frac{k}{ne^\epsilon}\Big)$$
$$\mathbb{E}\Big(\ell_1(\hat{\boldsymbol{p}}(\{\boldsymbol{y}^{(i)}\}_{i=1}^n), \boldsymbol{p}_U)\Big) = \Theta\Big(\frac{k}{\sqrt{ne^\epsilon}}\Big) \tag{13}$$

Proof. Since $\theta_{\epsilon,k} = \sqrt{\frac{e^\epsilon(e^\epsilon k - e^\epsilon + 1)}{k + e^\epsilon - 1}} = e^\epsilon\sqrt{\frac{k + \frac{1 - e^\epsilon}{e^\epsilon}}{k + e^\epsilon - 1}}$ and $\frac{1 - e^\epsilon}{e^\epsilon} \leqslant 0 \leqslant e^\epsilon - 1$, then

$$1 + \theta_{\epsilon,k} \leqslant \lceil 1 + \theta_{\epsilon,k} \rceil \leqslant \lceil 1 + e^\epsilon \rceil < 2 + e^\epsilon.$$

While the bivariate function $f(m, d)$ is defined as Eq. (8), we thus have $f(\lceil 1 + \theta_{\epsilon,k} \rceil, 1) < f(2 + e^\epsilon, 1)$, and

$$f(2 + e^\epsilon, 1) = \frac{4ke^\epsilon}{(e^\epsilon - 1)^2}\Big(1 + \frac{2e^\epsilon - 3 + \frac{k + 2e^\epsilon}{e^\epsilon(e^\epsilon + 1)}}{4k}\Big). \tag{14}$$

Besides, $\sum_{x=1}^{k} p_x^2 \geqslant \frac{\left(\sum_{x=1}^{k} p_x\right)^2}{k} = \frac{1}{k}$. Then, in the setting that $d = 1$ and $m = \lceil 1 + \theta_{\epsilon,k} \rceil$, we have

$$\mathbb{E}\left(\ell_2^2\left(\hat{\boldsymbol{p}}(\{\boldsymbol{y}^{(i)}\}_{i=1}^n), \boldsymbol{p}\right)\right) = \frac{1}{n}\left(f(\lceil 1 + \theta_{\epsilon,k} \rceil, 1) - \sum_{x=1}^{k} p_x^2\right)$$

$$< \frac{1}{n} f(2 + e^\epsilon, 1) - \frac{1}{nk} \tag{15}$$

and similarly,

$$\mathbb{E}\left(\ell_1\left(\hat{\boldsymbol{p}}(\{\boldsymbol{y}^{(i)}\}_{i=1}^n), \boldsymbol{p}_U\right)\right) < \sqrt{\frac{2k}{n\pi}\left(f(2 + e^\epsilon, 1) - \frac{1}{k}\right)} \tag{16}$$

By substituting Eq. (14) into (15) and (16), we can gain (10) and (11), respectively. Finally, the Eqs. (12) and (13) follow immediately.

4 Comparison

In this section, we compare our proposed mechanisms denoted by EDDE with Ye-Barg mechanisms theoretically and experimentally.

4.1 Theoretical Comparison

In this section, we compare EDDE with Ye-Barg mechanisms in the literature. In Ye-Barg mechanisms [14], it is shown that the estimated probability $\hat{p}_x$ is unbiased estimation of the real probability p_x, which is the same with our schemes EDDE, and the optimal choice of d for both the expected ℓ_2^2 risk and the expected worst-case ℓ_1 risk is given by either $\lceil \frac{k}{e^\epsilon+1} \rceil$ or $\lfloor \frac{k}{e^\epsilon+1} \rfloor$. However, when d is $\lceil \frac{k}{e^\epsilon+1} \rceil$ or $\lfloor \frac{k}{e^\epsilon+1} \rfloor$, it's difficult to specifically formulate the expected ℓ_2^2 risk and the expected worst-case ℓ_1 risk of Ye-Barg mechanisms. From Proposition (3), we know that when $d = 1$ and $\lceil m = 1 + \sqrt{\frac{e^\epsilon(e^\epsilon k - e^\epsilon + 1)}{k + e^\epsilon - 1}} \rceil$ or $\lfloor m = 1 + \sqrt{\frac{e^\epsilon(e^\epsilon k - e^\epsilon + 1)}{k + e^\epsilon - 1}} \rfloor$, the expected ℓ_2^2 risk and the expected worst-case ℓ_1 risk of our mechanisms EDDE obtain optimal value. Similarly, it's also difficult to specifically formulate the optimal expected ℓ_2^2 risk and expected worst-case ℓ_1 risk of EDDE. Hence, we attempt to compare the optimal expected ℓ_2^2 risk and expected worst-case ℓ_1 risk of EDDE and Ye-Barg mechanisms by plotting their graphs.

From [14], we obtain the expected ℓ_2^2 risk of Ye-Barg mechanisms as Eq. (17) and expected worst-case ℓ_1 risk as Eq. (18).

$$\mathbb{E}\left(\ell_2^2\left(\hat{\boldsymbol{p}}(\{\boldsymbol{y}^{(i)}\}_{i=1}^n)\right)\right) = \frac{1}{n}\left(\frac{(d(k-2)+1)e^{2\epsilon}}{(k-d)(e^\epsilon-1)^2} + \frac{2(k-2)e^\epsilon}{(e^\epsilon-1)^2} + \frac{(k-2)(k-d)+1}{d(e^\epsilon-1)^2} - \sum_{x=1}^{k} p_x^2\right). \tag{17}$$

$$\mathbb{E}\left(\ell_1\left(\hat{\boldsymbol{p}}(\{\boldsymbol{y}^{(i)}\}_{i=1}^n)\right)\right) = \frac{1}{e^\epsilon-1}\sqrt{\frac{2(k-1)}{n\pi}\left(e^\epsilon-1+\frac{k(d-1)e^\epsilon}{k-d}+k\right)\left(e^\epsilon+\frac{k-d}{d}\right)} + o(\frac{1}{\sqrt{n}}). \tag{18}$$

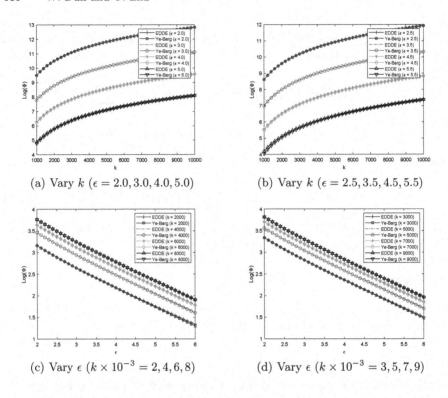

(a) Vary k ($\epsilon = 2.0, 3.0, 4.0, 5.0$)

(b) Vary k ($\epsilon = 2.5, 3.5, 4.5, 5.5$)

(c) Vary ϵ ($k \times 10^{-3} = 2, 4, 6, 8$)

(d) Vary ϵ ($k \times 10^{-3} = 3, 5, 7, 9$)

Fig. 1. Log(Φ) of EDDE mechanisms and Ye-Barg mechanisms with privacy budget ϵ and domain size k.

According to the expected ℓ_2^2 risk of EDDE Eq. (6) and the expected ℓ_2^2 risk of Ye-Barg mechanisms Eq. (17), we note that they all include $\frac{1}{n}$ and $(-\sum_{x=1}^{k} p_x^2)$ so that we can omit them in the process of comparison and obtain Eq. (19) and Eq. (20), respectively.

$$\Phi_{EDDE}(d, k, \epsilon, m) = \frac{k(e^\epsilon d + m - d)^2}{(m-d)d(e^\epsilon - 1)^2} + \frac{(m - 2d)(e^\epsilon d + m - d)}{(m-d)d(e^\epsilon - 1)}. \tag{19}$$

$$\Phi_{Ye-Barg}(d, k, \epsilon) = \frac{(d(k-2)+1)e^{2\epsilon}}{(k-d)(e^\epsilon - 1)^2} + \frac{2(k-2)e^\epsilon}{(e^\epsilon - 1)^2} + \frac{(k-2)(k-d)+1}{d(e^\epsilon - 1)^2}. \tag{20}$$

If we can get the relationship between Φ_{EDDE} setting $d = 1$ and $\lceil m = 1 + \sqrt{\frac{e^\epsilon(e^\epsilon k - e^\epsilon + 1)}{k + e^\epsilon - 1}} \rceil$ or $\lfloor m = 1 + \sqrt{\frac{e^\epsilon(e^\epsilon k - e^\epsilon + 1)}{k + e^\epsilon - 1}} \rfloor$ and $\Phi_{Ye-Barg}$ setting $d = \lceil \frac{k}{e^\epsilon + 1} \rceil$ or $d = \lfloor \frac{k}{e^\epsilon + 1} \rfloor$, we will get the relationship between Eq. (6) and Eq. (17). In practice, if given k and ϵ, the values of m in EDDE and d in Ye-Barg mechanisms are sole by rounding $m = 1 + \sqrt{\frac{e^\epsilon(e^\epsilon k - e^\epsilon + 1)}{k + e^\epsilon - 1}}$ and $d = \frac{k}{e^\epsilon + 1}$ to the nearest integer which is equal or greater than 1. Hence, we plot the graphs of Log(Φ_{EDDE}) and Log($\Phi_{Ye-Barg}$) under fixing privacy budget $\epsilon = 2.0, 2.5,$

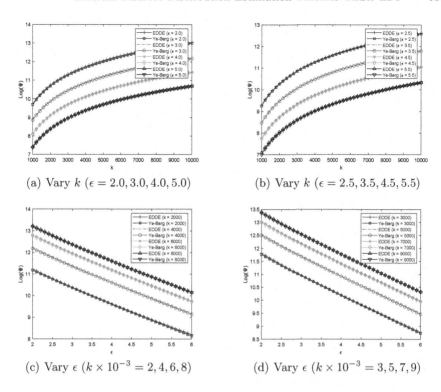

(a) Vary k ($\epsilon = 2.0, 3.0, 4.0, 5.0$)

(b) Vary k ($\epsilon = 2.5, 3.5, 4.5, 5.5$)

(c) Vary ϵ ($k \times 10^{-3} = 2, 4, 6, 8$)

(d) Vary ϵ ($k \times 10^{-3} = 3, 5, 7, 9$)

Fig. 2. Log(Ψ) of EDDE mechanisms and Ye-Barg mechanisms with privacy budget ϵ and domain size k.

3.0, 3.5, 4.0, 4.5, 5.0, 5.5 and varying the domain size k from 1000 to 10000 to obtain the Fig. 1(a) and 1(b). When we fix the domain size $k = 2000, 3000, 4000,$ 5000, 6000, 7000, 8000, 9000 and change privacy budget ϵ from 2.0 to 6.0, we plot the graphs of Log(Φ_{EDDE}) and Log($\Phi_{Ye-Barg}$) to get Fig. 1(c) and 1(d). From Fig. 1(a), 1(b), 1(c) and 1(d), we notice that the Log(Φ) of EDDE mechanisms and Ye-Barg mechanisms are almost identical regardless of ϵ and k when $1 \ll e^{\epsilon} \ll k$, i.e. in the medium privacy regime. Hence, the optimal expected ℓ_2^2 risks of EDDE and Ye-Barg mechanisms are almost the same in the medium privacy regime.

Similar to ℓ_2^2 risk, we omit $\sqrt{\frac{2}{n\pi}}$ and $o(\frac{1}{\sqrt{n}})$ in the expected worst-case ℓ_1 risk of EDDE Eq. (9) and the expected worst-case ℓ_1 risk of Ye-Barg mechanisms Eq. (18) to get the Eq. (21) and (22), respectively.

$$\Psi_{EDDE}(d, k, \epsilon, m) = \sqrt{k\left(\frac{k(e^{\epsilon}d + m - d)^2}{(m-d)d(e^{\epsilon} - 1)} + \frac{(m-2d)(e^{\epsilon}d + m - d)}{(m-d)d(e^{\epsilon} - 1)} - \frac{1}{k}\right)}.$$

$$(21)$$

Table 1. The input parameters of $DataGen$

Parameter	Description
n	The number of users in dataset
k	The domain size of user's discrete value
ζ	The distribution of user's discrete value

$$\Psi_{Ye-Barg}(d, k, \epsilon) = \frac{1}{e^\epsilon - 1}\sqrt{(k-1)\left(e^\epsilon - 1 + \frac{k(d-1)e^\epsilon}{k-d} + k\right)\left(e^\epsilon + \frac{k-d}{d}\right)}. \tag{22}$$

We also aim to prove the relationship between Ψ_{EDDE} and $\Psi_{Ye-Barg}$ to get the relationship between Eq. (9) and Eq. (18). The setting of d and m in EDDE and d in Ye-Barg mechanisms are the same to which of ℓ_2^2 risk comparison. Then, we plot the graphs of $\text{Log}(\Psi_{EDDE})$ and $\text{Log}(\Psi_{Ye-Barg})$ under fixing privacy budget $\epsilon = 2.0, 2.5, 3.0, 3.5, 4.0, 4.5, 5.0, 5.5$ and varying the domain size k from 1000 to 10000 to obtain the Fig. 2(a) and 2(b). When we fix the domain size $k = 2000, 3000, 4000, 5000, 6000, 7000, 8000, 9000$ and change privacy budget ϵ from 2.0 to 6.0, we plot the graphs of $\text{Log}(\Psi_{EDDE})$ and $\text{Log}(\Psi_{Ye-Barg})$ to get Fig. 2(c) and 2(d). From Fig. 2(a), 2(b), 2(c) and 2(d), we notice that the $\text{Log}(\Psi)$ of EDDE and Ye-Barg mechanisms are almost identical regardless of ϵ and k when $1 \ll e^\epsilon \ll k$, i.e. in medium privacy regime. Generally speaking, the optimal worst-case expected ℓ_1 risks of EDDE and Ye-Barg mechanism are almost the same in the medium privacy regime.

Through the above theoretical analysis, we know that the optimal expected ℓ_2^2 risks and worst-case expected ℓ_1 risks of our schemes EDDE and Ye-Barg mechanisms are almost the same regardless of ϵ and k in the medium privacy regime. Besides, we note that Ye-Barg mechanisms give order-optimal performance in the medium to high privacy regime. More specifically, when ϵ is small and k is large, the ℓ_2^2 risk is approximately $\frac{4k}{n\epsilon^2}$, and the ℓ_1 risk is approximately $\frac{2k}{\epsilon}\sqrt{\frac{2}{\pi n}}$. To compare our schemes with Ye-Barg mechanisms in the medium to high privacy regime, let ϵ be small and k be large. According to Eq. (10), (11) and (12), the ℓ_2^2 risk of our scheme is approximately $\frac{4k}{n\epsilon^2}$ and the ℓ_1 risk is approximately $\frac{2k}{\epsilon}\sqrt{\frac{2}{\pi n}}$, which are exactly the same as those of Ye-Barg mechanisms. Furthermore, when $1 \ll e^\epsilon \ll k$, the ℓ_2^2 risk of Ye-Barg mechanisms is $\Theta\left(\frac{k}{ne^\epsilon}\right)$ and the ℓ_1 risk of them is $\Theta\left(\frac{k}{\sqrt{ne^\epsilon}}\right)$ which are also exactly the same as those of our schemes according to Eq. (13). Hence, our schemes also are order-optimal in the medium to high privacy regime.

4.2 Experiment Comparison

In this section, we empirically evaluate the utility of EDDE and Ye-Barg mechanisms on synthetic datasets. We use the logarithm based two of Mean Square Error (MSE) to quantify their utility.

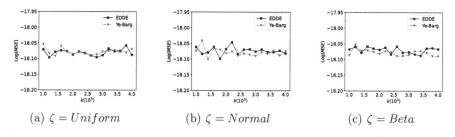

Fig. 3. Log(*MSE*) of EDD mechanisms and Ye-Barg mechanisms from datasets of different distribution with $\epsilon = 2.0$ and k varying from 1000 to 4000

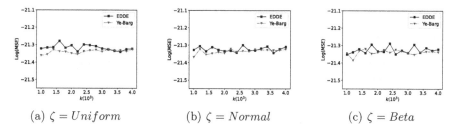

Fig. 4. Log(*MSE*) of EDD mechanisms and Ye-Barg mechanisms from datasets of different distribution with $\epsilon = 4.0$ and k varying from 1000 to 4000

$$\text{MSE} = \frac{1}{k} \sum_{j \in [k]} (\hat{p}_j - p_j)^2 \tag{23}$$

We design a dataset generator DataGen to generate datasets of different discrete distribution according to the input parameters as shown in Table 1. In order to make the utility of both mechanisms more better and avoid errors due to insufficient data, we set $n = 200000$ in the following experiments. In dataset generator DataGen, we first generate all numeric values of each distribution and obtain their maximum and minimum, then transform them to discrete numbers in $\{1, 2, \cdots, k\}$. Without losing generality, ζ is chosen from three distributions, i.e. Uniform, Standard Normal and Beta distribution (with distribution parameters $\alpha = 2.0$ and $\beta = 5.0$). All experiments are performed fifty times and we use the average of the results for demonstration.

In the first experiment, we generate different datasets by varying the domain size k when ζ is Uniform, Normal or Beta and $n = 200000$. Then, we fix $\epsilon = 2.0$ or $\epsilon = 4.0$ and compare the utility of our mechanisms EDDE and Ye-Barg mechanisms on these datasets to obtain Fig. 3 and Fig. 4. From Fig. 3 and Fig. 4, we can know that the datasets' distribution and the domain size k have little influence on the utility of EDDE and Ye-Barg mechanisms. Besides, it can be known that our schemes EDDE have almost the same utility as Ye-Barg mechanisms when the domain size changes when $1 \ll e^\epsilon \ll k$.

In the second experiment, we generate six different datasets whose size n is still 200000 when ζ is Uniform, Normal or Beta and k is 2000 or 3000. Then,

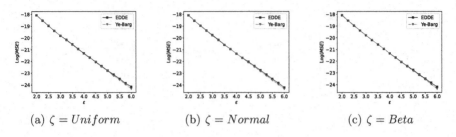

Fig. 5. Log(MSE) of EDDE mechanisms and Ye-Barg mechanisms from datasets of different distribution with $k = 2000$ and ϵ varying from 2.0 to 6.0

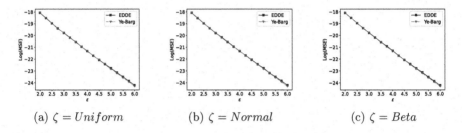

Fig. 6. Log(MSE) of EDDE mechanisms and Ye-Barg mechanisms from datasets of different distribution with $k = 3000$ and ϵ varying from 2.0 to 6.0

we compare the utility of EDDE and Ye-Barg mechanisms on datasets when k is 2000 and ζ is Uniform, Normal, Beta with ϵ varying from 2.0 to 6.0 to get Fig. 5. Similarly, we get Fig. 6 when k is 3000 and ζ is Uniform, Normal, Beta with ϵ increasing from 2.0 to 6.0. From the results in Fig. 5 and Fig. 6, we can get that the distribution of datasets does not affect the utility of EDDE and Ye-Barg mechanisms which is related to ϵ. The bigger the privacy budget ϵ, the better the utility of EDDE and Ye-Barg mechanisms. Furthermore, the utility of EDDE is almost the same to that of Ye-Barg mechanisms no matter what the privacy budget ϵ is when $1 \ll e^{\epsilon} \ll k$.

5   Related Work

The notion of differential privacy was introduced by Dwork in [1], which has been the widely-used standard for protecting privacy in data collection. Differential privacy has caught much attention from miscellaneous fields such as machine learning [15], data management [16], and so on. During the initial period, the models of differential privacy [17–19] depended on a trusted third party, called centralized differential privacy, which adds noise to the aggregated results so that the amount of revealed information for individuals is bounded and can't threaten their privacy security.

In recent years, local differential privacy (LDP) [3,4] has been proposed. The major difference between LDP and DP is that the security of user privacy under LDP does not depend on a trust third party which probably doesn't exist in real life. LDP has been deployed by many companies such as Google [5,6], Apple [7], and Microsoft [8]. There are many types of research about LDP in the academic community. Holohan *et al.* [12] provide the selection of the optimal parameters in randomized response mechanism for binary frequency estimation under LDP. Wang *et al.* [13] propose a pure LDP protocol framework to compare multiple discrete distribution estimation schemes, theoretically optimize some of them and result in two new protocols (i.e., Optimized Unary Encoding and Optimized Local Hashing) which can substantially reduce the expected estimation error. Subsequently, Ye and Barg [14] proposed another discrete distribution estimation schemes under LDP which can significantly reduce the expected estimation error in the medium privacy regime when $1 \ll e^{\epsilon} \ll k$. Based on Ye-Barg mechanisms, we propose our efficient discrete distribution estimation schemes which reduce the communication cost to less than $O(\log(2 + e^{\epsilon}))$ without sacrificing utility.

On the basis of discrete distribution estimation under LDP, frequent itemset mining under LDP, heavy hitters identification under LDP, and range query under LDP also have a lot of related research work. Wang *et al.* [20] propose a Prefix Extending Method under LDP to identify heavy hitters when the domain of user's input data is particularly large (e.g., 2^{128}). Qin *et al.* [21] propose the LDPminer method to estimate heavy hitters when the user's input data is a set not only one number. Cormode *et al.* [22] propose two types of methods for range query under LDP, which are derived from hierarchical histograms [23] and Haar wavelet transform [24], respectively. In addition, Xue *et al.* design effective and high-efficiency mechanisms under LDP for set intersection and union in [25] and propose a novel joint distribution scheme under LDP which can be used to train a Naive Bayes classification in [26].

Besides, there is lots of related work for numerical number mean estimation under LDP. The mean estimation schemes under LDP can be constructed by adding noise with mean 0 to private real data through Laplace mechanism [19] or Gaussian mechanism [19,27]. Duchi *et al.* [28] propose a LDP mechanism to support the mean estimation of multidimensional numeric tuples. Wang *et al.* [29] propose a novel one-dimensional mean estimation scheme under LDP that is at least not worse than the existing mean estimation scheme, and extends the scheme to multidimensional data. Recently, some methods for conserving the privacy of users using machine learning techniques have been proposed in [30,31].

6   Conclusion

In this paper, we proposed a family of new efficient discrete distribution estimation schemes under local differential privacy, which obtained order-optimal performance in the medium to high privacy regime when $\epsilon \ll k$. Our schemes reduced the communication cost between user and data collector from $O(k)$ to less than $O(\log(2 + e^{\epsilon}))$ and obtained almost the same expected estimation loss as Ye-Barg mechanisms under ℓ_2^2 metric and ℓ_1 metric in the medium privacy regime when $1 \ll e^{\epsilon} \ll k$. Finally, we compared our proposed schemes with Ye-Barg mechanisms theoretically and experimentally and confirmed our conclusion.

Acknowledgment. This work is partly supported by the National Key Research and Development Program of China (No.2017YFB0802300), and the Research Fund of Guangxi Key Laboratory of Trusted Software (No. kx201906).

References

1. Dwork, C.: Differential privacy: a survey of results. In: Agrawal, M., Du, D., Duan, Z., Li, A. (eds.) TAMC 2008. LNCS, vol. 4978, pp. 1–19. Springer, Heidelberg (2008). https://doi.org/10.1007/978-3-540-79228-4_1
2. Chen, R., Li, H., Qin, A.K., Kasiviswanathan, S.P., Jin, H.: Private spatial data aggregation in the local setting. In: 2016 IEEE 32nd International Conference on Data Engineering (ICDE), pp. 289–300. IEEE, Helsinki (2016)
3. Kasiviswanathan, S.P., Lee, H.K., Nissim, K., Raskhodnikova, S., Smith, A.: What can we learn privately? In: 49th Annual IEEE Symposium on Foundations of Computer Science, pp. 531–540. IEEE, Philadelphia (2008)
4. Kasiviswanathan, S.P., Lee, H.K., Nissim, K., Raskhodnikova, S., Smith, A.: What can we learn privately? SIAM J. Comput. **2**(3), 793–826 (2011)
5. Erlingsson, Ú., Pihur, V., Korolova, A.: RAPPOR: randomized aggregatable privacy-preserving ordinal response. In: Proceedings of the 2014 ACM SIGSAC Conference on Computer and Communications Security, pp. 1054–1067. ACM, New York (2014)
6. Fanti, G., Pihur, V., Erlingsson, Ú.: Building a RAPPOR with the unknown: privacy-preserving learning of associations and data dictionaries. Proc. Priv. Enhanc. Technol. **2016**(3), 41–61 (2016)
7. Cormode, G., Jha, S., Kulkarni, T., Li, N., Srivastava, D., Wang, T.: Privacy at scale: local differential privacy in practice. In: Proceedings of the 2018 International Conference on Management of Data, pp. 1655–1658. ACM, New York (2018)
8. Ding, B., Kulkarni, J., Yekhanin, S.: Collecting telemetry data privately. In: Advances in Neural Information Processing Systems, pp. 3571–3580. Curran Associates, New York (2017)
9. Wang, T., et al.: Answering multi-dimensional analytical queries under local differential privacy. In: Proceedings of the 2019 International Conference on Management of Data, pp. 159–176. ACM, New York (2019)
10. Bassily, R., Smith, A.: Local, private, efficient protocols for succinct histograms. In: Proceedings of the Forty-Seventh Annual ACM Symposium on Theory of Computing, pp. 127–135. ACM, New York (2015)
11. Wang, S., et al.: Mutual information optimally local private discrete distribution estimation. arXiv preprint arXiv:1607.08025 (2016)
12. Holohan, N., Leith, D.J., Mason, O.: Optimal differentially private mechanisms for randomised response. IEEE Trans. Inf. Forensics Secur. **12**(11), 2726–2735 (2017)
13. Wang, T., Blocki, J., Li, N., Jha, S.: Locally differentially private protocols for frequency estimation. In: 26th USENIX Security Symposium, pp. 729–745. ACM, New York (2017)
14. Ye, M., Barg, A.: Optimal schemes for discrete distribution estimation under locally differential privacy. IEEE Trans. Inf. Theory **64**(8), 5662–5676 (2018)
15. Bassily, R., Nissim, K., Stemmer, U., Thakurta, A.G.: Practical locally private heavy hitters. In: Advances in Neural Information Processing Systems, pp. 2288–2296. Curran Associates, New York (2017)

16. Krishnan, S., Wang, J., Franklin, M.J., Goldberg, K., Kraska, T.: PrivateClean: data cleaning and differential privacy. In: Proceedings of the 2016 International Conference on Management of Data, pp. 937–951. ACM, New York (2016)

17. Dwork, C., McSherry, F., Nissim, K., Smith, A.: Calibrating noise to sensitivity in private data analysis. In: Halevi, S., Rabin, T. (eds.) TCC 2006. LNCS, vol. 3876, pp. 265–284. Springer, Heidelberg (2006). https://doi.org/10.1007/11681878_14

18. McSherry, F., Talwar, K.: Mechanism design via differential privacy. In: 48th Annual IEEE Symposium on Foundations of Computer Science (FOCS 2007), pp. 94–103. IEEE, Providence (2007)

19. Dwork, C., Roth, A.: The algorithmic foundations of differential privacy. Found. Trends Theor. Comput. Sci. 9(3–4), 211–407 (2014)

20. Wang, T., Li, N., Jha, S.: Locally differentially private heavy hitter identification. IEEE Trans. Dependable Secure Comput. (2019). https://doi.org/10.1109/TDSC.2019.2927695

21. Qin, Z., Yang, Y., Yu, T., Khalil, I., Xiao, X., Ren, K.: Heavy hitter estimation over set-valued data with local differential privacy. In: Proceedings of the 2016 ACM SIGSAC Conference on Computer and Communications Security, pp. 192–203. ACM, New York (2016)

22. Cormode, G., Kulkarni, T., Srivastava, D.: Answering range queries under local differential privacy. Proc. VLDB Endow. 12(10), 1126–1138 (2019)

23. Qardaji, W., Yang, W., Li, N.: Understanding hierarchical methods for differentially private histograms. Proc. VLDB Endow. 6(14), 1954–1965 (2013)

24. Xiao, X., Wang, G., Gehrke, J.: Differential privacy via wavelet transforms. IEEE Trans. Knowl. Data Eng. 23(8), 1200–1214 (2010)

25. Xue, Q., Zhu, Y., Wang, J., Li, X., Zhang, J.: Distributed set intersection and union with local differential privacy. In: 2017 IEEE 23rd International Conference on Parallel and Distributed Systems (ICPADS), Shenzhen, pp. 198–205 (2017)

26. Xue, Q., Zhu, Y., Wang, J.: Joint distribution estimation and Naïve Bayes classification under local differential privacy. IEEE Trans. Emerg. Top. Comput. (2019). https://doi.org/10.1109/TETC.2019.2959581

27. Balle, B., Wang, Y.X.: Improving the Gaussian mechanism for differential privacy: analytical calibration and optimal denoising. arXiv preprint arXiv:1805.06530 (2018)

28. Duchi, J.C., Jordan, M.I., Wainwright, M.J.: Minimax optimal procedures for locally private estimation. J. Am. Stat. Assoc. 113(521), 182–201 (2018)

29. Wang, N., et al.: Collecting and analyzing multidimensional data with local differential privacy. In: 2019 IEEE 35th International Conference on Data Engineering (ICDE), pp. 638–649. IEEE, Macao (2019)

30. Sangaiah, A.K., Medhane, D.V., Han, T., Hossain, M.S., Muhammad, G.: Enforcing position-based confidentiality with machine learning paradigm through mobile edge computing in real-time industrial informatics. IEEE Trans. Ind. Inf. 15(7), 4189–4196 (2019)

31. Sangaiah, A.K., Medhane, D.V., Bian, G.B., Ghoneim, A., Alrashoud, M., Hossain, M.S.: Energy-aware green adversary model for cyberphysical security in industrial system. IEEE Trans. Ind. Inf. 16(5), 3322–3329 (2019)

Privacy Prediction of Lightweight Convolutional Neural Network

Shiyin Yang, Yongbiao Li, Dehua Zhou[✉], Linfeng Wei, and Qingqing Gan

Department of Computer Science, Jinan University, Guangzhou, China
mable@stu2018.jnu.edu.cn, {liyongbiao,tzhoudh,twei}@jnu.edu.cn,
gan_qingqing@foxmail.com

Abstract. The growing popularity of cloud-based deep learning raises a problem about accurate prediction and data privacy. Previous studies have implemented privacy prediction for simple neural networks. Since more complex neural networks require more computational overhead, existing privacy prediction schemes are inefficient. To tackles the above problem, this paper introduces a privacy prediction method for lightweight convolutional neural network (CNN) that can be applied to encrypted data. Firstly, the complex CNN is pruned into a lightweight network without compromising the original accuracy, which can realize secure prediction efficiently. Secondly, the FV homomorphic encryption scheme is adopted to encrypt the user's sensitive data and each layer in CNN is calculated on the ciphertext, so as to protect user's data privacy. Finally, the security analysis and experiment results demonstrate the privacy-preserving property and practicability of the proposed scheme, where the complex CNN on the MNIST data set can achieve more than 98% accuracy.

Keywords: Convolutional neural network · Homomorphic encryption · Network pruning · Privacy protection · Neural network prediction

1 Introduction

In recent years, there has been an increasing interest in machine learning and deep learning. Due to the blowout of data volume, breakthroughs in computing power and algorithms, deep learning has achieved great success in various fields, such as medical diagnosis [6,11], face recognition [5,22] and credit risk assessment [1,4]. Since the law *Health Insurance Portability and Accountability Act (HIPAA)* was passed by Congress in 1996, the issue that user's privacy has been attracting more and more attention. Subsequently, various countries promulgated *Privacy Act Of 1974*, *General Data Protection Regulation* and other bills to protect user's data privacy. In the context of big data, users worry that their private information will be collected, and service providers will also worry about the leakage of models. Therefore, it is an important issue to realize data analysis based on deep learning while ensuring the data privacy of both parties.

© Springer Nature Singapore Pte Ltd. 2020
G. Xu et al. (Eds.): FCS 2020, CCIS 1286, pp. 524–537, 2020.
https://doi.org/10.1007/978-981-15-9739-8_39

As for the neural networks, several privacy-protecting schemes have been extensively studied based on cryptographic tools such as homomorphic encryption, secure multi-party computing and differential privacy. Among them, homomorphic encryption allows computation on ciphertexts to generate an encrypted result, the result of which is the same as the result of their execution in plaintexts after decryption. However, the current homomorphic encryption schemes have many limitations. For example, they only support integer data, require a fixed multiplication depth or cannot perform addition and multiplication operations indefinitely. Due to the limitations of homomorphic encryption algorithms, they cannot be directly used in machine learning or deep learning to support the operations of comparison and maximum value. Secure multiparty computing is another privacy-preserving tool that distributes functions to multiple parties, and each party cannot obtain the data of other parties. The earliest secure multiparty computation was Millionaires' Problem in 1986 by Andrew Yao [27].

Convolutional neural network is one of common supervised machine learning algorithms, which usually proceed in two phases: training phase and inference phase. In the training phase, the user's sensitive data should not be leaked to the server who execute the model training, while in the inference phase, user's sensitive data which he want to predict should not be leaked to the server, and the deep learning model owned by the server should not be leaked to the user. Similarly, secure convolutional neural network also include the above two phases when they are applied on sensitive information such as medical data. Nowadays, there are various privacy prediction schemes for convolutional neural network to achieve secure training [17,26] and secure inference [9,21]. However, more complex neural networks incur heavier computational overhead, existing privacy prediction schemes are not suitable for practical application.

1.1 Main Contribution

In order to realize secure and efficient privacy prediction, we propose a novel privacy prediction approach with lightweight convolutional neural network (CNN). We consider this problem in the context where a patient wants to classify private images using a complex CNN trained by the hospital server. The main contribution is summarized as follows.

- Inspired by Li et al.'s scheme [15], we prune the complex CNN into a lightweight CNN with negligible influence on accuracy, which can support data prediction efficiently.
- We leverage the FV homomorphic encryption scheme [7] to encrypt the patient's private images so as to protect the privacy of sensitive data. And each layer in CNN is calculated on the ciphertext except the softmax layer.
- Finally, we analyze the security of the proposed privacy prediction scheme in CNN and conduct the experiment to show the practicability that the complex CNN on the MNIST data set can reach 98% accuracy.

1.2 Related Work

In the past few years, several privacy prediction schemes for convolutional neural network are proposed to achieve secure training. A method proposed by Shokri and Shmatikov [24] allows the parties to train their own neural network models locally and selectively share the gradients of some parameters with the central server. Security training also allows each data owner to secretly share training data to two (or more) non-conflicting servers, such as SecureML [17] or SecureNN [26]. Both of these schemes are based on homomorphic encryption, garbled circuit [27] and secret sharing [2,23]. SecureML uses a custom activation function, which is more effective for training neural networks using secure computing protocols.

Secure inference for a trained neural network has also been the main research direction. The CryptoNets [9] proposed by Microsoft uses leveled homomorphic encryption, which can realize a certain number of ciphertext multiplications. Considering the support of non-polynomial activation functions and pooling operations, Rouhani et al. [21] proposed the DeepSecure framework, which uses garbled circuits as its main encryption algorithm. In view of the characteristics of different secure computing protocols, many security prediction frameworks have been proposed based on hybrid protocols. For instance, the MiniONN framework [16] is proposed based on the garbled circuit protocol to perform nonlinear activation functions, and adopt the secret-sharing-based protocol to perform linear operations. The Chanelemon framework [20] uses the GMW protocol [10] for low-order nonlinear activation functions, and leverages the garbled circuit protocol to calculate more complex nonlinear activation functions.

2 Preliminary

2.1 Homomorphic Encryption

Homomorphic encryption is an important cryptographic technique, and its implementation is based on the computational complexity theory of mathematically difficult problems. Homomorphic encryption can be divided into three categories: partially homomorphic encryption (PHE), leveled homomorphic encryption (LHE) and fully homomorphic encryption (FHE). In 2009, Gentry [8] constructed the first FHE scheme by leveraging the "Bootstrapping" operation to reduce the ciphertext noise generated by the homomorphic operation. Their scheme can support more layers of homomorphic multiplication operations, but the "Bootstrapping" operation is not efficient. On this basis, many FHE schemes have constructed to improves the computational efficiency, such as integer-based FHE and (Ring) learning-with-error-based FHE.

The encryption scheme used in this paper is the FV homomorphic encryption scheme [7], which optimizes the FHE scheme proposed by Gentry to improve the efficiency of the "Bootstrapping" operation and reduce the increase in noise in the ciphertext. FV homomorphic encryption scheme mainly includes five algorithms: key generation, encryption algorithm, decryption algorithm, homomorphic addition and homomorphic multiplication operation.

For the key generation algorithm, the user randomly selects a polynomial sk from the ring R_2^n as the secret key: $sk \leftarrow R_2^n$, we use $a \leftarrow R_c^b$ to denote a is a uniformly distributed random vector in the polynomial ring R_c^b and $a \leftarrow \chi$ to denote a is a random vector subject to Gaussian distribution with standard deviation. The public key in the FV scheme consists of two parts, $pk = (pk_0, pk_1) = ([-(as + e)]_q, a)$, where $a \leftarrow R_q^n$, $e \leftarrow \chi$. The evaluation key consists of two parts $evk = (evk_0, evk_1) = ([-(a_i \cdot s + e_i) + T^i \cdot sk^2], a_i), i \in [0, l]$, where $a_i \leftarrow R_q^n$, $e_i \leftarrow \chi$, T_i is the base of FV scheme, $l = \lfloor log_T q \rfloor$.

The plaintext space of FV homomorphic encryption is $R_t^n = Z_t[x]/(x^n + 1)$. To encrypt a message $m \in R_t^n$, the ciphertext contains two elements on the polynomial ring $c \in R_q^n$ shown as follows:

$$c = (c_0, c_1) = ([\lfloor q/t \rfloor \cdot m + pk_0 \cdot u + e_1]_q, [pk_1 \cdot u + e_2]_q) \tag{1}$$

where $u \leftarrow R_2^n$, $e_1, e_2 \leftarrow \chi$.

Decryption is done by computing:

$$m = [\lfloor t/q \cdot [c_0 + c_1 \cdot s]_q \rfloor]_t \tag{2}$$

The addition operation over two ciphertexts $c_a = (c_a^0, c_a^1)$ and $c_b = (c_b^0, c_b^1)$ in R_q^n can be supported by:

$$c' = c_a + c_b = (c_a^0 + c_b^0, c_a^1 + c_b^1) \tag{3}$$

To multiply two messages $c_a = (c_a^0, c_a^1)$ and $c_b = (c_b^0, c_b^1)$, we need compute:

$$C_0 = [\lfloor t/q \cdot c_a^0 \cdot c_b^0 \rfloor]_q \tag{4}$$

$$C_1 = [\lfloor t/q(c_a^0 \cdot c_b^1 + c_a^1 \cdot c_b^0) \rfloor]_q \tag{5}$$

$$C_2 = [\lfloor t/q \cdot c_a^1 \cdot c_b^1 \rfloor]_q \tag{6}$$

The ciphertext consists of two parts, and the above three variables need to be relinearized:

$$c' = (c_0', c_1') = ([C_0 + \sum_{i=0}^{l} evk_0^i \cdot C_2^i]_q, [C_1 + \sum_{i=0}^{l} evk_1^i \cdot C_2^i]_q) \tag{7}$$

The decryption result of c_a is the operation result of the plaintext corresponding to c_a and c_b. For more details, please refer to [7].

2.2 Convolutional Neural Network

Neural network is a complex model which consists of many different layers of neurons, with each layer receiving inputs from previous layers, and passing outputs to further layers. In 1962, Hubel and Wiesel [13] conducted a systematic study of cat vision. Inspired from it, Lecun [14] proposed Convolutional Neural Network (CNN) in 1989. CNN is one of the classic algorithms of deep learning with a wide application in image recognition, face recognition, speech recognition and natural language processing. CNN usually contains the five layers: convolutional layer, pooling layer, activation layer, fully connected layer and softmax layer.

Convolutional Layer. The role of the convolutional layer is to extract the features of the input data, which is composed of a set of feature maps formed by multiple neurons. The filter performs a convolution operation with the feature map of the previous layer to generate the feature map of the next layer. Each neuron in the filter corresponds to a weight parameter and a bias vector. We use X_i to denote the i-th feature map in the convolutional layer. The l-th layer convolution layer receives n_l feature maps as input, and generates n_{l+1} feature maps after the convolution operation. The operation of the convolutional layer can be expressed as:

$$Y_i = \sum_{j=1}^{n_l} X_j \otimes W_{ij} \qquad (i = 1, 2, \ldots, n_{l+1}) \tag{8}$$

where $\otimes$ denotes convolution operation, W_{ij} denotes the connection weight between the j-th neuron and the i-th neuron.

Pooling Layer. The pooling layer usually follows the convolutional layer. Like the convolutional layer, the pooling layer is also composed of multiple feature maps. The difference is that each feature map in the pooling layer corresponds uniquely to the feature map of the previous layer. Currently there are two main pooling operations: maximum pooling and average pooling. The maximum pooling is to select the maximum value in the local connection domain, and the average pooling is to take the average value of the local connection domain.

Activation Function. In a deep neural network, there is usually a mapping relationship between neurons in two adjacent layers. This mapping relationship is called an activation function. Common activation functions include Sigmoid [12], tanh [3] and ReLU functions [18]. The output layer of this layer in the neural network will be passed to the next layer of neurons.

Fully Connected Layer. In CNN, after combining multiple sets of convolutional layers and pooling layers, it usually contains several fully connected layers. A fully connected layer is where each neuron in two adjacent layers is fully connected. The operation of the fully connected layer can be expressed as:

$$Y_i = \sum_{j=1}^{n_l} X_j W_{ij} \qquad (i = 1, 2, \ldots, n_{l+1}) \tag{9}$$

Where n_l denotes the number of input neurons, and n_{l+1} denotes the number of output neurons.

Softmax Layer. The CNN relies on a fully connected network to classify the extracted features, and the output value of the fully connected layer is passed to a softmax layer for classification. The softmax function maps k real numbers in $(-\infty, +\infty)$ into k real numbers in $(0, 1)$, while ensuring that their sum is 1.

3   Privacy Prediction Scheme of Lightweight CNN

In this paper, we design a lightweight CNN prediction scheme with privacy protection, focusing on the secure CNN inference phase. Our proposed scheme mainly includes two entities: users and cloud servers. Here we consider a realistic scenario between a patient and a hospital: the patient sends his personal encrypted health information to the hospital, and the hospital uses the trained prediction model to predict the encrypted health information; then the encrypted prediction result is returned to the patient, who decrypts it and obtains the final diagnosis result. During this process, the hospital cannot obtain the patient's private information. At the same time, because the patient has not used the deep learning model, the model is also protected for the hospital.

3.1   CNN Pruning

Inspired by Li et al.'s scheme [15], we prune the CNN without compromising the original accuracy. In each filter, the smaller the sum of the absolute values of the convolution kernels of each channel, the lower the importance of the filter. Each layer selects the m least important filters for pruning. The pruning method is to remove some less important filters from a trained model while minimizing the accuracy loss, so as to improve the calculation efficiency. For the CNN pruning, the most important point is how to choose the filter that needs pruning, and how to judge whether the weight is redundant.

Each filter contains one or more channels, and each channel represents a convolution kernel. The importance of this filter is measured by the sum of the absolute values of the convolution kernels of all channels in each filter. For the p-th channel of a filter, the sum of the absolute value of each weight in the convolution kernel of can be expressed as:

$$K_p = \sum_{i=1}^{k \times k} |w_i| \tag{10}$$

Where k denotes the size of the convolution kernel, w_i denotes each weight in the convolution kernel.

The sum of the absolute values of the convolution kernels of all channels for the j-th filter in the l-th layer can be expressed as:

$$F_j^l = \sum_{p=1}^{n_i} K_p \tag{11}$$

Where n_i denotes the number of channels of the filter in the l-th layer.

In the l-th convolutional layer, there are a total of n_{l+1} filters, which sorts the order of $S_j^l (j \leq n_{l+1})$ from small to large, and selects m filters with the smallest absolute value to prune. The above describes the construction method of single layer convolutional layer. When pruning the filters of multiple convolutional layers, each layer is regarded as independent, that is, each layer is pruned according to the method of a single layer filter.

3.2 Preprocessing Stage

The data type of the parameters in CNN is usually real numbers, such as the MNIST data set. When used as the input layer, the pixels of each picture are located between [0, 255] or converted into floating point numbers between [0, 1]. However, the plaintext space of the FV homomorphic encryption scheme is not an integer field or a real number field, but a polynomial quotient ring $R_t^n = Z_t[x]/(x^n+1)$, and the ciphertext space is $R_q^n = Z_q[x]/(x^n+1)$. To use FV homomorphic encryption, we need to encode input data and model parameters, and map integers or floating-point numbers into plaintext space.

Integer Coding. Choosing $B = 2$, we can encode the integer of $-(2^n - 1) \leq a \leq 2^n - 1$. First of all, $|a|$ is represented by n-bit binary representation as $a_{n-1} \dots a_1 a_0$. The specific coding formula is as follows:

$$IntegerEncode(a, B = 2) = sign(a) \cdot (a_{n-1}x^{n-1} + \cdots + a_1 x + a_0) \quad (12)$$

Floating Point Encoding. We multiply the real number by a scaling factor S, convert the decimal to an integer, and then encode by the same way as the integer above. The specific formula is as follows:

$$\begin{aligned} FracEncode(a, S, B = 2) &= IntegerEncode(\lfloor a \cdot S \rfloor, B = 2) \\ &= IntegerEncode(a', B = 2) \quad (13) \\ &= sign(a') \cdot (a'_{n-1}x^{n-1} + \cdots + a'_1 x + a'_0) \end{aligned}$$

CRT Batching. In homomorphic encryption schemes, a batch processing technique called Single Instruction Multiple Data (SIMD) [25], is often used. In general, it packs n integers with modulo t into a plaintext polynomial. The batch operation requires a polynomial order n and a plaintext space coefficient modulus t, requiring t to be prime and $t \equiv 1 (mod\ 2n)$. If the polynomial is selected as x^n+1, it means that n integers with modulo t can be packed in a polynomial. This method is called Chinese Remainder Theorem Batching (CRT batching) [19].

3.3 CNN Ciphertext Calculation

The original CNN is trained to obtain a pruned CNN, and the lightweight CNN is used for privacy prediction. Because only the filter is pruned, it is similar to the ordinary CNN, and is still composed of a convolutional layer, an activation layer, a pooling layer, and a fully connected layer. Note that in the prediction phase, we do not use the softmax layer because it does not affect the prediction results. Then we will explain the ciphertext calculation process by different layers. Since the plaintext and ciphertext spaces of FV homomorphic encryption are both polynomials, before the prediction of the ciphertext, the input samples have been encoded and encrypted, while the neural network parameters are only encoded.

Convolutional Layer. The ciphertext calculation on the convolutional layer, the input is the encrypted picture. Each element in the picture encrypted with FV is denoted by $[\cdot]$, and the weight is denoted by w_i. The convolution operation on the ciphertext can be expressed as:

$$[Y_i] = \sum_{j=1}^{n_l}([X_j] \otimes W_{ij}) \qquad (i = 1, 2, \ldots, n_{l+1}) \tag{14}$$

where $\sum$ denotes ciphertext accumulation operation, $\otimes$ denotes convolution operation. X_j is the input j-th feature map, Y_i is the output i-th feature map, and W_{ij} denotes the convolution kernel used in the convolution operation. The client encrypts and uploads the picture $[X]$ to the server, and the server performs the convolution operation on the ciphertext.

Activation Function. In CNN model, the convolutional layer and the fully connected layer are both linear layers, and perform linear operations. If there is no nonlinear function, the effect of the network approximation is the same no matter how deep the neural network is. Commonly used activation functions include Sigmoid, ReLU, tanh functions, and some of their variants, but they are all non-linear operations, and homomorphic encryption algorithms cannot be calculated. Our scheme chooses the square function as the activation function. The square function is a nonlinear function and a low-order polynomial, which can improve efficiency.

$$[X_i] \leftarrow [X_i][X_i] \tag{15}$$

Pooling Layer. Maximum pooling and average pooling are two common pooling operations in CNN, but they are both non-linear and cannot be operated using homomorphic encryption schemes. A special pooling layer is selected in CryptoNets [9], which can replace the operation of the largest pooling layer. The maximum function can be expressed as:

$$max(x_1, x_2, \ldots, x_k) = \lim_{d \to \infty} (\sum_i x_i^d)^{1/d} \tag{16}$$

The operation corresponding to the ciphertext can be expressed as follows:

$$max([x_1], [x_2], \ldots [x_k]) = \lim_{d \to \infty} (\sum_i^k [x_i]^d)^{1/d} \tag{17}$$

where k denotes the number of ciphertext pixels corresponding to the size of the filter.

In order to reduce homomorphic multiplication operations, d should be kept as small as possible, and the meaningful minimum value is $d = 1$. The result at this time is the scalar multiple of the average pooling function, that is, the sum of ciphertexts in the sliding window. In homomorphic encryption operations, division operations cannot be performed. To obtain average pooling results. When averaging, we consider multiplying by a factor instead of division. The pooling operation can be expressed as:

$$[Y] = P[\lfloor \frac{1}{k} \cdot S \rfloor] \odot \sum_{i \in D} [x_i]) \tag{18}$$

$\lfloor \cdot \rfloor$ denotes the round down function, and $P[\cdot]$ denotes CRT batch coding of the processed real factor. The pooling layer operation after scaling includes only ciphertext addition and multiplication of ciphertext and plaintext, and the FV encryption algorithm can be executed.

Fully Connected Layer. In CNN, after combining multiple sets of convolutional layers and pooling layers, it usually contains several fully connected layers. In a fully connected layer, each neuron in two adjacent layers is fully connected. The operation of the fully connected layer can be expressed as:

$$[Y_i] = \sum_{j=1}^{n_l} [X_j] W_{ij} \qquad (i = 1, 2, \ldots, n_{l+1}) \tag{19}$$

4   Security Analysis

The model scenario involves two entities: user and server. The user has the original data, and the server owns the weighted parameters in CNN. In this scenario, the structure of the CNN model, the types of activation functions and pooling layers are not protected. That is to say, the type of each layer of the neural network and the number of neurons are already public. For the user, his input information should not be disclosed, but the size of the input is not protected. For the cloud server, he does not want his model parameters to be leaked.

The user first encodes the original data, and then uses the FV full homomorphic encryption scheme [7] to encrypt the encoded data, finally uploading the encrypted data to the cloud server. The cloud server has the trained CNN in advance and the CNN has been pruned. Then the cloud server performs the CNN prediction operation. Since the data input by the user has been kept in the ciphertext state during the cloud server calculation process, the user's input content is protected by FV homomorphic encryption. All operations on the neural network designed in this scheme are based on the FV homomorphic encryption scheme and are protected in cryptography. After the cloud server predicts the encrypted data, the result is returned to the user. The user decrypts with his private key, and gets the final result. During the entire process, the user does not need to perform calculations, and naturally cannot know the parameters in the model of the cloud server, and thus the CNN on the server has been protected.

5   Experiment Results

We implemented the CNN prediction scheme under FV homomorphic encryption through two sets of experiments with different parameters, and compared it with the CryptoNets [9].

5.1   Fully Trained CNN

We use the MNIST dataset[1], which contains 70,000 gray scale handwritten digital pictures, of which 60,000 are used for training and 10,000 for testing. Each picture is a sample picture with 28×28 pixels and channel is 1. Each sample includes 784 features, and the value of each feature is between $[0, 255]$. The computer used for the experiment is the Windows 10 operating system, with a 3.5 GHz Intel(R) Core(TM) i3-4150 CPU and 4 GB RAM. When fully trained, the CNN we use is as follows:

(1) *Convolutional Layer 1*: The size of the input image is $1 \times 28 \times 28$. The convolution kernels are of size $1 \times 3 \times 3$, the stride of $(1, 1)$, and the mapcount of 5. The output of this layer is $5 \times 28 \times 28$.
(2) *Average Pooling Layer 1*: This layer has 2×2 windows, and the output of this layer is $5 \times 14 \times 14$.
(3) *Activation Layer 1*: A square activation function is used in this layer, and the output size is the same as the input size, both are $5 \times 14 \times 14$.
(4) *Convolutional Layer 2*: The input size is $5 \times 14 \times 14$. The convolution kernels are of size $5 \times 3 \times 3$, and a mapcount of 8. The output of this layer is $8 \times 14 \times 14$.
(5) *Average Pooling Layer 2*: This layer has 2×2 windows, and the output of this layer is $8 \times 7 \times 7$.
(6) *Convolutional Layer 3*: The input size is $8 \times 7 \times 7$. The convolution kernels are of size $8 \times 3 \times 3$, and a mapcount of 10. The output of this layer is $10 \times 7 \times 7$.
(7) *Activation Layer 2*: The activation function uses a square function, and the output size is the same as the input size, both are $10 \times 7 \times 7$.
(8) *Fully Connected Layer 1*: The input size is $10 \times 7 \times 7$, and the output size is 100×1.
(9) *Fully Connected Layer 2*: The input size is 100×1, and the output size is 10×1.
(10) *Softmax Layer*: Classification and normalization in multi-classification tasks.

When using the MNIST dataset, set the batchsize to 64, epoch to 20, and the learning rate to 0.01. Use pytorch to store the trained model and the size of the initial training CNN model is 46 KB. The accuracy on the training and set test set is 98.33% and 97.52%, respectively. The CNN shown in Fig. 1 is the convolutional neural network before pruning.

---

[1] http://yann.lecun.com/exdb/mnist/.

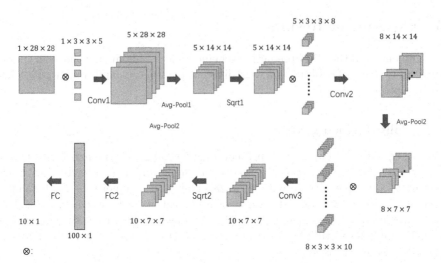

Fig. 1. Convolutional neural network suitable for FV encryption.

5.2   CNN Pruning Process

The second step is to prune the model trained in the previous step, pre-set the convolutional layers to be pruned, and each convolutional layer is pruned with 2, 3, and 3 filters in sequence. The number of prunes required for each convolutional layer is to satisfy FV homomorphic encryption, which will not generate excessive noise when performing ciphertext operations, and avoid the situation of being unable to decrypt. The filter number of each convolutional layer pruning is shown in Table 1. Then, Fig. 2 shows the pruned CNN.

Table 1. The pruning filter number of each convolutional layer.

Layer	Number of pruned	Pruned neurons
Convolution layer 1	2	[3, 1]
Convolution layer 2	3	[3, 5, 4]
Convolution layer 3	3	[2, 8, 6]

After pruning the CNN, the accuracy on the test set is 79.23%. We also need to fine-tune the weights, and then train to get the final CNN. Fine-tuning training uses epoch = 10, and the learning rate is 0.01. The fine-tuned CNN model size is 28 KB, the accuracy on the train set is 98.11%, and the accuracy on the test set is 98.64%.

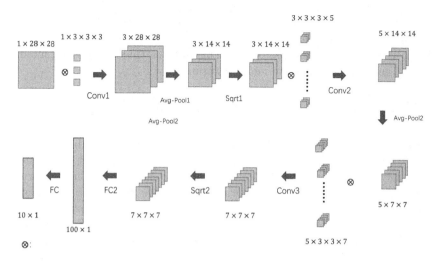

Fig. 2. Pruned convolutional neural network.

5.3 Ciphertext Image Prediction

In the prediction stage, the softmax layer is not used and it does not affect the prediction result. Before performing ciphertext image prediction, it is necessary to preprocess the input data and model parameters. Set the polynomial modulus n, coefficient modulus q, and plaintext modulus t. Due to the different selection of parameters in the FV scheme [7], the efficiency of homomorphic operation will be different. Choose two sets of different parameters to experiment separately. And the CryptoNets scheme [9] is reproduced in the same experimental environment, and a comparative experiment is carried out.

The first set of parameters is: $n = 4096$, and sets of (q, t) pairs are: $(2^{191} - 2589751, 40961), (2^{191} - 491527, 65537), (2^{191} - 2232751, 114689), (2^{191} - 2309565, 147457), (2^{191} - 15131401, 188417)$. When we use CRT batching, we need to set the batch size to 4096, that is, process 4096 sample pictures at the same time. The second set of parameters selects a larger n, $n = 8192$, $t_1 = 109951122689$, $t_2 = 1099512004609$, $q = 2^{383} - 2^{33} + 1$. The experimental results are shown in Table 2.

Table 2. Comparison with related scheme.

Data set	Scheme	Accuracy	Times		Number of network layers
			n = 4096	n = 8192	
MNIST	CryptoNets [9]	98.95%	335.6 s	682.4 s	1Conv+2sqrt+1Avg Pool+1FC
	Our scheme	98.64%	425.2 s	764.8 s	3Conv+2sqrt+2Avg Pool+2FC

Compared with the CryptoNets [9], our scheme uses a more complex CNN. The prediction accuracy of the scheme is similar to the CryptoNets scheme, but the prediction time is slightly increased. Because of the complexity of CNN, the homomorphic operations in the FV encryption scheme will increase, but this scheme is suitable for complex CNN. The features that can be extracted are complex and the functions are more powerful.

6   Conclusion

To solve the privacy problem of convolutional neural network prediction by cloud servers, we propose a privacy prediction scheme of lightweight convolutional neural network structure suitable for homomorphic encryption, using the pruning ideas of Li et al. to prune the neural network. We adopt FV homomorphic encryption to design a calculation method for the ciphertext operation of each layer in the convolutional neural network. Compared with the existing work, our proposed scheme tends to be more secure and practical.

Acknowledgment. This work is supported by Science and Technology Project of Guangzhou city (No. 201707010320).

References

1. Angelini, E., di Tollo, G., Roli, A.: A neural network approach for credit risk evaluation. Q. Rev. Econ. Finance **48**(4), 733–755 (2008)
2. Blakley, G.R.: Safeguarding cryptographic keys. In: 1979 International Workshop on Managing Requirements Knowledge (MARK), pp. 313–318. IEEE (1979)
3. Bradley, R.E., D'Antonio, L.A., Sandifer, C.E.: Euler at 300. Mathematical Association of America, Washington DC (2007)
4. Chopra, S., Yadav, D., Chopra, A.: Artificial neural networks based Indian stock market price prediction: before and after demonetization. J. Swarm Intell. Evol. Comput. **8**(174), 2 (2019)
5. Deng, J., Guo, J., Xue, N., Zafeiriou, S.: ArcFace: additive angular margin loss for deep face recognition. In: Proceedings of the IEEE Conference on Computer Vision and Pattern Recognition, pp. 4690–4699 (2019)
6. Esteva, A., et al.: Dermatologist-level classification of skin cancer with deep neural networks. Nature **542**(7639), 115–118 (2017)
7. Fan, J., Vercauteren, F.: Somewhat practical fully homomorphic encryption. IACR Cryptology ePrint Archive 2012/144 (2012)
8. Gentry, C.: Fully homomorphic encryption using ideal lattices. In: Proceedings of the Forty-First Annual ACM Symposium on Theory of Computing, pp. 169–178 (2009)
9. Gilad-Bachrach, R., Dowlin, N., Laine, K., Lauter, K., Naehrig, M., Wernsing, J.: CryptoNets: applying neural networks to encrypted data with high throughput and accuracy. In: International Conference on Machine Learning, pp. 201–210 (2016)
10. Goldreich, O., Micali, S., Wigderson, A.: How to play any mental game, or a completeness theorem for protocols with honest majority. In: Providing Sound Foundations for Cryptography: On the Work of Shafi Goldwasser and Silvio Micali, pp. 307–328. ACM (2019)

11. Gulshan, V., et al.: Development and validation of a deep learning algorithm for detection of diabetic retinopathy in retinal fundus photographs. JAMA **316**(22), 2402–2410 (2016)
12. Han, J., Moraga, C.: The influence of the sigmoid function parameters on the speed of backpropagation learning. In: Mira, J., Sandoval, F. (eds.) IWANN 1995. LNCS, vol. 930, pp. 195–201. Springer, Heidelberg (1995). https://doi.org/10.1007/3-540-59497-3_175
13. Hubel, D.H., Wiesel, T.N.: Receptive fields of single neurones in the cat's striate cortex. J. Physiol. **148**(3), 574–591 (1959)
14. LeCun, Y., et al.: Backpropagation applied to handwritten zip code recognition. Neural Comput. **1**(4), 541–551 (1989)
15. Li, H., Kadav, A., Durdanovic, I., Samet, H., Graf, H.P.: Pruning filters for efficient convnets. arXiv preprint arXiv:1608.08710 (2016)
16. Liu, J., Juuti, M., Lu, Y., Asokan, N.: Oblivious neural network predictions via minionn transformations. In: Proceedings of the 2017 ACM SIGSAC Conference on Computer and Communications Security, pp. 619–631 (2017)
17. Mohassel, P., Zhang, Y.: SecureML: a system for scalable privacy-preserving machine learning. In: 2017 IEEE Symposium on Security and Privacy (SP), pp. 19–38. IEEE (2017)
18. Nair, V., Hinton, G.E.: Rectified linear units improve restricted Boltzmann machines. In: ICML (2010)
19. Pei, D., Salomaa, A., Ding, C.: Chinese Remainder Theorem: Applications in Computing, Coding. Cryptography. World Scientific, Singapore (1996)
20. Riazi, M.S., Weinert, C., Tkachenko, O., Songhori, E.M., Schneider, T., Koushanfar, F.: Chameleon: a hybrid secure computation framework for machine learning applications. In: Proceedings of the 2018 on Asia Conference on Computer and Communications Security, pp. 707–721 (2018)
21. Rouhani, B.D., Riazi, M.S., Koushanfar, F.: DeepSecure: scalable provably-secure deep learning. In: Proceedings of the 55th Annual Design Automation Conference, pp. 1–6 (2018)
22. Schroff, F., Kalenichenko, D., Philbin, J.: FaceNet: a unified embedding for face recognition and clustering. In: Proceedings of the IEEE Conference on Computer Vision and Pattern Recognition, pp. 815–823 (2015)
23. Shamir, A.: How to share a secret. Commun. ACM **22**(11), 612–613 (1979)
24. Shokri, R., Shmatikov, V.: Privacy-preserving deep learning. In: Proceedings of the 22nd ACM SIGSAC Conference on Computer and Communications Security, pp. 1310–1321 (2015)
25. Smart, N.P., Vercauteren, F.: Fully homomorphic SIMD operations. Des. Codes Crypt. **71**(1), 57–81 (2014). https://doi.org/10.1007/s10623-012-9720-4
26. Wagh, S., Gupta, D., Chandran, N.: SecureNN: 3-party secure computation for neural network training. Proc. Priv. Enhanc. Technol. **2019**(3), 26–49 (2019)
27. Yao, A.C.: Protocols for secure computations. In: 23rd Annual Symposium on Foundations of Computer Science (SFCS 1982), pp. 160–164. IEEE (1982)

Privacy-Preserving and Outsourced Density Peaks Clustering Algorithm

Shaopeng Liang[1], Haomiao Yang[1,2(✉)], Qixian Zhou[1], and Minglu Zhang[1]

[1] School of Computer Science and Engineering,
University of Electronic Science and Technology of China, Chengdu, China
haomyang@uestc.edu.cn
[2] State Key Laboratory of Cryptology, P.O. Box 5159, Beijing 100878, China

Abstract. With the powerful platform of cloud, it is attractive for an organization with massive data to outsource to a cloud provider. However, the data owner may have concerns about the privacy of its data. In this paper, we propose a privacy-preserving and outsourced density peaks clustering algorithm over encrypted data (**PPODP** for short) in the cloud, which can achieve efficient density peaks clustering without revealing privacy. However, since the ciphertext distances under homomorphic encryption cannot be compared, we introduce an order-preserving encryption scheme that enables the cloud provider to compare encrypted distances. To guarantee the efficiency of the algorithm, we develop three optimization modules to ensure that **PPODP** runs efficiently. In addition, these optimization modules can be widely applied to other similar privacy-preserving machine learning algorithms. Finally, formal security analysis and extensive evaluation demonstrate that our **PPODP** achieves similar performance and efficiency while preserving data privacy compared with density peaks clustering over plaintexts.

Keywords: Density peaks clustering · Homomorphic encryption · Order-preserving encryption · Accelerated computing

1 Introduction

Data privacy-preserving concern has become a core issue in machine learning research, especially in sensitive areas involving cloud platforms, such as personal finance, medical health, etc. As we all know, cloud computing provides significant potential solutions for machine learning with massive data. However, due to incomplete credibility of the cloud platform, it is imperative to design a machine learning algorithm, which is privacy-preserving and outsourced for cloud platforms.

Homomorphic encryption (*HE*) allows operations over encrypted data [10]. This property has powerful applications, e.g., in outsourced (cloud) computation scenarios the cloud provider can use this to guarantee customer data privacy in the presence of both internal (malicious employee) and external (outside

© Springer Nature Singapore Pte Ltd. 2020
G. Xu et al. (Eds.): FCS 2020, CCIS 1286, pp. 538–552, 2020.
https://doi.org/10.1007/978-981-15-9739-8_40

attacker) threats. For example, in IEEE S&P 2018 and ACM CCS 2017, based on *HE*, the problem of private information retrieval and the private set intersection are well solved [2]. In this consideration, it is natural to think that homomorphic encryption can possibly provide a solution for privacy-preserving machine learning. As early as 2012, Graepel et al. proposed research based on homomorphic encryption [11], which exhibits using *HE* to secure machine learning. In the framework of *HE*, subsequently, there has been a long line of research focusing on privacy-preserving and outsourced classification algorithms, such as [5,14,21], etc. On the other hand, order-preserving encryption (*OPE*), which is an encryption scheme whose ciphertext sort order matches the corresponding plaintext order. As we all know, most machine learning algorithms, especially unsupervised clustering algorithms, involve many comparison operations. According to this consideration, order-preserving encryption is a practical solution. Agrawal et al. proposed the first complete order-preserving encryption system in 2004 [1]. After the formal definition of *OPE*, the order-preserving encryption has undergone several stages of development, and related research has [18,19], etc.

In 2014, Alex Rodriguez and Alessandro Laio proposed a density peaks clustering algorithm [20], which immediately attracted the attention of scholars with its excellent performance and few parameters. For untrusted outsourced cloud computing scenarios, if we can design a good privacy-preserving density peaks clustering algorithm, then we can have its excellent performance while ensuring its security. And our proposed framework can be extensive to other machine learning algorithm to provide privacy protection.

To our knowledge, there are few works to involve privacy-preserving for density peak clustering. Accordingly, in this paper, we proposed a privacy-preserving and outsourced density peaks clustering (**PPODP** for short) to solve the privacy issue in the cloud scenario.

In this paper, aiming at **PPODP**, we firstly analyze standard density peaks clustering (**SDP** for short) proposed in [20], as depicted in *Algorithm* 1. At first glance, it seems that *HE* can be directly applied to **SDP**, and **PPODP** can be trivially achieved. After carefully checking **PPODP**, there are three challenges as follows: (1) One essential operation in density peaks clustering is to compare distances between any two data items; (2) It is necessary to compare densities of every single data item; (3) It is also necessary to guarantee our algorithm **PPODP** achieve almost the same performance as the original algorithm **SDP**. After all, for the purpose of privacy protection, **SDP** has been somewhat adapted to fit with *HE*. As is known, in machine learning, datasets usually contain numerous data items, each of which has multiple attributes, and thus a data item can be treated as a vector. Hence, it is naturally thought of that we can exploit SEAL [7] to encrypt a data item into a single ciphertext in a batch manner, thereby significantly reducing computational and communication overhead. Especially, by ingeniously designing, we can also compare encrypted distances. Specifically, we use the order-preserving encryption scheme proposed in [18] to implement the ciphertext comparison operation in **PPODP**. Finally, we present

---

Algorithm 1. Standard density peaks clustering

Input: plaintext dataset $\boldsymbol{Dis} = \{dis_{ij} | 1 \leq i \leq n-1, i+1 \leq j \leq n\}$
Output: cluster assignments

1: Sort(dis_{ij})
2: Compute the cutoff distance d_c
3: Compute the density $\rho_i = \sum_{j \neq i}^m \chi(d_{ij} - dc)$

$$\chi(x) = \begin{cases} 1, & x < 0 \\ 0, & x \geq 0 \end{cases}$$

4: Compute the minimum distance $\delta_i = \min\limits_{j:\rho_j > \rho_i} (d_{ij})$
   Specially, for the point with highest density, $\delta_i = \max_j(d_{ij})$
5: Select k cluster centers manually
6: **repeat**
7:    Assign each remaining node to the same cluster of its nearest neighbor of higher density
8: **until** no remaining nodes
9: **return** $\{(i,j) | \boldsymbol{x}_i \in \boldsymbol{D}_j, i = 1, ..., n, 1 \leq j \leq k\}$

---

a **PPODP** algorithm, which can guarantee privacy while maintaining accuracy and performance. Different from existing works, our contributions are as follows.

- Firstly, we integrate *HE* and *OPE* into the density peaks clustering algorithm for better security than the original algorithm.
- Secondly, we propose a new **PPODP** algorithm by reconstructing **SDP** in encrypted domains. Security analysis proves that **PPODP** protects data privacy. Performance evaluation indicates that **PPODP** achieves the same accuracy and efficiency, as **SDP** over plaintexts.
- Thirdly, we develop an optimization strategy for **PPODP**, which consists of pairwise parallel acceleration, binary tree rotate for inner product and disjoint set.

2   Related Works

In the section, we briefly review some related works on privacy-preserving machine learning, clustering algorithms and density peaks clustering.

Privacy-Preserving Machine Learning. Machine learning algorithms are being widely used in various fields that process personal privacy data [13,17,23]. Due to the nature of machine learning and its need for massive data, outsourced machine learning algorithms is a common choice for researchers [16]. Machine learning is mainly divided into supervised learning and unsupervised learning. Due to unsupervised learning requires less human intervention and de-tagging, it is widely used in machine learning algorithms [15]. In massive data application scenarios, most data is unlabeled. For such data sets, classification algorithms cannot be used, but clustering algorithms can perform well on unlabeled data.

Homomorphic Encryption and Order-Preserving Encryption. With the rapid development of homomorphic encryption (*HE*) and order-preserving encryption (*OPE*), a large number of privacy-preserving machine learning algorithms have been proposed based on *HE*, *OPE*, or both [15,19,21]. In general, the application of homomorphic encryption to machine learning algorithms is quite mature, and the order-preserving encryption is still in the stage of rapid development.

Density Peaks Clustering. Compared with the traditional clustering algorithm, the density peaks clustering algorithm has the following advantages: (1) The algorithm separates the selection of cluster centers from the assignment of other points and improves the clustering accuracy; (2) The algorithm is suitable for clustering of pictures and non-spherical point sets; (3) The algorithm is less complex and less modulating. The privacy-preserving researches on other traditional clustering algorithms are rich and complete [3] etc. To our best knowledge, there is no research about the privacy-preserving density peaks clustering algorithm [22]. Given this, we design a scheme that guarantees the excellent performance of the density peaks clustering algorithm in the outsourced scenario while ensuring the security of the overall algorithm. And in the experimental part, we will compare our scheme with the proposed in [22], which called **SHOCFS**.

3   Problem Statement

3.1   System Model

Our model concentrates on how to achieve secure density peaks clustering over encrypted data in outsourced environments. It mainly consists of two entities: the data owner and the cloud. Note that the cloud is considered as an "honest-but-curious" service provider. As shown in Fig. 1. The system has two interactions. In the first round of interaction, let $D' = \{c_i | i = 1, 2, \ldots, n\}$ be the homomorphic encrypted of the dataset $D = \{x_i | i = 1, 2, \ldots, n\}$. Then, the data owner uploads D' to the cloud. Next, the cloud performs the first step of density peaks clustering over D', and returns the computation result of the *HE* distances $Dis' = \{d'_{ij} | 1 \le i \le n - 1, i + 1 \le j \le n\}$ to the owner. The owner decrypts the *HE* distances as plaintext, which is $Dis = \{d_{ij} | 1 \le i \le n - 1, i + 1 \le j \le n\}$.

In the second round of interaction, in order to compare the distance between every two data items, order-preserving encryption (*OPE*) will be used to encrypt the distances. Let $Dis'' = \{d''_{ij} | 1 \le i \le n - 1, i + 1 \le j \le n\}$ be the *OPE* distances of Dis. Then the data owner uploads Dis'' to the cloud. Next, the cloud performs the remaining steps of the algorithm and returns cluster assignments to the owner.

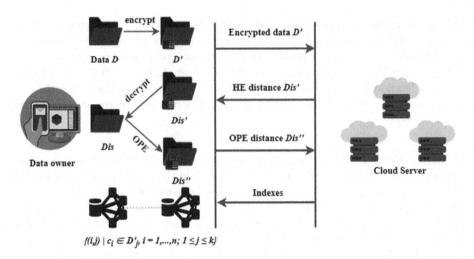

$\{(i,j) \mid c_i \in D'_j, i = 1,...,n; 1 \leq j \leq k\}$

Fig. 1. System model

3.2 Threat Model

In this paper, to develop a secure and efficient algorithm, assume that the cloud is "honest-but-curious".

Given such considerations, the execution phase typically includes inputs, outputs, and messages that are transmitted during the execution of the algorithm. To prove that the agreement is safe under the semi-honest model, the implementation of the agreement will not reveal any private information.

3.3 Design Goals

The overarching goal is to implement privacy-preserving and outsourced density peaks clustering. Therefore, the following requirements need to be fulfilled.

- Accuracy: First, the density peak clustering algorithm in the outsourced ciphertext domain should achieve the same performance as the standard density peaks algorithm.
- Security: Second, **PPODP** must ensure the security of the entire execution process, including data and distance will not disclose any private information.
- Efficiency: Third, when processing massive data, **PPODP** can still perform efficiently.

4   SEAL-BFV Scheme and Order-Preserving Encryption

The original FV scheme [9] has still suffered from efficiency weakness. Microsoft Research Institute optimizes the problem of low efficiency of ciphertext for BFV scheme and proposed SEAL homomorphic encryption library, which has the large advantage of performance compared with the original FV scheme [7]. We use the order-preserving encryption scheme from [18] and modify it to apply to the density peaks clustering algorithm.

4.1 Notations

The notations are listed in Table 1. In this paper, the scalar is represented by lowercase letters and the vector is represented by lowercase bold letters (e.g. x is a scalar, $\boldsymbol{x}$ is a vector).

Table 1. Notation used throughout this document

q	Coefficient modules
t	Plaintext modulus
R	The ring $Z[x]/(x^n + 1)$
R_a	The ring $Z[x]/(x^n + 1)$ with coefficients reduced modulo a
Δ	Quotient on division of q by t, or $\lfloor q/t \rfloor$
χ	Error distribution (a truncated discrete Gaussian distribution)

4.2 Scheme Description

In this part, we introduce the BFV homomorphic encryption scheme implemented by SEAL and our order-preserving encryption scheme. These algorithms are described below.

Homomorphic encryption (HE):

- **SKGen(λ):** Sample $s \leftarrow R_2$ and output $sk = s$
- **PKGen(sk):** Set $s = sk$, sample $a \leftarrow R_q$, and $e \leftarrow \chi$. Output $pk = ([-(as + e)]_q, a)$.
- **EvaKeyGen(sk, ω):** For $i \in \{0, ..., \ell\}$, sample $a_i \leftarrow R_q$, $e_i \leftarrow \chi$. Output $evk = ([-(a_i s + e_i) + \omega^i s^2]_q, a_i)$
- **Enc(pk, m):** For $m \in R_t$, let $pk = (p_0, p_1)$. Sample $u \leftarrow R_2$, and $e_1, e_2 \leftarrow \chi$. Compute $ct = ([\Delta m + p_0 u + e_1]_q, [p_1 u + e_2]_q)$
- **Dec(sk, ct):** Set $s = sk$, $c_0 = ct[0]$, and $c_1 = ct[1]$. Output $[\lfloor (t/q)[c_0 + c_1 s] \rceil]_t$
- **Add(ct_0, ct_1):** Output $(ct_0[0] + ct_1[0], ct_0[1] + ct_1[1])$.
- **Mult(ct_0, ct_1):** Compute $(ct_0[0] + ct_0[1]X)(ct_1[0] + ct_1[1]X) = e_0 + e_1 X + e_2 X^2$, output $ct_{mult} = (\lfloor te_0/q \rceil, \lfloor te_1/q \rceil, \lfloor te_2/q \rceil)$

Order-preserving encryption (OPE):

- **KGen(seed):** Randomly generate key, two integer pairs $k = (a, b)$, $a > 0$. Let $\boldsymbol{D}$ be the set of all input values. The *sensitivity* of $\boldsymbol{D}$ is the minimum element in the set $\{|x_1 - x_2| \| x_1, x_2 \in \boldsymbol{D}, x_1 \neq x_2\}$.
- **Enc(k, x):** Given the key k and the sensitivity $sens$, compute $c = ax + b + noise$, where $noise$ is randomly sampled from the range $[0, a \times sens)$.

5 Proposed PPODP

5.1 Density Peaks Clustering over Ciphertexts

In this part, we propose a **PPODP** algorithm by reconstructing the standard density peaks clustering process as described in *Algorithm* 1. Our algorithm can be divided into four phases: *Preparation, Computation, Clustering and BackResults*.

- *Preparation*(D). The dataset D is taken as the input, and the data owner constructs **BatchEncoder**, **Encryptor** and **Decryptor**. Then the owner encrypts $D = \{x_i | i = 1, 2, \ldots, n\}$ into $D' = \{c_i | i = 1, 2, \ldots, n\}$ and uploads D'.
- *Computation*(D'). Upon receiving D', the cloud calculates the direct Euclidean distance between every two points, as described in *Algorithm* 2 Stage 1. After securely computing the distances, the cloud returns the *HE* distance Dis' to the data owner.
- *Clustering*(Dis''). The data owner get the *HE* distance $Dis' = \{d'_{ij} | 1 \leq i \leq n-1, i+1 \leq j \leq n\}$ and decrypt the distance into $Dis = \{d_{ij} | 1 \leq i \leq n-1, i+1 \leq j \leq n\}$ by using **Decryptor**. Then the data owner encrypts Dis into $Dis'' = \{d''_{ij} | 1 \leq i \leq n-1, i+1 \leq j \leq n\}$ by using order-preserving encryption and uploads Dis'' to the cloud. Finally, the cloud performs the Stage 2–3 as described in *Algorithm* 2, which is securely computing ρ & δ of each data item and securely assigning.
- *BackResults*. The cloud returns cluster assignments $\{(i, j) | x_i \in D_j, i = 1, \ldots, n, 1 \leq j \leq k\}$ to the owner.

5.2 Correctness

An important observation is that **PPODP** can simulate **SDP**. As a result, **PPODP** can ensure correctness only if **SDP** guarantees such merits.

Theorem 1. *PPODP perfectly simulates SDP in the following sense: when the two algorithms are executed on the same clustering setting and the same dataset, PPODP can get the same assignments as SDP.*

Proof. By using homomorphic encryption, **PPODP** can compute the Euclidean distances, which are exactly the same as **SDP**. While by using order-preserving encryption, **PPODP** can obtain the same ρ of each data item as **SDP**, and due to the noise in the order-preserving encryption, **PPODP** can obtain different but order-preserving δ. Moreover, ρ & δ corresponding to **PPODP** do not affect the cluster centers selection and remaining points allocation. Comparing *Algorithm* 2 (**PPODP**) with *Algorithm* 1 (**SDP**), almost all the steps are the same except for the choice of clustering centers. According to Step 5, if k clustering centers are selected, then there are top-k γ_i to be taken. Due to order-preserving encryption, the choice of top-k is unaffected. As a consequence, **Theorem** 1 is turned out to be right.

A consequence of **Theorem** 1 is that correctness guarantees for **SDP** can equally apply to **PPODP**.

Algorithm 2. Privacy-preserving and outsourced density peaks clustering

---

Input: plaintext dataset $D = \{x_i | 1 \le i \le n\}$, cluster number k

Output: cluster assignments

1: {Stage 1: Distance computation}
2: The data owner encrypts $D = \{x_i | i = 1, 2, \ldots, n\}$ into $D' = \{c_i | i = 1, 2, \ldots, n\}$ and uploads D' to the cloud
3: **for** $i = 1$ to $n - 1$ **do**
4:     **for** $j = i + 1$ to n **do**
5:         The cloud securely computes the distance $dis_{ij} = d(c_i, c_j)$ accelerated by *Algorithm 3* and *Algorithm 4*
6:     **end for**
7: **end for**
8: The cloud returns the encrypted distances to the data owner
9: {Stage 2: ρ and δ computation}
10: The data owner decrypt the distances then encrypt Dis into Dis'' and uploads Dis'' to the cloud
11: The cloud sorts Dis''
12: The cloud computes the cutoff distance d_c
13: The cloud computes the density $\rho_i = \sum_{j \ne i}^m \chi(d_{ij} - d_c)$

$$\chi(x) = \begin{cases} 1, & x < 0 \\ 0, & x \ge 0 \end{cases}$$

14: The cloud computes the minimum distance $\delta_i = \min\limits_{j:\rho_j > \rho_i} (d_{ij})$
    Specially, for the point with highest density, $\delta_i = \max_j (d_{ij})$
15: {Stage 3: Assignment}
16: The cloud generates cluster centers as
        $\gamma_i = \rho_i \times \delta_i$ take top-k γ_i as cluster centers
17: **repeat**
18:     The cloud assigns each remaining node to the same cluster of its nearest neighbor of higher density by using *Algorithm 5*
19: **until** no remaining nodes
20: **return** $\{(i, j) | x_i \in D_j, i = 1, \ldots, n, 1 \le j \le k\}$

5.3   Security

Security for Computing Distances. As described in Stage 1 of *Algorithm 2*, the distance of every two data items can be securely computed, which can be supposed by the SEAL-BFV scheme. The only information revealed is the index of each data item. Hence, for the cloud server, only the index can be obtained, and it does not pose a threat to data privacy.

Security for Calculating the ρ and δ. As observed in Stage 2 of *Algorithm 2*, all comparison of distances, which can be supposed by order-preserving encryption. The only information revealed is each point's density ρ and minimum distance δ to other points. The cloud can not infer any privacy information about the original data.

Security for Assignments. As observed in Stage 3 of *Algorithm* 2, all assignments are performed in the ciphertext domain, which can be supported by Stage 1–2. Thus, no information leaks at this stage. The only information that the cloud can obtain at the end of the algorithm is the index of the cluster to which each point belongs, which is exactly what the data owner wants.

6   Algorithm Optimization

In this section, we develop three modules for optimizing **PPODP**, pairwise parallel acceleration, binary tree rotate for inner product and disjoint set for assignment. Besides, we will introduce these three modules and evaluate their efficiency.

6.1   Pairwise Parallel Acceleration

Since the time complexity of the distances computation step is $O(kn^2)$, it will be the most consumed part of the algorithm. Note that the computation of any pair of distances is independent of each other, so parallel operations can be used. Based on efficient parallel methods, OpenMP [6] and MapReduce [8], we propose parallel acceleration for **PPODP**, which can efficiently run in a single-machine multi-threaded process pool and cluster distributed case. The specific process is shown in *Algorithm* 3.

Algorithm 3. Pairwise parallel acceleration

1: **At Muti-thread version:**
2: **for** $i = 1$ to $n - 1$ **do**
3:     **for** $j = i + 1$ to n **do**
4:         task_pool.add($\{i, j\}$)
5:     **end for**
6: **end for**
7: **for** each thread **do**
8:     **if** task_pool is NOT empty **then**
9:         lhs, rhs = task_pool.pop()
10:        $distance_{lhs,rhs}$ = getDistance($\boldsymbol{x}_{lhs}, \boldsymbol{x}_{rhs}$)
11:    **end if**
12: **end for**
13: **At Muti-node version:**
14: Map($index$):
15: **for** $ext = index + 1$ to n **do**
16:     Emit($\{index, ext\}$)
17: **end for**
18: Reduce(lhs, rhs):
19: $\boldsymbol{x}_{lhx}, \boldsymbol{x}_{rhs}$ = getCipher($\{lhs, rhs\}$)
20: $distance_{lhs,rhs}$ = getDistance($\boldsymbol{x}_{lhs}, \boldsymbol{x}_{rhs}$)

6.2 Binary Tree Rotate for Inner Product

Due to the non-bitable nature of the SEAL library, the direct summation method cannot be used, but the "equal element status" vector is constructed by means of the "cyclic displacement" operation supported in the library to achieve the summation of the vector elements. In other words, assuming $V = (v_1, v_2, ..., v_d)$ the final vector need to be constructed as $V' = (v_1 + v_2 + ... + v_d, v_2 + v_3 + ... + v_d + v_1, ..., v_d + v_1 + ... + v_{d-2} + v_{d-1})$. Since the direct rotate is very expensive, we use binary tree rotate instead of direct rotate to calculate inner product, the method we design only needs to perform the $\log d$ rotates, which can reduce the time complexity from $O(d)$ to $O(\log d)$. The specific process is shown in *Algorithm* 4.

Algorithm 4. Binary tree rotate for inner product

Input: two ciphertexts' lhs and rhs
Output: Inner product of two vectors

1: $result = Square(Sub(lhs, rhs))$
2: $temp = result, k = 1$
3: **while** $k < len(result)$ **do**
4:     $temp = Rotate(result, k)$
5:     $result = Add(result, temp)$
6:     $k = k \times 2$
7: **end while**

6.3 Disjoint Set for Assignment

In the data item assignment stage of the algorithm execution, the clustering label is assigned to each data item. For the remaining nodes except the cluster centers, each point is assigned to the same cluster of its nearest neighbor of higher density until there are no remaining nodes. During this stage, the time complexity of the overall assignment is $O(n^2)$. Obviously, there are many duplicate queries in the link process of each point, which seriously reduces the efficiency of the algorithm. Therefore, we propose a disjoint set structure to efficiently distribute labels in the stage of assignment and the overall time complexity is $O(n)$. The specific process is shown in *Algorithm* 5.

7 Evaluation of Performance and Accuracy

In this section, we evaluate the proposed algorithm in terms of validity, computation cost, comparison cost and communication overhead. Besides, in terms of validity assessment, we use *internal criteria* (Accuracy) and *external criteria* (S_Dbw) [12] to evaluate clustering effects separately.

Algorithm 5. Disjoint Set for Assignment

Input: cluster centers $Center = \{C_j | 1 \le j \le k\}$ dataset $D = \{x_i | 1 \le i \le n\}$
Output: each point's label

1: **for** each x_i **do**
2:     MAKE-SET(i)
3: **end for**
4: **for** each x_i NOT in C_j **do**
5:     sp = False
6:     **for** each C_j **do**
7:         **if** $density_{x_i} == density_{C_j}$ and $distance_{x_i, C_j} \le d_c$ **then**
8:             UNION(x_i, C_j)
9:             sp = True
10:        **end if**
11:    **end for**
12:    **if** NOT sp **then**
13:        Find x_k is the smallest one of all $distance_{x_i, x_k}$ that satisfies condition $density_{x_i} > density_{x_k}$
14:        UNION(x_i, x_k)
15:    **end if**
16: **end for**
17: **for** each x_i **do**
18:    $lable_{x_i}$ = FIND-SET(x_i)
19: **end for**

7.1 Experiment Environment

To perform simulations, we use a laptop with i5-5200U CPU @ 2.20 GHz and 8 GB RAM, running Windows 10, and a laptop with i5-8259U CPU @ 3.60 GHz and 16 GB RAM, running Windows 10. In the experiment, the first laptop acts as the data owner, and the other laptop acts as the cloud provider.

Besides, in the cloud provider, we build a single-core single-thread environment for evaluating plaintext and ciphertext algorithms, and we also build a multi-core multi-thread environment for evaluating ciphertext algorithm with proposed optimization methods. For more details, please see Sect. 7.4.

In experiments, the performance will be evaluated with varying values of parameter k, n and m, denoting the number of data items, attributes and clusters respectively. To exhibit the feasibility of our algorithm, different real datasets are used to verify the practicability of our algorithm, regarding widely varying values of k, n or m.

7.2 Complexity Analysis

Considering the cost of cloud computing and the characteristics of the semi-honest cloud security framework, this section theoretically analyzes the computation and communication cost of the proposed scheme.

Let the number of elements in the dataset be n, and the number of attributes of each element, that is, the vector dimension of each piece of data is d.

Table 2. Performance evaluation on UCI datasets

Dataset	k	n	m	Time (ms)		Accuracy (%)		S_Dbw	
				plaintext	ciphertext	plaintext	ciphertext	plaintext	ciphertext
Seeds	3	210	7	148	1730	90.9	85.0	1.157	1.536
Flame	2	240	2	142	1812	84.2	78.8	1.726	1.771
Breast cancer	2	699	9	362	19261	93	92.9	1.571	1.571
Spiral	3	312	2	303	2900	94.9	94.9	1.693	1.693
Iris	3	150	4	56	765	96.7	95.6	0.763	0.529
Wine	3	178	13	98	1392	94.4	94.4	1.177	1.218

Computation Cost. The distance computation step is the most consumed part of the algorithm, and its time complexity is $O(kn^2)$. In the distance computation step, we optimize the computation method of the vector inner product, and the time complexity is $O(\log d)$. In the data item allocation stage of the algorithm execution, we propose a disjoint set to assign labels with overall time complexity of $O(n)$. Therefore, the total computation time complexity is $O(kn^2 \log d + n)$, which is much smaller than the scheme in [22].

Communication Cost. The main communication overhead comes from transmitting encrypted dataset D', HE distance Dis' and OPE distance Dis''. Besides, the bandwidth of D' and Dis' are determined by the *poly_modulus* and Dis'' is determined by real number pair (a, b), which described above. Compared with the scheme in [22] that needs to download $(n + 1)s$ (s is the Paillier encryption key size) message from the cloud, our communication cost is negligible.

7.3   Encryption Time

To ensure the privacy of the data, the data needs to be encrypted during the interaction between the client and the cloud server. To measure the influence of dataset size on encryption time, the client encrypts the dataset with 40, 80, 120, 160 and 200 items and evaluates their respective time consumption. The encryption time is shown in Fig. 2. The encryption time of our scheme grows linearly from 0.002 s to 0.008 s, which is negligible compared to the scheme in [22]. Besides, the client only performs encryption (including homomorphic encryption and order-preserving encryption) once in the whole process. Therefore, our scheme is very lightweight.

7.4   Execution Time

As aforementioned, our algorithm consists of four phases: *Preparation, Computation, Clustering* and *BackResults*. It is noteworthy that each phase only runs once. To evaluate time cost, the computation time under plaintext, ciphertext and ciphertext with multi-thread are compared for different numbers of data items with 11 dimensions. Running time is shown in Fig. 3. It can be seen from

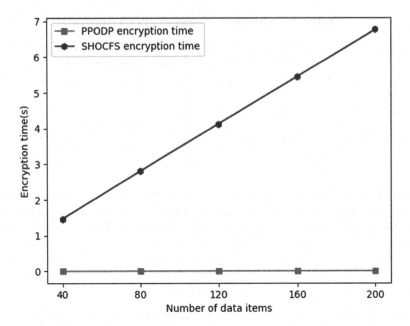

Fig. 2. Encryption time

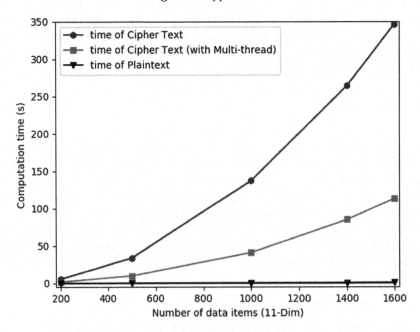

Fig. 3. Time cost

the figure that the optimization method proposed can effectively improve the computational efficiency under ciphertext.

7.5   Clustering Accuracy

In this section, **PPODP** runs on multiple real datasets retrieved from the UCI repository [4]. The clustering performance is evaluated with *Accuracy* and *S_Dbw*. Table 2 summarizes our results, which provides the overall clustering time, accuracy and S_Dbw with greatly varying values of k, n, m. We note that for all of the datasets, compared with density peaks clustering over plaintexts, our clustering method over ciphertexts can achieve similar performance and accuracy while preserving data privacy. Moreover, it possesses important merit of privacy-preserving that is imperative to securely perform density peaks clustering in cloud environments.

8   Conclusion

In this paper, we proposed an efficient and secure density peaks clustering algorithm over outsourced encrypted data by using SEAL-BFV and order-preserving encryption. Especially, we have proposed three acceleration modules to make our algorithm run efficiently. We have also improved the density peaks clustering algorithm so that it can automatically select the cluster center. In future work, we will further extend privacy protection to other machine learning algorithm. For instance, we will perform target detection, computer vision and deep learning in a privacy fashion.

References

1. Agrawal, R., Kiernan, J., Srikant, R., Xu, Y.: Order preserving encryption for numeric data. In: Proceedings of the 2004 ACM SIGMOD International Conference on Management of Data, pp. 563–574. ACM (2004)
2. Angel, S., Chen, H., Laine, K., Setty, S.: PIR with compressed queries and amortized query processing. In: 2018 IEEE Symposium on Security and Privacy (SP), pp. 962–979. IEEE (2018)
3. Anikin, I.V., Gazimov, R.M.: Privacy preserving DBSCAN clustering algorithm for vertically partitioned data in distributed systems. In: 2017 International Siberian Conference on Control and Communications (SIBCON), pp. 1–4. IEEE (2017)
4. Bache, K., Lichman, M.: UCI machine learning repository (2013)
5. Bourse, F., Minelli, M., Minihold, M., Paillier, P.: Fast homomorphic evaluation of deep discretized neural networks. In: Shacham, H., Boldyreva, A. (eds.) CRYPTO 2018. LNCS, vol. 10993, pp. 483–512. Springer, Cham (2018). https://doi.org/10.1007/978-3-319-96878-0_17
6. Chandra, R., Dagum, L., Kohr, D., Menon, R., Maydan, D., McDonald, J.: Parallel Programming in OpenMP. Morgan kaufmann (2001)
7. Chen, H., Laine, K., Player, R.: Simple encrypted arithmetic library - SEAL v2.1. In: Brenner, M., et al. (eds.) FC 2017. LNCS, vol. 10323, pp. 3–18. Springer, Cham (2017). https://doi.org/10.1007/978-3-319-70278-0_1

8. Dean, J., Ghemawat, S.: MapReduce: simplified data processing on large clusters. Commun. ACM **51**(1), 107–113 (2008)

9. Fan, J., Vercauteren, F.: Somewhat practical fully homomorphic encryption. IACR Cryptology ePrint Archive 2012, 144 (2012)

10. Gentry, C., et al.: Fully homomorphic encryption using ideal lattices. In: STOC, vol. 9, pp. 169–178 (2009)

11. Graepel, T., Lauter, K., Naehrig, M.: ML confidential: machine learning on encrypted data. In: Kwon, T., Lee, M.-K., Kwon, D. (eds.) ICISC 2012. LNCS, vol. 7839, pp. 1–21. Springer, Heidelberg (2013). https://doi.org/10.1007/978-3-642-37682-5_1

12. Halkidi, M., Vazirgiannis, M.: Clustering validity assessment: finding the optimal partitioning of a data set. In: Proceedings 2001 IEEE International Conference on Data Mining, pp. 187–194. IEEE (2001)

13. Jordan, M.I., Mitchell, T.M.: Machine learning: trends, perspectives, and prospects. Science **349**(6245), 255–260 (2015)

14. Khan, A.N., Fan, M.Y., Malik, A., Memon, R.A.: Learning from privacy preserved encrypted data on cloud through supervised and unsupervised machine learning. In: 2019 2nd International Conference on Computing, Mathematics and Engineering Technologies (iCoMET), pp. 1–5. IEEE (2019)

15. Kim, H.J., Chang, J.W.: A privacy-preserving k-means clustering algorithm using secure comparison protocol and density-based center point selection. In: 2018 IEEE 11th International Conference on Cloud Computing (CLOUD), pp. 928–931. IEEE (2018)

16. Liang, J., Qin, Z., Ni, J., Lin, X., Shen, X.S.: Efficient and privacy-preserving outsourced SVM classification in public cloud. In: 2019 IEEE International Conference on Communications (ICC), ICC 2019, pp. 1–6. IEEE (2019)

17. Ni, J., Lin, X., Shen, X.: Toward privacy-preserving valet parking in autonomous driving era. IEEE Trans. Veh. Technol. **68**(3), 2893–2905 (2019)

18. Popa, R.A., Li, F.H., Zeldovich, N.: An ideal-security protocol for order-preserving encoding. In: 2013 IEEE Symposium on Security and Privacy, pp. 463–477. IEEE (2013)

19. Quan, H., Wang, B., Zhang, Y., Wu, G.: Efficient and secure top-k queries with top order-preserving encryption. IEEE Access **6**, 31525–31540 (2018)

20. Rodriguez, A., Laio, A.: Clustering by fast search and find of density peaks. Science **344**(6191), 1492–1496 (2014)

21. Sun, X., Zhang, P., Liu, J.K., Yu, J., Xie, W.: Private machine learning classification based on fully homomorphic encryption. IEEE Trans. Emerg. Top. Comput. (2018)

22. Zhao, Y., Yang, L.T., Sun, J.: A secure high-order CFS algorithm on clouds for industrial internet of things. IEEE Trans. Ind. Inf. **14**(8), 3766–3774 (2018)

23. Zhu, L., Li, M., Zhang, Z., Qin, Z.: ASAP: an anonymous smart-parking and payment scheme in vehicular networks. IEEE Trans. Dependable Secure Comput. (2018)

The Socio-economic Impacts of Social Media Privacy and Security Challenges

Feras Al-Obeidat[1], Anoud Bani Hani[1], Oluwasegun Adedugbe[2], Munir Majdalawieh[1], and Elhadj Benkhelifa[2(✉)]

[1] Zayed University, Dubai, UAE
Feras.Al-Obeidat@zu.ac.ae
[2] Cloud Computing and Applications Research Lab, Staffordshire University,
Stoke-on-Trent, UK
e.benkhelifa@staffs.ac.uk

Abstract. Privacy and Security are two major challenges faced by users on social media today. These challenges are experienced in diverse ways and forms by different types of users across the web. While technological solutions are usually implemented to address them, the effects have proven to be limited so far. Despite continuous deployment of technological solutions, the need to evaluate socio-economic impacts of these challenges have also become more imperative. Hence, this paper provides a critical review and analysis of socio-economic impacts of these social media challenges. The research findings reveal significant levels of negative socio-economic impacts and provides an evaluation framework towards defining the scope, thereby identifying appropriate measures for both addressing the challenges and curbing the socio-economic impacts. The findings also demonstrate the need for solutions beyond the use of technology, to employing and deploying solutions from social sciences which deals with behavioral issues and how to address them.

Keywords: Privacy · Security · Social network · Social media · Social data analysis

1 Introduction

The connectivity level among humans today has reached extraordinary levels, with over a billion users of internet social media such as Facebook, Google, Twitter, Instagram, and YouTube. The vast amount of data that is provided and disseminated on social networks includes user's personal details, location, address, email, usernames, and interests. Users also offer updates in the form of status information which includes what they think or what they wish to contribute in an online discussion. All these convey vital data about social network users that may be of interest to several groups of people. As a result, several unfavorable incidents occur on social media which breaches privacy of users [1]. The importance of user confidentiality has been greatly discussed both in the media and academia, with many initiatives put in place to enlighten users not to disclose so

© Springer Nature Singapore Pte Ltd. 2020
G. Xu et al. (Eds.): FCS 2020, CCIS 1286, pp. 553–563, 2020.
https://doi.org/10.1007/978-981-15-9739-8_41

much personal data and propose technical solutions to protect user confidentiality [2]. Additionally, information on social media is now being co-related with physical location of users, allowing for real-time interaction between user preferences and social relationships with the environment they are in. The fusion of internet social media with mobile computing in real world has also resulted in the creation of many applications with unique requirements and implications that are yet to be fully understood [3]. These systems, however, sometimes pay little consideration to the privacy and security concerns that are associated with revealing user's personal data on the ubiquitous internet environment. The two major challenges facing social media include privacy and security issues, generating significant impacts for users and service providers [1]. From the users' perspective, possible effects include improper sharing of personal information; leakage and exploitation of personal details through active mining [4]. For social media service providers, there is the disruption of appropriate services as well as damage to reputation by these threats.

The activities of mining user data from social media is majorly fueled by the massive amount of data available on the platforms. Facebook usage has grown exponentially to include a wide variety of users. According to the statistics page of Facebook.com, it has over 2.5 billion active users, with over 1.6 billion of them logging in daily. This, when compared with Statista's statistics of internet usage globally would imply that about 33% of the total users of the internet log on to Facebook daily and that the number of its active users real-time is higher than the internet population of any country [5]. With advancements in information technology infrastructure, such as internet of things, semantic technologies and cloud computing, capacity for collecting, analyzing, and sharing data poses a considerable threat to the privacy and security of social media users. While the major entities with social media can be identified as users, service providers, third-party applications as well as advertisers, users and service providers can be regarded as the primary entities while third-party applications and advertisers as secondary. There are interactions among users within a social media platform and oftentimes, most users do not know each other. Levels of user interaction are defined by service providers. These relate to storage and processing of user data as well as management of user activities, in relation to services provided on the platform. In addition, users utilise third-party social applications for different purposes and advertisers place ads for users to click. This process creates huge potentials for leaking vital personal data. With the lack of academic papers specifically on socio-economic impacts of these challenges in relation to social media, this research focuses on guidelines towards identifying appropriate measures for both addressing the challenges and curbing the socio-economic impacts. Section 2 of this paper would critically review and analyse privacy challenges and Sect. 3 would focus on security challenges. Section 4 would evaluate socio-economic impacts of the challenges with an evaluation framework for understanding the impacts. The framework also constitutes an initial step towards modelling of the discourse space to provide context and better understanding of the domain. Section 5 concludes the paper with a summary of the research and recommendations for further research in the domain.

2 Privacy Challenges

The management of user privacy on social media has emerged as a major challenge over the years. The primary issue, as stated by [6], is the willingness by users to express concerns about their privacy on social media, but seldom act in ensuring it is protected. [7] also stated that inaction of users to protect private information is what is known as a "privacy paradox", based on the concept that while users are concerned about invasion of their privacy, many freely give up data on social media, largely due to naivety of the risks. The privacy challenge is also supported by [8], who argue that lack of awareness and structure in enforcing privacy on social media drastically increases the challenge. [2] also supports the idea by identifying different types of privacy risks and classifying them into three, multimedia, traditional and social threats. Multimedia threats pose the highest level of risk, based on the "privacy paradox" by [7]. Such threats include content exposure, transparency, metadata, static data and tagging; occurring in content that includes images, videos, and other forms of non-textual data. These threats lead to privacy breaches such as profiling, data ownership loss and unwarranted information disclosure not anticipated or consented to by users. Traditional threats include cyber-attacks, spamming, malware and phishing while social threats include bullying, espionage, stalking and other abuses of privacy that may lead to loss of reputation on a personal or organisational scale, harassment, information leakage and profiling [2]. Furthermore, it can be generally observed that privacy concerns on social media can be defined based on three different dimensions. These are concerns with data sharing, concerns based on specific social media platform policies and ones relating to location-based services.

2.1 Social Media Data Sharing

Sharing services on social media allows generation of different types of content by users, revealing physical and social contexts about a subject. [9] analysed the issues and conducted studies on considerations and patterns of privacy on web and mobile, claiming that the rising number of personal contents is exposing users to a new set of concerns relating to privacy. Digital cameras and smartphone cameras which can directly upload video and photo content to the web have made publishing of private content a lot easier. The privacy concerns are particularly acute in multimedia collections since they reveal so much about private and social environments of users. Users are often unaware about risks involved when sharing content on social media. According to [10], the decision to share content is momentary, and in the world of today, content shared is available to many other social media users. Users tend to believe that content shared online is private between them and the intended recipients, which is usually not the case.

2.2 Social Media Policies

Often, social media users are unaware of the reality that their privacy has been compromised and are therefore not taking measures to protect their private information from being used by other parties [11]. Social media sites create central repositories of private information which are cumulative and persistent [12]. With machine learning algorithms which can be maliciously utilised for inference attacks, this constitutes a potential privacy breach for users. This has led to criticisms of popular social media platforms in recent times, regarding policies about online privacy, hate speech and child safety, among several other privacy concerns.

2.3 Location-Based Services

Location-based services are made possible by GPS which tracks location of users coupled with other vital features such as instant messaging [13]. Location-based services on social media are commonly referred to as geosocial networking. Furthermore, they not only imply adding GPS features to a social media platform but also comprises of a new social structure made up of users linked by the interdependency that comes from their physical locations together with media content that are location-based via IDs such as videos, texts, and photos [14]. The link between users further goes beyond sharing of physical locations to involving sharing common interests, activities, and opinions. Without appropriate usage policies, such persuasive tools pose a challenge to privacy. Users of location-based services also face situations where information shared could be used in tracking them, by stalkers for example. Advocates for privacy fear that geolocation applications are exposed to data scraping activities; monitoring user activities and building a rich database from private users' data. Hence, insurgence of applications meant for information aggregation potentially pose a major threat to location-based services and privacy of social media users [15].

3 Security Challenges

Security on social media focuses on protection of data and resources against attacks as well as protection against network impropriety. Security threats can be categorised into two; classic threats which social media inherited from the web and modern threats, which have become more synonymous with social media than with the web generally.

3.1 Classic Threats

These are threats that expose both social media users and other online users to security threats. Such threats pre-date social media and include malware, spam, phishing, and cross-site scripting attacks. While these are being addressed in diverse ways, they still constitute significant threats till date. They aim at extracting user personal data to attack and target peers of victims too [16]. Malware refers to malicious software which is created with the sole intent to access user private data. Malware attacks are easier on social media compared to other platforms due to social media nature and the high level of user interaction on them [17]. Phishing is another classic threat whereby cybercriminals acquire user personal data by posing as legitimate third parties using a false identity. Spam on the other hand, is generally unwanted messages. With social media, spam is particularly more of a threat than email spam because users spend more time on social media. Spam messages normally contain adverts or malicious links that may redirect users to malware or phishing sites. They generally emanate from false profiles or spam applications, but significant amounts also spread from compromised accounts [16]. Cross-site scripting is among the most common and serious security issues affecting internet applications. A cross-site scripting attack allows cybercriminals run malicious codes on the web browser of targeted users, which compromises their data or results in theft of data stored as cookies or other forms of confidential data [17].

3.2 Modern Threats

These are threats more specific to social media and its users due to exploitation of social media infrastructure and security mechanisms. Modern threats mainly focus on obtaining private data of users or of their social network of friends. If users have their privacy settings on social networking sites as public, this information can easily be accessed by other parties. In this case, attackers can create a similar social network profile and send friend requests to targeted users, disclosing their private information to the hackers once the friend request is accepted. A summary of such threats is presented in Table 1.

Table 1. Modern security threats on social media

Security threats	Description
Sybil attacks	Creation of multiple fake identities for malicious purposes such as sending messages to legitimate users with the goal of collecting private data only accessible to friends
User profiling	Analysis of routine user activity by social platforms, which can pose a threat when accessed by a cyber-criminal
Social engineering	Deceiving users to reveal or disclose confidential data through various social devices and mechanisms
Identity theft	Attempts to collect personal data for impersonation and obtaining benefits or harming users. They are possible using various strategies, such as when users share account details with others; download malicious apps and low privacy settings
Clickjacking	Use of malicious techniques for prompting users to click on a link that they had not intended to click
Compromised accounts	Hijacking accounts by malicious users, thereby having access to users' social media data repository
Inference attacks	Utilization of data mining mechanisms to collect sensitive information through analysis of available and authorized data, drawing inferences from the data
De-anonymization attacks	It can be regarded as a form of inference attack, whereby identities of users are inferred based on a set of mobility traces

4 Socio-economic Impacts of the Challenges

To enhance sustenance of social media, users require conviction regarding security for personal data and protection of their privacy. Users are becoming increasingly concerned about privacy and security in an era when cybersecurity incidents, data breaches and controversies over social media have gained prominence. The most direct threat to user trust is a negative personal experience. According to NTIA Survey, 19% of social media users have been affected by online security breaches within the last year [18]. Security breaches are seemingly more common among most intensive social media users. Social media users also pointed out identity theft as a major concern related to privacy and security on the platforms [19]. Other common concerns commonly shared included card and banking frauds, tracking and collection of data by online services, loss of private data, tracking by both governmental and non-governmental agencies, as well as other threats to privacy [1–3]. The apparent fallout from concerns of privacy and security on social media extends beyond commerce to several social vices. For instance, a significant percentage of social media users expressed concerns about private data collection preventing them from expressing opinions that were seemingly controversial or political [20]. Based on these and analysis of privacy and security challenges described in Sects. 2 and 3, Fig. 1 presents an illustration of different social media components and their inter-relationships, building towards socio-economic impacts for social media

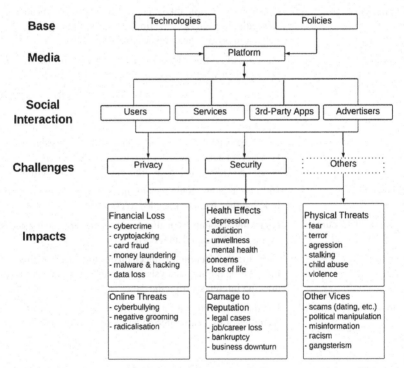

Fig. 1. Socio-economic impacts of privacy and security challenges on social media represented via interconnectivity between different social media components

privacy and security challenges. The figure demonstrates the role of technologies and policies for building and running social media platforms. These platforms facilitate social interactions between users, advertisers, services and diverse third-party applications. The current very high level of interactions between these for varying purposes has resulted into several challenges, with privacy and security being the most prominent ones.

4.1 Financial Crimes

Over the past few years, there has been a rapid increase in number of reported data breaches with cybercriminals continuing to conduct financial crimes for profit from consumer and business data mined from social media. These financial losses come from diverse activities, such as cryptojacking, malware sales, hacking services and money laundering. According to [21], available evidence shows certain obvious trends in the utilization of social media platforms in crime. The researcher's study shows that crimes enabled by social media generate a minimum worldwide revenue of $3.25bn for the international cybercrime economy yearly. Open criminal activities such as credit card fraud also thrives, with data hacking and selling. Furthermore, botnet and booter hires were discovered to be available on social media platforms with costs at an average of $10 per month or $25 for a lifetime rental. According to data from CIFAS, the utilization of social media in recruiting money mules below 21 years of age has increased by 36% since 2016 [21]. Many existing research efforts are towards the estimation of cybercrime value according to costs incurred by organisations due to breaches and data theft. However, [22] noted that it is better to consider the impact of cybercrime based on revenues obtained from the activities involved as it describes what motivates actions of cybercriminals and assists in tracking and likely disrupting criminal activity. The average cost of data breach in 2019 was a whopping $3.92 million, constituting 12% increase from the last five years [23]. Financial implications are not only recorded as a one-time cost, but rather felt from when a breach occurs all the way to when the breach is contained.

4.2 Cyber Threats

Cyber threats in this context refers to threats to social media users that are non-physical in nature. These include cyberbullying, radicalization, and all forms of negative grooming online. Social media have continuously come in handy for instigating cyberbullying. Cyberbullying is an aggression towards anyone through electronic means, and specifically via social media [24]. It has become almost impossible to avoid social media trolls. Most reported cases of cyberbullying have direct connections with social engineering, cybersecurity, and social media. Often, those who engage in cyberbullying conceal their identity and impersonate other individuals, through false identities towards terrorizing their victims. A study by [24] revealed that about 20 to 35% of adolescents said they either bullied someone or were bullied, or both. A British study also showed that one out of four children reported to have experienced cyber bullying. These have led to critical mental scars in teenagers and have resulted to cases of teen suicides [25]. Online threats among children also emanate from gaming on social media with cases of using force or pressure to obtain personal data from others [26]. Generally, it can be observed that online threats are being extensively utilised by social engineers to destabilize cybersecurity while undermining digital autonomy and privacy.

4.3 Physical Threats

Physical threats emanate online to become threats within a physical environment; instigating physical threats from social media which can result in loss of physical property or lives [27]. Such threats include terror, aggression, child abuse, stalking and societal violence. Social media facilitates spreading of information across borders without limits posed by physical boundaries. They also enhance creation of new forms of technology that enhance anonymity. Factors such as absence of proper security and privacy measures, trigger an extensive use of compromised data to achieve the desired anonymity [28]. This explains the use of such loopholes by terror groups to accelerate their activities. Terror groups have perfected skills required to reach their audiences through social media, recruiting, raising funds and training users among several other cybercrimes. These then leads to several types of physical attacks such as kidnappings, rape, and robbery [29]. With the wide use of location-based services on social media, failure to have private location-based data kept secure can also adversely affect personal safety of a user. Relaxed privacy and security settings foster terror-related activities, as users can be targeted based on their geolocation.

4.4 Other Social Vices

Several other social vices emanate from privacy and security challenges on social media. These include dating scams, political manipulation, misinformation, racism and gangsterism. Democratic processes have been observed to be crafted to suit specific narratives through manipulation on social media. The United States, among other countries, has reported political campaigns marred by the spread of misinformation. This is fueled by the fact that people are highly dependent on social media for news. People release fake news to social media platforms and without verifying authenticity of such information, others continue to disseminate it, usually resulting into other vices such as racism and gangsterism. National security is threatened in the process, as numerous individuals instantly react to the dissemination of such news, attacking each other based on ethnicity, religion, and tribe, among others. Likewise, such news instantly promotes fear, tensions, and violence in the society [29] which have been identified under physical threats. This also demonstrates interlinkage between the various socio-economic impacts.

4.5 Health Issues

Several health issues also arise from privacy and security challenges on social media. These include depression, addiction, stress, mental health concerns and even loss of life. These usually stem from other socio-economic impacts such as financial loss and online threats. Victimization because of cyberbullying plays a major role in this case. Currently, bullying victimization is linked to growing risk of suicidal behaviors, and growing risk of mental health problems [30]. Likewise, financial and data loss could lead to depression.

Furthermore, with another online threat: negative grooming comes the development of anti-social behaviors, which over time, leads to addiction. These include addiction to drugs and other harmful substances. Stress also develops with conflicting opinions in real world with those received online via grooming activities and with time, this degenerates into more severe medical conditions.

4.6 Reputational Damage

Social media platforms provide huge capabilities for connecting users in new ways and coming up with new methods of social interaction. Hence, cybercriminals find social media platforms quite attractive. According to [21], available evidence reveals trends in the utilization of social media platforms for crime. ICC's data obtained by the researcher noted an increase in the number, by more than 300 of reported crimes related to social media from 2015 to 2017 in the United States, while in the UK, police data revealed four times increment in crime enabled by social media from 2013 to 2018. Furthermore, data of more than 1.3 billion social media users had been compromised in the previous five years and from 45 to 50% of illegal trading of data between 2017 and 2018 might be related to breaches of social media platforms. It was discovered that there are diverse methods on social media platforms through which malware can be delivered to users, such as via updates or shares, add-ons and plug-ins, compared to sources like ecommerce, media or culture-oriented websites. In addition, infected ads are responsible for about 30 to 40% of social media infections and a minimum of 20% of social media infections come from add-ons or plug-ins for social media [21]. When it comes to fraud on social media, estimates suggest that a significant percentage of leading brands' social media accounts are fake [31], and these accounts are frequently utilised by criminals to conduct cybercrimes, as well as malware distribution or the development of phishing emails on the basis of user information and preferences. Likewise, the target of firm executives with high visibility on social media is a worrying development. These and many more results into reputational damage for both individuals, organisations and social media platform providers. Several other impacts also emerge from such damage such as legal cases, job or career loss, financial bankruptcy, and business downturn.

5   Conclusion

This paper focused on identifying and analyzing socio-economic impacts of two major social media challenges, privacy, and security. From the critical analysis of these challenges, a wide range of socio-economic impacts were identified and classified based on type. While these provide a basis for further understanding the challenges and their impacts, it also illustrates roles of different entities and fosters modelling for the network. Furthermore, it provides guidelines towards appropriate measures for addressing them; both from technical and non-technical perspectives. Recommended further research in this domain would focus on identifying and analyzing other potential major challenges for social media as well as considering integrated solutions, which include both technical and non-technical components. In addition, research towards a semantic transformation of the evaluation framework is suggested, providing a model to semantically describe instances of social media socio-economic impacts and drawing implicit insights and reasoning from multiple instances towards addressing socio-economic impacts of all major challenges defined.

References

1. Kayes, I., Iamnitchi, A.: Privacy and security in online social networks: a survey. Online Soc. Netw. Media **3**, 1–21 (2017)
2. Rathore, S., Sharma, P.K., Loia, V., Jeong, Y.-S., Park, J.H.: Social network security: issues, challenges, threats, and solutions. Inf. Sci. **421**, 43–69 (2017)
3. Sowmya, H.S., Kavitha, M., RuhiKhanum, P.C., Asha Rani, M.: Compatible and confidentiality-preserving friend matching in mobile cloud. In: 3rd National Conference on Image Processing, Computing, Communication, Networking and Data Analytics, p. 127 (2018)
4. Heravi, A., Mubarak, S., Choo, K.-K.R.: Information privacy in online social networks: uses and gratification perspective. Comput. Hum. Behav. **84**, 441–459 (2018)
5. Statista: Facebook - Statistics and Facts. https://www.statista.com/topics/751/facebook/. Accessed 06 Mar 2020
6. Nesi, J.: The impact of social media on youth mental health: challenges and opportunities. N. C. Med. J. **81**(2), 116–121 (2020)
7. Wu, P.F.: The privacy paradox in the context of online social networking: a self-identity perspective. J. Assoc. Inf. Sci. Technol. **70**(3), 207–217 (2019)
8. Kramer, N.C., Schawel, J.: Mastering the challenge of balancing self-disclosure and privacy in social media. Curr. Opin. Psychol. **31**, 67–71 (2020)
9. Pham, V.V.H., Yu, S., Sood, K., Cui, L.: Privacy issues in social networks and analysis: a comprehensive survey. IET Netw. **7**(2), 74–84 (2017)
10. Ham, C.-D., Lee, J., Hayes, J.L., Bae, Y.H.: Exploring sharing behaviors across social media platforms. Int. J. Market Res. **61**(2), 157–177 (2019)
11. Aghasian, E., Garg, S., Gao, L., Yu, S., Montgomery, J.: Scoring users' privacy disclosure across multiple online social networks. IEEE Access **5**, 13118–13130 (2017)
12. Alshaikh, M., Zohdy, M., Olawoyin, R., Debnath, D., Gwarzo, Z., Alowibdi, J.: Social network analysis and mining: privacy and security on Twitter. In: 2020 10th Annual Computing and Communication Workshop and Conference (CCWC), pp. 0712–0718. IEEE (2020)
13. Sun, G., Xie, Y., Liao, D., Yu, H., Chang, V.: User-defined privacy location-sharing system in mobile online social networks. J. Netw. Comput. Appl. **86**, 34–45 (2017)
14. Kylasa, S.B., Kollias, G., Grama, A.: Social ties and checkin sites: connections and latent structures in location-based social networks. Soc. Netw. Anal. Min. **6**(1), 1–14 (2016). https://doi.org/10.1007/s13278-016-0404-3
15. Palos-Sanchez, P., Saura, J.R., Reyes-Menendez, A., Esquivel, I.V.: Users acceptance of location-based marketing apps in tourism sector: an exploratory analysis. J. Spat. Organ. Dyn. **6**(3), 258–270 (2018)
16. Veni, R.H., Hariprasad Reddy, A., Kesavulu, C.: Identifying malicious Web links and their attack types in social networks. Int. J. Sci. Res. Comput. Sci. Eng. Inf. Technol. **3**(4), 1060–1066 (2018)
17. Ali, S., Islam, N., Rauf, A., Din, I.U., Guizani, M., Rodrigues, J.J.P.C.: Privacy and security issues in online social networks. Future Internet **10**(12), 114 (2018)
18. Jain, R., Jain, N., Nayyar, A.: Security and privacy in social networks: data and structural anonymity. In: Gupta, B.B., Perez, G.M., Agrawal, D.P., Gupta, D. (eds.) Handbook of Computer Networks and Cyber Security, pp. 265–293. Springer, Cham (2020). https://doi.org/10.1007/978-3-030-22277-2_11

19. Wang, C., Yang, B., Cui, J., Wang, C.: Fusing behavioral projection models for identity theft detection in online social networks. IEEE Trans. Comput. Soc. Syst. **6**(4), 637–648 (2019)
20. NTIA: Internet Use. https://www.ntia.doc.gov/blog/2016/first-look-internet-use-2015. Accessed 06 Mar 2020
21. McGuire, M.: Social media platforms and the cybercrime economy: the next chapter of into the web of profit. Bromium Report (2019)
22. McGuire, M.: Into the web of profit: Understanding the growth of the cybercrime economy. Bromium Report (2018)
23. Stahl, B.C., Wright, D.: Ethics and privacy in AI and big data: implementing responsible research and innovation. IEEE Secur. Priv. **16**(3), 26–33 (2018)
24. Bannink, R., Broeren, S., van de Looij-Jansen, P.M., de Waart, F.G., Raat, H.: Cyber and traditional bullying victimization as a risk factor for mental health problems and suicidal ideation in adolescents. PloS One **9**(4), e94026 (2015)
25. Baruah, H., Dashora, P., Parmar, A.: Impact of cyberbullying on psychological health of adolescents. Int. J. Hum. Soc. Sci. (IJHSS) **6**(4), 137–144 (2017)
26. Du, J., Jiang, C., Chen, K.-C., Ren, Y., Vincent Poor, H.: Community-structured evolutionary game for privacy protection in social networks. IEEE Trans. Inf. Forensics Secur. **13**(3), 574–589 (2017)
27. Palvia, P., Baqir, N., Nemati, H.: ICT for socio-economic development: a citizens' perspective. Inf. Manag. **55**(2), 160–176 (2018)
28. Jegede, A.E.: Modern information technology, global risk, and the challenges of crime in the era of late modernity. In: Impacts of the Media on African Socio-Economic Development, pp. 18–33. IGI Global (2017)
29. Nsudu, I., Onwe, E.C.: Social media and security challenges in Nigeria: the way forward. World Appl. Sci. J. **35**(6), 993–999 (2017)
30. Beheshti, A., Hashemi, V.M., Yakhchi, S.: Towards context-aware social behavioral analytics. In: Proceedings of the 17th International Conference on Advances in Mobile Computing & Multimedia, pp. 28–35 (2019)
31. Chen, Z.F., Cheng, Y.: Consumer response to fake news about brands on social media: the effects of self-efficacy, media trust, and persuasion knowledge on brand trust. J. Product Brand Manag. (2019)

Program Analysis

Automatic Repair of Semantic Defects Using Restraint Mechanisms

Yukun Dong[✉], Li Zhang, Shanchen Pang, Hao Liu, Wenjing Yin,
Mengying Wu, Meng Wu, and Haojie Li

College of Computer Science and Technology, China University of Petroleum,
Qingdao, Shandong, China
dongyk@upc.edu.cn

Abstract. Program defect repair faces serious challenges in that such repairs require considerable manpower, and the existing automatic repair approaches have difficulty generating correct patches efficiently. This paper proposes an automatic method for repairing semantic defects in Java programs based on restricted sets which refers to the interval domains of related variables that can trigger program semantic defects. First, the program semantic defects are summarized into defect patterns according to their grammar and semantic features. A repair template for each type of defect pattern is predefined based on a restricted-set. Then, for each specific defect, A patch statement is automatically synthesized according to the repair template, and the detected defect information is reported by the static detection tool (DTSJava). Next, the patch location is determined by the def-use chain of defect-related variables. Finally, we evaluate the patches generated by our method using DTSJava. We implemented the method in the defect automatic repair prototype tool DTSFix to verify effect of repairing the semantic defects detected by DTSJava in 6 Java open-source projects. The experimental results showed that 109 of 129 program semantic defects were repaired.

Keywords: Automatic program repair · Program semantic defect · Defect pattern · Restricted-set · Patch synthesis

1 Introduction

With the development of information technology, the Internet of Things (IoT) has made breakthrough progress in smart transportation, smart home, public safety, etc., and extended it to satellites, airplanes, submarines and other areas. The number and complexity of IoT security defects have increased significantly. Program defects that threat the IoT security may cause operational errors under certain conditions, producing abnormal results or behaviors, or even large irreparable losses in severe cases. Generally, developers are busy implementing of algorithms and functions, which makes it easy to miss hidden semantic defects.

© Springer Nature Singapore Pte Ltd. 2020
G. Xu et al. (Eds.): FCS 2020, CCIS 1286, pp. 567–583, 2020.
https://doi.org/10.1007/978-981-15-9739-8_42

These missed defects subsequently result in substantial workloads to find and repair the defects during the testing and maintenance stages.

Nowly, static analysis to identify common program defects and automatic program repair (APR) becomes the main apporaches to strengthen the security of IoT applications. APR is gradually becoming a hot spot in software engineering research due to its advantages in helping developers find and repair defects more efficiently. APR techniques, which reduce the onerous burden of debugging and preserve program quality, are of tremendous value. Depending on the targets of the repair, APR techniques can be classified into the following two families: functional defect repair [1–3] and semantic defect repair [4–8]. Functional defect repair focuses on repairing defects that fail to meet the functional requirement specifications, while semantic defect repair is intended to repair defects that violate program security semantics. Functional defect repair usually relies on test cases or assertions, but test suites coverage issues and patch overfitting problems severely impede repair precision and efficiency. Qi et al. [9] performed manual inspections to repair to 105 real defects in GenProg [1] and AE [10] and found that only two of the GenProg repair results, and only three of the AE repair results were semantically correct. The program semantic defect repair not only guarantees the function-required implementation but also ensures the correctness of the program semantics. Defect repair based on program semantics can narrow the search space, ensure the correctness of the program semantics after repair, and improve the repairs success rate. However, existing program semantic defect repair methods do not combine defect information during the defect detection process. Thus, the repair is not targeted, and the success rate of repairs is still low.

By comparing the repair effect of different repair methods, we found that repair methods for specific defect patterns is more targeted and the success rate of repairs are higher. This paper proposes a automatic program repair method using restraint mechanisms for defect pattern. With the help of the static analysis, the program semantic defects in the program are automatically repaired to improve the quality of IoT program and security assurance. Similar to our prior work [11,12], we utilize the static detection tool DTSJava to obtain semantic defect information, including defect type, defect-related variable, etc. DTSJava is a static analysis tool based on defect patterns that can detect potential defects in programs, such as null pointer dereferences. Our work focuses on repairing variable-related defects that refer to a problem, error, or hidden defect caused by a variable value that damages the normal operation of the computer software or the program. In severe cases, the system may exit or crash abnormally. The current variable-related defects mainly include null pointer dereferences, out-of-bounds, illegal calculations, and so on.

First, we extract the defect information, such as the defect file name, defect pattern, defect location, to guide the repair process. Aiming at different defect patterns [12], we summarize six common defect repair templates and propose a unified repair method for semantic defects. Next, a corresponding predefined repair template is selected for each specific defect based on the defect pattern.

And the patch condition is automatically synthesized by the defect-related variables based on a restricted-set denoting the defect semantic constraints. Then, the patch location is determined based on the principle of minimum program modification, and the patch statement is applied to the location. Finally, the generated patch is retested by DTSJava to ensure that the patch is both correct (i.e., the defect was repaired) and safe (i.e., no new defect was induced). This approach fully utilizes the defect information reported by DTSJava to synthesize the precise condition and determine the patch location, avoiding blind automatic program repairs and improving the repair precision and efficiency.

In summary, the main contributions of this paper are as follows:

- An automatic program repair method that utilizes defect information detected by the static analysis tool DTSJava.
- Two algorithms of conditional synthesis are proposed based on a restricted-set and patch location to achieve multi-point repair.
- An analysis of the repair results for 129 defects in a real-world program after applying the method proposed in this paper is provided.

We have implemented our approach as a Java program repair system, DTS-Fix, and evaluated DTSFix on six open-source Java project. Our approach achieves an optimal balance in scalability (repairing the large-scale real-world projects), repairability (repairing more types of semantic defects detected by DTSJava), and repair quality (obtaining a functionally equivalent patch). And the approach we proposed can repair the 84.5% semantic defects, and achieve the functional-equivalence repair.

2   Related Work

At present, related researches on automatic repair of program semantic defects is mainly divided into three main categories: program semantic defect repair based on constraint solving, program semantic defect repair based on program specifications, and template-based program semantic defect repair.

The program semantic defect repair method based on constraint solving refers to acquiring program runtime information via symbol execution, generating the constraint conditions required for solving, and using conditional synthesis to complete the program repair. Hoang et al. [13] proposed an automatic repair method, called SemFix, that was based on symbolic execution, constraint solving and program synthesis. Constrained by a given test suite, the constraint is solved by iteratively repairing the hierarchical space of the expression, and finally the repair condition is synthesized. Specific to Java programs, Xuan et al. [14] proposed an automatic repair method for defect conditional statements, called Nopol, which uses the concept of angelic value pair positioning to determine the expected value of the condition during test execution and encodes the runtime trace collection variable and its actual value as an instance of satisfiability modulo theories (SMT). Finally, the solution is transformed into a code patch. Xuan-Bach et al. [15] inferred semantic constraints via Symbolic PathFinder, a well-known symbolic execution engine for Java programs and utilize conditional synthesis to implement semantic repair of Java programs.

Program semantic defect repair based on program specifications refers to the use of a series of expected behaviors, namely, the program specifications, to achieve automatic program repair. This process is divided into incomplete-specification repair and complete-specification repair issues. Mechtaev et al. [16] introduced the idea of using a reference program to alleviate the overfitting problem and provided a new idea to alleviate the overfitting problem in incomplete-specification repair issues. Gao Qing et al. [17] focused on memory leak in C code, by summing up the program specifications that must be satisfied when no memory leak is present, and proposed a memory leak repair method based on these complete-specifications.

Template-based program semantic defect repair refers to a generic template summarized by the prior repair experience and patch data. Chen Liu et al. [18] combined historical fix templates, machine learning techniques, and semantic patch generation techniques to fix defects automatically. Benoit Cornu et al. [19] designed nine repair strategies by predefining two major types of repair templates, and implemented runtime fixes for null pointer references in Java projects. Dongsun Kim et al. [20] studied existing human-written templates to obtain the 8 general repair templates, analyzed the synthetic repair conditions, and achieved automatic defect repair. Kui et al. [8] used a repair template for defective codes after static analysis as part of a patch generation effort to implement the AVATAR system. This system complemented other template-based repair methods. To address the inaccuracies of the existing methods, Xiong et al. [21] achieved the precise conditional synthesis of program repair by variable sorting, API document analysis and predicate mining; and the accuracy of this system reached 78.3%, which improved the patch repair rate.

3   Program Semantic Defects

3.1   Program Semantic Defect Patterns

Definition 1 Semantic Defect. During the programming process, the code is fully compliant with the specifications of the computer language, and no compile/link errors occur, but logic errors may exist. This defective code may cause a program exception at runtime, and could even cause the system to crash.

The semantic defects related to variables are caused by the value of variables. During the static analysis process, for the current real domain, and the restricted domain of the variable γ_v^l, if $\theta_v^l \cap \gamma_v^l \neq \varnothing$, a program semantic defect may be generated.

Definition 2 Defect Pattern. A defect pattern refers to a class of semantic defects that have a commonality, where the same grammatical or semantic feature describes a program property, the root cause or the same solution. This paper summarizes semantic defects into defect patterns.

Definition 3 Restricted-set. Variables may violate the sets of intervals of the legal value range in the program. The restricted interval domain is defined as a restricted-set.

Let D be the interval domain of the variable, including $\varnothing$. The set of connectors is denoted as $C = \{\wedge, \vee\}$. If both two operands of the restricted operation violate the range of values, the connector $\wedge$ will be used; otherwise it is $\vee$. The restricted rule defined by the restricted-set is a quadruple $R = <e, domain_1, c, domain_2>$, where $domain_1$ represents the restricted interval domain of the first relevant operational expression, e represents the defect expression, and $domain_2$ represents the restricted interval domain of the second relevant operation expression. $domain_1 \subseteq D$, $domain_2 \subseteq D$, $c \in C$. This paper specifies that the operational expression is divided into a pre-expression operator (preoperator) and post-expression operator (postoperator). For example, in the expression $c = a/b$, the operator is the arithmetic division, and the preoperator and postoperator are a and b respectively. From the restricted rule of the division operator, the divisor cannot be zero, therefore the restricted set of $Defect_{var}(d)$ in the restricted-set of the b is $[0,0]$ in this example.

For example, the program shown in Fig. 1 is the PolarPlot.java file of the Java open-source project **jfreechart**. The program initializes the variable *state* to null at line 1399, and $axes.size()$ in line 1398 may return 0, the statement in the next for loop fail to execute, and causing the code in line 1411 to be executed immediately. However, when the variable *state* is used in line 1417, its value is still null; therefore, a null pointer dereference occurs at that point. The defect pattern in Fig. 1 is a null pointer dereference, and according to the repair template, a null check statement should be inserted. The restricted-set of the variable *state* is determined and the patch condition **state!=null** is synthesized. Then, the def-use chain analysis is used to determine the patch insertion location, which adds a null check before line 1417.

```
1398:  int axisCount = this.axes.size();
1399:  AxisState state = null;
1400:  for(int i = 0;i<axisCount; i++){

        ......
1405:      AxisState s = this.drawAxis(axis, location, g2, dataArea);
1406:      if(i ==0){
1407:          state = s;
1408:      }
1409:  }

        ......
1416: +  if(state != null){
1417:          drawGridlines(g2, dataArea, this.angleTicks, state.getTicks());
1418: +  }
```

Fig. 1. Example of defect program repair

3.2   Semantic Defect Detection

In this paper, the static detection [11] tool for specific defect patterns, DTSJava, can be used to detect various defects through static analysis of program source code. The defect information includes the main details regarding the defect, such as the name of the defect file, the defect type, the defect location, and the restricted-set of defects, etc. The specific defect information outputted in the defect report is illustrated by the defective program in Fig. 1, as shown in Table 1.

Table 1. Example of defect report output

Defect feature	Defect information	Example
Defect	defect type	The defect type in line 1417 is "fault"
Category	defect pattern	The defect pattern in line 1417 is "null pointer dereference"
Id	defect point ID	The unique number of the defect point in AST, 52
File	location of defect file	The absolute path of the defect file, e.g., D:\testprogram\test.java
Variable	related variable	The variable related to the defect in line 1417: state
StartLine	start line	The declaration line for the state variable: line 1399
IPLine	defect line	The defect line: line 1417
IPLineCode	code in defect line	The code in the defect line: drawGridlines(g2,dataArea,this.angleTicks,state.getTicks());
Restrictset	restricted set	The interval set over which variables may violate the legal range of values in the program

The static detection tool DTSJava enables accurate analysis of Java projects, using field-sensitive and context-sensitive program analysis to obtain accurate defect information. The synthesis of patch statements depends on the information in the defect report, which help make the repair more targeted and helps developers find the specific causes and defect information that leads to defects. DTSFix does not need to generate a large number of candidate patches, which reduces the overhead of generating and filtering invalid patches.

To facilitate the description of the program semantic defect repair method proposed in this paper, the following symbols are used to represent the various attributes of the defect record, where d refers to a specific defect:

$Defect_{pattern}(d) :=$ defect pattern
$Defect_{id}(d) :=$ The unique number of the corresponding node in the abstract syntax tree
$Defect_{file}(d) :=$ defect file
$Defect_{op}(d) :=$ operator in defect point

$Defect_{var}(d) :=$ defect-related variable
$Defect_{line}(d) :=$ defect line
$Defect_{rst}(d) :=$ defect restricted-set
Various properties of the repair record:
$Patch_{syn}(d) :=$ patch synthesis condition
$Patch_{startloc}(d) :=$ patch start location
$Patch_{endloc}(d) :=$ patch end location

4   Program Semantic Defect Repair

Upon receiving a defect report, we execute DTSFix, analyze the defect report, determine the defect pattern, and generate possible patches to repair the defect. First, a repair template is selected according to the defect pattern. Then, a patch statement is obtained based on the restricted-set. Next, the patch location is determined. Finally, the patch condition and the patch location are synthesized to generate the patch, achieving automatic repair of defective programs.

4.1   Repair Template

The goal of our repair strategy is to ensure that the state of repaired program never transfers to the *error* state [22]. What we want to do is to make conditions that can transfer to *error* state unsatisfiable by adding check statements. The patch statements usually have the following forms:

$$\varphi_{ps} \stackrel{\text{def}}{=} (\text{ if}(c) \text{ return } Ret;) \vee (\text{ if}(c) \{s_1;\})$$
$$\vee (\text{ if}(c) \{s_1; s_2; ...; s_n;\} (n{>}1))$$
$$\vee (\text{ if}(c) \text{ throw } e)$$

where c, Ret, s and e represent the patch condition, expected return value, program statements and object of exception class respectively. The value of n is determined by the patch location.

When the value of the variable is not within the permissible range, a variable-related defect will be generated. Before a variable is used, the value of that variable needs to be checked to ensure it is legal. Therefore, these semantic defects can be repaired by inserting a check statement or a statement that legalizes the value of the variable. For variable-related defects, the effects after repairing the defects are as follows: the string or object is initialized; the variable is not null when it is used; when the variable is declared, its value does not exceed the maximum or minimum range specified by the data type on the computer platform; array index does not exceed the initialized upper-bound.

To satisfy the above conditions and repair the semantic defects of Java programs, we summarize the common repair templates from experience gained during manual repairs and developer-patches. As shown in Table 2, a unified repair method is given for program semantic defect features, which improve the efficiency of program repair.

Table 2. Semantic defect repair template

Defect pattern	Repair template
Null pointor dereference	Add null checker
Variable not initialization	Initializate the object
Out-of-bounds	Add array boundary check
Illegal calculation	Add a variable to the legal scope check in the computer
Integer overflow	

According to the repair templates, this paper implements a more accurate program repair method (automatic program repair method for program semantic defects based on restricted-set). When a new defect report is submitted, the method first reads the defect information, and then selects the corresponding defect repair template based on the defect pattern. Then, the patch condition is synthesized using information such as $Defect_{var}(d)$. Subsequently, following the principle of minimum program modification, we can utilize the AST structure and def-use chain analysis to find the location of the defect node. The nearest-distance rule of the statement block states that beginning with the block where $Defect_{var}(d)$ is located, the first definition of $Defect_{var}(d)$ is found when checking each block from inside to outside. Then, the location of the patch statement is determined. Finally, a patch is generated, and the patch is retested by DTSJava. A patch both repaired the original defect and does not cause in a new program defect, it is considered to be a correct patch. A patch verified as correct is inserted into the original program code, and a defect repair report is output, that includes the number of defect repairs, the repair template for the defect, and any conditional statements. Figure 2 shows the defect repair framework of this paper.

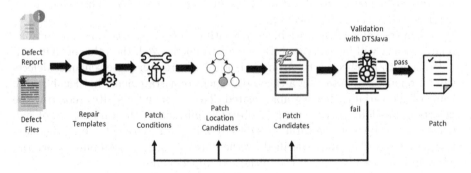

Fig. 2. The Framework of DTSFix

4.2 Patch Condition Synthesis Based on Restricted-Set

We can obtain the defect report output by DTSJava. If a defect is detected, $Defect_{pattern}(d)$ and $Defect_{op}(d)$ are first determined according to the defect report information, and $Defect_{rst}(d)$ is determined by the following constraint rule. The specific content of the restricted rules and the corresponding $Patch_{syn}(d)$ are shown in Table 3.

Table 3. Restricted rule

Defect pattern	Related expression	Operator	Restricted sets	Synthesis condition
Null pointer dereference	e_1	e_1.f()	<e_1,null,∨,∅>	e_1!=null
Illegal calculation	e_1,e_2	/, /=, %, div(), ldiv(), fmod()	<e_2,∅,∨, [0,0]>	e_2!=0
	e_1	log(), log10(), sqrt(), _logb(),_y0(), _y1()	<e_1, [Min,0],∨,∅>	e_1>=0
	e_1	asin(), acos()	<e_1, [Min,0]∪[1,Max],∨,∅>	e_1>=0&&e_1<=1
	e_2	atan2()	<e_2,∅,∨,[0,0]>	e_2!=0
	e_1,e_2	pow()	<e_1∪e_2,[0,0],∧, [Min,0]>	e_1!=0&&e_2>=0
	e_1,e_2	_jn(), _yn()	<e_1∪e_2, [Min,0],∧, [Min,0]>	e_1>0&&e_2>=0
Out-of-bounds	e_1	array[e_1]	<e_1,[array.length(),Max],∨,∅>	e_1<array.length()
Variable uninitialization	e_1	Variable uninitialization before use	<e_1,[0,0]∪null,∨,∅>	e_1=new classnameofe$_1$()

For some common program semantic defects, the proposed method can select a predefined repair template based on the defect pattern, $Defect_{pattern}(d)$, and then use the defect information to analyze the variable-related defect to obtain the restricted-set of the defect, $Defect_{rst}(d)$. Finally, the patch synthesis condition, $Patch_{syn}(d)$, is synthesized using $Defect_{var}(d)$ as the synthesis ingredients of the patch condition according to $Defect_{rst}(d)$.

Algorithm 1. Patch synthesis condition in DTSFix

Input:A Specific Defect, d
Ouput:$Patch_{syn}(d)$
1 ResultSet←Defect Information from Defect Report order by File
    // Read the defect information into the result set in the order of $Defect_{file}(d)$
2 $Defect_{pattern}(d)$← Category in ResultSet
3 Apply the repair-template for $Defect_{pattern}(d)$
4 Rebuild the AST of $Defect_{file}(d)$
5 **while**$(Defect_{file}(d).hasDefect())$ // Defects still exist in a defect file
6   defectNode← ASTraverse $(Defect_{id}(d))$
7     $Defect_{op}(d)$←operator on the currentNode
8     $Defect_{rst}(d)$←the rational variable restricted set by $Defect_{op}(d)$
9     $Patch_{syn}(d)$←synthesis condition by restricted set
10 **return** $Patch_{syn}(d)$

Based on the restricted-set, an algorithm is proposed to obtain the synthesized patch condition $Patch_{syn}(d)$. Another defect file performs the synthesis of the patch statement successively according to Algorithm 1 until all the defect file information has been read. Algorithm 1 implements a patch condition solver based on the restricted-set. First, the process reads the defect report, sorts each row of the defect report according to $Defect_{file}(d)$, and obtains $Defect_{var}(d)$. Then, the Abstract Syntax Tree (AST) of $Defect_{file}(d)$ is reconstructed. According to the unique $Defect_{id}(d)$ of the defect point on the AST, the corresponding tree node on the AST is returned by breadth-first traversal of the AST.Thus, $Defect_{op}(d)$ will be determined. $Defect_{rst}(d)$ is obtained from $Defect_{op}(d)$ according to the restricted rules, and finally, $Patch_{syn}(d)$ of the patch is obtained. For instance, in the program code shown in Fig. 1, line 1417 is detected as NPD. The first template selected involves adding a null check, and $Defect_{op}(NPD)$ is a reference to a variable that may be null. Then, the restricted set of $Defect_{var}(NPD)$ is obtained (here the variable *state* is determined to be null), and its composition condition is determined **state!=null**.

4.3   Patch Location Based on the Def-Use Chain

Given a program variable v and statement s, if v is used as input in s, it becomes a use point of v, denoted as $U(s, v)$. If v is assigned in s, it becomes a definition point of v, denoted as $D(s, v)$. The def-use chain is introduced to represent the def-use relationship, where U and D are the use point and definition point of the same variable v respectively, and the def-use chain U-D is used to denote that D is the last assignment of v before it is used at U. The assignment of the definition point determines the value of V at the use point U.

Algorithm 2. Repair Location in DTSFix

Input: AST of $Defect_{file}(d)$, Defect Information of $Defect_{file}(d)$
Ouput: list$[<Patch_{syn}(d), Patch_{startloc}(d), Patch_{endloc}(d)>]$
1 Update Defect Information of ASTNode in AST
   // ASTNode represents a node on the abstract syntax tree
2 **while** (ASTNode != null)
3   defectNode ← ASTraverse $(Defect_{id}(d))$
4   push defectNode to the stack
5   set flag of each Element in the stack to false
6 $Patch_{startloc}(d), Patch_{endloc}(d)$ ← topE.defloc()
   // topE represents the top element of the stack, defloc represents the
                              //definition point of the defect-related variable
7 **while**(!stack.isempty())
8   **while**(stack.nextElement())
9   **if** (flag == true)
10   pop topEm
11   **else if** (topEm. $Defect_{pattern}(d)$ == nextEm.Defect$_{pattern}(d)$
                     &&(topEm. $Defect_{var}(d)$ == nextEm.Defect$_{var}(d)$)
   // nextEm represents the next element in the stack
12   analyze the ASTNode by def-use chain
13   **if** (topEm.defloc() <nextEm.loc())
   // loc indicates the location of the defect
14                 $Patch_{startloc}(d)$ ← nextEm.loc()
15                 $Patch_{endloc}(d)$ ← topEm.defloc()
16   set the flag of the nextEm as true
17   **else** $Patch_{startloc}(d), Patch_{endloc}(d)$ ← topEm.defloc()
18   get the $Defect_{syn}(d)$ of topEm
19   pop topEm
20 **return** list$[<Patch_{syn}(d), Patch_{startloc}(d), Patch_{endloc}(d)>]$

To increase the readability of the program, the patch insertion location is set according to the principle of minimum program modification, and the same defect patterns in the same statement block are preferentially analyzed. If the defect pattern appears in a statement block and $Defect_{var}(d)$ are the same, and there is no redefinition or a statement that affects it, the location where the statement block starts is determined as the insert location of patch statement. In other cases, the defect location is considered the insertion location.

For example, if there are multiple defects in the **for** loop of line 1400 in Fig. 1, the null pointer dereference exception caused by *state* is null, and *state* is not redefined and no subsequent statement affects it, then it will still be null, and the check statement is placed before the **for** loop.

The defect files in the Java project are sequentially repaired. Algorithm 2 determines the patch location of all the defects in a file. We can obtain the patch synthesis conditions and the defect patch location, and uniformly repair the defects in the file. During the repair, the information in the defect report is read, then breadth-first traversal of AST is performed, and the information on the ASTNode is marked on the AST based on $Defect_{pattern}(d)$ and $Defect_{var}(d)$. Algorithm 2 is the algorithm that determines the specific location for all the defect repairs in a file.

When a variable triggers only one defect, we apply the signal-point repair, i.e. one patch statement repairs only one defect. But when a variable causes multiple identical defect patterns, we choose the multi-point analysis method. Algorithm

2 shows the idea of identifying the patch location following the principle of minimum program modification. The implementation of Algorithm 2 is based on the def-use chains and the patch synthesis condition obtained from Algorithm 1. Algorithm 2 determine the real patch location. First, the defect information is read. According to the unique $Defect_{id}(d)$ of the defect point on the AST, all the defect nodes are pushed into the stack by traversing the AST. The patch start and the end locations are initialized to the location of the top element of the stack. The top elements of the stack are compared with $Defect_{pattern}(d)$ and $Defect_{var}(d)$ and with other remaining elements sequentially until the bottom of the stack is reached. If $Defect_{pattern}(d)$ and $Defect_{var}(d)$ are the same, the definition point of $Defect_{var}(d)$ of the currently accessed element need to be checked by the def-use chain. If the definition point of the top element is prior or the same as the location of the current element $Defect_{var}(d)$, we update the patch start location(the start location of the block statement where the current element is located).

The end location of the patch remains unchanged, and the current element access update flag is set; otherwise, both start and end locations of the patch remain unchanged. The bottom element of the stack is accessed and a repair triplet is returned $<Patch_{syn}(d), Patch_{startloc}(d), Patch_{endloc}(d)>$. Then, the top element of the stack is popped.

We need to check whether an updated access token exists. If there is one, the algorithm continues to pop items; otherwise, repeats the above steps, and the updated access token is no longer compared until the stack is empty. The algorithm uses the list to record the repair triple $<Patch_{syn}(d), Patch_{startloc}(d), Patch_{endloc}(d)>$ for all the defects in a defect file.

4.4   Verification of Functional Equivalence of Programs

Automatic program repair can modify bug code, but functional test cases may not be sufficient to ensure that the function of the program after repair is consistent with the original. Although program semantic defect repair can repair bugs, it may lead to functional differences with the original program. Thus, it is necessary to verify whether the repaired program with the original one is functionally equivalent.

Definition 4 Functional Equivalence. If the same outputs are generated before and after repair for any inputs, then it is called functional equivalence.

$$\frac{Exec(BRP)(input) = output, Exec(ARP)(input) = output}{BRP^f = ARP^f}$$

where the BRP, ARP and f indicate the before-repair program, after-repair program and function of original program respectively.

Program function can be regarded as a set of program paths. Therefore, if we can ensure that each path producing the same output for the same input before and after repair, we can consider the path equivalent. Given a program S with semantic defects, in which exists program statement s and defective statement s', the control flow graph is obtained by program S, and corresponding defective statement is marked as unsafe node γ on control flow graph. Traversing control flow graph, the program path set $P<input, path, output>$ is obtained, where *input* records program input and *path* records program execution path. The path containing γ is called unsafe path nSP, and the path without γ is called safe path SP. According to the output result of the same input of the defective program and the repaired program, it verifies whether the program change with semantics preservation and the program automatic repair with functional equivalence are realized.

In order to avoid triggering γ, security constraints are imposed on nSP by adding constraints (synthesis conditions) entering nSP. Semantic defects of nSP are repaired by code changes, such as adding statements, deleting statements, modifying statements.

5   Experimental Evaluation

To analyze the repair effect of our program repair method for semantic defects, we conducted a program repair comparison experiment using the defect repair algorithm and the program semantic defect automatic repair method based on the restricted-set proposed in this paper. We scanned 6 large Java open-source projects and verified the effect of repairs using DTSJava. Aiming at the defects detected by DTSJava, we compared with the state-of-the-art approach based on the repair template (PAR [19]). The patch generation results are shown in Table 4.

Statistics suggest that the density of program semantic defects is 3–5/kloc. Thus, improving the repair efficiency of program semantic defects has high value for software development. These experiment results demonstrate that we can repair the most of variable-related semantic defects, and effectively improve the program quality.

The number of repairs required for different defect patterns is different. In this paper, the repair consequences of various types of defects in the experiment are counted to verify the repair effect of the proposed method on different types of defect patterns. The statistical results are listed in Table 5.

Because NPD generation is closely related to the value of the variable, we can obtain the $Defect_{var}(d)$ detected by the static defect detection tool DTSJava. Thus, by relying on DTSJava, DTSFix can repair all the NPD defects. For example, a null pointer dereference exception in the ChartPanel.java file under the **jfreechart** project was repaired as shown in Fig. 3.

Table 4. Comparison of experimental result

Subject	#Size (line)	#Bugs	#Bugs repaired by PAR	#Bugs repaired by DTSFix
rhino	51001	24	9	21
log4j	27855	24	5	20
math	121168	34	6	28
lang	54537	22	3	19
collections	48049	9	1	8
jfree-chart	130300	16	13	8
Total	432910	129	33	109

Table 5. Repair effect of different defect patterns

Defect pattern	Number of defects	Number of repaired defects
Null pointer dereference	75	75
Illegal calculation	34	32
Variable uninitialization	0	0
Out-of-bounds	3	2

```
  if (option == JFileChooser.APPROVE_OPTION) {
      String filename = fileChooser.getSelectedFile().getPath();
      if (isEnforceFileExtensions()) {
+         if(filename!=null){
          if (!filename.endsWith(".png")) {
              filename = filename + ".png";
          }
+         }
      }
  }
```

Fig. 3. Code comparison before and after null pointer dereference repair

We can repair over half the illegal calculation, even achieve the multi-point repair,such as the defect shown in Fig. 4 (an illegal calculation exception in the FastCosineTransformer.java file under the **commons-math** project). However, in some cases, we cannot repair these defects, for example, when the returned value of the function involved in the illegal calculation.

Most of the out-of-bounds defects can be repaired by DTSFix in a manner similar to the repair to TokenStream.java in the **rhino-mirror** project shown in Fig. 5. DTSFix determines the defect location accurately based on the defect static analysis; therefore, the repair effect is more dependable.

```
      for (int i = 1; i < (n >> 1); i++) {
          final double a = 0.5 * (f[i] + f[n - i]);
   +      if(n!=0){
              final double b = FastMath.sin(i * FastMath.PI / n) * (f[i] - f[n - i]);
              final double c = FastMath.cos(i * FastMath.PI / n) * (f[i] - f[n - i]);
   +      }
          ......
      }
```

Fig. 4. Code comparison before and after illegal calculation

```
      if (ungetCursor != 0) {
          cursor++;
   +      if(0<=ungetCursor && ungetCursor <3){
              return ungetBuffer[--ungetCursor];
   +      }
      }
```

Fig. 5. Code comparison before and after arrays out of bound repair

The experimental data show that our tools have the following advantages for the repairing of program semantic defects:

1. We repaired 6 Java open-source programs and achieved high repair rate especially for NPD defects.
2. Because the method proposed in this paper can be combined with the defect detection process, the repair is targeted, and does not need to generate large numbers of candidate patches; thus, it substantially reduces the repair time.
3. Compared with other approaches which assume that the repair is successful if the patch program can pass all of the test cases (but where the program may actually still contain program semantic defects), our method utilizes DTSJava to assure the semantic correctness of the repaired program, which avoids invalid repairs.

Although the method we proposed possesses the advantages listed above, the following threats to validity still exist:

1. The proposed method can repair variable-related defects, but it does not currently the repair non-variable related defects, such as multi-thread related or concurrent correlation defects.
2. The proposed method mainly repairs the defects based on prior defect detection information generated by DTSJava. When defects cannot be detected by DTSJava, the proposed method lacks the necessary reference information.In such cases, the versatility of the repair method is limited.

6   Conclusion

This paper analyzed the advantages and disadvantages of current automatic program repair methods and proposed a semantic defect repair method for Java program. Compared with existing other semantic defect repair methods, our approach avoids the blind repairs, and does not generate any invalid patches, which reduces the development costs. The repair effect achieved on the semantic defects of six large Java open-source projects showded that the proposed method is highly targeted and yields a high repair rate.

In future work, we plan to formulate additional general repair templates from manual defect repair experiences and from data mining of repair reports and add the associated repairable defect patterns. We also plan to apply DTSFix to more Java open source programs to verify the effectiveness of the proposed method. Finally, we also plan to use machine learning and other data mining algorithms to learn the relationship between defect patterns and repair strategies, train a generalizable repair model, and improve the repair efficiency.

References

1. Goues, C.L., et al.: GenProg: a generic method for automatic software repair. IEEE Trans. Softw. Eng. **38**(1), 54–72 (2012)
2. Goues, C.L., et al.: A systematic study of automated program repair: fixing 55 out of 105 bugs for $8 each. In: International Conference on Software Engineering, pp. 3–13 (2012)
3. Qi, Z., et al.: Efficient automatic patch generation and defect identification in kali. In: International Symposium on Software Testing and Analysis (ISSTA) (2015)
4. Li, B., et al.: Automatic program repair: key problems and technologies. J. Softw. **30**(2), 244–265 (2019)
5. Xiong, Y.F., et al.: Identifying patch correctness in test-based program repair. In: Proceedings of the 40th International Conference on Software Engineering, pp. 789–799 (2018)
6. Durieux, T., Monperrus, M: DynaMoth: dynamic code synthesis for automatic program repair. In: International Workshop on Automation of Software Test (2016)
7. Le, X.B.D., et al.: S3: syntax- and semantic-guided repair synthesis via programming by examples. In: Joint Meeting on Foundations of Software Engineering (2017)
8. Liu, K., et al.: Avatar: fixing semantic bugs with fix patterns of static analysis violations. In: 2019 IEEE 26th International Conference on Software Analysis, Evolution and Reengineering (SANER), pp. 1–12 (2019)
9. Qi, Z., et al.: An analysis of patch plausibility and correctness for generate-and-validate patch generation systems. In: International Symposium on Software Testing & Analysis (2015)
10. Weimer, W., Fry, Z.P., Forrest, S., et al.: Leveraging program equivalence for adaptive program repair: models and first results. In: Automated Software Engineering, pp. 356–366 (2013)
11. Yukun, D.: Illegal computing defect detection by static analysis for C program. Comput. Eng. Appl. **52**(19), 31–36 (2016)

12. Dong, Y., Gong, Y., Jin, D.: Null pointer dereference defect detected based on region-based memory model. Acta Electronica Sinica **42**(09), 1744–1752 (2014)
13. Nguyen, H.D.T., et al.: SemFix: program repair via semantic analysis. In: 2013 35th International Conference on Software Engineering (ICSE) (2013)
14. Xuan, J., et al.: Nopol: automatic repair of conditional statement bugs in java programs. IEEE Trans. Softw. Eng. **43**(1), 34–52 (2017)
15. Le, X.B.D., et al.: JFIX: semantics-based repair of java programs via symbolic pathfinder. In: International Symposium on Software Testing and Analysis (2017)
16. Mechtaev, S., et al.: Semantic program repair using a reference implementation. In: The 40th International Conference. IEEE Computer Society (2018)
17. Gao, Q., et al.: Safe memory-leak fixing for C programs. In: IEEE/ACM 37th IEEE International Conference on Software Engineering (ICSE). IEEE Computer Society (2015)
18. Liu, C., Yang, J., Tan, L., et al.: R2Fix: automatically generating bug fixes from bug reports. In: 2013 IEEE Sixth International Conference on Software Testing, Verification and Validation (ICST) (2013)
19. Cornu, B., et al.: NPEFix: automatic runtime repair of null pointer exceptions in java. Comput. Sci. (2015)
20. Kim, D., et al.: Automatic patch generation learned from human-written patches. In: IEEE/ACM 37th IEEE International Conference on Software Engineering (ICSE). IEEE Computer Society (2013)
21. Xiong, Y.F., et al.: Precise condition synthesis for program repair. In: IEEE/ACM 39th International Conference on Software Engineering (ICSE), pp. 416–426 (2017)
22. Zhang, D., et al.: Optimizing static analysis based on defect correlations. Ruan Jian Xue Bao/J. Softw. **25**(2), 386–399 (2014)

Code Property Graph-Based Vulnerability Dataset Generation for Source Code Detection

Zhibin Guan$^{(\boxtimes)}$, Xiaomeng Wang, Wei Xin, and Jiajie Wang

China Information Technology Security Evaluation Center, Beijing, China
zhi_bin_guan@163.com

Abstract. Most existing deep learning-based source code vulnerability detection methods focus on the design of different deep learning algorithms to improve the accuracy of source code vulnerability detection, ignoring the obvious problems: firstly, lack of sufficient source code vulnerability data; secondly, lack of high-quality code data for deep learning algorithms. Therefore, we propose a code attribute graph-based data generation method for deep learning based source code vulnerability detection. The proposed method tries to represent source code based on code attribute graph, which is used to extract the control flow information and data flow information of source code sequentially. And the code data can be generated by retrieval-matching method. The advantage of this method is that it can extract rich semantic information of source code, and the generated code slices can be used for deep learning algorithms directly. Experimental results show that the proposed method can generate a large number of high-quality code data, which can provide data for deep learning-based source code vulnerability detection.

Keywords: Vulnerability dataset generation · Code property graph/Code attribute graph · Data flow · Control flow · Source code vulnerability detection · Deep learning

1 Introduction

Source code vulnerability detection (SCVD) is an attractive research in the field of information security and has attracted widespread attention, which focused on detecting various vulnerability contained in the source code, such as sensitive API/functions, malicious code. It is of great significance for ensuring user information security and preventing malicious attacks.

Benefiting from the successful application of deep learning in various fields, including image classification, object detection, etc., many researchers and engineers tried to identify source code vulnerability by using deep learning (DL)

Supported by National Natural Science Foundation of China (NSFC) under Grant [U1736110], [U1836209], [U1936211], [U1836113], partially supported by the National Key Research and Development Program of China under Grant [2018YFB0804101].

[13,16]. Source code is essentially a text language. Most text analysis algorithms in the field of natural language processing can be used for vulnerability analysis and detection of source code.

In most DL-based SCVD methods [4,14], researchers mainly focused on two directions: 1) extracting the structural information and semantic information in the source code by using different code representation methods, such as abstract syntax tree (AST) or program dependency graph (PDG); 2) designing DL models with different structures to achieve SCVD, such as Long Short Term Memory, tree-based Long Short-Term Memory networks (Tree-LSTM) [15], etc.

However, most training data for DL-based SCVD comes from Software Assurance Reference Dataset (SARD) [12]; a few data is generated from real source code such as National Vulnerability Database (NVD) [11]. The source code in SARD is relative simple, which is essentially a type of test cases. The shortcoming of NVD data is that there are few real vulnerability source code, which cannot provide sufficient data for the training of DL methods.

In this paper, we proposed a new code property graph-based vulnerability data generation method for source code detection to solve the problem discussed earlier. The proposed method is based on code property graph (CPG), which is a novel and comprehensive source code representation form. As opposed to other methods, the proposed method tried to generate large amounts of code data based on real source code; and the generated code data can be directly used as input for DL-based methods. In addition, the source code used in this paper not only comes from SARD or NVD, but also come from some open source projects. The language types of source code involved in this paper are C or C++.

2   Related Work

2.1   AST-Based Methods

AST refers to represent the syntax structure information of source code through a tree, and it is widely used in vulnerability detection of source code. When an AST is used for SCVD, the relationship between nodes in AST usually represents the syntax structure of source code.

In paper [2], AST is utilized to represent static source code, and an AST-based recursive neural network is proposed for code clone detection. This research can be regarded as a method with high exploration value, because the researchers not only explored the influence of model selections and hyperparameters, but also studied the impact of different AST representation methods, such as binary trees. The drawback is that it attempted to transform the initial AST into a binary tree, which would increase the depth of AST, and lose some association information between different nodes in AST.

Similar, authors in [3] proposed a Tree-LSTM network to detect vulnerabilities in source code. The difference is that researchers tried to build ASTs at source file level, that is, each source code file has an corresponding AST. In addition, considering the original AST may be too large, which leads to the loss of long-term dependencies between nodes, researchers in [15] split each large

AST into code statements sequences, and applied bidirectional recurrent neural network (BRNN) to process the code statement sequence. The contribution of this method is that it can recursively encode statements to vectors.

Because the AST of source code is relatively complicated in structure, when applying DL algorithms for feature extraction, it is likely to cause the loss of some important semantic information, such as data flow relationship. Consequently, most researchers tried to utilize PDG to represent static source code.

2.2 PDG-Based Methods

Different from AST, a PDG of source code can clearly represent the data flow relationship and control flow relationship. There are two commonly used PDG: control flow graph (CFG) and data flow graph (DFG).

Considering that the PDG can extract rich semantic information of source code, authors in [1] tried to directly encode the PDG to vectors and designed the graph-based DL methods, which were built upon Graph Neural Networks [7].

In vulnerability detection of C/C++ source code, researchers tried to construct CFGs at function level, which means that each function has a corresponding CFG [5]. In [8], CFGs and DFGs were used for source code representation simultaneously, but the actual influences of CFGs was not explored. Inspired by the impressive contributions of DL in image processing, authors in [9] explored to extract features of source code through DL-based methods.

We can observe that the process of DL-based SCVD methods can be broadly divided into two parts: the presentation of source code; and the vulnerability detection of source code. The problem of existing DL-based SCVD methods is that the training data mainly comes from SARD or NVD, which cannot provide sufficient data for DL algorithms. Our method focuses on generating the code data of real source code, which can be directly used as training data for DL-based SCVD.

3   CPG-Based Vulnerability Dataset Generation Method

The source code contains many miscellaneous information, such as comments, repeated code, etc. If the source code is only regarded as a collection of code statements, the rich semantic information of source code cannot be extracted. Therefore, it is a more appropriate strategy to represent the source code through graphs so that the sufficient semantic information can be maintained clearly. The main contribution of this proposed method is that it can extract syntax of semantic information through graphs, such as ASTs, CFGs, and DFGs. The framework of the proposed method can be seen in Fig. 1.

3.1   CPG Extraction of Source Code

In this method, we firstly attempted to generate the CPG of source code. CPG is a novel and comprehensive source code representation form, which not only

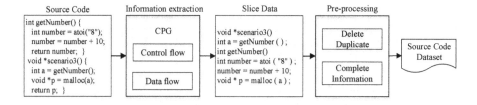

Fig. 1. The framework of CPG-based vulnerability dataset generation method.

contains AST, but also integrates CFG and DFG to form a joint data structure. In this paper, Joern [6] is utilized to generate CPG of C/C++ source code. Meanwhile, the generated CPG is stored in a Neo4j graph database [10]. Joern is an open source tool which can parsing C/C++ source code, and Neo4j is a high-performance graph database for storing structured data on graphs. As shown in Fig. 2, a simplified CPG of the source code in Fig. 1 is given.

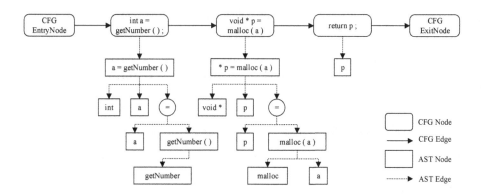

Fig. 2. The simplified CPG of the program in Fig. 1.

Since CPG contains a large amount of semantic information, we can retrieve different types of code statements in source code, including definition statement, expression statement, parameter list, etc.

3.2 Extraction of CFG Information Based on CPG

Based on the generated CPG, the CFG corresponding to each function can be extracted according to the type of edge "FLOWS_TO". As shown in Fig. 3, the control flow relationships of function "scenario3" and function "getNumber" are given respectively. The definition of the control flow relationships in source code is given as Eq. 1:

$$CFG(src) = \{cfg(f_1), cfg(f_2), ..., cfg(f_n)\}, \tag{1}$$

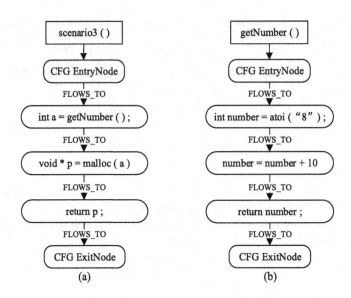

Fig. 3. The diagram of control flow relationship of source code.

where "src" represents each source code file, and f_i means the user-defined function in file "src", such as "scenario3", "getNumber". It is worth noting that the system built-in functions are not included, such as "malloc".

3.3   Extraction of DFG Information Based on CPG

Similarly, based on the generated CPG, the data flow corresponding to different variables can be extracted according to the type of edge "REACHES". The DFG of function "scenario3" and function "getNumber" are respectively given

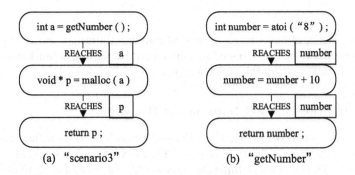

Fig. 4. The diagram of data flow relationship of source code.

in Fig. 4. And the definition of the data flow relationship in source code is given as Eq. 2:

$$DFG\left(src\right) = \{dfg\left(f_1\right), dfg\left(f_2\right), ..., dfg\left(f_n\right)\}. \tag{2}$$

In each DFG, an edge is usually pointed by an assignment statement to the statement that needs to be calculated, and the name of parameter is pointed out by the corresponding edge. As shown in Fig. 4 (a), for parameter "a", its data flow relationship is from assignment statement "int a = getNumber()" to the statement where parameter "a" needs to be calculated, that is, "void *p = malloc(a)".

4   Experimentation

4.1   Experiment Setting

In CFGs and DFGs, each node records the required syntax or semantic information: the line number of code, code statements, and types of statements. Code statements including definition statements, assignment statements, etc. In this paper, the graph search algorithm is utilized to extract slice datas of source code based on CFGs and DFGs. Since CFGs and DFGs are both directed graphs, the graph search algorithms utilized in this research are mainly forward traversal and backward traversal according to identifiers. The search identifiers are usually some sensitive functions, such as "memcpy", "strcpy", etc.

4.2   Results and Discussion

The CPG-based dataset generation method proposed in the paper is different from existing methods. In terms of data sources, the proposed method not only used SARD and NVD, but also involved other real source code from open source repositories, such as Firefox, Chromium, and Domoticz, referring to Table 1.

Table 1. The number of slice data generated by our proposed method.

SourceCode	sensitiveAPI	ArrayUsage	PointerUsage	ExpressionStatement	Total
SARD	144,260	20,420	73,271	2,566	240,571
NVD	3,414	2,515	11,404	1,936	19,269
Firefox	14,333	5,167	33,572	4,230	57,302
Chromium	7,483	5,601	83,147	6,939	103,170
Domoticz	3,539	1,472	816	332	6,159

The generated code slices including four categories: sensitive API calls, pointer usage, array usage, and arithmetic expressions [9]. And the number of slice data generated by the proposed method is around 426,471.

For different source code, the above four categories of slice data are generated. It is worth noting that in the data statistics given in Table 1, each code slice is different from other code slices, which means that the generated code slices in different categories can be directly summarized and utilized for DL-based methods.

```
int getNumber() {
    int number = atoi("8");
    number = number + 10;
    return number;  }
void *scenario3() {
    int a = getNumber();
    void *p = malloc(a);
    return p;  }
```

```
void *scenario3()
int a = getNumber ( ) ;
int getNumber()
int number = atoi ( "8" ) ;
number = number + 10;
void * p = malloc ( a ) ;
```

(a) Source Code   (b) Slice Data

Fig. 5. Result of slice data generated by our proposed method.

Furthermore, one sample result of source code slices was displayed in Fig. 5. It can be observed that the syntax and semantic information of source code are extracted, and the generated slice data retains rich semantic information, which can be directly used as input for DL-based SCVD methods. Experimental results show that the proposed method can extract data flow relationship and control flow relationship between functions to a certain extent. However, the relationship between different source code files cannot be extracted yet, and further research is needed.

5   Conclusion

In this research, we tried to solve a problem in existing methods, i.e., that the most training data used for DL-based SCVD methods was coming from SARD or NVD, which cannot provide sufficient data for the application of DL algorithms.

We propose a CPG-based dataset generation method for vulnerability detection of source code, which can solve the aforementioned problem. The proposed method first generated the CPG of source code, which can be utilized to extract semantic information of source code. Then, the relationships of control flow and data flow were extracted based on CPG.

We validated our proposed method with several open source code, including chromium, firefox, and so on. The experimental results show that the proposed method can generate large scale of slice data for DL-based SCVD methods, which is significant in application of real world source code detection.

This paper only consider C/C++ source code, which can be extend to more languages. In the future work, we will take more types of source code languaage, like Java, PHP, etc. into account to generate more sufficient data for DL-based SCVD methods.

References

1. Allamanis, M., Brockschmidt, M., Khademi, M.: Learning to represent programs with graphs. CoRR abs/1711.00740 (2017)
2. Büch, L., Andrzejak, A.: Learning-based recursive aggregation of abstract syntax trees for code clone detection. In: 2019 IEEE 26th International Conference on Software Analysis, Evolution and Reengineering (SANER), pp. 95–104 (2019)
3. Dam, H.K., et al.: A deep tree-based model for software defect prediction. CoRR abs/1802.00921 (2018)
4. Duan, X., et al.: Vulsniper: focus your attention to shoot fine-grained vulnerabilities. In: Proceedings of the Twenty-Eighth International Joint Conference on Artificial Intelligence, IJCAI 2019, pp. 4665–4671 (2019)
5. Harer, J.A., et al.: Automated software vulnerability detection with machine learning. CoRR abs/1803.04497 (2018)
6. Joern. https://joern.readthedocs.io/en/latest/index.html
7. Li, Y., Tarlow, D., Brockschmidt, M., Zemel, R.S.: Gated graph sequence neural networks. CoRR abs/1511.05493 (2016)
8. Li, Z., Zou, D., Tang, J., Zhang, Z., Sun, M., Jin, H.: A comparative study of deep learning-based vulnerability detection system. IEEE Access **7**, 103184–103197 (2019)
9. Li, Z., et al.: Sysevr: a framework for using deep learning to detect software vulnerabilities. CoRR abs/1807.06756 (2018)
10. Neo4j. https://neo4j.com/
11. NVD. https://nvd.nist.gov/
12. SARD. https://samate.nist.gov/SRD/index.php
13. Xiaomeng, W., Tao, Z., Runpu, W., Wei, X., Changyu, H.: Cpgva: code property graph based vulnerability analysis by deep learning. In: 2018 10th International Conference on Advanced Infocomm Technology (ICAIT), pp. 184–188 (2018)
14. Xiaomeng, W., Tao, Z., Wei, X., Changyu, H.: A survey on source code review using machine learning. In: 2018 3rd International Conference on Information Systems Engineering (ICISE), pp. 56–60 (2018)
15. Zhang, J., Wang, X., Zhang, H., Sun, H., Wang, K., Liu, X.: A novel neural source code representation based on abstract syntax tree. In: Proceedings of the 41st International Conference on Software Engineering, ICSE 2019, pp. 783–794. IEEE Press, Piscataway (2019)
16. Zou, D., Wang, S., Xu, S., Li, Z., Jin, H.: vuldeepecker: a deep learning-based system for multiclass vulnerability detection. IEEE Trans. Dependable Secure Comput. 1 (2019)

References

Quantum Cryptography

A Hybrid Quantum Secret Sharing Scheme Based on Mutually Unbiased Bases

Dan-Li Zhi, Zhi-Hui Li$^{(\boxtimes)}$, Li-Juan Liu, and Zhao-Wei Han

College of Mathematics and Information Science, Shaanxi Normal University,
Xi'an 710119, Shaanxi, China
`lizhihui@snnu.edu.cn`

Abstract. With the advantages of both classical and quantum secret sharing, many practical hybrid quantum secret sharing schemes have been proposed. In this paper, we propose a hybrid quantum secret sharing scheme based on mutually unbiased bases and monotone span program. First, a dealer sends the shares in the linear secret sharing to the participants in the authorization set via a secure channel. Then, the dealer and participants perform unitary transformation on a d-dimensional quantum state sequentially, and the dealer publishes the measurement result confidentially to the participants in the authorization set to recover the secret. The verifiability of the scheme is guaranteed by the Hash function. Next, the correctness and security of the scheme are proved and our scheme is secure against the general eavesdropper attacks. Finally, a specific example is employed to further clarify the flexibility of the scheme and the detailed comparisons of similar quantum secret sharing schemes also show the superiority of our proposed scheme. The scheme realizes quantum secret sharing under the access structure with one qudit and different influence of the participants, which saves quantum resources and makes it more flexible and convenient in practical applications.

Keywords: Quantum secret sharing · Mutually unbiased bases · Verifiability · Access structure

1 Introduction

As a combination of cryptography and quantum mechanics, quantum cryptography plays an important role in cryptography. Compared with classical cryptography on the basis of computational complexity, quantum cryptography based on the laws of quantum physics can achieve unconditional security. Many branches of quantum cryptography have been developed, such as quantum key distribution (QKD) [1,2], quantum key agreement (QKA) [3–5], quantum secure direct communication (QSDC) [6,7], quantum teleportation [8,9], quantum signature [10,11], quantum authentication [12,13,13], quantum secret sharing (QSS) [14–29] and so on.

© Springer Nature Singapore Pte Ltd. 2020
G. Xu et al. (Eds.): FCS 2020, CCIS 1286, pp. 595–607, 2020.
https://doi.org/10.1007/978-981-15-9739-8_44

Quantum secret sharing (QSS) is an important research field in quantum cryptography, which means that the dealer divides a secret into several shadows and sends them to multiple participants. Only the participants in authorized sets can recover the secret, and the participants in unauthorized sets can not recover the secret. Since Hillery et al. [14] proposed the first quantum secret sharing scheme by using GHZ state in 1999, a growing number of QSS schemes [15–29] have been proposed. For example, Williams et al. [21] described and experimentally demonstrated a three-party quantum secret sharing protocol using polarization-entangled photon pairs. Tsai et al. [22] used the entanglement property of W-state and proposed the first three-party SQSS protocol. Song et al. [23] demonstrated a (t, n) threshold d-level quantum secret sharing scheme. A verifiable (t, n) threshold quantum secret sharing scheme was proposed using the d-dimensional Bell state and the Lagrange interpolation by Yang et al. in Ref. [24]. Hao et al. [25] put forward a secret sharing scheme using the mutually unbiased bases on the p^2-dimensional quantum system. Bai et al. [26] proposed the concept of decomposition of quantum access structure to design a quantum secret sharing scheme. In Ref. [27], Liu et al. study the local distinguishability of the 15 kinds of seven-qudit quantum entangled states and then proposed a (k, n) threshold quantum secret sharing scheme. A new improving quantum secret sharing scheme was proposed by Xu et al. [28], in which more quantum access structures can be realized by the scheme than the one proposed by Nascimento et al. [29].

Although many schemes have been proposed, the verifiability and the flexibility of the schemes are also important issues worthy of consideration. In this paper, we propose a hybrid and verifiable quantum secret sharing scheme based on mutually unbiased bases and monotone span program, with the application of the linear secret sharing, which focuses on transmitting a d-dimensional quantum state among the dealer Alice and participants. Each participant in a authorization set can perform a unitary transformation on the received particle and send it to the next one until the last one sends it to Alice. They can recover the secret by the linear secret sharing and the measurement value sent by Alice. Verifiability ensures that the secret recovered in each authorization set is the original one, and it also ensures that once a dishonest participant appears, he will be found. Compared with the threshold scheme, the quantum secret sharing scheme based on the access structure realizes the different influences of participants in the process of recovering secrets, thereby achieving the flexibility of the scheme.

By comparison, our scheme shows all the advantages of the previous QSS and the unique advantages, such as,

(1) It uses a d-dimensional state(qudit) instead of a 2-dimensional state(qubit).
(2) The participants can check the authenticity of the recovered secret.
(3) It needs fewer quantum resources and quantum operations.
(4) It has general access structure.
(5) It reduces the communication costs and computation complexity.

This paper is organized as follows. In Sect. 2, we illustrate the preliminary knowledge related to the proposed scheme. The new proposed scheme is introduced in Sect. 3. Section 4 give a proof of the correctness, verifiability and security of the proposed scheme. In Sect. 5, we give an example to further illustrate our proposed scheme. Finally, the comparison and conclusion is given in Sect. 6 and Sect. 7.

2 Preliminaries

In this section, we introduce the preliminary knowledge of our scheme.

2.1 Access Structure

Definition 1. Let $\mathcal{P} = \{P_1, P_2, \cdots, P_n\}$ be a set of participants, an access structure $\Gamma \subseteq 2^{\mathcal{P}}$ is a family of authorized sets of participants.

Definition 2. If Γ is the access structure on $\mathcal{P}$, then any set in Γ is called the authorization subset on $\mathcal{P}$, which is called the authorization set for short. If $A \in \Gamma, A \subseteq B \subseteq \mathcal{P}$, then $B \in \Gamma$. The family of the unauthorized sets is called an adversary structure, that is to say, $\Gamma^c = \Delta$.

Example 1. Let $\mathcal{P} = \{P_1, P_2, P_3, P_4\}, \Gamma = \{A_1, A_2, A_3\}$, where $A_1 = \{P_1, P_2, P_3\}$, $A_2 = \{P_1, P_2, P_4\}$, $A_3 = \{P_1, P_2, P_3, P_4\}$. So

$$\Delta = \left\{ \begin{matrix} \emptyset, \{P_1\}, \{P_2\}, \{P_3\}, \{P_4\}, \{P_1, P_2\}, \{P_1, P_3\}, \{P_1, P_4\}, \\ \{P_2, P_3\}, \{P_2, P_4\}, \{P_3, P_4\}, \{P_1, P_3, P_4\} \{P_2, P_3, P_4\} \end{matrix} \right\}.$$

2.2 Monotone Span Program

Monotone span program was introduced in Ref. [30] by Karchmer and Wigderson as a model of computation to design the linear secret sharing scheme.

Definition 3. $\mathcal{M}(\mathcal{F}, M, \psi, \boldsymbol{\xi})$ is a monotone span program(MSP), where M is a $k \times l$ matrix over a finite field $\mathcal{F}$, $\psi : \{1, 2, \cdots, k\} \to \mathcal{P}$ is a surjective labeling map, $\boldsymbol{\xi} = (1, 0, \cdots, 0)^T \in \mathcal{F}^l$ is defined as the target vector. For any $A \subseteq \mathcal{P} = \{P_1, P_2, \cdots, P_n\}$, there is a corresponding eigenvector $\boldsymbol{\delta}_A = (\delta_1, \delta_2, \cdots, \delta_n) \in \{0, 1\}^n$ if and only if $P_i \in A, \delta_i = 1$. The Boolean function $f : \{0, 1\}^n \to \{0, 1\}, f(\delta_A) = 1$ represents the corresponding ε rows of M, where $\psi(\varepsilon) \in A, \varepsilon \in \{1, 2, \cdots, k\}$.

Definition 4. A monotone span program (MSP) is called a MSP for access structure Γ, if it can be satisfied that $\forall A \in \Gamma, \exists \boldsymbol{\lambda}_A \in \mathcal{F}^k \Rightarrow M_A^T \boldsymbol{\lambda}_A = \boldsymbol{\xi}$, and $\forall A \in \Delta, \exists \boldsymbol{h} = (1, h_2, \cdots, h_l) \in \mathcal{F}^l \Rightarrow M_A \boldsymbol{h} = \boldsymbol{0} \in \mathcal{F}^m$.

Example 2. $\mathcal{M}(\mathcal{F}, M, \psi, \boldsymbol{\xi})$ is an MSP of access structure Γ as shown in example 1, where $\mathcal{F} = \mathcal{Z}_5$, $\psi(i) = Bob_i, i \in \{1, 2, 3, 4\}$, $\boldsymbol{\xi} = (1, 0, 0, 0)^T$,

$M = \begin{pmatrix} 1 & 0 & 3 & 4 \\ 0 & 0 & 2 & 1 \\ 3 & 4 & 1 & 0 \\ 1 & 2 & 4 & 0 \end{pmatrix}$. Therefore, $\boldsymbol{\lambda}_{A_1} = (1, 1, 0)^T, \boldsymbol{\lambda}_{A_2} = (1, 1, 0)^T, \boldsymbol{\lambda}_{A_3} = (1, 1, 3, 4)^T$.

2.3 Linear Secret Sharing

Monotone span program is utilized to design the linear secret sharing scheme, which is aimed that the dealer Alice shares a secret s among k shareholders $Bob_1, Bob_2, \cdots, Bob_k$ according to the MSP for access structure Γ. It includes the following two phases as follows.

Distribution Phase
Alice prepares a random vector $\boldsymbol{\rho} = (s, \rho_2, \cdots, \rho_l)^T \in\ ^l$ and computes $\boldsymbol{s} = M\boldsymbol{\rho} = (s_1, \cdots, s_k)^T$. Then, she sends s_i to $\psi(i)$ via a secure channel.

Reconstruction Phase
Let $\boldsymbol{s}_A$ be indicated the vector for the authorized set A. The participants in A restore the secrets cooperatively as follows.

$$\boldsymbol{s}_A^T \boldsymbol{\lambda}_A = (M_A \boldsymbol{\rho})^T \boldsymbol{\lambda}_A = \boldsymbol{\rho}^T \left(M_A^T \boldsymbol{\lambda}_A \right) = \boldsymbol{\rho}^T \boldsymbol{\xi} = s. \tag{1}$$

2.4 Necessary Quantum Properties

Definition 5. Mutually unbiased base is defined that two sets of standard orthogonal bases $A_1 = \{|\varphi_1\rangle, |\varphi_2\rangle, \cdots, |\varphi_d\rangle\}$ and $A_2 = \{|\psi_1\rangle, |\psi_2\rangle, \cdots, |\psi_d\rangle\}$, which defined over a d-dimensional complex space C^d in Ref. [31,32], if the following relationship is satisfied

$$|\langle \varphi_i | \psi_i \rangle| = \frac{1}{\sqrt{d}}. \tag{2}$$

If any two of the set of standard orthogonal bases $\{A_1, A_2, \cdots, A_m\}$ in space are unbiased, then this set is called an unbiased bases set. Besides, it can be found $d + 1$ mutually unbiased bases if d is an odd prime number.

Definition 6. The computation base is expressed as $\{|k\rangle\ |k \in D\}$, and the remaining groups can be expressed as:

$$\left| v_l^{(j)} \right\rangle = \frac{1}{\sqrt{d}} \sum_{k=0}^{d-1} w^{k(l+jk)} |k\rangle, \tag{3}$$

where $\left| v_l^{(j)} \right\rangle$ represents the l-th vector in the j-th bases, $w = e^{\frac{2\pi i}{d}} l, j \in D, D = \{0, 1, \cdots, d-1\}$. These mutually unbiased bases satisfy the following conditions:

$$\left| \left\langle v_l^{(j)} \middle| v_l^{(j')} \right\rangle \right| = \frac{1}{\sqrt{d}}, j \neq j'. \tag{4}$$

Definition 7. In Ref. [33], the two unitary transformations X_d and Y_d that we need to use in this paper can be expressed as:

$$X_d = \sum_{m=0}^{d-1} w^m |m\rangle \langle m|, Y_d = \sum_{m=0}^{d-1} w^{m^2} |m\rangle \langle m|. \tag{5}$$

Implementing (5) on $\left|v_l^{(j)}\right\rangle$ in turn, we can obtain:

$$X_d^x Y_d^y \left|v_l^{(j)}\right\rangle = \left|v_{l+x}^{(j+y)}\right\rangle. \tag{6}$$

For the convenience of expression, $X_d^x Y_d^y$ is denoted as $U_{x,y}$, that is,

$$U_{x,y} \left|v_l^{(j)}\right\rangle = \left|v_{l+x}^{(j+y)}\right\rangle. \tag{7}$$

3 Proposed Scheme

In this section, we construct a verifiable quantum secret sharing scheme that includes a dealer Alice and n shareholders $Bob_1, Bob_2, \cdots, Bob_n$. The access structure Γ can be expressed as $\Gamma = \{A_1, A_2, \cdots, A_r\}$, where $A_i(i = 1, 2, \cdots, r)$ is a authorization set. For the convenience of description, the authorization set is recorded as $A_i = \left\{Bob_1^{(i)}, Bob_2^{(i)}, \cdots, Bob_m^{(i)}\right\}, (1 \le m \le n)$. Without losing generality, it is assumed that the participants in the authorization set $A_i = \left\{Bob_1^{(i)}, Bob_2^{(i)}, \cdots, Bob_m^{(i)}\right\}$ want to recover the secret s. The specific steps of the scheme are as follows.

3.1 Distribution Phase

Alice implements the following steps.

3.1.1. Select a random vector $\boldsymbol{\rho} = (S_i, \rho_2, \rho_3 \cdots, \rho_l)^T$ according to authorization set A_i.

3.1.2. Calculate $\boldsymbol{s} = M_{n \times l} \boldsymbol{\rho} = \left(s_1^{(i)}, s_2^{(i)}, , \cdots, s_n^{(i)}\right)^T, i = 1, 2, \cdots, r$ and send $s_j^{(i)}$ to $\psi(j) = Bob_j (j = 1, 2, \cdots, n)$ through the quantum secure channel.

3.1.3. Compute and publish $H_1 = h(S_i)$, $H_2 = h(s)$, where $h()$ is a public Hash function.

3.1.4. Prepare a quantum state $|\phi\rangle = \left|\varphi_0^0\right\rangle = \frac{1}{\sqrt{d}} \sum_{j=0}^{d-1} |j\rangle$ and perform a unitary operation $U_{p_0^{(i)}, q_0^{(i)}}$ to get the quantum state $|\phi\rangle_0^{(i)} = U_{p_0^{(i)}, q_0^{(i)}} \left|\varphi_0^0\right\rangle = \left|\varphi_{p_0^{(i)}}^{q_0^{(i)}}\right\rangle$, where $p_0^{(i)} = s$ is the secret, $q_0^{(i)}$ is a secret value known only to Alice. Then, she sends the performed quantum state $|\phi\rangle_0^{(i)}$ to the first participant $Bob_1^{(i)}$ in the authorization set A_i.

3.2 Reconstruction Phase

Participants in $A_i = \left\{ Bob_1^{(i)}, Bob_2^{(i)}, \cdots, Bob_m^{(i)} \right\}, (1 \leq m \leq n)$ can recover the secret by the following steps.

3.2.1. After receiving the quantum state $|\phi\rangle_0$, the first participant $Bob_1^{(i)}$ performs unitary operates $U_{p_1^{(i)}, q_1^{(i)}}$ on it and gets the quantum state $|\phi\rangle_1^{(i)} = U_{p_1^{(i)}, q_1^{(i)}}$ $\left| \varphi_{p_0^{(i)}}^{q_0^{(i)}} \right\rangle = \left| \varphi_{p_0^{(i)}+p_1^{(i)}}^{q_0^{(i)}+q_1^{(i)}} \right\rangle$. Next, the quantum state $|\phi\rangle_1^{(i)}$ is sent to the second participant $Bob_2^{(i)}$ in the authorization set A_i, where $p_1^{(i)} = \lambda_1^{(i)} s_1^{(i)}, q_1^{(i)} = \lambda_1^{(i)}$.

3.2.2. The other participants $Bob_j^{(i)} (j = 2, 3, \cdots, m)$ in the authorization set A_i perform the same operation as in step 3.2.1, which means that after receiving the quantum state $|\phi\rangle_{j-1}^{(i)}$, $Bob_j^{(i)}$ performs unitary operation $U_{p_j^{(i)}, q_j^{(i)}}$ on it and

gets the quantum state $|\phi\rangle_j^{(i)} = U_{p_j^{(i)}, q_j^{(i)}} \left| \varphi_{\sum_{k=0}^{j-1} p_k^{(i)}}^{\sum_{k=0}^{j-1} q_k^{(i)}} \right\rangle = \left| \varphi_{\sum_{k=0}^{j} p_k^{(i)}}^{\sum_{k=0}^{j} q_k^{(i)}} \right\rangle$, and then sends

it to the next participant $Bob_{j+1}^{(i)}, (j = 2, 3, \cdots m - 1)$ until the last participant $Bob_m^{(i)}$ in the authorization set A_i completes the operation and sends the final quantum state to Alice, where $p_j^{(i)} = \lambda_j^{(i)} s_j^{(i)}, q_j^{(i)} = \lambda_j^{(i)}$. For the authorization set A_i, when all the participants act and transmit, the final quantum state is

$$|\phi\rangle_m^{(i)} = \prod_{k=0}^{m} U_{p_k^{(i)}, q_k^{(i)}} |\varphi_0^0\rangle = \left| \varphi_{\sum_{k=0}^{m} p_k^{(i)}}^{\sum_{k=0}^{m} q_k^{(i)}} \right\rangle. \tag{8}$$

3.2.3. When Alice receives the final quantum state $|\phi\rangle_m^{(i)}$, she can know that it satisfies the following condition on account of $q_0^{(i)}, q_1^{(i)}, \cdots, q_m^{(i)}$,

$$q_0^{(i)} + q_1^{(i)} + \cdots + q_m^{(i)} = q_i. \tag{9}$$

She selects the measurement bases $M_{q_i} = \left\{ \left| \varphi_j^{(q_i)} \right\rangle \mid j \in D \right\}$ to measure it, and then infers the following condition should be established in the authorization set A_i

$$p_0^{(i)} + p_1^{(i)} + \cdots + p_m^{(i)} = p_0^{(i)} + S_i = r_i \tag{10}$$

If it is established, Alice checks whether H_1 of the participants are equal to the published one. If so, the measurement results r_i will be sent to all participants in the authorization set A_i through the secure channel and then it move to the next step. If not, the scheme is terminated.

3.2.4. In order to reconstruct the secret, each participant in authorization set A_i can recover the secret by calculating $s = p_0 = r_i - \sum_{i=1}^{m} p_i = r_i - S_i$.

4   Correctness, Verifiability and Security

In this section, the provability of the correctness, verifiability and security of our scheme is given.

4.1   Correctness

Theorem 1. If a d-dimensional quantum state in mutually unbiased bases is $\left|v_l^{(j)}\right\rangle = \frac{1}{\sqrt{d}} \sum_{k=0}^{d-1} w^{k(l+jk)} |k\rangle$, and a unitary operation $U_{x,y} = X_d^x Y_d^y$ is performed on it, then it will become another state $\left|v_{l+x}^{(j+y)}\right\rangle$, that is, $U_{x,y}\left|v_l^{(j)}\right\rangle = \left|v_{l+x}^{(j+y)}\right\rangle$.

Proof. When implementing Y_d^y, X_d^x on $\left|v_l^{(j)}\right\rangle$ in turn, we can obtain,

$$
\begin{aligned}
X_d^x Y_d^y \left|v_l^{(j)}\right\rangle &= X_d^x \left(\sum_{m=0}^{d-1} w^{ym^2} |m\rangle \langle m|\right) \left(\frac{1}{\sqrt{d}} \sum_{k=0}^{d-1} w^{k(l+jk)} |k\rangle\right) \\
&= \frac{1}{\sqrt{d}} \sum_{m=0}^{d-1} w^{xm} |m\rangle \langle m| \sum_{k=0}^{d-1} w^{k(l+(j+y)k\ )} |k\rangle \\
&= \frac{1}{\sqrt{d}} \sum_{k=0}^{d-1} w^{k[(l+x)+(j+y)k]} |k\rangle \\
&= \left|v_{l+x}^{(j+y)}\right\rangle .
\end{aligned}
\tag{11}
$$

This completes the proof.

Lemma 1. *In the secret sharing scheme, according to Theorem 1, the initial state selected by Alice is $|\phi\rangle = \left|\varphi_0^0\right\rangle = \frac{1}{\sqrt{d}} \sum_{j=0}^{d-1} |j\rangle$, and the unitary operation $U_{p_k^{(i)},q_k^{(i)}} = X_d^{p_k^{(i)}} Y_d^{q_k^{(i)}}, k = 0, 1, \cdots, m$ is performed on the states sequentially by Alice and all the participants in the authorization set A_i, then the final state is $|\phi\rangle_m^{(i)} = \left(\prod_{u=0}^m U_{p_u,q_u}\right) |\phi\rangle$, that is, $|\phi\rangle_m^{(i)} = \prod_{k=0}^m U_{p_k^{(i)},q_k^{(i)}} \left|\varphi_0^0\right\rangle = \left|\varphi_{\sum_{k=0}^m p_k^{(i)}}^{\sum_{k=0}^m q_k^{(i)}}\right\rangle$. When Alice announces the measurement result r_i via the quantum secure channel to the participants in A_i, they can restore the secret $s = p_0 = r_i - \sum_{k=1}^m p_k^{(i)} = r_i - S_i$.*

4.2   Verifiability

On one hand, before Alice sends the measurement result, she can check H_1 to ensure that the secret value recovered by linear secret sharing is correct, which provides a prerequisite for participants to recover the correct secret. On the other hand, each participant can check

$$
H_2 = h(s),
\tag{12}
$$

to ensure that the recovered secret is the original one.

4.3 Security

We analyze the security of our scheme against the general attacks here.

Entangle and Measure Attack. We assume that eavesdropper Eve intercepts the particles sent among Alice and the participants and then uses a unitary operation U_E to entangle an ancillary state $|E\rangle$ on the transmitted particle. In order to steal secret information by measuring the ancillary state, Eve act the unitary operator U_E on $|E\rangle$ and the transmitted particle. To simplify the description, we consider the bases corresponding to $j = 0$, namely, $\left|v_l^{(0)}\right\rangle = \frac{1}{\sqrt{d}}\sum_{k=0}^{d-1} w^{kl}|k\rangle$, so

$$U_E|k\rangle|E\rangle = \sum_{h=0}^{d-1} a_{kh}|h\rangle|e_{kh}\rangle, \tag{13}$$

$$
\begin{aligned}
U_E\left|v_l^{(0)}\right\rangle|E\rangle &= U_E\left(\frac{1}{\sqrt{d}}\sum_{k=0}^{d-1} w^{kl}|k\rangle\right)|E\rangle \\
&= \frac{1}{\sqrt{d}}\sum_{k=0}^{d-1} w^{kl}\left(\sum_{h=0}^{d-1} a_{kh}|h\rangle|e_{kh}\rangle\right) \\
&= \frac{1}{\sqrt{d}}\sum_{k=0}^{d-1}\sum_{h=0}^{d-1} w^{kl}a_{kh}\left(\frac{1}{\sqrt{d}}\sum_{m=0}^{d-1} w^{-hm}\left|v_m^{(0)}\right\rangle\right)|e_{kh}\rangle \\
&= \frac{1}{d}\sum_{k=0}^{d-1}\sum_{h=0}^{d-1}\sum_{m=0}^{d-1} w^{kl-hm}a_{kh}\left|v_m^{(0)}\right\rangle|e_{kh}\rangle,
\end{aligned}
\tag{14}
$$

where $w = e^{\frac{2\pi i}{d}}$, $|E\rangle$ is the initial state of the auxiliary space, $|e_{kh}\rangle$ are pure ancillary states determined uniquely by the unitary operation U_E, so

$$\sum_{h=0}^{d-1}|a_{kh}|^2 = 1, k \in \{0, 1, \cdots, d-1\}. \tag{15}$$

For the sake of avoiding the rising error rate, Eve has to set $a_{kh} = 0$, $k, h \in \{0, 1, \cdots, d-1\}, k \neq h$. Therefore, (13) and (14) can be simplified to

$$U_E|k\rangle|E\rangle = a_{kk}|k\rangle|e_{kk}\rangle, \tag{16}$$

$$U_E\left|v_l^{(0)}\right\rangle|E\rangle = \frac{1}{d}\sum_{k=0}^{d-1}\sum_{m=0}^{d-1} w^{k(l-m)}a_{kk}\left|v_m^{(0)}\right\rangle|e_{kk}\rangle. \tag{17}$$

Similarly, to avoid the eavesdropping check, Eve has to set

$$\sum_{k=0}^{d-1} w^{k(l-m)}a_{kk}|e_{kk}\rangle = 0, \tag{18}$$

where $m \in \{0, 1, \cdots, d-1\}, m \neq l$. For any $l \in \{0, 1, \cdots, d-1\}$, we can obtain $d-1$ equations

$$a_{00} |e_{00}\rangle = a_{11} |e_{11}\rangle = \cdots = a_{d-1,d-1} |e_{d-1,d-1}\rangle. \tag{19}$$

So, whatever quantum state Eve uses, he can only get the same information from the auxiliary particles. Similar analysis can be used for the other quantum states $\left| v_l^{(j)} \right\rangle = \frac{1}{\sqrt{d}} \sum_{k=0}^{d-1} w^{k(l+jk)} |k\rangle$, so the entanglement measurement attack is invalid in our scheme.

Intercept and Resend Attack. The eavesdropper Eve intercepts the transmitted particles among Alice and the participants and resends some forged particles. For a simple description, we suppose that the eavesdropper Eve intercepts the quantum state $|\phi\rangle_k$ sent by $Bob_k^{(i)}$ to $Bob_{k+1}^{(i)}$. However, he does not know any information about the measurement bases and only chooses the correct measurement bases with the probability of $\frac{1}{d}$ to get measure outcome

$$p_0 + \sum_{i=1}^k p_i. \tag{20}$$

Even if the result is measured with the probability of $\frac{1}{d}$, the secret information cannot be obtained because $p_i, i \in \{k+1, \cdots, m\}$ is unknown. If Alice shares n secret information, the probability that eavesdropper succeed will be $\left(\frac{1}{d}\right)^n$. With the increase of the number of n, there will be $\lim_{n \to \infty} \left(\frac{1}{d}\right)^n = 0$. The other is that Eve intercepts the s_i sent by Alice to the participants, but the s_i does not carry any information of the secret. In short, Eve cannot obtain the secret in intercept-and-resend attack.

Forgery Attack. If Alice shares a fake s_t to $Bob_t^{(i)}$, the secret s will not be restored by the participants in A_i. If one or some of the participants perform the false unitary operation, they will be found by Alice because the measurement result will be inconsistent with Alice's expectation. What's more, even if some dishonest participants performed the fake unitary transformation and Alice successfully measured the expected result, there is no use for this attack. Because the recovered secret s' with $H_2' = h(s') \neq H_2 = h(s)$ guaranteed. So, the forgery attack is useless.

Collusion Attack. If the participants in $B_i, B_i \subseteq A_i$ collude to restore the secret, they must obtain the $s_k^{(i)}$ and $\lambda_k^{(i)}$ of each participant in the authorization set A_i to recover S_i. When $B_i \subseteq A_i$, they can not get the other's secret share information, so this attack is unsuccessful.

5 Example

Here, we explain our scheme more clearly by giving an example.

Example 3. According to the MSP and the access structure Γ in the example 2, assuming Alice wants to share secret $s = 3 \in \mathcal{Z}_5$ among the four participants $Bob_1, Bob_2, Bob_3, Bob_4$, she prepares a random vector $\boldsymbol{\rho} = (4, 1, 0, 2)^T$ firstly and then computes $\boldsymbol{s} = M\boldsymbol{\rho} = (s_1, s_2, s_3, s_4)^T = (2, 2, 1, 1)^T$. Next, she sends s_i to Bob_i, $(i = 1, 2, 3, 4)$ via a secure channel and publishes $H_1 = h(4)$, $H_2 = h(3)$. Without losing generality, we assume that the participants in A_1 want to restore the secret. The dealer Alice prepares a state $|\phi\rangle = |\varphi_0^0\rangle = \frac{1}{\sqrt{5}} \sum\limits_{i=0}^{4} |i\rangle$ and performs $U_{p_0,q_0} = U_{3,2}$ on it to obtain $|\phi\rangle_0 = U_{3,2} |\varphi_0^0\rangle = |\varphi_3^2\rangle$, where $p_0 = s = 3$ is the secret, $q_0 = 2 \in \mathcal{Z}_5$ is a randomly selected secret value only known by Alice. Next she sends the quantum state $|\phi\rangle_0 = |\varphi_3^2\rangle$ to Bob_1. After receiving $|\phi\rangle_0 = |\varphi_3^2\rangle$, Bob_1 performs the unitary operation $U_{\lambda_1 s_1, \lambda_1} = U_{2,1}$ to get $|\phi\rangle_1 = |\varphi_0^3\rangle$ and sends it to Bob_2. When receiving $|\phi\rangle_1 = |\varphi_0^3\rangle$, Bob_2 performs the unitary operation $U_{\lambda_2 s_2, \lambda_2} = U_{2,1}$ to get $|\phi\rangle_2 = |\varphi_2^4\rangle$ and sends to Bob_3. After receiving $|\phi\rangle_2 = |\varphi_2^4\rangle$, Bob_3 performs $U_{\lambda_3 s_3, \lambda_3} = U_{0,0}$ to get $|\phi\rangle_3 = |\varphi_2^4\rangle$ and sends it to Alice. For the authorization set A_1, when all participants act and transmit particle, the final quantum state is

$$|\varphi\rangle_{final} = \left(\prod_{i=0}^{3} U_{p_i,q_i} \right) |\varphi_0^0\rangle = \left| \varphi_{\sum\limits_{i=0}^{3} q_i}^{\sum\limits_{i=0}^{3} p_i} \right\rangle = |\varphi_2^4\rangle. \tag{21}$$

In this case, Alice selects $M_4 = \left\{ \left| \varphi_j^{(4)} \right\rangle \big| j \in \{0, 1, 2, 3, 4\} \right\}$ to measure $|\varphi\rangle_{final} = |\varphi_2^4\rangle$ and records the measurement result r_1. Afterwards, Alice checks whether $r_1 = 2$ and $H_1 = h(4)$ are true. If not, the scheme is terminated. If they are established, the measurement result r_1 is sent to each participant in A_1 through a quantum secure channel. After the participant receives it, the secret s can be recovered as

$$s = p_0^{(1)} = r_1 - p_1^{(1)} - p_2^{(1)} - p_3^{(1)} = r_1 - \lambda_1^{(1)} s_1^{(1)} - \lambda_2^{(1)} s_2^{(1)} - \lambda_3^{(1)} s_3^{(1)}. \tag{22}$$

That is $s = 2 - (2 + 2 + 0) = 3$. Last but not least, they can check H_1 to make certain of the authenticity of the secret.

6 Comparisons

In this section, we give comparisons among our scheme and other similar d-dimensional QSS schemes [23,34,35] in terms of basic properties, computational complexity and communication costs. For these comparisons, we first introduce similar references, and then compare with our proposal from the two aspects. The schemes in Ref. [23,35] are the threshold QSS, however the scheme in Ref. [34] and ours are the general access structure QSS. The general access structure makes the level and influence of the participants different, making the scheme more flexible. They all use the Hash function to make the verifiability of the d-dimensional QSS scheme. The scheme proposed by Song et al. [23] shared a classical secret by utilizing polynomials according to the Lagrange interpolation formula. The transformation of the particles includes some operations such as d-level CNOT, QTF, Inverse QTF, and generalized Pauli operator. However, the general access structure QSS is far more flexible and practical than the threshold one. In Ref. [34], Mashhadi proposed a hybrid secret sharing based on the quantum Fourier transform and monotone span program, in which the participants recover the secret by means of measuring the entangled state. The number of unitary operators is not much different in the premise, while the number of required quantum states and the number of measurement operations are greatly reduced, which consumes less quantum resources and the scheme is more practical. Qin et al. [35] put forward a verifiable (t, n) threshold QSS using d-dimensional Bell state and they realize the authentication of quantum state transmission by adding some decoy particles. According to the Lagrange interpolation and the unitary operation, they can recover the secret with measuring the final Bell state. The Specific comparison of basic property among Ref. [23, 34, 35] and ours is given in Table 1. The comparison of the computational complexity and communication costs of the general access structure QSS[34] and the new is given in Table 2.

Remark 1. LI: Lagrange interpolation, MSP: Monotone span program, MUB: Mutually unbiased bases, LC: Linear computation, NQO: necessary quantum operation, QTF: Quantum Fourier Transform, QFT^{-1}: Inverse Quantum Fourier Transform, UO: Unitary operation, UT: Unitary transformation.

Table 1. Basic comparison among the QSS schemes

Property	Song [23]	Mashhadi [34]	Qin [35]	New
Model	(t, n)threshold	General	(t, n)threshold	General
Verification	Hash function	Hash function	Hash function	Hash function
Secret	Classic	Classic	Classic	Classic
Dimension	d	d	d	d
Method	LI	MSP,LC	LI	MSP,MUB,LC
NQO	QFT, QFT^{-1}, Pauli	QFT,Pauli	UO	UT

Table 2. Comparison of communication costs and computational complexity

Property	Mashhadi [34]	Ours
Number of message particles	$m - 1$	1
Unitary operation	m	$m + 1$
QTF	1	–
Measure operation	m	1
Hash function	2	2

7   Conclusions

The verifiable quantum secret sharing scheme based on the access structure is very useful in practice. In this paper, we construct a verifiable quantum secret sharing scheme based on the property of the mutually unbiased base and the monotone span program. The dealer and participants in the authorization set can restore secret through the transformation and transmission of a d-dimensional quantum state as well as linear secret sharing. In addition, the correctness, verifiability and security analysis of the scheme have been proved. Finally, a specific example and a comparison are given to further clarify the advantages and practicality of our scheme.

The verifiability of the scheme is analyzed from the view that the recovered secret is consistent with the original one in this paper. However, For the future work, the issue of mutual authentication among the participants in the authorization set is still worth studying.

Acknowledgements. We would like to thank anonymous reviewer for valuable comments. This work is supported by the National Natural Science Foundation of China under Grant No. 11671244.

References

1. Shor, P.W., Preskill, J.: Simple proof of security of the BB84 quantum key distribution protocol. J. Phys. Rev. Lett. **85**(2), 441–444 (2000)
2. Lo, H., Ma, X., Chen, K., et al.: Decoy state quantum key distribution. J. Phys. Rev. Lett. **94**(23), 230504–230504 (2005)
3. Chong, S.K., Hwang, T.: Quantum key agreement protocol based on BB84. J. Opt. Commun. **283**(6), 1192–1195 (2010)
4. Liu, B., Gao, F., Huang, W., et al.: Multiparty quantum key agreement with single particles. J. Quantum Inf. Process. **12**(4), 1797–1805 (2013)
5. Shukla, C., Alam, N., Pathak, A.: Protocols of quantum key agreement solely using Bell states and Bell measurement. Quantum Inf. Process. **13**(11), 2391–2405 (2014). https://doi.org/10.1007/s11128-014-0784-0
6. Deng, F., Long, G.: Secure direct communication with a quantum one-time pad. J. Phys. Rev. A **69**(5) (2004)
7. Wang, C., Deng, F., Li, Y.S., et al.: Quantum secure direct communication with high-dimension quantum superdense coding. J. Phys. Rev. A **71**(4) (2005)
8. Furusawa, A., Sorensen, J., Braunstein, S.L., et al.: Unconditional quantum teleportation. J. Sci. **282**(5389), 706–709 (1998)
9. Bouwmeester, D., Pan, J., Mattle, K., et al.: Experimental quantum teleportation. J. Nat. **390**(6660), 575–579 (1997)
10. Lee, H., Hong, C., Kim, H., et al.: Arbitrated quantum signature scheme with message recovery. J. Phys. Lett. A **321**(5), 295–300 (2004)
11. Fei, G., Sujuan, Q., Fenzhuo, G., et al.: Cryptanalysis of the arbitrated quantum signature protocols. J. Phys. Rev. A **84**(2) (2011)
12. Li, X., Barnum, H.: Quantum authentication using entangled states. J. Int. J. Found. Comput. Sci. **15**(04), 609–617 (2004)

13. Naseri, M.: Revisiting quantum authentication scheme based on entanglement swapping. J. Int. J. Theoret. Phys. **55**(5), 2428–2435 (2016)
14. Hillery, M., Buzek, V., Berthiaume, A., et al.: Quantum secret sharing. J. Phys. Rev. A **59**(3), 1829–1834 (1999)
15. Hsu, L.: Quantum secret-sharing protocol based on Grover's algorithm. J. Phys. Rev. A **68**(2) (2003)
16. Xiao, L., Long, G., Deng, F., et al.: Efficient multiparty quantum-secret-sharing schemes. J. Phys. Rev. A **69**(5) (2004)
17. Sun, Y., Wen, Q., Gao, F., et al.: Multiparty quantum secret sharing based on Bell measurement. J. Opt. Commun. **282**(17), 3647–3651 (2009)
18. Hsu, J., Chong, S., Hwang, T., et al.: Dynamic quantum secret sharing. J. Quantum Inf. Process. **12**(1), 331–344 (2013)
19. Rahaman, R., Parker, M.G.: Quantum secret sharing based on local distinguishability. J. Phys. Rev. A **91**(2) (2015)
20. Wang, J., Li, L., Peng, H., et al.: Quantum-secret-sharing scheme based on local distinguishability of orthogonal multiqudit entangled states. J. Phys. Rev. A **95**(2) (2017)
21. Williams, B.P., Lukens, J.M., Peters, N.A., et al.: Quantum secret sharing with polarization-entangled photon pairs. J. Phys. Rev. A **99**(6) (2019)
22. Tsai, C., Yang, C., Lee, N., et al.: Semi-quantum secret sharing protocol using W-state. J. Modern Phys. Lett. A **34**(27) (2019)
23. Song, X., Liu, Y., Deng, H., et al.: (t, n) threshold d-level quantum secret sharing. J. Sci. Reports **7**(1) (2017)
24. Yang, Y., Jia, X., Wang, H., et al.: Verifiable quantum (k, n)-threshold secret sharing. J. Quantum Inf. Process. **11**(6), 1619–1625 (2012)
25. Hao, N., Li, Z., Bai, H., et al.: A new quantum secret sharing scheme based on mutually unbiased bases. Int. J. Theor. Phys. **58**, 1249–1261 (2019)
26. Bai, C.-M., Li, Z.-H., Si, M.-M., Li, Y.-M.: Quantum secret sharing for a general quantum access structure. Eur. Phys. J. D **71**(10), 1–8 (2017). https://doi.org/10.1140/epjd/e2017-80286-3
27. Liu, C., Li, Z., Bai, C., et al.: Quantum-secret-sharing scheme based on local distinguishability of orthogonal seven-qudit entangled states. Int. J. Theor. Phys. **57**, 428–442 (2018)
28. Xu, T., Li, Z., Bai, C., et al.: A new improving quantum secret sharing scheme. Int. J. Theor. Phys. **56**, 1308–1317 (2017)
29. Nascimento, A.C., Muellerquade, J., Imai, H., et al.: Improving quantum secret-sharing schemes. J. Phys. Rev. A **64**(4) (2001)
30. Karchmer, M., Wigderson, A.: On span programs. In: Structure in Complexity Theory Annual Conference, pp. 102–111 (1993)
31. Ivonovic, I.D.: Geometrical description of quantal state determination. J. J. Phys. A **14**(12), 3241–3245 (1981)
32. Wootters, W.K., Fields, B.D.: Optimal state-determination by mutually unbiased measurements. J. Ann. Phys. **191**(2), 363–381 (1989)
33. Tavakoli, A., Herbauts, I., Zukowski, M., et al.: Secret sharing with a single d-level quantum system. J. Phys. Rev. A **92**(3) (2015)
34. Mashhadi, S.: General secret sharing based on quantum Fourier transform. Quantum Inf. Process. **18**(4), 1–15 (2019). https://doi.org/10.1007/s11128-019-2233-6
35. Qin, H., Dai, Y.: Verifiable (t, n) threshold quantum secret sharing using d-dimensional Bell state. J. Inf. Process. Lett. **116**(5), 351–355 (2016)

Steganography

A Novel Method to Improve Security and Imperceptibility of Image Steganography

Kymbat Taalaibekova, Xianjin Fang$^{(\boxtimes)}$, and Zhifeng Xu

School of Computer Science and Engineering, Anhui University of Science and Technology, Huainan 23100, Anhui, China
talaibekova31@gmail.com, {xjfang,2019200707}@aust.edu.cn

Abstract. Nowadays when photos, images and selfies are very popular, when we cannot imagine our lives without them in our daily life, security of images is our priority. Over the last year, the messenger Snapchat, which is popular among teenagers has become the target of hackers three times. And we also remind you about the hacking of the anti-doping administration and management system (ADAMS). Hackers gained access to the athletes' personal medical images and made publicly available images, the results of their doping tests, which indicated that athletes were taking illegal substances.

Securing images can be accomplished by cryptography and steganography. The combination of both techniques can enhance image security. The Arnold's transformation (ACM) in this paper has been combined with Elliptic Curve cryptography (ECC) based on new mapping method, which proposed to convert the pixels of the plain image into the coordinates on the curve. In addition, this paper also suggests combining ACM with ECC and subsequently integrating the result into a cover image with Least Significant Bit (LSB) steganography.

After a simulation test, efficiency of the proposed system is evaluated using peak signal to noise ratio (PSNR), histogram analysis, and entropy as parameters for obtaining quality of stego image and quality of cipher image. The proposed method recorded the highest PSNR of 59.22 dB, the highest entropy of stego image and cover images equaled 7.76. The simulation results show that a high level of security is offered by the proposed algorithm.

Keywords: Arnold's transformation · Elliptic curve cryptography · Image security · Least significant bit · Steganography

1 Introduction

In today's world image plays an essential role in everyone's life and have become an inescapable source of information. Millions of photos are transferred ordinary over the network. These days, internet multimedia is very popular; each second a vital amount of data is exchanged over an unsecured network that may not be safe. Subsequently, it is essential to protect the data from attackers.

How we mentioned above, popular messenger Snapchat, which approves that all messages, images disappearing immediately, has hacked three times, in 2019. For the

© Springer Nature Singapore Pte Ltd. 2020
G. Xu et al. (Eds.): FCS 2020, CCIS 1286, pp. 611–627, 2020.
https://doi.org/10.1007/978-981-15-9739-8_45

first time, the names and phone numbers of millions of users Snapchat hit the Internet. The next hacking happened after 1.5 months. This time hackers had get access to many combinations of mail addresses and passwords, but, fortunately, the attack turned out to be harmless. And in October, another leak occurred: this time, 100,000 user's photos hit the Internet.

At least 16 national and international sports and anti-doping organizations on three continents were the victims of hacker's attacks from Fancy Bear/APT28, which began on September 16. Some of these attacks were successful, but most were not. Fancy Bear/APT28 is not the first time targeted at such organizations. The group reportedly issued medical records, images and emails from sports organizations and anti-doping officials in 2016 and 2018, which resulted in a 2018 indictment in the U.S. federal court.

Cryptography is a very effective technique to protect highly confidential and valuable information from cyber criminals. But alone cryptography can't furnish a better protection strategy because the scrambled message is still accessible to the eavesdropper. There is a necessity of data hiding. So here we are using a combination of steganography and cryptography for improving the security.

Cryptography is the science of keeping the transmitted data secure. Before transmission, the encryption process is applied and after receiving the encrypted data, the decryption process is applied. Steganography is the science of hiding messages within a different digital content; it transmits the information by concealing it in other media such as picture or audio called the cover object. Before transmission, the data hiding process is applied and after receipt, the extraction process is applied.

The primary difference between cryptography and steganography based totally on the existence of the secret message. Cryptography encrypts the message and transmits it; absolutely everyone can see the encrypted message, however is very tough to be understood, particularly if it has been encrypted with strong cryptographic algorithm. Steganography conceals the secret message presence hiding it in a cover object. The cover object can be labeled as Text-based Steganography in which the message is embedded in a textual content file, audio Steganography to cover the secret message in audio and image steganography in which the secret information is embedded in an image.

Steganography system can be implemented using two techniques. Firstly, the spatial domain based steganography, where the least important bits of the cover object is changed through the secret message bits. Secondly, the steganography centered on the transform domain; in this case, the secret message is embedded with the coefficient of the cover object.

In order to improve the reliability of the communication system; cryptography and steganography can be combined to execute a sturdy and impervious system; in this case, the encryption and hiding are achieved in the transmitter, while the extraction and decryption are accomplished in the receiver.

To order to measure the difference between the cover image and the stego image, the PSNR is used. It is possible to calculate PSNR using:

$$PSNR = 10\log\frac{L^2}{MSE} \tag{1}$$

where, L is the maximum value the samples and MSE is the mean squared error.

The remainder of this article is structured as follows. Section 2 describes the related work. Preliminaries is outlined in Sect. 3. Sect. 4 discusses the proposed methods, experimental results and Sect. 5 concludes the article.

2 Related Work

Bendaoud, et al. [1] proposed an improved elliptic curve cryptosystem - ECC-based image encryption scheme by using Deoxyribo-Nucleic Acid computing. The plain image is mapped using the mapping methodology based on a map table and its ECC encrypted. The authors have shown that their proposed algorithm can withstand brute, mathematical, and differential attacks.

Bhargava, et al. [2] were using combination RSA encryption, LSB method and DWT. First they are using LSB method for hiding encrypted by RSA algorithm text message, then DWT for embedding and extracting message from stego image. Authors has proved that this method sustained the attack of brute force.

Budianto, et al. [3] were showing, that to secure identity data, particularly the data in the Indonesia Identity Card the ECC and LSB steganography are successfully implemented. The ECC is used here to secure personal information of person who came to apply for electronic Indonesian Identity Card. After the ECC, least significant bit steganography is used to insert the information (cipher text) into the image of the person. This method successfully implemented in the web-based application and guarantee the security and confidentiality of information.

Jain, et al. [4] suggested a secured method of steganography to hide multiple images, in this case 4 images within an image using the technique of LSB and Arnold Transformation. After hiding the secrete images they scramble the embedded image by using the Arnold transformation.

Kumar et al. [5], established a new method for RGB image steganography which can hide more than one RGB secret image (3 in this case) in a single RGB cover image. Here DCT and Arnold transform were used to improve secrecy. The proposed method has been thoroughly tested using various color images and the results of these experiments have been scrutinized via different quality metrics which prove the method's effectiveness.

Kushal Gurung, et al. [6] the RSA algorithm for data privacy and confidentiality was used in this system. Plain text message was encrypted and embedded in image. For this process, the LSB substitution method was employed. There were negligible changes in color of the image which could not be identified by human eyes.

Lakshmanan, et al. [7] proposed in this paper circular queue LSB substitutions based on crypto – stegno scheme to improve security in data communication. Firstly, an effective ECC-cryptosystem is used to encrypt text message content. Second, to conceal the presence of the message in a digital image, a powerful circular queue LSB substitutions based embedded approach is used. It is found that this scheme preserves the high degree of confidentiality in comparison with the other existing methods.

Mathur, et al. [8] had used pixel scrambling technique in this work, Arnold transformation, zigzag transformation, and double random-phase technique in fractional Fourier transform domain to increase key strength many times, which makes encryption technique more efficient. Simulation data show that the proposed algorithm exhibits both the strong security and the high efficiency.

Nair, et al. [9] proposed to use both stenographic and cryptographic methods to secure data from unauthorized access. Authors was combining pixel value differencing (PVD) and AES encryption. Authors affirming that this algorithm provides the data with multiple levels of security.

Patil, et al. [10] suggested the algorithm for calculating secret key value without sharing in network. The secret key value is created by ECC with coordinate system. The proposed system can avoid selected attacks on plaintext, man-in - the-middle attacks, etc. Authors have also proved that ECC algorithm provides the fastest security with minimum key value as compared to AES and RSA.

Shanthakumari, et al. [11] suggested algorithm of using ECC for encrypting and decrypting image, after embedding this image with LSB method within cover image. This method has been extensively tested by several stegoanalysis attacks and experimental result showed that this method is resistant to crypto attacks.

Zhang, et al. [12] proposed an asymmetric algorithm for the encryption of images based on ECC. The sender and recipient settle on an elliptic curve point based on the key exchange strategy used by the Diffie-Hellman public. The proposed algorithm makes key handling and transmission relatively simple and secure.

Liu, et al. [13] proposed a new model of digital image watermarking based on scrambling algorithm Logistic and RSA asymmetric encryption algorithm to ensure the security of secret data on the basis of large capacity for embedding, strong robustness and high computational performance.

K. Jiao, et al. [14] proposed a new image encryption scheme based on a generalized Arnold map and RSA. Authors proved that the encryption scheme proposed in this study is effective and has strong anti-attack capabilities and key sensitivity.

Having drawn conclusions from the above articles, we decided to improve the methods by combining three methods into one: ECC, ACM and LSB method to enhance image steganography. Thus, create the novel method which will have obvious practical significance in the field of image steganography and will show that the method have high security.

3 Preliminaries

3.1 Arnold's Transformation (ACM)

In 1960, Vladimir Arnold invented Arnold's Cat Map, also called Arnold's Transformation. This chaos system is a two dimensional map that produces values for new random coordinates (x', y') from real coordinates (x, y) in the image size of M × M. This transformation includes a and b (positive integers) and i as input values for multiple iterations to produce the new coordinates.

$$\begin{bmatrix} x' \\ y' \end{bmatrix} = \begin{bmatrix} 1 & a \\ b & ab+1 \end{bmatrix} \begin{bmatrix} x \\ y \end{bmatrix} \bmod M \qquad (2)$$

In Eq. (2) the determining value of the metrics containing a and b should be 1 to generate a new coordinate within the image. This equation is repeated i times. There is sometimes an iteration value returning the image to the original image. This value of repetition is called Arnold's period.

$$\begin{bmatrix} x \\ y \end{bmatrix} = \begin{bmatrix} 1 & a \\ b & ab+1 \end{bmatrix}^{-1} \begin{bmatrix} x' \\ y' \end{bmatrix} \mod M \tag{3}$$

Equation (3) shows the enciphering formula generating the original coordinates (x, y). The result of the metric inverse matrices containing a and b works with the cipher image's randomized coordinates.

3.2 Elliptic Curve Cryptography

An Elliptic curve is a cubic equation with the form (4):

$$y^2 = x^3 + ax + b \tag{4}$$

where, a and b are integers that satisfy (5) and p is a large prime number.

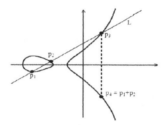

Fig. 1. Graph of an elliptic curve

Figure 1 demonstrates an elliptic curve on an elliptic curve over the real field R and point addition $(p1 + p2)$:

$$4a^3 + 27b^2 \neq 0 \;(\mathrm{mod}\; p) \tag{5}$$

Alice and Bob used an elliptic curve to encrypt a message and took an affine point (G) on the curve. Plaintext M is encoded into a point P_M. Alice has selected a random prime integer x and Bob has selected a random prime integer y, x and y are the private keys of Alice and Bob, respectively. Alice calculates (6) and Bob computes (7) to generate the public key.

$$P_A = xG \tag{6}$$

$$P_B = yG \tag{7}$$

Alice chooses another random integer k to encrypt a message point P_M for Bob, and uses Bob's public key (P_B) to compute the encrypted message P_C. P_C is a set of points (8):

$$P_C = [(kG), (P_M + kP_B)] \tag{8}$$

Alice is sending Bob the encrypted P_C message. He receives the ciphered message and multiplies his private key y with kG, and subtracts it to measure P_M from the second point in the encrypted message. The result corresponds to message M in plaintext (9):

$$P_M = [(P_M + kP_B) - [ykG]]$$
(9)

Additional operation over an elliptic group for two points P and Q; if $P + Q = (X_3, Y_3)$ is given by (10):

$$X_3 = \lambda^2 - X_P - X_Q \bmod p$$

$$Y_3 = \lambda(X_P - X_3) - Y_P \bmod p$$

$$\lambda = \begin{cases} \frac{Y_Q - Y_P}{X_Q - X_P} & \text{if } P \neq Q \\ \frac{3X_P^2 + a}{2Y_P} & \text{if } P = Q \end{cases}$$
(10)

Multiplication kP is determined by repeating the addition operation k times using (10) over an elliptic group. The reliability of an ECC-based cryptosystem depends on how difficult it is to figure out how many times G is applied to itself in order to get P_A.

3.3 Mapping Methodology

Each image is made up of pixels. Each pixel has an 8-bit value between 0 and 255 in gray scale images. A pixel is represented separately by 3 octet values in color images; indicate the Red, Green and Blue intensity.

Each pixel should be considered as a message to encrypt an image using ECC and mapped to a point on a predefined elliptic curve. The proposed method of mapping is based on a map table in this study. The elliptic group $E_p(a, b)$ is created first to construct this table, which is all possible points on the finite field, and then these points are put in 256 groups. Each group has $N = \lceil order\ of\ E/256 \rceil$ members. The index in the row starts with 0 and ends with 255. Each row stands for a pixel intensity value; however, for same values, there are multiple points. If N is not a multiple of 256, additional rows are filled with zero in the last column, and the last column is not considered for mapping.

The corresponding point with the intensity value in the table is mapped to this pixel from the first pixel in the plain image and continues to the last pixel. The next point in the corresponding row is selected for repeated intensity values. If all $N - 1$ points are selected for all intensities, then for next one we start from the first again.

The next step is to encrypt these points using the receiver's public key and Eq. (6) after mapping all pixels to their related point one by one. Encrypting a point on an elliptic curve results in a set of two points. In this case, for all pixels, the first point (kG) in (6) is the same, but the second point $(P_M + kP_B)$ for each pixel is different. After encrypting all pixels, the result can be shown as an image. The final step is releasing the encrypted points as an image. We refer to the mapping table, find out the current index according to each point and substitute it with the related value.

3.4 Histogram Analysis

An image histogram at each grey level is a graphic illustration of the distribution of pixels. If it is not completely changed after encryption, some important pieces of information can be extracted.

For instance, different people's facial image has a similar histogram or an image histogram can be used to determine whether or not it is a cartoon. Therefore, from its histogram, the meaning of an image is obtained. The histogram of an encrypted image should be drastically different from the original image in order to prevent leakage of information from a ciphered picture and usually contain a uniform distribution.

3.5 Entropy Analysis

Entropy is a quantity that shows the optimal length of the code assigned to a pixel in an image, according to Shannon's information theory. Entropy is a statistical scalar parameter determining the randomness of an input image in the image encryption analysis. A ciphered image's highest value of ~8 means that it has a random texture. Using the proposed method, entropy of an encrypted image is determined using (11) resulting in 7.76.

$$Entropy = \sum_{i=0}^{n} P_i * \log_2 P_i \tag{11}$$

3.6 LSB Steganography

LSB-Steganography is a technique of steganography in which we conceal messages within an image by replacing Least Significant Bit with the bits of message which have to be hidden.

LSB stands for Least Significant bit. The principle behind LSB embedding is that if we change a pixel's last bit value, there won't be much visible change in the color. 0 is black, for instance. Changing the value to 1 is not going to make a big difference as it is still black, just a lighter shade [14].

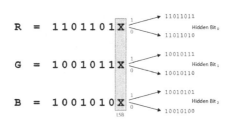

Fig. 2. How Least-Significant Bit Steganography works

4   Proposed Method

Initially, the secret image with size $M \times M$ is separated into the corresponding RGB color channels. After that, the result was encrypted using Elliptic Curve cryptography based on mapping method and Arnold's transformation is applied to it. The encryption result is embedded in a cover image using LSB steganography.

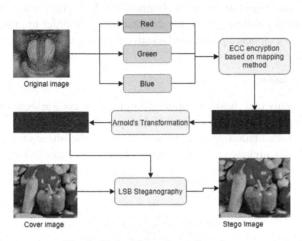

Fig. 3. Embedding scheme flowchart.

The process of embedding produces a stego image is as follows (see Fig. 3):

1. Input values for p and q (prime numbers). Also input secret image (M × M) and cover image (N × N).
2. The secret image with size M × M is separated into the corresponding RGB color channels.
3. From p and q, generate a key for encryption and decryption.
4. Encrypt each pixel of the image using ECC based on mapping method
5. Apply Arnold's transformation.
6. Insert the result of the previous step into the cover image (N × N). Each bits of the encryption result is embedded with LSB method.

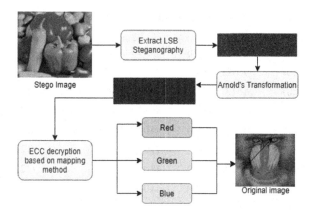

Fig. 4. Extracting scheme flowchart.

A flowchart of the extracting scheme is shown in Fig. 4. This scheme will produce the original image. The detailed steps for extracting the secret image are:

1. Input the stego image to extract the message bits.
2. Apply Arnold's Transformation
3. Do ECC decryption for each pixel using the key that has been inputted.
4. Rearrange the decryption result into an M × M image, i.e. the original image.

4.1 Implementation of ECC Based on Mapping Method

Now we will describe implementation of ECC based on mapping method in detail. For instance, we decided to use a simple elliptic curve E_{123457} *(5376, 2438)* to clearly show and describe the implementation steps that is represented by:

$$y^2 mod\,123457 = x^3 + 5376x + 2348mod\,123457$$

Table 1 shows some of the points generated. The first point is placed in row 0 to create the mapping table, which corresponds to the pixel with an intensity value of 0, and then proceeds with the next value to the next point. The next 256 points will be placed in the second column after putting the first 256 points in the first column of the table and start until the last point is reached. There are 123387 points on the curve in this case. Those points occupy 481 columns and the 482nd column's 250 rows entirely. The last column's remaining free spaces are filled with zeros.

Table 1. Mapping table

Index	1st Mapping	2nd Mapping	3rd Mapping	....	482nd Mapping
0	(42908,0)	(512, 47183)	(1033, 54418)	...	(122949, 838668)
1	(95914,0)	(513, 33718)	(1039, 9194)	....	(122951, 74732)
2	(108092,0)	(515, 24882)	(1039, 3322)	...	(122953, 121769)
3	(3, 31443)	(516, 49743)	(1041, 8203)	...	(122954, 66970)
4	(5, 11660)	(519, 6902)	(1043, 46883)	...	(122958, 73556)
5	(6, 2174)	(520, 20390)	(1044, 52089)	...	(122959, 84424)
6	(7, 58403)	(521, 20390)	(1046, 3610)	...	(122961, 71950)
7	(8, 29200)	(524, 59065)	(1049, 55356)	...	(122962, 91690)
....					
154	(305, 46853)	(824, 9038)	(1339, 50036)	...	(123276, 99876)
155	(306, 33458)	(825, 50433)	(1340, 25625)	...	(123277, 107283)
156	(307, 29631)	(831, 5746)	(1341, 37870)	...	(123279, 104846)
157	(312, 43431)	(832, 39441)	(1342, 48041)	...	(123280, 82736)
158	(314, 37257)	(834, 26653)	(1344, 60034)	...	(123285, 119446)
159	(315, 58283)	(835, 23727)	(1346, 20117)	...	(123287, 87751)
160	(317, 57467)	(836, 30492)	(1351, 35977)	...	(123288, 84108)
161	(318, 23904)	(840, 29931)	(1355, 30658)	...	(123289, 81841)
....					
250	(501, 10872)	(1020, 25923)	(1511, 61516)	...	(123456, 95491)
251	(504, 34198)	(1021, 52191)	(1514, 18629)	...	0
252	(508, 56806)	(1022, 35175)	(1515, 52722)	...	0
253	(509, 17779)	(1023, 21986)	(1525, 20628)	...	0
254	(510, 45297)	(1027, 4468)	(1530, 38375)	...	0
255	(511, 58316)	(1029, 53908)	(1531, 18176)	...	0

To encrypt the image, some parameters should be defined as follows, according to (6) and (7); $G = (2225, 75856)$ as a generator point, $y = 36548$ as the private key of the receiver, and $k = 23412$ as a random integer specified by the transmitter. Using these values, the public key of the receiver is determined according to (7) and the result is: $P_B = (30402, 35513)$.

All pixels are mapped to corresponding points using Table 1 before encrypting an image using this technique. Table 2's first row displays the Lena picture intensity value of 9 pixels in place (1, 1) to (1, 10). The results are displayed in the third row after encrypting all the points using (6).

The result of encrypting a point is two points. For all pixels, the first point is the same and will be sent once, but for each pixel, the second point is different. To represent the

Table 2. Results of mapping pixels to points, encryption and mapping encrypted points to pixels

Pixel value	161	159	157	158	161	159
Mapped Point	(318, 23904)	(315, 58283)	(312, 43431)	(314, 37257)	(840, 29931)	(835, 23727)
Encrypted Points	(117616, 24017)	(117616, 24017)	(117616, 24017)	(117616, 24017)	(117616, 24017)	(117616, 24017)
	(1222358, 40144)	(60803, 3943)	(11960, 81566)	(99326, 59783)	(8435, 79086)	(24718, 3745)
Encrypted Pixel	205	222	82	77	107	88

encrypted points as an image, we first construct a matrix of the same size as the image, find and point in Table 1 and then place the index of the row in the matrix equivalent. The last row in Table 2 contains the converted values for encrypting the value of the pixel from the encrypted points, which can then be displayed as an image.

4.2 Result and Testing

Windows 10 operating system was used with the MATLAB R2017b software to simulate the work. For Testing as a secret messages were used three images with size 64×64. Using the proposed scheme they were encrypted and embedded. However, the image size may also be different, as long as each side has a 2n pixel size and the image length is greater than or equal to the image width. After the encryption process, the encryption result is embedded in a cover image with size 512×512.

Figure 5 displays the secret images that the proposed scheme used to encrypt. Random Integer defined by sender and this number equals to 19, as receiver's private key chosen number 31.

Fig. 5. Secret images for testing 1) baboon.kg 2) lena.jpg 3) peppers.jpg

Figure 6 shows image baboon.png, which was encrypted using the mapping method of ECC. This cipher image was extended into binary form before ECC encryption. The process of expansion transforms each pixel into an 8-bit binary in each layer and then reconstructs this binary form into an image.

Fig. 6. Image baboon.jpg after ECC encryption

Next, ACM was used to randomize the image in Fig. 6. ACM can be implemented only on square images, every 64 blocks of the binary image has been scrambled, so it has been processed in 16 iterations. The result of ACM encryption is shown in Fig. 7.

Fig. 7. Image result after ACM encryption.

As shown in Fig. 8, in contrast with the original image's histogram (baboon.png), the histogram of the encrypted image and the histogram of the scrambled image are significantly different. The histogram result of the proposed encryption scheme has a flat pattern that decreases the chance of being attacked using a statistical method.

Compared to the method from [11] the entropy value of the proposed method is higher.

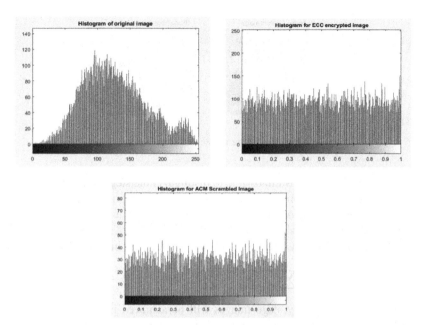

Fig. 8. Histograms of image baboon.png 1) original image 2) encrypted image 3) ACM scrambled image

The result is embedded in a cover image after the encryption method, as shown below. As a cover image we can use any image with any size. We used two images as a cover image here.

Fig. 9. Cover images 1) fruits.jpg 2) peppers.jpg

The encrypted and after scrambled image shown in Fig. 7 were embedded in the cover image peppers.jpg shown in Fig. 9. These cover images have the same size, i.e. 512×512. In the colored cover image, we inserted the secret image into the blue layer, because human vision is less sensitive to the color blue. The maximum payload that can be inserted using traditional LSB is only 262.144 bytes, with a cover image size equal to 512×512.

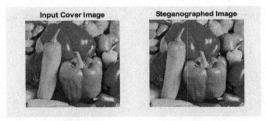

Fig. 10. Cover image and stego image

As shown in Fig. 10, it is impossible to distinguish the stego image from the cover image after the insertion process. This means that our proposed scheme has a good quality stego image. Embedding process results have been tested using mean square error (MSE) and peak signal to noise ratio (PSNR) which we can calculate using (12) and (1). MSE is used to measure the error between the cover image and stego image.

$$MSE = \frac{1}{M * N} \sum\nolimits_{x=1}^{x} \sum\nolimits_{y=1}^{y} \sum\nolimits_{z=1}^{z} \|C_i(x, y, z) - S_i(x, y, z)\|^2 \qquad (12)$$

From [10], good-quality stego images will be achieved if the value of PSNR is above 40 dB. The results we compared to existing method ECC using LSB [11] and image watermarking method using logistics, LSB and RSA encryption [13], as shown in Table 3.

Table 3. Comparison of MSE and PSNR of existing system and proposed system.

Image name	Mean Squared Error (MSE)			Peak Signal to Noise (PSNR)		
	Image embedding using Logistics and RSA [13]	Image Steganography using ECC and LSB [11]	Proposed technique	Image embedding using Logistics and RSA [13]	Image Steganography using ECC and LSB [11]	Proposed technique
Lena	N/A	0.75647	0.012725	48.03	48.13	59.2083
Baboon	N/A	0.804756	0.01319	44.75	48.13	59.2237
Peppers	N/A	0.976521	0.012802	46.2	47.5	59.2426

As shown in Table 3 by comparing the MSE and PSNR values of all the images, MSE of images used is less and PSNR of the images in proposed technique is higher than the existing techniques. To get an output image close to the input image, high PSNR value and low MSE value are required, thus giving the better result.

After getting results of RSNR and MSE we are calculating Entropy of the cover images and stego images using (11).

The obtained results of the entropy of the images shows that the entropy of the stego images is slightly larger than the images on the cover.

Table 4. Stego images' entropy and cover images' entropy.

Cover image	peppers. jpg		fruits.jpg	
Embedded image name	Entropy of stego image	Entropy of cover image	Entropy of stego image	Entropy of cover image
Lena	7.7626	7.7614	7.6758	7.6698
Baboon	7.6799	7.6721	7.6889	7.6625
Peppers	7.7505	7.7487	7.6903	7.6698

After calculating entropy we extracted original image from stego image. First we are extracting from stego image with LSB method ACM scrambled image (see Fig. 11).

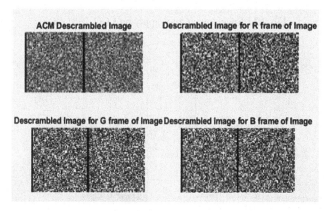

Fig. 11. Image result after using LSB steganography to extract ACM scrambled image from stego image

After getting ACM scrambled image we are applying ECC decryption to get original image (see Fig. 12).

If we will compare histogram of ACM scrambled image after extraction from stego image (Fig. 13, left) with histogram of ACM scrambled image (Fig. 8) and histogram of decrypted image (Fig. 13, right) with histogram of original image (Fig. 8), we can see that histograms are almost identical.

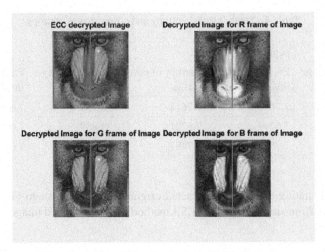

Fig. 12. Image result after applying ECC decryption

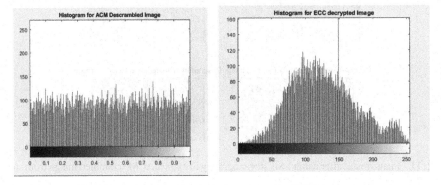

Fig. 13. Histogram of image baboon.png after ECC decryption

5 Conclusion

In this paper, a combined encryption and concealment method is proposed. Its encryption scheme, using a combination of ACM and ECC based on mapping method, produced encrypted images with better quality with a best entropy value of 7.7626. In addition, using LSB method with above mentioned combination of ACM and ECC produced stego images of good quality. This was proved by the recorded highest PSNR value for stego image −59.2426.

ECC new mapping method was introduced to convert a pixel's value to a point on an affine elliptic curve over a finite field $GF(p)$ using a map table. This mapping technique is fast, has low complexity and computation, also it's easy to implement.

After applying ECC encryption and ACM to embed image with LSB steganography we were able to safely hide our information. And after decryption, we could fully extract original image from stego image without any changes. The results show that the proposed method works better when compared with existing ones and set tasks for us accomplished.

References

1. Bendaoud, S., Amounas, F., El Kinani, E.H.: A new image encryption scheme based on enhanced elliptic curve cryptosystem using DNA computing. In: ACM International Conference Proceeding Series, Part F1481 (2019). https://doi.org/10.1145/3320326.3320361
2. Bhargava, S., Mukhija, M.: Hide image and text using LSB, DWT and RSA based on image steganography, pp. 1940–1946 (2019). https://doi.org/10.21917/ijivp.2019.0275
3. Budianto, C.D., Wicaksana, A., Hansun, S.: Elliptic curve cryptography and LSB steganography for securing identity data. In: Lee, R. (ed.) ACIT 2019. SCI, vol. 847, pp. 111–127. Springer, Cham (2020). https://doi.org/10.1007/978-3-030-25217-5_9
4. Jain, A.: A secured steganography technique for hiding multiple images in an image using least significant bit algorithm and arnold transformation. In: Hemanth, D.J., Shakya, S., Baig, Z. (eds.) ICICI 2019. LNDECT, vol. 38, pp. 373–380. Springer, Cham (2020). https://doi.org/10.1007/978-3-030-34080-3_42
5. Kumar, N., Mitra, S., Bhattacharjee, M., Mandal, L.: Multiple RGB image steganography using arnold and discrete cosine transformation, vol. 811 (2019). https://doi.org/10.1007/978-981-13-1544-2
6. Gurung, K., Azam, S., Shanmugam, B., Kannoorpatti, K., Jonkman, M., Balasubramaniam, A.: A novel approach for steganography app in Android OS. In: Abraham, A., Muhuri, Pranab Kr., Muda, A.K., Gandhi, N. (eds.) ISDA 2017. AISC, vol. 736, pp. 442–450. Springer, Cham (2018). https://doi.org/10.1007/978-3-319-76348-4_43
7. Lakshmanan, A., Devi, S.G., Nisha, M.M., Dhanalakshmi, M.: An efficient and enhanced mechanism for message hiding based on image steganography using ECC-cryptosystem (2019). https://doi.org/10.1007/978-981-13-3450-4
8. Mathur, A., Khunteta, A., Kumar Verma, A.: An efficient approach for image encryption using zigzag, arnold transformation and double random-phase encoding in fractional Fourier transform domain. In: Chaudhary, A., Choudhary, C., Gupta, M.K., Lal, C., Badal, T. (eds.) Microservices in Big Data Analytics. LNDECT, pp. 49–58. Springer, Singapore (2020). https://doi.org/10.1007/978-981-15-0128-9_5
9. Nair, K.C., Ratheesh, T.K.: A data security scheme using image steganography. In: Hemanth, D.J., Shakya, S., Baig, Z. (eds.) ICICI 2019. LNDECT, vol. 38, pp. 615–622. Springer, Cham (2020). https://doi.org/10.1007/978-3-030-34080-3_69
10. Banerjee, S., Patil, A.: ECC based encryption algorithm for lightweight cryptography, pp. 641–652 (2019). https://doi.org/10.1007/978-3-030-16657-1
11. Shanthakumari, R., Malliga, S.: Dual layer security of data using LSB inversion image steganography with elliptic curve cryptography encryption algorithm. Multimedia Tools Appl. (2019). https://doi.org/10.1007/s11042-019-7584-6
12. Zhang, X., Wang, X.: Digital image encryption algorithm based on elliptic curve public cryptosystem. IEEE Access **6**, 70025–70034 (2018). https://doi.org/10.1109/ACCESS.2018.2879844
13. Liu, Y., Tang, S., Liu, R., Zhang, L., Ma, Z.: Secure and robust digital image watermarking scheme using logistic and RSA encryption. Expert Syst. Appl. **97**, 95–105 (2018). https://doi.org/10.1016/j.eswa.2017.12.003
14. Jiao, K., Ye, G., Dong, Y., Huang, X., He, J.: Image Encryption Scheme Based on a Generalized Arnold Map and RSA Algorithm (2020)
15. https://www.cybrary.it/0p3n/hide-secret-message-inside-image-using-lsb-steganography/

Multi-resolution Steganalysis of JPEG Images Using the Contrast of DCT Coefficients

Jiang Yu, Changqi Zhang, Yudong Li, and Wen Si[✉]

Faculty of Business Information, Shanghai Business School, Shanghai 201400,
People's Republic of China
heroyujiang@163.com, zhangcq@sbs.edu.cn, lydmm_2002@163.com,
siwen@fudan.edu.cn

Abstract. This paper proposes a novel JPEG steganalytic scheme, which combines the designing of feature called as the Contrast of Discrete Cosine Transform (DCT) coefficients, multi-resolution decomposition. Unlike the conventional steganalytic schemes, without using the co-occurrence to show directly the correlation between the DCT coefficients, the original JPEG image is decompressed into spatial domain and, applying the Fast Discrete Curvelet Transform (FDCT), the spatial version is resolved into several multi-resolution subimages. After transforming all the spatial subimages into JPEG image, the contrast of two DCT coefficients is turned into an angle and the l_2 norm is used as the weight of the angle. Therefore, the new feature is seen as a union of the first-order statistics of weighted angle. On modern stegnographic algorithm JPEG Universal Wavelet Relative Distortion (J-UNIWARD), we demonstrate the proposed scheme achieves more accurate detection than Cartesian-calibrated feature (CFstar) and is superior to the Cartesian-calibrated JPEG Rich Model (CC-JRM) at lower embedding rate.

Keywords: Steganalysis · Multi-resolution · Contrast of Discrete Cosine Transform coefficients · Affine transformation

1   Introduction

Seganography is the art to secretly deliver messages by slightly embedding of cover images [1]. Generally, the effect of embedding is equivalent to add an independent noise-like signal to a cover [2–9]. For achieving higher security, the practical steganographic algorithms first define a distortion function to measure the risk of modification of each cover element [10, 11]. Then, a dual convolutional code equipped with the Viterbi algorithm named as syndrome trellis coding (STC) is employed to minimize the total risk generated by embedding operation [12, 13]. As the adversary of steganography, steganalysis aim to find covert communication by the statistic difference between cover and stego images.

With the rapid sharing and propagation of JPEG images on the Internet and in social networks, many researchers design steganographic algorithms of JPEG images. In the JPEG domain, based on the STC, the typical algorithm [14] is the uniform embedding

© Springer Nature Singapore Pte Ltd. 2020
G. Xu et al. (Eds.): FCS 2020, CCIS 1286, pp. 628–640, 2020.
https://doi.org/10.1007/978-981-15-9739-8_46

distortion (UED) which not use any side information denoted as rounding distortion with respect to the raw/uncompressed image. Currently, J-UNIWARD is the most secure embedding algorithm and the corresponding distortion function is defined as a sum of different directional changes of decompressed image [18, 19]. The mechnisem of above mentioned steganographic algorithms can preserve the statistics of transform coefficients or embed the data into the complex area to obtain better security [15, 16].

As discussed before, the goal of steganalysis is to detect the presence of secretly hidden data. Modern steganography detectors consist of two basic parts: a low-dimensional statistical model (statistical feature) and a machine learning tool (classifier). The statistical model is considered as a heuristic dimensionality reduction of the processed image and its sensitivity to steganographic changes is correlated with the detection accuracy [17]. The common method to enhance the sensitivity of feature is to supress the image content with diverse high-pass filters and effectively expose the steganographic changes. Moreover, the formed model can capture dependencies among individual pixels or DCT coefficients [29]. The machine learning tools, such as SVM [32] or ensembel classifier [30], can be trained based on the statistical difference of model between cover and stego images and the trained classifier can be used to detect the image is cover or stego one.

In this paper, we propose a novel scheme for JPEG steganalysis with multi-resolution decomposition and affine transformation. Firstly, the original JPEG image is decompressed to a spatial one. Then, the most powerful tool named as FDCT is applied to decompose the spatial image and, discarding different FDCT coefficients, we can obtain several spatial subimages with different resolution, such as complex or coarse subimage [31]. With the same quality factor, we can create the corresponding JPEG subimages. These operations can be seen as to suppress the smooth ingredient within the spatial domain and, moreover, the steganographic changes scatter in the original image is redistributed into all JPEG subimages with the non-linear pattern. In order to get the weak correlation between the DCT coefficients of obtained JPEG subimages, without using the co-occurrence matrix, we propose an alternative statistical description of co-occurrence matrix to indicate the joint probability statistic of DCT coefficients. Here, we turn the ratio of DCT coefficients into an angle and l_2 norm of coefficients is calculated as the weight of resulting angle. Finally, we use the weighted histogram of angle as the steganalytic feature named as the contrast of DCT coefficients (CoDC). The proposed scheme brings several advantages over the previous representation based on co-occurrence matrix. Since the quantization and truncation operation are not used, effective steganographic changes of long-range dependencies cannot be preserved. On the other hand, the dimension of the CoDC is linear with the corresponding parameters. Therefore, we can achieve a desired trade-off between detection accuracy and feature dimensionality. The proposed scheme is illustrated by the following flowchart Fig. 1.

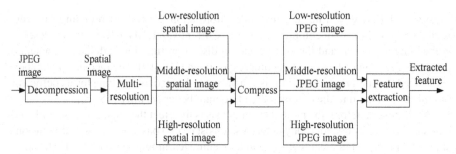

Fig. 1. Flowchart of proposed scheme

2 Related Work

In the most traditional steganalysis schemes of JPEG image, the main task to the steganalyzer is the designing of feature and, then, the proper ensemble classifier can be trained based on the feature difference between the cover and stego images. Generally, the steganalysis combines the training/testing process and the corresponding framework is shown in Fig. 2.

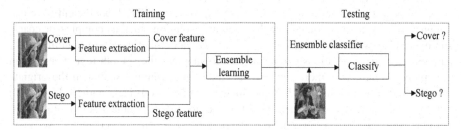

Fig. 2. Framework of typical steganalysis

For JPEG steganalysis, the statistical model (statistical feature) is key to capture the steganographic changes. In [20], the first feature-based steganalytic method for JPEG images using 23 statistical calculations is introduced. Currently, the feature sets for detection of steganography in JPEG images are classified into two categories. The first kind is based on the Markov model which is employed to reveal the weak correlation by sample intra- and inter-block co-occurrences of DCT coefficients. An typical feature based on the Markov model is PEV-274. Moreover, using the Cartesian calibration technique, the dimensionality of the extended version CC-PEV is 548. In [21], the features are designed based on the differential neighboring joint density on the absolute array of DCT coefficients between the original JPEG images and the calibrated versions. The final feature is the average of multiple calibrated features [22, 23]. Since the Markov model represented by the co-occurrence matrix is effective to many steganographic algorithms [24, 25], J. Kodovsky et al. proposed 7850-dimensional CFstar feature set using diverse DCT coefficients pairs. In [26], the absolute values of DCT coefficients in a JPEG image are viewed as weakly dependent parallel channels and the joint probability distribution of truncated differences between DCT coefficient pairs is represented by the co-occurrence matrix. This scheme is named as JPEG Rich Model (JRM) [27] and the dimensionality of Cartesian calibration version of JRM is 22510. With the aid of 64kernel of the DCT (the so-called undecimated DCT), the second kind of features DCTR (Discrete Cosine Transform Residual) is desinged as the first-order statistics of quantized noise residual computed from the decompressed JPEG image [28]. DCTR owing 8000-dimension and low computational complexity is seen as a counterpart to the projection spatial rich model.

3   Obtaining Multi-resolution JPEG Images

In this section, we introduce the processing of getting multi-resolution JPEG subimages with the multi-resolution decomposition technique. First, the original JPEG image is decompressed to the spatial domain with a quality factor. Then, after applying the multi-resolution decomposition, we can obtain the multi-resolution spatial subimages. Finally, all spatial subimages are recompressed to obtain the corresponding JPEG subimages with same quality factor.

3.1   Decompression

We note that the target of multi-resolution decomposition is the spatial image. Hence, the original JPEG image must be decompressed into the spatial domain. After applying the JPEG decompression algorithm, the spatial image is generated using standard quantization matrix and inverse DCT (IDCT).

Assume the size of given JPEG image $\mathbf{X}$ is $M \times N$. Given a block $\mathbf{D}_{xy}^{(i,j)} \in \mathbf{X}^{8 \times 8}$ of $\mathbf{X}$, with the 8×8 quantification matrix $\mathbf{Q}_{xy}$, the decompressed/unquantized spatial block is computed as

$$\tilde{\mathbf{Z}}_{xy}^{(i,j)} = \mathbf{D}_{xy}^{(i,j)} \cdot \mathbf{Q}_{xy}, \tag{1}$$

where (x, y) indicates the horizontal and vertical spatial frequencies in the (i, j)th 8×8 DCT block, $(x, y) \in \{0, 1, \ldots, 7\}^2$ and $i, j \in \left\{1, 2, \ldots, \lceil M/8 \rceil \cdot \lceil N/8 \rceil \right\}$. Then, the decompressed spatial block $\tilde{\mathbf{Y}}_i$ is calculated as

$$\tilde{\mathbf{Y}}_{xy}^{(i,j)} = \text{trunc}_T (\text{round}(\text{IDCT}(\tilde{\mathbf{Z}}_{xy}^{(i,j)}))), \tag{2}$$

where the operation $trunc(\cdot)$ truncates integers to a finite range, $round(\cdot)$ operation makes the undecimaed coefficients to the nearest integer and T is the threshold. Collecting all the blocks $\tilde{\mathbf{Y}}_{xy}^{(i,j)}$, the decompressed corresponding version $\mathbf{Y}$ of JPEG image $\mathbf{X}$ is obtained.

3.2   Multi-resolution Decomposition

To achieve diverse representation, the decompessed spatial image $\mathbf{Y}$ can be decomposited into sveral subimages according to the resolution of image. From the view of multi-resolution, to the best of our knowledge, the Fast Discrete Curvelet Transform is the best mathematical transform for decomposition of spatial image. In this paper, we use the FDCT($\cdot$) implemented as *fdct_wrapping* in Matlab when inputting pixels represented as 'double'. For the full description of FDCT, we limit this section to be brief description and refer the reader to the original paper for more details [30]. Below, we focus on the application of the FDCT.

Applying the FDCT, the transform coefficients are computed according to two different parameters denoted as direction and angle. Suppose the transform coefficient matrices are $C_{r,j}$, according to the scale parameter r, these coefficients can be classified into three categories, where $r \in \{1, 2, 3, 4, 5, 6\}$ and j stands for the direction parameter. $C_{1,j}$ is the low-frequency coefficient which could be used to form the coarse image. When $r \in \{2, 3, 4, 5\}$, the corresponding coefficients are called middle-frequency coefficient groups which are used to generate several detailed spatial image. In middle-frequency coefficients, each group contains multiple sub-coefficients which are created by diverse directional low- or high-pass filters. For example, if $r = 2$, 32 directional filters is employed and $C_{2,j}$ contains four coefficient matrices with different sizes. If r is equal to 6, we can use the third high frequency coefficient $C_{6,j}$ to form the fine image consisting of edge and texture ingredients of the decompessed spatial image Y. In Fig. 3, we show four subimages using different FDCT coefficients.

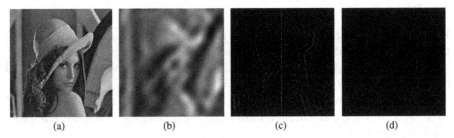

Fig. 3. (a) Original cover, (b) Coarse image (only C_1 is used), (c) Rough image (only C_3 is retained) and (d) Detailed image (only C_5 is employed).

We note that the main ingredient of normal spatial image is the smooth region. Therefore, for effectively suppressing the image content and exposing the steganographic changes distributed in the complex region, we discard the low- and middle-frequency coefficients gradually. Thus, the smooth and coarse components of image Y are removed and complex part is left. After the inverse FDCT operation, we can obtain diverse subimages. Clearly, unlike the usage of high-pass filters, this operation is interpreted as an alternative method to improve the signal to noise ratio. In the proposed scheme, six multi-resolution spatial images are calculated as following:

$$Y_1^{MR} = \text{IFDCT}(C_{r,j}), \ r \in \{1, 2, 3, 4, 5, 6\}, \tag{3}$$

$$Y_2^{MR} = \text{IFDCT}(C_{r,j}), \ r \in \{2, 3, 4, 5, 6\}, \tag{4}$$

$$Y_3^{MR} = \text{IFDCT}(C_{r,j}), \ r \in \{3, 4, 5, 6\}, \tag{5}$$

$$\mathbf{Y}_4^{MR} = \text{IFDCT}(\mathbf{C}_{r,j}), \ r \in \{4, 5, 6\}, \tag{6}$$

$$\mathbf{Y}_5^{MR} = \text{IFDCT}(\mathbf{C}_{r,j}), \ r \in \{5, 6\}, \tag{7}$$

$$\mathbf{Y}_6^{MR} = \text{IFDCT}(\mathbf{C}_{r,j}), \ r \in \{6\}, \tag{8}$$

where MR stands for the multi-resolution and IFDCT is inverse FDCT. Obviously, $\mathbf{Y}_1^{MR}$ is the smooth spatial subimages $\mathbf{Y}$, four subimages $\mathbf{Y}_2^{MR}, \mathbf{Y}_3^{MR}, \mathbf{Y}_4^{MR}, \mathbf{Y}_5^{MR}$ contain coarse ingredients of image and $\mathbf{Y}_6^{MR}$ is the fine subimage.

3.3 Compression

Assume the multi-resolution spatial subimages $\mathbf{Y}_g^{MR}$ is sized by $M \times N$, where $g \in \{1, 2, 3, \ldots, 6\}$. We use Matlab's '*imwrite*' with the same quality factors to create corresponding JPEG image. This way, we guarantee that six JPEG images $\mathbf{X}_g^{MR}$ were created with the same JPEG compressor.

4   Construction Contrast of DCT Coefficients (CoDC)

In this section, without using the co-occurrence matrix, we describe a new statistical feature set for the steganalysis of the JPEG images to get the joint probability distribution of DCT coefficients of intra- and inter-block. In the proposed scheme, the ratio of multiple DCT coefficients is transformed into an angle and the l_2 norm of coefficient pair is used as the weight of angle. Here, the new feature is called as contrast of DCT Coefficients (CoDC) combing the angle and weight.

4.1 DCT Coefficients Pairs

The DCT coefficient pairs of the proposed scheme are an existing set of JPEG coefficients pairs incorporated in the CC-JRM. All the coefficient pairs are generated from six matrices $\mathbf{A}^\times, \mathbf{A}^\rightarrow, \mathbf{A}^\downarrow, \mathbf{A}^\searrow, \mathbf{A}^\Rightarrow, \mathbf{A}^\Downarrow$ originated from a recompressed JPEG image $\mathbf{X}_g^{MR}$ and the corresponding matrices is defined as following:

$$\mathbf{A}_{i,j}^\times = \left| \mathbf{D}_{i,j} \right|, \quad i = 1, \ldots, M, j = 1, \ldots, N, \tag{9}$$

$$\mathbf{A}_{i,j}^\rightarrow = \left| \mathbf{D}_{i,j} \right| - \left| \mathbf{D}_{i,j+1} \right|, \quad i = 1, \ldots, M, j = 1, \ldots, N-1, \tag{10}$$

$$\mathbf{A}_{i,j}^\downarrow = \left| \mathbf{D}_{i,j} \right| - \left| \mathbf{D}_{i+1,j} \right|, \quad i = 1, \ldots, M-1, j = 1, \ldots, N, \tag{11}$$

$$\mathbf{A}_{i,j}^\searrow = \left| \mathbf{D}_{i,j} \right| - \left| \mathbf{D}_{i+1,j+1} \right|, \quad i = 1, \ldots, M-1, j = 1, \ldots, N-1, \tag{12}$$

$$\mathbf{A}_{i,j}^\Rightarrow = \left| \mathbf{D}_{i,j} \right| - \left| \mathbf{D}_{i,j+8} \right|, \quad i = 1, \ldots, M, j = 1, \ldots, N-8, \tag{13}$$

$$\mathbf{A}_{i,j}^{\Downarrow} = \left| \mathbf{D}_{i,j} \right| - \left| \mathbf{D}_{i+8,j} \right|, \quad i = 1, \ldots, M - 8, \, j = 1, \ldots, N. \tag{14}$$

Clearly, the elements of matrix $\mathbf{A}^{\times}$ are the absolute values of DCT coefficients. Three matrices $\mathbf{A}^{\rightarrow}$, $\mathbf{A}^{\downarrow}$, $\mathbf{A}^{\searrow}$ are the difference matrices calculated along the horizontal, vertical and diagonal directions, respectively. The ingredient of the left two matrices $\mathbf{A}^{\Rightarrow}$, $\mathbf{A}^{\Downarrow}$ is the inter-block differences. The proposed feature CoDC will be computed from the coefficient pairs extracted from the following six matrices $\mathbf{A}^{*}$, where $* \in \{\times, \rightarrow, \downarrow, \searrow, \Rightarrow, \Downarrow\}$.

Suppose two selected coefficients of one block $\mathbf{D}_{xy}^{(i,j)}$ are located at (x, y) and $(x + \Delta x, y + \Delta y)$, the corresponding coefficient pair is defined as $\left(e_{x,y}, e_{x+\Delta x, y+\Delta y} \right)$. Therefore, according to the mutual positions of coefficient of each matrix $\mathbf{A}^{*}$, we can create the coefficient pairs matrix $\left(\mathbf{E}_{x,y}^{*}, \mathbf{E}_{x+\Delta x, y+\Delta y}^{*} \right)$. To give diverse representation of correlation of multiple coefficients, we give ten modes as following:

$$H_1 = \{ (x, y, x + 0, y + 1) | 0 \le x; \ 0 \le y; \ x + y \le 5 \}, \tag{15}$$

$$H_2 = \{ (x, y, x + 0, y + 1) | 0 \le x; \ 0 \le y; \ x + y \le 5 \} \cup \{ (x, y, 1, -1) | 0 \le x \le y; \ x + y \le 5 \}, \tag{16}$$

$$H_3 = \{ (x, y, x, y + 2) | 0 \le x; \ 0 \le y; \ x + y \le 4 \}, \tag{17}$$

$$H_4 = \{ (x, y, y - x, x - y) | 0 \le x < y; \ x + y \le 5 \}, \tag{18}$$

$$H_5 = \{ (x, y, 2, 2) | 0 \le x \le y; \ x + y \le 4 \} \cup \{ (x, y, 1, -2) | 0 \le x < y; \ x + y \le 5 \}, \tag{19}$$

$$H_6 = \{ (x, y, -1, 2) | 1 \le x; \ 0 \le y; \ x + y \le 5 \}, \tag{20}$$

$$H_7 = \{ (x, y, 0, 8) | 0 \le x; \ 0 \le y; \ x + y \le 5 \}, \tag{21}$$

$$H_8 = \{ (x, y, 8, 8) | 0 \le x \le y; \ x + y \le 5 \}, \tag{22}$$

$$H_9 = \{ (x, y, -8, 8) | 0 \le x \le y; \ x + y \le 5 \}, \tag{23}$$

$$H_{10} = \{ (x, y, y - x, x - y + 8) | 0 \le x; \ 0 \le y; \ x + y \le 5 \}. \tag{24}$$

Obviously, for six modes H_1, H_2, H_3, H_4, $H_5 H_6$, the chosen coefficient pairs are within a DCT block. Therefore, these modes can capture the mutual relationship of the DCT coefficients of the 8×8 intra-block along the horizontal, vertical, diagonal and minor-diagonal directions. Meanwhile, the offset $(\Delta x, \Delta y)$ of other four modes H_7, H_8, H_9, H_{10} can make the selected coefficient pairs $\left(e_{x,y}, e_{x+\Delta x, y+\Delta y} \right)$ distribute into different DCT blocks along multiple directions. Hence, the generated pairs can be utilized to create the statistic feature to represent the jointly relationship of inter-blocks. In the propose scheme, based on the defined ten modes, 314 coefficient pairs are generated and the corresponding coefficient matrix pairs are denoted as $\left(\mathbf{E}_{x,y}^{*}, \mathbf{E}_{x+\Delta x, y+\Delta y}^{*} \right)$.

4.2 Proposed Feature

In this subsection, we describe the proposed feature CoDC to represent the jointly prob-ability statistic of coefficient pair. Firstly, two matrices $\mathbf{E}^*_{x,y}$ and $\mathbf{E}^*_{x+\Delta x,y+\Delta y}$ are seg-mented into several non-overlapping $r \times r$ smaller matrices and the generated coefficient matrix pairs is denoted as $\left(\bar{\mathbf{E}}^*_{x,y}, \bar{\mathbf{E}}^*_{x+\Delta x,y+\Delta y} \right)$. Then, the ratio matrix $\mathbf{RA}$ containing $r \times r$ elements is computed as

$$\mathbf{RA} = \frac{\bar{\mathbf{E}}^*_{x,y}}{\bar{\mathbf{E}}^*_{x+\Delta x,y+\Delta y}}. \tag{25}$$

Here, $r = 6$ is recommended. Applying the arctangent operation, we obtain the angle matrix

$$\mathbf{AN} = \arctan(\mathbf{RA}). \tag{26}$$

Assume the each element of $\mathbf{AN}$ is α_l, according the categories of matrices $\mathbf{A}^*$, each α_l is located within the region $\Psi = [0, 2\pi]$ or $\Psi = \left[0, \pi/2\right]$, where $l \in [1, 2, \ldots, r \times r]$. To give a proper statistical representation of α_l, we use the parameter β to segment the region Ψ into several non-overlapping domains and a set of quantization centroids are described as

$$\left\{ \beta, 2\beta, \ldots, \lfloor 2\pi/\beta \rfloor \right\}, \tag{27}$$

$$\left\{ \beta, 2\beta, \ldots, \lfloor \pi/(2 \cdot \beta) \rfloor \right\}. \tag{28}$$

Meanwhile, a quantizer Φ_Ψ is defined as

$$\Phi_{\Psi,\beta}(e_{x,y}) \triangleq \arg\min_{\beta \in \Psi} \left| e_{x,y} - \beta \right|. \tag{29}$$

Formally, the effect of Φ_Ψ makes a decimal angle to an integer. Here, we use the l_2 norm of $(e_{x,y}, e_{x+\Delta x,y+\Delta y})$ as the weight of the corresponding angle. Combing the weight and the angle α_l, the new feature CoDC is calculated as

$$\mathbf{F}(k\beta; \Psi) = \sum_{\alpha \in \mathbf{AN}} \left(e^2_{x,y} + e^2_{x+\Delta x,y+\Delta y} \right)^{1/2} \cdot \left[Q_{\Psi,\beta}(\alpha) = k\beta \right], \tag{30}$$

where $k \in \left(0, \lfloor 2\pi/\beta \rfloor \right)$ or $k \in \left(0, \lfloor \pi/(2 \cdot \beta) \rfloor \right)$. Formally, $[\cdot]$ is the Iversion bracket function. It implies that, if the statements S is 0, the Iversion bracket $[S] = 1$. However, if S is not equal to $0, [S] = 0$. Applying the Eqs. (29) and (30) to all the matrix pairs, we can obtain multiple subfeatures which will be averaged to form the ultimate feature. The flowchart of forming the CoDC feature is illustrated in Fig. 4.

Due to all the coefficients of the matrix $\mathbf{A}^\times$ are positive, the created angle α_l is distributed in the region $\left[0, \pi/2\right]$ and the scalar quantizer Φ_Ψ owns $\lfloor \pi/(2 \cdot \beta) \rfloor + 1$ bins. However, when $* \in \{\rightarrow, \downarrow, \searrow, \Rightarrow, \Downarrow\}$, the statistical region of angles generated from $\mathbf{A}^*$ is $[0, 2\pi]$. Therefore, once β is fixed, Φ_Ψ have $\lfloor 2\pi/\beta \rfloor + 1$ bins. In the proposed scheme, the parameter β is set to 18 and the dimensionality is 7 or 21. Here, the two

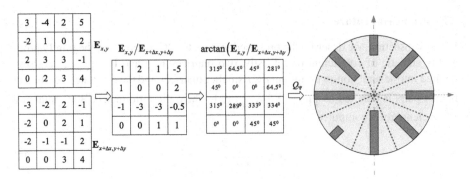

Fig. 4. The flowchart of forming the CoDC feature

marginal bins, such as 0 and 2π, will be emerged into one and the dimensionality of fused feature is reduced to 6 or 20. For controlling the total dimensionality, we fold the subfeature and the dimensionality will be changed into 3 or 10. When the feature extraction is applied on the created 314 DCT coefficients pairs and 6 recompressed JPEG images, the dimensionality of the acquired feature is 5181. Furthermore, we use the Cartesian calibration, which doubles the dimensionality to 10362.

5   Experimental Results and Analysis

In this section, we illustrate the detectability of the proposed scheme for the most security JPEG steganographic scheme J-UNIWARD. Meanwhile, two universal feature sets of JPEG domain named as CFstar and CC-JRM are used as the comparison methods. The test database BOSSbase 1.01 contains 10000 images with a fixed size 512×512. With the JPEG quality factor 75 and 95, we create JPEG images on a range of different relative payloads expressed in terms of bits per non-zero AC coefficient (bpnzac). All images are divided into two halves for training and testing with same number. The minimal total error P_E under equal priors achieved on the testing set is defined as

$$P_E = \min_{P_{FA}} \frac{1}{2}(P_{FA} + P_{MD}),\tag{33}$$

where P_{FA} and P_{MD} stand for the probabilities of false alarm and missed detection [30].

In Fig. 5, we show detection results with four kinds of subimages for quality factor 75 on 1000 images at 0.4 bpnzac. The mode 'low' is the subimage generated from the low-frequency coefficients. The 'middle' stands for the rough subimage formed with middle-frequency coefficients. The third mode 'high' represents the detailed subimage which is created with the high-frequency coefficients. The last mode 'middle+high' is the subimage containing the middle-frequency and the high-frequency coefficients.

Just as stated above, we obtain six spatial subimages $\mathbf{Y}_g^{MR}$, where $g \in \{1, 2, 3, \ldots, 6\}$. Here, in order to acquire best detection accuracy, we define eight composited modes of subimages to find optimal combination of the subimages. The test is carried on the 1000 images at 0.4 bpnzac.

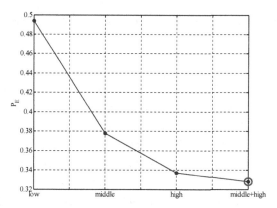

Fig. 5. Detection results for detecting J-UNIWARD with different coefficients.

For the mode 'F1', six subimages are used to extract the CoDC feature. Then, for the mode 'F2' to 'F6', each subimage is discarded one by one and the left subimages are used to extract feature. Using three subimages $\mathbf{X}_1^{MR}$, $\mathbf{X}_2^{MR}$ and $\mathbf{X}_3^{MR}$, the feature of mode 'F7' is formed. At last, the feature of mode 'F8' is the average of the individual features extracted from the subimages $\mathbf{X}_4^{MR}$, $\mathbf{X}_5^{MR}$ (Fig. 6).

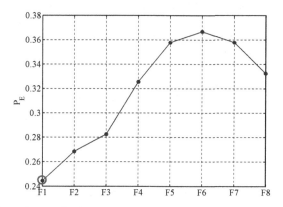

Fig. 6. Detection results for J-UNIWARD using different resolution image set.

Table 1 shows that, for quality factor 75, CoDC outperforms the CFstar by about 0.58% for four payloads on J-UNIWARD algorithm. Compared with another typical JPEG steganalytic algorithm CC-JRM, when the corresponding payload is smaller than 0.3 bpnzac, the proposed CoDC is spurious to CC-JRM by about 0.33%. However, when the payload is equal to 0.3 bpnzac, CoDC is slightly worse than CC-JRM. For another quality factor 95, it is obviously that, when the payload is smaller than 0.2 bpnzac, the proposed feature CoDC gives better detection accuracy. However, when the payload is larger than 0.2 bpnzac, CoDC is slight lower than the two compared methods. According to the full detection results, we must confirm that, for the typical modern content adaptive embedding algorithm J-UNIWARD, the proposed scheme can provide better detection accuracy than CFstar across a set of payloads and is superior to the CC-JRM at lower embedding rate.

Table 1. Performance comparison of three steganalytic schemes for detection J-UNIWARD

bpnzac	Detecting J-UNIWARD (QF 75)			Detecting J-UNIWARD (QF 95)		
	CFstar	CC-JRM	CoDC	CFstar	CC-JRM	CoDC
0.05	0.4900	0.4906	**0.4865**	0.5017	0.5006	**0.4962**
0.1	0.4714	0.4698	**0.4672**	0.4977	0.4966	**0.4913**
0.2	0.4206	0.4096	**0.4068**	0.4824	0.4792	**0.4820**
0.3	0.3554	0.3385	**0.3496**	0.4532	0.4508	**0.4634**

6   Conclusion

In this work, we propose a novel JPEG steganalysis scheme using the multi-resolution decomposition. In order to get optimal detection results for highly secure content-adaptive steganographic algorithms, applying the decompression and compression operations, the original JPEG image is transformed into several multi-resolution JPEG subimages with the same JPEG quality factor and FDCT. Then, the joint probability distribution of the DCT coefficients is changed into an angle and the l_2 norm of coefficients is denoted as the weight of angle. Finally, the ultimate feature is represented as the weighed histogram of angles. The steganographic changes of long-range dependencies is preserved perfectly and we hope the diversity of feature can be improved with other multi-resolution methods.

References

1. Sharp, T.: An implementation of key-based digital signal steganography. In: Moskowitz, I.S. (ed.) IH 2001. LNCS, vol. 2137, pp. 13–26. Springer, Heidelberg (2001). https://doi.org/10.1007/3-540-45496-9_2
2. Fridrich, J., Goljan, M., Du, R.: Reliable detection of LSB steganography in color and grayscale images. In: Proceedings of the ACM, Special Session on Multimedia Security and Watermarking, Canada, pp. 27–30, 5 October 2001
3. Ker, A.D.: Improved detection of LSB steganography in grayscale images. In: Proceedings of 7th International Workshop on Information Hiding, vol. 3200, pp. 97–115 (2004)
4. Ker, A.D.: Steganalysis of LSB matching in grayscale images. IEEE Signal Process. Lett. **12**(6), 441–444 (2005)
5. Eggers, J.J., Baeuml, R., Girod, B.: Communications approach to image steganography. In: Proceedings of SPIE Electronic Imaging, Security and Watermarking of Multimedia Content IV, vol. 4675, pp. 26–37 (2002)

6. Franz, E.: Steganography preserving statistical properties. In: Proceedings of 5th International Workshop on Information Hiding, vol. 2578, pp. 278–294 (2002)
7. Böhme, R., Westfeld, A.: Exploiting preserved statistics for steganalysis. In: Proceedings of 6th International Workshop on Information Hiding, vol. 3200, pp. 82–96 (2004)
8. Westfeld, A.: High capacity depsite better steganalysis: F5–a steganographic algorithm. In: Proceedings of 4th International Workshop on Information Hiding, vol. 2137, pp. 289–302 (2001)
9. Pevný, T., Fridrich, J.: Benchmarking for steganography. In: Solanki, K., Sullivan, K., Madhow, U. (eds.) IH 2008. LNCS, vol. 5284, pp. 251–267. Springer, Heidelberg (2008). https://doi.org/10.1007/978-3-540-88961-8_18
10. Fridrich, J., Filler, T.: Practical methods for minimizing embedding impact in steganography. In: Proceedings of SPIE, Electronic Imaging, Security, Steganography, and Watermarking of Multimedia Contents VI, San Jose, CA,vol. 6050, pp. 650502.1–15 (2007)
11. Filler, T., Fridrich, J.: Gibbs construction in steganography. IEEE Trans. Inf. Forensics Secur. 5(4), 705–720 (2010)
12. Filler, T., Fridrich, J., Judas, J.: Minimizing embedding impact in steganography using trellis-coded quantization. In: Proceedings of SPIE, Electronic Imaging, Media Forensics and Security XII, CA, San Jose, pp. 1–14, 18–20 January 2010
13. Filler, T., Judas, J., Fridrich, J.: Minimizing additive distortion in steganography using syndrome-trellis codes. IEEE Trans. Inf. Forensics Secur. 6(3), 920–935 (2011)
14. Guo, L., Ni, J., Shi, Y.-Q.: An efficient JPEG steganographic scheme using uniform embedding. In: Proceedings of Fourth IEEE International Workshop on Information Forensics and Security, Tenerife, Spain, 2–5 December 2012
15. Filler, T., Fridrich, J.: Design of adaptive steganographic schemes for digital images. In: Proceedings of SPIE, Electronic Imaging, Media Watermarking, Security and Forensics of Multimedia XIII, vol. 7880, San Francisco, CA, pp. 1–14, 23–26 January 2011
16. Holub, V., Fridrich, J.: Designing steganographic distortion using directional filters. In: Proceedings of 4th International Workshop on Information Forensics and Security, Tenerife, Spain, 2–5 December 2012
17. Li, B., Tan, S., Wang, M., Huang, J.: Investigation on cost assignment in spatial image steganography. IEEE Trans. Inf. Forensics Secur. 9(8), 1264–1277 (2014)
18. Holub, V., Fridrich, J.: Digital image steganography using universal distortion. In: EURASIP Journal on Information Security, Special Issue on Revised Selected Papers of the 1st ACM IH and MMS Workshop, pp. 59–68 (2013)
19. Holub, V., Fridrich, J., Denemark, T.: Universal distortion function for steganography in an arbitrary domain. EURASIP J. Inf. Secur. 2014(1), 1–13 (2014). https://doi.org/10.1186/1687-417X-2014-1
20. Fridrich, J.: Feature-based steganalysis for JPEG images and its implications for future design of steganographic schemes. In: Proceedings of 6th International Workshop on Information Hiding, vol. 3200, pp. 67–81 (2004)
21. Shi, Y., Chen, C., Chen, W.: A markov process based approach to effective attacking JPEG steganography. In: Proceedings of 8th International Workshop on Information Hiding, vol. 4437, pp. 249–264 (2006)
22. Pevný, T., Fridrich, J.: Merging markov and DCT features for multi-class JPEG Steganalysis. In: Proceedings of SPIE, Electronic Imaging, International Society for Optics and Photonics, vol. 6505, pp. 03–04 (2007)
23. Kodovský, J., Fridrich, J.: Calibration revisited. In: Proceedings of 11th ACM Workshop on Multimedia and Security, pp. 63–64 (2009)
24. Liu, Q.: Steganalysis of DCT-embedding based adaptive steganography and YASS. In: Proceedings of 13th ACM Workshop on Multimedia and Security, pp. 77–86 (2011)

25. Kodovský, J., Fridrich, J.: Steganalysis of JPEG images using rich models. In: Proceedings of SPIE, Electronic Imaging, Media Watermarking, Security, and Forensics of Multimedia XIV, vol. 8303, pp. 0A 1–13 (2012)

26. Holub, V., Fridrich, J.: Low complexity features for JPEG steganalysis using undecimated DCT. IEEE Trans. Inf. Forensics Secur. 10(2), 219–228 (2015)

27. Fridrich, J., Kodovský, J.: Rich models for steganalysis of digital images. IEEE Trans. Inf. Forensics Secur. 7(3), 868–882 (2012)

28. Holub, V., Fridrich, J.: Random projections of residuals for digital image steganalysis. IEEE Trans. Inf. Forensics Secur. 8(12), 1996–2006 (2013)

29. Kodovský, J., Fridrich, J., Holub, V.: Ensemble classifiers for steganalysis of digital media. IEEE Trans. Inf. Forensics Secur. 7(2), 432–444 (2012)

30. Li, F., Zhang, X., Cheng, H., Yu, J.: Digital image steganalysis based on local textural features and double dimensionality reduction. Secur. Commun. Netw. 9(8), 729–736 (2016)

31. Candès, E.J., Demanet, L., Donoho, D., Ying, L.: Fast discrete curvelet transform. Multiscale Model. Simul. 5(3), 861–899 (2006)

32. Vapnik, V.N.: The Nature of Statistical Learning Theory. Springer, New York (1995)

Web Security

A Key Business Node Identification Model for Business Process Based on AE-VIKOR Method

Lixia Xie[1]([✉]) [iD], Huiyu Ni[1] [iD], Guangquan Xu[2] [iD], and Jiyong Zhang[3]

[1] Civil Aviation University of China, Tianjin 300300, China
lxxie@126.com
[2] Tianjin University, Tianjin 300350, China
[3] Swiss Federal Institute of Technology in Lausanne, 1015 Lausanne, Switzerland

Abstract. Based on the research of information security and business continuity management, a key business node identification model for the business process based on AE-VIKOR (Analytic hierarchy process and Entropy weighting VIKOR, AE-VIKOR) method is proposed. Firstly, the business nodes are obtained based on the business process, and the importance decision matrix of business nodes is constructed by quantifying the evaluation attributes of nodes. Secondly, the attribute weight is improved from subjective and objective dimensions to form the combination weight decision matrix, and the AE-VIKOR method is used to calculate the business importance coefficient to identify the key nodes. Finally, when an information security event occurs in the system, the impact of key business nodes on business continuity is analyzed, and the business continuity risk value is calculated to evaluate the business risk to prove the effectiveness of the model. The experimental results of civil aviation departure control system show that the AE-VIKOR method can effectively identify key business nodes, and the impact of key business nodes on business continuity is analyzed, which further proves the efficiency and accuracy of the model.

Keywords: Key business nodes · AE-VIKOR · Business continuity · Risk assessment

1 Introduction

Nowadays, with the rapid development of the Internet, related research fields are more concerned about information security and business continuity management recently. The multi system cooperation of smart mobile devices is closely related to its business continuity. Therefore, when an information security event occurs in a system, it may lead to delay or stagnation of business execution, which will inevitably affect business continuity. Based on the management of business continuity, at present, there are many achievements in the research of business continuity security [1–5]. Key business node identification is very important for business recovery which is one of the research hotspots in the field of risk assessment for the business process. Based on information security risk

G. Xu et al. (Eds.): FCS 2020, CCIS 1286, pp. 643–653, 2020.
https://doi.org/10.1007/978-981-15-9739-8_47

assessment and business continuity management, Torabi et al. [6] put business continuity risk management into the framework of information security risk assessment through business continuity risk analysis. Belov et al. [7] proposed a risk value calculation of the business completion rate by studying the situation of the business resource completion rate and quantitatively assessed the business system risk. Hariyanti et al. [8] proposed a new ISRA (Information security risk assessment) model based on the business process to improve the model based on the organization's assets. VIKOR (Vise Kriterijumska Optimizacija I Kompromisno Resenje in Serbian) is one of the common methods of multi attribute decision making which is often used in risk assessment [9], economics, management and other hot fields.

The contributions of this paper can be summarized as follows. A key business node identification model for the business process based on AE-VIKOR is proposed. The model mainly focused on as follows: 1) The combined weighting from the subjective and objective dimensions is used to improve the attribute weights of the VIKOR method of multi attribute decision-making. 2) When information security events occur in the system, the model can analyze the impact of key business nodes on business continuity, calculate the risk value of business continuity.

The organization of this paper is described as follows: In Sect. 2, data preparation module and data operation module are described in detail. Decision module and analysis module are expounded in Sect. 3. In Sect. 4, the effectiveness of the model is verified by analyzing the business continuity of the departure business and the loading business. Conclusion is given in Sect. 5.

2 Data Preparation Module and Data Operation Module

The key business node identification model is composed of four modules: data preparation module, data operation module, decision module and analysis module (see Fig. 1). Data preparation module and data operation module are described in detail in Sect. 2.

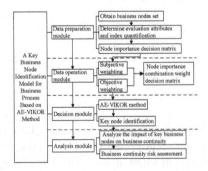

Fig. 1. Key business node identification model

2.1 Data Preparation Module

Through the analysis of the business process, this model extracts all businesses into nodes to form the business node set to be evaluated, which is recorded as $M = \{n_1, n_2,$

$n_3 \ldots n_m$}. Three factors are used to evaluate business importance, which are business node relevance, business user, and business priority. The specific process of indicator quantification of the business node importance attribute is as follows.

According to node centrality theory [10], business relevance can be measured according to the direct relationship between other business nodes and the business node, the value of business node relevance is calculated in Eq. (1). The larger the value is, the more important the business node is. In Eq. (1), g_i is the ratio of connected nodes number of business node i to total nodes number except for it. h_i means nodes number directly connected to node i. m is the total number of business nodes.

$$g_i = h_i / (m - 1) \tag{1}$$

In this paper, business user types are divided into staff, ordinary users, both staff and ordinary users, and 1, 2, 3 level is used to assignment for business user types. The larger the value is, the more important the business is. The importance levels for business user types are defined in Table 1.

Table 1. Importance level of business user type

Category	Value
Ordinary users	1
Staff member	2
Both staff and ordinary users	3

The higher business priority level, the higher the importance of business. The business priority assignment is based on the service characteristics and application types of the business. The business priority level is divided into 1, 2, 3, and 4 levels. The assignment table is shown in Table 2.

Table 2. Business priority table

Business	Service	Application type	Business priority
Background	Without time delay	No special requirement transmission time	1
Interactive	On demand response	Online data interaction and request response mode	2
Flow pattern	Time delay	Real time business and low interaction	3
Conversation	Time delay strictly	Real time business and high quality interaction	4

The data preparation module forms the node importance decision matrix X through the quantification of attributes and the nodes obtained. The matrix X is normalized by

Eq. (2) for comparison. Where, $x_j^{max} = \max\{ x_{i1}, x_{i2}, x_{i3}\}, x_j^{min} = \min\{ x_{i1}, x_{i2}, x_{i3}\}$. The standardized matrix is R.

$$R = \begin{bmatrix} r_{11} & r_{12} & r_{13} \\ r_{21} & r_{22} & r_{23} \\ \vdots & \vdots & \vdots \\ r_{m1} & r_{m2} & r_{m3} \end{bmatrix}$$

$$r_{ij} = (x_{ij} - x_j^{min}) / (x_j^{max} - x_j^{min}) \tag{2}$$

2.2 Data Operation Module

This paper uses the combined weighting to determine the attribute weight to eliminate some subjective influence of attributes and enhance the accuracy of the model.

Table 3. Comparison of business importance assessment attribute indexes

Meaning	Value
Attribute i has the same effect as attribute j	1
Attribute i has a stronger influence than attribute j	3
Attribute i is an absolutely stronger influence than attribute j	5

AHP is used to calculate the subjective weight. Firstly, the business relevance is the local attribute of the business nodes, and its impact is relatively low. Users' impact is stronger than that of the business relevance, and the impact of the business type is greater than others. Therefore, the comparison of the attribute of node importance evaluation is shown in Table 3. Where, 2, 4 indicates that the influence degree of attribute i and attribute j is between 3, 5. According to the subjective influence of business attributes on business importance, an initial comparison matrix A is constructed. Matrix A is normalized to form matrix B according to Eq. (3) Calculate the sum of each row of matrix B and get the set S is $\{0.3185, 0.7815, 1.9000\}$. The set is standardized to get the other set S_1 is $\{0.1062, 0.2605, 0.6333\}$. The element of set S_1 is the subjective weight. After the consistency test, the calculation of consistency test index CI is shown in Eq. (4)–(5). After testing, the subjective weight assignment conforms to the consistency test index. Therefore, the subjective weight of each attribute is obtained which are $w_1^A = 0.1062$, $w_2^A = 0.2065$, $w_3^A = 0.6333$.

$$B = A_{ij} / \sum_{j=1}^{3} A_{ij} \tag{3}$$

$$A = \begin{bmatrix} 1 & \frac{1}{3} & \frac{1}{5} \\ 3 & 1 & \frac{1}{3} \\ 5 & 3 & 1 \end{bmatrix} \quad B = \begin{bmatrix} \frac{1}{9} & \frac{1}{13} & \frac{3}{23} \\ \frac{3}{9} & \frac{3}{13} & \frac{5}{23} \\ \frac{5}{9} & \frac{9}{13} & \frac{15}{23} \end{bmatrix}$$

$$CI = (\lambda_{\max} - n)/(n - 1) \tag{4}$$

$$AW = \lambda_{\max} W \tag{5}$$

Using entropy value to modify the objective weight provides a more reliable basis for the evaluation of business importance. The objective weight is calculated in Eq. (6)–(8).

$$S_{ij} = r_{ij} \bigg/ \sum_{i=1}^{m} r_{ij} \tag{6}$$

$$e_j = -k \sum_{j=1}^{n} S_{ij} \ln S_{ij}, \, j = 1, 2 \cdots, n \tag{7}$$

$$w_j = 1 - e_j \bigg/ \sum_{j=1}^{n} (1 - e_j) \tag{8}$$

Where S_{ij} is the proportion of each indicator of each node in Eq. (6). In Eq. (7), e_j is the information entropy of the j-th index. The objective weight of each attribute is obtained, which are defined as w_1^A, w_2^A, w_3^A.

Combined weight combines subjective weight and objective weight Firstly, weight matrix Y is constructed based on the subjective and the objective method. The combined weight of attributes is calculated by (9)–(11), which is defined as w_z^A, w_z^A, w_z^A.

$$Y = \begin{bmatrix} w_1^A & w_1^O \\ w_2^A & w_2^O \\ w_3^A & w_3^O \end{bmatrix}$$

$$[(R^T Y)^T (R^T Y)]X^* = \lambda_{\max} X^* \tag{9}$$

$$W^* = YX^* \tag{10}$$

$$w_i^z = \left(w_1^* \bigg/ \sum_{j=1}^{3} w_j^*, \, w_2^* \bigg/ \sum_{j=1}^{3} w_j^*, \, w_3^* \bigg/ \sum_{j=1}^{3} w_j^* \right) \tag{11}$$

$$C = w_i^z \times R \tag{12}$$

$\lambda_{\max}$, X^* are the largest eigenvalue and the largest eigenvector of respectively in the Eq. (9).The standardized decision matrix C of node importance combined weight is calculated by Eq. (12).

3   Decision Module and Analysis Module

3.1   Decision Module

The business importance coefficient is calculated and sorted based on the AE-VIKOR method in the module. AE-VIKOR method improves the evaluation attribute weight of the VIKOR method by combined weighting in the data operation module. VIKOR method is one of the common methods of the multi attribute decision model. The method considers both the maximum group utility and the minimum individual regret effect of the object, it focuses on ranking and selecting from a set of alternatives, and determines compromise solutions for a problem with conflicting criteria, which can help the decision-makers to reach a final decision. TOPSIS (Technique for Order Performance by Similarity to Ideal Solution) [11] is also one of the classic multi attribute evaluation methods. AE-VIKOR and TOPSIS are compared by experiments. The maximum group utility value is measured by U_i, the minimum individual regret effect value is calculated by K_i, and Q_i is decision value calculated by the Eq. (13)–(15), v is the coefficient of decision-making mechanism, $v = 1/2$.

$$U_i = \sum_{i=1}^{3} w_i^z c_{ij} \tag{13}$$

$$K_i = \max_i(w_i^z c_{ij}) \tag{14}$$

$$Q_i = v(U_i - U^*)/(U^- - U^*) + (1 - v)(K_i - K^*)/(K^- - K^*) \tag{15}$$

Where $U^* = \min_i U_i, U^- = \max_i U_i, K^* = \min_i K_i, K^- = \max_i K_i$.

AE-VIKOR method is also a compromise ranking method, the feasible solution of which is closest to the ideal solution. Therefore, the AE-VIKOR method is without loss of generality to meet the following two conditions: Condition 1: Acceptable advantage. The first two nodes in sorting are Q_i, Q_j. The conditions shown in formula (16) need to be met. Condition 2: Acceptable stability. The importance coefficients of key business nodes rank first in U_i, K_i. If the above two conditions are met at the same time, the model recognition results are considered valid. Where m is the number of business nodes.

$$Q_i - Q_j \geq 1/(m - 1) \tag{16}$$

The value of Q_i calculated based on the AE-VIKOR method is the business importance coefficient. The key business node is the largest business importance coefficient. Through the calculation of the AE-VIKOR method, the business importance coefficient is between [0, 1].

3.2   Analysis Module

Information security is closely related to business continuity management in the Internet era. The relationship between information security and business continuity is shown in Fig. 2.

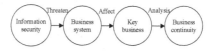

Fig. 2. Relationship between information security and business continuity

The business continuity risk value is calculated by combining the importance coefficient of key business according to business user number, business average execution time of, and resource utilization in this paper. The maximum of business user's numbers, average execution time and resource utilization are respectively set as $u_{max}, t_{max}, r_{max}$. When an information security event occurs, the number of business users, business execution time, and resource utilization rate at i time are defined as u_i, t_i, r_i and the business continuity risk value is calculated by Eq. (17)–(19).

$$P_i = 1 - \frac{1}{3} \sum (u_i, r_i, t_i) / (u_{max}, r_{max}, t_{max}) \tag{17}$$

$$\Delta P = P_1 - P_2 \tag{18}$$

$$L = Q_i * \Delta P \tag{19}$$

Where, the business importance coefficient is Q_i, L is the business continuity risk value. ΔP is between 0 and 1, and the business importance coefficient is between 0 and 1, business continuity risk is classified according to business continuity risk value. When the risk value of business continuity is higher than 0.15, it is considered that business continuity is at higher risk. The business risk value is between 0 and 0.15, so the business continuity risk level table is shown in Table 4 below.

Table 4. The risk level of business continuity

Business continuity risk value	Business continuity risk level
0–0.05	Low
0.05–0.10	Medium
0.10–0.15	High
$L \geq 0.15$	Higher risk

4 Experimental Results and Analysis

4.1 Calculate the Business Importance Coefficient

The civil aviation industry is one of the key industries of information security. Therefore, the experimental object is the civil aviation departure control business process. Its business process is shown in Fig. 3.

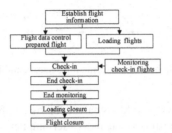

Fig. 3. Departure control business

Table 5. Assignment table of the important attribute index of departure business nodes

Node	Business relevance	Business user	Business priority
n_1	0.2500	3	1
n_2	0.3750	2	1
n_3	0.2500	3	2
n_4	0.5000	3	3
n_5	0.1250	2	2
n_6	0.2500	2	2
n_7	0.1250	2	1
n_8	0.2500	1	1
n_9	0.2500	2	1

All businesses in the departure business process are extracted into nodes to form the business node set to be evaluated, which is recorded as $N = \{n_1, n_2, n_3, n_4, n_5, n_6, n_7, n_8, n_9\}$.respectively represents every business in departure control system in Fig. 3. The decision matrix of node importance is formed by the node and the attributes of each node. According to the assignment of node attribute indicators in the data module, the assignment of departure business node importance attribute indicators is shown in Table 5 The standardized node importance decision matrix R is formed as follows.

$$R = \begin{bmatrix} 0.2917 & 0.4330 & 0.1961 \\ 0.4376 & 0.2887 & 0.1961 \\ 0.2917 & 0.4330 & 0.3922 \\ 0.5835 & 0.4330 & 0.5883 \\ 0.1459 & 0.2887 & 0.3922 \\ 0.2917 & 0.2887 & 0.3922 \\ 0.1459 & 0.2887 & 0.1961 \\ 0.2917 & 0.1443 & 0.1961 \\ 0.2917 & 0.2887 & 0.1961 \end{bmatrix}$$

The subjective weight is $w^A = \{0.1062, 0.2605, 0.6333\}$, which calculated by the AHP method. According to the objective weight calculated by the Entropy method in Sect. 2.2 is $w^O = \{0.3273, 0.3298, 0.3429\}$, the combined weight of the two is $w^Z = \{0.2228, 0.2756, 0.5016\}$. The importance coefficient of departure business node is calculated as $D_i = \{0.1975, 0.1464, 0.5199, 1.000, 0.4844, 0.4947, 0.1048, 0.057, 0.1176\}$ by the AE-VIKOR. It can be seen that the most important factor of n_4 the node is that check-in is the key business of the departure control system.

4.2 Business Continuity Analysis and Risk Assessment

The maximum number of business users, average execution time, and resource utilization rate of the passenger check-in system at T_0 time are respectively corresponding to 1000, 10 s, and 90%. After the information security event occurs in the check-in system at T_0 time, the check-in system data within 1 h can be obtained through monitoring. The loading system is specially monitored and obtained to compare with the check-in system. Table 6 shows the execution of the check-in business system after the information security event.

Table 6. Execution of the check-in business system after an information security event

Business	Check-in			Loading fights		
Execution	Users	Average execution time/s	Resource utilization	Users	Average execution time/s	Resource utilization
T_0	1000	10.0	90%	100	5.0	98%
T_1	800	10.5	85%	80	6.5	81%
T_2	550	12.0	65%	55	7.2	69%
T_3	300	12.5	50%	30	7.8	50%
T_4	100	13.0	25%	10	8.0	28%

It can be seen from Fig. 4 that the business continuity risk value of check-in business increases rapidly after T_0 time, while that of the loading business is relatively slow compared with the check-in business. At T_4 time, the check-in business continuity risk is close to the higher risk, and the loading business continuity at T_4 time is medium. Therefore, the experiment further proves the validity and accuracy of the model.

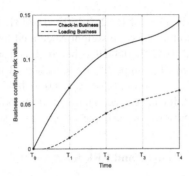

Fig. 4. Business continuity analysis of check-in and loading business

4.3 Comparison of Key Business Identification Methods

In this paper, the AE-VIKOR method is compared with the other four methods. The calculation method and business node ranking of business nodes are shown in Fig. 5 As can be seen from Fig. 5, the AE-VIKOR method is more accurate than the other four methods.

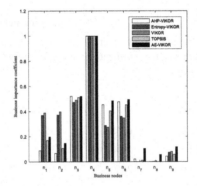

Fig. 5. Different methods used to calculate nodes importance

A combined weight to improve the attribute weight in the AE-VIKOR method used to calculate the business importance coefficient to ensure the accuracy of the results to facilitate the analysis and management of business continuity.

5   Conclusion

The attribute weight is improved by the combined weight and the AE-VIKOR method is used to identify the key business node in this paper. Business continuity risk assessment is carried out by analyzing the key business node's impact on business continuity. The experimental results show that the key business node identification model based on the AE-VIKOR method is more accurate, and the business continuity risk assessment is carried out reasonably. The next step is to analyze the impact of key business on business recovery priority after information security events occur in the system, and further improve the recognition ability and adaptive ability of the model.

References

1. Moldagulova, A., Uskenbayeva, R.K., Satybaldiyeva, R.Z., Kamennova, M.S., Kalpeeva, Z.B., Bektemyssova, G.U.: On identification of hybrid business processes for effective implementation in the form of cloud services. In: 2019 19th International Conference on Control, Automation and Systems (ICCAS), pp. 51–54, IEEE, Jeju (2019)
2. Sherzod, G., Abdukhalil, G., Viktoriya, V.: Formalization of the business process security. In: 2019 International Conference on Information Science and Communications Technologies (ICISCT), pp. 1–3. IEEE, Tashkent (2019)
3. Ming, Q., Songtao, L.: Overview of system wide information management and security analysis. In: 2017 IEEE 13th International Symposium on Autonomous Decentralized System (ISADS), pp. 191–194, IEEE, Bangkok (2017)
4. Stergiopoulos, G., Dedousis, P., Gritzalis, D.: Automatic network restructuring and risk mitigation through business process asset dependency analysis. Comput. Secur. **96**, 101869 (2020)
5. Matulevičius, R., Norta, A., Samarütel, S.: Security requirements elicitation from airline turnaround processes. Bus. Inf. Syst. Eng. **60**, 3–20 (2018)
6. Torabi, S., Giahi, R., Sahebjamnia, N.: An enhanced risk assessment framework for business continuity management systems. Saf. Sci. **89**, 201–218 (2016)
7. Belov, V.M., Pestunov, A.I., Pestunova, T.M.: On the issue of information security risks assessment of business processes. In: Proceedings of the 14th International Scientific-Technical Conference on Actual Problems of Electronics Instrument Engineering APEIE, pp. 136–139. IEEE, Piscataway (2018)
8. Hariyanti, E., Djunaidy, A., Siahaan, D.O.: A conceptual model for information security risk considering business process perspective. In: 2018 4th International Conference on Science and Technology (ICST), pp. 1–6. IEEE (2018)
9. Yang, J., Han, J., Zhang, X.: Information system security risk assessment based on IDAV multi-criteria decision model. In: 2018 12th IEEE International Conference on Anti-counterfeiting, Security, and Identification (ASID), pp. 121–127. IEEE, Xiamen (2018)
10. Shen, Y., Gu, C., Zhao, P.: Structural vulnerability assessment of multi-energy system using a pagerank algorithm. Energy Procedia **158**, 6466–6471 (2019)
11. Piwowarski, M., Danuta, M., Małgorzata, Ł., Mariusz, B., Kesra, N.: TOPSIS and VIKOR methods in study of sustainable development in the EU countries. Procedia Comput. Sci. **126**, 1683–1692 (2018)

An Adaptive Utility Quantification Strategy for Penetration Semantic Knowledge Mining

Yichao Zang[1], Tairan Hu[1(✉)], Rongrong Cao[2], and Junhu Zhu[1]

[1] National Key Laboratory of Mathematical Engineering and Advanced Computing, Zhengzhou 450001, China
aipteamzhouty@aliyun.com
[2] Political College of National Defense University, Shanghai 200433, China

Abstract. Penetration semantic knowledge mining plays an important role in automated penetration testing. The loss of external utility makes it hard to employ high utility itemset mining algorithms to retrieve the knowledge. To overcome this problem, this paper proposes an adaptive utility quantification strategy which could differentiate and quantify external utility of item effectively. Further, incremental high utility pattern tree structure is adopted to maintain utility information for incremental database so as to facilitate the calculation of external utility. The experimental result turns out that high utility itemsets mining algorithms with proposed adaptive utility quantification strategy could mine penetration testing semantic knowledge from raw penetration testing data effectively and efficiently.

Keywords: Penetration semantic knowledge · High utility itemsets mining · Automated penetration testing · Frequent itemsets mining

1 Introduction

With the rapid development of computer network, the security problem becomes much more prominent than ever. Penetration testing shows great advantages in improving security level. It interleaves scanning and vulnerability exploitation actions where scanning action offers information such as operating systems, services etc. based on which security experts choose corresponding vulnerability exploitation program and correct vulnerability exploitation program could motivate further information gathering. Figure 1 shows typical penetration testing scenario where attack path is composed of three steps ①②③, and each step is pair of host information and common vulnerability and exposure exploitation(cve), such as <tomcat 7.0.56, cve-2017-12615>, <windows 7 sp1, cve-2018-0121> etc. The quality or effectiveness of penetration testing depends heavily on security experts' experience and it becomes a hot research topic to automate penetration testing, for which mining penetration semantic knowledge is an essential prerequisite.

© Springer Nature Singapore Pte Ltd. 2020
G. Xu et al. (Eds.): FCS 2020, CCIS 1286, pp. 654–666, 2020.
https://doi.org/10.1007/978-981-15-9739-8_48

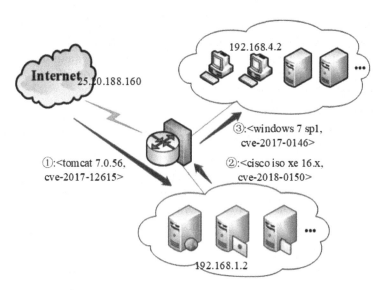

Fig. 1. Typical penetration testing scenario where attack path is composed of three steps ①②③, and each step is pair of host and vulnerability exploitation information.

Penetration semantic knowledge is a kind of mapping relationship {*software:version → vulnerability*} which means that the specific *version* of *software* may cause the *vulnerability*, based on which we could choose corresponding *vulnerability* exploitation program when faced with specific *version* of *software*. Existed researches extract semantic knowledge from penetration testing data through transforming specific vulnerability database [1] such as metasploit framework. Taking *vulnerability*, numbered cve-2019-0708, for example, the affected platforms include windows 7 sp1, windows server 2003 sp2, windows server 2008 sp2, so there are three individual penetration semantic knowledge, namely {windows 7 sp1 → cve-2019-0708}, {windows server 2003 sp2 → cve-2019-0708}, {windows xp sp3 → cve-2019-0708} meaning that when host owns one of the above operating systems, there is great possibility that it owns vulnerability numbered cve-2019-0708, so that we could use corresponding vulnerability exploitation program to control the host. There are two disadvantages for this kind of approach, one is that the semantic knowledge extracted from specific vulnerability database could not match information gathered through scanners, the other is that the penetration semantic knowledge becomes tedious without considering information gathered through multiple scanners. Table 1 shows an example of application, operating system and vulnerability information gathered by Nmap [2] and Shodan [3] scanner. The mapping relationship {Apache httpd:2.4.29 → cve-2018-7584} is our interested penetration knowledge which owns high utility because vulnerability numbered cve-2018-7584 is caused by Apache httpd:2.4.29. The aim of penetration semantic knowledge mining is to discover all of penetration semantic knowledge which owns high utility from raw penetration testing data. High utility itemsets mining algorithms (HUIM) seem could solve the problem but fail because the loss of external utility for each item. To solve this problem, we proposed an adaptive utility quantification strategy ARUQ, which could measure importance of item automatically to achieve penetration semantic knowledge mining.

Table 1. Transactions of application, operating system and vulnerability information for each individual host.

IP	Application	Operating system	Vulnerability
171.3.13.3	OpenSSH:7.2 Apache httpd:2.4.29	Linux kernel:2.6.32	cve-2018-7584 cve-2018-10547
11.4.1.63	OpenSSH:7.4 BIND:9.11 Apache httpd:2.4.29	Linux kernel:2.6.32	cve-2018-7584 cve-2018-10547
41.3.5.175	MySQL:5.5.55, Apache httpd:2.4.29	Linux kernel:2.6.32	cve-2018-7584 cve-2018-10547
121.5.7.15	MySQL:5.7	Linux kernel:2.6.32	

The remainder of the paper is organized as follows. Section 2 presents background knowledge of high utility mining and penetration semantic knowledge mining. Section 3 presents our proposed adaptive utility quantification strategy for each item in penetration testing transaction. Section 4 analyses details of penetration testing data and compares performance of high utility itemsets mining algorithms with proposed strategy on these data with frequent itemsets mining algorithms. Section 5 summarizes our study and points out some future research issues.

2   Background

As penetration semantic knowledge mining could be transformed into high utility itemsets mining problem. It is necessary to introduce some preliminaries and background knowledge of high utility itemsets mining first.

2.1   Preliminaries

Definition 1 (Transaction Database). *Given set I, transaction database D is a set where each item satisfies $T_i \subseteq I, T_i \in D$. For example, the penetration testing transaction database is composed of all records shown in Table 1. A positive value $p(s)$ is called external utility for each item $s \in I$, and the number of s in T_i is called internal utility of item s, represented in $q(s, T_i)$.*

Definition 2 (Utility of item in transaction/database). *The utility of item s in transaction T_i is the product of internal utility and external utility, represented in $u(s, T_i) = p(s) * q(s, T_i)$, the utility of item s in database D is the sum of item s in all transactions belonging to D, represented in $u(s, D) = \sum_{i=1}^{|D|} u(s, T_i)$.*

Definition 3 (Utility of set in transaction/database). *The utility of set X in transaction T_i is the sum of all item utility in the transaction, represented in $u(X, T_i) = \sum_{s \in X} p(s) * q(s, T_i)$, the utility of set X is the sum of all items in database, represented in $u(X, T_i) = \sum_{s \in X} \sum_{i=1}^{|D|} u(s, T_i), X \subseteq T_i$.*

Definition 4 (High Utility Itemsets Mining). *Given a user-specified utility threshold ξ, high utility itemsets mining aims to discover all itemsets X from database D which satisfies $u(X, D) \geq \xi$. In Table 1, the high utility itemset is {Apache httpd:2.4.29, cve-2018-7584} because it is the penetration semantic knowledge we want to mine from transaction database.*

Definition 5 (Penetration Semantic Knowledge Mining). *Penetration semantic knowledge is a collection of itemset $\{item_{causal}, item_{effect}\}$ where $item_{causal}$ is precondition item and $item_{effect}$ is result item. Vividly, we could regard $item_{effect}$ as a bucket and each item appeared together with $item_{effect}$ in a transaction is put into the bucket, and the process of penetration semantic knowledge mining is to filter all irrelevant items, the left items with $item_{effect}$ is final interested penetration semantic knowledge. $\{item_{causal}, item_{effect}\}$ denotes that when $item_{causal}$ occurs, $item_{effect}$ occurs with great possibility. We want to find all $item_{causal}$ which could result in $item_{effect}$, and this process could be formalized as a special kind of high utility itemsets mining problem, which owns the following characteristics:*

- *The external utility for each item is unknown.*
- *The internal utility for each item in each transaction equals 1.*
- *Items appeared frequently for each bucket contribute to high utility.*
- *Items appeared frequently for multiple buckets contribute not to high utility.*
- *The effect item in a transaction must appeared in each individual final high utility itemset.*
- *Every itemset without effect item must not be high utility itemset.*

Penetration semantic knowledge mining aims to discover all causal related itemsets within each individual bucket. The transactions with same effect item are in same bucket, taking Table 1 for example, transactions 1, 2, 3 are in same bucket because all of their effect items include cve-2018-7584. Items Apache httpd:2.4.29 and linux kernel:2.6.32 appeared frequently in the bucket, but Apache httpd:2.4.29 contributes more to discover knowledge {Apache httpd:2.4.29, cve-2018-7584} than linux kernel:2.6.32 because linux kernel:2.6.32 appeared frequently in other buckets, illustrating that linux kernel:2.4.29 is a common item than causal related item in the knowledge. And the result high utility itemset is {Apache httpd:2.4.29, cve-2018-7584}. Penetration semantic knowledge mining aims to discover all of these causal related high utility itemsets.

2.2   High Utility Itemsets Mining

Enough works have been done to accelerate high utility itemset mining [4,5], which could be divided into three categories, namely candidate based algorithms, without candidate based algorithms and other algorithms. Two-Phase algorithm [6] is a famous and classical candidate based high utility itemset mining algorithm which is composed of two phase, the first phase prunes search space and generates candidates by proposed transaction weight downward closure property while the second phase scans database to filter high utility itemsets from high transaction weight utility itemsets identified in phase I. Amhed et al. proposed $IHUP_{twu}$ (Incremental High Utility Pattern) tree structure [7] to maintain information of incremental databases for exact utility calculation instead of scanning database. Vincent et al. proposed an algorithm named UP-Growth [8] to mine high utility itemsets, which could construct utility pattern tree from database based on DGU (Discarding Global Unpromising items), DGN (Discarding Global Node utility), DLU (Discarding Local Unpromising items), DLN (Discarding Local Node utility) strategies to prune search space. Even though lots of tricks are proposed to prune search space, there are still a lot of candidate itemsets waiting to be tested in phase II which consumes huge memory and time. To overcome these problems, Liu et al. proposed an algorithm called HUI-Miner [9] to mine high utility itemsets without generating candidates. HUI-Miner uses a novel structure, called utility-list, to store both utility information and heuristic information of itemset for pruning search space. Based on utility-list, the high utility itemsets could be mined by joining utility lists instead of scanning database, which shrinks much mining time. Further, Krishnamoorthy et al. proposed an algorithm called HUP-Miner [10] which employs two novel pruning strategies, namely partitioned utility pruning and lookahead utility pruning to prune search space. Peng et al. proposed a modified HUI-Miner(mHUIMiner) [11], which utilizes IHUP tree structure to guide the itemset expansion process to avoid considering itemsets that are nonexistent in the database. Liu et al. proposes a novel algorithm d^2HUP [12] which could mine high utility patterns in a single phase without generating candidates, the novelties lies in a lookahead strategy to avoid enumeration and a linear structure CAUL (Chain of Accurate Utility Lists) for scalable representation of utility information. Fournier-Viger et al. proposed a utility list based fast high-utility miner (FHM) [13] algorithm. The algorithm could reduce join action of utility lists effectively after analyzing co-occurrences property of items. Zida et al. proposed a algorithm named EFIM (Efficient high-utility Itemset Mining) [14] to mine high utility itemsets effectively. EFIM outperforms both in terms of execution time and memory through novel database projection and transaction merging techniques. Considering huge memory consumption problem caused by utility-list intersection/join operation, Duong et al. proposed an improved utility-list structure called utility-list buffer to reduce the memory consumption and speed up the join operation. This structure is integrated into a novel algorithm named ULB-Miner [15]. Rather than pruning search space by monotonic properties, there are also some works integrating evolutionary computation algorithms into mining high utility itemsets. Kannimuthu and Premalatha firstly adopted the genetic algorithm into high utility itemsets mining, proposed two algorithms HUPEumu-GRAM and HUPEwumu-GRAMs with/without specified minimum utility threshold separately [16]. Lin et al. adopted particle swarm optimization to mine high utility itemsets and proposed an algorithm called HUIM-BPSO$_{sig}$ [17], the algorithm encodes particles as binary variables and takes utility function as fitness function to achieve evolutionary optimization. Wu et al. adopted ant colony optimization into high utility itemsets mining and proposed HUIM-ACS algorithm [18], which could map completed solution space into routing graph to mine high utility itemsets as well as to avoid generating unreasonable solutions.

3   Methodology

To Achieve penetration semantic knowledge mining, we proposed an adaptive utility quantification strategy for individual item whose external utility in bucket m is calculated as follows:

$$p_m(i) = \alpha \frac{N_m}{N} \tag{1}$$

where N_m is the number of transactions containing item i in bucket m, N is the number of transactions containing item i in whole database and α is coefficient to differentiate external utility for item in the bucket. This formula conveys the idea that the external utility of item gets higher when it appeared frequently in the bucket and less in whole database, satisfying characteristic 3 and 4 in Sect. 2.1. After quantifying external utility for each item, all of the classical high utility itemsets mining algorithms could be adopted to mine penetration semantic knowledge which owns high utility.

Even though it seems easy to implement the calculation of external utility, it has to rescan whole database again to update utility for each item when new transactions appear, which consumes huge time. To facilitate high utility mining for incremental database, the IHUP$_{aruq}$ tree structure is proposed, whose construction method is similar to IHUP$_{twu}$ [19]. IHUP$_{aruq}$ is composed of three parts, namely global header table (GHT), local header table (LHT) and local IHUP$_{aruq}$ tree. Element in GHT is composed of three fields, including item_name, count, link, where item_name is the name of item, count is the number of item appeared in whole database and link is pointer to link corresponding item in each local table sequentially. Element in LHT is also composed of three fields, item_name, count, and link, where item_name is the name of item, count is the number of item appeared in the bucket and link is pointer to link corresponding item in IHUP$_{aruq}$ tree sequentially. IHUP$_{aruq}$ tree is constructed for each bucket in adaptive utility descending order. The details of constructing IHUP$_{aruq}$ tree is shown in Algorithm 1 described as follows:

Step1: Scan database to calculate the adaptive external utility for each item in bucket k. Create local header table for items of the bucket in adaptive utility descending order and reorganize transactions of each bucket in utility descending order. Set the count field of each element in LHT_k to the number of item in the bucket. Finally add each item to GHT.

Step2: Create local tree for each individual bucket, the item_name of root node is denoted as effect item. Insert each reorganized transaction into local IHUP_{aruq} tree with prefix share strategy. And increase the number of shared prefix node by 1 or create new branches to maximal share prefix path with increasing node in maximal shared prefix path by 1 and setting the count of items in new branches to 1.

Step3: For each item in GHT, link the pointer field to each LHT with same item sequentially and set the count field in GHT to the sum of count field in each linked LHT, finally reorganize GHT in count descending order to finish the creation of IHUP_{aruq} tree. Based on constructed IHUP_{aruq} tree for each bucket, the high utility itemsets could be retrieved by depth first search method to discover all of those items whose external utility is higher than user specified threshold.

Further, in order to facilitate high utility mining process for incremental database, we could adjust IHUP_{aruq} tree structure instead of creating new one as follows:

Algorithm 1. IHUP_{aruq} tree construction algorithm

Input: original database db
Output: GHT, LHTs, IHUP_{aruq}

1: **for** $transaction \in db$ **do**
2:     $m \leftarrow$ check_bucket($transaction$)
3:     buffer$_m$.append($transaction$)
4:     **for** $item$ in $transaction$ **do**
5:         $\text{LHT}_m(item) \mathrel{+}= 1$
6:         $\text{GHT}(item) \mathrel{+}= 1$
7: **for** k = 1, ... n **do**
8:     **for** $item$ in buffer$_k$ **do**
9:         $p(item) = \text{LHT}_k(item)/\text{GHT}_k(item)$
10:     r-buffer$_k \leftarrow$ reorganize(buffer$_k$, p)
11:     $\text{IHUP}^k_{aruq} \leftarrow$ create_tree(r-buffer$_k$)
12: **return** LHTs, GHT, IHUP_{aruq}

Supposing the incremental database for bucket m is denoted as db'_m, and we could scan db'_m to count the number of each item i as N'_i, also we could resort to LHT and GHT for item i appeared in whole database and bucket m represented as N and N_i respectively. So the new external utility for item i in bucket m could be updated as follows:

$$p'_m(i) = \alpha \frac{N_i + N'_i}{N + N'_i} \tag{2}$$

After updating new external utility for each item in bucket m, we could got new utility descending order, based on which we could compare with the old one to find those pairs that need to be exchanged through bubble sorting algorithm. Then we could update information in LHT_m, GHT and adjust those exchange required paths in IHUP_{aruq} tree whose pairs need to be exchanged to keep in new utility descending order. Finally, after updating IHUP_{aruq} tree, we could discover all itemsets whose utility is higher than user specified threshold through depth first search method, and these itemsets are final penetration semantic knowledge which owns high utility. The detail of IHUP_{aruq} update algorithm is shown in Algorithm 2.

Algorithm 2. IHUP_{aruq} update algorithm

Input: incremental database db_k^+, LHT_k, GHT, IHUP_{aruq}^k
Output: output u-GHT, u-LHT_k, u-IHUP_{aruq}^k

1: **for** $item$ in db_k^+ **do**
2:      $N_{item} \leftarrow \text{count}(db_k^+, item)$
3:      $p'(item) \leftarrow (\text{LHT}(item) + N_{item})/(\text{GHT}(item) + N_{item})$
4:      $\text{GHT}(item) \leftarrow \text{GHT}(item) + \text{count}(item)$
5:      $\text{LHT}_k(item) \leftarrow \text{LHT}_k(item) + \text{count}(item)$
6: $pairs \leftarrow \text{exchange}(p', p)$
7: r-$db_k \leftarrow \text{reorganize}(db_k, p')$
8: **for** $path$ in IHUP_{aruq}^k **do**
9:      **for** $< n_1, n_2 >$ in $pairs$ **do**
10:          $path \leftarrow \text{adjust}(path, < n_1, n_2 >)$
11: $\text{IHUP}_{aruq}^k \leftarrow update\_tree(\text{r-}db_k)$
12: **return** LHT_k, GHT, IHUP_{aruq}^k

---

4 Experiment

In this section, we verified the effectiveness of our proposed adaptive utility quantification strategy by comparing high utility itemsets mining algorithms with three classical frequent itemsets mining algorithms on four datasets. The experiment aim is to illustrate that our proposed strategy could quantify item utility effectively to make high utility itemsets mining algorithms available in mining penetration semantic knowledge.

4.1 Metric and Datasets

Experiment datasets are gathered through penetration testing on four common services, including Apache, IIS, MySQL and nginx. The experiment compares performance of four high utility itemsets mining algorithms, Two-Phase, FHM, EFIM and HUI-Miner with proposed adaptive utility quantification strategy. Also, there are three frequent itemsets mining algorithms, Apriori [19], LCM-Freq [20] and PrePost+ [21] are implemented to compare performance. The threshold of algorithms ranges from 0.1 to 0.9. The metric adopted in the experiment is true positive ratio (TPR) and false positive ratio (FPR) whose calculation formula is shown as follows:

$$TPR = \frac{|D \cap P|}{|P|} \times 100\%, \quad FPR = \frac{|D \cap N|}{|N|} \times 100\% \tag{3}$$

where P is set of correct penetration semantic knowledge, N is set of wrong knowledge and D is set of discovered knowledge. ROC (Receiver Operating Characteristic curve) is adopted to integrate TPR and FPR metric to describe the performance of algorithm under different algorithm parameter.

4.2   Result and Analysis

The experiment result is shown in Fig. 2, which describes ROC performance of algorithms on four datasets, among which (a)(c)(e)(g) are intact picture of algorithms and (b)(d)(f)(h) are local detail picture (enlargement of black box) for observing performance of algorithms on datasets. From Fig. 3, we could see that the high utility itemsets mining algorithms, Two Phase, FHM, EFIM and HUI_Miner with proposed ARUQ strategy outperformed comparative ones, the area under curve (AUC) is larger than others, proving the effectiveness of our proposed strategy. Detaily, Fig. 2(a) shows that the high utility itemsets mining algorithms with ARUQ strategy shares similar performance on Apache dataset and the highest ratio reaches 85% while Apriori, LCMFreq and PrePost+ algorithms reaches 22.5% at most which is less than those high utility itemsets mining algorithms with our proposed ARUQ strategy. Also, we could conclude from the performance on the other three datasets that Two Phase algorithm with ARUQ strategy achieves best performance and the true positive rate of all frequent itemsets mining algorithms are less than 40% on the former three dataset. Further, we could see from (b)(d)(f)(h) that apriori algorithm shows good performance than other frequent itemsets mining algorithms in mining penetration semantic knowledge, but still far less than the comparative high utility itemsets mining algorithms with ARUQ strategy. To sum up, we could conclude from the experiment result that high utilities itemsets mining algorithms with proposed ARUQ strategy could mine penetration semantic knowledge from raw dataset effectively.

To better understand the performance of algorithms in mining penetration testing knowledge, we compare the CPU and memory consumption performance of algorithms on Apache dataset, and curves in each subfigure shows the details of algorithms in mining penetration semantic knowledge from Apache dataset. "Bottom points" in each curve is used to differentiate algorithm parameter. From Fig. 3 we could see that high utility itemsets mining algorithms consumes

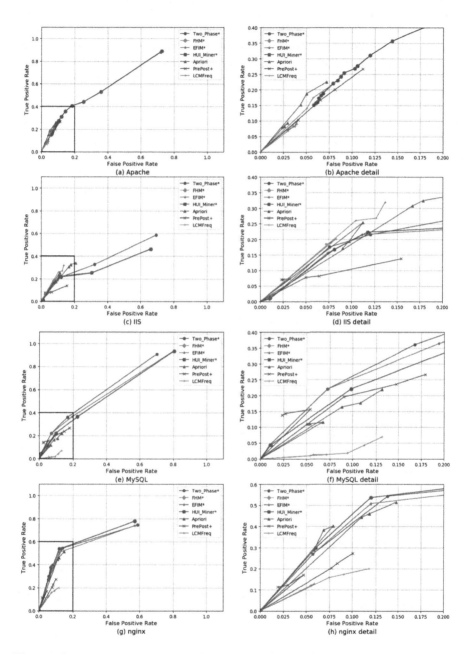

Fig. 2. The receiver operating characteristic curve and locally enlarged receiver operating characteristic curve of algorithms on each experiment dataset.

much CPU time than frequent itemsets mining algorithms in mining penetration semantic knowledge. The average CPU consumption ratio for high utility itemsets mining algorithms with proposed ARUQ strategy is 15000% (overfrequency) while those frequent itemsets mining algorithms are all below 10%. This phenomenon demonstrates that high utility itemsets mining algorithms with proposed ARUQ strategy is much more computation intensive. In contrast, we also could find from Fig. 3 that those high utility itemsets mining algorithms consume far less memory than comparative Apriori, LCMFreq and PrePost+ algorithm because there is no generated candidates for knowledge mining in high utility itemsets mining algorithms, so that they consume similar less memory. In conclusion, the experiment results tell us that high utility itemsets mining algorithms with our proposed adaptive utility quantification strategy outperform frequent itemsets mining algorithm in both accuracy and memory consumption performance.

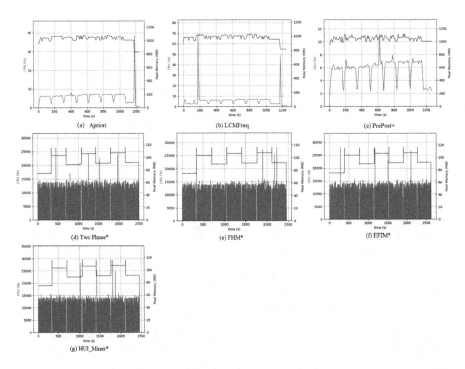

Fig. 3. The comparison of memory and CPU consumption for each data mining algorithm under Apache dataset.

5   Conclusion

In this paper, we have proposed a novel adaptive utility quantification strategy for penetration semantic knowledge mining and construct IHUP$_{aruq}$ tree structure to maintain utility information. Adaptive utility quantification strategy could quantify external utility for each item effectively but avoid rescanning database which saves a lot of time. Experimental results show that high utility itemsets mining algorithms with adaptive utility quantification strategy achieve significant performance improvement over these algorithms in both accuracy and memory consumption.

References

1. Sarraute, C.: Automated attack planning. arXiv preprint arXiv:1307.7808 (2013)
2. Lyon, G.: Nmap security scanner. Nmap.org [En linea] (2014). http://nmap.org/. Accessed 20 Apr 2015
3. Genge, B., Enachescu, C.: ShoVAT: Shodan-based vulnerability assessment tool for Internet-facing services. Secur. Commun. Netw. **9**(15), 2696–2714 (2016)
4. Zhang, C., et al.: An empirical evaluation of high utility itemset mining algorithms. Expert Syst. Appl. **101**, 91–115 (2018)
5. Gan, W., et al.: A survey of incremental high utility itemset mining. Wiley Interdisc. Rev. Data Min. Knowl. Discov. **8**(2), e1242 (2018)
6. Liu, Y., Liao, W., Choudhary, A.: A two-phase algorithm for fast discovery of high utility itemsets. In: Ho, T.B., Cheung, D., Liu, H. (eds.) PAKDD 2005. LNCS (LNAI), vol. 3518, pp. 689–695. Springer, Heidelberg (2005). https://doi.org/10.1007/11430919_79
7. Ahmed, C.F., et al.: Efficient tree structures for high utility pattern mining in incremental databases. IEEE Trans. Knowl. Data Eng. **21**(12), 1708–1721 (2009)
8. Tseng, V.S., et al.: UP-Growth: an efficient algorithm for high utility itemset mining. In: Proceedings of the 16th ACM SIGKDD International Conference on Knowledge Discovery and Data Mining (2010)
9. Liu, M., Qu, J.: Mining high utility itemsets without candidate generation. In: Proceedings of the 21st ACM International Conference on Information and Knowledge Management (2012)
10. Krishnamoorthy, S.: Pruning strategies for mining high utility itemsets. Expert Syst. Appl. **42**(5), 2371–2381 (2015)
11. Peng, A.Y., Koh, Y.S., Riddle, P.: mHUIMiner: a fast high utility itemset mining algorithm for sparse datasets. In: Kim, J., Shim, K., Cao, L., Lee, J.-G., Lin, X., Moon, Y.-S. (eds.) PAKDD 2017. LNCS (LNAI), vol. 10235, pp. 196–207. Springer, Cham (2017). https://doi.org/10.1007/978-3-319-57529-2_16
12. Liu, J., Wang, K., Fung, B.C.M.: Mining high utility patterns in one phase without generating candidates. IEEE Trans. Knowl. Data Eng. **28**(5), 1245–1257 (2015)
13. Fournier-Viger, P., Wu, C.-W., Zida, S., Tseng, V.S.: FHM: faster high-utility itemset mining using estimated utility co-occurrence pruning. In: Andreasen, T., Christiansen, H., Cubero, J.-C., Raś, Z.W. (eds.) ISMIS 2014. LNCS (LNAI), vol. 8502, pp. 83–92. Springer, Cham (2014). https://doi.org/10.1007/978-3-319-08326-1_9
14. Zida, S., Fournier-Viger, P., Lin, J.C.W., Wu, C.W., Tseng, V.S.: EFIM: a highly efficient algorithm for high-utility itemset mining. In: Sidorov, G., Galicia-Haro, S. (eds.) MICAI 2015. LNCS, vol. 9413, pp. 530–546. Springer, Cham (2015). https://doi.org/10.1007/978-3-319-27060-9_44
15. Duong, Q.-H., et al.: Efficient high utility itemset mining using buffered utility-lists. Appl. Intell. **48**(7), 1859–1877 (2018). https://doi.org/10.1007/s10489-017-1057-2

16. Kannimuthu, S., Premalatha, K.: Discovery of high utility itemsets using genetic algorithm. Int. J. Eng. Technol. (IJET) **5**(6), 4866–4880 (2013)
17. Lin, J.C.-W., et al.: Mining high-utility itemsets based on particle swarm optimization. Eng. Appl. Artif. Intell. **55**, 320–330 (2016)
18. Wu, J.M.-T., Zhan, J., Lin, J.C.-W.: An ACO-based approach to mine high-utility itemsets. Knowl. Based Syst. **116**, 102–113 (2017)
19. Agrawal, R., Srikant, R.: Fast algorithms for mining association rules. In: Proceedings of the 20th International Conference on Very Large Data Bases, VLDB, vol. 1215, pp. 487–499 (1994)
20. Uno, T., Asai, T., Uchida, Y., et al.: LCM: an efficient algorithm for enumerating frequent closed item sets. In: Workshop on Frequent Itemset Mining Implementations, FIMI 2003. DBLP (2003)
21. Deng, Z.H., Lv, S.L.: PrePost+: an efficient N-lists-based algorithm for mining frequent itemsets via Children–Parent Equivalence pruning. Expert Syst. Appl. **42**(13), 5424–5432 (2015)

RF-AdaCost: WebShell Detection Method that Combines Statistical Features and Opcode

Wenzhuang Kang[1](✉), Shangping Zhong[1], Kaizhi Chen[1], Jianhua Lai[2], and Guangquan Xu[3]

[1] College of Mathematics and Computer Science,
Fuzhou University, Fuzhou 350100, Fujian, China
kangkangajax@163.com, {spzhong,ckz}@fzu.edu.cn
[2] Fujian Institute of Scientific and Technological Information, Fuzhou 350003, Fujian, China
laijh@heidun.net
[3] Tianjin Key Laboratory of Advanced Networking (TANK), College of Intelligence and Computing, Tianjin University, Tianjin 300350, China
losin@tju.edu.cn

Abstract. WebShell is called a webpage backdoor. After hackers invade a website, they usually mix backdoor files with normal webpage files in the WEB directory of the website service area. Then, they use a browser to access the backdoor and obtain a command execution environment to control the website server. WebShell detection methods have stringent requirements because of the flexibility of the PHP language and the increasing number of hidden techniques used by hackers. The term frequency–inverse document frequency (TF-IDF) used in the existing random forest–gradient boosting decision tree (RF-GBDT) algorithm does not consider the distribution information and classification capabilities of feature words among classes, and no balance exists between false negative and false positive rates. This work proposes a PHP WebShell detection model called RF-AdaCost, which stands for random forest–misclassification cost-sensitive AdaBoost, based on RF-GBDT. We used the statistical characteristics of PHP source files, including information entropy and index of coincidence, and extracted the opcode sequences of PHP source files, thus merging statistical features and opcode sequences to improve the detection efficiency of the WebShell. Experimental results show that the RF-AdaCost algorithm demonstrates better performance than the RF-GBDT algorithm.

Keywords: WebShell detection · RF-GBDT · TF-IDF · Statistical features · Opcode sequence · RF-AdaCost

1 Introduction

WebShell is essentially a script file written in various languages, such as ASP, JSP, and PHP. It resides in the publicly accessible directory of a web server, and attackers can directly access it by using a browser or customized client software. WebShell provides remote access to various key functions, such as executing arbitrary commands, traversing

© Springer Nature Singapore Pte Ltd. 2020
G. Xu et al. (Eds.): FCS 2020, CCIS 1286, pp. 667–682, 2020.
https://doi.org/10.1007/978-981-15-9739-8_49

file directories, viewing and modifying arbitrary files, enhancing access permissions, sending spam, and phishing emails [1]. Statistics [2] show that PHP accounts for 78.4% of web server programming languages. This study focuses on PHP types, and the proposed detection method can be extended to other WebShell types.

By detecting traffic, listening to network traffic to extract WebShell or upload or execute http requests, and paying attention to payload characteristics, WebShell detection cannot establish potential dangers in advance. In addition, extremely heavy traffic affects server performance. Log detection involves detecting WebShell by analyzing whether the page request and response characteristics recorded in the web log contain relevant malicious behavior after the file is executed. However, the attack has already occurred at this time; hence, this type of detection is suitable for use as an auxiliary detection method. With regard to file detection, due to the flexibility of the PHP language, various detection tools can be fooled through special transformation methods to avoid detection and killing. Currently popular WebShell killing systems are implemented through the principle of rule matching or a single statistical principle. Each time a new WebShell appears, these systems need to be updated after a certain period to achieve killing. A zero-day WebShell does not achieve good results. Regular expressions of WebShells are widely used in web application firewall on the border of the web server, but regular expressions are easily confused and bypassed [3] and can only detect known WebShell. Current research generally focuses on the extraction of WebShell statistics (information entropy, coincidence index, longest word, file compression ratio, and dangerous function) or n-gram segmentation of the source file extraction opcode sequence to extract term frequency–inverse document frequency (TF-IDF) features. Current algorithms rarely use the two together. In addition, research on logs and traffic cannot fundamentally ensure that no WebShell script exists on the server, that is, no backdoor file is present after the attack on the server.

Cui et al. [4] proposed the random forest–gradient boosting decision tree (RF-GBDT) algorithm, trained the model by using TF-IDF [5] and HASH vectors, predicted the dataset, used the prediction results as features, and combined the statistical features to obtain a model that uses integrated learning. This method is more accurate than models trained with statistical features or opcodes alone. The TF-IDF used in the algorithm does not consider the distribution information and classification capability of feature words among classes [6], which affect model performance. Moreover, the model does not consider the cost of WebShell underreporting in practical applications. Hence, reducing the underreporting rate as much as possible under the condition that the false alarm rate is acceptable is worth studying.

With reference to RF-GBDT, this study proposes a WebShell detection method based on RF-AdaCost. First, an opcode is extracted from a WebShell file, and n-gram segmentation is performed [7]. Second, the TFIDF–chi feature is extracted [8], and RF [9] is used for training. Third, the predicted results are utilized as a feature after obtaining the model. Lastly, combined with the statistical characteristics of the WebShell, AdaCost [10] (misclassification cost-sensitive AdaBoost) is used for training to obtain the final model.

The main contributions of this work include the following:

(1) An improved TFIDF–chi feature is used to extract WebShell opcode features;
(2) AdaCost is adopted to reduce the underreporting rate and verify the effectiveness of the proposed model.

The rest of the paper is organized as follows. Related technologies are discussed in the second section. The algorithm and framework used in this study and comparative tests are presented in the third section. The experimental methods and results are given in the fourth section. The final section concludes the study and discusses future research directions.

2 Related Work

Hu et al.'s study [11] on WebShell detection methods based on Bayesian theory has similarities with our study, such as the use of common statistical characteristics (e.g., information entropy, coincidence index, and compression ratio). However, this previous study has certain disadvantages. First, the researchers used only 600 samples. The samples were too few to guarantee the generalization performance of the experiment. Second, the features the researchers selected could not clearly reflect the PHP WebShell, that is, the features were also suitable for detecting other WebShell, such as JSP or ASP. Our method is different. To ensure the reliability of the experiment, we collected 5000 samples for training and extracted the characteristics of the PHP file opcode sequence to reflect the characteristics of the PHP file effectively.

The text vector-based PHP WebShell detection method proposed by Zhang et al. [12] uses n-gram and TF-IDF algorithms to convert the opcode sequence generated during the execution of the PHP script into a text vector, with the text vector as the input feature. The researchers used the limit gradient lifting algorithm XGBoost [13] to classify the PHP script through the judgment of the classification results to achieve WebShell detection. The experimental results showed that the proposed method can effectively detect the WebShell and improve the accuracy of WebShell detection. However, this detection model has disadvantages. The TF-IDF used in the algorithm does not consider the distribution information and classification capability of feature words among classes, which affect model performance. In addition, the statistical characteristics of the utilized WebShell are disregarded. The experimental results showed that the added statistical characteristics are improved.

Tu et al. [14] proposed a WebShell recognition method based on the optimal threshold of malicious signatures, malicious function samples, and longest file characters. By scanning and searching for malicious code in each file of the web application, the administrator provides a list of suspicious files and a detailed log analysis table for each suspicious file for further inspection. In view of the shortcomings of traditional machine learning algorithm-based detection models, Yan et al. [15] proposed the application of convolutional neural networks [16] to WebShell detection. Deep learning models do not require complex artificial feature engineering. Model features trained through model learning can enable attackers to avoid targeted bypass in WebShell detection. With the accumulation of training samples, the accuracy of the detection model in different application environments gradually improves. This method has obvious advantages compared with traditional machine learning algorithms. However, this method is applicable to all types of WebShell, and it does not flexibly apply text classification to WebShell detection. Obviously, it does not use PHP-type opcode, and the model's accuracy still has room for improvement.

Cui et al. [4] developed a WebShell detection method based on the RF-GBDT algorithm for detecting PHP web pages. The developed method is a two-layer model that combines RF and GBDT [17]. At the first layer, preliminary prediction results are obtained with the RF classifier by using the characteristics of the opcode sequence. Then, the statistical characteristics of the PHP file are combined with the preliminary prediction results of the first layer, participate in the training of the next layer on the basis of the GBDT classifier, and produce the final prediction results. Effective features, such as information entropy, coincidence index, compression ratio, and text features of the opcode sequence, were selected, and the trained model achieved good prediction performance. However, the model has several problems. The TF-IDF used does not consider the distribution information and classification capability of feature words among classes. In addition, its failure to consider WebShell underreporting in applications can cause serious problems.

Different from these previous researchers, we adopted the advantages of WebShell detection in previous work, improved RF-GBDT, and proposed the RF-AdaCost model. The model uses the statistical characteristics of WebShell and pays attention to the opcode sequence of the PHP WebShell. To reduce the false negative rate of the WebShell, we introduced AdaCost and added cost sensitivity while sacrificing the false positive rate, reducing the false negative rate, and minimizing the loss.

3   Method

We proposed RF-AdaCost, which is shown in Fig. 1. RF-AdaCost, which merges RF and AdaCost, is a two-layer model. At the first layer, we obtained preliminary prediction results on the basis of the opcode sequence of the random forest classifier. Then, we merged the statistical characteristics of the PHP file and its preliminary prediction results to participate in the next training layer with the AdaCost classifier to generate the final prediction result.

RF is an ensemble learning method that consists of many decision tree classifiers. It was proposed by Tin Kam Ho [18] and subsequently developed by Leo Breiman [9]. It constructs many child datasets of the original dataset, conducts sampling with replacement, and leverages the child datasets to build a decision tree. The final prediction results are obtained based on the majority of the predictions produced by all decision trees. RF has two key points: randomness and forestry. Randomness means that the process of building child datasets is completely random, that is, every feature and every sample may contribute to the growth of a decision tree. Forestry means that RF generates its prediction from many decision trees that can form a forest. RF can process a large amount of information within a short time, has high accuracy, and usually has better

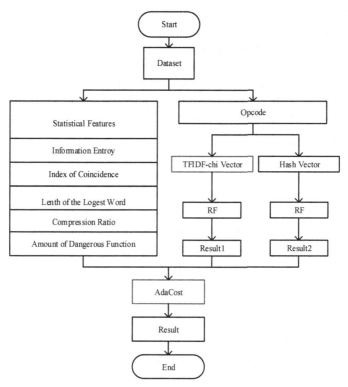

Fig. 1. RF-AdaCost is the fusion of RF and AdaCost. The red box shows the different parts of the model and RF-GBDT. TF-IDF and AdaBoost are used in RF-GBDT. (Color figure online)

performance than decision trees. Therefore, it has a wide range of applications in science and technology.

AdaBoost, which was introduced by Freund et al. [19], learns many "weak" hypothetical high-precision voting sets. Generally, each hypothesis outputs a prediction and the confidence of the prediction. Each hypothesis is trained on the same dataset, but the distribution is different. Different assumptions are made in different booster wheels. In each round, AdaBoost increases the weight of incorrectly classified training instances and decreases the weight of correctly predicted instances. AdaBoost allows arbitrary initial distribution. For classification errors, each example has an equal weight. Costly examples can be given a higher weight than the other examples to reduce the accumulated cost of misclassification. AdaBoost reduces the weighting error of the initial distribution. Schapire et al. [20] provided different weights to false positives and false negatives when applying AdaBoost in text filtering. Karakoulas et al. [21] used a similar method. However, the misclassification cost is not used in the weight update rule of AdaBoost. In AdaCost [10], the weight update rule actively increases the weight of cost misclassification but conservatively reduces the weight of correct cost classification. This condition is achieved by introducing a misclassification cost adjustment function in the weight update formula. Under this update rule, the weight of expensive examples is high, and the weight of cheap examples is low. Each weak hypothesis correctly predicts an expensive example of this distribution. The final voted ensemble also correctly predicts expensive examples. The AdaCost algorithm is shown in Algorithm 1. The red box shows the different parts of AdaCost and AdaBoost.

Algorithm 1   AdaCost[10]

- input: $T = \{(x_1, y_1), \dots, (x_N, y_N)\}, \quad x_i \in \mathcal{X}, \quad y_i \in \{-1, +1\};$
- output: $G(x)$
- Initialize D_1

$$D_1 = (w_{11}, \dots, w_{1i}, \dots, w_{1N}), \quad w_{1j} = \frac{1}{N}, i = 1, 2, \dots, N$$

- For $m = 1, \dots, M$:

  1. Use the training data set with weight distribution D_m to learn and get the basic classifier:

$$G_m(x): \mathcal{X} \rightarrow \{-1, +1\}$$

  2. Calculate the classification error rate of $G_m(x)$ on the training data set:

$$e_m = P(G_m(x_i) \neq y_i) = \sum_{i=1}^{N} w_{mi} I(G_m(x_i) \neq y_i)$$

  3. Calculate the weight of $G_m(x)$:

$$\alpha_m = \frac{1}{2} \log \frac{1 - e_m}{e_m}$$

  4. Update the weight distribution of the training data set:

$$D_{m+1} = (w_{m+1,1}, \dots, w_{m+1,i}, \dots, w_{m+1,N})$$

$$w_{m+1,i} = \frac{w_{m,i}}{Z_m} \exp(-\alpha_m y_i G_m(x_i) \boxed{\beta(i)}, i = 1, 2, \dots, N$$

  where $\beta(i)$ is a cost-adjustment function. Z_m is a normalization factor chosen so that D_{m+1} will be a distribution.

- Get $G(x)$:

$$f(x) = \sum_{m=1}^{M} \alpha_m G_m(x)$$

$$G(x) = \text{sign}(f(x)) = \text{sign}(\sum_{m=1}^{M} \alpha_m G_m(x))$$

3.1 Feature Extraction

We extracted the statistical features, including information entropy, index of coincidence, length of the longest word, compression ratio, and dangerous function, of the PHP file samples. By combining these typical features, we obtained a five-dimensional feature vector. With regard to the PHP file, the text features can be used effectively. Therefore, we extracted the opcode sequence from each PHP sample and determined the text feature TF-IDF–chi and hash vector of the opcode sequence.

1) Information Entropy

Information entropy was introduced by Shannon [22] to represent the disorder and uncertainty of given information by measuring the average uncertainty of all possible information sources. The greater entropy is, the messier the information is. In general, to achieve ambiguity, a WebShell is encrypted and encoded, and several random strings are introduced, leading to an increase in information entropy. Therefore, the value of information entropy can be used to identify WebShell. Information entropy is calculated as

$$Entropy = -\sum_{i=1}^{255} p_i \log p_i, \tag{1}$$

where $p_i = \frac{X_i}{S}$, S is the total number of characters, X_i is the i-th ASCII code that appears in the file, and $i \neq 127$. Given that 127 is a space, it is not counted.

2) Index of Coincidence

The index of coincidence is also known as IC and was developed by W.F. Friedman [23]. It can evaluate the probability of finding two identical letters by randomly selecting two letters from a given text. Given that the randomness of the encrypted text is improved, the IC value of a WebShell is lower than the IC value of ordinary files, thus providing us new evidence to identify the WebShell. IC is calculated as

$$IC = \frac{\sum_{i=1}^{c} n_i(n_i-1)}{N(N-1)}, \tag{2}$$

where N is the length of a given text and n_i is the frequency of letter i in the text. Notably, the text has c different letters.

3) Length of the Longest Word

We resort to the proof that an encrypted WebShell may have several abnormal words or strings with an extremely large length. Thus, by measuring the length of the longest word from a given text, we can determine whether it is suspicious and a WebShell.

4) Compression Ratio

Data compression reduces the size of a file by using fewer codes instead of the original presentation. The compression ratio is the ratio of the uncompressed size of the file to the compressed size, as shown in Formula (3). By assigning short codes to high-frequency characters and mapping long codes to low-frequency characters, data compression eliminates the unbalanced distribution of specific characters [24]. A compression algorithm makes the characters of the original file uniform; thus, the more unevenly the bytes are used, the greater the proportion of compression is. After a series of steps, such as WebShell or small encryption, the internal bytes become uneven and thus cause the compression ratio of the WebShell to increase. The compression ratio of the file can therefore be used as one of the characteristics of checking WebShell.

$$Compression\,Ratio = \frac{UncompressedSize}{CompressedSize} \tag{3}$$

5) Dangerous Function

WebShell usually has functions that accidentally appear in normal files, including eval, python eval, and base64 decode. We can calculate the number of characters that can match these functions in each test file and use this number as a feature to help identify the WebShell.

6) TFIDF–chi vector

PHP opcodes are part of machine language instructions and used to specify the operations that need to be performed [25]. Compared with extracting text features directly from PHP source files, extracting text features from opcode sequences is more effective because opcodes can filter some noise in the PHP source code, such as comments. In our experiments, we extracted the opcode sequence of all samples and used it to extract the text features from the opcode sequence, namely, the TFIDF–chi vector [8].

TF-IDF
In the TF-IDF algorithm, IDF represents inverse document frequency, and its characteristics are as follows: if the number of documents containing the same word is large, then the classification capability of the feature word is poor. For example, although several pronouns appear frequently, they do not have the capability to distinguish text. IDF is calculated as

$$idf_i = log\left(\frac{N}{n_i} + 1\right), \tag{4}$$

where N represents the total number of text in the entire training sample and n_i represents the number of text containing the feature word t_i.

Term frequency refers to the frequency of words appearing in the file and is usually expressed as TF. In TF, if the feature word appears frequently in an article, then the feature can effectively express the main information of the text and is suitable for text classification. Keywords appear often in the text, that is, the number of words and the importance of words have a certain positive correlation. However, regardless of the importance of words, a long document may have more words than a short document. TF is the normalization of the number of words to prevent bias toward long files. TF is calculated as

$$tf_{ij} = \frac{n_{ij}}{\sum_k n_{kj}}, \tag{5}$$

where n_{ij} represents the number of times that word t_i appears in document d_j and $\sum_k n_{kj}$ represents the sum of all words in document d_j.

In the traditional TF-IDF calculation method, the TF word frequency statistical method is used to describe high-frequency features, and these high-frequency features are often noise words that are not helpful for text classification. Several low-frequency words that can represent text information well because of the low frequency of occurrence are ignored. IDF enhances the weight of feature words with a low frequency of occurrence to make up for the shortcomings of TF [26]. The TF-IDF weighting method combines the two methods, as follows:

$$W_{ij} = tf_{ij} * idf_i. \tag{6}$$

TF-IDF does not consider the distribution of feature words within categories [8]. Under normal circumstances, feature words with an unstable distribution should be given a lower weight than feature words with a relatively stable distribution. Similarly, if a feature word only appears in a certain type of text, then the word does not help in text classification and should be given a low weight. This scenario is not reflected in the traditional TF-IDF.

Advanced TF-IDF algorithm [8]: TFIDF–chi

The chi-square statistical algorithm is used to measure the deviation degree of two variables, in which the theoretical and actual values are independent of each other. A large deviation means that the two variables are independent of each other. Yang et al. [27] showed that the chi-square statistic is one of the most effective feature selection methods in existing text classification. The greater the chi-square value of a feature item in a category is, the more distinctive the feature vocabulary is. However, this statistic has disadvantages. For example, the traditional chi-square does not consider the situation where the feature words are evenly distributed within the category. Specifically, the chi-square statistical formula does not reflect the large weight that feature words should be given when they appear uniformly in a certain type of document; it only focuses on the procedure of giving weights when the frequency of other types of feature words is high and when the frequency of this type is low. The calculation formula of chi-square statistics is

$$chi = \frac{N(AD-BC)^2}{(A+C)(B+D)(A+B)(C+D)}, \tag{7}$$

where A is the frequency of documents containing the feature word t and belonging to category c, B is the frequency of documents that contain the feature word t but do not belong to category c, C is the frequency of documents that belong to category c but do not contain the characteristic word t, D is the frequency of documents that neither belong to c nor contain the characteristic word t, and N is the total number of documents.

The traditional TF-IDF weight calculation method ignores the difference in the distribution of feature words between categories, but the chi-square statistic of feature words can effectively describe the distribution information of feature words between categories. Specifically, the classification capability of the characteristic vocabulary is proportional to its chi-square value. In view of this situation, we introduced chi-square statistical methods to improve the classification capability of feature words between classes. The calculation formula of the feature word weight improvement algorithm based on chi-square statistics is

$$Tfidf - chi = W_{ij} * chi. \tag{8}$$

7) Hash vector

A hash vector can map arbitrary data blocks to a fixed number of locations, and the values of TF are added to these locations. It can almost ensure that the same input produces the same output and that different inputs produce different outputs. This vector is also called a hashing trick, which means that it can use the hash function to determine the index position of the eigenvector and does not need to create a large dictionary. The advantage of this trick is what the TF-IDF method lacks. The TF-IDF method has to create a dictionary, which may require a large memory space. Mathematically, if the hash function hashes the i-th feature to position j, i.e., $h(i) = j$, then the TF value of the j-th original feature $\phi(i)$ will be added to the TF value of j-th feature $\bar{\phi}(j)$, as follows:

$$\bar{\phi}(j) = \sum_{i \in J; h(i)=j} \phi(i), \tag{9}$$

where j is the dimension of the original feature.

3.2 Algorithm

Given this background, this study developed a WebShell detection method that combines statistical features and an opcode, as shown in Algorithm 2.

Algorithm 2   RF-AdaCost

1. Prepare the php webshell data set, and randomly divide the data set into a training set and a test set in a 7:3 ratio.

2. Extract the statistical characteristics of each WebShell, such as information entropy, index of coincidence, length of the longest word, compression ratio and danger function. Record as $D = \{d_1, d_2, ..., d_N\}$, D is the WebShell training set, where d_i is the i-th WebShell file. $d_i = \{x_{i1}, x_{i2}, x_{ij} ..., x_{i5}\}$, x_{ij} is the j-th dimension feature of the i-th webshell.

3. Extract the 146-dimensional Tfidf-Chi vector in the D dataset, and the i-th data is recorded as $d_i' = \{\alpha_{i1}, \alpha_{i2}, \alpha_{ij} ..., \alpha_{i146}\}$, RF classifier is used for training to obtain an intermediate model, and then d_i' is input to this model, and the prediction result is used for the sixth dimension feature x_{i6} of d_i.

4. Extract the 200-dimensional hash vector in the D dataset, and the i-th data is recorded as $d_i'' = \{\beta_{i1}, \beta_{i2}, \beta_{ij} ..., \beta_{i200}\}$, RF classifier is used for training to obtain an intermediate model, and then d_i'' is input to this model, and the prediction result is used for the seventh dimension feature x_{i7} of d_i.

5. Dataset $D = \{d_1, d_2, ..., d_N\}$, $d_i = \{x_{i1}, x_{i2}, x_{ij} ..., x_{i5}, x_{i6}, x_{i7}\}$ .Use   AdaCost   classifier （Algorithm 1） ,   and set different cost factors β for training.

END FOR

3.3 Analysis of the Algorithm

The proposed RF-AdaCost algorithm is a fusion of RF and AdaCost. In this algorithm, the opcode of the WebShell is obtained, and the TFIDF–chi and hash vectors are extracted. The RF classifier is then used to train and predict the results, and the statistical characteristics of the WebShell are ignored. Current detection models cannot detect encrypted variant files well, so this study proposed the RF-AdaCost algorithm, which improves the indicators of the model on the basis of sacrificing time and space. The following experimental results verify this improvement. Using RF to train the opcode of WebShell, the complexity of time and space is O (n). Using AdaCost to train the statistical feature of WebShell, the time and space complexity is O (m). Through analysis, the time and space complexity of RF-AdaCost proposed in this paper is O (m + n).

4 Experiment

The main aim of the experiment was to use the proposed RF-AdaCost model in detecting WebShell and compare it with a model without improvement and other models to verify the effectiveness of the proposed method.

4.1 Dataset and Evaluation Method

The dataset used in this experiment was from Fujian Strait Information Technology Co., Ltd. Given that some data may be repeated, the content is the same, but the file name is different. Thus, the dataset needed to be de-duplicated by message-digest algorithm 5 (MD5) to obtain 2162 WebShell samples and 2236 normal samples at a training set: test set ratio of 7:3. Each group of experiments was repeated thrice, and the average value was obtained. Accuracy, Recall, Precision, FNR, and FPR were used to evaluate performance.

4.2 Data Handling

MD5 deduplication calculates the MD5 value of each file in accordance with the content of the file. If the MD5 value is the same, then the file is considered to be the same and deduplication is performed. After a careful analysis of the PHP file, we found that comments exist in the file. If the comments are also included in the statistical features, then they will affect the extracted features and cause errors in the various indicators of the model results. Regular expressions are therefore required to eliminate comments. An opcode is an intermediate language after the PHP script is compiled. It includes operators, operands, instruction formats and specifications, and data structures that store instructions and related information. PHP script execution has four stages, namely, lexical analysis, grammatical analysis, opcode compilation, and opcode execution. The compiler binds the opcode with the corresponding parameter or function call in the third stage. Even if the WebShell dangerous function is confused and encrypted, the opcode statement will be different from the normal file compilation result during compilation. Therefore, according to this feature, an opcode can be used to distinguish between Web-Shell and normal files, and the detection of files can be converted into the detection of opcode sequences. This work uses the PHP plug-in logic extension module (Vulcan logic dumper or VLD) to compile and obtain the PHP files' opcode.

4.3 Experiment Results

The experimental environment is a Windows 7 64-bit operating system, python3.6. The processor is Intel Core i5-4570 CPU at 3.20 GHz, and the memory is 16 GB.

4.3.1 Effect of Advanced TFIDF-Chi on the Results

A set of comparative experiments was designed specifically to verify that the opcode's TFIDF–chi vector can represent WebShell features better than the TF-IDF vector can. The experimental results are shown in Table 1.

Table 1. Effect of advanced TFIDF–chi on the results

Feature	Algorithm	Accuracy	Precision	Recall	FNR	FPR
TF-IDF	RF	92.26%	92.66%	91.51%	8.11%	7.01%
TFIDF-chi	RF	93.55%	93.51%	93.36%	6.41%	6.27%

4.3.2   Comparison with the Method Before Fusion

To verify the effectiveness of the RF-AdaCost model, we compared the experimental results of the method before fusion and the method in this study, as shown in Table 2. First, we extract the statistical features of WebShell, and then use AdaCost classifier to train. Then we use opcode of WebShell to extract TFIDF-chi and Hash vectors, and then use RF classifier to train them. Compare these experimental results with our method, and the experimental results are shown in Table 2.

Table 2. Comparison with the method before fusion

Feature	Algorithm	Accuracy	Precision	Recall	FNR	FPR
Statistical features	AdaCost	87.17%	87.13%	86.73%	12.78%	12.39%
TFIDF-chi	RF	93.55%	93.51%	93.36%	6.41%	6.27%
HASH	RF	91.58%	92.15%	90.59%	8.96%	7.46%
Statistical features, TFIDF-chi, HASH	RF-AdaCost	95.30%	95.36%	95.06%	4.76%	4.48%

4.3.3   Comparison with Other Machine Learning Models

To verify that the RF-AdaCost model is better than other methods, we compared it with Hu's method [11] and Zhang's method [12]. In addition, we made a comparison with RF-GBDT. The experimental results are shown in Table 3.

Table 3. Comparison with other machine learning models

	Accuracy	Precision	Recall	FNR	FPR
RF-AdaCost	95.30%	95.36%	95.06%	4.76%	4.48%
RF-GBDT	94.39%	94.70%	93.83%	5.92%	5.07%
Hu Method	85.28%	85.33%	84.82%	14.26%	14.78%
Zhang Method	92.41%	90.90%	93.49%	8.58%	6.12%

4.3.4   Influence of β Factor on the Experimental Results of RF-AdaCost

The effect of setting different cost factors β (Algorithm 1) in RF-AdaCost on various indicators of the experimental results is shown in Table 4.

4.3.5   Comparison with Popular Detectors on the Internet

To verify the performance of RF-AdaCost, we downloaded several popular advanced WebShell detectors from the Internet, namely, D-Shield, SHELLPUB, and WEBDIR+

Table 4. Influence of β factor on the results of RF-AdaCost

RF-AdaCost	Accuracy	Precision	Recall	FNR	FPR
β = 1	95.30%	95.36%	95.06%	4.76%	4.48%
β = 1.2	95.14%	94.51%	95.68%	4.23%	5.37%
β = 1.5	94.84%	93.15%	96.60%	3.41%	6.87%
β = 1.8	94.01%	92.76%	96.91%	3.17%	8.81%

[28–30], and used the same test set as the model of this article for scanning detection and measurement. The experimental results are shown in Table 5. D-Shield demonstrated good performance in terms of precision and false positive rate. But in other ways, its performance not as good as ours.

Table 5. Comparison with popular detectors on the Internet

Detector	Accuracy	Precision	Recall	FNR	FPR
D Shield	94.92%	96.33%	93.21%	6.37%	3.43%
SHELLPUB	89.98%	93.73%	85.34%	13.05%	5.52%
WEBDIR+	92.26%	95.81%	88.12%	10.66%	3.73%
RF-AdaCost	95.30%	95.36%	95.06%	4.76%	4.48%

4.4 Analysis of Experimental Results and Reasons

The experimental results in Sect. 4.3.1 indicate that the overall performance of TFIDF–chi was better than that of TF-IDF, and the recall rate increased by 1.85%. The reason may be that the TF-IDF weight calculation method based on chi-square statistics makes up for the defect of not considering the distribution of feature words among classes and provides a low weight to words that are evenly distributed among classes but do not have a classification capability. To a certain extent, it improves the traditional calculation method, effectively enhances the accuracy of weight calculation and text classification, and can extract word vectors with classification capability.

The experimental results in Sect. 4.3.2 show that the statistical characteristics of the PHP WebShell alone were not good, and the accuracy was less than 90%. In addition, the TFIDF–chi and hash vectors were better than the statistical characteristics. We conclude that the opcode feature of PHP can effectively reflect the essence of WebShell, but statistical features can also be used as a basis for judging WebShell.

The experimental results in Sects. 4.3.3 and 4.3.5 reveal that the proposed RF-AdaCost model exerted a better overall effect in comparison with the other machine learning algorithms and detectors. Specifically, the accuracy rate of D-Shield is 96.33%, but it is not as good as our model in terms of Recall and FNR, which are aspects that enterprises attach great importance to. In addition, our model has advantages over other models. We can try our best to reduce the false negative rate according to an acceptable range of the false positive rate. Section 4.3.4 shows that the best performance was observed when $\beta = 1.5$. When the β value increased again, the false positive rate increased by 1.94%, and the false negative rate only decreased by 0.24%.

5 Conclusion

In the detection of WebShell, we should pay attention to essential features and use text features, both of which can improve the detection efficiency of WebShell. In practice, the omission of WebShell is disastrous to enterprises. The rate of omission must be reduced under the condition that the rate of false positives is acceptable.

With the development of deep learning, text detection can be used to detect WebShell. If we apply the idea of text detection to WebShell detection, then the essential characteristics of WebShell will be ignored. The combination of the essential characteristics of WebShell with deep learning is worth studying.

Acknowledgments. This work is supported by the National Natural Science Foundation of China (NSFC) under Grant 61972187, the Scientific Research Project of Science and Education Park Development Center of Fuzhou University, Jinjiang under Grant 2019-JJFDKY-53 and the Tianjin University-Fuzhou University Joint Fund under Grant TF2020-6.

References

1. Kim, J., Yoo, D.H., Jang, H., et al.: WebSHArk 1.0: a benchmark collection for malicious web shell detection. J. Inf. Process. Syst. **11**(2), 229–238 (2015)
2. WEB TECHNOLOGY SURVEYS: Usage statistics of server-side programming languages for websites [EB/OL]. https://w3techs.com/technologies/overview/programming_lan-guage. Accessed 15 May 2020
3. Argyros, G., Stais, I., Kiayias, A., et al.: Back in black: towards formal, black box analysis of sanitizers and filters. In: 2016 IEEE Symposium on Security and Privacy (SP). IEEE (2016)
4. Cui, H., Huang, D., Fang, Y., et al.: Webshell detection based on random forest–gradient boosting decision tree algorithm. In: 2018 IEEE Third International Conference on Data Science in Cyberspace (DSC), pp. 153–160. IEEE (2018)
5. Salton, G., Yu, C.T.: On the construction of effective vocabularies for information retrieval. ACM **9**(3) (1973)
6. Debole, F., Sebastiani, F.: Supervised term weighting for automated text categorization. In: Sirmakessis, S. (ed.) Text Mining and its Applications. Studies in Fuzziness and Soft Computing, vol. 138, pp. 81–97. Springer, Berlin (2004). https://doi.org/10.1007/978-3-540-452 19-5_7
7. Cavnar, W.B., Trenkle, J.M.: N-gram-based text categorization. In: Proceedings of SDAIR-94, 3rd Annual Symposium on Document Analysis and Information Retrieval, p. 161175 (1994)
8. Ying, Ma., Hui, Z., WanLong, L.: Optimization of TF-IDF algorithm combined with improved CHI statistical method. Appl. Res. Comput. **9**, 2596–2598 (2019)
9. Breiman, L.: Random forests. Mach. Learning **45**(1), 5–32 (2001)

10. Stolfo, W.F.S.J.: AdaCost: misclassification cost-sensitive boosting. In: Sixteenth International Conference on Machine Learning. Morgan Kaufmann Publishers Inc. (1999)
11. Biwei, H.: Research on webshell detection method based on Bayesian theory. Sci. Mosaic (2016)
12. Hewei, Z., Xiaojie, L.: PHP webshell detection method based on text vector. Data Commun. **04**, 16–21 (2019)
13. Chen, T., Guestrin, C.: XGBoost: a scalable tree boosting system. In: ACM SIGKDD International Conference on Knowledge Discovery & Data Mining. ACM (2016)
14. Truong, T.D., Cheng, G., Guo, X.J., et al.: Webshell detection techniques in web applications In: International Conference on Computing, Communication and Networking Technologies (ICCCNT). IEEE (2014)
15. Lv, Z.-H., Yan, H.-B., Mei, R.: Automatic and accurate detection of webshell based on convolutional neural network. In: Yun, X., et al. (eds.) CNCERT 2018. CCIS, vol. 970, pp. 73–85. Springer, Singapore (2019). https://doi.org/10.1007/978-981-13-6621-5_6
16. Kim, Y.: Convolutional neural networks for sentence classification. In: Proceedings of the 2014 Conference on Empirical Methods in Natural Language Processing (EMNLP). Doha, pp. 1746–1751 (2014)
17. Friedman, J.H.: Greedy function approximation: a gradient boosting machine. Ann. Stat. **29**(5), 1189–1232 (2001)
18. Ho, T.K.: Random decision forests. In: 1995 Proceedings of the third International Conference on Document Analysis and Recognition. IEEE Computer Society (1995)
19. Freund, Y., Schapire, R.E.: A decision-theoretic generalization of on-line learning and an application to boosting. J. Comput. Syst. Sci. **55**, 119–139 (1999)
20. Schapire, R., Singer, Y., Singhal, A.: Boosting and Rocchio applied to text filtering. In: International ACM SIGIR Conference on Research & Development in Information Retrieval. ACM (1998)
21. Karakoulas, G., Shawe-Taylor, J.: Optimizing classifiers for imbalanced training sets. In: Annual Conference on Neural Information Processing Systems, pp. 253–259 (1999)
22. Shannon, C.E.: A mathematical theory of communication. Bell Labs Tech. J. **27**(4), 379–423 (1948)
23. Friedman, W.F.: The index of coincidence and its applications in cryptology. Department of Ciphers. Publ 22. Geneva, Illinois, USA: Riverbank Laboratories (1922)
24. Bell, T.C., Cleary, J.G., Witten, I.H.: Text Compression. Prentice Hall, Upper Saddle River (1990)
25. Sklar, D.: "Understanding PHP Internals" Essential PHP Tools: Modules, Extensions, and Accelerators, pp. 265–274. Apress, Berkeley (2004)
26. Xue, X.B., Zhou, Z.H.: Distributional features for text categorization. IEEE Trans. Knowl. Data Eng. **21**, 428–442 (2006)
27. Yang, Y., Pedersen, J.O.: A comparative study on feature selection in text categorization. In: Proceedings of the Fourteenth International Conference on Machine Learning (ICML), pp. 412–420. Morgan Kaufmann Publishers Inc., San Francisco (1997)
28. D shield takes the initiative to protect your website[CP/DK]. http://www.d99net.net/. Accessed 15 May 2020
29. SHELLPUB.COM Focus on killing[CP/DK]. https://www.shellpub.com/. Accessed 15 May 2020
30. Next generation webshell detection engine[CP/DK]. https://scanner.baidu.com/. Accessed 15 May 2020

Author Index

Printed in the United States
By Bookmasters